The Economics of Social Justice and Societal Evolution

Emil Dinga

The Economics of Social Justice and Societal Evolution

An Epistemological Approach

palgrave
macmillan

Emil Dinga
Financial and Monetary Research
Center; Academy of Romanian
Scientists
Romanian Academy
Bucharest, Romania

ISBN 978-3-032-24054-5 ISBN 978-3-032-24055-2 (eBook)
https://doi.org/10.1007/978-3-032-24055-2

This Palgrave Macmillan imprint is published by the registered company Springer Nature Switzerland AG
The registered company address is: Gewerbestrasse 11, 6330 Cham, Switzerland

To my wife, Paula—the amazing garden where I flourished!

Contents

Abbreviations

AEM	Automatic Self-Escalating Mechanism
AM	Automatic Mechanism
ARFIS	Arising-Regulation-Finality-Impact-Signification
ASM	Automatic Self-Stabilizing Mechanism
BCG	Biases Contingently Gained
BNG	Biases Necessarily Gained
CC	Cryptocapillarity
CEE	Capillarity Externally Induced
CIG	Capillarity Internally Generated
CMR	Capillary Model of Rationality
CT	Capabilities Theory
DAM	Discretionary Adjustment Mechanism
DM	Discretionary Mechanism
DPA	Dominant Protective Association
EIH	Entropic Interaction Horizon
ET	Entitlement Theory
FT	Fairness Theory
GDP	Gross Domestic Product
KDFR	Knowledge—Democracy—Freedom—Responsibility
KDFRS	Knowledge—Democracy—Freedom—Responsibility—Sustainability
LMEG	Law of the Minimal Entropic Gradient
MEG	Minimal Entropic Gradient
PLC	Plenary Life Chain
PT	Proceduralist Theory
RC	Regular Capillarity
RT	Resilience Theory

SAM	(Re)structuring Adjustment Mechanism
SEM	Structural Evolutionary Model
SEP	Stanford Encyclopedia of Philosophy
UMS	Ultra-Minimal State
VLC	Viable Life Chain

List of Figures

Chapter 1

Chapter 2

Chapter 3

Chapter 4

Chapter 5

Chapter 6

Chapter 7

Chapter 8

Chapter 9

Chapter 10

List of Tables

Chapter 6

Chapter 7

Chapter 8

Chapter 9

Chapter 10

PART I

Evolutionary Paradigm of the Society

CHAPTER 1

Society as a Symbolic Species

1 What a Species Is It?

Scientists have "organized" the living world in a systematic way, so that a global hierarchy of all living entities, from microscopic to macroscopic, is now available for researchers. In our book, we will be interested only in two layers in that arborescence, namely individuals and species.

An individual is an objectified living entity that cannot be divided without losing its identity. Abstractly, a species is a set of individuals sharing a criterion (or many) that is (are) considered relevant for a given scientific or practical interest. Starting from the biological case, a species puts together the individuals capable of mating among them and generating viable off-springs—that is, off-springs capable of mating among them and generating viable off-springs.

But the biological case is only the first (and, for this, most known) one in matter of species. Elsewhere, we discuss more analytically about three categories of species: (a) biological species; (b) symbolical species; (c) logical species. *Nota bene*: the symbolical species and logical species can be grouped in a supra-species called artefactual species. Consequently, we need a much more general definition of the concept of species than that of biological species.

E. Dinga, *The Economics of Social Justice and Societal Evolution*,
https://doi.org/10.1007/978-3-032-24055-2_1

1.1 *The Sufficiency Predicates of a Species*

By sufficiency predicates (or, equivalently, sufficient predicates) we understand a (minimal) set of consistent, convergent, and complete characteristics/attributes of a population of individuals so that they form a species. Our proposal for the sufficiency predicates is as follows:

- (*S*1) a *group of individuals*,[1] indiscernible among them from a structural point of view

Comment:

(i) it does not matter the number of those individuals, it could be a single individual (as in the case of symbolical species—see point 1.1.2), or a myriad of individuals, even extended at infinity (e.g., ants, bacteria, rational numbers);
(ii) the same structure causes the same functions, that is, the same role, so it is presumed that the individuals of a species are not discernible among them from a functional point of view, too;
(iii) extra-structural differences among the individuals do not matter for excluding some individuals from a given species; these (possible) differences are peripherical and, consequently, non-decisive for the membership to that given species.

- (*S*2) a given common *ontological substrate* of the individuals' structure

Comment:

(i) any structure needs a material/substantial (ontological) substrate aimed at sustaining that structure and allowing its functioning. The concrete nature of such a substrate is very different, but it must be common for the individuals presumed to belong to a given species;
(ii) so, although it is possible to meet two individuals with the same structure (or, more exactly, with structural isomorphism between them), if the substrates of those structures are different, they do not belong to the same species—e.g., a brain and a computer, *grosso*

modo, have the same structure (or, at least, some of their functions seem to indicate a structural isomorphism between them) but their substrates are different: the brain has a biological substrate, while the computer has a technological one);

- (*S*3) a *principle of autopoiesis*. This predicate of sufficiency addresses the following issue: the maintaining of the species in time.[2] This temporal maintaining can take the following forms:
  - (*S*3/1) *perpetuation* as such: the individuals are conserved/ preserved, as they are, in one way or another, in the long or very long term (*Nota bene*: of course, an infinite duration is not conceivable, as we know by now)[3];
  - (*S*3/2) *reproduction*, by particular processes, of individuals: a well-known example here is the individual's reproduction in biological systems. It is to be mentioned that the reproduction does not "deliver" identical individuals with those replaced, but only "promises" that, in favourable conditions, the reproduced individuals will become identical with their "models". This form of autopoiesis is common in the natural living worlds[4];
  - (*S*3/3) *replication*, by copying, of individuals: this is the case in which the individuals are substituted, when and where they end their existence, with identical individuals;
  - (*S*3/4) *re-conditioning* of individuals: the individuals who loss or are at the point to loss one or more crucial attributes to belong to a species are "repaired" in order to re-establish the full membership to that species.

Comment:

(i) as the name says, the principle of autopoiesis must be internal to that species, that is, it must act internally, based on internal signals that trigger (inside algorithms that the species owns), the maintaining process, of any type of the four ones mentioned;

(ii) the four forms of the principle of autopoiesis can coexist—for example, in the case of reproduction, some individuals need "reparations", provided by medicine, or instructions, provided by school, etc., so the reproduction coexists with re-conditioning;

(iii) this principle is the active and regulative one, while the previous two principles are only constitutive.

1.2 *The Triangle of Species*

There are three categories of species. Based on the sufficiency predicates established at point 1.1.1, we shortly provide some considerations about the three types. More exactly, we shall particularize each principle for each type/category of species, so as to build clear differences among them.

(a) Biological species

- ($S1/B$) the individuals are *biologically living* entities. For the moment we shall say that a living entity must be understood as a dissipative entity, i.e., an open entity (system, process, etc.) liable to operate entropic exchange with its environment. It is to be mentioned that biologically living entities are belonging to Popper's world 1;
- ($S2/B$) the ontological substrate of biological species is *organic*.[5] In other words, the ontological substrate is natural or naturally generated[6];
- ($S3/B$) the principle of autopoiesis is *reproduction*—$S3/B/2$. As shown above, scientists established even an empirical criterion for belonging to a species: the capacity of viable reproduction among the individuals in the case, so that, the off-springs belong, too, to that given species.

Nota bene: reproduction needs a period we can call *the period of adequacy*, for the reproduced individuals to reach the state of adulthood. The individuals of biological species cease to be individuals either in a natural way (natural death) or in different non-natural ways.

(b) Symbolical species

- ($S1/S$) the individuals are *artefactual* entities. An artefactual entity must be understood as an entity that is an effect of the human being's action. In many cases, an artefact is the result of a combination between human action and natural "action" (e.g., agricultural activity), so, whenever there is a human intervention in a process, that process must be considered artefactual. As has already resulted, the artefactual property subsists no matter if there is an intention (deliberativeness) in a human intervention.[7] It is to be mentioned that artefactual entities are belonging to Popper's world 3;

- ($S2/S$) the ontological substrate is *institutional*. The word institutional, here, must be considered in its most extended sense, from the non-codified habit to the largest public organization. An institution is a shared habit or behaviour (so, something objectified) in some degree within a given population, no matter if it is or is not codified in imperative norms;
- ($S3/S$) the principle of autopoiesis is *replication* – $S3/S/3$. The individuals are, generally, clones[8]; they are replicated whenever and wherever it is needed, in the quantity that is required.

(c) Logical species

- ($S1/L$) the individuals are *artefactual* entities. The logical individuals are of the same nature as the symbolic ones, i.e., are instituted in the reality by humans;
- ($S2/L$) the ontological substrate is *cognitive*. This time, the ontological substrate of the individuals is knowledge. A question could be asked: can information be an ontological substrate? In our opinion, the answer is negative: only knowledge (cognizance), namely that information that is already integrated into knowledge[9] can constitute the substrate under discussion;
- $S3/L$) the principle of autopoiesis is *re-conditioning*—$S3/L/4$. The cognitive individuals are always only corroborated (not yet rejected), so they are always under the sign of (empirical) falsifiability or (methodological) reconstruction, no matter it is talking about sciences, arts, religion, politics, and so on.

2 Why Need We the Concept of Species?

The concept of species is an embedding one, throwing a layer of intelligibility on reality (objective, subjective, or objectified). Without a mark of intelligibility, we cannot understand anything. Usually, such a mark of intelligibility is provided by our theories, myths, or simple conjectures but, locally and temporarily, even isolated concepts could deliver an understandability. Regarding the concept of species, its cognitive functions are as follows:

- segments the reality in "bigger slices", easier to see and comprehend and, this way, easier to be captured into behavioural patterns, either logical or pragmatical;
- allows the process of evolution, in its both objectivity and comprehensibility. Indeed, at an individual level (for example, in the biological case) there is only a development process until the individual reaches adulthood. The dynamic transformation of the individuals, i.e., the evolution, happens at the species level only, and it is observable just at the species level. This is also valid for the symbolic and logical species, *mutatis mutandis* (namely, excluding the period of individual's growing towards its phase of adulthood);
- generally, the finality works at the species level—the individuals are "used" to accomplish the species' survival,[10] and the individuals disappear (usually, they die[11]) exactly for the species continue to live. The supra-individual signification of finality is decreasing with the level of consciousness but it remains, still, a basic way things are going;
- although the species does not exist per se (only particulars, e.g., individuals, have reality, in any of the three "species" of reality), the concept in the case has a strong power to intelligibilize the world and, for scientific purposes, its role is invaluable.

3 Symbolic Species—Additional Developments

So, the "portrait" of a generic symbolic species is: constituted by artefactual individuals, having the institution as an ontological substrate (support), and evolving through replication. In this paragraph, we bring some details on the general phenomenology of symbolic species, in order to prepare the introduction of the society as a (*sui generis*) symbolic species.

3.1 *On the Individuals*

An artefact is an output (outcome), either intended or not intended, of an action, either act or abstention, produced by a human being, either as a person or a group, which are objectified.[12] The defining feature of an artefact is, so, its non-natural character. A question can be asked here: the outputs (outcomes) of other biological living entities, except the humans, could they be also considered as artefacts? The answer is not too easy to deliver. Our positioning is as follows:

- the key issue, here, is establishing the "border" between nature and culture. In our opinion, nature "passes" into culture when the capacity for representation is born. By capacity of representation must be understood the capacity of perception without the necessary presence, *in actu*, of the object of that perception (e.g., an anticipation/prediction, a phantasm, a remember, and others similar);
- the "substrate" of the capacity of representation is the consciousness. In the light of today's knowledge, consciousness is owned by human beings only. Although we do not yet know what is the consciousness (for the moment it is a simple label for the "outcome" of brain functioning), it is almost certain that the border between nature and culture is provided by this crucial phenomenon in the life evolution, called consciousness emergence.

Based on the above, the artefacts must be outputs (outcomes) of the living entities endowed with consciousness (i.e., with a capacity of representation). It results that only humans (and human groups, including human societies) are "credited" with the potential to objectify artefacts. For example, the birds' nests, or beavers' lairs, or, generally, the animals' shelters, are edified based on instincts, which, probably, is the antechamber of the consciousness. These outputs (outcomes) have a... natural nature, and the non-human animals are totally immersed in nature.[13] Of course, the non-human animals know that they edify a shelter, but they do not know that they know this. This is the key difference between instinct and consciousness.

So, to conclude, an artefact implies two sufficiency predicates: (a) (C) an entity endowed with consciousness (or, equivalently, with a capacity of representation) (b) (O) an objectifying, in one way or another, of a purpose of the entity in the case. Although the majority of artefacts put together common purposes of many human beings, it is possible that an artefact be a purpose's objectifying of a single person. If the artefact is noted with A, then we can write:

$$A \leftarrow (C) \wedge (O)$$

3.2 *On the Ontological Substrate*

We said that the ontological substrate of the symbolical species is the institution. It is time to define the concept of institution. By institution must be understood a voluntary agreement between at least two persons, regarding a rule of functioning or behaviour. For example, the "how do you do" formula is an institution. Being a voluntary agreement, any institution is a contract.[14] In fact, society (societal) life unfolds almost in totality,[15] under institutions, in the most general sense.

In this large sense, the concept of institution grounds any artefact, since any artefact is an objectifying of a purpose, so it does require the agreement of at least another person. So, the institution can be defined as that artefact that implies at least two persons. If we note the requirement of "at least two persons" agreeing on an artefact with T, , then the institution (I) could be formalized as:

$$I \leftarrow (A) \wedge (T)$$

or

$$I \leftarrow (C) \wedge (O) \wedge (T)$$

3.3 *On the Membrane*

The membrane[16] of symbolic species is of institutional nature, too. The institutional membrane can be, in its turn, of three kinds: (a) normative (M_N); (b) customary/habitual (M_H); (c) aspirational (M_A).

(a) The normative membrane

The normative membrane (M_N) is the symbolic species' most used and visible membrane. It consists in stipulating a norm (most usually, codified, i.e., integrated into Codes[17]) that describes the respective membrane. A normative membrane establishes, for a given symbolic species, at least three borders (limits):

- spatial borders (limits)—its extension;
- temporal borders (limits)—its duration;
- actional borders (limits)—its functionality and behaviour.

The more common (i.e., of a more extended social utility) sharing of a symbolic species, the more normativity is used to implement that symbolic species. This is why, in society, we have different degrees of normativity, which are directly proportional to the communitarian usefulness of the symbolic species. For example, the national defence is more regulated than the access to a library.

The Codes into which the normative membranes are stipulated can be public or private. While the public normative membrane is perfectly transparent,[18] the private one is, usually, known by the individuals who are directly involved in that symbolic species (*Nota bene*: according to the law, some aspects of those membranes must be provided for public awareness).

(b) The customary/habitual membrane

The customary/habitual membrane (M_H) is a membrane that is established between at least two persons, by voluntary agreement. This membrane is, in turn, of two kinds: (i) of general use (ii) of idiosyncratic use.

(i) customary/habitual membrane of general use: addresses the non-formal social interactions and arises, most often, as a necessary result of exactly these interactions—e.g., the daily courtesy greeting, giving a seat in the bus to the elderly, opening the door, by men, for women, to enter. Although they are informal, these cases completely verify the semantic content of the concept of institution;

(ii) customary/habitual membrane of idiosyncratic usage: this kind of membrane can be either formal or informal and addresses the relationships between two (or more) persons so that it is inapplicable to other non-involved persons—e.g., contracts.

The customary/habitual membranes constitute, of course, the vast majority of membranes regarding the symbolic species. Their ventilation is the most rapid and has the largest spread, the rate of birth and death being the biggest within the society. At the same time, this type of membrane is the least predictable among all types of membranes, since they are almost totally at the latitude of the free will of people. It is possible, also, that some customary/habitual membranes become normative ones.

(c) The aspirational membrane

The aspirational membrane addresses those membranes that embed individuals sharing the same visions, purposes, and so on, without existing normative or customary/habitual membranes. Such membranes act, especially, in the political field but, also, in cultural and social fields. The aspirational membranes are more difficult to identify. At the same time, these membranes are very volatile, they rapidly change or disappear and re-appear, embedding other individuals. Although most aspirational membranes are rather local and temporary, cases in which they have extended geographical space and duration can exist. It is possible, also, that some aspirational membranes become normative ones.

3.4 On the Replication

The replication of the individuals inside a symbolic species has some peculiarities as follows:

- it is *deliberative*: since the symbolical species is instituted by an external active principle (generally, this principle is held by a person or a group of persons, sometimes by the society as a whole), any changes (including the replication of individuals) on the symbolical species in the case are decided and objectified by that person (or group) "responsible" of it;

- it, generally, provides *clones*: replication means copying a new individual, similar (when not identical) to other individuals of the involved species. The difference from identical copying is caused by (small) differences in roles or functions that a new individual must accomplish. So, principled, the new individual replicated is a clone;
- occasionally, it provides non-clones: namely, when the species is instituted (is "born") or when radical changes in that species (regarding the role, the functions, the spatial spread, etc.) are needed, so, when different individuals are required. The rapport (rate) between clones and non-clones in the replication process depends on the context, it is, so, an empirical issue, not a theoretical one;
- is made directly to the *adulthood* level: the replication, by contrast to reproduction, delivers individuals directly to the adult stage, ready to accomplish the role/function for which they are "born". So, they do not require a period to grow until the adulthood stage.

3.5 On the General Phenomenology of Symbolic Species

The phenomenology of symbolic species can be synoptically illustrated as shown in Fig. 1.

<u>Discussion</u>

- symbolic species is always an artefact, and it is the result of the desirability of an individual, group, or, at the limit, of society as a whole. Consequently, its arising is "decided" by a purpose, having a teleological (*causa finalis*) ground;
- the purpose always belongs to human being only, so it must be "translated" into the finality of the symbolic species. This is required since a symbolic species, as artefact, has not its own consciousness,[19] so it is mandatory to define a finality of the symbolic species in the case;
- the finality must materialize (objectify) by manifesting a role in the environment of that symbolic species. Consequently, the finality is "translated" into the role of that symbolic species;

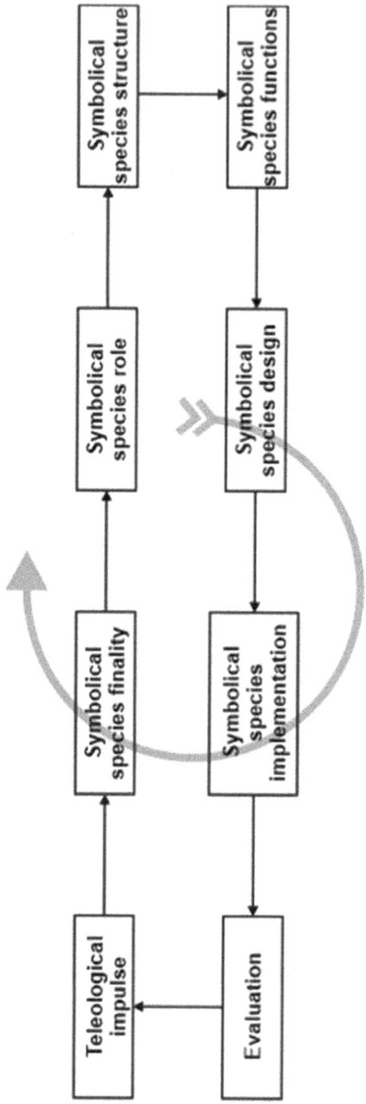

Fig. 1 General phenomenology of symbolic species (*Source* author)

- accomplishing a role is possible based on an internal structure, so, starting from the described role, the set of sufficient[20] structural components of the symbolic specie is designed;
- a role is a set of inter-correlated functions, so the role be achieved with certainty, in an efficient[21] way; consequently, the set of the minimal number of functions to be operated by the symbolic species is designed and put in place;
- after all of the above, the symbolic species is completely designed and the next step is to norm the new entity so it can come into existence inside the society (societal system);
- the functioning of the symbolic species is permanently under monitoring and periodically under evaluation, so that the needed improvements be operated (*Nota bene*: in fact, the symbolic species enters a process of evolutionary path, as the book will show and prove next).

4 A Typology of Symbolic Species

To get a (general) typology of symbolic species it is needed, firstly, to find the set of criteria that can discriminate among different classes/categories of those species.

4.1 Criteria to Discriminate Among Symbolic Species

A set of discriminatory criteria must verify some properties (predicates of sufficiency), as follows:

- delivers clarity, i.e., non-ambiguity in the process of discrimination—it cannot be the case in which a given symbolic species seems to belong to two (or more) different classes based on same criterion[22];
- considers basic/crucial (i.e., definitory) aspects of symbolic species—it cannot be the case in which peripherical features are viewed as discriminators;
- exhausts, as much as possible, the perspectives from which the classes of symbolic species could be established—this sufficiency predicate is the most difficult to accomplish, especially caused by the state of science (or philosophy of science, or methodology of science, or logic of science) at the moment when that set of criteria is proposed;

- guarantees the consistency among the criteria—it cannot be the case in which any two criteria are contradictory between them.

Based on the above conditions (sufficiency predicates) of the criteria, we propose the following distinct criteria to classify symbolic species, namely the ARFIS (arising-regulation-finality-impact-signification) set of criteria:

(i) (C_1) *arising* (entering the real existence)—addresses the mechanism through which the symbolic species comes into reality;
(ii) (C_2) *regulation*—addresses the mechanism through which the symbolic species evolves;
(iii) (C_3) *finality*—addresses the end passively expected or actively established, after the case, according to the purpose (i.e., teleology) involved;
(iv) (C_4) *impact*—addresses the basic effect[23] of a symbolic species functioning, which, usually, is described and contained in the purpose (respectively, finality) of a given symbolic species;
(v) (C_5) *signification*—addresses the subjective (in most cases, strongly idiosyncratic) meaning[24] for the individual, group, or the entire society, after the case, of the functioning, finality, and impact of a given symbolic species.

4.2 Classes of Symbolic Species

According to the criterion C_1, can exist the following (classes of) symbolic species:

- ($SS_1^{C_1}$) symbolic species generated by *invisible hand*—the symbolic species are instituted in an impersonal way, by the simple play of the individual autonomous purposes. The unintended result of such an interaction is a symbolic species which will evolve in the same way, namely impersonally, i.e., non-deliberatively (e.g., the economic system in a free society,[25] most often called free market economy);
- ($SS_2^{C_1}$) symbolic species generated by *individual deliberativeness*—the symbolic species is instituted by an individual, in an intentioned way, in order to get an own objective/purpose, within society (e.g., a private enterprise in the economic, social, cultural, etc., field);

- ($SS_3^{C_1}$) symbolic species generated by *collective deliberativeness*—the symbolic species is instituted by a group of individuals, in an intentional way, in order to get a common objective or purpose of that group (e.g., a trade union within the labour market);
- ($SS_4^{C_1}$) symbolic species generated by the *state*—the symbolic species is instituted by the state (in fact, by different state institutions or organizations), in an intentional way, in order to accomplish the public objective/purpose, generally to provide the public goods.

Discussion

- the majority of symbolic species classes generated by criterion C_1 are of deliberative type. Generally, the spontaneous symbolic species arise at the most general level (e.g., at the societal level), while the deliberative ones could appear at any level;
- among the deliberatively generation of symbolic species, the majority is of $SS_4^{C_1}$ type;
- the set of symbolic species of $SS_2^{C_1}$ and $SS_3^{C_1}$ types constitutes what is generally called civil society (non-governmental organizations – NGOs).

According to the criterion C_2, can exist the following (classes of) symbolic species:

- ($SS_1^{C_2}$) symbolic species regulated through *co-evolution*—those symbolic species that are endowed with autopoiesis and enter the co-evolutionary process with their environment. This way, the symbolic species in this case regulate their path in space and time. For example, this is the very case of the symbolic species of type $SS_1^{C_1}$, that self-regulates by permanent interactions with its environment—we have here what can be called *spontaneous* stabilizers;
- ($SS_2^{C_2}$) symbolic species regulated through *strategy/program*—those symbolic species that, initiated either by invisible hand or by visible hand, once real, are regulated based on deliberativeness, namely following strategies/programs on long term or, at least, medium term (the regulators can be either individuals, group or individuals, or the state); we have here what can be called *discretionary programs*;

- ($SS_3^{C_2}$) symbolic species regulated through ***stabilizers***—those symbolic species that are regulated by ***mixed*** stabilizers. The mixed stabilizers are those stabilizers that are discretionarily introduced (as in the case $SS_2^{C_2}$ but which automatically work (as in the case $SS_1^{C_2}$);

Discussion

- the spontaneous stabilizers are not too... spontaneous—a free market economy plays based on background regulation, at the principle level, not in an anomic way; somewhat, basically, spontaneous stabilizers cannot exist but, theoretically, they can be conceived;
- the most stabilizers in the symbolic species chreods are of mixed category. In fact, the mixed type of a generic stabilizer is the very final purpose of any legislation/regulation in the societal system.

According to the criterion C_3, can exist the following (classes of) symbolic species:

- ($SS_1^{C_3}$) symbolic species with an *economic finality*: are aimed at performing the production and distribution of goods and services needed for the society as a whole;
- ($SS_2^{C_3}$) symbolic species with a *social finality*: are aimed at getting the social purposes of the society (as they are embedded into the adequate symbolic species)—quality of life, social justice (with the freedom accompanied by responsibility), and, generally, social harmony[26];
- ($SS_3^{C_3}$) symbolic species with a *cultural finality*: are aimed at providing the capabilities (namely, the needed and sufficient infrastructures, structures, and supra-structures) for education, cultural life, and others of the same, targeting the realization of (individual) life;
- ($SS_4^{C_3}$) symbolic species with an *ecological finality*: are aimed (especially, in the contemporary era, with its global existential challenges) at delivering the needed and sufficient means and actions to protect the ecological (non-anthropogenic) environment, so that it to be in adequacy with the human general action and life;

- ($SS_5^{C_3}$) symbolic species with a ***political finality***: are aimed at conducting, in a legitimate[27] way, the societal path, according to its desirability and to the Constitution.[28]

Discussion

- the classes of symbolic species according to the criterion of finality express the basic macro-purposes (i.e., aggregated purposes at the societal system level), as they are designed and implemented (i.e., objectified) into those classes;
- the classes of symbolic species have, of course, a historical (i.e., local—spatially and temporally) hypostasis/occurrence, so passing from the level of species to the level of individuals;
- there are no hierarchy of importance/relevance among the classes of symbolic species according to the criterion of finality, those classes try only to exhaust the macro-purposes of a generic societal system.

According to the criterion C_4, can exist the following (classes of) symbolic species:

- ($SS_1^{C_4}$) symbolic species with a ***normative*** impact: introduces into the societal system new norms (rules) of behaviour or functioning, after the case, so completing the normative framework of the society;
- ($SS_2^{C_4}$) symbolic species with a ***functional*** impact: introduces into the societal system new actors (operators) regarding the societal interactions (e.g., new institutions, new organizations, etc.);
- ($SS_3^{C_4}$) symbolic species with a ***cognitive*** impact: introduces into the societal system new institutional agents aimed at producing/improving the knowledge, of any type (scientific, philosophical, metaphysical/theological, artistical, etc.);
- ($SS_4^{C_4}$) symbolic species with an ***axiological*** impact: introduces into the societal system new values and new evaluators in the axiological field, including ethics, aesthetics, social capital, social justice, etc.

Discussion

- the impact of a symbolic species is, of course, very different from its finality—for example, the impact could be different from the designed (i.e., desired) finality, or even contrary to it; or, equally, it could be more than expected, even in the correct arrow/direction of the finality in the case;
- as in the case of the criterion of finality, the classes of symbolic species based on the criterion of impact are aimed at exhausting the basic categories of possible impact (and, equally, desired/expected/designed) at the (generic) societal level, and then, from these categories following to be particularized historical (i.e., local) individuals of such symbolic species;

According to the criterion C_5, can exist the following (classes of) symbolic species:

- ($SS_1^{C_5}$) symbolic species signifying *stable/sustainable order* at the societal level: are those symbolic species that have the (normative and operational) power to monitor, control, and adjust the societal processes and phenomena so that they remain (or become, after the case) stable, i.e., in a small and smooth oscillation around the equilibrium. On a superior level, the stability could be transformed into sustainability, namely, in a stability along medium or long term;
- ($SS_2^{C_5}$) symbolic species signifying *defence of freedom, self-esteem, and reciprocity* within the societal system: are those symbolic species aimed at providing, guaranteeing, and defending the individual freedom of choice, in the largest sense, as well as the general conditions for self-esteem and reciprocal respect in all the subsystems of the societal system;
- ($SS_3^{C_5}$) symbolic species signifying *equal chances for a deserved quality of life*: the equality of chances in the societal kinematics is the basic issue of the concept of liberty implementation. The freedom must lead the individuals to the same potential opportunities[29];
- ($SS_4^{C_5}$) symbolic species signifying the *augmentation of the social capital*[30] within the society: much more than the physical or financial capital, the social capital—for example, the mutuality—is desirable at the societal level. After a given level of the average standard of

life is reached, the social capital "production" becomes the highest purpose of individuals and society as a whole.

Discussion

- it must be said that the perception of a phenomenon is much more important than the phenomenon as such. The decision and the behaviour (actions, either acts of abstentions, after the case) are primarily based on the perception. But the perceptions lead exactly to the signification, as this concept is defined in this study;
- by contrast with the other criteria, the signification introduces a hierarchy among the classes established. The decreasing order of relevance is just that of notations (from 1 to 4), so the most relevant symbolic species is $SS_1^{C_5}$—because no one of the other symbolic species can plenary objectify without the societal order;
- the freedom and self-esteem is more important, relevant, and desirable than the quality of life, which, in turn, is more relevant than the social capital, since the individuals must firstly survive, then they will develop the social capital subspecies.

4.3 A Little Formalism

Based on the five criteria we can identify 20 classes of relevant and distinct symbolic species within the societal system. As previously said, a given symbolic species can belong to one, two, or more criteria, as it is suggested in Annex 1.

Starting from the findings in Annex 1, any classes of symbolic species can be written, formally, as follows:

$$SS_x^y = \left[C_{k(\alpha)}^{\alpha} | C_{k(\beta)}^{\beta}; C_{k(\gamma)}^{\gamma}; C_{k(\delta)}^{\delta}; C_{k(\varepsilon)}^{\varepsilon} \right]$$

where

- $y \in \{1, 2, 3, 4, 5\}$
- $\alpha, \beta, \gamma, \delta, \varepsilon$: indicate one of the five criteria for establishing the classes of symbolic species;

- the criterion at the left of the constant "|" is considered the basic criterion of belonging, and the criteria at the right of that constant are considered secondary criteria of belonging.

Nota bene: in fact, if the values for x and y are given, then $k(\alpha) = x$, and $\alpha = y$.

For example, if $x = 2$, and $y = 3$, then:

$$SS_2^3 = \left[C_2^3 | C_{3,4}^1; C_2^2; C_1^4; C_3^5\right]$$

Namely, the classes of symbolic species with a social finality arise either by collective deliberativeness or is generated by the state, is regulated through a strategy/program, has a normative impact, and signifies providing equal chances for a deserved quality of life.

This formalism brings some value added in examining and handling the concept and typology of symbolic species as follows:

(i) allows a quasi-comparability among symbolic species, by the integrated set of criteria proposed;
(ii) highlights the advantages and disadvantages of a given symbolic species, compared with other symbolic species;
(iii) makes it possible to improve a given symbolic species, by enhancing its positioning related to one criterion or other;
(iv) allows the concatenation (either serially or parallelly) of different symbolic species so that a given objective be reached—so building up a *sui generis* logic of symbolic species in causal chains.

4.4 Some Formal Developments

The symbolic species can be either coexistent or successive to one another. Based on the formalism of symbolic species, proposed above, we think it can be discussed further three issues: (a) behavioural interactions between symbolic species; (b) co-evolutive pre-dispositions of symbolic species; (c) generative propensities of some symbolic species.

(a) Behavioural interactions

The behaviour consists of the set of possible (not actual only) relationships between a system and its environment, that is, between a symbolic species and all the other symbolic species that compose the environment of the first one.

The behaviour is allowed just through the compatibilities identified in Annex 1 regarding the criteria grounding the typology of symbolic species. Let us presuppose two symbolic species with the following formal expression, as randomly chosen from Annex 1:

$$SS_2^4 = \left[C_2^4 | C_{1,2}^1; C_{1,3}^2; C_1^3; C_1^5\right]$$

that is, a symbolic species with a functional impact (C_2^4), and

$$SS_1^3 = \left[C_1^3 | C_{1,2}^1; C_{1,3}^2; C_2^4; C_1^5\right]$$

that is, a symbolic species generated by a collective deliberativeness.

There are five compatibilities between the two symbolic species, as follows:

- regarding the criterion 1 (way of arising): both symbolic species can arise based either on invisible hand or individual deliberativeness ($C_{1,2}^1$)—two compatibilities;
- regarding the criterion 2 (way of regulation): both symbolic species can be regulated either by co-evolution or by stabilizers ($C_{1,3}^2$)—two compatibilities;
- regarding the criterion 5 (signification): both symbolic species have the same signification, namely the stability of societal order—one compatibility.

The more the points (criteria) of compatibility, the more the probability to be developed behavioural interactions between two (or more) symbolic species. Probably, that probability is directly proportional with the number of criteria of compatibility but such a quantitative measure must be tested further. At any rate, that proportionality will be rather non-linear than linear.

(b) Co-evolution pre-dispositions

The co-evolution of the symbolic species is, in considering the basic objective of the present book, the most interesting phenomenon linked to the concept of symbolic species.

(i) some preliminaries

Evolution (as a process) is understood as a state change of an entity, no matter its nature, under the pressure of either itself or (most often) its environment. The pressure is manifested as selection (or rejection, after the case) of the new state, while the new state is "proposed" by mutation exerted on that entity (*Nota bene*: in fact, as it will be shown later, the mutation is exerted on what is called genotype of the entity in the case). In reality, mutations can appear not only in the entity but, also, in the entity's environment or both of them. Consequently, any evolution is, essentially, a co-evolution—both the entity and its environment change relative to one another. In such circumstances, the entity plays the role of environment for the... environment, while the environment plays the role of entity for the... entity. In what follows, we shall consider, of course, only co-evolution processes.

(ii) about the co-evolution pre-dispositions

Since co-evolution means a reciprocal influence of an entity on another entity (*Nota bene*: of course, more than two entities can be, also, engaged in a co-evolutionary process), we must find the connection points, that is, the possibilities of some (co-evolutionary) synapses. We believe that the co-evolutionary pre-dispositions of symbolic species are held among the criteria that led to the symbolic species typology. In Fig. 2, this idea is synoptically developed.

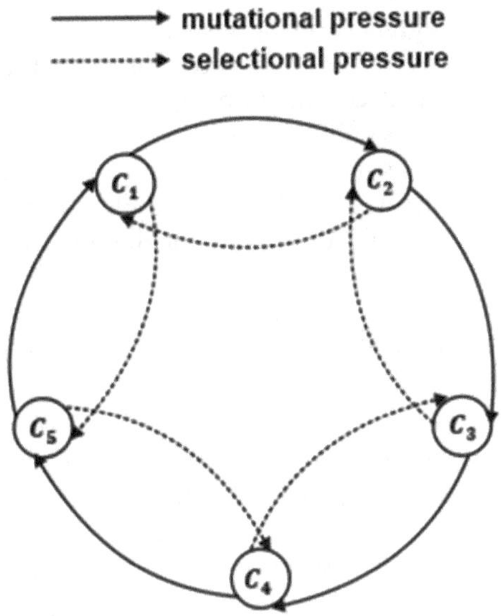

Fig. 2 Possible co-evolutionary synapses of symbolic species (*Source* author)

Discussion

- the way in which a symbolic species arises (C^1) can trigger mutations on the way in which a symbolic species is regulated (C^2); reciprocally, the way of regulating in a symbolic species can select the way in which a symbolic species arises;
- the way in which a symbolic species is regulated (C^2) can trigger mutations on the way in which a symbolic species accomplishes its finality[31] (C^3); reciprocally, the finality of a symbolic species can select the way in which a symbolic species is regulated;
- the way in which a symbolic species achieves its finality (C^3) can trigger mutations on the nature of the impact that a symbolic species introduces into the reality (C^4); reciprocally, the impact of a symbolic species can select the way in which a symbolic species achieves its finality;
- the nature (and, of course, the size, the intensity, and other parameters of interest) of the impact of a symbolic species (C^4) can trigger mutations on the signification (*Nota bene*: not of the meaning!) that a symbolic species bears for the human being (C^5); reciprocally, the

signification of a symbolic species can select the nature (together with other parameters of it) that a symbolic species exerted on the involved human being;

- the signification that a symbolic species bears (C^5) can trigger mutations on the way in which a symbolic species arises (C^1); reciprocally, the way in which a symbolic species arises can select the signification which is of interest for the involved human being.

(iii) basic assessment of co-evolution pre-dispositions

Firstly, it can be said that, in any discussion about the co-evolutionary pre-dispositions of symbolic species, in the background always stays the human being (person) which initiated and/or is entitled with handling the symbolic species in the case.

Secondly, it seems to exist a circular (i.e., indefinite resuming) of the co-evolutionary process among the categories of symbolic species as they are generated by the criteria established. This could suggest that there is an internal (perhaps, of autopoietic nature) mechanism for a co-evolutionary entanglement of those categories of symbolic species. In fact, in what follows, exactly this (presumed) property of the set of symbolic species working inside a given society will guide us to propose an evolutionary model of the societal system.

Thirdly, some formal examinations can identify, in a more analytical way, the co-evolutionary pre-dispositions of symbolic species. A sketch in this matter is provided below—we shall exemplify only for the pair ($C^1 - C^2$), leaving the reader to develop the rest of analyses, based on the model presented.

The set of C_1 classes of symbolic species is: $C^1 = \left\{SS_1^{C_1}, SS_2^{C_1}, SS_3^{C_1}, SS_4^{C_1}\right\}$, and the set of C_2 classes is: $C^2 = \left\{SS_1^{C_2}, SS_2^{C_2}, SS_3^{C_2}\right\}$. According to Annex 1, the two vectors of classes for the two criteria are:

$$C^1 = \begin{pmatrix} SS_1^1 = [C_1^1 | C_1^2; C_1^3; C_2^4; C_1^5] \\ SS_2^1 = [C_2^1 | C_1^2; C_1^3; C_2^4; C_1^5] \\ SS_3^1 = [C_3^1 | C_2^2; C_2^3; C_1^4; C_3^5] \\ SS_4^1 = [C_4^1 | C_2^2; C_2^3; C_1^4; C_2^5] \end{pmatrix}$$

$$C^2 = \begin{pmatrix} SS_1^2 = \left[C_1^2 | C_{1,2}^1; C_1^3; C_2^4; C_1^5 \right] \\ SS_2^2 = \left[C_2^2 | C_{3,4}^1; C_2^3; C_1^4; C_3^5 \right] \\ SS_3^2 = [C_3^2 | C_1^3; C_2^4; C_1^5] \end{pmatrix}$$

Two issues should be examined here: (1) if there is something like a co-evolutionary mark of two symbolic species; (2) what could be the meaning of such a co-evolutionary mark.

(1) about co-evolutionary mark

By the co-evolutionary mark we should understand something as the chance or, somehow, probability of a pair of (or, in some cases, many) categories[32] of symbolic species to interact between them so that generating in each other both mutations and selective action. Based on the simple formalism in writing a symbolic species, we propose that such a co-evolutionary mark be determined as the number of coincidence between the compatibilities of the two (or more) categories of symbolic species considered. For example, for the classes C^1 and C^2, we can count the coincidences of the compatibilities, as follows (Table 1). *Nota bene*: inside parentheses are written the coincidence of category, and outside parentheses are written the coincidences of classes. The coincidences at level of classes will be quantified as "1", while the coincidences at level of category will be quantified as "0.5". At total will be the sum.

Discussion

- at category level, between C^1 and C^2, the evolutionary mark is 26.5;
- at class level, the maximum evolutionary mark is 3 (for five cases) and the minimum evolutionary mark is 1.5 (in six cases); a distinct value is 2.5 (between C_2^2 and C_4^1);

Table 1 Calculating the (absolute) evolutionary mark

C^1 C^2	$SS_1^1 \equiv C_1^1$	$SS_2^1 \equiv C_2^1$	$SS_3^1 \equiv C_3^1$	$SS_4^1 \equiv C_4^1$	*Total*
$SS_1^2 \equiv C_1^2$	C_1^3; C_2^4; C_1^5 – **3**	C_1^3; C_2^4; C_1^5 – **3**	(C^3); (C^4); (C^5) – **1.5**	(C^3); (C^4); (C^5) – **1.5**	6 + 3 = 9
$SS_2^2 \equiv C_2^2$	(C^3); (C^4); (C^5) – **1.5**	(C^3); (C^4); (C^5) – **1.5**	C_2^3; C_1^4; C_3^5 – **3**	C_2^3; C_1^4; (C^5) – **2.5**	5 + 3.5 = 8.5
$SS_3^2 \equiv C_3^2$	C_1^3; C_2^4; C_1^5 – **3**	C_1^3; C_2^4; C_1^5 – **3**	(C^3); (C^4); (C^5) – **1.5**	(C^3); (C^4); (C^5) – **1.5**	6 + 3 = 9
Total	6 + 1.5 = 7.5	6 + 1.5 = 7.5	3 + 3 = 6	2 + 3.5 = 5.5	26.5

Source author

- to make comparable the values of evolutionary marks, perhaps a normalization at the real interval [0, 1] could be of usefulness:
  - the maximum possible value for the evolutionary mark at classes level is 4 (all the four criteria are coincident), while the minimum value is 0 (no criteria is coincident)
  - the formula of normalization of normalization is:

$$\overline{e}_M = \frac{e_M^e - e_M^{min}}{e_M^{max} - e_M^{min}}$$

where $\overline{e}_M$ is the normalized evolutionary mark, e_M^e is the effective (measured) evolutionary mark, e_M^{min} is the minimum value or evolutionary mark ($e_M^{min} = 0$), e_M^{max} is the maximum value of evolutionary mark ($e_M^{max} = 4$).

So,

$$\overline{e}_M = \frac{\overline{e}_M}{4}$$

- this way, the normalized values of the evolutionary marks for the pair (C^1, C^2) are the following (Table 2).

Table 2 Calculating the (normalized) evolutionary mark

C^1 / C^2	$SS_1^1 \equiv C_1^1$	$SS_2^1 \equiv C_2^1$	$SS_3^1 \equiv C_3^1$	$SS_4^1 \equiv C_4^1$	*Total*
$SS_1^2 \equiv C_1^2$	0.75	0.75	0.375	0.375	2.25
$SS_2^2 \equiv C_2^2$	0.375	0.375	0.75	0.625	2.125
$SS_3^2 \equiv C_3^2$	0.75	0.75	0.375	0.375	2.25
Total	1.875	1.875	1.5	1.375	6.625

Source author, based on Table 1

Discussion

- the chances to happen evolutionary interactions between the classes of symbolic species are directly proportional with the normalized evolutionary mark (NEM);
- the most probable such interactions could take place between the following pairs of classes of symbolic species: (C_1^1, C_1^2); (C_2^1, C_1^2); (C_3^1, C_2^2); (C_1^1, C_3^2); (C_2^1, C_3^2);
- the most improbable such interactions could take place between the following pairs of classes of symbolic species: (C_3^1, C_1^2); (C_4^1, C_1^2); (C_1^1, C_2^2); (C_2^1, C_2^2); (C_3^1, C_3^2); (C_4^1, C_3^2);
- an intermediate case is the pair (C_4^1, C_2^2).

Nota bene: Of course, the same analysis can be done for all the pairs of interest in Fig. 2, so a "map" of the co-evolutionary pre-dispositions for the (generic) item called symbolic species can be obtained. Since the very procedure to do that was presented above, we leave it to the reader's option to complete the analysis in the matter.

(2) functioning of co-evolutionary mark

Now, we should describe the functioning of the co-evolutionary mark. The following considerations provide a sketch about how the symbolic species (could) interact in an evolutionary way:

- the co-evolutionary interaction takes place at the level of classes of symbolic species, not at the category (i.e., criteria) level;
- regarding the categories, the co-evolutionary process unfolds in a cascade manner:
  - the highest NEM triggers a first mutation, according to the specifications in Fig. 2—for example, as considering the classes SS_1^1 and SS_1^2 (between which NEM is 0.75), a mutation will be induced by SS_1^1 into SS_1^2, and the last will select (or not) that mutation;
  - concomitantly or successively, depending on the particular context, SS_2^1 can initiate a mutation in SS_1^2 (between which NEM is, also, 0.75), with the response, regarding selection, from SS_1^2;
  - the next possible co-evolutionary interaction is between SS_3^1 and SS_2^2 (with NEM equal to 0.75), with a mutation from the first class to the second one;
  - the process will continue with the pairs (SS_1^1, SS_3^2 – NEM is 0.75) (SS_2^1, SS_3^2 – NEM is 0.75), then the next values of NEM enter the co-evolutionary process: (SS_4^1, SS_2^2 – NEM is 0.625), (SS_3^1, SS_1^2 – NEM is 0.375) and so on, with all remained NEMs with the value 0.375.

Additional comment—the keystone species

Recently, scientists have introduced the concept of keystone species in the debate. A keystone species (KS) is considered a species that, in a given ecosystem, has the determinant role in surviving that ecosystem as such and, correlatively, all the other species. More precisely, a KS provides the basic principles and mechanisms in a given ecosystem for that ecosystem to maintain its sustainability (NeSmith, 2021; Pongen, 2024). Although the concept of KS was proposed for the biological species, it is easily expandable to informational species and (what is interesting for us) to symbolic species. In the biological ecosystems, the KS is identified by counterfactual experiments—the presupposed species as being a KS is eradicated from a given ecosystem and, if the ecosystem collapses (including other species contained), then it is concluded that the eradicated/extracted species is the very KS. Since the counterfactual experiment acts as a corroborative or non-corroborative (i.e., rejective) test, this way of establishing the KS is the falsifiability testing, so it is scientific. In what follows, the concept of KS will play a significant role regarding, this time, the symbolic species, especially the societal symbolic species.

(c) Generative propensities

We saw at point (b) above that the co-evolutionary pre-dispositions of the categories of symbolic species reside in the criteria established for the symbolic species typology. This time, namely, regarding the generative propensities of the symbolic species, we thing these propensities should be searched inside each criterion, more precisely, among the classes identified by each criterion. It is talking about the possibility (or, in fact, probability, since the propensity[33] is a species of objective probability assignable to a singular event, that is, without an archive of past events which can provide a distribution of probabilities, i.e., a pattern of behaviour) that a class of symbolic species inside a given criterion be able to generate another class of symbolic species, inside the same criterion.[34]

Let us consider the above C^1 criterion (arising, i.e., way of emergence). The formal expression of this category is:

$$C^1 = \left\{SS_1^1, SS_2^1, SS_3^1, SS_4^1\right\}$$

where SS_1^1 means symbolic species generated by invisible hand, SS_1^2 means symbolic species generated by individual deliberativeness, SS_1^3 means symbolic species generated by collective deliberativeness, SS_1^4 means symbolic species generated by the state.

We propose a *sui generis* quantification of the propensity of a given symbolic species inside criterion C^1 to generate another symbolic species of the classes inside the same criterion, by assigning natural numbers to the relationships between the four classes.[35] *Nota bene*: the highest propensity has the number 1, and the weaker propensity, the greater the number. In fact, such a quantification looks as x/y, where x means the propensity, and y means the type of propensity, so that $x \in \mathbb{N}$, and $y \in \{r, i, m\}$, where r means "through regulation", i means "through imitation", m means "through multiplication". Figure 3 suggests such a phenomenology.

<u>Discussion</u>

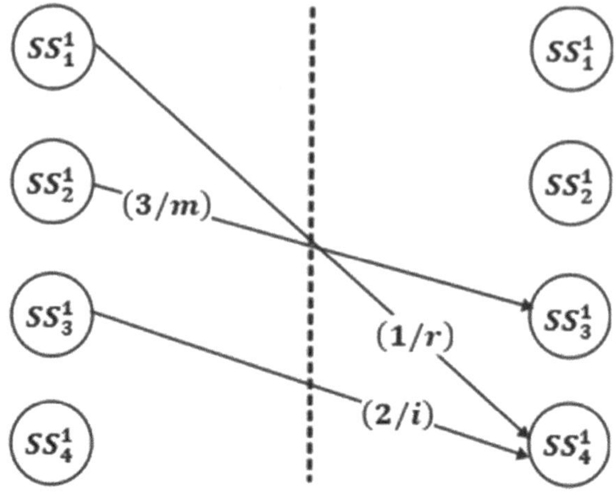

Fig. 3 Generating propensities inside the criterion C^1 (*Source* author)

- a symbolic species generated by the invisible hand (SS^1_1) is, generally, of interest to the state, since it could produce adverse (or even perverse[36]) effects; consequently, the state is willing, most often, to proceed to the regulation of such symbolic species, i.e., to build up SS^1_4;
- a symbolic species generated by individual deliberativeness (SS^1_2) is observed and imitated by other individuals so, in the medium or long term, it can be transformed into a new class of symbolic species collectively deliberated, namely SS^1_3;
- a symbolic species generated by collective deliberativeness (SS^1_3) becomes observable from the state side and, like in the case of SS^1_1, the state will proceed to regulate this symbolic species, so transforming it in SS^1_4.

Nota bene: of course, based on the above method, all the other 19 cases of symbolic species classes can be analysed. This way, a general map of generational propensities can be identified—they are of great relevance in deciphering the evolutionary background of the symbolic species.

5 Society as a Symbolic Species

5.1 The Genesis of Society

A society is generated by the arising of a structure of system type, in a set of generic elements. A structure of system type is characterized by emerging, from the elements embedded inside a membrane of some kind, of two qualitatively opposed components: (a) a leading component, from which orders/commands regarding the functioning and behaviour are transmitted to the rest of components; (b) driven components, from which reports regarding the accomplishing of the orders/commands are transmitted to the leading component.

The above considerations are valid for any social arrangements of living entities of any kind. In other words, not every social arrangement is a systemic one—the non-systemic arrangements are of network type, not systemic ones. In a network, all components of the set in the case are equal vertically among them (there are no hierarchies), although, usually, they are not identical (or similar) horizontally. Even if in a social arrangement there are actions of cooperation among the components, that is, there are convergent actions to a common target. This cooperation is spontaneous, non-regulated by an instance within that social arrangement—for example, as happens, for example, the convergent actions in an ants social network, or as happens in the case of the invisible hand in the economic field of mankind. So, a social arrangement is always of network type. A network becomes a system when the components separate into the two sorts of components above mentioned. We can say that a system arises from a network by this separation of roles/functions (*Nota bene*: in the case of humans, historians, sociologists, or anthropologists talk about separation of power, no matter its nature).

In the case of human social arrangement, the leading component is called *the state* (with its institutions, authorities, and agencies)—Annex 2 provides some details regarding the most considered theories in the matter of the mechanisms through which a state arises from social arrangements. Although the "hidden" target is to explain the concept of social justice, in its whole generality and necessity, the theories in the case must discuss the process of the state birth from a given social arrangement—the social arrangement is considered, in the three approaches presented, as... natural, i.e., generated by the human nature and the needs of surviving and evolution.

5.2 *The Necessary Character of the State's Birth*

From Annex 2, the necessary (i.e., mandatory, inevitable, without alternative) character of the state's birth is obvious enough. However, two issues should be analysed in this point: (i) the contingent character of leading components arising in a social arrangement; (ii) the special nature of the state as a leading component in the mankind system.

(i) The leading component as a contingent entity

The initial (originary) position, in Rawls's theory of state emerging, and the agglutination of a dominant association aimed at preserving individual freedom, in Nozick's theory of state emerging, are, both, possible but non-necessary, i.e., they are contingent. There are many sets of living entities in Nature that remained, for eons, at the social mode of organizing, that is, inside networks.

However, some reasoning could shake this opinion. We shall make some considerations:

- in the non-teleological worlds (e.g., social groups of animals), there is, almost always, an α-individual, which leads the group in their behaviour: defence of the territory, searching food and water, ensuring the best genes in the biological reproduction, etc. In fact, the α-individual is a kind of leading component of that set (group) of individuals;
- as the group in the case is, as said, a non-teleological one, the α-individual constitutes a self-entitlement as such, based on a kind of power, namely (in this case) the physical power (an α-individual is the biggest and strongest individual)[37];
- the two mentions above contain an indication about a quasi-necessity of emerging the leading component in a given set of individuals, that is, a necessary character of passing from network to system.[38]

(ii) The special nature of the state

The state, as a leading component (i.e., an individual) arising in a social network of humans, stays in a special world among the living entities worlds, since:

- the social network of humans is a teleological one, i.e., the individuals inside the network make choices (take decisions and initiate actions) based on purposes. So, both the original position (Rawls) in which the basic structure of the society/state is established, and the dominant association (Nozick) aimed at defending individual freedom are results of (free) deliberativeness;
- we usually say, regarding the social entities purpose based, that they are artefacts. The entire social construction (institutions, organizations, rules/norms of behaviour, and other of the same)—including, of course, the state—constitutes artefacts. Any artefact is an objectification of a purpose, either individual or collective (communitarian)[39];
- the state—the α-component of the social system[40]—like in the non-teleological worlds, can be dethroned, regularly by political elections (but, also, by force, like revolutions or coups d'état);
- we think that, by its characteristics, the state, as leading component in a social/societal system has a necessary nature, that is, at a moment in its historicity, a social network of humans will generate a state, no matter its particular way of being and functioning, more or less complicated or more or less performative.

It can be formulated a (symmetrical) question: if the state arising is (somewhat) necessary, what about its disappearing? We provide some short considerations in that matter:

- there are, of course, in the social/political philosophy, theories or conjectures regarding the disappearing of the state—*Nota bene*: by the vanishing of the state, the social system becomes, from a logical point of view, a social network—for example, the Marxist theory (anchored, however, to the capitalist stage of the mankind political and economic organizing, so considering the state of supra-structural device to exploit the people) but, also, the relentless and somewhat blind insistence of libertarians regarding the uselessness of the state in a society that tends towards prosperity;
- in our opinion (coming from, as we think, a universal principle of organizing the worlds), the increasing of the complicatedness of the generic worlds (communities of living entities) necessarily causes a

"preference" for systems to the detriment of networks. This "principle of preference" leads to a necessary way of maintaining (at least inside the teleological worlds, like the humans one) the state as leading component. Of course, the historical context (including the technological one,[41] or the ethical commandments) will necessarily lead us to large (possible, radical) change in the structure, role, and functions of the state in future, but, logically, the state will "survive";
- in conclusion, we think the disappearing of the state, in its conceptual bases, is not a necessary process, although its form could be, in the long term, unrecognizable.

5.3 *What Kind of Species Is the Society?*

As we have seen before, the society arises when, in the human social network, one component becomes the leading one, so transforming the network into a system. That leading component is just the state, and the human social system endowed with a state is called society (or a societal system). In other words, a social system becomes a societal one with the sufficient condition that its leading component be/becomes a state. It is problematic if, in Nature, when, regularly, there are social systems, the leading components (i.e., the so-called alpha-individual, or alpha-family) function as a state, i.e., as a general regulator and guardian of the rules imposed regarding the both functionality and behaviour of the rest of individuals and sub-groups.[42] From an anthropological perspective on the concept of state, we think it is hazardous (and, perhaps, not too productive) to introduce the state in the non-human social systems.

Returning to the topic of this paragraph, we shall proceed further to examine if the society (societal system) as it was built previously verifies, from a logical point of view, the attributes/sufficient predicates of a symbolic species. Our intuition, based on the general considerations regarding the concept of symbolic species, tells us yes, but any intuition must be corroborated by rationality.

Let us remember the set of sufficiency predicates of a generic symbolic species (see point 1.1.2):

- ($S1/S$) the individuals are *artefactual* entities;
- ($S2/S$) the ontological substrate is *institutional*;
- ($S3/S$) the principle of autopoiesis is *replication.*

6 Discussion

(1) about the sufficiency predicate *S1/S*

We have here to discuss the most important issue in society as a symbolic species. We said that a generic symbolic species contains individuals of artefactual nature. Since the artefacts are produced by humans (as either individuals or communities) for humans' use, it results that, inside a symbolic species, there are, alongside the artefacts, even the humans themselves. In fact, it must be concluded that a symbolic species in human societies contains two basic categories of individuals: (a) human beings; (b) artefacts. *Nota bene*: of course, a symbolic species contains also: (c) living non-human entities; (d) non-anthropogenic entities (Nature) but the last two components are not basic, they are complementary, both structurally and functionally. Consequently, the sufficiency predicate *S1/S* must be reformulated as: the individuals are both humans and artefacts. This means that the symbolic species inside the human society (at the limit, the society itself, as a whole) must be considered to have a mixed character, referring to both humans and artefacts. With this clarification, we think the society verifies the sufficiency predicate *S1/S* of the concept of symbolic species, based on the *a fortiori* argument.

(2) about the sufficiency predicate *S2/S*

This sufficiency predicate operates a separation inside the "population" of artefacts. So, some artefacts are of institutional nature, while other artefacts are of a non-institutional nature. We must say that an institution does not need to be codified, that is, to be included in a norm which is opposable to tertiary individuals (in fact, to the entire society). For example, the "thank you" is a norm of behaviour, i.e., an institution which is not codified as such, while the fiscal policy is a (macro)norm, i.e., an institution which is codified. When we talk about society, of course, we talk about a codified institution. Consequently, the society, as a whole, constitutes an institution, i.e., it has, as an ontological substrate, the institution. In this context, we appreciate that the society, as codified as an institutional artefact, verifies the second sufficiency predicate of a symbolic species, namely *S2/S*.

Nota bene: as the ontological substrate of the society is of institutional type, it peremptorily results that the membrane which separates the society from non-society must be, also, of institutional type.[43]

(3) about the sufficiency predicate *S3/S*

We have shown that a generic symbolic species has, as an autopoietic (species of) principle, the replication (*S3/S/3* – see point 1.1.2). Let us examine if the society (the societal system) verifies this sufficiency predicate.

- replication, by contrast to reproduction, produces directly adult individuals. This means that the individuals do not need a period of growing, educating, etc., they are capable, once replicated, to accomplish the tasks pre-established inside the system concerned. When we refer to the society, we see that its components (and it as a whole) are replicated at the very moments they are required by the functionality and behaviour of that society, directly as "adults";
- replication implies some deliberativeness in designing and performing the new versions of the components. But the society, as an artefact, and its components as well are deliberatively created and replicated, so it seems that the society verifies this sufficiency predicate, too;
- however, just like in the case of the sufficiency predicate *S1/S*, here we have a mixture, since, alongside the replication, another sort of autopoiesis can work in the case of society, namely the re-conditioning. Indeed, we must accept that a given component inside the society, which does not anymore accomplish its tasks at the required standards (either quantitative or qualitative), can be improved without eliminating it, at least for the moment, so that this improvement brings that component at the established standards. In fact, the autopoiesis in the case of the society acts by these two actional vectors: replication and re-conditioning. It is expected that, when a problem arises, the first step to perform is the re-conditioning and, if this step does not repair according the requirements, the next step is that of replication—*Nota bene*: of course, replication is, from the beginning, made at the required standards.

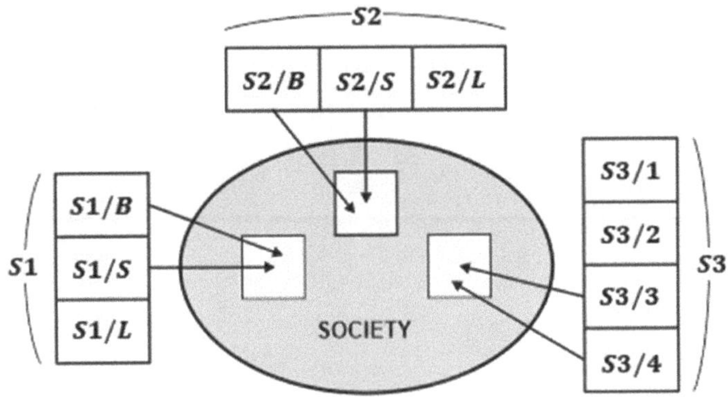

Fig. 4 Society (societal system) as symbolic species (*Source* author)

Based on the previous, we conclude that the society verifies the S3/S sufficiency predicate and more exactly, verifies a mixed sufficiency predicate: $(S3/S/3) \wedge (S3/S/4)$. Figure 4 shows, synoptically, the society (societal system) as a symbolic species.

Annex 1: A Topology of Classes of Symbolic Species

See Table (1.3)

Annex 2: The Binomial "State–Society"

The concept of state and the concept of society are inseparable—the state and society appear simultaneously, neither of them is a cause for (or effect of) the other, they exist or do not exist simultaneously, in tandem. With a term increasingly used (taken from the terminology of Quantum Physics), they represent entangled concepts that are found in a phenomenon of causal, structural, and functional correlation as strong as it is mysterious.

The Social

We will start from the concept of social. This concept, which has the nature of an attribute or predicate, that is, of a property, refers to the state of any system, "endowed" with living entities, contemporary with each other, either human or non-human, who live together, in terms of

Table 3 Multiple belonging of some classes of symbolic species

		C_1				C_2			C_3					C_4				C_5			
		$SS_1^{C_1}$	$SS_2^{C_1}$	$SS_3^{C_1}$	$SS_4^{C_1}$	$SS_1^{C_2}$	$SS_2^{C_2}$	$SS_3^{C_2}$	$SS_1^{C_3}$	$SS_2^{C_3}$	$SS_3^{C_3}$	$SS_4^{C_3}$	$SS_5^{C_3}$	$SS_1^{C_4}$	$SS_2^{C_4}$	$SS_3^{C_4}$	$SS_4^{C_4}$	$SS_1^{C_5}$	$SS_2^{C_5}$	$SS_3^{C_5}$	$SS_4^{C_5}$
C_1	$SS_1^{C_1}$					x			x						x			x			
	$SS_2^{C_1}$					x			x						x			x			
	$SS_3^{C_1}$						x			x				x						x	
	$SS_4^{C_1}$						x			x				x					x		
C_2	$SS_1^{C_2}$	x	x						x						x			x			
	$SS_2^{C_2}$			x	X					x				x						x	
	$SS_3^{C_2}$								x						x			x			
C_3	$SS_1^{C_3}$	x	x			x		x							x			x			
	$SS_2^{C_3}$			x	X		x							x						x	
	$SS_3^{C_3}$															x					x
	$SS_4^{C_3}$													x				x			
	$SS_5^{C_3}$													x					x		
C_4	$SS_1^{C_4}$			x	X		x			x		x	x							x	

			C_1				C_2			C_3				C_4				C_5			
	$SS_2^{C_4}$	x	x			x		x	x									x			
	$SS_3^{C_4}$										x									x	
	$SS_4^{C_4}$																				x
C_5	$SS_1^{C_5}$	x	x			x		x	x			x			x						
	$SS_2^{C_5}$				X								x								
	$SS_3^{C_5}$			x			x			x				x		x					
	$SS_4^{C_5}$										x						x				

Source author

physical area, targeted resources, and carried out actions, those entities belonging to the same species. We do not develop the concept of species[44] here, but we insist on saying that social is a property of a community of living entities belonging to the same species. Therefore, the social characterizes this living together, within a species, which implies a certain structure of the community in question, including a division of the activities carried out, often this division of activities being reflected in a somatic division of the individuals comprising the species in question. It should be noted that the social implies, in addition to the structure supporting communal living, specific to the community in question, a set of rules of interaction between the members of that community, which arise spontaneously, generated by the interactions between individuals, through the "trial-and-error" method.[45] Therefore, the social implies only a mutual horizontal positioning between the members of the respective community, and the spontaneity (at the community level), even if there is deliberation at the individual level, dominates that phenomenology.

The Societal

The social, that is, the property of the social, does not yet constitute (or establish) a society. It only "ensures" a community of living, including access to resources, based on self-established rules, originating from the own functioning (own interactions) of that community. Society appears when an individual or a group of individuals in the community concludes that that community must be led based on an "intellectual project". We use the phrase "intellectual project" in its modern sense, because in any community that becomes a society (as we will show below), the emergence of such an "intellectual project" is needed. Essentially, an intellectual project is a representation, in the consciousness of an individual (or a group of individuals) of the desirable state of the community of which that individual (or that group) is a part. Today, we would say, it is a dream, in the social, not psychological, sense of the term, shared by a (relatively) restricted group in a given social community. Here, the theory proposed by Nozick (1997) regarding the emergence of the state (the ultra-minimal state, respectively the minimal state) is interesting (see below).

The State

There are three modern theories regarding the emergence of the state: (a) John Rawls' theory (*fairness* theory), which is a procedural contractarianism; (b) Robert Nozick's theory (*entitlement* theory), which is a resilient contractarianism; (c) Martha C. Nussbaum's theory (*capabilities* theory), which is a non-contractarianist theory.[46]

(1) Procedural contractarian theory

The basic elements of this theory are discussed below. Rawls considers that the determining element (in the structural sense) of a theory of the state is that of social justice, and the determined element (in the causal sense) of social justice is the *basic structure* of society, by which he understands the set of axioms/principles that deductively underpin the normative canvas (both formal and informal) of society. It should be noted that Rawls treats the concept of society in the most generic (abstract) sense, which is understandable from the perspective of his goal of providing a general theory of justice.[47] The theory proposed by Rawls also generates its contractarian-proceduralist nature.[48]

The entire theoretical construction is based on a social state (a state in which society finds itself) that Rawls calls a *well-ordered society*.[49] In his impeccable logical manner, the author defines the concept of a well-ordered society through two sufficiency predicates: (a) each individual accepts (and knows that other individuals accept) the same principles of justice; (b) social institutions satisfy (and all individuals know this) the principles of justice. Obviously, if at least one of these sufficiency predicates is violated, that society is not well ordered. The main working hypotheses, of a methodological type, on the basis of which Rawls builds his theory of the state are the following:

(1.a) generalities

- society is considered to have the capacity to allocate/re-allocate resources (of any kind), according to the chosen principles—this capacity resides, of course, in the basic structure built, from a normative point of view, on the basis of the chosen principles in what is called the original position;

- the key word (present sometimes explicitly, often implicitly) in Rawls's entire theoretical development is that of *adequacy*: the concept of adequacy is not made explicit, in turn, being considered, of course, a primitive concept (just like the concept of social cooperation); it seems that the "label" represented by the term fairness has many family similarities (as Wittgenstein would say) with the concept of adequacy[50];
- Rawls firmly positions the concept of justice by relating it to the Platonic/Aristotelian concept of *pleonexia*: pleonexia[51] (Greek: πλεονεξία) designates, in the "soft" sense, greed, avarice, and in the "hard" sense, the desire to appropriate what rightfully belongs to others; more precisely, (the attitude of) justice is conceptually opposed to (the attitude of) pleonexia;
- from a technical point of view, Rawls seems to remain an adherent of *methodological individualism*. This conclusion results both directly from the structural proceduralism[52] of the Rawlsian conception itself and from the fact that, as seen below, the basic principles are assumed, in the original position, not through mediation among the participants,[53] but through their consensus[54]; it should be noted that utilitarianism (against which Rawls strongly speaks out) does not fall, despite appearances, into methodological individualism[55];
- the theory of justice must be an irreducible part of the *theory of social decision*. Rawls, therefore, considers the theory of justice to be of the type of social decision, requiring that no theory of social decision (or, equivalently, of public choice) lacks a "module" on justice (more precisely, on justice as fairness[56]).

(1.b) the logical model

In this paragraph, a set of general coordinates of the Rawlsian theory of justice will be given, as the dominant theory today in the topic of state theory.

- any connection between the concept of justice (as equity) and that of utilitarianism is broken. The concept of utility has no relevance in the (contractarian, therefore proceduralist) establishment of justice, the only "criterion" for choosing the basic structure of society being the acceptability from the perspective of the participants in the conclusion on the social contract[57];we mention that utilitarianism is a conception based on result/finality, not on proceduralism and, in addition, utilitarianism does not have a contractarian basis, but an emergent one[58];
- it seems that Rawls's vision is a *deontological* one, although it separates (like the teleological vision, typical of utilitarianism) the predicate of *right* from the predicate of *good* (without putting them in a contradictory relationship or even in a contrariety one), a separation that is typical of teleological theories. This coordinate of Rawlsian theory results, clearly enough, from the fact that, in the original position, the general, principled positioning of the individuals of the future society is "discussed", better said, is forged by choosing the basic principles not in relation to utility (which carries the predicate of *good*), but in relation to equity (which carries the predicate of *right*); we mention that utilitarianism[59] ignores the differences between individuals, while equity is based precisely on these inter-individual differences. In this context, law (i.e., the distribution of justice) cannot be annulled;
- the distinction (and, moreover, the separation) that Rawlsian theory makes between the predicate *good* and the predicate *right* is echoed in another distinction, which makes the transition from predicates to narratives: thus, Rawls distinguishes (and separates) the problematic/narrative of wellbeing, whether individual or social, from the problematic/narrative of individual freedom,[60] by asserting that right[61] cannot be annulled by the requirement of increasing or maintaining or repairing wellbeing. The distinction between contractarianism and utilitarianism reappears: while contractarianism distinguishes between wellbeing and justice, giving logical and axiological priority to justice in relation to wellbeing, utilitarianism does not make this distinction, seeming to suggest that the achievement of wellbeing can be a proxy for the achievement of justice.[62] However, the irrefutable demonstration of the fact that, in the original position, participants choose the principle of justice "cleansed" of any utilitarianism has not yet been made;

- given the procedural character of Rawlsian contractarianism, justice cannot be removed from the realm of social calculation, which brings the theory in question closer to utilitarianism, which, in turn, is a species of social calculation (or social or public choice). There is, however, a crucial difference between the natures of the two types of social calculations: while utilitarianism aims at substantive utility, Rawlsian procedural contractarianism aims at symbolic utility. This (latent) maintenance of the link between Rawlsian contractarianism and utilitarianism constitutes a deviation from Rawls's (manifest) anti-utilitarian;
- Rawlsian theory is based (to a significant extent) on the intuitionist model of "rationality".[63] Indeed, in the original position, the (eligible) participants not only know very little about what the future society will be, respectively, about each of the other participants, but they do not have any model of rationality at their disposal, because the (logical/axiomatic) bases of such a model of rationality are not identified, they (i.e., the basic principles) are exactly the result of the "deliberation" that takes place in that original position. The intuitionist position[64] of the Rawlsian theory of social justice is, moreover, in the hypotheses and purposes envisaged by the author, the only possible and productive one.[65] However, the intuitionist emphasis should not be exaggerated with regard to Rawls, because he does not accept, as we have already mentioned, the sacrifice of justice for the sake of the common good—which intuitionism does on the basis of the distinction it operates between aggregative and distributive. Moreover, from an epistemological (and even methodological) point of view, Rawls allows intuition only as a first moment (as a first "shot") of the original position—that of establishing the basic principles of social justice, since, and after this moment, the entire model will function completely deductively or, as we prefer to say, procedurally. Limiting intuitionism to a single (first) moment of the process of establishing the basic structure of the future society is also important from another perspective: intuitionism opposes, as is known, constructivism. Now, the deductivism of Rawlsian theory presupposes a massive and generalized intuitionism, once the basic axioms/principles have been chosen/established;
- there is, therefore (or it can be presumed, consequently), a certain incommensurability (so to speak, that is, not quite an incompatibility) between the secondary character of moral principles (in

relation to the basic principles chosen in the original position) and the distributive essence of the proceduralism specific to Rawlsian theory;

- the problem of the rapport between reason and emotion is also an important one in the theory of state (or of social justice) proposed by Rawls. Moreover, from a logical point of view, it is also a consequence of the secondary nature of the moral mark in relation to the rational mark in the choice of the basic principles of society. The author introduces an interesting concept (we can call it a methodological concept of conduct, given the role that is conferred on it in the economy of the theory in question), which he calls *reflective equilibrium*.[66] Individuals called to participate in the original (or initial)[67] position must manifest, within the *veil of ignorance*, a certain attitude, namely that of reflective equilibrium, by which is meant a state in which the mutual adjustment of the principles of justice and our carefully considered judgements are possible.[68] We observe that the coverage of the term "equilibrium" is made by the requirement of the mutual adjustment of the principles of justice (we are obviously talking about what is called basic principles), and the coverage of the term "reflective" is made by the requirement of producing carefully considered judgements. The semantic content of the expression "carefully considered judgments" refers directly and indisputably to the rational component of the "deliberation" that takes place in the original position in the context of choosing the basic principles of the future society. And then, is there still room for emotion in the original position? In connection with this aspect, we make the following considerations:

  - under the veil of ignorance, no participant in the original position is "allowed" to have clear images of his/her own interests and the place he/she wants to occupy in the future society, just as he/she does not have such information about the rest of the participants;
  - this "informational restriction" and desirability in the original position, however, obviously leaves room for intuition, by reducing the area of manifestation of rationality (rational calculation)—of course, intuition is not entirely emotion, but it is, in any case, opposed to rationality. This is the sense in which we believe that, in the theory proposed by Rawls regarding the

state or, equally, the social justice (more precisely, the theory of justice), there is or is (tacitly) allowed a mix of emotion/intuition—rationality in the functioning of the original position;

- the issue of the *negotiability* nature of basic principles is one of the most difficult issues to elucidate in Rawls's theory of state/justice. *Prima facie*, it would seem that the "constituent assembly" (more precisely, the "pre-constituent assembly"[69]) that takes place in the original position would essentially create the fundamental law of the future society, as it is also called the Constitution. However, the author repeatedly draws attention to the fact that in the original position only the basic principles of justice (i.e., the essence of the future state of the society) are agreed upon. The question is how exactly is this agreement achieved between the participants in the original position? Strange as it may seem, the author expresses the disconcerting idea that "rights secured on the basis of justice are not negotiable". Here we consider that the following specific analyses should be made:
  - if even the rights secured on the basis of justice (that is, from a logical point of view, the rights that are inferred, by valid methods, from the principles of justice chosen in the original position) are not negotiable, then, *a fortiori*, the principles in question are not negotiable. But, in this case, how exactly do the participants in the original position in order to choose those principles of justice? The conclusion is related to the considerations made previously regarding the concept of reflective equilibrium, namely: a) there is no actual (authentic) negotiation of the basic principles, in the sense that the participants—each or only some of them—would propose one or more principles, and the other participants would subject these proposals to pertinent questions in order to reach consensus[70]; b) it is assumed (more precisely, the author assumes) that the veil of ignorance, under which all participants in the original position are,[71] makes the basic principles, somehow, "float in the air", towards that reflective equilibrium invoked as an all-encompassing methodological device;
  - therefore, the basic principles are not chosen through negotiation (even if this were to be finalized exclusively by consensus),

but through an esoteric "birth" of them which are, concomitantly, chosen without objection by the participants. This emergence (which was evoked, from another perspective, above, in connection with the relationship between reason and emotion) could lead to the conclusion that the basic principles are chosen, in the original position, by what we could call *reaping the obvious*;

- the issue of the *priority* of basic principles is a problem that must, of course, be solved almost simultaneously with the issuance, respectively the "approval" of these principles, in the original position. It refers to the case where, for the construction and functioning of the future state/society, a number of basic principles greater than one is necessary (which is the case in Rawls's theory of justice). We develop some considerations in this direction:
  - the problem of priority always generates a more primitive problem, called the problem of prioritization criteria. The criteria have a justificatory role; therefore, they can be replaced by models of rationality that also deliver such justifications of ordering or prioritization;
  - in the original/initial position (especially as an effect of imposing the veil of ignorance of the participants), there is no model of rationality. The explanation for this fact is simple: the original position, through the basic principles it has to choose from, provides exactly such a model of rationality, so we are faced with a vicious circle: a model of rationality is needed to order (and to extract, moreover) the basic principles, on the one hand, and, on the other hand, these very principles (which, for now, do not exist) generate the model of rationality that is needed;
  - there is only one solution, and Rawls has no choice here: he must "decree" not only the basic principles but also their order of priority, which, of course, he does by using the so-called lexicographic ordering. We will examine the two actions that are carried out in the original position and that must be carried out in the absence of a pre-existing model of rationality:
- *choosing* the basic principles: the principles needed for the design and functioning of the future state/society are chosen on the basis

of intuition (under the veil of ignorance), therefore outside of any rationality (i.e., in the absence of discursiveness);

- *ordering* the basic principles: in the absence of criteria for ordering the basic principles, they are ordered/prioritized on lexicographic grounds, that is, by establishing (also based on intuition or, as is possible, on the basis of a prejudice in the matter). Lexicographic ordering is, as known, an a-criterial ordering. Since, however, a justification of the respective ordering is needed, this justification is given from a purely logical perspective;
- such a perspective for justifying the lexicographic order contains the following "ingredients":
  - the "prime" principle must, first of all, be of the greatest possible generality in the matter of interest, and, secondly, necessarily possess two attributes: (a) institutive role; (b) regulative role. The institutive role is a role, par excellence, constructivist, in the sense that it must be demonstrated that the principle in question is a sufficient logical condition for the generation/causing/institution of the intended ideal object (artefact), i.e., the state, while the regulative role is called upon to ensure the maintenance of the other basic principles under the conceptual "umbrella" of the first principle; it is obvious that the first principle represents the "legislative" device of the system of principles in question;
  - the other principles must, in turn, necessarily possess two attributes: a) be of lower generality than that of the first principle but possess the greatest possible generality with respect to the condition set for the first principle; b) have the potential to represent the "executive" device of the system of principles in question.

(2) Contractarian theory of entitlement

The most plausible hypothesis of the emergence of the state within human society seems to be the theory proposed by Robert Nozick (1997). This theory could be considered, at the limit, as a contractarian theory (although the author does not explicitly speak of a social contract, as Rawls does), namely a theory of resilient contractarianism, as we will show below. A brief presentation of this theory is given below.

(a) the emergence of the ultra-minimal state

Nozick starts from the natural state of the individual, by considering, as a basic assumption, that the natural state can be described, in the most adequate way, as a state of anarchy.[72] The natural state is considered to be of the type of fundamental potential explanation[73] (*Nota bene*: by fundamental potential explanation is meant the explanation which, if correct, would encompass the entire domain of reference[74]). Starting from the natural state, Nozick considers the following conditions regarding the emergence of the state, that is, of a form of civil government:

- the problem of civil government arises only after the natural state exhausts its own possibilities/potentialities for voluntary management of the community of individuals (*Nota bene*: this condition had already been set by Locke);
- the most… natural phenomenon that occurs in the natural state is the emergence of concentrations (hubs) of common interests of individuals, which can be called voluntary associations of individuals;
- the primary interest (which can also encompass other interests) is that relating to survival, therefore these associations are, in fact, in their intentionality and purpose, *protective associations*. Protection can be directed towards any common "enemy": natural phenomena, aggression from other individuals (or just the anticipated risk of such aggression), etc. However, protection associations may have their own problems and risks of functioning:
  - *internal conflicts (intra-association)*: the emergence of subgroups within the association or, at the limit, the emergence of protection associations within the protection association. This possibility is exactly of the same nature (therefore has the same probability of occurrence) as the emergence of a protection association in general, if some categories of interests coalesce smaller groups within a given protection association;
  - *cases in which the intervention of all is not needed*: although some dangers or risks can be managed without the mediation of a protection association, these associations nevertheless appear, constituting, from a structural point of view, a redundancy at the level of society;

- *abuse of calling for help*: once a protection association is established, it can be used excessively to resolve situations that could be resolved (perhaps better, as contemporary fundamentalist libertarians argue) at an individual, unstructured level;
- *conflict between protection associations (or agencies)*: just as individuals can generate inter-individual conflicts, protection agencies, when there are more than one (and, from a logical point of view, nothing prevents the existence of a multitude of such associations at a given time), can also generate such conflicts. The resolution of such conflicts can be done, in Nozick's vision, in the following alternative ways:

  one of the associations/agencies wins (in this case, all the clients of the losing agency go to the winning agency);

  each agency wins in its geographical area of "competence"—the borders between the associations/agencies are maintained;

  a system of rules emerges that arbitrates conflictual situations (including overall protection agencies). Obviously, this is the germ of the emergence of what, ultimately, will be called the state.[75]

- conflicts that may arise at the level of protection associations (especially inter-association/agency conflicts) will lead, *eo ipso*, to the self-selection[76] of a ***dominant*** protection association.[77] Such a conflict can be resolved by one of the three solutions mentioned above. It should be noted, therefore, that, whatever the solution adopted, one of the associations (although, regarding the second solution, there may be two or more such associations) becomes dominant or more attractive than the others;
- the question arises, at this point, whether the dominant protection association, thus formed, is a state. Nozick offers the following reasoning[78] in this matter:

  - two possible consequences of the dominant protection association must be eliminated:

    to allow some individuals to assert their rights—in this case, the association could not protect those who are not allowed to assert their rights;

    to have individuals who are not defended (*Nota bene*: we could add—but who cannot defend themselves)—in this case, the association would not fulfil its definitional, so to speak prerogatives;

- the *necessary condition*[79] for the existence of the state: to announce that it will punish anyone who uses force without the permission of the state:

  but protection associations do not announce anything like that;

  therefore, they do not have a monopoly on the use of force, so they do not constitute themselves as a state;

- in addition, only those who pay have protection (and there are different degrees of protection, depending on the payment);

  it seems that from this point of view, the protection association cannot be a state either;

- in conclusion, the dominant protection association cannot be a state. The solution that Nozick finds and proposes is to logically add a predicate to those already held by the concept of dominant protective association in order to obtain what he calls the *ultra-minimal state*. We will summarize the author's considerations in this regard:

- the additional sufficiency predicate introduced by Nozick to make the logical transition from the dominant protective association (DPA) to the ultra-minimal state (UMS) is the following: *holding the monopoly of the use of force* in defence of the members of the DPA[80];
- UMS will only consider collateral constraints.[81] By collateral constraints we mean those constraints that are not generated by the goal, but by the means of achieving the goal, that is, by the operationalized action in achieving the goal[82] (*Nota bene*: there are also internal constraints, which are contained in/generated by the goal)[83];
- it should be noted that the genesis of the UMS from the DPA, although governed by the invisible hand mechanism, is not a process based on moral principles but, as is known, on selfish principles. Moreover, morality (or moral principles) implies a "centre" of monitoring and, possibly, sanctioning (as we will see in the case of the minimal state), and the invisible hand is an impersonal paradigm (or model of rationality).[84]

Note bene: libertarians, as befits any fundamentalist, extend the prohibition of constraints to collateral constraints, that is, to the means of achieving goals, which nullifies not only the minimal state, which they have in mind in particular, but also the ultra-minimal state which, as defined by Nozick, would have no reason to be... anti-libertarian, since its main prerogative (i.e., reason for existing) is precisely the defence of individual freedom.

(b) the emergence of the minimal state

The causality of the emergence of the minimal state lies in the ultra-minimal state. More precisely, the minimal state is obtained, from a logical point of view, by adding an additional sufficiency predicate to the set of sufficiency predicates of the ultra-minimal state, namely that of *redistribution*.[85] Of course, the meaning of the concept of redistribution is, in this context, a general, abstract one, not limited to the material/economic aspect (dominant aspect in current discussions on the subject): more precisely, redistribution refers (or must refer) to primary goods, in the sense accepted by Rawls, that is, to freedom.[86] Nozick shows that the meaning of the redistribution carried out by the minimal state is from the clients of the ultra-minimal state (i.e., individuals who buy protection) to individuals who are not clients of the ultra-minimal state.[87] The process unfolding from anarchy (the natural state) to the minimal state can be represented synoptically as in Fig. 5 (*Nota bene*: the shape of the anarchy dis-agglutination curve is our proposal, Nozick not referring to this issue).

Comment

The curve that correlates the variation of the degree of non-anarchy (*Nota bene*: increasing non-anarchy degree[88] signifies reducing anarchy and vice versa), as an exogenous/independent variable of the transition of social organization from one category of association to another, as an endogenous/dependent variable, is of the logistic type, having the following meaning/interpretation:

- the agglutination of the common interests of individuals (or of a part of individuals) is relatively accelerated in the initial moments

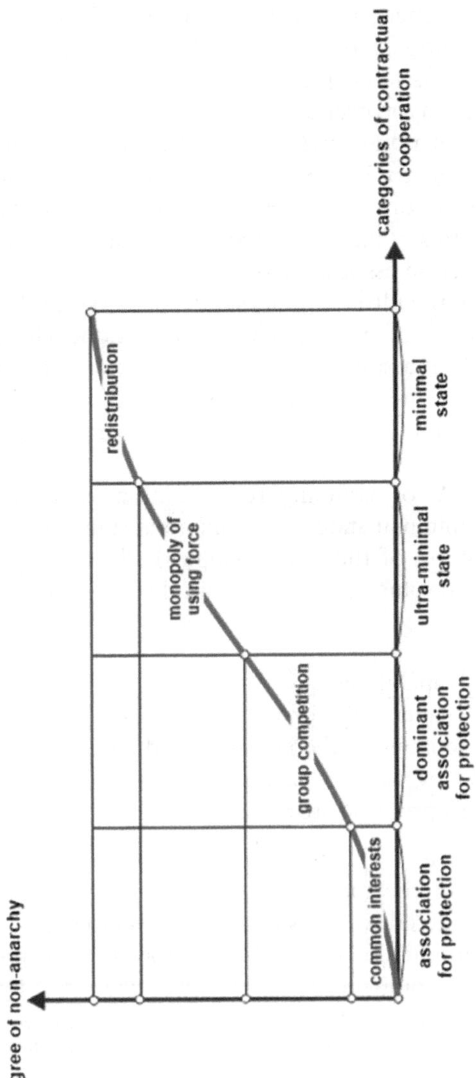

Fig. 5 Path from anarchy to the minimal state (*Source* author)

(of awareness of the common interest of defence against aggression exercised against economic property, especially). This means that the pressure for the emergence of the association/associations for the protection of rights/freedoms is quite high from the beginning[89];

- the competition between protection associations or between subgroups in a given protection association also agglutinates, from the perspective of non-anarchy, in a relatively accelerated manner, leading, according to Fig. 5, to the emergence of the dominant protection association (*Nota bene*: obviously, there can only be, at the end of this stage of non-anarchy agglutination, only one dominant protection association);
- the formation of the ultra-minimal state is achieved under conditions of a deceleration[90] of non-anarchy agglutination, which signifies a certain difficulty in assuming (and recognizing this assumption) the monopoly of the use of force in ensuring the protection of the rights and freedoms of the members of the dominant protection association;
- further, the speed of assuming redistribution—that is, of moving from the ultra-minimal state to the minimal state—is reduced even more, this function of the state asymptotically tending towards its desirable/feasible value at the maximum degree of non-anarchy.

(3) The theory of capabilities

The most challenging theory of the state (implicitly of social justice) is the capabilities theory, suggested by Amartya Sen (1999) and developed by Martha C. Nussbaum (2012).[91] The essential elements of this proposal are presented below.

- Amartya Sen
  - one of the major shortcomings of economic theory is considered to be its distance from ethics;
  - economic theory should pay more attention to the ethics of economic behaviour, not just its rationality;
  - Sen distinguishes between *wellbeing*-type behaviour and *agency*-type behaviour; he also distinguishes between distributive justice and broader evaluations of the individual and the group;

- economic analysis must move away from the approach based on individual egoism;
- in economic theory, norm and behaviour must be put together;
- in Sen's view, utilitarianism is a combination of three elements: (a) *welfarism*: the good state of a situation depends only on information about the utility of that state; (b) *additivity*: information about the state can only be evaluated by summing all the utilities involved; (c) *consequentialism*: any choice is evaluable by its effect on the state (*Note bene*: Pareto optimality only targets the first component—welfarism, although, from a logical point of view, consequentialism is also involved);
- Sen proposes five criteria for establishing the capabilities of the individual: (a) the importance of real freedoms in assessing a person's advantage; (b) individual differences in the ability to transform resources into valuable activities; (c) the multi-variable nature of activities that give rise to happiness (*Note bene*: Aristotelian eudaimonism, not simple hedonism); (d) a balance of material and non-material factors in assessing human wellbeing; (e) concern for the distribution of opportunities within society.

- Martha Nussbaum
  - the capabilities theory/approach aims at the good life of the individual as an effect of the social or political framework or arrangement in the (historical) society in question. Therefore, it is not a matter of a natural state, but of a social (cultural) state;
  - the capabilities theory (CT) is an "axiomatic" theory, in the sense that it starts from positional or positioning statements that are not disputable (although, obviously, they can be rejected, but, as long as they are not rejected *ab ovo*, they function as axioms);
  - the capabilities theory is, like the equity/fairness theory (FT) and the entitlement theory (RT), respectively, a normative theory, not simply positive one;
  - the capabilities theory (as a result, among other things, of the fact that it is sharply distinct from proceduralist

theories—such as Rawls's theory) is a *finalist* theory. It claims that the finalities of the application of the theory of social justice be known in advance, by each individual and by the entire society, and guaranteed in terms of their effective accessibility;

- from a distributional point of view, CT *does not claim redistribution*. This conclusion is based, of course, on the fact that, since the list of capabilities that must be ensured/guaranteed through a specific social arrangement (of a normative type, obviously) is given, no deviation from it is possible, in principle, i.e., it is not possible to block any individual's access to any of the listed capabilities;
- the so-called capabilities (which represent the potentialities of the individual's functioning in the direction of his/her wellbeing) are qualitative, not quantitative concepts, i.e., a size (quantum, value, frequency, etc.) that must be objectified in relation to each capability is not established. Moreover, the individual is not required, from a normative point of view, to use the capability in question, he/she still has the latitude/freedom to decide whether or not to use that capability that is guaranteed but is not mandatory—it is, in other words, a right, without a correlative obligation;
- Nussbaum takes up and integrates Sen's concept of consequentialism, which she correlates with the concept of finality (finalism) of the capability's theory.

The positioning of the three theories of the state (seen through the prism of the theory of social justice) can be done from four perspectives: a) historicism/contextualism vs. logicality/abstraction; b) rigidity vs. flexibility; c) Lamarckism vs. Darwinism; d) feedback vs. feedforward, and is presented in Fig. 6 (we make the following notations: PT—proceduralist theory, of Rawls; RT—resilience theory, of Nozick; CT—capabilities theory, of Nussbaum).

General comment

Although, of the three theories presented, the capabilities theory does not directly target the emergence (formation) of the state, it is obvious that this theory, referring to the state's obligation to

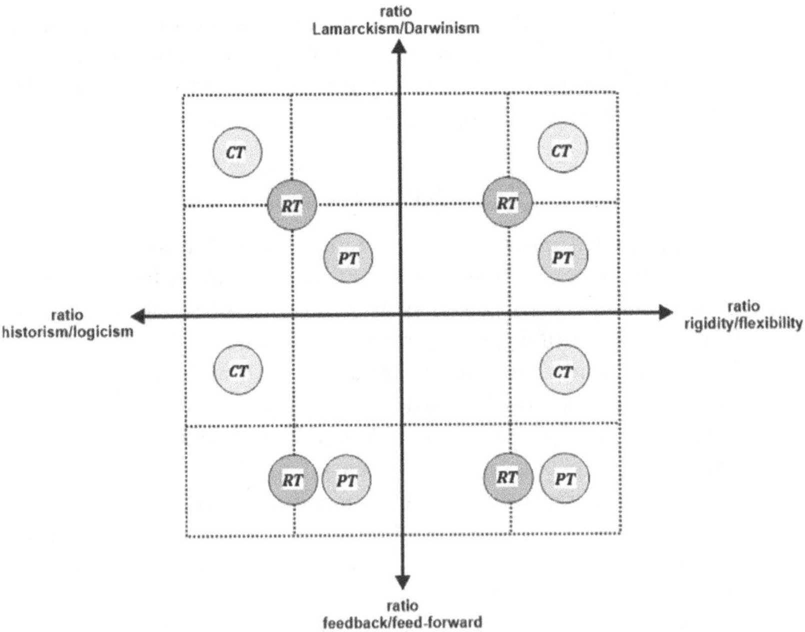

Fig. 6 Quadrilateral positioning of the three theories of the state (*Source* author)

ensure capabilities, as well as equal access to them, also has in mind a certain profile of the state.

As for Rawls' theory, and Nozick's theory, respectively, they directly target the emergence (formation) of the state and, as a necessary (obligatory) consequence, the establishment of social justice. Since the present book targets the structural and functional link between the state and social justice, this latter issue is of utmost importance and relevance in the economics and logic of this study.

The problem of the state can, of course, be examined from very different perspectives, any of them having its own relevance and, possibly, even epistemological urgency. In the present book, the approach to the problem will be a logical one, considering that only this approach ensures/offers maximum rigour and abstract analyticity in studying such a complicated subject, with so many determinations of the most different natures: historical, epistemological, methodological, generally philosophical, ethical, and even aesthetic,[92] and with so many challenges related to freedom (free will), democracy, the flourishing of the person, etc.

Notes

1. Here, the term *individual* must be understood in its most general and abstract sense—e.g., the number 4 is an individual of the natural numbers set, a star is an individual of a galaxy, a person is an individual of a given human population.
2. It must be said that a system exists as long as its individuals, no matter how many or few exist.
3. Generally, this principle of autopoiesis is "confiscated" by the natural entities (e.g., a stellar system).
4. In the case of reproduction, the individuals need a process, called growing (which requires a period/duration), to get the statute and functions of a valid individual of the species (the growing lasts till the state of adulthood is reached).
5. In the sense provided by Chemistry for the concept *organic*.
6. Of course, the genetic engineering, artificial intelligence, and transhumanism complicate the affairs regarding the ontological substrate.
7. For example, the invisible hand in the economic field (even more extended, at the social level) is a (macro)artefact, but it is non-intended.
8. Some small differences, required by locality and other contexts, compromise the quality of (pure) clone but, principled, the autopoiesis act by replication (*Nota bene*: as in the case of biological species, re-conditioning can co-exist with replication).
9. Integration of information into knowledge is both a logical and psychological process: the probability of such an integration is directly proportional to the resemblance of the new information with the existent knowledge (*Nota bene*: something like in Wittgenstein's syntagma of family resemblance).
10. See Dawkins's assertion about the gene that "uses" the organism to perpetuate itself (Dawkins, 1976).

11. Of course, in the case of symbolic and logical, respectively, the concept of death has particular forms, but conceptually, it is talking about death in all cases.
12. Logically, it becomes an inhabitant of Popper's third-world. If the objectifying is not happened, we cannot talk about an artefact.
13. Regarding the human being itself, it (he/she) has a mixed character: a natural part and a cultural part. Evolutively, the part of the cultural mark is increasing, and the part of the natural mark decreases. The artificial intelligence (the transhumanism) will accelerate the process above mentioned.
14. The written/signed form of such a voluntary agreement (contract) is, obvious, superfluous.
15. There is, of course, the subjective life—this does not require institutions, as they are defined here, although each person has his/her own idiosyncratic "institutions" for the internal monologues.
16. A membrane has a quantitative nature; it separates the species in the case from the environment. Of course, regarding the consequences of such separation, some qualitative meanings can appear.
17. The primary (logically, and chronologically) Code in a society is the Constitution. All the other norms must be done in applying the Constitution and cannot be under the sanction of invalidity (namely, for non-constitutionality) contradictory with the Constitution.
18. Obviously, we talk here about a free and democratic society. In an authoritarian one, the state of affairs is different enough.
19. The purpose cannot appear and subsist other than inside a consciousness. Wherever it does not exist consciousness, we have finalities only, never purposes.
20. Namely, the minimal number of different functions that, in their completeness and interactions, can get the role, without manifesting either their incompleteness or redundancy.
21. Efficiency is an optimum between cost (economicity) and efficacy in getting finality (purpose).
22. But, of course, a given symbolic species can belong to two or more criteria, at the same time. In fact, as we shall see, each symbolic species can be described, formally, exactly based on its spectrum of criterial belonging.

23. A basic effect can be accompanied by some secondary effects (spillovers), many of them being non-intentioned, unexpected, and unanticipated.
24. Here, a clarification is needed: by *meaning*, one must understand an explanation (i.e., a causal justification), while by *signification*, one must understand an idiosyncratically filtered meaning. In other words, the signification is what the particular/concrete individual perceives, so that if the meaning is generally invariant (the same for all individuals), the signification is different for different individuals.
25. The democratic feature of that society is not required (i.e., it is not a sufficiency predicate) for the symbolic species called economy.
26. As we will see further (see Chapter 7), it is talking about social... æsthetics.
27. We mention that the legitimacy of an action is not the same thing as the legality of that action—for instance, a perfectly legal action can be illegitimate, that is, it can violate the rights and liberties of individuals in an unjustified way and degree, no matter that a law supports, formally, that action.
28. According to the state theory (with its social contract topic), the structural base of a generic society resides in the principles stipulated in the law of laws, i.e., the Constitution.
29. In the theory of social justice, the opportunities are called, usually, capabilities (Nussbaum, 2007).
30. An analytical examination of the concept of social capital is done in Dinga (2014).
31. We remember that the finality is of the symbolic species but the purpose to which that finality corresponds belongs to the human person "responsible" for initiating and administering the symbolic species in the case.
32. We remember that a category of symbolic species means the criterion to classify the symbolic species, and a class of symbolic species is the set of symbolic species generated by a category. So, we have five categories of symbolic species, and, for example, the category 2 (C_2 has. three classes of symbolic species. Of course, each class of symbolic species will generate individuals of that symbolic species.
33. An analytical exposure of the concept of propensity is provided in Dinga et al. (2022), alongside a short discussion in the matter.
34. In the terminology of algebra, we have a closed operation.

35. As above, the reader is invited to replicate this reasoning for the other four criteria, *mutatis mutandis.*
36. The distinction between adverse and perverse effects is the following: adverse effects are effects contradictory with (or, at least, opposed to) the expected effects but are predictable, while perverse effects have the same attributes as the adverse ones but are unpredictable (*Nota bene*: the famous unintended consequences on which Popper attracted attention regarding the policy-makers' decisions).
37. There are, also, cases in which not only an individual is self-instituted as α. ndividual, but the entire family, including the off-springs that will inherit the leading position at their maturity—e.g., for the human society: hereditary monarchy.
38. In a metaphorical way (one could say: in a metaphysical way), even the non-living worlds proceed to get a leading component: for example, a stellar system (as our solar system) has a star that, inside the gravitation field, exerts the role of a ... leading individual. The same can be said about the black holes driving the galaxies.
39. It is talked about social construction as a macro-artefact.
40. It is to be observed that, once the state has emerged, the social network has become a social system (*Nota bene*: better said, a societal system).
41. See, here, the presumed impact of artificial intelligence on the decision-making process, including the public choice.
42. It is crucial to mention here that the emergence of the state requires teleology. As we know by now, non-human living entities do not have consciousness, so they are not capable of teleology.
43. We shall discuss elsewhere, in the book, the strange proposal of Niklas Luhmann, in its autopoietic social theory, to eliminate from the social exactly the humans, i.e., the origin/cause of communication—*Nota bene*: in Luhmann's theory, the communication is exactly the phenotype of the species called society.
44. We do this elsewhere, showing, moreover, that the state (like society) represents species of symbolic type.
45. The phrase *trial and error* has been introduced by the American psychologist Edward Lee Thorndike, as a component of connectionism, integrated into a theory of learning. Later, the mechanism was taken up by Burrhus Frederic Skinner (who, however, eliminated the punishment for not achieving the goal pursued by the

experimenter, because it suppresses unwanted behaviour without reinforcing the desired one). *Nota bene*: this idea was raised to the rank of principle by Daniel Kahneman, who introduced it in his behaviourist theory applied to economic behaviour. Of course, there is an essential connection of this phrase with Pavlov's experiments.

46. A scrupulous analysis of this theory will find enough elements of contractarianism, because in society any agreement of will, regarding any common (public) good, has the nature of a contract.
47. We mention that Rawls uses the term *justice*, which is quite ambiguous, being able to mean both justice and righteousness. The difference between justice and righteousness lies in the fact that justice mainly aims at verifying the positive norm that regulates the human condition, while righteousness mainly aims at verifying the moral norm that regulates the human nature. *Nota bene*: for the concept of righteousness we propose the term rightness. We must remember that Rawls himself uses, for the concept of righteousness, the term *fairness*.
48. Moreover, Rawls mentions, *expressis verbis*, that justice has three fundamental features: a) it is the first virtue of social institutions; b) it cannot be defeated even by the wellbeing of all (*Nota bene*: here is the origin of the rejection of the concept of global utility); c) the rights ensured by the implementation of justice are not negotiable (again the deductive, proceduralist character of Rawlsian theory appears).
49. In the author's conception, a well-ordered society is equivalent, from a referential point of view, to a just society (in the terminology used: a society that verifies the *fairness* predicate).
50. It is possible that Rawls deliberately left these two concepts—adequacy and fairness—unclear (to some extent), more precisely in order to leave the possibility of an intuitive rather than discursive understanding of his approach, especially since, being a Kantian in his intellectual structure, he was sensitive to Kant's maxim according to which *many books would be much clearer if they did not strive to be so clear*. Although Rawls is a consummate logician (not necessarily in the sense of logical formalism), in this case, he left intuition much more room for manifestation, with the associated risks, of course.

51. The concept and term *pleonexy* appear in Plato (then taken up by Aristotle), in the work The Republic. Later, Christianity took over the term in its philosophical (theological) bases.
52. From an epistemological point of view, proceduralism functions as a dynamic law (*Nota bene*: a law—whether natural or positive—is qualified as dynamic if its application is identical for each individual in the population involved), in the sense that a result/finality desired by an individual is generated by the procedure in question for any other individual who would manifest the same desire.
53. In its deepest sense, election by vote (e.g., by majority vote) represents a mediation—some participants may reject the majority decision, but the decision is made in favor of the latter.
54. Consensus is (theoretically) the least likely choice. This is why, recently, at the proposal of the President of France, Emmanuel Macron, the President of the European Commission (Ursula von der Leyen), and the President of the European Council (Charles Michel) are calling for the revision of the two Treaties on the European Union (TEU, TFEU respectively) in order to eliminate the consensus procedure in decision-making on certain issues. As is known, Romania (and a number of other 12 Member States) opposes this revision which could, in principle, lead to the promotion of a two-speed Europe, in which emerging Member States would be disadvantaged by Community decisions.
55. It is sufficient to recall, in support of this statement, the following "facts": (1) utilitarianism does not consider the utility of each individual, but an average utility (usually associated with an average individual called a representative agent, which is, of course, an artificial statistical construction); (2) utilitarianism also calculates a so-called total or global utility, at the level of society.
56. Rawls deals analytically with what he calls the principle of equity: *a person has an obligation to contribute as required by the rules of a just institution, once he has accepted the benefits of that institution*. Thus, the principle of equity comprises two parts: (a) how we acquire the obligations (by accepting the benefits); (b) the condition that the institution is just.
57. Here is an important place where Rawls says, almost explicitly, that solving the justification of the conception of justice is done by solving a decision problem.

58. We mention that there are positions in the theory of social justice that claim to be based on utilitarianism (or the concept of utility)—for example, the conception of Henry Sidgwick, see his work *The Methods of Ethics* (first published in 1874), Hackett Publishing, 1981, in which it is argued that a society is just if it ensures, through its institutions, the greatest satisfaction for all individuals (or for as many of them as possible). It is worth noting, on the margin of proceduralism, that such a conception emerges from the consensual decision, typical of Rawls. *Nota bene*: it would be interesting to analyse the (logical) causal relationship from consensualism to proceduralism (an aspect that we ignore, however, here).
59. For example, Friedrich Hayek (2011) seems to be a utilitarian when he argues that economic inequality is a state of society that is in the interest of everyone.
60. Like the overwhelming majority of theorists in the field of freedom, Rawls does not accept collective rights (regardless of the degree of community aggregation in mind). We mention that there is such a theory (which, by the way, is the "headquarters" of potential dangers even for freedom and, moreover, for democracy)—*consociationalism* (the division of power, sometimes found in the phrase *consociational democracy* or *consociationalism* (Lijphart, 1999).
61. The "replacement" of freedom with justice (i.e., of free will with law) is not as arbitrary as it seems *prima facie*, because the free manifestation of the individual is possible only by granting, recognizing, guaranteeing, and protecting (including restoring) the right. It should be noted that, even in the specialized jargon, the phrase "rights and freedoms" is used (analogously, *mutatis mutandis*, with the phrase, in the fiscal field, "taxes and duties").
62. This causal-deterministic utilitarian relationship also constitutes the institution of damages (or compensation): the granting of substantive compensation (for example, a sum of money) for the violation of a right.
63. We cannot refer here to phenomenology: indeed, the aspiration of phenomenology (especially in Husserl's original version) is to constitute itself as an intuitive science, in which, through the operation of transcendental reduction: *epoché*—gr. ἐποχή, transliterated *epokhē*—(bracketing, suspension of the natural attitude and of judgment/discursiveness) it abstracts from any antecedent rationality

and attempts to constitute the *eidos* (pure essence) of the intentional object exclusively from the perspective of the pure intuition offered by consciousness.

64. We specify that the intuitionist position is both teleological and deontological, being, therefore, compatible both with the deontological dominance of Rawls's theory and with some teleological remnants of this theory (which evokes, as we have shown, utilitarianism through symbolic utility).
65. As far as we know at the time of writing this study, there are no (notable) phenomenological approaches to the theory of social justice (and even less to Rawlsian theory), although, for the economic field, an interesting and promising trend of a phenomenological economy (as a theory) is already forming (Düppe, 2009).
66. The author defines the judgement in reflective equilibrium as follows: the judgement that is issued after weighing the various theories that support the judgement. *Nota bene*: offering the entire set of theories that could change the initial judgement (instead of just a subset) is analogous to the verificationist testing of scientific truth (see Vienna Circle), but a criterion such as falsifiability should also be sought: for example, one could make a lexically ordered list of theories in order of their restrictive power (or their generality). There arises (as in the problem of economic modeling) the issue of heterogeneity vs. homogeneity of individuals who issue judgements in reflective equilibrium. Is the concept of representative agent needed here too? It seems that we need a theory of how judgements in reflective equilibrium vary according to the evolution of the theories that support them, that is, the problem of the transition from static (as Rawls does) to dynamic (probably the variable that introduces the dynamic character here is the learning).
67. Leaving aside an inevitable mystical, esoteric air that emerges from the way in which this original position is described—almost an act of initiation or passage, if we make certain approximations to the mythology and mysticism of the history of human society. We will see that this impression is completely absent in both resilient contractarianism and capabilities theory—the other two theories of the state/social justice that are examined in this research.

68. Moreover, explicitly, *carefully considered judgement* is defined as that judgement in which moral capacity is expressed undistorted (e.g., in a way undistorted by personal interests).
69. As we will see later, the Constitution is to be drafted only after the completion of the original position moment in which only the basic principles are chosen (i.e., the normative backbone—the basic structure—of the future society is created).
70. We recall that the basic principles chosen in the original position are not subject to a vote, based on any type of majority that can be imagined. Since we are talking about consensus, the degree of vulnerability of such a choice to veto is, obviously, maximum.
71. In this sense, it must be assumed that the original position takes place very early related to the establishment of the community in question, since no community can subsist without a state (*Nota bene*: here, by state is meant the simplest and purest form of political structure, knowing that wherever common interests or the risk of conflict related to these interests arise, a state is needed), but, of course, fulfilling this condition is not at all difficult, at least from a theoretical point of view, and Rawls seems to assume it tacitly and unproblematically.
72. Of course, in this context, the concept of anarchy does not have the pejorative meaning it has acquired in the meantime, through semantic demonetization, but maintains its primary etymological content: the absence of centres (individuals, groups, instances of any kind) of power. *Nota bene*: by power is understood the capacity/right to impose one's own goal on another and to be able to force that person to fulfill it.
73. We recall that epistemology (more precisely, meta-epistemology) "forbids" that the fundamental explanation for a domain use concepts/terms from that domain.
74. A typology of the concept of potential explanation is given by the logician Carl Hempel: (a) nomic-incomplete potential explanation: the major premise is false; (b) factual-incomplete potential explanation: the minor premise is false; (c) processual-incomplete potential explanation: there is no conclusion, that is, the phenomenon cannot be explained (it is neither nomic-incomplete nor factual-incomplete); (d) fundamental potential explanation: explanation that, if it were effective, would encompass the entire domain (it produces clarification even if it is not the correct explanation).

75. From a logical point of view, it must be shown that this third way of resolving the conflict between protection agencies is of a necessity character, that is, no matter how many conflicts are resolved through the first two ways, in the end (or, even, precisely as a result of the resolution through the first two ways) the third way is inexorably imposed, sooner or later. This finality of voluntary protection associations in the very constitution of the state represents, of course, the core of Nozickian theory of social justice.
76. Here, then, is an interesting phenomenon of evolution (more precisely, of co-evolution) in the impersonal process of the emergence of the state.
77. It is easy to see that we are dealing, at this point, with the so-called *hub* effect (Barabási, 2002).
78. The reasoning is based on the use of the concept of the *invisible hand*, as previously mentioned.
79. It is worth noting that this condition of necessity operates, logically, after the emergence of the dominant protective association, otherwise it would be a condition of sufficiency.
80. Except for self-defense, but excluding private revenge (vendetta, etc.).
81. Any constraint on an individual is generated by the rights of other individuals within social cooperation.
82. The reference to the Kantian maxim: *man is always an end, not just a mean*, is immediate.
83. It can be said that UMS is cultivating a utilitarianism of rights (*Nota bene*: obviously, from here to symbolic utility—specific to the minimal state—is a small step, which Nozick takes).
84. We recall that state intervention (whether ultra-minimal or minimal) falls under the paradigm (model of rationality) of the… visible hand type.
85. It should be noted that redistribution is a species of rights protection (protection implies: defending, guaranteeing, restoring the initial state). From this point of view, informed and honest libertarians would have no reason to rebel against the concept and procedure of redistribution.
86. Redistribution does not, therefore, involve simple Friedmanian vouchers, but refers to a more general approach.
87. In our opinion, the phenomenon of buying protection, that is, of being included in the "population" of the minimal state, in

Nozick's theory, is equivalent to the phenomenon of choosing basic principles in the original position, in Rawls's theory. We have, here, of course, another argument in favor of our contractarianist positioning regarding Nozick's theory of social justice, therefore an additional support to speak, with justification, about Nozick's conception as being a resilient contractarianism.

88. From a logical point of view, the increase in the degree of dis-agglutination of anarchy signifies the decrease in social entropy (Dinga et al., 2020).
89. Here there are no significant/relevant differences from Rawls's position which, although without explicitly expressing this, implied that the original position is urgent, being a *conditio sine qua non* for the functioning of society as a game of inter-individual cooperation.
90. The transition point from an accelerated course of the curve to a decelerated course is, as is known, given by the solution of the second derivative of the logistic function (in which the categorical transition of the organization of society is the exogenous variable, and the variation of the degree of dis-agglutination of anarchy is the endogenous variable). Of course, from another perspective, equally plausible, the two variables can be substituted for each other.
91. There are, however, a number of remarkable precursors throughout the history of culture: (1) Aristotle—he did not present a coherent theory on the issue of social justice, but he has references to what can be called distributism (in Aristotle it is called eudaimonism) or as a distributional theory, especially in *Politics* and *Nicomachean Ethics*; (2) Adam Smith—attenuates his principle of egoism by using the phrase *common prudence*, through which he denotes the unity between motivation and understanding and which also implies group altruism, see his work *The Theory of Moral Sentiments*; (3) Karl Marx—the human being must live in dignity—where dignity is understood as the availability of true human functioning; in addition, human dignity cannot be defined before and independently of human capabilities, but simultaneously and in interconnection with them; (4) Hillary Putnam and Vivian Walsh—there is a need to abandon the strict dichotomy between facts and values, which is a dichotomy recommended by logical positivism that (still) underlies the mainstream in the field of economic theory (*Nota bene*: see the *homo œconomicus* model);

in this sense, there is talk of the disappearance or eclipse (Ostapiuk, 2020) of value-free economics.

92. We recall Schiller's suggestion regarding *social aesthetics*—a type of harmony within society, that is, at the level of social interactions (today we would say: societal), which is added to social ethics (i.e., to morality).

References

Barabási, A. -L. (2002). *Linked: The New Science Of Networks Science Of Networks*. Perseus Books Group.

Dawkins, R. (1976). *The Selfish Gene*. Oxford University Press.

Dinga, E., Tănăsescu, C. R., Ionescu, G. -M. (2020). *Social Entropy and Normative Network*. Entropy, Special Issue: Information Theory and Economic Network.

Dinga, E., Oprean-Stan, C., Tănăsescu, C. R., Brătian, V., Ionescu, G. -M. (2022). *Financial Market Analysis and Behaviour. The Adaptive Preference Hypothesis*. Routledge—Taylor & Francis Group.

Dinga, E. (2014). *Social Capital and Social Justice*. Procedia Economics and Finance, no. 8/2014.

Düppe, T. (2009). *The Phenomenology of Economics. Life-World, Formalism, and the Invisible Hand*, Haveka BV, Alblasserdam, The Netherlands.

Hayek, F. (2011). *The Constitution of Liberty*. Chicago University Press.

Lijphart, A. (1999). *Patterns of Democracy. Government Forms and Performance in Thirty-Six Countries*. Yale University Press.

NeSmith, R. A. (2021). *Keystone species: Nature's Maintenance Managers (Love of Nature)*. Applied Principles of Education & Learning.

Nozick, R. (1974). *Anarchy, State, and Utopia*. Basic Books.

Nussbaum, C. M. (2007). *Frontiers of Justice: Disability, Nationality*. Harvard University Press, Belknap Press.

Ostapiuk, A. (2020). *'The Eclipse of Value-Free Economics*. Publishing House of Wroclaw University of Economics and Business.

Pongen, R. (2024). Keystone species: Ecological architects of biodiversity and stability—Review. *International Journal of Science and Research Archive, 11*(1).

Rawls, J. (1999). *A Theory of Justice*. The Belknap Press of Harvard University Press.

Sidgwick, H. (1981). *The Methods of Ethics*. Hackett Publishing.

CHAPTER 2

Evolutive Change of the Society

1 Preamble

Principled, as the (presumed) deepest theory of the world—Quantum Theory—states, all entities in Universe are entangled, i.e., have subtle links among them, set at the Big Bang, of different nature and intensities, not always observable or conceivable. This entanglement must be viewed at two levels, or through two layers: (a) at non-anthropic entities layer; (b) at anthropic entities (social artefacts) layer.[1] Each layer, in turn, contains both non-living entities and living entities (Table 1).

Since the concept of non-living entities within the anthropic layer is disputable, we shall provide a short logical discussion in this matter.

(i) the concept of automaton

Among the three distinct entities possible in the Universe (things, properties, relations), the automaton (A) is a thing. As a thing, it has, of course, a series of properties, respectively generates a series of relations. We will refer to these, in the following, as its sufficiency predicates, i.e., the minimum number of attributes/characteristics that, by cumulative verification, qualify the entity in question as an automaton:

- (A^I) there is a device (its ontological nature does not matter) that ensures the attributes of intelligence, i.e., it has an internal capacity

E. Dinga, *The Economics of Social Justice and Societal Evolution*,
https://doi.org/10.1007/978-3-032-24055-2_2

Table 1 Two layers of reality

	Non-anthropic layer	*Anthropic layer*
Non-living entity	ex.: mountains, rivers	ex.: institutions
Living entity	ex.: animals, plants	ex.: humans

Source author

for choice, in a deductive/inferential manner (calculation). In other words, an automaton must contain ***intelligence*** (more precisely, naked, non-conscious intelligence);

- (A^P) there is an ***autopoietic capacity***—by autopoietic capacity we mean an internal capacity (i.e., operationally closed to the environment) to maintain the state (robustness, resilience, antifragility) in relation to disturbances, either internal or external, that occur or are likely to occur to the entity in question. Autopoietic capacity implies the existence of a ***self-controllable operational program*** (A^O)—as a result of operational closure to the environment—which allows both the functionality and the behaviour of the entity in question.[2] From a logical point of view, it must be accepted that the autopoietic capacity includes both the ***capacity for self-replication*** (A^R) and the ***capacity for self-controllable operation*** (A^O), i.e.:

$$A^P \rightarrow A^R \bigwedge A^O$$

$$\overline{A}^P \rightarrow \overline{A^R \bigwedge A^O} \leftrightarrow \overline{A}^R \bigvee \overline{A}^O$$

- (A^D) there is a ***dissipative capacity*** (potential)—by dissipative capacity we mean the capacity of an entity to maintain or reduce its level of entropy. The concept of a dissipative system was introduced by Ilya Prigogine and I. Stengers (1984), and by entropy we mean the level/degree of order (of some kind, i.e., from the perspective of a pre-established criterion—the degree of order is greater the closer the actual state is to the state required by the criterion in question).

From a formal point of view, therefore, we can write:

$$A = \left(A^{I}\right) \bigwedge \left(A^{P}\right) \bigwedge \left(A^{D}\right)$$

Automaton has been built, by computer programs, in a wide variety of types (differentiated, as a rule, by the internal operational program—the set of operating rules), usually called *cellular automata.* Cellular automata were discovered as early as 1940 (Stanislaw Ulam and John von Neumann), but the concept was developed, especially in the one-dimensional case, by Stephen Wolfram (2002). But, of course, we will not develop the analysis of the concept of automaton further.

Comment: the capacity for self-controllable operation implies what we call the capacity (or potential) of reaction, either in response to internal actions or in response to external (trans-membrane) ones. We mention that by reaction it must be understood a very wide spectrum of interactions, either between the component elements of the entity in question or with the environment of that entity:

- *ex post evaluative reactions*: the ability to examine, measure, characterize, predict (in different measures, from case to case) past actions, to which it can oppose a response action (which we call reaction)—these evaluative reactions may be (or not) of an action type;
- *ex ante evaluative reactions*: the ability to examine, measure, characterize, predict (in different measures, from case to case) future actions, to which it can oppose a current response action (which we call reaction, too)—these evaluative reactions may be (or not) of an action type;
- *classificatory reactions*: reactions consisting in the creation of typologies/nomenclatures of entities in the environment of the entity in question, so that a "map" of the environment is built from the perspective of criteria of interest for the respective entity (the primary interest being that of survival);
- *definitional reactions*: reactions consisting of conceptualizations (regardless of the degree of cognitive sophistication) regarding the entities in the environment of the entity in question—particular forms of conceptualizations are: naming, establishing predicates of

sufficiency (or necessity, as the case may be), definitions, interpretations of various natures and various degrees of cognition, etc.

- *(ii) the logically living (LL)*

In a manner analogous to that in which the definition of the automaton was carried out, we will also proceed to define the logically living system (or, equivalently, of life in the logical sense). The sufficiency predicates of the logically living (LL), or of a logically living system (or, still, living in the logical sense) are the following:

- (L^A) it is an *automaton*: it verifies the three sufficiency predicates, described previously, for the existence of an automaton;
- (L^E) it is an *evolutionary* entity: an evolutionary entity is an entity that undergoes changes in the direction of the fitness required by its environment (*Nota bene*: rigorously, any evolution is a co-evolution), that is, an entity capable of designing and carrying out reactions that have an "arrow", where the arrow is represented by fitness itself.[3]

Then we can write:

$$LL = \left(L^A\right) \bigwedge \left(L^E\right)$$

(iii) species of logical living things

In our opinion, there can be three species (types, categories, classes) of logically living, as defined above: (a) (BL) biologically living; (b) (IL) informationally living[4]; (c) (SL) symbolically living. We will specify the additional sufficiency predicates for each of these species, so to define them within the species called logically living (LL). It must be said that this additional sufficiency predicate refers to the ontological substratum that supports each species of logically living. Therefore, the concept of logically living constitutes the pattern (general model or genus) starting from which the three species of living are defined and individualized. In other words, the logically living must be considered the genus, and the three identified species of living must be considered species of this genus. As a species is differentiated from the genus to which it belongs by adding an attribute/predicate of sufficiency, we will add, for each one, that required attribute. As we have already said, the additional sufficiency predicate will identify the ontological substratum of each species of living.

- (iii.1) biologically living

The ontological substrate of the biologically living species (BL) is the biological organism (from the biological cell to the human). If we denote the ontological substrate of the biological type with S^B, , then biologically living (or biological life) is formally described as follows:

$$BL = (LL) \bigwedge (S^B)$$

Biologically living is the best-known (and most studied) species of logically living, we ourselves—humans—representing a concrete-historical hypostasis of this species. It should be noted that biologically living develops what we usually call a ***natural intelligence***, with a substrate also biological, since the brain is a biological entity (based on carbon). In the case of non-human biologically living entities, it is considered, at least until the time of writing this study, that they do not develop awareness, that is, they do not have the capacity for representation. Instead, man developed such a capacity for representation, so he/she acquired awareness and, as a result of a remarkable effect of the capacity for representation (which we usually call culture), humans also developed consciousness.[5]

- (iii.2) informationally living

The ontological substrate of the informational life (IL) is information. The question arises: why is not this substrate directly the knowledge or cognition (and, thus, let us talk about the cognition living, not the informationally living)? We formulate our answer to this question:

- knowledge implies understanding, and understanding implies awareness (and, on a higher level, consciousness). Now, if the ontological substrate were knowledge or cognition, this would mean that most of the entities that can process information but cannot process knowledge/cognition would be prohibited from experimenting with the devices that we call informational life;

- here, more precisely, in the issue of cognition, we are outside the paradigm of the so-called Santiago School[6] regarding cognition, which claims that this capacity (cognitive capacity) subsists in any living entity, regardless of the level of development of the brain, therefore of intelligence, meaning, simply, the capacity of that entity to access the niche in the environment that is favourable to its survival.[7] We consider that cognition, that is, that capacity to transform information into knowledge, implies a minimum *conditio sine qua non*, namely intelligence, which, however, does not constitute a sufficient condition. In order for information to become knowledge, it is necessary to move from explanation (logical-deductive foundation) to understanding, that is, to extracting significance, not only meaning, from the explanation—in principle, this process involves the intellect (a superior product of intelligence), respectively reason (a superior product of intellect).

Therefore, the informationally living is that logically living that is based on the ontological substrate that we call information. If we denote this substrate by S^I, then we can write:

$$IL = (LL) \bigwedge (S^I)$$

- (iii.3) symbolically living

First of all, the issue of the name, symbolically living, must be clarified, because the following question may arise: is not the informationally living, also, a symbolically living, since information is susceptible to symbolization? We answer this question as follows:

- in fact, information is not susceptible to symbolization, that is, it does not have the capacity (property) to symbolize per se. The essence of information is to remove, through semantic content (through denotation or, as it is also called in semiotics, through referential) an uncertainty or incompleteness in the receiver of the information in question. This effect of information can manifest itself both on a human receiver and on a non-human receiver—animal, computer, or other imaginable device for receiving and processing information;

- therefore, information does not represent any symbolization—for example, it does not symbolize its denoted/referential, but simply stands for it or in its place[8]—although, of course, any information can be associated with a certain symbolization, through an external symbolic code;
- the association of symbols with information is a cultural act, it is possible only in the presence of cultural subjects, that is, of man (society, more generally) and, moreover, it is a result of the action of man (or society as a whole);
- if we had called the informationally living as cognitive living, then things would have changed, because for information to become knowledge, it is necessary, among other conditions (including the psychological one, in the presence of awareness, respectively, of consciousness), precisely this symbolization. Moreover, as we will have the opportunity to see further, a cognitive living is a subspecies of the symbolic living, not of the informational one.

2 The Society State, Kinematics, and Dynamics

2.1 A General Map of Change[9]

To frame the society change, we need a general (abstract) scheme of change in the world (Universe). To this end, we shall take over the scheme we proposed in (Dinga et al., 2023) Fig. 1.

Discussion

The evolution is a category of change of matrix type, which takes different forms, depending on the context in which evolution takes place:

- if evolution is driven by growth, then it is called *development* (evolution of type A);
- both growth and development are part of the group of first-order changes—that is, changes that do not involve goals or values established by cultural subjects;

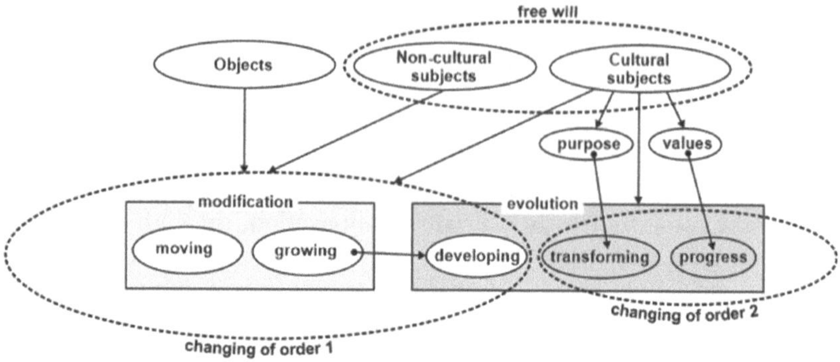

Fig. 1 General (abstract) scheme of changes in the world. (*Source* author)

- if evolution is guided by the goals of cultural subjects, we call this type of change *transformation* (evolution of type B);
- if evolution is guided by the values of cultural subjects, we call this type of change *progress* (evolution of type C);
- it should be noted that both transformation and progress are part of the group of second-order changes—that is, which involve goals or values established by cultural subjects.

Consequently, we have three categories of evolution: (a) evolution as development; (b) evolution as transformation; (c) evolution as progress. In terms of assigning to the individual, species, or genus the different forms that evolution takes, our view is that the following systematization can be made (Table 2).

The society is affected by any of the three types of evolution. As we shall see in the present research, the social justice is not possible than in

Table 2 Types of evolution

Type of evolution	*Name of evolution*	*Unity of evolution*	*The cause of evolution*	*Finality of evolution*
A	development	individual	growth	survival
B	transformation[10]	species	purpose/goal	adaptation[11]
C	progress	society	value	realization

Source author

the type C (progress) of societal evolution, for which the types A and B, respectively, constitute structural (type A) and functional (type B), respectively, bases. So, principled, the society change/evolution is plenary observed and has relevant significance only within the type C of evolution.

2.2 The State Vector of Society

To build up a state vector of society, we must, of course, identify the components of such a vector. Consequently, firstly, we shall discuss such issue.

Criteria to Identify the Components of the State Vector of Society

We propose the following set of criteria aimed at identifying the components of the state vector of society:

- (C_1^S) the *purpose* (conscious finality) of the societal system: addresses the rational way of designing the target of the society as a whole in a desirable and feasible time horizon, according to the social contract;
- (C_2^S) the legitimate *means* to achieve the purpose: addresses the effective way (resources, processes, strategies, social organization, political conducting, etc.), i.e., the path, which are adequate to get, with a sufficient probability and accuracy, the proposed purpose;
- (C_3^S) the sufficient and legitimate *control*, on the societal level, on the correlation between purpose and the associated means.

The Components of the State Vector of Society

By (abstractly) applying of the established criteria to identify the components of the state vector of society, the following such components can be identified formulated:

- (S_1): this component is generated by the criterion C_1^S and can be formulated as follows: the plenary life realization of each and all individuals, by providing all the needed capabilities as well as the freedom of accessing them, according to the individual decision and choice. We can call this component as: the *individual life plenary realization*;
- (S_2) this component is generated by the criterion C_2^S and can be formulated as follows: *free society*—this means that the societal

system is free, i.e., a society inside which freedom is the supreme value the state is charged to accomplish. It is implicitly understood that a free society is the most general and powerful mean to achieve the mentioned purpose S_1;

- (S_3) this component is generated by the criterion C_3^S and can be formulated as follows: the best way/mode to causally and functionally correlate, in both space and time, the purpose and the mean is a *democratic society*.[12]

General comment

(i) the problem could be put: is freedom the supreme value in the human being axiological set? Namely, is not, in fact, survival a more primitive value than freedom? Or, alternatively, is not, in fact, self-esteem even a more primitive value than freedom or survival? Our position is as follows:

- self-esteem seems to be the most fundamental value for the contemporary human being, i.e., for the individual with a high level of culture, morality, and sociality;
- however, the self-esteem is extremely difficult to be quantified because its incredible idiosyncrasy—this means, generally, that an inter-individual as well as an inter-temporal comparison in the matter of self-esteem is almost impossible;
- survival is, without doubt, the primary value from the perspective of human nature, but, from the perspective of human condition it not so—history shows many examples according to which individuals preferred death when their freedom or self-esteem was in danger;
- to conclude, from an operational point of view, freedom "qualifies" as the primary value to be reached in the societal system (at least in its contemporary understanding).

(ii) freedom cannot be established per se as the purpose of the society (or of individuals), since individual has a single life and, for he/she, the fundamental target in the life is the plenary realization as being[13];

(iii) the problem of democracy as regulative instance to correlate the purpose and the mean is, as known, infinitely complicated, so only some general considerations will be provided here:

- democracy is nothing more and nothing less than a mechanism to make public decisions (*Nota bene*: this means that from democracy cannot be validly inferred the freedom—the democratic public decision can also be taken in an authoritarian society);
- in a democratic society, the individuals have the (legal) possibility to allocate the necessary resources or capabilities to get the purpose—this mechanism is of a regulative action between the purpose and means for that purpose;
- it is worth to mention that the means (i.e., the capabilities) are not narrowed to the public goods (see Annex 1) because they also contain private goods, so the public decision, based on the democracy, does not cover all the relationships between purpose and means.

The State Vector of Society

Noting the state vector of society with S, and a given moment with t, then we can write:

$$S^t = \begin{pmatrix} S_1^t \\ S_2^t \\ S_3^t \end{pmatrix}$$

2.3 The Propensity Vector of Society

Criteria to Identify the Components of the Propensity Vector of Society

We propose the following set of criteria aimed at identifying the propensity of the state vector of society:

- (C_1^P) the *trend*—indicates the direction in which the components of the state vector go. So, the components could increase, decrease, or remain constant; operationally, if a continue function models those components kinematics, then the increase is given by the positive value of the first-order differential of that function, a negative value gives the decrease, and a null value gives the constancy;

- (C_2^P) the *speed*—indicates a marginal measure of the trend related to time, i.e., shows the size with which the numerical values of the state vector components modify in each time unity;
- (C_3^P) the *acceleration*—indicates a marginal measure of the speed related to time, i.e., shows the size with which the numerical values of the speed modify in each time unity.

The Components of the Propensity Vector of Society.
By (abstractly) applying of the established criteria to identify the components of the state vector of society, the following such components can be identified:

- (P_1) the *societal arrow*—is that component of the propensity vector of society regarding the ***direction*** in which that society is engaged. P_1 concerns all the three components of the state vectors, so we have: P_{11} which addresses S_1, P_{12} which addresses S_2, and P_{13} which addresses S_3;
- (P_2) the *societal kinematics*—is that component of the propensity vector of society regarding the *pace* with which the societal arrow unfolds. Also, we have here three cases: P_{21} which addresses S_1, P_{22} which addresses S_2, and P_{23} which addresses S_3;
- (P_3) the *societal gravitation*—is that component of the propensity vector of society regarding the rhythm of pace with which the societal arrow unfolds. The same, we have here three cases: P_{31} which addresses S_1, P_{32} which addresses S_2, and P_{33} which addresses S_3.

Nota bene: the societal gravitation should be understood as a hub effect, i.e., a self-catalysing process. Once society starts to move in a direction, with a given speed and acceleration, a kind of inertia installs, and that society is "led" by internal forces (which we shall discuss more analytically next), to go into the direction and with the propensities already got. As we shall see at point 2.2.6, such a behaviour is conducted by a set of forces and mechanisms of great importance, relevance, and significance for the main purpose of this book: sketching of the evolutionary dynamics of the societal system in correlation with the social justice.

So, the vector of propensity at societal level, at a given moment t, is:

$$P^t = \begin{pmatrix} P_1^t \\ P_2^t \\ P_3^t \end{pmatrix}$$

or

$$P^t = \begin{pmatrix} P_{11}^t & P_{21}^t & P_{31}^t \\ P_{12}^t & P_{22}^t & P_{32}^t \\ P_{13}^t & P_{23}^t & P_{33}^t \end{pmatrix}$$

2.4 *The Situational Vector of Society*

By situational vector of society, we understand the simultaneous qualification of that society from the state vector and propensity vector perspectives. If we note with SV^t the situational vector of the society at the moment t, then we have:

$$SV^t = \begin{pmatrix} S_1^t/(P_{11}^t, P_{21}^t, P_{31}^t) \\ S_2^t/(P_{12}^t, P_{22}^t, P_{32}^t) \\ S_3^t/(P_{13}^t, P_{23}^t, P_{33}^t) \end{pmatrix}$$

Discussion

- each component of the state vector is a three-dimensional space (with the three coordinates of the propensity vector: P_{i1}^t, P_{i2}^t, P_{i3}^t, where $i = 1$ for S_1, $i = 2$ for S_2, $i = 3$ for S_3). So, abstractly, the societal space is a nine-dimensional one or, more exactly, a phase space with nine coordinates (see Fig. 2);
- for each moment of time, a situational vector of society can be built, so, for a given time horizon, we can have time series for each of the state vector's components.

2.5 *Short Note on Kinematics Versus Dynamics*

The situational vector of society can be observed per se, along the time series assigned, without interest for the cause involved in its profile and

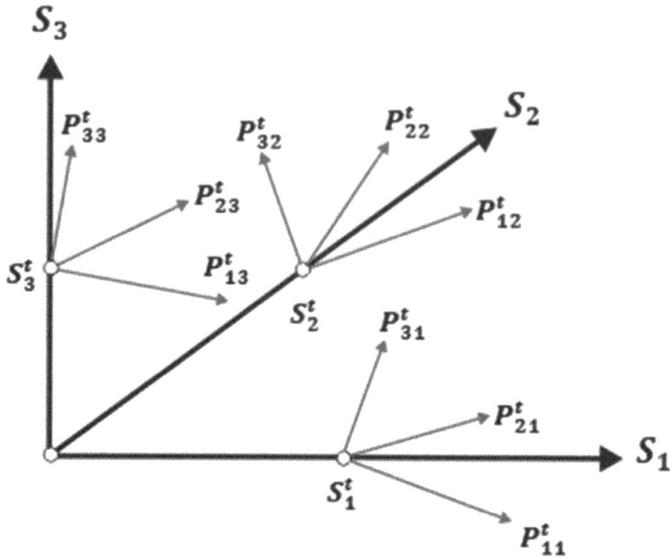

Fig. 2 (Abstract) phase space of the situational vector of society. *Source* author

unfolding, or can be observed together with the (at least presumptive) cause/s of its change in time. The first type is called kinematics, and the second type is called dynamics (*Nota bene*: such a distinction was proposed even by Newton). Obviously, there are cases in which we are interested by the trajectory (i.e., the chreod) only of the situational vector, as may be cases in which the cause involved in unfolding the trajectory is of clear interest. Consequently, the kinematics or dynamics of the situation vector of society—both describing the chreod of that situational vector—will be appealed alternatively, related to the goal of research. In what follows, we shall be interested in the dynamics of the situational vector of society.

2.6 *The Forces Involved into the Societal Change*

In an abstract way, we can identify the forces that move the societal system (i.e., the society as such). (*Nota bene*: in fact, we shall identify binomials of forces which, on the one part, must balance inside that binomial—static equilibrium—and, on the other part, must balance with the rest of binomials—dynamic equilibrium).

It must be mentioned that, at the societal level, all actions, societal forms (institutions, organizations and so on), and results of actions and societal forms are artefacts, namely based on deliberativeness and teleology—even in the case of the so-called invisible hand, i.e., an impersonal force at macro-level containing individual forces at micro-level.[14] The term force (that involuntarily evokes Newtonian Mechanics) has the general and abstract meaning of cause/impulse, either in the efficient cause (*causa eficiens*) or in the final cause (*causa finalis*) framework. In what follows, we shall propose the categories of such forces that have the nature of societal forces, with a succinct description for each of them—these descriptions will be of usefulness in the next chapters where we shall treat, analytically enough, the phenomenon of evolutionism at societal level, combined with the social justice. To be mentioned a critical issue here: the societal forces, as identified and presented below, are not in vertical relationships among them (i.e., we have not, here, a hierarchy), but in a horizontal one (i.e., in the structure of a network). Consequently, our list of societal forces should not be correlated, at any rate, with the social reductionist theories (as, for instance, Marxism, Hegelianism, Theologism, etc.).

We think there are four societal forces, each of them constituted as a binomial which must balance itself before to enter the macro-societal balance among them, namely: (i)F_1: binomial *population—resources*; (ii)F_2: binomial *science—social construction*; (iii)F_3: binomial *humanities—art*; (iv)F_4: binomial *realization of human being—social justice*. From the causality perspective, the four societal forces are integrated through the four generic causes: materialis, eficiens, formalis, and finalis (Fig. 3.)

(i) (F_1) *binomial* "population – resources"

This is the "material", i.e., objective binomial, and it immediately evokes the coordinate of economic production, within the society, but, also, the technological dimension of the society, related to using/recovering/creating the sufficiency resources aligned to the population's dimension, necessities, and consumption. The societal force F_1 acts at the level of

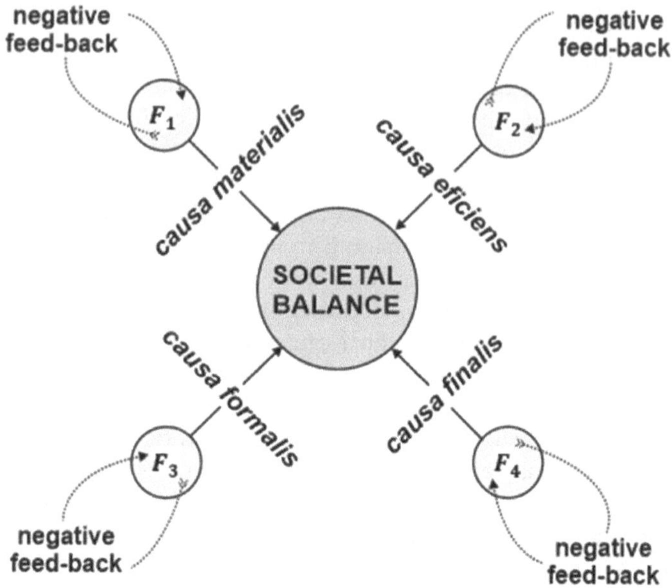

Fig. 3 Supra-binomial societal forces—generis causality. (*Source* author)

the *societal structure* and constitutes the *causa materialis* of the societal change.

(i.1) (F_1^R) the role of F_1 is: to ensure, in a sustainable, permanent, and continuous way, at a sufficient level, structure, and quality (according to the societal axiological matrix), the biological (as species) survival of human beings and their non-anthropogenic environment.

(i.2) (F_1^f) the functions F_1 must accomplish inside the societal system are:

- (F_1^{f1}) function: *demographic sustainability*, i.e., ensuring at least the minimum rate of "replacing" the human beings by natural reproduction; of course, the issues of immigration vs. emigration must be taken into consideration related to this societal function;

- (F_1^{f2}) function: *ecological sustainability*, i.e., ensuring that population needs that are satisfied based on the non-anthropogenic environment do not cause an irreparable impact on it that, further, will compromise the very survival of the population; here are comprised, as well, the so-called global problems: global heating, global pollution, and so on;
- (F_1^{f3}) function: *cosmic and non-human life sustainability*, i.e., although this function seems, prima facie, to overlap with the function F_1^{f2}, we want to list it separately because it has great relevance in an era of extra-terrestrial activities of mankind, as well as, of the rise of artificial intelligence that threats the biological life equally on Earth and in Cosmos;
- (F_1^{f4}) function: *economic sustainability*, i.e., an economic process verifying the two fundamental sufficiency predicates of the concept of sustainability: (a) *circularity*: any economic input must be recovered quantitatively, structurally, and qualitatively, in an accessible duration, from the very economic output—usually, at the national or international level but, also, at micro-economic level; (b) *inputability*: any economic output must become integrally, in an accessible duration, an economic input.

The four functions of the force F_1 are correlated among them according to Fig. 4.

Figure 5 exposes a synoptic graph of the force F_1 (modelled by the curve PR) in the societal system (with ED is noted the variable economic demand; with T, the variable time; with P, the variable population; with R, the variable resources; with PR the curve population—resources).

Discussion

- *quadrant II*: the curve $PR = g_{PR}(R)$ indicates the logistic unfolding of the economic demand related to resources (of any kind). The economic demand is presupposed to peak an asymptote;
- *quadrant III*: the equilibrium between P and R is represented by the bisector (of 45^0) of the right angle $(P - R)$;
- *quadrant IV*: the curve $P = g_P(T)$, indicating the logistic unfolding of the population related to the time. The population is presupposed,

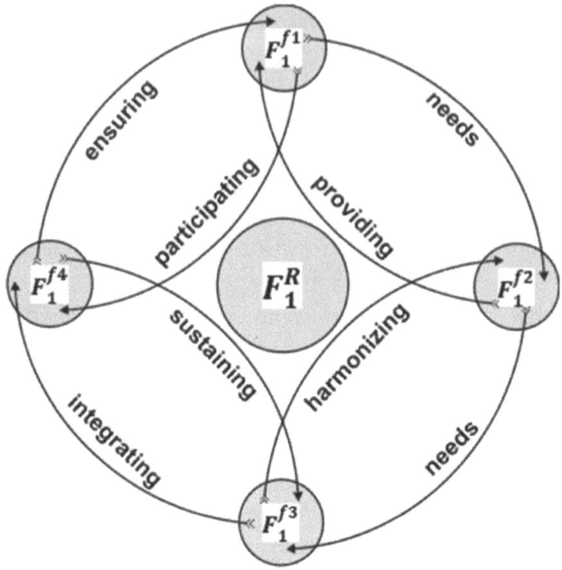

Fig. 4 Contributions of functions to the role of force F_1. (*Source* author)

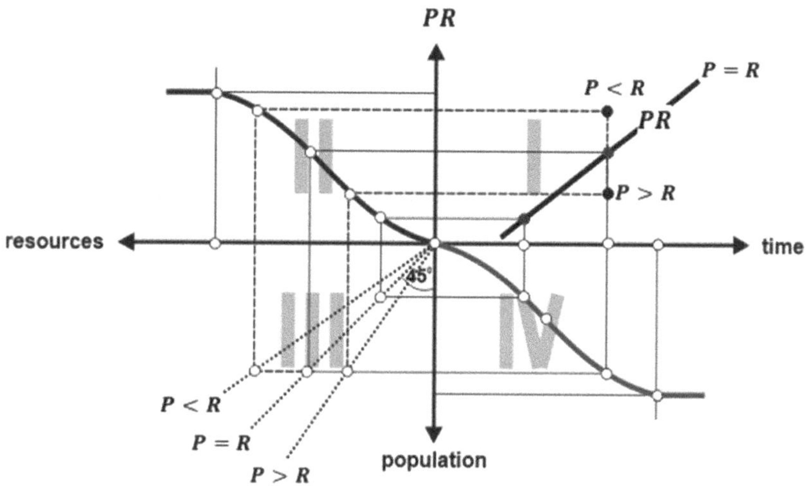

Fig. 5 Force F_1 in the societal change. *Source* author

also, to peak an asymptote, i.e., it presupposes a stabilization of the population size;
- *quadrant I*: based on verifying the quadrants II-IV, the curve (in fact, a straight line) is drawn—an increasing line of PR related to the time: $PR = h_{PR}(T)$;
- if, instead of condition $P = R$, in quadrant III, we take the condition $P < R$, the verification of the quadrants II-IV leads us, in quadrant I, above the curve PR, so any point in the semi-space above the curve PR means that $P < R$, i.e., there is not a pression of population over resources;
- if, instead of condition $P = R$, in quadrant III, we take the condition $P > R$, the verification of the quadrants II-IV leads us, in quadrant I, below the curve PR, so any point in the semi-space below the curve PR means that $P > R$, i.e., there is a pression of population over resources.

So:

$$g_{PR}(R) = h_{PR}(T)$$

$$T = h_{PR}^{-1}[g_{PR}(R)] = \left(h_{PR}^{-1} \circ g_{PR}\right)(R)$$

$$T = g_P^{-1}(P)$$

$$PR = h_{PR}\left[g_P^{-1}(P)\right] = \left(h_{PR} \circ g_P^{-1}\right)(P), \text{ etc.}$$

(ii) (F_2) *binomial* "science – social construction"

The force F_2 constitutes the *causa eficiens* of the societal change. The concept progress overcomes the growth, the development, and the transformation (see Fig. 1), being an evolution of society triggered and directed by values, i.e., the axiological matrix of society. Indeed, at the *societal infrastructure* level, the science and, correlatively, technology supported by science constitutes the very engines.

(ii.1) (F_2^R) the role of F_2 is: to provide the knowledge on the world (natural and social/societal) so that the society to be edified based on both natural laws and social laws,[15] in a harmonized way and mutual corroboration between the two categories of laws.

(ii.2) (F_2^f) the functions F_2 must accomplish inside the societal system are:

- (F_2^{f1}) function: ***knowing the objective world***, i.e., elaborating principles, theories, hypotheses, and conjectures regarding the general relationships of object–object type. This function constitutes a theoretical elucidation of the world, either natural or social;
- (F_2^{f2}) function: ***grounding the social construction***, i.e., elaborating visions, models, strategies, programs aimed at objectifying the communitarian desirability regarding the society it wants;
- (F_2^{f3}) function: ***modelling the co-habitation*** between the objective world and the objectified world (i.e., social construction), to mutual advantages, and based on societal values (axiology);
- (F_2^{f4}) function: *ensuring the self-sustainability of the social construction*, from the both scientific and axiological points of view.

Figure 6 exposes a synoptic graph of the force F_2 in the societal system.

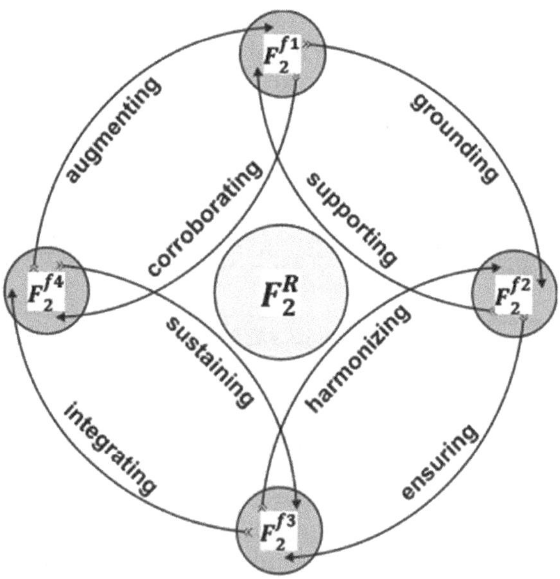

Fig. 6 Contributions of functions to the role of force F_2. (*Source* author)

Figure 7 exposes a synoptic graph of the force F_2 (modelled by the curve SC) in the societal system (with T is noted the variable time; with S, the variable scientific solutions; with C, the variable social construction; with SC the curve scientific solutions–social construction).

Discussion

- *quadrant II*: the curve $SC = g_{SC}(S)$ indicates the exponential unfolding of the pair scientific solutions–social construction related to the scientific solutions provided (or, after the case, required). The SC pair is presupposed to go to an asymptote;
- *quadrant III*: the equilibrium between S and C is represented by the bisector (of 45^0) of the right angle ($S - C$);
- *quadrant IV*: the curve $S = g_S(T)$, indicating the concave parable unfolding of the social construction related to the time. The social construction is presupposed, also, to peak an asymptote, i.e., it is presupposed a stabilization of such social construction;
- *quadrant I*: based on verifying the quadrants II-IV, the curve (in fact, a straight line) is drawn—an increasing line of SC related to the time: $SC = h_{SC}(T)$;

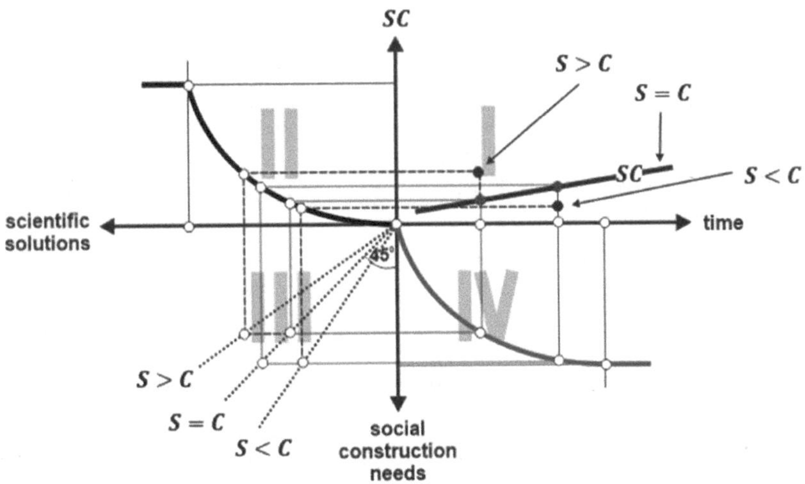

Fig. 7 Force F_2 in the societal change. (*Source* author)

- if, instead of condition $S = C$, in quadrant III, we take the condition $S < C$, the verification of the quadrants II-IV leads us, in quadrant I, below the curve SC, so any point in the semi-space below the curve SC means that $S < C$, i.e., there is not a pression of social construction over scientific solutions for such a social construction;
- if, instead of condition $S = C$, in quadrant III, we take the condition $S > C$, the verification of the quadrants II-IV leads us, in quadrant I, above the curve SC, so any point in the semi-space above the curve SC means that $S > C$, i.e., there is a pression of social construction over scientific solutions for such a social construction.

So:

$$g_{SC}(S) = h_{SC}(T)$$

$$T = h_{SC}^{-1}[g_{SC}(S)] = \left(h_{SC}^{-1} \circ g_{SC}\right)(S)$$

$$T = g_S^{-1}(S)$$

$$SC = h_{SC}\left[g_S^{-1}(S)\right] = \left(h_{SC} \circ g_S^{-1}\right)(S), \text{ etc.}$$

(iii) (F_3) *binomial* "humanities – art"

The force F_3 constitutes the *causa formalis* of the societal change. It acts at the *societal suprastructure* level.

(iii.1) (F_3^R) the role of F_3 is: to provide the knowledge of the human being, in both its generality and idiosyncrasy, and from both the scientific/philosophic/theological side and art(istical) side.

(iii.2) (F_3^f) the functions F_3 must accomplish inside the societal system are:

- (F_3^{f1}) function: *formation of the ethical* (exemplary) *profile* of the person
- (F_3^{f2}) function: *formation of the aesthetical* (exemplary) *profile* of the person[16]
- (F_3^{f3}) function: *formation of the communitarian* (canonical) *profile* of the person

- (F_3^{f4}) function: *formation of axiological* (exemplary) *profile* of the person

Figure 8 exposes a synoptic graph of the force F_3 in the societal system.

Figure 9 exposes a synoptic graph of the force F_3 (modelled by the curve HA) in the societal system (with T is noted the variable time; with H, the variable humanities development; with A, the variable art development; with HA, the curve humanities–art).

Discussion

- *quadrant II*: the curve $HA = g_{HA}(H)$, indicates the concave increasing of the HA binomial development related to the humanities findings provided (or, after the case, required). The HA pair is presupposed to go to an asymptote;
- *quadrant III*: the equilibrium between H and A is represented by the bisector (of 45^0) of the right angle ($H - A$);

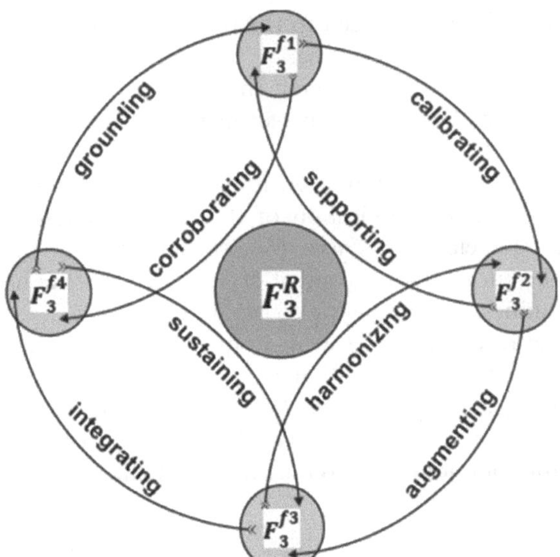

Fig. 8 Contributions of functions to the role of force F_3. (*Source* author)

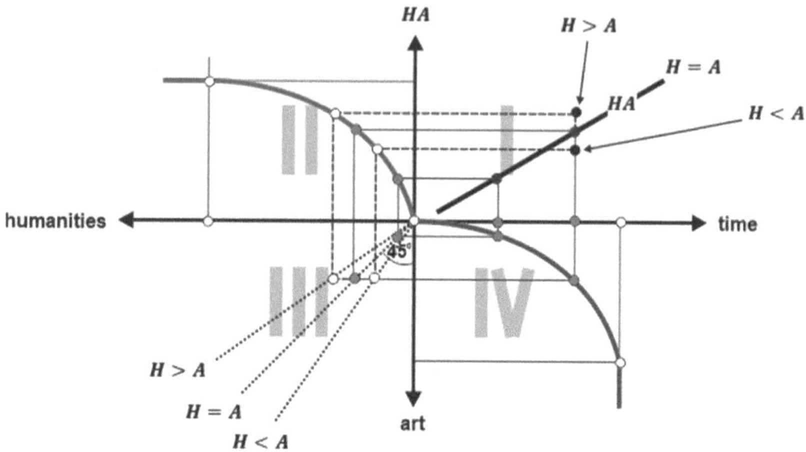

Fig. 9 Force F_3 in the societal change. (*Source* author)

- *quadrant IV*: the curve $A = g_A(T)$, indicating the convex parable unfolding of the art related to the time. The art progress is presupposed to be unlimited in time;
- *quadrant I*: based on verifying the quadrants II-IV, the curve (in fact, a straight line) is drawn—an increasing line of HA related to the time: $HA = h_{HA}(T)$;
- if, instead of condition $H = A$, in quadrant III, we take the condition $H < A$, the verification of the quadrants II-IV leads us, in quadrant I, below the curve HA, so any point in the semi-space below the curve HA means that $H < A$, i.e., there is not a pression of humanities development over art development;
- if, instead of condition $H = A$, in quadrant III, we take the condition $H > A$, the verification of the quadrants II-IV leads us, in quadrant I, above the curve HA, so any point in the semi-space above the curve HA means that $H > A$, i.e., there is a pression of humanities development over art development.

So:

$$g_{HA}(H) = h_{HA}(T)$$

$$T = h_{HA}^{-1}[g_{HA}(H)] = \left(h_{HA}^{-1} \circ g_{HA}\right)(H)$$

$$T = g_A^{-1}(A)$$

$$HA = h_{HA}\left[g_A^{-1}(A)\right] = \left(h_{HA} \circ g_A^{-1}\right)(A), \text{ etc.}$$

(iv) (F_4) *binomial* "realization of human being – social justice"

The force F_4 constitutes the *causa finalis* of the societal change. It acts also at the level of *societal structure*, as the force F_1.

(iv.1) (F_4^R) the role of F_4 is: to deliver and put in place, fully functional and accessible, all the capabilities allowed by the other three forces (F_1, F_2, and F_3), so the society's members to experiment and enjoy of the best possibilities throughout their life;

(iv.2) (F_4^f) the functions F_4 must accomplish inside the societal system are:

- (F_4^{f1}) function: fully *providing of the freedom of individual choice*, in any forms and fields (including human rights)
- (F_4^{f2}) function: *defending of the life, health, and guaranteeing of completely flourishing*, for individuals and community
- (F_4^{f3}) function: providing the *equality of individuals* before positive law and societal's opportunities
- (F_4^{f4}) function: *defending society against monopolization* of political power (through ensuring democracy), economic power (through ensuring social justice), and cultural power (by preserving the cultural identity of individuals and communities)

Figure 10 exposes a synoptic graph of the force F_4 in the societal system.

Figure 11 exposes a synoptic graph of the force F_4 (modelled by the curveRJ) in the societal system (with T is noted the variable time; with$R$, the variable realization of human being; with$J$, the variable social justice; withRJ, the curve realization of human being–social justice).

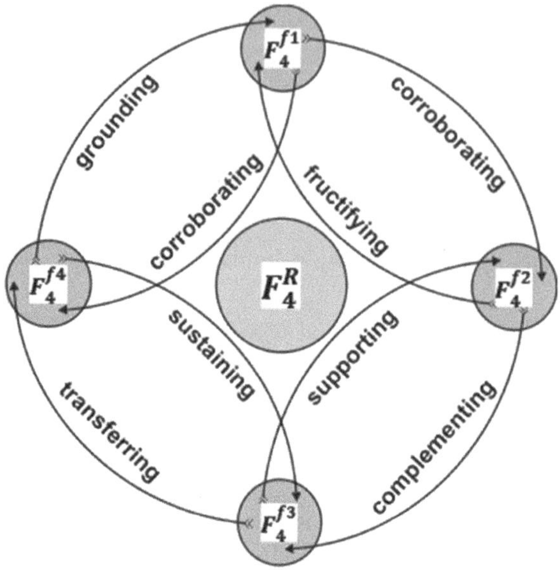

Fig. 10 Contributions of functions to the role of force F_4. (*Source* author)

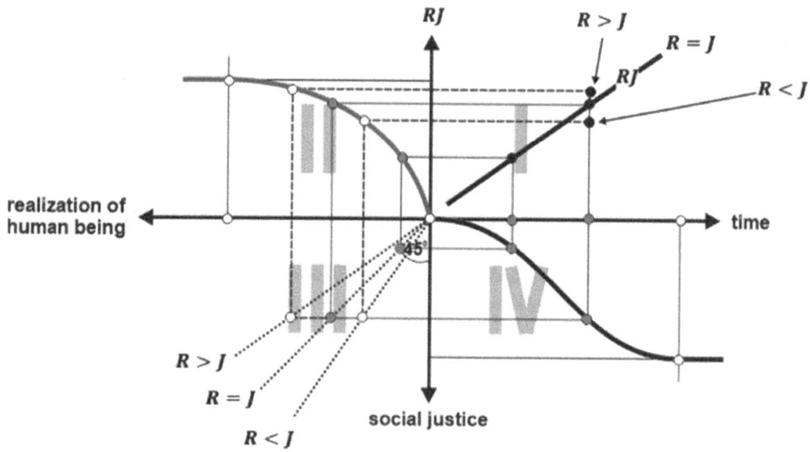

Fig. 11 Force F_4 in the societal change. (*Source* author)

Discussion

- *quadrant II*: the curve $RJ = g_{RJ}(R)$, indicates the concave increasing of the RJbinomial development related to the humanities realization of human being findings provided (or, after the case, required). The RJ pair is presupposed to go to an asymptote;
- *quadrant III*: the equilibrium between R and J is represented by the bisector (of 45^0) of the right angle $(R - J)$;
- *quadrant IV*: the curve $J = g_J(T)$, indicating the logistic unfolding of the social justice related to the time. The social justice progress is presupposed to go to an asymptote in time;
- *quadrant I*: based on verifying the quadrants II-IV, the curve (in fact, a straight line) is drawn—an increasing line of RJ related to the time: $RJ = h_{RJ}(T)$;
- if, instead of condition $R = J$, in quadrant III, we take the condition $R < J$, the verification of the quadrants II-IV leads us, in quadrant I, below the curve RJ, so any point in the semi-space below the curve RJ means that $R < J$, i.e., there is not a pression of realization of human being development over social justice development;
- if, instead of condition $R = J$, in quadrant III, we take the condition $R > J$, the verification of the quadrants II-IV leads us, in quadrant I, above the curve RJ, so any point in the semi-space above the curve RJ means that $R > J$, i.e., there is a pression of realization of human being development over social justice development.

So:

$$g_{RJ}(R) = h_{RJ}(T)$$

$$T = h_{RJ}^{-1}[g_{RJ}(R)] = \left(h_{RJ}^{-1} \circ g_{RJ}\right)(R)$$

$$T = g_J^{-1}(J)$$

$$RJ = h_{RJ}\left[g_J^{-1}(J)\right] = \left(h_{RJ} \circ g_J^{-1}\right)(J), \text{ etc.}$$

So, we can write the functional matrix (FM) of a generic societal system as:

$$FM = (F_1, F_2, F_3, F_4) = \begin{pmatrix} F_1^{f1} & F_2^{f1} & F_3^{f1} & F_4^{f1} \\ F_1^{f2} & F_2^{f2} & F_3^{f2} & F_4^{f2} \\ F_1^{f3} & F_2^{f3} & F_3^{f3} & F_4^{f3} \\ F_1^{f4} & F_2^{f4} & F_3^{f4} & F_4^{f4} \end{pmatrix}$$

Based on the four forces of the societal changing, we can now represent (Fig. 12) the generic state of a societal system. *Nota bene*: we consider a random case (for didactical use) for the slopes of forces but, of course, in concrete analysis the representation will take over the real case.

Discussion

We can separate 11 bi-dimensional regions with the following signification:

- region (1): $(P < R) \bigwedge (S > C) \bigwedge (H > A) \bigwedge (R > J)$
- region (2): $(P > R) \bigwedge (S < C) \bigwedge (H < A) \bigwedge (R < J)$

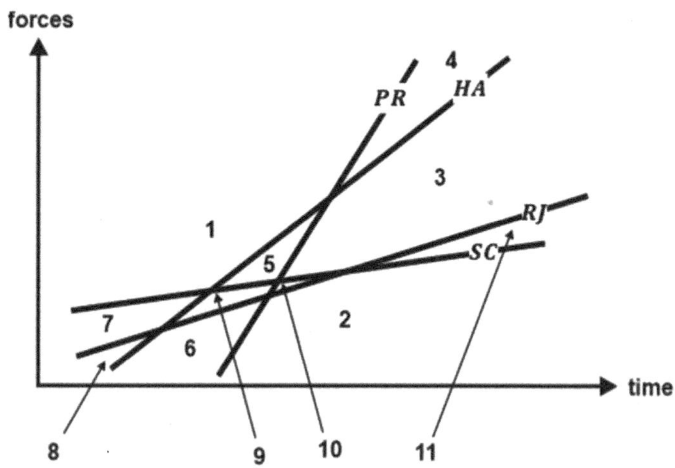

Fig. 12 A didactical case of societal forces coexistence. (*Source* author)

- region (3): $(P > R) \bigwedge (S > C) \bigwedge (H < A) \bigwedge (R > J)$
- region (4): $(P > R) \bigwedge (S > C) \bigwedge (H > A) \bigwedge (R > J)$
- region (5): $(P > R) \bigwedge (S > C) \bigwedge (H < A) \bigwedge (R > J)$
- region (6): $(P < R) \bigwedge (S < C) \bigwedge (H < A) \bigwedge (R < J)$
- region (7): $(P < R) \bigwedge (S > C) \bigwedge (H > A) \bigwedge (R < J)$
- region (8): $(P < R) \bigwedge (S < C) \bigwedge (H > A) \bigwedge (R < J)$
- region (9): $(P < R) \bigwedge (S > C) \bigwedge (H < A) \bigwedge (R > J)$
- region (10): $(P > R) \bigwedge (S < C) \bigwedge (H < A) \bigwedge (R > J)$
- region (11): $(P > R) \bigwedge (S > C) \bigwedge (H < A) \bigwedge (R < J)$

In the case of equilibrium at the societal level among the four forces, we have the following graph (Fig. 13).

Discussion

- region (A): $(P < R) \bigwedge (S > C) \bigwedge (H > A) \bigwedge (R > J)$
- region (B): $(P > R) \bigwedge (S > C) \bigwedge (H > A) \bigwedge (R > J)$
- region (C): $(P > R) \bigwedge (S > C) \bigwedge (H < A) \bigwedge (R > J)$
- region (D): $(P > R) \bigwedge (S > C) \bigwedge (H < A) \bigwedge (R < J)$
- region (E): $(P > R) \bigwedge (S < C) \bigwedge (H < A) \bigwedge (R < J)$
- region (F): $(P < R) \bigwedge (S < C) \bigwedge (H < A) \bigwedge (R < J)$
- region (G): $(P < R) \bigwedge (S < C) \bigwedge (H > A) \bigwedge (R < J)$
- region (H): $(P < R) \bigwedge (S < C) \bigwedge (H > A) \bigwedge (R > J)$

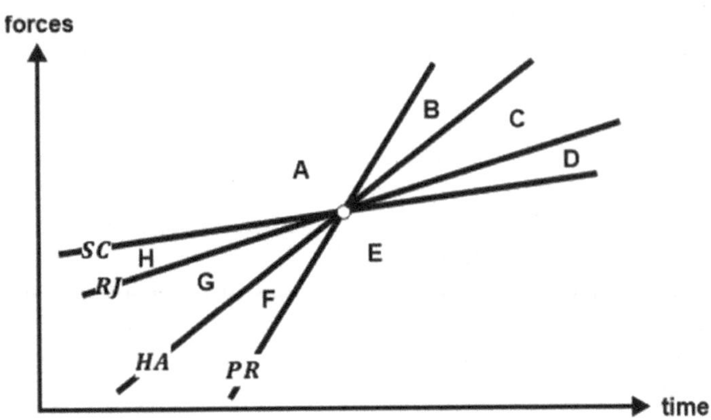

Fig. 13 General societal equilibrium. (*Source* author)

Nota bene: in the intersection point of all the forces, the societal state is described as:

$$(P = R) \bigwedge (S = C)(H = A) \bigwedge (R = J)$$

3 The Mixed Causality of Symbolic Species

We saw (see Chapter 1) what is a symbolic species. We are now interested if the causality implied in both the emergence of these symbolic species and the functioning/working of them.

3.1 Emergence of the Causality of Symbolic Species

Any symbolic species is an artefact, so, principled, it is a result of human action (either act, or abstention[17]). While the causal origin of symbolic species is the human action, the way in which this causality[18] works is of two kinds: (a) impersonal; (b) personal.

(a) Impersonal causality

The impersonal causality is generated by the autonomous and (relatively) independent actions of myriad individuals in the societal functioning—for example, the well-known ***invisible hand***, introduced in the economic field (but valid, also, for the larger societal field) by Adam Smith. The impersonal causality is characterized by the following attributes:

- it is an aggregate causality, namely it is a result of combining, in different ways, the individual "unknown" but deliberative actions (each of them with its own personal causality—see point (b) below);
- although the individual actions are autonomous, they are not totally but only relatively autonomous[19];
- it is not independent[20] from the actions of other individuals (either contemporary or not contemporary), since many of the decisions/actions of an individual could be just reactions to the decisions/actions of other individuals;
- it is related, for each involved individual, to his/her purpose, which could be (and, generally, is) very different from the purposes of other individuals;

- it leads to an aggregate result that could correspond to the purposes of some individuals and could not correspond to the purposes of other individuals;
- the individual agents can reverse his/her already implemented previous action, without having the certitude of the new effect occurring, exactly as in the case of the initial action;
- generally, the impersonal causality has an aggregate result that constitutes in a macro-order from micro intended orders and possible disorders—something analogous to Prigogine's order through fluctuations (Prigogine, 1984).
- Personal causality

The personal causality addresses the cases in which a given and identifiable individual or group (institution, organization, authority, etc., including the state) develops an action that generates an artefact (for example, a symbolic species[21]). Personal causality differs from the impersonal one only by the punctually identifiable origin of the causality, while the effect of the two causalities is commensurable, and even (in some cases) identical. So, the main attributes of personal causality seem to be the following:

- it has a "known" origin, that is, a given individual or group/institution/authority;
- it has a deliberative nature (like the impersonal causality);
- it targets a purpose assigned either to the very agent of action or to a larger community, including the national one;
- the agent of an action can reverse the previous one, this time having the certitude of producing the expected effect of the reversed action;
- if the impersonal causality is mandatorily aggregated into a macro-causality, the personal one just can be aggregated, not mandatorily is;
- it is autonomous, like in the case of impersonal causality;
- aggregation of the personal causality is problematic enough: it can be the case in which more personal actions combine their effects but, equally, can be the case in which those actions do not combine among them.

A well-ordered society, i.e., a sustainable society, will be all the time attentive to the impersonal causality, to transform it into a personal causality, usually by intermediation of codified normativity. So, the personal causality can be of two kinds:

(i) autonomous personal causality: does not consider the impersonal causality;
(ii) derived personal causality: does consider the impersonal causality.

Nota bene: we do not discuss the nature of the causality, that is, if it is or is not ontological. According, for example, to Hume (1992), causality consists in our mind's perceptions about the precedency and contiguity that characterize two observed entities (either real or nonreal), so the causality is either an impression or an idea. This leads us to the conclusion that causality is not objective but subjective. This state of affairs can reduce much enough the distinction between correlation and causality in the economic/social field.

3.2 Functioning/Working of the Causality of Symbolic Species

Based on the above, we can now examine the structure of causality regarding the symbolic species. We think there are three categories of causes (or causalities[22]): (a) personal causality; (b) impersonal causality (*Nota bene*: these two kinds of causality form the contingent causality); (c) necessary causality.

(i) Inter-conditioning of causalities

In the case of symbolic species, in an (apparent) paradoxical way, not the necessary causality is the trigger of certain processuality, but the contingent one. This statement is based on the fact that any action, either of constituting a symbolic species or of its functioning, starts from a purpose (final cause) which always belongs to the human individual or human community (organization, institution, state) and, of course, establishing a purpose is a contingent fact. However, in the very phenomenology of the economy, there are many processes that are non-anthropic and, consequently, unfold in a necessary way—we call such episodes of necessary processuality as intra-contingent necessity (Dinga, 2025).

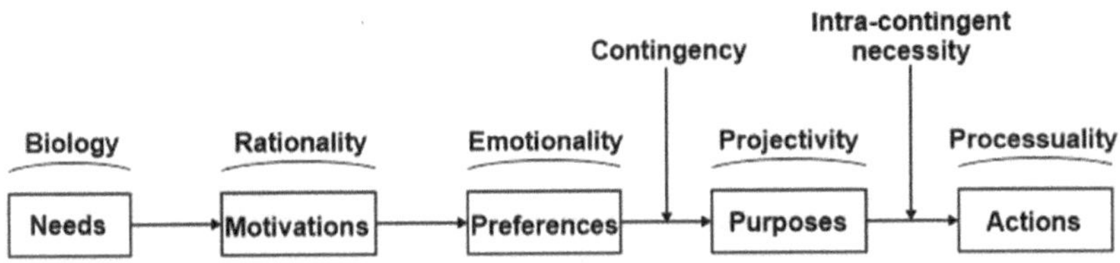

Fig. 14 Inter-conditioning of causalities in symbolic species processuality. (*Source* author)

The general inter-conditioning of the causalities in the case of symbolic species is shown in Fig. 14.

(ii) Hierarchy of causalities

Above, it was shown that the starting point in the symbolic species functioning is a contingent causality, namely establishing of the purpose. This primordiality in the causality functioning is not just a chronological primitivity but, essentially, a logical primitivity. In this context, we thing we must accept a hierarchy of the causalities in the symbolic species functioning. Such a hierarchy should verify the following "principles":

- the contingent causality is the highest level of primitivity in the general causality assigned to symbolic species;
- inside the contingent causality, personal causality is more primitive than impersonal causality[23];
- the necessary causality is, in fact, an intra-contingent necessity—that is, episodes (islands) of necessity within the general (ocean of) contingency;
- inside the necessary causality, there is a socially necessary causality, based on the social necessity (for example, the norms at the societal level), and a naturally necessary causality, based on the natural (non-anthropic) processes/phenomena involved in the societal processuality;
- between the two species of necessary causality, the natural causality is hierarchically supra-ordered related to the social causality.

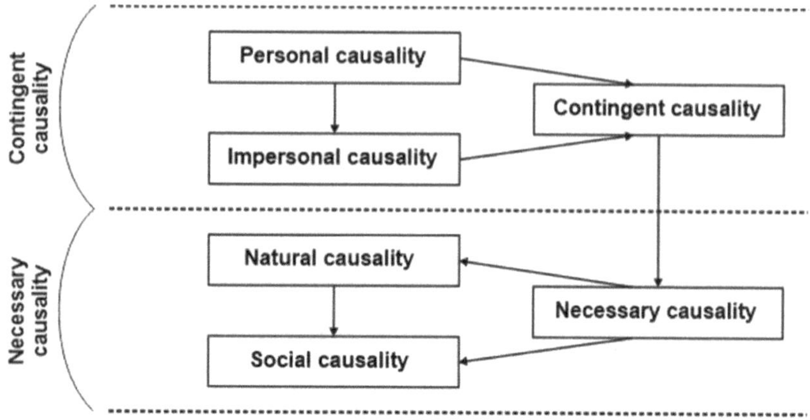

Fig. 15 Hierarchy of causalities in symbolic species phenomenology. (*Source* author)

A synoptic view on the issue of hierarchy of causality in the case of symbolic species is provided in Fig. 15.

4 Evolutive Movement of Society and *Causa Sui* Hypothesis

The necessary causality can have two origins: (a) from the anthropic space – will shall call it endogenous causality; (b) from the non-anthropic space – will shall call it exogenous causality.

(a) The endogenous causality

The endogenous necessary causality addresses the societal constraints, usually expressed by the normative framework of that society, either codified as positive norms or non-codified (for example, the ethical/ moral norms, traditions, culture—including religion—imitations). We can call the endogenous necessary causality, together with the contingent causality (*Nota bene*: of course, any contingent causality is endogenous): *causa sui*[24] causality, since it does not come from outside of the society, but from inside.

(b) The exogenous causality

The exogenous causality is located inside the society but, somewhat, acts from outside it.[25] Since it is obvious that such causality functions, however, within the society, some considerations to explain its qualification as exogenous are required, as follows:

- Nature (i.e., non-anthropogenic space) is structurally and functionally integrated into the society working. For example, the economic process[26] cannot occur without the "participation" of the non-anthropogenic space[27];
- despite this inevitable operational "community" of Nature and Society, from a logical point of view, Nature is non-Society, so the necessary causality coming from Nature (for example, chemical or biological processes) must be considered an exogenous causality.

Since the natural necessary causality occurs only as intra-contingent necessity, so being a relative occurring, namely to the contingent causality called above *causa sui*, we can consider that in society (societal system) there is a *causa sui causality*. In all further developments of our research, we shall have before eyes this hypothesis—namely, the *causa sui hypothesis*—in describing, analysing, and interpreting the kinematics/dynamics of the society from the perspective of its evolutionary path or "destiny". This means that the societal movement, of any kind, will be considered in its absolute coordinates, based on *causa sui*, although at least in its incipient historical stages, the human society was under the (large) imperium of Nature.

5 An Evolutionary Model of the Society

Based on previous findings, in this paragraph we try to sketch, at a logical level, i.e., a general and abstract one, an evolutionary model of the society.

5.1 Preamble

The actants of societal dynamics are the four forces identified above (see the point 2.2.6), and the general framework in which the forces act is the situational vector of society (see the point 2.2.4). We resume the two components of societal dynamics (movement):

(1) The societal forces
- (F_1) *binomial* "population – resources"
- (F_2) *binomial* "science – social construction"
- (F_3) *binomial* "humanities – art"
- (F_4) *binomial* "realization of human being – social justice"

(2) The situation vector of society

$$SV^t = \begin{pmatrix} S_1^t/(P_{11}^t, P_{21}^t, P_{31}^t) \\ S_2^t/(P_{12}^t, P_{22}^t, P_{32}^t) \\ S_3^t/(P_{13}^t, P_{23}^t, P_{33}^t) \end{pmatrix}$$

where S_i^t is the state vector i ($i = 1$: the *individual life plenary realization*; $i = 2$: *free society*; $i = 3$: *democratic society*); and P_{ji}^t is the component j of the propensity vector of society, assigned to the i component of the state vector of society ($j = 1$: *societal arrow*; $j = 2$: *societal kinematics*; $j = 3$: *societal gravitation*).

The forces and the situational vector generate a dynamics process in three steps which are shaped not in a spiral[28] but in a logistic chreod, i.e., targeting the stabilization/sustainabilization.

The three steps are driven, each of them, by three principles, as follows:

- the *constitutive* principle of societal movement: this principle is "responsible" for forming each of the four forces as such within the societal system; it governs the balance inside each of the four forces, ensuring the development of the very forces involved. The equilibrium or dis-equilibrium inside the binomial of any force will affect how the forces interact, then, among them, as we shall see further. Somewhat, the entropic gradient of each force will measure the size and intensity of the impulse that a force exerts (or could exert) on the other forces;
- the *institutive* principle of societal movement: here we have a very suggestive illustration of our idea regarding the criterion of (general) interaction in the Universe, namely the minimum entropic gradient. In the case under discussion here, entropy is viewed under two

aspects: (a) as the level of balance inside the binomial of the societal forces"the perfect equilibrium denotes maximum entropy, while the deterioration of the equilibrium denotes a decrease in entropy[29]; (b) as the level of balance between societal forces. Since the signification of the concept of entropy, as discussed in this research, is opposite to the "orthodox" one, and, more, since the concept of entropy used here is a species of social entropy, we ask the reader to agree to call "our" entropy as *sentropy* (from social entropy). Hence, we shall use only the term sentropy when we refer to social entropy.

Nota bene: we would call the sentropy that happened inside the forces binomials *micro-sentropy* (mE), and the sentropy that happened among the forces (see point 2.5.2) *macro-sentropy* (ME). So, there are the following micro-sentropies: mE_1, of force F_1; mE_2, of force F_2; mE_3, of force F_3; mE_4, of force F_4. Also, we note the sentropic gradient of the micro-sentropy as follows: $g(mE_1)$ for force F_1; $g(mE_2)$ for force F_2; $g(mE_3)$ for force F_3; $g(mE_4)$ for force F_4. We mention that in calculating the micro-sentropy gaps is important to specify a kind of "algebraic sign" of those gaps, because it is relevant if the first member of the binomial is "in excess", or the second one (detailed mentions will be provided in the right place below). In an analogical way, we can note the six cases (C_4^2) of the gradients of macro-sentropy, as follows:

- ✓ $g(ME_{12}) = g(mE_1) - g(mE_2)$;
- ✓ $g(ME_{13}) = g(mE_1) - g(mE_3)$;
- ✓ $g(ME_{14}) = g(mE_1) - g(mE_4)$;
- ✓ $g(ME_{23}) = g(mE_2) - g(mE_3)$;
- ✓ $g(ME_{24}) = g(mE_2) - g(mE_4)$;
- ✓ $g(ME_{34}) = g(mE_3) - g(mE_4)$.

To be observed that $g(ME_{pq}) = -g(ME_{qp})$, for $p, q \in \{1,2,3,4\}$, and $p \neq q$, so the algebraic sign of the macro-sentropy gap is relevant in extracting the impulse will be delivered in the societal system.

- the *regulative* principle of societal movement: this principle shows if the interactions among the four societal forces improve (or do not improve) the situational vector of the society, for the three components of the state vector, respectively for the three components of the propensity vector. In fact, the regulative principle will generate feedbacks (either positive or negative, after the case) which adjust the next movement of the societal system.

5.2 *Some Qualitative Considerations*

(a) as we shall see further, when the gap of micro-sentropy is null for a given force, the impulse transmitted from that force to the other ones is null, which means that, in the case in which all the four gaps of micro-sentropy are null, the society does not move in any way. This conclusion is logically correct but, factually, we think the following issues are equally relevant:

- inside each force there is an "arms race", so the binomial factors stimulate each another, so, principled, the perfect equilibrium between them is never accomplished. Consequently, always the gap of the micro-sentropy is non-null in any of the four forces;
- however, as the society unfolds and improves its forces (which means, of course, reducing the micro-sentropy gaps), the respective gaps narrow more and more, although not in the same size or rhythm in all the four forces—this is the reason for which we have conjectured above that the society movement has the "necessary" tendency to an asymptote (see below). It is something analogous to a passing to limit in mathematical calculus;

(b) the interactions among the four societal forces are driven by a sentropic gap of second order, that is, a macro-sentropic gap of the micro-sentropic gaps, as will be shown below.

5.3 *The Evolutionary Model—Gross Lines*

We shall begin the (logical) construction of the evolutionary model of the societal system by a graph (Fig. 16).

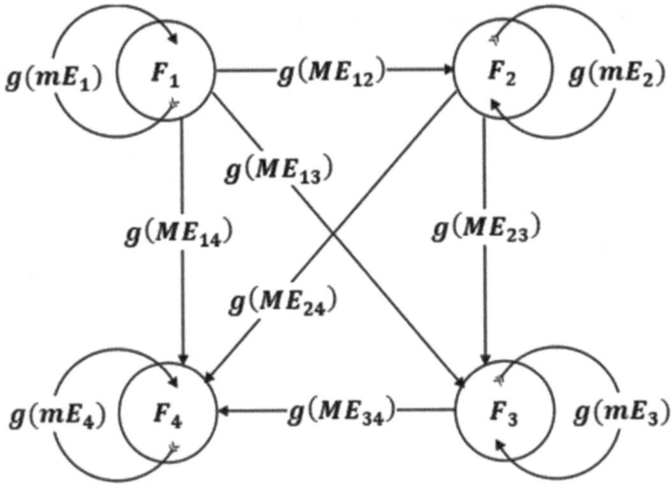

Fig. 16 Evolutionary model of the societal system – I. (*Source* author)

Discussion

(a) General issues

- in an independent way, each societal forces "calculates"[30] its own micro-sentropy gap,$g(mE_i)$, based on respective definitory binomial;
- in a correlated way, for every pair (the six pairs) of societal forces, the macro-sentropy gaps are determined, to establish which are the dominant impulses in the societal system dynamics (movement);

(b) Special issues

Let us note the left component of each binomial societal forces with x, and the right component with y. So, we have the following correspondence of notation:

- force F_1: for population, F_1^x, and for resources, F_1^y
- force F_2: for science, F_2^x, and for social construction, F_2^y
- force F_3: for humanities, F_3^x, and for art, F_3^y

- force F_4: for realization of human being, F_4^x, and for social justice, F_4^y

Conventionally, in order to provide a symmetric evaluation of the sentropy gaps, we can consider the following algebraic signs of the micro-sentropy gaps (we introduce the following logical constant: $\dashv$, meaning "dominates"). For example, if in the societal force F_i, F_i^x is scanty in relation to F_i^y, then we write $F_i^x \dashv F_i^y$. The signification[31] is that the pression to movement inside the societal force i comes from the component F_i^x, that is, the internal arrow of dynamics is caused by the more (relatively) scanty component.

The above result is important both for each of the four societal forces and for the macro-sentropy gaps between those forces, as follows:

- if $F_i^x \dashv F_i^y$, then, inside the societal force i it is to do actions so that the micro-sentropy gap be reduced or (at limit) cancelled. This result is somewhat counter-intuitive related to the current understanding of the entropy signification (not meaning!). Indeed, the dissipative systems (as symbolic species are) try to reduce the internal entropy, while in our case, by the contrary, the dynamics targets to increase entropy. Such reversing of "purpose" is caused by the very definition of the entropy in the present research. Shortly, in the sentropy case, as it is that considered here, the internal homogeneity denotes a good state of affairs, so the maximum of social entropy is... desired.[32]

A more analytical evolutionary model of the societal system is shown in Fig. 17

Discussion

- we propose to identify four ages in the societal unfolding: childhood, youth, adulthood, and wisdom. The ages approximately overlap the historical path (chreod) of the human society as other theoretical perspectives accept or propose;
- in every age of the society, another societal force is at the very origin of the society movement (at limit, progress[33]). This force is exactly the most significant one for the society in case at that age or, in other words, the most restrictive binomial tension in the societal system in case.

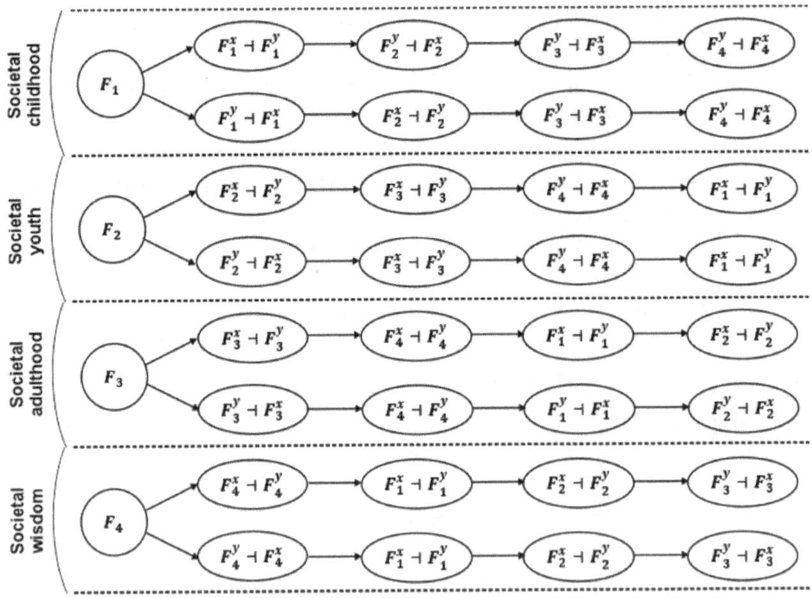

Fig. 17 Evolutionary model of the societal system – II. (*Source* author

 - for the childhood age: F_1
 - for youth age: F_2
 - for adulthood age: F_3
 - for wisdom age: F_4

- in the childhood age, the starting point in the societal evolution is force F_1(binomial "population – resources"), and it could proceed in two opposite cases, based on the algebraic sign of the micro-sentropic gap:
  - if the initial state is$F_1^x \dashv F_1^y$, i.e., there is a constraint of the population on resources (for example, there is a resources scarcity), then the impulse transmitted to F_2 is on improving the social construction (F_2^y); further, solving the social construction arrearage, the impulse passes to forceF_3, namely to stimulate the humanities development which is, in turn, under-developed related to the art and, finally, the impulse

passes to force F_4, to develop social justice, as previously the realization of human being was pushed by F_3^y;
- if the initial state is $F_1^y \dashv F_1^x$, i.e., there is a constraint of resources on population (for example, a resources abundance), then the impulse transmitted to F_2 is to develop the science (F_2^x) so to solve the resource constraint; further, as the humanities is served by pushing on F_2^x, the art becomes a constraint inside the force F_3, what directs the impulse to the component F_3^y, and finally, the impulse travels to force F_4, namely to push on the F_4^y(social justice improvement) because this component remains back when the realization of human being (F_4^x) is already augmented by F_3^y.

The reader is invited to follow the logic for the other three ages of the societal system, and to establish the chains of impulses. *Nota bene*: the chains must be closed among the four forces, so that, at the societal level, to continuously function the stimulation of the eight components in Fig. 17, and, this way, to provide the reason for societal development and progress.

Observation: the causal changes in Fig. 17 are of qualitative nature, because, in fact, the impulse among the societal forces circulates based on the macro-sentropy gap, namely choosing that force with which the force expected to provide the impulse registers the minimum sentropic gradient. Figure 17 has been drawn considering this criterion of interaction, but only in a qualitative/intuitive way—in a real process, the macro-sentropic gap must be determined related to all the other three societal forces by choosing the destination of the impulse so it is generated by the new macro-sentropy gap.

5.4 *The Evolutionary Model—Analytical Lines*

Based on the above reasoning, we can now build a more analytical scheme of the evolutionary model of the society (societal system).

Some Precautionary Preparations

There are many differences between the standard Darwinian evolutionary theory, which is applicable to biological species, and a possible evolutionary theory applicable to symbolic species. However, in the general view, the intrinsic logic is the same, since it seems Darwin (and his adepts and followers) identified the crucial "ingredients" that can move a species on its path (chreod) in both time and space. In what follows, we presume the fundamentals of the evolutionary theory assigned to biological species are known and, consequently, the analysis will be focused on the differences brought by the entrance of the symbolic species (as social constructs/artefacts) on the stage.

The symbolic species considered is the society as a whole (namely, the societal system[34]). The ground on which our proposal will be edified is represented by the four societal forces above examined. Before starting an analytical examination of the proposal, some remarks are, we think, required, regarding the concept of societal forces, in order to prevent some misunderstandings.

(i) a societal force is not an objective/historical force, as some social theories or philosophies claim (for example, Marxism). An objective/historical force has necessity, i.e., its actions (either by acting or abstaining) occur without the humans' free will or desire. Although, as we shall see, a societal force is, more exactly, an objectified force, namely, it is opposable to each and all of individuals or groups, since it, itself, is the result of the contingency and, in majority of cases, of the deliberativeness (i.e., it has the nature of an intellectual project);

(ii) the objectified character of a societal force "sends" it into Popper's third world, namely into the world of the inter-subjective content of thought.

(iii) there is a so-called minimum distance between the societal force as necessity and the societal force as contingency, namely the impersonal construction of the societal forces. Let us take the famous invisible hand, i.e., the societal force acting in the economic field (*Nota bene*: we have in my mind a free market economic system, of course)—there are many individual (or of small groups) purposes, most of them contradictory to each other, and these purposes enter either the competition or cooperation (together with the means/resources required to their accomplishment) and, as a result, on long term and in average, the society experiences a sufficient harmony, i.e., order to go on. As some scientists said (remember Prigogine), we have order from fluctuations or, in other words, a macro-order from micro-disorders. Such a state of affairs is met in both Nature and society[35];

(iv) although the societal forces have no necessary character, each of them "governs" the established binomials under the constraint of equilibrium (what is called micro-sentropy). This finality (*Nota bene*: the purpose is an internalization of finality into the conscious) confers to the four societal forces sufficient power in influencing (at limit: driving) the societal system on its path (chreod) so to be justified the term of force. In fact, the societal forces constitute four different and correlated societal tensions (gradients) inside the society, aimed at guiding and moving that society. As we shall see next, the societal forces enter a *sui generis* evolutionary process, where neither the perfect micro-equilibrium nor the perfect micro-chaos are tolerated.

Basic Structural Elements of the Evolutionary Model.
(a) Genotype

The genotype is that entity that contains the "program" of the future phenotype. In contrast to the biological species, in the case of the symbolic species, the genotype can be (and usually is) outside the very phenotype. It is located at the individual (or group, organization, institution, authority, etc.) responsible for the phenotype associated. For example, the genotype of the symbolic species called fiscal policy is constituted by the fiscal strategy of the Government. By definition, the genotype is the place where occur the mutations aimed at affecting the next generations of the phenotype.

The genotype is located (principled but not mandatorily) inside the societal force that is positioned at the left edge of the causal chain of societal evolution, i.e., in the starting point, as suggested in Fig. 17. So, for the childhood age, the genotype of the symbolic species in the case is located inside force F_1, for the youth age, inside the force F_2, for the adulthood age, inside the force F_3, and for the wisdom age, inside the force F_4.

Also principled, the genotype exhibits, somehow, both the size (intensity) of the micro-sentropy gap inside the respective societal force and the algebraic sign associated with that gap. As we shall see, the mutation affects both the size and the sign of the micro-sentropic gap.

(b) Phenotype

The phenotype is the "adult" individual of the species called society (societal system). As the genotype, the phenotype differs according to the age of society taken into consideration. Principled, the phenotype is the state of society as this is represented by the societal force positioned at the right edge of the causal chain of the society (age) in the case. Consequently, never the genotype and the phenotype reside in the same societal force. This is a crucial conjecture of our research.

It is to be mentioned that there is a crucial difference between the phenotype in the symbolic species case and the phenotype in the biological species: the symbolic phenotype is born directly as an adult; it does not need to grow or develop in a way or another.

Essentially, the phenotype is exactly the societal forces placed on the right edge of the society. So:

- for the childhood age of the society: the phenotype is the force F_4;
- for the youth age of the society: the phenotype is the force F_1;
- for the adulthood age of the society: the phenotype is the force F_2;
- for the wisdom age of the society: the phenotype is the force F_3.
- Mutation

The mutation is always exerted on the genotype and represents an alteration of that genotype, of different kinds and sizes/intensities. In contrast to the mutation regarding the biological species, in the case of symbolic species, the mutations hold some peculiarities as follows:

- is not random (except rare cases as: natural catastrophes, wars, pandemics, social revolutions, etc.);
- as a consequence, it is, in the overwhelming measure, deliberative, either according or not to a strategy/program—so, we can say that the mutation in the case of symbolic species is, almost always, of the purpose nature;

- it gravitates around, i.e., produces its impact, on the binomial component of the societal force involved which "plays" the role of the constraint, that is, under-developed comparing with the second component in that binomial. For example, in the adulthood age of the society (see Fig. 17), in the case $F_3^y \dashv F_3^x$, the (eventual) mutation will exert its impact on the component F_3^y.
- Transcription

Transcription of mutation means a set of changes operated, following the mutation, in the strategy or program assigned to the paired components of the force impacted by that mutation. Of course, the changes signify the taking over of the mutation's suggestions in the strategy/program in the case.[36]

(e) Translation

Translation of mutation means elaboration of a set of norms (within the normative framework of the society) aimed at codifying the transcription already operated in the strategy/program assigned to the societal force involved as "depository" of the genotype.[37]

Before continue the discussion, it is useful to provide a graphical scheme of mutation phenomenology (Fig. 18).

(f) Fitness

The concept of fitness addresses (as in the case of biological species) the degree and way through which an individual of symbolic species meets the

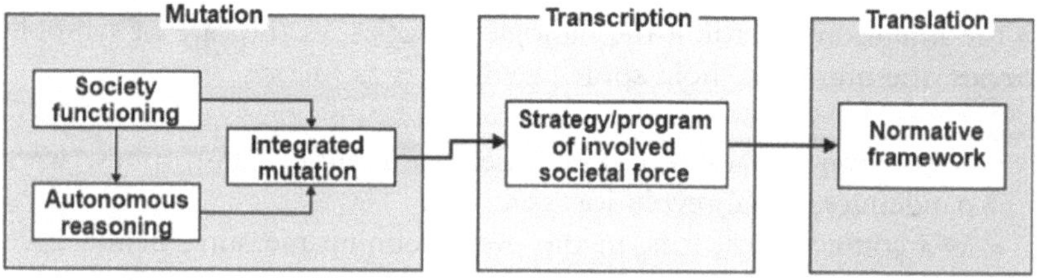

Fig. 18 From mutation to translation in the evolutionary path of symbolic species. (*Source* author)

constraints of the environment (*Nota bene*: in the environment is included the other individuals of that species and the other species, as well).

The main characteristics of the fitness in the symbolic species case are the following:

- in contrast to the case of biological species, the fitness of symbolic species is not primarily a response/reaction to the environment (whatever this might mean), but to the internal gap of micro-sentropy of the societal force involved. Of course, as shown before, the dynamics of the micro-sentropy gap will influence, in turn, the other forces in the causal chain suggested in Fig. 17, but this happens just in a second instance;
- so, by fitness must be understood always the internal equilibrium of the paired components of binomials that constitute each societal force, namely:
  - the more punctualized the internal equilibrium, that is, the smaller the gap of micro-sentropy, the better the fitness assigned;
  - logically, the fitness in the symbolic species case targets rather a kind of "adaptation" to the internal affairs of each societal force than an adaptation to the requirements of the environment at the societal level;
  - it results that it appears an intermediary step in validating the fitness and, then, in the selection process, in contrast to the biological species case—this intermediary step is the internal equilibrium of the societal forces involved;
  - this fitness realization in two steps or two stages is a peculiarity of the symbolic species dynamics in its evolutionary process;
- a new issue arises in the case of symbolic species (which is unknown because it is irrelevant in the case of biological species), namely regarding the *representative fitness*. To introduce the concept of representative fitness, some extra considerations are useful:
  - according to the general/abstract scheme shown in Fig. 17, each of the four societal forces holds its own fitness, namely the equilibrium between the binomial components or, the same, the micro-sentropy gap;

- so, a question can be put in such a context: which of the four individual fitnesses is concluding and significant for the evolutionary process of the societal system? My positioning here is as follows:
    - the representative fitness of a causal episode in societal evolution is always the state of affairs exhibited by the societal force placed on right edge in the given causal chain, as we have already mentioned at point (b) above;
    - as we shall see below (point (g)), the selection of the mutation is always done on the representative fitness, not on the intermediary fitnesses placed to left of the representative fitness.

- Selection

The selection is the very process by which the mutation that occurred in the societal system is or is not accepted by the environment. First of all, we have to clarify the concept of environment in the case of symbolic species.

(1) The environment

The environment of the phenotype—*Nota bene*: now we can introduce the concept of *representative phenotype*, as being that phenotype that corresponds to the representative fitness considered—is constituted by the following entities:

- the other three (non-representative) phenotypes, associated with the other three societal forces;
- the responsible individuals (or groups, organizations, authorities) that monitor and decide on the society's evolution.

The environment "examines" the representative phenotype and decides on accepting or rejecting the mutation(s) that led to that phenotype.

(2) The selection process

The selection of the representative phenotype is a selection based on reference/benchmark, namely: if the micro-sentropy gap inside the ultimate societal force in the causal chain is under a threshold, then the mutation is accepted (validated, selected), if not, then the mutation is rejected.

(3) The threshold of selection

The issue of the threshold to be considered in the selection process here discussed is, of course, an exogenous variable. It is established by the individuals (or groups, organizations, authorities) responsible for the selection process based on autonomous considerations, preferably of an axiological nature. As said before, the perfect (punctualized) equilibrium between the components of the binomials of any societal force is not only (practically) impossible but also undesirable. The following considerations are useful to be provided:

- about impossibility
  - inside any of the four societal forces, the "engine" is exactly the tension (the micro-sentropy gap) between the two components of the own binomial. Accepting the perfect equilibrium, that is, the null sentropy gap means the force concerned becomes inert, uncapable of any advance in future—such a state is impossible, since the mutual dynamics of the components of binomial contains unpredictable oscillations;
  - the micro-sentropy gap is a human measurement, which is liable of objective imprecisions, on the one part, and of subjective evaluations, on the other part. Moreover, the two components of the binomial are inextricably enough joint, so it is possible to have, for any societal force, a sort of *Heisenberg's imprecision*: the more precisely we measure one component, the more imprecisely we measure the other component[38];
- about undesirableness
  - it is obvious that neither society wishes to stop the movement (perhaps, the progress) of the societal forces. Even if, hypothetically, we would have perfect equilibrium inside a societal force, the society should unbalance that force to forge new developments.

The Logical Analytical Scheme of the Societal Evolution
In the final of this chapter, we shall design a more analytical scheme of the societal evolution, based on the above mentioned (Fig. 19).

(a) some preliminaries

- let us consider a generic societal force, F_k, as the beginner force (at the left edge of the causal chain in Fig. 17), so the representative phenotype, based on which the fitness will be measured and the selection will be made, is the societal force F_{k+3} ($k = 1,2,3,4$), modulo 4:
  - for $k = 1$, the representative phenotype is F_4 (4 modulo 4)
  - for $k = 2$, the representative phenotype is F_1 (5 modulo 4)
  - for $k = 3$, the representative phenotype is F_2 (6 modulo 4)
  - for $k = 4$, the representative phenotype is F_3 (7 modulo 4)
- the minimum macro-sentropy gradient is arbitrarily presumed to be registered between two societal forces, which I choose myself[39];
- in this research I do not propose methods to measure either the micro-sentropy gaps within the societal forces or the minimum macro-sentropy gap among societal forces—such engagements will be postponed for (probably) a scientific article in near future.

Nota bene: it is more and more obvious that the society ages proposed above are generic enough, since today, dis-equilibriums between binomial components of all the societal forces arise in all societies, no matter their age. This leads us to consider any of the four causal chains in Fig. 17 to design the analytical logical scheme of the society's evolutionary path. In fact, for example, we can consider the second causal chain, where the starting societal force is F_2, and the final societal force is F_1, without losing the generality of examination.

(b) the logical scheme

The logical scheme of the analytical path of the evolutionary becoming of the society is sketched in Fig. 19 (notations: T_k^{mE} is the critical threshold

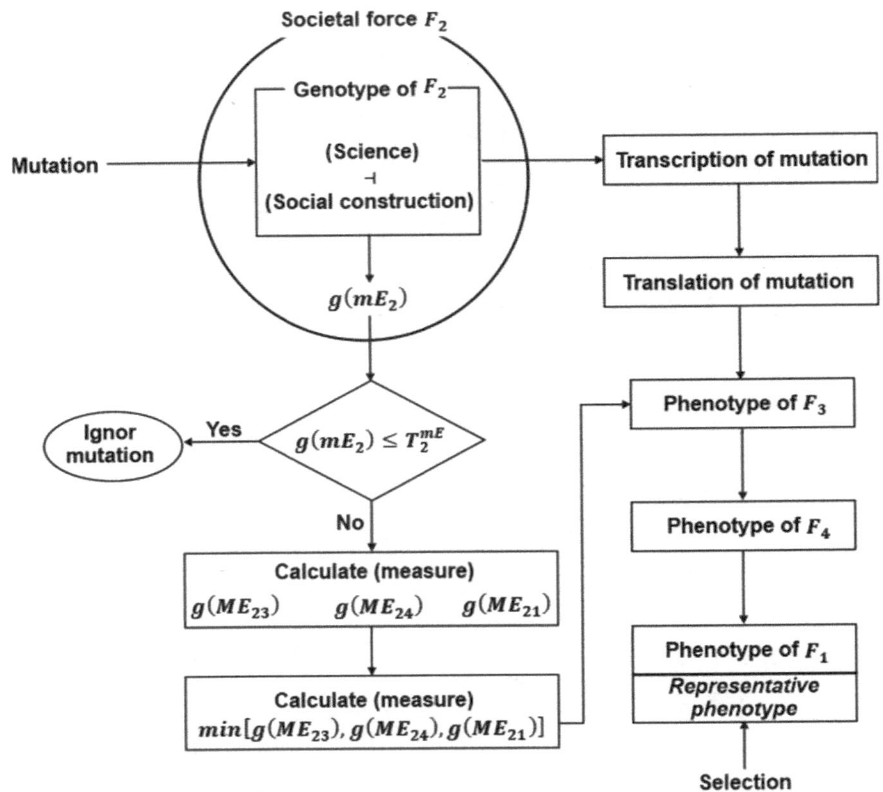

Fig. 19 Analytical (logical) scheme of societal evolutionary process. (*Source* author)

of the micro-sentropy gap for the societal force F_k; $T_{k/q}^{ME}$ is the macro-sentropy gap between the societal forces k and q—see the formalization at point 2.5.1. (2). It is presupposed, for the sake of discussion, that $g(ME_{23}) \leq g(ME_{24}) \geq g(ME_{21}), g(ME_{34}) < g(ME_{31})$).

Discussion

- the mutation, as it is generated according to Fig. 2. 18, occurs in the societal force F_2, in the case $F_2^x \dashv F_2^y$, i.e., science registered an under-development related to social construction needs;
- the responsible for this genotype (e.g., the minister of research) calculates the micro-sentropy gap, namely $g(mE_2)$;
- a decision block is used to compare $g(mE_2)$ with the pre-established T_2^{mE}:
  - if $g(mE_2) \leq T_2^{mE}$, the tension between the two components of the binomial host by F_2 is insufficient to take over the mutation—as consequence, the mutation is ignored;
  - if else (i.e., $g(mE_2) > T_2^{mE}$, the procedure continue by calculating the macro-sentropies $g(ME_{23}), g(ME_{24}), g(ME_{21})$;
- according to the presuppositions made above, we proceed to calculate the minimum value of the macro-sentropy gaps $min[g(ME_{23}), g(ME_{24}), g(ME_{21})]$, and we shall find the value $g(ME_{23})$;
- as result, the impulse will pass from F_2 to F_3;
- parallelly, the mutation occurred into F_2 is transcribed and translated according to the above-presented procedures;
- next, the impulse will circulate from F_3 to F_4, respectively from F_4 to F_1;
- finally, the representative phenotype is the micro-sentropy $g(mE_1)$, and the selection will be exerted on this phenotype;
- if $g(mE_1) > T_1^{mE}$, the entire process will be resumed, this time by starting from the societal force F_1.

Annex 1: About Public Goods

1. Generalities

The generic term public goods refers to those goods and services that are necessary and useful for a given community, that is, for each individual and for the community as a whole, but which goods and services cannot be produced by individuals themselves, either individually or through voluntary cooperation between individuals. In this (working) definition, several ideas appear that need to be clarified in order to be able to move forward with the concept of public good:

(a) firstly, it is about the expression public goods—although, as has now been shown, this includes both goods and services,[40] the generic name used is that of public goods. We will not pedantically dismantle this already established expression, although, as we will see, the largest part of public goods is constituted exactly by public services;
(b) secondly, it is about the necessary character of public goods—the phrase necessary character has, here, its very meaning from logic, that is, it refers to something that cannot be missing, that is, something essential for a given purpose;
(c) thirdly, it is about the usefulness of public goods—the public goods must resolve some needs, of established sorts (usually, by the Constitution), so they cannot exist, i.e., they cannot be produced and distributed if no assignation to a need (either individual or communitarian) is possible—however, a normative list for the public goods allowed or required is difficult to be established;
(d) fourthly, it is about the fact that public goods are necessary and useful both for each individual and for the community as a whole[41]—indeed, the two targets of public goods must be maintained in their conjunction, because a public good necessary for a community but which does not maintain its necessity for each individual component of that community is unlikely to maintain its presence in the long term. On the other hand, a public good necessary for each individual may or may not be necessary for the community as such. We therefore believe that, for the rigorous definition of the concept of public good, the aforementioned conjunction of necessity (both for each individual and for the community as such) must be preserved;
(e) fifthly, there is the issue of the utility of public goods—for example, an individual who has a physical impairment that prevents him from travelling on public roads might consider that the public road is not

useful to him and might claim not to be involved (from a cost point of view—see further on the issue of the costs of public goods) in the design and production of this type of public good;

(f) sixthly, there is the "property" of public goods that they cannot be produced by individuals themselves, either individually or through voluntary cooperation between individuals (of course, within a given community).[42] The following considerations may be of utility:

- the impossibility of producing public goods at the level of individuals refers to an economic impossibility, not a technological one: the price of such public goods would be exorbitant and, obviously, completely prohibitive—for example, it would mean that each individual would have to produce his/her own army, his/her own police, his/her own gendarmerie unit, his/her own highway, etc.;
- the cooperation of individuals in the production of public goods is also questionable—in a small community the public goods that are needed could not be produced, no matter how much voluntary cooperation was involved, there simply are not enough resources for this. In addition, in two close communities conflicts would certainly arise, for example, between police forces, or regarding roads/highways, etc.;
- the only possibility of solving the problem is inter-individual cooperation at the most extensive level of the community—usually the national or state community, as we will discuss in the following chapters. Cooperation at the level of the maximum extended community has several necessary (mandatory) particularities:
  - it involves specialization: a certain contingent of individuals, trained precisely in the production and distribution of public goods, will be normatively tasked with this activity (we call this the public sector)[43];
  - it involves the participation, from the perspective of costs, of the entire society in the production and distribution of public goods (we call this concept as tax);
  - of course, in this context the problem of individual agreement to bear the costs of production and distribution of public goods reappears; although the moral

issue remains, not yet receiving a generally accepted/ acceptable justification, from a constitutional point of view it has received the resolution of legal (normative) support;

(g) *seventhly*, the production and distribution of public goods involve (as indirectly follows from the above) a decision, somehow, taken by an elite group, which decision, however, concerns the entire community. Indeed, this elite (ultimately, it is the state) determines both the necessity and the utility of public goods and, of course, the structure, quality, and quantity of their production and distribution to the community. This decision is not, however, entirely discretionary—we bring, in support of this assertion, the following arguments:

- the state (which arises with human society[44]) appears either as a result of a founding act (the choice of first or basic principles, in the original position—see Rawls' theory), or as a result of the actions of the invisible hand, through the spontaneous aggregation of an association for the defence of individual rights of any kind, as they are "stipulated" by natural law—see Nozick's theory. So, in both cases (*Nota bene*: in a third case, Nussbaum does not present a mechanism for the emergence/ formation/institution of the state, but focuses on the role and functions of the state, which actually interferes, in the most substantial part, with the two theories mentioned), the state represents an objectification of individual options, as they are aggregated in one way or another. Somehow, what the state is going to do—among other things, the establishment, production, and distribution of public goods—is approved, through a founding act, by the very individuals who make up a generic community;
  - therefore, it cannot be said that there is a rupture of purpose between the founding individuals of the state (i.e., of society) and the individuals called upon, after the emergence of the state (in fact, perpetually[45]), to decide and ensure the production and distribution of public goods at the community level. We can accept, however, that, regarding the means of achieving the goal assumed at the time of the emergence/institutions of the state,

there may be "novelties" that were not anticipated at the time in question but the goal remains unaltered in its essence[46];

- goals formulated by that elite (i.e., the state) may also appear, which goals were not considered by individuals who participated, from a historical point of view (but, especially, from a logical point of view) in the emergence/institution of the state. This possibility resides in the course of the historical evolution of the community, when new challenges arise and, therefore, the stability of new goals is needed. However, the stability of new goals cannot depart from the general principle requiring that the goals of the state aim at safeguarding individuals and the community as such, of which the individuals are part. The (possible) deviation from this sacrosanct principle is fined precisely through the electoral mechanism, when representatives who care to deviate (or intend to deviate) from the respective principle can be withdrawn from the state structure (institutions, agencies, agencies).[47]

2. Methodological issues

In this paragraph, we will examine, in a more analytical way, the concept of public good and we will establish, based on some criteria, a taxonomy[48] of them, thus obtaining, in this way, the classes of public goods that can exist in a generic community (more precisely, society).

(a) Criteria for taxonomy of public goods

Two criteria for classifying (at the taxonomy level) public goods are of interest:

(i) the way in which public goods are distributed at the level of society (it being established, with sufficient clarity, that their production is the prerogative of the state—through institutions, agencies, and specialized organizations);

(j) the nature of the public good, or the type of social need that public goods satisfy.

(b) Classes of public goods

According to the criterion that verifies the distribution method, public goods can be:

- (BP_1^1) distributed by the state through the public sector: for example, national defence;
- (BP_2^1) distributed by the state through the private sector of the state: for example, free or subsidized electricity granted by the state to its private domain;
- (BP_3^1) distributed by the private sector, under a subsidy granted by the state: for example, food for students or for people with deficiencies/disabilities/handicap[49];
- (BP_4^1) distributed by the state sector in a complementary manner with similar private goods and services: for example, education or health.

According to the criterion that verifies the nature of the public goods, they can be[50]:

- (BP_1^2) public goods aimed at biological survival;
- (BP_2^2) public goods aimed at individual freedom;
- (BP_3^2) public goods aimed at the full integration of the individual into society/community;
- (BP_4^2) public goods aimed at the safety and security of life;
- (BP_5^2) public goods aimed at the intellectual development of the human being;
- (BP_6^2) public goods aimed at the harmony between the individual (community) and the non-anthropic environment;
- (BP_7^2) public goods aimed at the preservation and adaptation[51] of community identity;
- (BP_8^2) public goods aimed at the emotional development of the human being (art, religion);
- (BP_9^2) public goods aimed at the harmony between the human being and artificial intelligence;
- (BP_{10}^2) public goods aimed at the formation and protection of self-esteem.

Of course, the two criteria can be combined, so that they act simultaneously, thus resulting in a number of 40 theoretically possible classes of public goods (Table 3).

Discussion

- first, let us note the incompatibilities between the two criteria, i.e., the combined classes of public goods that "cannot exist":
    - the incompatibilities refer to the public good BP^2_2 (individual freedom)—this public good is too important (probably, the most important—we say probably, because the public goodBP^2_{10}, self-esteem, could also "compete" for this title) to let the private sector, whose general behavioural criterion is to obtain profit, if possible, at its maximum level, manage it, either independently or in cooperation with the public sector;
- second, let us make the following observations:
    - public goods provided only by the state aim at freedom and the achievement of harmonious "symbiosis" between the human being and artificial intelligence;
    - the greatest overlap of providers of public goods occurs in the case of public goods offered (not produced, as shown) by the private sector based on state subsidies in 8 cases out of 10

Table 3 Classes of double-classified public goods

Criterion 2 \ Criterion 1	BP^1_1	BP^1_2	BP^1_3	BP^1_4
BP^2_1		x	x	x
BP^2_2	x			
BP^2_3		x	x	x
BP^2_4				x
BP^2_5			x	x
BP^2_6		x	x	x
BP^2_7		x	x	x
BP^2_8			x	
BP^2_9	x	x	x	x
BP^2_{10}		x	x	

Source author

possible; in second place are goods offered in a complementary manner by the state and the private sector, 7 cases, and in third place are public goods offered through the state's private domain, 6 cases.

Notes

1. Here we have the very concept of social construction, i.e., the "population" of Popper's third-world.
2. We recall that functionality is understood as the possible set (not just the current one) of interactions between the components of an entity (seen as a system), and behaviour is understood as the possible set of interactions (not just the current one) between the components of the entity, on the one hand, and the environment of that entity, on the other hand. Of course, there is a mutual causal determination between functionality and behaviour, but, from a theoretical (and methodological) point of view, they constitute different concepts.
3. Not only does the entity adapt to the environment, but the environment also adapts to the entity—this pressure of the entity towards modifying the environment according to its own requirements is called *enaction*.
4. For example, automatons experienced in computers have the characteristics of the informational living.
5. We must operate a clear, non-ambiguous distinction between awareness and consciousness—while awareness is a generical capacity of representation (namely, it belongs to human nature), consciousness is the effect of the culture on awareness (namely, the consciousness belongs to the human condition). So, while the awareness is, somewhat, a-temporal, the consciousness is historical, i.e., it is a historical hypostasis of the awareness.
6. Founded by the famous Chilean biologists, Humberto Maturana and Francisco Varela, creators of the concept of *autopoiesis* (Maturana, 1975); (Maturana; Varela, 1980).
7. The constructal law, which claims a great novelty, is, obviously, a generalization of the very concept of the Santiago School on the cognition.
8. We specify that this description rigorously corresponds to the concept of sign in semiotics or linguistic theory.

9. This paragraph is taken over from (Dinga et al., 2023).
10. In the field of living things, the change that concerns the species is called evolution—in our opinion, keeping this term, when necessary, we will have to use either the term transformation or the term progress, as the case may be, for the evolution of the human species or symbolic species as: language, routines, communication, norms (or normative systems), strategies, etc.
11. In the case of the human being, finality acquires either the "look" of the goal (*Nota bene*: the goal is a consciously predetermined finality), as in the case of evolution as transformation, or the "look" of value (axiological finality), as in the case of evolution as progress.
12. A free society can generate a democratic one, but a democratic society is not necessarily (from the logical point of view) liable to causally generate a free society. Consequently, this component of the state vector of society must contain a conjunction between a free society and a democratic one.
13. See, here, the theses of existentialism, especially at Heidegger.
14. Something that Prigogine named order through (or from) fluctuations.
15. Natural laws are originated in necessity, while social laws are originated in contingency (the so-called positive laws). This is why freedom (or free will) manifests only related to the positive laws, never to natural laws.
16. There is not only an individual/personal æsthetic profile but also a social aesthetic profile (see Schiller, here).
17. It is, somehow, counter-intuitive that an abstention (a lack of act) could create/generate an artefact. The question is analogous to that of the very abstention as a species of action, alongside the act (to do). To abstain from creating or generating an artefact is equivalent to creating, in reality, an artefact, namely exactly to the absence of that artefact.
18. I remind that any change in the world is causal—either it is necessary or contingent, and either it is deterministic, stochastic, or random. It is worth noting that the stochastic events require/allow a probability distribution as behaviour pattern, while the random events do not allow such a probability distribution (no matter the kind of probability—enerally, however, a Kolmogorov probability).
19. Something like in a large network of *sui generis* unintentional duopolies or, better said, oligopolies.

20. I remind that autonomy is different from independence: while autonomy implies the "right" to elaborate and follow own rules of decision/behaviour, independency implies no relationships (either, causal or functional) with tertiaries. This means that it could exist autonomy without independence, but it could not exist independence without autonomy.
21. The logical relationship between artefact and symbolic species is the following: the symbolic species is a… species of the genus called artefact, namely that artefact capable of evolution (or co-evolution or self-evolution).
22. Of course, there is a crisp difference between cause and causality: causality is a principle, while the cause is a local (i.e., spatio-temporal, contextual) hypostasis of causality. The causality always acts through local causes, so the causes are always local, while the causality is general/universal. From a logical perspective, the causality is the general, and the cause is the particular. I am a nominalist, so I consider that the causality is *an ideal*, while the cause is *a real*.
23. To some extent, the impersonal causality could be considered (with required precautions) as a necessary causality, but a social necessity (see next, in the main text body), not a natural (non-anthropic) one.
24. Essentially, *causa sui* (Lat.) is an autonomous causality, namely a cause by itself—e.g., God).
25. The case is analogous to that provided by Niklas Luhmann in its autopoietic social theory (1995): the human being, although living inside the society, is considered to be located outside of it, from the perspective of the social phenotype called communication.
26. The economic process is a praxiological process (see Chapter 1), i.e., it implies the relationships between subject and object, which, in turn, imply the entropic exchange between the human being/society and the non-anthropic environment.
27. It is true, however, that technological progress narrows more and more non-anthropogenic space so that more and more that space (Nature) becomes… physical capital, under the definition provided by economists for the concept of capital.

28. The spiral is a Marxist proposal for… infinite progress—but infinite progress is inconceivable from any perspective, including the limitations of both human beings (as possibilities and aspirations) and of Earth (as opportunities, restrictions, and sustainability).
29. Using the terminology of Romanian-French logician and Philosopher Stephane Lupasco, the maximum entropy is equivalent to the maximum homogenization, while the decrease of entropy is signalled by the increase of heterogenization—homogenization and heterogenization go in opposed directions by the difference from "1", namely the sum between the relative homogenization and the relative heterogenization is 1.
30. It is obvious that both micro-sentropy gaps and macro-sentropy gaps are evaluated by the individuals, organizations, or institutions normatively empowered to do that.
31. The signification is different from meaning: while meaning expresses the denotation (or definition) of something, signification expresses the (idiosyncratic) perception, by the generic individual, of the meaning (Dinga, 2025).
32. Let us, for example, consider the case of economic polarization (inequality) in society—it seems the greater polarization the greater diversification (heterogeneity), so the smaller entropy. But, as signification, it is obvious that the smaller economic polarization is desirable for the society's benefit, so, in fact, from a social perspective, the entropy must… increase—exactly this type of entropy I shall call *sentropy*.
33. In contrast to other measurements at the societal level (growth, development), the progress is not standardly measurable by objective indicators. It is subject to evaluation/hermeneutic, fundamentally from an axiological perspective. In my opinion, the most adequate such perspective is the social justice accomplishment.
34. I remind that by the predicate *societal*, it must be understood the logical combination between the predicate *social* and the predicate *statal*, i.e., a social system endowed with a state. Consequently, there are many social systems (for example, ant social systems) but a single societal system: the human society.
35. An example from Thermodynamics (the science that "exported" the concept of entropy to the societal working—*Nota bene*: what I called before with the term sentropy) is the following: from the

disorder of electrons random movement we see, at the "surface", that is, at macro-level, the temperature.

36. To be observed the (logical) analogy of the transcription in symbolic species case with the transcription in biological species case: in the last case, the transcription comes from DNA to RNA, while in the former case, the transcription comes from the individual/group responsible with the societal force involved to the strategy/program assigned to that force. *Nota bene*: do not forget that any mutation, no matter its source (the society itself or the autonomous reasoning of the responsible individual), grows and maturates in the "head" of the individual/group.
37. The equivalent in the biological case is, as known, the protein synthesis based on ARN transcription (more exactly, the information transcribed in RNA is transmitted to ribosomes, where the protein synthesis happens).
38. A formal/mathematical development of this conjecture is, I think, of scientific and practical interest enough.
39. So, the scheme is rather didactical/illustrative, without reducing the validity of reasoning by this.
40. For economists, the difference between good and service is clear: a good is a result of human activity (i.e., an artefact) for which the moment of production and the moment of consumption differ between them, while a service is (also) an artefact for which the two mentioned moments coincide. An intermediate position in this taxonomy is occupied by durable goods (which can be called, with equal justification, durable services). Further considerations regarding these concepts will be made, as appropriate.
41. Here, the term community must be considered in its most general sense, that is, it can refer to any dimension or criterion within which a set of individuals coagulate and live together, from certain points of view—for example, it can be a village, a region, a country, or a multi-state integrative system (federal or intergovernmental), or it can be a scientific or professional community or a social category (like a Kuhnian paradigm).
42. More exactly, they cannot be produced (generally, from economic causes) by what is known as private sector.
43. We make the following conceptual clarifications: economic property is of two broad categories: (a) private property; (b) state property. Private property can be (a1) individual private property;

(a2) associative private property—e.g., through shares, actions, and the like. State property can be: (b1) public property—which, as we will see, produces public goods; (b2) private property of the state—e.g., national companies—which produces private goods, i.e., distributed through the market.

44. Let us recall that, conceptually, the societal is defined as society "applied" to a social group. But the societal is the result of the emergence of society, and society is the result of the emergence (i.e., self-instituting of) of the state.
45. There are no convincing theories for the "death" of the state, as there are (at least relatively convincing) for the death of God—see Nietzsche—or for the death of the subject—see Foucault—or for the death/end of history—see Fukuyama. The Marxist theory of the necessary disappearance of the state has proven inconsistent, and other theories with at least as solid a foundation have not yet been developed.
46. Not else happens with the things in the case of representative democracy that functions today in the vast majority of contemporary societies: individuals freely choose their representatives in state decision-making institutions and authorities, based on the intended purpose, but the means of objectifying those purposes are left (inevitably, from a technical/operational point of view) to the discretion of the elected officials themselves.
47. We recall that not only moments of political elections can play this role of "political hygiene", but there are mechanisms and procedures also between moments of ordinary elections, for example the institution of referendum or, in exceptional cases, the intervention of criminal law, ministerial responsibility or, where the state is authentic, the institution of dismissal of persons unworthy of the position and responsibilities of a public servant.
48. Even though it seems pedantic, there is a difference between taxonomy and typology: taxonomy is based on theoretical (generic) criteria, while typology is based on empirical criteria.
49. The three characteristics are conceptually distinct: (a) impairment is the absence of a natural functionality of the person; (b) disability is the inability of the person to perform a function/role required for his/her social integration; (c) handicap is the disability that brings to the person in question negative discrimination within society. Nota bene: it is not necessary that impairment becomes disability

or that disability becomes handicap, but it is contingent fact that such transitions of meaning occur.

50. There is an interesting proposal of 10 capabilities that the state should ensure for the full functioning of the person, proposed by Nussbaum (2006): 1. life, 2. bodily health, 3. bodily integrity, 4. senses, imagination and thinking, 5. emotions, 6. practical rationality, 7. affiliation capacity, 8. other animal species, 9. play, 10. control over one's own environment—but we consider that they do not exhaust the needs for public goods and, in any case, not on the proposed structure. For example, $${BP}_{1}^{2}$$ targets three of the capabilities proposed by Nussbaum: life, bodily health, and bodily integrity. Freedom is not even provided as a capability (except, partially, for practical rationality, respectively for affiliation capacity—possibly also for play), etc. And as for capability no. 10 (Control over your own environment), we find it hard to believe that this should be left to (or required from) the individual/person and not be assumed by the state.
51. It seems curious to combine the action of preserving community identity (usually national identity) with the action of adapting community identity—in our opinion, we are not dealing with an internal contradiction here, because both socio-historical conditions and inter-community relations (usually at international level) lead to the need for a reconfiguration of community identity, of course, preserving the background of tradition but not neglecting social evolution.

References

Dinga, E., Oprean-Stan, C., Tănăsescu, C.R., Brătian, V., Ionescu, G.-M. (2023). *Co-Evolution of Symbolic Species in the Financial Market. A Framework for Economic and Political Decision-Making*. Palgrave Macmillan – Springer Nature.

Dinga, E. (2025). *Economic Resilience During Overlapped Crises – Antifragility, Sustainability and Autopoieticity*. Palgrave Macmillan – Springer Nature.

Hume, D. (1992). *Treatise on Human Nature*. Prometheus.

Kant, I. (1998). *Critique of Pure Reason*. Cambridge University Press.

Luhmann, N. (1995). *Social Systems*. Stanford University Press.

Maturana, H., & Varela, F. (1980). *Autopoiesis and Cognition*. Reidel Publishing Company.
Maturana, H. (1975). The organization of the living: A theory of the living organization. *International Journal of Man-Machine Studies*.
Prigogine, I., & Stengers, I. (1984). *Order out of Chaos: Man's New Dialogue with Nature*. Flamingo Edition.
Nussbaum, M. C. (2006). *Frontiers of Justice: Disability, Nationality*. Harvard University Press, Belknap Press.
Wolfram, S. (2002). *A New Kind of Science*. Wolfram Media.

CHAPTER 3

Societal Order and Evolutive Process

1 Preamble

Any human activity takes place within a cultural framework—whether it refers to customary traditions (including rituals, myths, or even magical practices) or to institutions, as is the case in modern societies today. This general cultural framework forms what we can call the order of that activity or, more precisely, the ordering principles because order is an effect (result) of ordering principles. One of the most significant orders in the world is, of course, the social order. This chapter aims to propose a theoretical, conceptual framework regarding the social order.

The concept of order is an extremely abstract one and involves considerations that can range from the purest transcendentalism (such as a phenomenological perspective) to the most radical materialism (such as a Marxist perspective). Of course, in this chapter, the concept of order will not be approached from these philosophical perspectives, but from a much more modest one, namely from a logical and praxiological perspectives.

In general, human action is of three categories: (a) theoretical action—concerns object/object interaction (e.g., physics or mathematics); (b) practical action—concerns subject/subject interaction (e.g., politics or religion); (c) praxiological action—concerns subject/object interaction (e.g., economic activity). Of course, there are no pure "versions" of any of the three categories of action, theoretical action involves interactions

E. Dinga, *The Economics of Social Justice and Societal Evolution*, https://doi.org/10.1007/978-3-032-24055-2_3

with the subject, practical action involves interactions with the object, and praxiological action involves both object/object interactions and subject/subject interactions. However, the distinction of the three categories of human action can be made based on the dominance of one of the three relations that can occur within the society. In this conceptual context, we suggest that any action targeting the society as a whole is a praxiological type of human action—what often is called social construction (see Chapter 2, regarding the four societal forces). At least two important arguments can be brought in the direction of the acceptability of this suggestion:

(a) The social has as its reason the ensuring of the principles of survival of individual[1] and groups, including the society as a whole. The current individual[2] is a natural individual of biological type who is connected, from an entropic perspective, with the non-anthropic natural environment. This means that the ensuring of the principles of biological existence of the individual claims, as a crucial function, the interaction between the (generic) individual and the natural environment—but exactly this is the very definition of human action of praxiological type, that is, the interaction of subject-object;
(b) The social constructs, at the same time, require the means to achieve the goals (in general, the acquisition of neg-entropy) that involve non-anthropic environment. The social interaction of the individuals generally involves two types of means: (1) anthropic means—that is, interactions with other individuals, generated mainly by the social division of activity (or labour) which, in turn, necessarily leads to the exchange of activities with other individuals; (2) non-anthropic means—that is, interactions with the non-anthropic natural environment.[3] The category of non-anthropic means, indispensable in the social process (at least for the moment), therefore forms the second argument in favour of considering social life as a praxiology.[4]

Common language (natural or "civil" language) has, of course, a definition of the concept of order—this is considered a configuration, either spatial or temporal or (most often) a combination of the two, which characterizes a phenomenon and which is detectable as such a configuration, that is, it is intelligible to the empirical observer, without he/she having special skills for this observation. In other words, the "common" order is, simply, a pattern, static or kinematic, that the ordinary observer "throws" over a real phenomenon (either objective, subjective, or objectified) and that pattern "fits" the reality in question. Two aspects seem important at this point: (a) what is the "method" by which the pattern in question is detected; (b) what is the potential for truth (more specifically, for true prediction) of that pattern. I provide some considerations here:

(a) It is quite obvious that, in the common understanding of the term, the order observed at the non-specialized empirical level is of the inductive type. The observer notes regularities, periodicities, and other replicability characteristics of a phenomenon and, through inductive inference, that is, through generalization, constructs the order in question (the reader will acknowledge here the Hume-ian position). Of course, inductive inference is susceptible to falsification[5]; therefore the common concept of order is a vulnerable concept[6];

(b) In terms of the potential to allow the formulation of true predictions, the common concept of order is extremely deficient. Of course, predictions can be made, but they are true (i.e., the previous predictive statement coincides with the subsequent descriptive statement) only by chance.[7] The explanation lies in the fact that the generalization has an enormous probability of being local (both temporally and spatially), while the truth of a prediction is "governed" mainly by the universal character of the major premise, not only by its general character.[8] Therefore, the common understanding of the concept of order consists of considering reality as it appears to the non-specialized (or, the same, innocent) observer and inferring causality (and therefore the order pattern) through generalization, that is, through induction.[9]

2 Order—An Analytical Approach

2.1 Sufficiency Predicates of Order as General Concept

In a social entity, the question arises regarding the existence (or not) of a specific order, which we call social order. We denote the concept of social order with *SO*, then it can be written, from a logical point of view, that social order is given by the logical conjunction of the four sufficiency predicates[10]:

- (S_1^O) *sensory observability*: the phenomenon that will underlie the observation (or non-observation[11]) of an ordered configuration must be observable at the sensory level,[12] even if, of course, subsequently to the sensory sensation, other three processes could arise: perception, conceptualization, and judgement (reasoning), which, ultimately, lead to the formulation, through universalization, of the order in question;
- (S_2^O) *intellectual observability*: if S_1^O involves the natural senses of the cognitive subject, S_2^O involves the intellect of that subject. As is known, perception represents the form that consciousness gives to sensation.[13] For the formation of concepts and the preparation of judgments, the intellect of the subject is needed, which transforms perception into a concept. Conceptualization is the crucial stage in the deductive identification of order[14];
- (S_3^O) *psychological intuition*: the order is a binary construction, that is, it comes from two directions: one based on the perception and reasoning (which could be called *substantial emerging*) and one based on the individual idiosyncrasy (which could be called *emotional emerging*). In fact, we think that all decisions taken by individuals are based, prima facie, on the perception of order, more precisely, of the social (or, narrower, economic) order. All the other factors or conditionalities are secondary (or tertiary, after the case[15]) and rather shape irrelevant features of those decisions/actions;
- (S_4^O) *catalog registration*: the application of the first two sufficiency predicates leads only to the possibility of perceiving an order. The effective perception of order occurs only if the result of applying S_2^O and/or S_3^O is found in the already existing catalog of possible orders, which catalog is, of course, accessible to the cognitive subject in question.[16]

So, logically, there is an order, in its general/abstract understanding if the following conjunction occurs:

$$o \leftarrow \left(s_1^o\right) \wedge \left(s_2^o\right) \wedge \left(s_3^o\right) \wedge \left(s_4^o\right) = \bigwedge_{i=1}^{4} s_i^o$$

A brief discussion may be useful here:

(a) How does the cognitive subject come into possession of the catalog containing the list of already known orders (with the basic, defining characteristics, to ensure the recognizability of each one)? Obviously, only as a result of previous experience, so it will have to be accepted that this catalog is an a posteriori one;

(b) How is the comparison of the conceptual outline of the new possible order with the catalog records actually carried out? Someone could ask, here, to postulate a fourth predicate of sufficiency that would guarantee this operational capacity. We consider, however, that this predicate would be redundant[17]; therefore we will assume that the cognitive subject has this intellectual capacity simply on the basis of his/her quality as a cultural subject;

(c) If the cognitive subject does not find, in the catalog, the order that seems to him/her to be identifiable on the basis of the first two predicates of sufficiency, how does he/she proceed? Here two alternative options should be mentioned:

(c.1.) he/she "decrees" that there is no order in the phenomenon in question; here there is a type 1 error—the rejection of a true hypothesis;

(c.2) he/she completes the catalog with the new presumed order, with distinguishing characteristics from those already existing in the catalog; here there is a type 2 error—the admission of a false hypothesis. From a logical point of view, if we do not accept an a priori nature of the catalog of orders,[18] the catalog is formed, over time, namely for each cognitive subject in particular, exclusively by practising type 2 errors;

(d) Are there also catalogs of orders that are supra-subjective (supra-individual)? The answer is, obviously, affirmative: in society does function (and is admitted at the level of all individuals) a common (social, community) catalog of orders. Their inclusion in the common catalog is done by democratic "vote"[19] (for, example, a democratic society, or a free market economy);

(e) Both the catalogs of orders of individuals and those at the community (social) level are, in turn, divided into domains of interest or typological domains: ontological orders, gnoseological orders, axiological orders, praxiological orders, political orders, religious orders, etc.

2.2 A Logical Definition of the Concept of Order

Based on the three sufficiency predicates established above, a logical definition of the concept of order can now be formulated: *the order is a configuration, either spatial or temporal, or (most often) a combination of the two, that characterizes a phenomenon and is detectable as such a configuration, that is, it is intelligible to the cognitively and performatively competent empirical observer*. A synthesis of all considerations regarding the concept of order from a logical perspective is provided, synoptically, by Fig. 1 (Dinga, 2025).

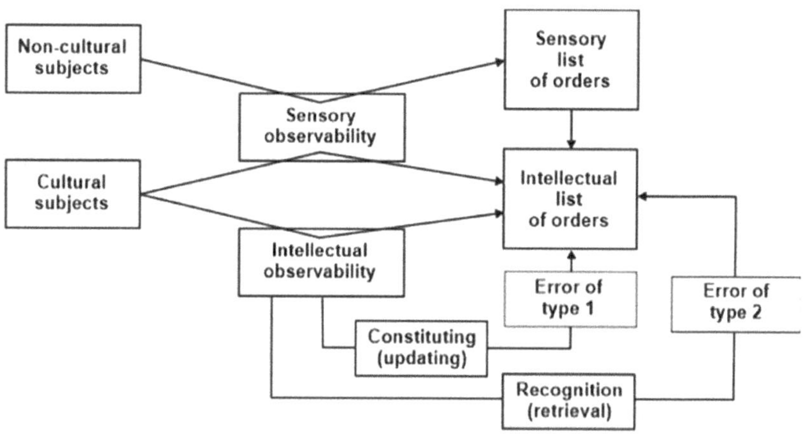

Fig. 1 Mechanism of constituting the list of orders (*Source* author)

2.3 *Revealing of Order*

The revelation of order refers to the acquisition of the conviction, at the level of the empirical observer, that there is an order in the entity that is the object of observation. As it has already been shown, the revelation of order is operated by the intellectual ascertainment of the existence of the type of order detected observationally in the pre-existing list of orders. At least two questions result from this way of defining the revelation of order: (a) what happens if the order is not revealed; (b) what happens if the empirical observation reveals a single order; (c) what happens if the empirical observation reveals more than one order. We will examine them in turn.

(a) The revelation does not indicate any order

As said above, if the result of the empirical observation does not overlap with any existing order in the list of orders, the subject will "decree" that, in the observed entity (thing, phenomenon, process), there is no order. The absence of an order does not prohibit praxiology in the entity in question, but this praxiology will either be operationalized "blindly"[20] or be based on the imposition of a *sui generis* order, generated by the operationalized praxiology itself.[21] The second alternative—the imposition of a *sui generis* order—will inscribe a new order in the list of orders, by the modality of a type 1 error.

(b) The revelation indicates a single order

This is the standard case, in which the cognitive (and praxiological) subject identifies an overlap between the empirically observed order and an entry (and only one) in the previous list of orders. This is a conservative and unproblematic case.

(c) The revelation indicates more than one order

Finding more than one entry in the list of orders following empirical observation is much more problematic than the two cases previously discussed, for the following reasons:

- How will the order that will govern the praxiological action[22] be "chosen"? In this situation, the concept of adequacy is useful. This concept has a vagueness generated by its use in common ("civil") language; therefore we will have to associate a rigorous meaning with it. We propose that, by praxiological adequacy of the revealed order, we understand the property of the order in question to be located at the smallest "logical distance" from the intrinsic logic implied by the expected praxiological action.[23] It is pedantic (and useless) to formulate models of "choosing" the appropriate order, since the real actor will never use such models (either because he/she does not know them, or because the transaction cost of using them is prohibitive). We believe that each actor will perceive, on intuitive grounds but, above all, using past experiences, which particular order among those revealed is the most appropriate[24];
- Could the lexicographic ordering of the pre-known orders from the list of orders available to the observer provide a criterion for choosing the most appropriate order? We believe that the answer here should be negative. A lexicographic ordering (i.e., essentially, an a-criterial one) will be of no use, because each praxiological situation in particular has its own description of the intrinsic logic which is, as proposed above, decisive in choosing the most appropriate order.

2.4 Order and Entropy

The concept of entropy[25] is a concept of maximum generality, having a triple meaning:

- *Ontological* (more precisely, ontical): parameter of a real existential entity (objective or subjective, or objectified);
- *Epistemological*: cognitive significance for the subject (indicates the level of order of the entity);
- *Methodological*: selects the procedure by which the subject "interrogates" the object.

The referential (denotate) of the concept of entropy is a state of an existential entity (system, phenomenon, process). This state is of the nature of order. Entropy is a parameter that "moves" inversely proportional to order, more precisely: the magnitude of entropy is inversely proportional to the degree of ordering of the entity in question. It should be noted that entropy is non-static: in a closed system (e.g., our Universe) entropy increases permanently, namely spontaneously[26]; in other words, the global entropy is irreversible: in a closed system entropy cannot decrease or remain constant.[27]

Among the characteristics of entropy, we mention:

- It is a *state quantity* (function); in addition, the value of the entropy variation does not depend on the intermediate stages (of "path dependence"), but only on the initial and final points[28];
- It is a *macroscopic quantity*; more precisely, it signifies a macroscopic irreversibility derived from a microscopic (possible) reversibility[29];
- It is a *statistical quantity* (based on the phenomenological formulation of Thermodynamics); this fact justifies the appearance of probability in the analytical formula of entropy from statistical thermodynamics (since probabilities can only model the average of a population)[30];
- It is an *additive quantity*.

Based on the above, entropy can be seen as an orderer of reality (either objective or subjective or objectified). The most effective proxy in perceiving/identifying the order of reality seems to be the structure of the entity intentionally targeted. There are two categories of primitive, ontological structures of order:

- *Causality structure*: it is "responsible" for explanations/predictions and for altering the identity of the entity[31];
- *Coexistence structure*: it is "responsible" for functions/outcomes and for preserving the identity of the entity.

The preferential direction of change in the entities of objective reality is given by necessity, which is the only "arrow" of finality. Necessity is "projected" exclusively by physical laws (biological or chemical "laws" are ultimately reduced to considerations of Quantum Physics).[32]

The increase in global entropy is a macro-need (enveloping need), which is fed by local needs (including those in dissipative systems), although here a problem arises: even if we admit the comparability of static structures with each other, how can we compare a static structure (a spatial configuration) with a functional structure, in order to decide on the level of order?[33]

Based on the concept of entropy and the entropic mechanism, let us examine the relationships that could exist between it and the concept of order. The following suggestions seem relevant to us:

- According to its meaning in Thermodynamics,[34] entropy signifies a tendency towards homogeneity, undifferentiation, of a process or system. In this sense, the idea that the increase in entropy indicates an increase in disorder is risky—any spatio-temporal, causal, or functional configuration can signify an order. For example, financial stability is perceived as signifying a high degree of economic order, although it is characterized by a greater homogeneity of the financial process (by reducing the number or amplitude of monetary shocks);
- In our opinion, the use of the concept of entropy to identify, "measure" or evaluate order should be done with great caution. We believe that, from a performative point of view, this concept does not bring much added value to the debate on the concept of order;
- In the case of dissipative systems (as is the case of economic or social systems, which are the "targets" of this chapter) the concept of entropy can play a role but, probably, only in terms of an exotic label for phenomena/events that either already have their own associated terms or can be named without resorting to the term entropy.

3 The Concept of Economic Order

3.1 Defining the Economic Order

We need additional sufficiency predicates for the concept of economic order as a species of the (general) order. For the order perceived on the basis of the four above-mentioned sufficiency predicates to be an economic one, the order in question must verify two more sufficiency predicates,[35] namely:

- (S_5^O) the *social nature* of the phenomenon: the phenomenon in question must be a phenomenon that does not exist (does not appear) otherwise than through social interaction. As is known,

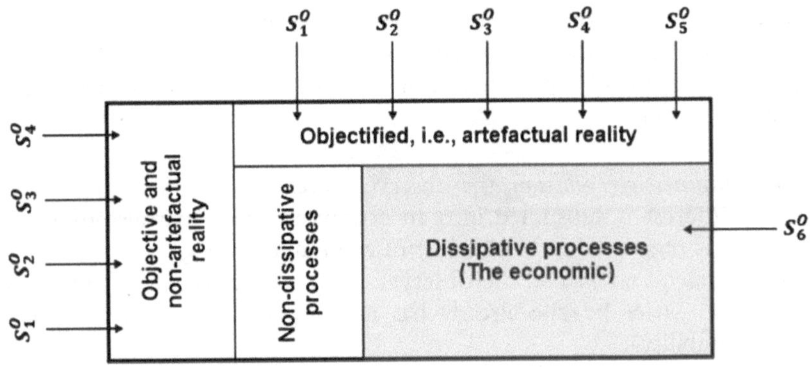

Fig. 2 Logical genesis of the economic order (*Source* author)

social "objects" do not exist unless and to the extent that they represent artefacts, that is, they are results of the action (more precisely, of the interaction) of individuals. A social "object" disappears if the social interaction that gave rise to it ceases;

- (S_6^O) the *entropic nature* of the social phenomenon in question: as is known, the property of economic refers to the property of involving entropic exchange between the individual (or collectivity, considered as a set of individuals) and non-artefactual nature.[36]

Therefore, to have an economic order, the six sufficiency predicates must be verified simultaneously (Fig. 2 summarizes the emergence of the concept of economic order).

Logically, the economic order (EO) is defined by the following conjunction of sufficiency predicates:

$$EO \leftarrow \left(S_1^O\right) \wedge \left(S_2^O\right) \wedge \left(S_3^O\right) \wedge \left(S_4^O\right) \wedge \left(S_5^O\right) \wedge \left(S_6^O\right) = \bigwedge_{i=1}^{6} S_i^O$$

3.2 *Revealing the Economic Order*

Applying it to an economic "object" (we have seen that an economic "object" is a social "object" that has a dissipative nature, that is, it involves entropic exchange between the individual and non-artefactual nature), the revelation of the economic order is subject to the same commandments to which the revelation of any order is subject. We would like to add here the idea that, in principle, there can be three types of revelation of the economic order:

- *Anamnestic revelation*: the observer notes that the economic entity of interest is subsumed into an economic order that already exists and is registered in his/her list of economic orders;
- *Pareidolic revelation*: the observer sees an order seemingly identical to an order he/she already has in mind (often, as an emotional desirability);
- *Projective revelation*: the observer, who is always theoretically loaded (even if this closure is, for example, of the prejudice type), is therefore prepared and inclined to identify in the examined reality the order that he/she foresees as "necessary". The overlap between the observer's intellectual desirability and the spatio-temporal configuration of the economic reality examined leads to the inclusion in the list of economic orders of an economic order—the one just "discovered";
- *Phantasmatic revelation*: the observer does not find any overlap between the economic reality examined and his/her list of orders and, at the same time, his/her intellectual baggage (his/her theoretical loading) does not lead him/her to identify an economic order either. In this case, the observer can imagine an economic order either according to his/her current desires or according to a certain interest.[37]

3.3 Economic Order and Economic Entropy

Economic "objects" (phenomena, events, processes, systems) are dissipative objects, that is, objects that maintain (or decrease) their entropy due to the entropic exchange with the non-artefactual or artefactual environment—dissipative objects extract low entropy, or bound energy (also called neg-entropy) from the non-artefactual environment and eliminate high entropy or free energy in the non-artefactual or artefactual environment.[38]

It seems, therefore, that, with regard to the economic order, the connection with entropy is much more obvious and, it seems, necessary. In this sense, we will keep the following considerations in mind:

- In the economic field, the concept of entropy should refer to the degree to which economic freedom[39] is self-testable. By economic self-testability we propose to understand the self-regulation of the economic system without generating in society negative externalities that are untreatable (either in nature, in terms of quantity, or in terms of the speed of their production) or treatable with unacceptable costs that can cause unsustainable situations;
- Therefore, no mention of the aspects of volatility, disorganization or the like, which semi-educated economists enthusiastically introduce under the label of entropy (especially in the financial field);
- It follows that, from the perspective of economic policy, a government intervention must necessarily occur whenever economic freedom becomes entropic beyond a certain degree. This intervention will provide exactly those "ingredients", which take the form of mandatory norms, which will help the economic system (the market) to reduce its production of negative externalities beyond the limit admissible from the perspective of sustainability;
- Of course, such a concept of economic entropy must simply be developed from scratch, and not necessarily from a simply instrumental perspective, but from a much broader and more grounded—namely, from the perspective of social philosophy.

3.4 Criteria of Classifying Economic Order

The theoretical evaluation of a typology of economic order is, of course, an extremely vast and necessarily interdisciplinary undertaking. Therefore, in this paragraph, only an outline will be presented which, possibly, could constitute, for other researchers, a starting point for more extensive and substantiated developments. The importance of the classification of economic order, however abstract it may be (and perhaps, the more abstract, the more useful!), cannot, in our opinion, be overestimated.

Criteria for Choosing... Criteria

Any classification is possible only as a result of a system of classification criteria. In order to choose the system of classification criteria, we need... criteria for choosing these criteria. Regression to infinity is not acceptable here, because it is a question of a *sui generis* order that the subject introduces into the artefactual world, not into the objective world (we recall that the artefactual world is an objectification of inter-subjectivities). We therefore believe that only one step of regression is sufficient, namely the step in which the criteria for choosing the criteria for classifying the generic economic order are established. In this sense, we make the following proposal for the set of these second-order criteria:

- (C_1^C) *abstract character*: the criteria for classifying the economic order must be of the greatest generality, to allow the identification of classes of such an order so that be generally valid. It should not be understood from this that the criteria in question must be an-historical—as we have shown, the economic is generated by human action which is necessarily historically qualified—but only that those criteria that "force" the typology of economic order to be subsumed into our current, or recent experience, or, even worse, that could not contain future states of order, namely which have not been experienced so far, must be avoided;
- (C_2^C) *relevant character*: the criteria for classifying economic order must avoid unnecessary, redundant, or theoretically insignificant multiplication of the classification of economic order.[40] The relevance of these criteria must, of course, be theoretical, so that C_2^C is compatible with C_1^C;
- (C_3^C) *closed character*: the criteria for classifying economic order must allow the inclusion of all known species of economic order. It is not admissible that some such species do not fall into any class permitted by the respective criteria. The closed nature of the criteria for classifying economic order does not, of course, mean that possible species of economic order (which humanity has not yet experienced, but which are possible in principle) cannot enter the respective classes, but only that the criteria in question do not prohibit the inclusion of any species of past, present, or future economic order. Therefore, this criterion for choosing criteria does not prohibit the entry, but rather prohibits the omission.

Criteria to Classify the Economic Order

Respecting the criteria for choosing the criteria, as mentioned above, we propose the following "battery" of criteria for classifying the economic order:

- (C_1^{EO}) *degree of self-sufficiency*: the criterion refers to the way in which the economic activity satisfies the economic needs of the individuals or communities in question—with or without economic exchange (exchange of activities, i.e., goods and services);
- (C_2^{EO}) *market–state relationship*: the criterion refers to the normative, institutional, or effective relations between the market, considered as the "environment" in which generic economic activity is carried out, and the state, considered not as an economic actor, but as an institutional subject invested with the constitutional authority to issue norms regulating[41] economic activity;
- (C_3^{EO}) *level of intermediation of interactions*: the criterion refers to the way in which the "chain" of economic activities is concatenated from a structural and functional point of view in order to achieve their goal: satisfying the economic needs of individuals and communities. The level of intermediation of interactions is understood as a quantitative parameter that describes the intensity of the indirect nature of social interaction, either between individuals or between groups of individuals, as the case may be;
- (C_4^{EO}) *level of intermediation of the economic impulse*: the criterion refers to the structural, functional but, above all, causal relationship between real economic flows and nominal economic flows;
- (C_5^{EO}) *finality of economic action*: the criterion refers to the purpose of the economic action/activity. In principle, this purpose is reduced to satisfying economic needs and, consequently, to satisfying the other types of needs in Maslow's pyramid that are conditioned by the purchasing power ensured by satisfying economic needs—purchasing power having, from a praxiological point of view, the quality of a mean. However, through a positive feedback effect encouraged by the formation of a perverted axiological matrix, the acquisition of purchasing power has transformed itself from a means to an end as such—it seems that the contemporary type of capitalism has necessarily[42] entered this "logic".

3.5 Typologies of Economic Order

Based on the criteria previously described, we can make the following proposal for classes of economic orders.

(a) Based on C_1^{EO} (degree of self-sufficiency)

- ($K_1^{C_1}$) *autarchic economic order*: it is that economic order functioning at the lowest level of social aggregation (e.g., family, tribe, or a limited inter-tribal community) in which there is no praxiological specialization (i.e., division of labour), and therefore no economic exchange (exchange of activities). As a rule, such an economic order is associated either with a low level of technological endowment or with a low level of social interaction, but, from a logical point of view, such associations are not mandatory;
- ($K_2^{C_1}$) *local cooperative economic order*: it is that economic order that involves praxiological specialization (division of labour) and, consequently, economic exchange (exchange of activities). Local cooperative economic orders can be of two types:
- ($K_{2/N}^{C_1}$) *localized national cooperative economic order*[43]: is that economic order that operates within institutional "membranes"called national political boundaries. It is relatively conservative economic order, and the political entity under which it operates acts, vis-à-vis other similar political entities, as individuals;
- ($K_{2/I}^{C_1}$) *internationalized local cooperative economic order*: is that economic order that operates in an integrative system, by including a number of nation-states, based on association/integration treaties that homogenize the same economic order at the international level involved. The best known (and, in fact, the only one that verifies the definition of such a type of economic order) internationalized local cooperative economic order is the one related to the European Union;
- ($K_3^{C_1}$) *global cooperative economic order*: is that economic order that operates at a planetary/global level, that is, it encompasses all political-economic entities constituted at a global level. From a logical point of view, although there is much

discussion about globalization (especially in the economic field, and in this field, especially in the financial sub-field), there is still no global cooperative economic order proper said. In order for such an order to exist, global institutions are needed, therefore, which have an institutional and regulatory vocation at a planetary level, which is not the case today (the international organizations such as the IMF, WHO, World Bank, WTO, etc., are...international organizations, not global).

(b) Based on C_2^{EO} (market–state relationship)

- ($K_1^{C_2}$) *decentralized economic orders*: are those economic orders in which state intervention is characterized by two attributes: (1) it ensures a relatively invariant normative framework capable of organizing, based on the principles of economic freedom, the economic activity belonging to autonomous economic actors; (2) it limits its interventionist measures to cases, or areas, or moments characterized by the inability of the market to self-test, respectively to self-regulate[44];
- ($K_2^{C_2}$) *centralized economic orders*: economic orders in which the state arrogates legal rights (which are not necessarily legitimate) to establish imperatively the conditions (both general and specific—by branches, sub-branches, sectors of activity) in which economic activity, i.e., the functioning of the market, must take place. Here a problem arises related to the concept of economic property, which makes this type of economic order have two distinct species:
- ($K_{2/W}^{C_2}$) *weakly centralized economic orders*: economic orders characterized by the following attributes: (1) the market functions as in the case of decentralized economic orders; (2) the state reserves for itself, to a significant extent,[45] sectors, branches, sub-branches, or areas in which economic activity is carried out by the state (the so-called private domain of the state).[46] It should be noted that in the case of these economic orders, private property is provided, guaranteed, and defended by the state;

- $(K^{C_2}_{2/S})$ *strongly centralized economic orders*: economic orders in which the economic market is not free. This means that economic choice is imposed by the state (for example, the structure of supply, demand, employment, export, import, price level, wages, interest rates or exchange rate). The limitation (or even liquidation[47]) of private property is the institutional basis on which the reduction (or liquidation, as the case may be) of the economic freedom of the market is built.

(c) Based on C^{EO}_3 (level of intermediation of interactions)

- $(K^{C_3}_1)$ *weakly intermediated economic orders*: these are economic orders in which the exchange of activities is carried out according to the nature of the results of the activities that enter the exchange process—the established name is, in this case, barter. Through barter, activities (more precisely, the products/results of activities) are exchanged as such, based on an empirical, conjunctural exchange relationship, with ad hoc significance, without universal value;
- $(K^{C_3}_2)$ *moderately intermediated economic orders*: these are economic orders in which there is a commodity, established either institutionally or "naturally", which is used as a means of intermediation of exchange for any products/activities, being accepted by all participants in economic exchange (the best-known such commodity is the gold) and therefore acting as a universal medium of exchange. In addition, this universal medium of exchange has intrinsic value, verifiable by each participant in economic exchange;
- $(K^{C_3}_3)$ *highly intermediated economic orders*: these are economic orders in which there is also a universal medium of exchange, and this no longer has intrinsic value, but one that is assigned to it by a monetary authority—it is called currency. This universal medium of exchange is accepted by participants in economic exchange on the basis of trust (which is why this universal medium of exchange is also called fiduciary currency). Of course, within this type of economic order there are "internal" degrees of intermediation, but we consider

that we are dealing with differences in degree, not type of order—e.g., electronic currency, virtual currency.

(d) Based on C_4^{EO} (level of intermediation of the economic impulse)

- ($K_1^{C_4}$) *financial economic orders*: these are economic orders in which the exchange of real economic flows is mediated by financial economic flows, completely causally and structurally dependent on real economic flows; in these economic orders, nominal flows are, however, relatively dependent on real and financial flows;
- ($K_2^{C_4}$) *nominal economic orders*: these are economic orders in which both real and financial economic flows are accompanied by nominal economic flows. In this type of economic order, nominal flows become dominant in relation to the other two types of economic flows and, in addition, acquire an increasing autonomy, until they are completely broken from the dynamics of the other two flows mentioned. Crises of economic systems, which are, originally, exclusively nominal crises, can only occur in nominal economic orders (Dinga, 2025).

(e) Based on C_5^{EO} (finality of economic action):

- ($K_1^{C_5}$) *economic orders of the means type*: these are economic orders in which the result of economic activity (materialized, ultimately, in purchasing power) is considered as a means to satisfy individual (or group, especially family) needs, on all levels—primary, secondary, tertiary needs, etc. We can say that this type of economic order is the desirable type, adequate and in accordance with the values of sustainability, intra-and inter-generational solidarity and moral values;
- ($K_2^{C_5}$) *economic orders of the end type*: these are economic orders in which the result of economic activity—purchasing power—is pursued in itself, having a weak connection with its role as a mean in ensuring the quality of life and becomes, increasingly, an end pursued as such. We can say that this type of economic order is the undesirable (perverted), inadequate

type and which, sooner or later, self-undermines itself through its own logic.

A given economic order can fall into several classes, as they were established above. Of course, it is a question of the compatibility of the criteria in question—depending on how the criteria are compatible with each other, they allow the integration of a given economic order into several classes. In our opinion, the following situations have logical consistency—the marked cells (Table 1).

Table 1 Compatibility of economic order classes

		C1				*C2*			*C3*			*C4*		*C5*	
		$K_1^{C_1}$	$K_{2/N}^{C_1}$	$K_{2/I}^{C_1}$	$K_3^{C_1}$	$K_1^{C_2}$	$K_{2/W}^{C_2}$	$K_{2/S}^{C_2}$	$K_1^{C_3}$	$K_2^{C_3}$	$K_3^{C_3}$	$K_1^{C_4}$	$K_2^{C_4}$	$K_1^{C_5}$	$K_2^{C_5}$
C1	$K_1^{C_1}$	x					x		x						x
	$K_{2/N}^{C_1}$		x			x			x						x
	$K_{2/I}^{C_1}$			X			x			x	x	x		x	
	$K_3^{C_1}$				x	x					x	x		x	
C2ara>	$K_1^{C_2}$		x		x	x			x			x		x	
	$K_{2/W}^{C_2}$	x		X			x					x		x	
	$K_{2/S}^{C_2}$							x	x						
C3	$K_1^{C_3}$	x	x			x		x	x						
	$K_2^{C_3}$			X						x		x			
	$K_3^{C_3}$			X	x						x		x	x	
C4	$K_1^{C_4}$			X	x	x	x			x		x		x	
	$K_2^{C_4}$										x		x		x
C5	$K_1^{C_5}$			X	x	x	x				x	x		x	
	$K_2^{C_5}$	x	x										x		x

(*Source* author)

3.6 *Mechanisms in the Economic Order*

Preliminaries

The economic order, of whatever class it may be, operates on the basis of an internal mechanism that has its origin, of course, in the basic principle of that order, stated in the description of the respective classification criterion. However, from a theoretical point of view, it is important to analyse whether there are "standard" mechanisms of the economic order considered in its generic meaning. In this paragraph, we will formulate some opinions on this matter.

In general, by mechanism of the economic order we understand an internal "logic" or, more technically, an "algorithm" of that order, which describes, at a principle level, the way in which the economic order in question functions. Before proceeding to develop the subject, we will make some considerations that we consider fundamental in the analysis of the mechanism of economic order (and even of the concept of economic order itself).

- The economic order (including the autarchic economic order) is institutionally grounded. It does not matter, of course, whether we are talking about formal or informal institutions. This characteristic is an immediate logical consequence of the fact that, with the exception of the singular individual (although the "case" of Robinson Crusoe seems to be an exception to... exception), any human group interacts, in all aspects, not only from an economic perspective, on institutional bases[48];
- The economic order evolves under the impact of two causes that inter-relate: (a) spontaneous "mutations"induced by the teleology of economic actors acting under the empire of the economic order, followed by validation/invalidation, also spontaneous,[49] which generates an implicit evolutionary process; (b) discretionary changes, induced by political decision-makers—models, visions, social philosophies, etc. Both causes are of an institutional nature, except that the first are informal (more precisely, they are uncodified), while the others are formalized (codified). The effects of the spontaneous cause can, in turn, be formalized, when they are appreciated as being valuable for the improvement of the economic order in question. Symmetrically, the effects of the discretionary

cause can be eliminated (through opposite rules—the so-called de-regulation), when they are considered harmful to the improvement of the respective economic order.

The Concept of Mechanism of Economic Order

By mechanism of the economic order we will understand a logical device for the generation, functioning, and evolution of the economic order. Such a mechanism is "endowed" with three mandatory components: (a) an institutive component; (b) a regulatory component; (c) an evolutionary component.

(a) The institutive component

It refers to the principle able to initiate a certain economic order, to give it personality, and to make it distinct from other possible economic orders. The institutive component can also be called, according to its content, the *generative* component or the causal component.

(b) The regulatory component

It refers to the principle that ensures the continuous maintenance of the institutive component. Essentially, the regulatory component has the role of making corrections in cases where the functioning of the economic order itself or external disturbances could lead to the deviation of the economic order in question from its institutive principle.[50]

(c) The evolutionary component

It refers to the "acquisitions" that the functioning of the economic order in question generates, so that "mutations" occur in the institutive component, and some mutations are validated (or invalidated, as the case may be) so that an evolution of the economic order occurs. In other words, the evolutionary component consists of what the regulatory component does not "return" in cases where the functioning of the economic order leaves the tunnel of acceptability of the institutive component.

Fig. 3 explains, from a synoptic perspective, these considerations.

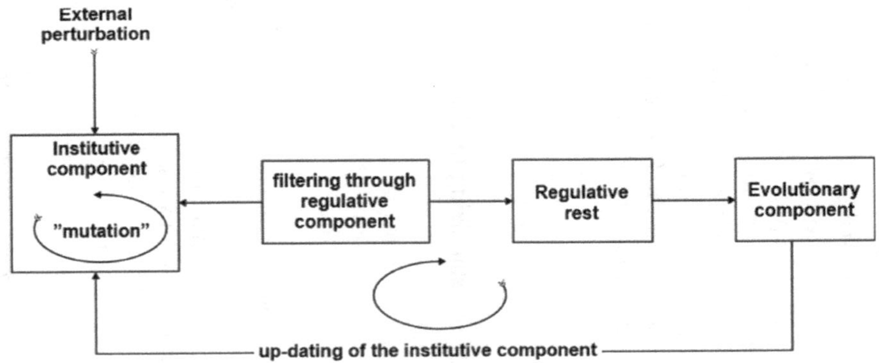

Fig. 3 Functioning of the components of the economic order mechanism (*Source* author)

Classes of Economic Order Mechanisms

We consider that there are two classes of mechanisms in the functioning of the economic order, each of them with a dichotomous typology.

1. (*AM*) Automatic mechanisms

They are mechanisms that are established by themselves, as a necessary result of social interaction (more specifically, of economic interaction). They can also be called implicit mechanisms, because they are characterized by emergence (i.e., by non-deliberativeness). One of the fundamental characteristics of this class of mechanisms of the economic order is its synergistic character—the quantity, structure, and quality of economic actors that interact within the framework of economic actions lead, through this very interaction, to the emergence of the component elements of this class of mechanisms. Automatic mechanisms of the economic order contain two species: (a) automatic self-stabilizing mechanisms; (b) automatic self-escalating mechanisms.

(1.1) (*ASM*) automatic self-stabilizing mechanisms

Automatic self-stabilizing mechanisms are characterized by the dominance of negative feedback in the interactions of economic actors. Although, in any economic order, negative feedback and positive feedback coexist, in the case of the economic order in which automatic self-stabilizing mechanisms operate, negative feedback dominates. We can also say that the net difference between the "amount" of negative feedback and the "amount" of positive feedback in these mechanisms has a positive algebraic sign. Automatic self-stabilizing mechanisms are specific to the free economic market—for example, the mechanism for forming the transaction price on the free economic market is self-stabilizing.[51]

- The institutive component of *ASM*: *competition*.[52] By competition we mean the dispute, between economic actors, under more or less specified or implemented institutional-normative conditions, of the same generic economic resource.[53] The conditions of the dispute, as well as the dispute as such, have an internal origin, that is, they are generated by the economic actors involved themselves;

- The regulatory component of *ASM*: *negative feedback.* Negative feedback is understood as a reaction from the output to the input of the same system,[54] based on the assessment of the gap between the projected (desirable) output and the actual (actual) output, and with the aim of returning the new input to the level that will lead the system to the projected output. In other words, negative feedback is stabilizing[55];
- The evolutionary component of *ASM*: *own profit*. Own profit is understood, theoretically, as the difference between the economic actor's own income and own expenses. It is important to refer to own profit because, in a real economic order, there are incomes that are not own (for example, subsidies received from the government) and expenses that are not own (for example, taxes paid to the government). The main argument for considering own profit is the following: obtaining own profit is a process under the direct control of the economic actor in question, while the other elements that affect profit by affecting income or expenses are not under the direct control of the economic actor, but are external elements (according to the examples mentioned, they are under the control of the government).

(1.2) (*AEM*) automatic self-escalating mechanisms

Automatic self-escalating mechanisms are characterized by the dominance of positive feedback in the interactions of economic actors. We can also say that the net difference between the "amount" of negative feedback and the "amount" of positive feedback in these mechanisms has a negative algebraic sign. Automatic self-escalating mechanisms are also specific to the free economic market—for example, the mechanism of forming the price-wage relationship or the mechanism of monopolization (or, symmetrically, of monopsonization).

- The institutive component of the *AEM*: *cooperation.*[56] By cooperation we mean the distribution, between the economic actors involved, under more or less specified or implemented institutional-normative conditions, of the use of the same generic economic resource. The conditions of distribution, as well as the distribution as such, have internal origins, that is, they are generated by the economic actors involved themselves;

- The regulatory component of the *AEM*: *positive feedback*. Positive feedback is also understood as a reaction from the output to the input of the same system (as in the case of negative feedback), based on the assessment of the gap between the projected (desirable) output and the effective (actual) output, but with the purpose of amplifying the observed gap. In other words, positive feedback is destabilizing, or, as we have called this type of mechanism, self-escalating;
- The evolutionary component of *AEM*: *own profit* (similarly to the case of *ASM*).

2. (*DM*) Discretionary mechanisms

They are mechanisms that are not established by themselves, but are introduced, through imperative norms, by the political component of the entity in which the economic order in question operates (for example, a national economic system). Although there is a difference between the term policy and the term politics, the norms introduced discretionarily through public policy measures are, in fact, expressions of the political objectives of the discretionary factor (for example, of the party holding governmental power). Discretionary mechanisms of the economic order contain two species: (a) discretionary adjustment mechanisms; (b) discretionary (re)structuring mechanisms.

(2.1) *(DAM)* discretionary adjustment mechanisms

Discretionary adjustment mechanisms are intended to introduce corrective impulses into the functioning of the economic order, in cases where it deviates from the specific benchmark. For example, a phenomenon of collusion, which affects the free formation of prices, will attract, once identified, intervention with discretionary measures to eliminate the phenomenon in question. Most situations where discretionary adjustment measures are needed occur in the nominal economy—for example, massive exchange rate depreciations or capital market manipulations.

- The institutive component of *DAM*: *market failure*. Market failure refers to the inability of the free market to self-test the trends of the main macroeconomic variables. In essence, discretionary adjustment mechanisms are "required" by automatic self-escalating mechanisms. It can be shown that state intervention is legitimate only in areas and in relation to macroeconomic variables that are not self-testable (or self-regulating) at the free market level (see Chapter 5);

- The regulatory component of *DAM*: *stability*. Stability refers to the property of a system (or process) to return to its "cruising" position after being disturbed by a shock (internal or external, real or nominal).[57] The adjustment intervention applied in a discretionary manner by the state aims at the stability of the targeted economic system (or process).[58] The most suggestive example, in this case, may be that of the economic cycle—the state intervenes through discretionary adjustment measures of an anti-cyclical type (aiming at "returning" of the economic process from its self-catalysing tendency);
- The evolutionary component of *DAM*: *learning*. By learning is meant the integration, in the spontaneous functioning of the economic market, of discretionary adjustment interventions. It is a *sui generis* phenomenon of reverse moral hazard.[59]

(2.2) (*SAM*) (re)structuring adjustment mechanisms

Discretionary structuring (or restructuring) mechanisms are intended to introduce impulses that modify the very structure of the functioning of the economic order. Some economists call them structural measures or policies. These interventions of the political factor in the economic order are extremely important because, in principle, they can change the economic order itself—for example, the discretionary introduction of imperative norms regarding economic property can cancel a certain economic order and establish another. In general, however, this type of measures aims to stabilize/consolidate the functioning of a given economic order by ensuring their structural basis (either of the real economy or of the nominal economy). The most important such structural basis is, of course, the normative basis.

- The institutive component of the *SAM*: *state failure*. By state failure is meant the property of discretionary adjustment interventions of not being effective, that is, of not "turning back" the targeted economic system (process) within the range of variation of the defining parameter that defines the state of stability;

- The regulatory component of the *SAM*: *sustainability*. Sustainability is understood as the property of a system (or process) to record variations in the defining parameter exclusively in a quantitative tunnel (with extension in time), without requiring discretionary adjustment interventions. This property is, to a certain extent, acquired "naturally" through the *ASM*-type mechanisms discussed above, but, in a safety way, it must be introduced by discretionary means at the structural level of the economic system (process). Since the function of an economic system (process) is generated by its structure, it is understandable why sustainability, as a regulatory principle of this type of mechanism of the economic order, must be implemented in the very structure of the system (process) in question. Of course, here too, the most effective method is the normative one, which refers to the introduction, in the structure of the system, of elements that necessarily, permanently, and continuously lead to the desirable functioning of that system (process);
- The evolutionary component of the *SAM*: *fetality*. Fetality[60] refers to the property of structural changes generated by discretionary structuring intervention to be "accepted" by the pre-existing functioning structure of the economic order in question and, thus, to integrate it into the subsequent functioning of that economic order.

4 The Concept of Social Order

4.1 Again, about the Concept of Social

To define the concept of social, we will use a property, namely the property of sociality. In turn, to define the property of sociality, we will use a more primitive property, namely the property of communitarianity.[61] By communitarianity we mean the property that the component elements of an entity (we denote by *IC*—internal connections—the set of connections among the component elements of an entity, for example, of a system) develop a limited number of functions that are common to all elements of that entity. Therefore, the sufficiency predicate *IC* must be separated into two components: IC_p, i.e., the set of inter-component connections with a "private" character, namely autonomous (individual, even idiosyncratic), and IC_c, i.e., the set of inter-component connections with a common or "public" character, namely non-autonomous ones, which involve all components of the system.[62] Consequently, we have the property of social (or sociality) whenever we have, in a given entity, connections of the class IC_c. In our world there are many cases of entities (systems) endowed with subjects (cultural or non-cultural) in which there are connections of the class CI_c: bees, ants, humans, and some species of animals (lions, wolves). It should be noted that, in relation to entities that are not "endowed" with subjects, the problem of sociality does not arise. Therefore, a definition of the social could be formulated as follows: *an entity (system) has a social character if the subset IC_c is not empty.*

4.2 Defining the Social Order

Generally, the social order is the genus for the economic order. So, to get the social order, we must reject one (or more, as the case may be) of the sufficiency predicates that define the economic order. In our opinion, the sufficiency predicate that should be rejected is S_6^O, namely the property involving entropic exchange between the individual (or collectivity, considered as a set of individuals) and non-artefactual nature (see point 3.3.1). Consequently, the societal order (noted SO) is defined by the logical conjunction:

$$SO \leftarrow \left(S_1^O\right) \bigwedge \left(S_2^O\right) \bigwedge \left(S_3^O\right) \bigwedge \left(S_4^O\right) \bigwedge \left(S_5^O\right) = \bigwedge_{i=1}^{5} S_i^O$$

or, equivalently:

$$SO \leftarrow EO \setminus \left(S_6^O\right)$$

4.3 Revealing the Social Order

The revealing of social order is, to a significant extent, more complicated (and, hence, more uncertain) than the revealing of economic order. The fundamental cause of this difference lies in the very definition of the social, that is, in the fact that, within the internal connections of the system in question (the set of connections denoted IC) there inherently[63] develops a subset of connections (denoted IC_c) that refers to those connections between the component elements that involve all the component elements of the system. In connection with this issue, we make the following brief considerations:

- Common (or public) connections refer to values or interests that are shared or affect all individuals of a given social system. The existence of a subset of connections denoted IC_c is "guaranteed" by the very existence of society, an existence that logically implies the existence of the state. For example, the existence of the state necessarily generates such a set of common values and interests through the way it appears and is established,[64] thus generating society itself;
- Unlike the connections in the subset IC_p, which are necessarily conscious and are generated voluntarily at the individual level (even with idiosyncratic meanings), the connections in the subset IC_c may not be fully conscious except by the most educated and most involved members in the affairs of society. However, there are criteria (usually of an institutional nature[65]) that help us build this subset IC_c;

The revealing of the social order is, for the members most involved in the affairs of society, a direct revealing (especially since the members we are referring to here may be the very members who propose the coordinates of the social order in question); instead, for the rest of the members of society, the revealing of social order can be indirect:

- Through behavioural contagion (memes)—for example, behaviour in the community or in relation to a certain general problem can be induced by the behaviour of opinion leaders or praxiological leaders, either from the close community or at the national level[66];
- Through imperative norms (obligation, respectively prohibition);
- Through stimulating norms (rewards or cancellation of the sanction).

4.4 *Social Order and Social Entropy*

In the social domain, the concept of entropy is much more problematic than that related to the economic domain. If we consider the original meaning of the concept of entropy (that of Thermodynamics, the only authentic concept of entropy, in our opinion), we will have to accept that, in a system, we have an increase in entropy whenever in that system we have an increase in homogeneity, from a given point of view. We believe that, at the social level, the criterion on which we should rely when evaluating the degree of homogeneity (or, its antonym, the degree of heterogeneity) is the criterion of normativity. By normativity we will understand the fabric of norms, of any kind, that regulates the life of a society, however not this fabric in itself, but correlated with the freedom of individuals in that society. In this sense, we will examine the polar categories of a society that deviate from the "average" society, i.e., the nomic society: a) quasi-anomic society; b) supra-nomic society.

(a) (*QaNS*) quasi-anomic society

By quasi-anomic[67] society we mean a society in which the normative framework is minimal, referring only to the strictly necessary set of social interactions. In addition, as a rule, quasi-anomic society does not have, mandatorily, a formal (codified) normative framework but, rather, an implicit (tacit) one. Very important is the fact that quasi-anomic society is characterized by a very low degree of social (including economic) sophistication—it is specific to autarchic societies. From a theoretical point of view, however, of course, such a type of society has a "right" to exist even if there were no more copies anywhere on the planet today.

(b) (*SNS*) supra-nomic society

By supra-nomic society we mean a society in which the normative framework is maximal, or rather, in which this normative framework has two fundamental characteristics: (a) it regulates behaviours or actions that can be (and, usually, are) regulated by the individuals involved in those behaviours/actions themselves; (b) regulates beyond level "1" of regulation (or beyond primary legislation). There is, of course, a threshold that should not be exceeded in terms of the regulatory framework, so that societies remain standard nomic societies (*NS*). In fact, there are two categories of thresholds that should not be exceeded in the process of social norming:

(i) The threshold of *competence*: here the principle of subsidiarity must operate— there is no regulation where regulation is more effective if it is self-regulation;
(ii) The threshold of *redundancy*: here the principle of sufficient reason must operate—there is no regulation of regulation.

Based on the establishment of the three categories of societies from the perspective of the degree of nomicity (*CaNS*, *SNS*, *NS*—*Nota bene*: *NS* society is exactly the benchmark of the society's *nomicity*), we will make the following considerations regarding the relationship between social order and social entropy:

- The concept of entropy has, in Thermodynamics, the meaning of the degree of homogeneity. Adapting this meaning to the social domain, we can concede that by the concept of social entropy (Dinga et al., 2020) we understand the degree of nomicity of the social system in question;
- Based on this meaning of the concept of social entropy (degree of nomicity) we can develop the following judgements:
- A society has two meanings regarding social entropy: social entropy is high both in the case of *CaNS* (quasi-anomic societies) and in the case of *SNS*. This means that nomic homogeneity has the same meaning from an entropic perspective both in the case where nomicity is very low (*CaNS* case) and in the case where nomicity is very high (*SNS* case). We are therefore talking, in the social domain, about both an entropy of normative scarcity and an entropy of normative excess (or redundancy);
- The question of the correlation between freedom and social entropy arises. It would seem that, in the case of *CaNS*-type societies, individual freedom is greater, as a result of the normative scarcity. In reality, freedom is less in the case of normative scarcity because, as is known, the freedom of an individual must be correlated with the freedom of other individuals in the community. To a certain extent, this inter-individual harmonization of freedom is achieved tacitly, through informal ad hoc norms, but their effectiveness is

very low. The biggest shortcoming, in this case, is the fact that there is no social contract through which the state—or the concrete-historical substitute of the state, for example, the tribal chief, or the monarch—can defend the interference of a private individual in the formulation of the goals of another private individual (i.e., to defend the content of the concept of freedom). The social contract appears above a threshold of normativity, more precisely when the Constitution appears. This is the reason why the shortage of normativity signifies a high degree of social entropy:

- At the other pole, that of excess of normativity (*SNS*-type societies), freedom appears as restricted as in the case of *CaNS*-type societies, but from a different perspective, namely from the perspective of public power interference. Here a conceptual problem arises: as shown above, freedom is defined (apophatically), in the most general sense, as the absence of private interference in the formulation of an individual's private goals. As a result, the interference of public power in the formulation of an individual's private goals would not represent a limitation (or suspension) of individual freedom. Since the excess of normativity makes public interference in the formulation of private goals plausible (or probable), we have a problem of consistency. Our interpretation is as follows: public interference (i.e., interference of public power) in the formulation of individuals' private goals is illegitimate (although it may be legal), that is, it has the potential to limit or suspend individual freedom, when the individuals concerned have the capacity and ability to formulate their own private goals (for example, whether to conclude full-time or part-time employment contracts, whether to marry or not, whether to have one or more children or none, and the like). However, in the case where private individuals cannot formulate their own private goals, the interference of public power is no longer illegitimate, and therefore is no longer limitative or suspensive regarding individual freedom (for example, the formulation of the goal of participating in a war to defend threatened national sovereignty). In the case of *SNS*-type societies, however, it is precisely the extreme analyticity of the normative framework that creates, with a high probability, the risk of illegitimate interference of public power in the extension, and intensity of freedom. As a result, we consider that, also in the case of *SNS*-type societies, we have a high social entropy;

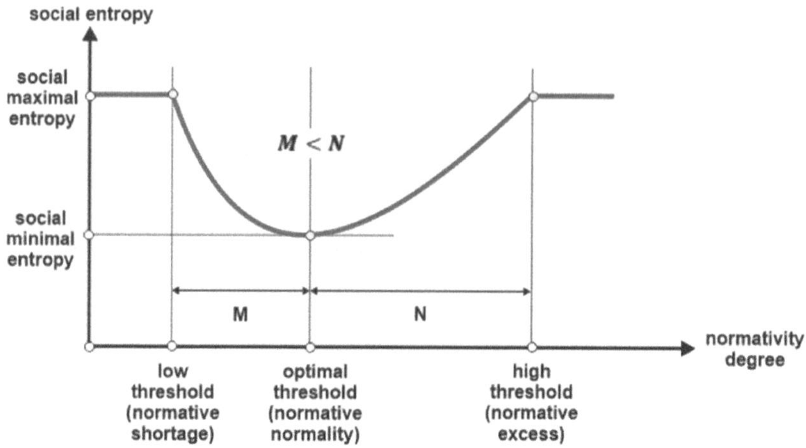

Fig. 4 Asymmetric non-linear curve of social entropy depending on the degree of social normativity (*Source* author)

- It follows that we will have lower social entropies in *NS*-type societies. Indeed, according to the logic followed so far, in *NS* societies we do not have too much shortage of normativity, nor too much excess of normativity. Of course, in the case of *NS*-type societies, inter-societal comparability is perfectly possible, that is, we can estimate the degrees of social entropy. We could probably accept a reduction in entropy when moving from *CaNS*-type societies to *NS*-type ones and, symmetrically, an increase in social entropy when moving from *NS*-type societies to *SNS*-type ones. Figure 4 presents, in a synoptic manner, the considerations regarding the relationship between the type of society and the size of social entropy.

5 The Concept of Societal Order

5.1 The Concept of Societal

The predicate societal is generate by the logical conjunction of two predicates, namely social and state. In other words, the societal is that social endowed with a state or that social that generates a society. Logically, we have here to add a new sufficiency predicate to the social, namely the predicate formulated as follows: *forming a society*. If we note this new sufficiency predicate with S_7^O, then the societal order (SSO) is defined as:

$$SSO \leftarrow (SO) \bigwedge \left(S_7^O\right)$$

As is known, in systems theory it is stated that the set of connections between the component elements of a system generates what is called the functionality of that system. So, the set IC is "responsible" for the functionality of the system. At the same time, the connections between the component elements of the system, on the one part, and the environment of that system, on the other part, generate what is called the behaviour of the system. So, the set EC (denoting the environment connections) is "responsible" for the behaviour of the system. We have seen that sociality (the attribute of social) refers only to the set IC (more precisely, to the subset IC_c, where

$$IC = (IC_c) \bigcup (IC_{p.})$$

We will also have to separate the EC set into two subsets: EC_p through which we distinguish the subset of "private" (autonomous) connections between the component elements of the system (entity) and the environment of that system (entity), respectively EC_c, through which we distinguish the subset of "public" (common, non-autonomous) connections between the component elements of the system (entity) and the environment of that system, of course with the logical closure condition:

$$EC = \left(EC_p\right) \bigcup \left(EC_p\right)$$

The logical features of the four subsets and the correlations between them are as follows:

$$IC = (IC_c) \bigcup (IC_p)$$

$$EC = (EC_c) \bigcup (EC_p)$$

$$(IC_c) \bigcap (IC_p) = \varnothing$$

$$(EC_c) \bigcap (EC_p) = \varnothing$$

$$IC_c \bigcap EC_c \neq IC_c$$

$$IC_c \bigcap EC_c \neq EC_c$$

$$IC_p \bigcap EC_p \neq IC_p$$

$$IC_p \bigcap EC_p \neq EC_p$$

$$IC_c \bigcap EC_c \neq \varnothing$$

Therefore, a definition of the societal could be formulated thus: *an entity (system) has societal character if and only if the subset EC_c is not empty*. It should be noted that an entity cannot be societal if it is not a social entity first. So, the set of societal entities (SSE) is included in the set of social entities (SE). The question arises whether there can be social societies that are not societal. The answer is, of course, negative, therefore the distinction between social and societal is rather methodological in nature, and we will not insist too much on it. A synoptic representation of these logical developments is made in Fig. 5.

Based on the brief description of the concept of societal order, we will now formulate the list of sufficiency predicates for such a societal order to exist:

- (SO) existence of a social order: a societal order implies the existence of a social order, that is, an order that implies the existence of the set of connections IC_c. In a system that does not "have" social order, it is unlikely (or even impossible) to form the set of connections EC_c, of course, as previously shown;
- (S) the existence of the state: this predicate ensures on the fact that, inside the social order, a society arises;
- (S_7^O) the existence of system-environment co-evolution: in order for the set of connections EC_c to exist, it is necessary for the system in question (more precisely, the set of connections IC_c to become "aware" of the fact that the system and the system's environment influence each other and that, in fact, the interaction between them is not only inherent, but also co-evolutionary). A short discussion is needed to provide additional clarifications:

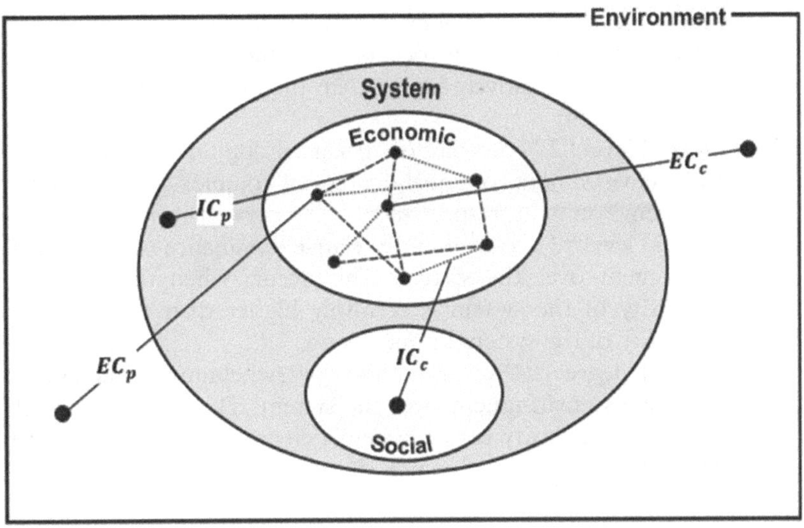

Fig. 5 Logical construction of the concepts of social and societal (*Source* author)

- There is (or can be postulated[68]) an invariance of the total complexity[69] of a system: the logical sum between the internal complexity of a system and the complexity of its environment (or the external complexity of that system) is constant (i.e., it is an invariant);
- Based on the invariance of the total complexity of a system, we can conclude that we have the most intense process of co-evolution when the degrees of internal and external complexity are relatively equal. If the two degrees of complexity are relatively unbalanced, co-evolution decreases in intensity, but still works. In fact, we can propose a typology of the co-evolution system–environment, as follows:

(a) ($CoE/0$) level "0" co-evolution: overwhelming dominance of the system over its environment. This occurs when the degree of complexity of the system related to the degree of complexity of its environment is very high;

(b) ($CoE/1$) level "1" co-evolution: relative dominance of the system over its environment. This occurs when the degree of complexity of the system is relatively higher than the degree of complexity of its environment;
(c) ($CoE/2$) level "2" co-evolution: balanced dominance of the system and its environment, or equal degrees of complexity of the system and its environment, respectively;
(d) ($CoE/3$) level "3" co-evolution: relative dominance of the system's environment over the system. This occurs when the degree of complexity of the system is relatively higher than the degree of complexity of the system in question;
(e) ($CoE/4$) degree "4" co-evolution: overwhelming dominance of the system's environment over the system. This occurs when the degree of complexity of the system's environment is very high in relation to the degree of complexity of the system.

So, the logical formulation of the societal order (SSO) can be as follows:

$$SSO \leftarrow (SO) \bigwedge (S) \bigwedge \left(S_7^O\right)$$

$$SSO \leftarrow \left(S_1^O\right) \bigwedge \left(S_2^O\right) \bigwedge \left(S_3^O\right) \bigwedge \left(S_4^O\right) \bigwedge \left(S_5^O\right) \bigwedge (S) \bigwedge \left(S_7^O\right)$$

A visualization of these typologies of the co-evolutionary process is presented in Fig. 6 (TC means total complexity, i.e., the logical sum of internal complexity and external one—*Nota bene*: it is obvious that TC is an indifference curve).

5.2 *Revealing of the Societal Order*

The revealing of societal order is not much different from the detection of social order. However, a few nuances (i.e., specificities) should be highlighted:

- Unlike the observation and recognition, in the detection of social order, of the set of connections IC_c, this time the set of connections EC_c must be observed and recognized. Since there are relations between IC_c and EC_c that can strongly influence the detection of societal order, we make some considerations in this regard:

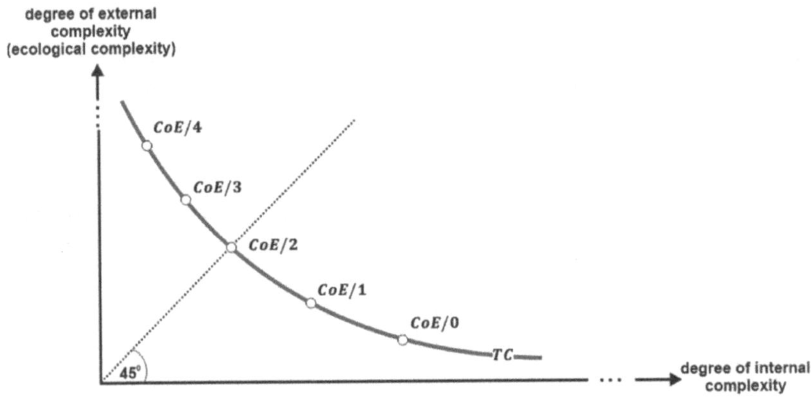

Fig. 6 Basic cases of system-environment co-evolution (*Source* author)

- It is not necessary that $EC_c \subset IC_c$, in other words, there can be common connections between the component elements of the system and its environment (i.e., connections of the behavioural type), without them coinciding with the common connections between the elements of the system with respect to the system itself (i.e., connections of the functional type);
- Since the possibility of some overlaps between the two sets of connections cannot be excluded either, the logical expression of the relations between IC_c and EC_c should be:

$$\left[IC_c \bigcap EC_c \neq \varnothing\right] \bigwedge \left[IC_c \bigcap EC_c \neq IC_c\right] \bigwedge \left[IC_c \bigcap EC_c \neq EC_c\right]$$

There may be a transition of some elements from the set IC_c to the set EC_c and vice versa. This possibility is explained as follows: some common connections within the system IC_c will "come to" the conclusion that those connections depend, in terms of their stability or even relevance, on their membership in the set EC_c. Let us consider for example the common social connection that we call solidarity. In the event of an external danger (such as the danger of an armed attack that would threaten the sovereignty of the community in question), the common social connection of the solidarity type is transformed into the common societal connection of the patriotism type, that is, into a connection that belongs to the set EC_c. Conversely, a common societal connection of the feeling of belonging to an integrative political-economic structure (such as the European Union), a connection from EC_c, can be transformed into a common social connection of the national interest type, which belongs to the set IC_c;

The greater the openness of a social system to the international environment, the more common social connections become common societal connections and vice versa, the closure of a social system to the international environment will lead to the transformation of common societal connections into common social connections.

Based on the above, we can say the following about revealing societal order:

- More than in the case of "accessing" connections in the set IC_c, accessing connections in the set EC_c is more difficult both informationally (for example, foreign intelligence services will not make all connections in EC_c transparent to the entire population, for obvious reasons), and cognitively (observing, understanding, and evaluating connections in EC_c requires a much more specialized prior instruction than observing, understanding, and evaluating connections in IC_c);
- In principle, there will be a specialized category of individuals, usually included in institutions that are also specialized, who will benefit from revealing societal order (for example, in addition to foreign intelligence services, this also includes the Ministry of Foreign Affairs, the Parliament—sometimes only members of the parliamentary committee on foreign policy and/or European affairs, the head of state, as the holder of foreign policy prerogatives).

5.3 *Societal Order and Societal Entropy*

We saw, previously, the concept of social entropy, as correlated with the concept of social order. Social order, measured by social entropy, concerns the status/normative framework of society. It is obvious that part of this normative framework will concern behavioural connections between the society in question and its external environment (economic, political, military, and, of course, the external normative environment, for example international law), that is, what we noted above with EC_c. The question arises whether the concept of societal order, respectively the concept of societal entropy, can exist. In our opinion, the concept of societal order and the correlative one of societal entropy have no right to intellectual "citizenship", in the sense that neither one nor the other brings significant added value to the concepts of social order, respectively social entropy. Consequently, societal order will be a component of social order that will target the connections in the set EC_c, and societal entropy will be the social entropy that will measure the normative framework that targets the connections in EC_c.

5.4 *Criteria of Classifying Societal Order*

The problem of classifying societal order[70] is more difficult than classifying social order (and even than classifying types of system-environment co-evolution, presented above based on the concept of co-evolution and the principle of invariance of total system-environment complexity), for the following reasons:

- Societal systems are "immersed" in each other, i.e., in super-systems, respectively subsystems of a given system; this means that clear boundaries must be established between the system under consideration, on the one hand, and the environment that is targeted for that system, on the other hand (for example, a member state of the European Union is a system that is part of the supra-system called the eurozone—Economic and Monetary Union—but, in turn, the eurozone is a system that is part of a supra-system called the European Union which, in turn…, etc.);
- The borders discussed previously are also of different types: they can be economic borders (for example, the economic border of a member state of the European Union extends to the economic border of the Union, while the economic border of a non-member state of the European Union usually coincides with its territorial/political border), political borders, cultural borders (of ethos), etc.;
- The perspective from which a certain system is seen in relation to its environment depends on the interest in knowledge (e.g., social philosophy), the praxiological interest (e.g., economic exchanges), or the practical interest (e.g., political or religious relations).

We propose the following criteria for classifying societal order:

1. (S_{SSO}) *subsumption*: refers to the relations between the system and its environment. Here, we accept a narrower view of the societal system than Luhmann (who considers, for example, that the social system does not have a social environment, because, if it were so, then the environment, being social, should enter the system[71]), so we will consider that any societal system can be considered a subsystem, from the perspective of the extensive sphere, of a broader societal system. Obviously, this inclusion is made on the logical relationship individual–species (the species is obtained by eliminating a sufficiency predicate from the individual's definition, respectively the individual is obtained by adding a sufficiency predicate to the species' definition);
2. (I_{SSO}) *interaction*: refers to the relations between societal systems. Although each societal system "plays" the role of environment for another societal system, not every societal system (in any case, not with logical necessity) has as its environment also another societal system. As a rule, the environment of a societal system can be a *sui generis* combination of societal systems and non-societal systems[72] (among non-societal systems, natural systems are the most frequent);
3. (A_{SSO}) *self-sufficiency*: refers to the capability of a societal system to subsist with a minimum of "import" of resources from its environment (including from other societal systems). Since it might seem that this criterion is not independent of the first two proposed above, we will make some brief considerations in this regard:

- The self-sufficiency criterion is not dependent on the subsumption criterion, since the first one refers to a different objective (the autonomy) compared to the objective targeted by the second one (the integrativity);
- The self-sufficiency criterion is not dependent on the interaction criterion, because the former refers to a different means (internalization of replication operations) compared to the means targeted by the latter (externalization of replication operations).

5.5 A Typology of Societal Order

1. According to the subsumption criterion (S_{SSO}):

- (*CSSO*) *closed societal order*: the societal order in a system that has few integrative (subsumption) relations with its environment. This includes, for example, closed societies from antiquity or those in contemporary times that have a more "relaxed" closure (e.g., China, North Korea, Russia);
- (*OSSO*) *open societal order*: the societal order in a system that has numerous integrative (subsumption) relations with its environment. In general, here we can have three distinct classes of societal orders:
- (*OSSO/S*) *symmetric open societal order*: the open societal order in which the "strength" of the initiative in the subsumption relation is approximately equal between the society in question and its environment;
- (*OSSO/A*) *asymmetric open societal order*: the open societal order in which there are imbalances in the origin of the "initiative" of subsumption between the system and the environment. There can be two sub-classes here:
- (*OSSO/AI*) *internally oriented asymmetric societal order*: asymmetric societal order in which most of the subsuming connections between the system and the environment are initiated by the environment; this includes societies that are not sufficiently autonomous in relation to their environment (which includes, of course, other societal systems, not as such, but as component elements of the environment); this is the case of societies that could be considered rather passive;
- (*OSSO/AE*) *externally oriented asymmetric societal order*: asymmetric societal order in which most of the subsuming connections between the system and the environment are initiated by the system; this includes societies that have a relatively high degree of autonomy in relation to their environment that they try to subsume to their goals and objectives; this is the case of societies that could be considered rather active.

2. According to the criterion of interaction (I_{SSO}):

- (*SSOC*) *societal order of completeness*: the societal order in a system that develops interactions with other societal systems for reasons of completeness—for example, resource shortage (of any kind, not just economic); these are societies that, by geographical location, are faced with the absence of basic material resources, thus being forced to develop international economic exchange relations (e.g., Japan);
- (*SSON*) *societal order of niche*: the societal order in a system that develops interactions with other societal systems for reasons of maximizing its own capacities, compared to the situation in which it would not develop such interactions—for example, the national economic specialization based on the absolute/comparative/competitive advantage;

3. According to the criterion of self-sufficiency (A_{SSO}):

- (*ASSO*) *autonomous societal order*: the societal order in a system that fulfils the sufficient character of replicating the respective order exclusively based on the internal principles of normative organization and cultural framework[73];
- (*DSSO*) *dependent societal order*: the societal order in a system that does not verify the conditions of the autonomous societal order.

5.6 A Qualitative Analysis of Societal Order Classes

The three criteria for classifying societal order, although logically independent, interact with each other, leading to different types of societal trajectories (chreods), which we will briefly refer to below. First, the possible relationships (both structurally and functionally or kinematically) between the three classification criteria and, consequently, between the classes of societal orders resulting from the global action of the respective classification criteria must be established. In Table 2, we present the basic types of possible relationships between the criteria, respectively the classes of societal orders.

The concept of societal order trajectory/chreod can be extracted by further conceptualizing the inter-conditioning relations described in Table 1. To approach this concept, some preliminary considerations are helpful. In fact, we will have to answer in these preliminary considerations,

Table 2 Inter-conditioning relations between classes of societal orders

				S_{SSO}				I_{SSO}		A_{SSO}	
				CSSO	OSSO			SSOC	SSON	ASSO	DSSO
					OSSO/S	OSSO/A					
						OSSO/AI	OSSO/AE				
A_{SSO}		*CSO*		–	↮	↮	↮	↮	↮	↮	↮
	OSO	*OSO/S*		↮	–	↔; ↓	↔; ↓	↔; ↓	↔; ↓	↮	↮
		OSO/A	*OSO/AI*	↮	↔; ↑	–	↮	↔; ↑	↔; ↑	↔; ↻	↔; ↻
			OSO/AE	↮	↔; ↑	↮	–	↔; ↑	↔; ↑	↔; ↻	↔; ↓
I_{SSO}		*SOC*		↮	↔; ↑	↔; ↓	↔; ↓	–	↔; ↓	↮	↔; ↓
		SON		↮	↔; ↑	↔; ↓	↔; ↓	↔; ↑	–	↮	↔; ↓
S_{SSO}		*ASO*		↮	↮	↔; ↻	↔; ↻	↮	↮	–	↮
		DSO		↮	↮	↔; ↻	↔; ↑	↔; ↑	↔; ↑	↮	–

Legend: ↔: compatibility; ↮: incompatibility; ↑: cause for; ↓: effect of; ↻: ambiguous relationship (*Source* author)

several questions: (a) are there desirable orders (lexicographic or based on external criteria) within the classification of societal order? (b) are there desirable orders (lexicographic or based on external criteria) within the classifications generated by each of the three assumed criteria? (c) can the ordering of societal orders be "concatenated" in such a way that we have an "evolutionary arrow" of these orders, so that the arrow can then suggests the trajectories/chreods of societal order, which we assume? We will express our opinions in relation to these questions.

(a) The question refers to the possibility that, among the three criteria for classifying societal order, which have, of course, their own independence in the respective group of criteria, there may nevertheless be an "order" of importance or relevance. Of course, in attempting to establish such an order, a criterion for classifying the criteria (i.e., a meta-criterion) is needed. We do not consider that the problem, thus formulated, has too great relevance in the economy of this chapter; therefore we will propose a lexicographic order (i.e., an order that does not need an external criterion). Thus, we consider that the order of these criteria should be the following:

- (I) The criterion of self-sufficiency; (II) the criterion of interaction; (III) the criterion of subsumption. Our arguments (which are *post factum*, i.e., after the ordering has already been done) are the following:

- The structure of a societal system fundamentally determines its functions (both those that refer to internal operations—functionality, and those that refer to relations with the environment—behaviour. This means that the properties of self-sufficiency are decisive in the positioning and activism of a given societal system; in other words, the criterion of self-sufficiency must be prior (in importance, significance, and relevance) to the criterion of interaction;
- Both the genesis and the evolution of societal systems are caused by their presence (and interactions) with other societal systems; moreover, the environment of a societal system is, in quasi-totality, formed by other societal systems, so the criterion of interaction must come before the criterion of subsumption.

A synoptic representation of this argumentation of necessity is given in Fig. 7.

(b) Since we are talking about lexicographic orders (thus, which do not "claim" logical ordering criteria), we can, of course, accept or establish such orders. In our opinion, regarding the three criteria for classifying societal order, the following internal orderings could be accepted:

- Within the classification generated by the subsumption criterion:

– (*OSSO/AE*) *externally* oriented asymmetrical societal order;
– (*OSSO/AI*) *internally* oriented asymmetrical societal order;
– (*OSSO/S*) *open* symmetrical societal order;
– (*CSSO*) *closed* societal order;

- Within the classification generated by the interaction criterion:

– (*SSOC*) societal order of *completeness*;
– (*SSON*) *niche* societal order;

- Within the classification generated by the self-sufficiency criterion:

– (*ASSO*) *autonomous* societal order;
– (*DSSO*) *dependent* societal order.

If we would have to identify a "criterion" that lies behind these proposals for lexicographic ordering of societal orders within each criterion, my opinion is that this would be a criterion of adequacy to contingent (i.e., social-historical) conditions of the contemporary era. However, from the perspective of the objectives of this chapter, this issue does not have a particular significance.

(c) This is a difficult, but relevant question, so we will develop some specific considerations below. To this end, we will use both the lexicographic ordering of the three categories of societal orders (related to the three proposed classification criteria, see Fig. 7), and the

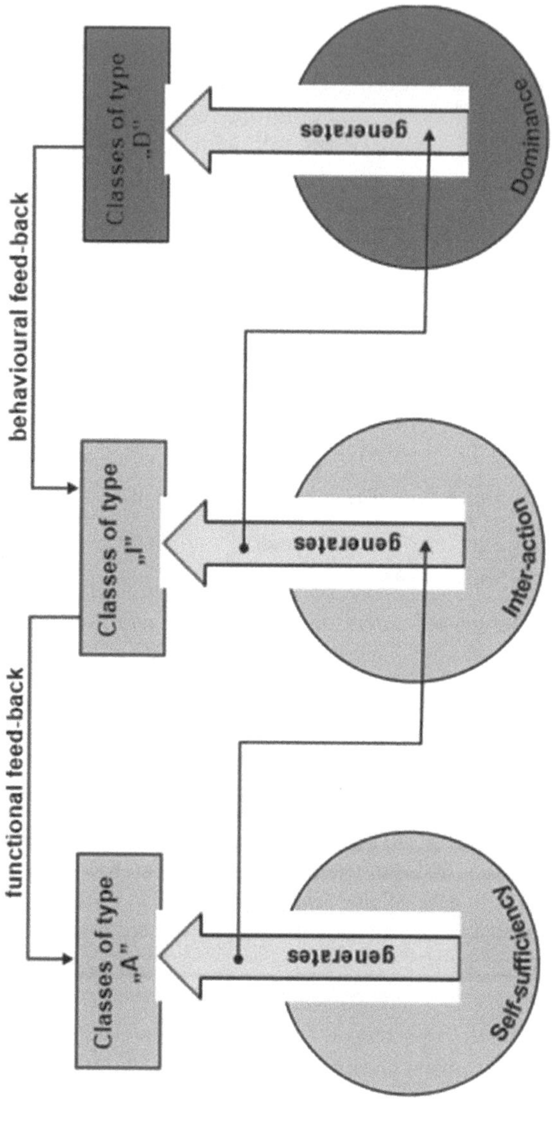

Fig. 7 Lexicographic order of the criteria for classifying societal order (*Source* author)

opinion expressed in point (b) above. We will also capitalize on the suggestions given in Table 1.

- For there to be an "evolutionary arrow" from the perspective of societal order, there must be a "reason" for society to go in the direction indicated by that arrow. In other words, a criterion must be found that any society will respect or seek in its self-organization, without this criterion having too much contextual dependence (if possible, it should even be...a-contextual);
- In this framework, we consider useful to discuss the concept of propensity (Dinga et al., 2022):

- An entity (object, event, process) has an internal inclination, a disposition, a tendency to pass from one state to another;
- This tendency is a property of that entity, a property called propensity[74];
- Propensity is not an absolute property; it manifests itself, objectively, in the singular case, only in accordance with the conditions in which the event unfolds;
- Propensity thus considered is the (objective) probability of the singular case (event);
- Absolute propensity (which cannot be known as such, but only through its manifestation as a disposition of the entity in question) is invariant precisely as a result of its "declaration" as absolute. The problem that arises here is that, being invariant, even if the derivation of the objective probability of the singular case from the relative propensity is accepted, we cannot return from probability to propensity;
- Based on the concept of propensity it can be said that, objectively, there should be a tendency that materializes in the kinematics of the societal order. This tendency has, over time, been identified with various causalities[75]:
- *Divine will*: explanation used especially in theological metaphysics—the tendency and change in the societal order are introduced by God, based on a plan inaccessible to man and to which man, too, cannot oppose (*Nota bene*: the content, here, is that of Theism, not Deism);

- *Historical laws*: explanation used, under the influence of Marxist philosophy, by materialist approaches to history (the so-called historical materialism). Being laws, historical laws are credited with having an objective character, therefore as functioning independently of the subject[76];
- *Role of personality*: explanation used by various theories regarding heroes and heroism in history[77];
- *Role of the state*: explanation used by institutional approaches of the societal dynamics;
- *Evolutionary arrow*: explanation based on the three concepts of evolution (see Fig. 1). This arrow seems the most realistic and plausible explanation. Its scientific character is done by the large spectrum of possible predictions and, correlatively, of possible factual falsifiability.

Notes

1. Although social action has always been socially organized (for reasons of effectiveness and, in the case of the current paradigm of optimality, for reasons of efficiency), its ultimate goal has been the biological existence of the individual or group. The social is an epistemological category, not an ontological one—more precisely, the social is an objectified reality (Popper's 3rd world), while the individual is an objective category (Popper's 1st world; *Nota bene*: do not confuse the individual as object with the individual as subjectivity—the latter falls into Popper's 2nd world).
2. We ignore here, as irrelevant from the perspective of the study, the concept (and presumed process) of transhumanism which, as the name suggests, transgresses the biological individual through technical technology (*Nota bene*: there are other types of technology—educational technology, social technology, political technology, etc., although, in common parlance, these types of non-technical technologies are called methodologies).
3. Increasingly, as a result of the globalized (and globalizing) economic process, the natural environment becomes an anthropic "natural" environment, meaning it is "filled" with anthropic products (this is not just about residues/wastes that are incompletely

or not at all recyclable naturally, but even high-tech products—the entire physical infrastructure or space objects that already orbit the planet).

4. Although not necessarily from a logical perspective, as we do here, the suggestion that the economy (and, larger, the social action) is a praxiological activity is not new in economic philosophy (and, more generally, in social philosophy). We recall only the theory most clearly oriented in this perspective, namely the economic theory proposed by Ludwig von Mises (2012) (taken over, more or less systematically, by what is called the Austrian School of Economics). *Nota bene*: the Praxiology, as distinct field of knowledge, was initiated by Polish philosopher and logician Tadeusz Kotarbiński.
5. As many logicians have shown (among whom we mention Bertrand Russell—see Russell's hen; and Carl Hempel—see Hempel's raven).
6. Deductive inference, which we will refer to immediately, is no less susceptible to falsification, but it is a different kind of falsification from a logical point of view (see, here, Popper's factual falsifiability).
7. The reader is invited to note the scientific "culture", encouraged by many false mentors, that today's young researchers so uncritically adopt, namely the enthusiastic and self-sufficient belief that econometric modeling can (or, even worse, must) be used for predictions—from an epistemological point of view, here generality is confused with universality in the statement of the major premise of the implied syllogism (see the footnote immediately following).
8. Universality (at least hypothetical) is ensured only by deductive inference. This, by the way, is the logical difference between inductive and deductive truth: in the case of inductive truth the major premise of the syllogism is a law of general coverage, while in the case of deductive truth the major premise of the syllogism is a law of universal coverage.
9. We specify, for the sake of intellectual honesty, that all scientific knowledge uses induction, but not in its uncritical form, which we have discussed above, but in the form of abduction—i.e., the most plausible explanation, prima facie, obtained inductively but subsequently subjected to the deductive mechanism.
10. This paragraph and the next are adapted from the conceptual construction provided in Dinga (2025).

11. From an epistemological (but not ontological!) perspective, the failure to observe an order is equivalent to the non-existence of order, since order exists only in association with a subject. From this point of view, phenomenology is very close to the opinion expressed here.
12. This condition is mandatory because the phenomenon, by definition, is what appears to a cognitive subject after being "filtered" through the existential constitution of that subject—that is, through his/her natural senses (it is not relevant and does not change the validity of the reasoning the case in which the natural senses are either augmented or supplemented with artificial "senses" of a technological nature—the so-called exo-somatic organs, as opposed to the endo-somatic ones, of a biological type—because, ultimately, any observation can only be made translated into the "language" of the natural senses). *Nota bene*: in Quantum Mechanics, this "translation"refers to the transfer of indirect observations (with the help of exo-somatic technology) into direct perceptions or what has been called the information transfer from the microscopic (quantum) to the macroscopic (human) level.
13. The senses perceive only primary qualities, so sensation occurs at the level of these primary qualities (for example, the wavelength of electromagnetic radiation). Perception is what consciousness "does" with sensation (consciousness provides the so-called secondary qualities—the primary qualities as transformed by consciousness—for example, the color red, which corresponds to the spectrum of electromagnetic radiation of light located between 630 and 670 nanometers, that is, between $630 \bullet 10^{-9}$ and $670 \bullet 10^{-9}$ metres.
14. It is worth noting that sensory observability is common to non-cultural and cultural subjects, even if the former cannot reach the concept of order. However, empirically (and especially with the help of memetic learning), non-cultural subjects can access a certain static (and even kinematic) "map" of the space and temporal interval in which they live their life.
15. Probably, the coming in cascade of the causes/conditionalities in generating the decisions and actions could not be reasonably rejected.
16. We exclude the case in which the subject is cognitively or performatively incompetent (performative incompetence implies the

inability to operate cognitive competence—someone who knows a foreign language is cognitively competent in that language, but if they do not have enough dexterity to speak that language, they are performatively incompetent in relation to the language in question).

17. The list of sufficiency predicates for defining a concept must itself verify three sufficiency predicates: a) the elements in the list must be independent of each other, two by two; b) the elements in the list must be consistent (i.e., non-contradictory) with each other, two by two; c) the elements in the list must be complete, i.e., ensure the formulation of the expected definition (*Nota bene*: that is why they are called sufficiency predicates, and not necessary predicates). The first sufficiency predicate of the list of sufficiency predicates refers precisely to redundancy, i.e., to the absence of independence—in the sense that one of the predicates can be logically inferred from another.
18. This research direction is not without interest, but the aspects in question are rather of a general philosophical and epistemological nature; therefore we will not develop it here.
19. For example, the second law of Thermodynamics (the law of entropy, which we will refer to below) is imposed by the "vote" of the scientific community (mostly qualitative physicists). The same thing happens in economy, with the difference that, this time, we no longer expect unanimity, but only majorities (which are, over time, reversible).
20. We call a "blind" praxiological operation that action that is not based on known causalities (either deterministic or statistical regularity).
21. Here we have a behaviour based on the "seeing and doing" principle, generally used in management.
22. It is not acceptable for praxiological action to take place within two or more orders simultaneously, because each order has, as we have shown above, its own "logic". Operating under several orders simultaneously not only introduces incoherence (or even inconsistency) in the action, but can even evade rationality as such, given that a certain order is unambiguously associated with a certain model of rationality.
23. We draw attention to the fact that the adequacy of the revealed order does not refer to the adequacy of this order to the purpose

of the praxiological action involved, but to the "means" of that action, that is, as we said, to the intrinsic logic of the action in question.

24. The question arises: will selecting the most appropriate order from two or more revealed orders influence the performance of the intended praxiological action? The answer is, of course, affirmative, but in most real cases—which are non-counterfactual—one will not be able to perceive the "gain" or "loss" from choosing the most appropriate order (of course, ingenious speculations, but without any psychological or praxiological foundation, can be made at any time, for the purpose of writing "scientific" articles).
25. (Gr.) εντροπία, formed from "εν"—towards, and "τροπή"—turn, turning) means to turn towards..., to transform in the direction of... Therefore, the meaning is that of a necessary propensity in an unambiguous direction.
26. The continuous vs. quantum (discrete) aspect of entropy variation is not yet fully elucidated. As a personal opinion, I believe that since the variation of order in a system is perceived/measured quantumly, we can infer a quantum variation of entropy (under the assumption of an entropy–order bijectivity).
27. This feature seems to be of the nature of vitalism, în Bergson's sense (Boltzmann tried to introduce a reversibility of entropy in closed systems, but the issue is still unclear, including from a mathematical point of view).
28. Dependence on intermediate stages leads to process quantities (functions). It is possible that, in economics (or, more generally, in the social field), many process quantities are falsely considered to be state quantities—e.g., the criteria for economic convergence, both nominal and real, with the European Union.
29. See, here, the considerations of Boltzmann, in his Statistical Mechanics. Also, the issue of the devil of Maxwell.
30. In reality, Boltzmann does not have in mind probabilities in their usual sense (i.e., inductively derived, as is the case, for example, of objective probabilities or Kolmogorov's probabilities) but rather possibilities: by possibilities we understand states (or events), either necessary or contingent, without any connection to a previous archive of states or to a subjective desirability of the observer.
31. Explanation and prediction are logically equivalent and chronologically substitutable.

32. Except in the case of living reality, where materialistic reductionism is inapplicable.
33. Static structures check for points/axes/planes of symmetry (they are comparable from this perspective), but functional ones do not (e.g., the human physical body is only symmetrical in a few superficial aspects).
34. The only "legal" meaning, although economists in particular, but also researchers from other social fields, have demonetized the concept, as they usually do with other concepts taken from the natural sciences.
35. These two sufficiency predicates are not cumulative, as the first three are, but they are applied "in cascade" as follows: the first applies to the result of the cumulative application of the first four, and the second applies to the result of the application of the first of these last two.
36. Although the economic, along the lines indicated by Lionel Robbins, is still considered to be that property related to the scarcity of resources in relation to needs (along this line, the ridiculous neoclassical economic quantitative modeling is developing and not only), the definition of the economic must be restricted to entropic processes (see, in this context, also the important suggestions made by the Romanian-American economist Nicholas Georgescu-Roegen (1976)).
37. For example, dictatorships are very inclined not to observe reality as it is (they are often helped in this direction by the obedient bureaucracy) and then they imagine the economic order closest to their desires or interests, and the decisions made for the economy are subsumed into the imagined economic order, and not the real economic order (notorious cases in recent history refer to communist dictatorships).
38. The standard case, which refers directly to Thermodynamics (as is, in our opinion, correct), is the increase in the entropy of the non-artefactual environment by transforming bound energy (for example, the energy stored in oil) into heat. It should be noted that, always, the high entropy removed into the environment is greater than the low entropy extracted from the environment, which leads to the idea of accelerating the entropy of the Universe (which is a closed system) in the presence of dissipative systems (the most "entropically active" dissipative systems are living systems).

39. The closest proxy here seems to be the free functioning of the market.
40. Here the well-known sorting rule called Occam's razor applies.
41. So-called deregulation is, of course, a species of regulation, just as economic decline is a species of economic growth, and deflation (not disinflation!) is a species of inflation.
42. One of the authors who peremptorily explain this conclusion is Hyman Minsky (2008), without mentioning Marx's analyses, although carried out under different historical conditions and for a different stage of capitalism.
43. We also include here the historical case of city-states.
44. Examples of the market's inability to self-regulate (which falls under the so-called market failure) are: (a) monopolization of supply or monopsonization of demand; (b) production of negative externalities; (c) impossibility of producing public goods; (d) impossibility of social responsibility actions (in our opinion, the phrase corporate social responsibility is an oxymoron—logically it is a *contradictio in adjecto*).
45. The question of the meaning of the expression "to a significant degree" is difficult and requires specific and dedicated analyses. For the moment, we cannot produce a systematic argument on the matter, but we believe that reaching a lower limit of 20% of the total economic activity (for example, as a share in GDP) could qualify the economic order in question as a weakly centralized economic order.
46. The distinction made here between the public sector and the private domain of the state is the well-known one: (a) the public sector produces public goods (goods that are distributed in a non-market system); (2) the private domain of the state produces private goods (which are distributed through a market system).
47. As was the case with the socialist economies of Eastern Europe, the former Soviet Union, and the Soviet Union's satellite states outside Europe.
48. In this sense, institutionalism, as a paradigm of the economic process, has missed an essential aspect of that process—namely, its evolutionary basis—although, as we have already mentioned, institutionalism is an essential aspect of any human interaction. In our opinion, institutionalism should be "captured" in a broader and more coherent theory, namely evolutionarism.

49. For example, spontaneous validation/invalidation can be done by the social "device" known as the invisible hand.
50. Generally, we call these corrections on the path as negative feedbacks.
51. See here the *cobweb model* of the oscillation of the transaction price around the equilibrium price. More recently, in chaos theory, this result is found based on the concept of attractors.
52. The essential issue in the concept of competition is the following: competition takes place exclusively between (in our case) economic actors of the same type, that is, with the same economic role—thus, competition takes place between producers, or between consumers, or between investors, but never between producers and consumers, for example.
53. It is understood that we only have competition in conditions of *scarcity* of resources.
54. Of course, it's about the output at time i and the input at time $(i + 1)$.
55. From a mathematical point of view, the gap analyser will calculate the algebraic modulus of the difference between the projected output and the actual output, thus ignoring the direction in which the deviation occurs.
56. Like competition, cooperation only takes place between economic actors of the same type.
57. As it can be observed, stability is the very result of the structural property called resilience—which is enthusiastically confused with the property called robustness (Dinga, 2025).
58. We have referred, on other occasions, to the conceptual distinction that must be made regarding three concepts that are interconditioned but distinct from each other: *stationarity* (maintaining the defining parameter of a system/process at a point level), *stability* (maintaining the defining parameter of a system/process at an quantitative interval level), *sustainability* (maintaining the defining parameter of a system/process at a tunnel level—the tunnel is a quantitative interval extended in time).
59. Which, from a scientific point of view, should be examined in detail, because, for example, a mirror effect of adverse selection could be discovered.
60. The concept of fetality refers, of course, to the concept of economic graft, but the latter concept is only a species of discretionary

structuring intervention (it refers, for example, to the "import" of normative components from other types of economic orders or from the same type of economic order but held by other socio-cultural spaces).

61. The concept of communitarianity implies three defining attributes: a) spatial coexistence; b) hierarchy of power; c) non-empty intersection of individual/group interests; d) non-empty intersection of resources usable/used by each individual/group.
62. To exemplify human society, market relations are connections that belong to the class IC_p, while relations that relate to national defense are connections that belong to the class IC_c.
63. The question of whether this inherent development is emergent or deliberative is important and will be discussed immediately.
64. In relation to this issue, we adhere to John Rawls' contractarianist point of view regarding the emergence of the state (Rawls, 1999).
65. This is one place (among many others) where social behaviourism (and even psychological behaviourism) fails "successfully". Nothing can be deduced from an individual's behaviour regarding the degree to which he/she is aware of his/her membership in the subset of connections IC_c. An example of an institutional criterion that helps us in constructing this subset is the constitutional criterion—the Constitution exclusively includes connections from the category IC_c. Also, the publication of laws (i.e., norms of general and impersonal applicability) in a dedicated official publication is another such criterion.
66. Here also arises the problem of behavioural models—exceptional people (the heroes that Thomas Carlyle spoke of)—either contemporary or (most often) non-contemporary, who inspire values, attitudes, behaviours, and actions.
67. It is completely unproblematic to state that an a-nomic society is impossible—the crucial argument for this statement is the non-empty character of the set IC_C in any society, by the very definition of the social.
68. The only justification for such a postulation is methodological in nature—it is simpler to give an explanation under the postulated conditions [obviously, we are dealing here with the famous hypothesis *as if*, from Germ. *Als Ob* (Vaihinger, 2021)].

69. In fact, it is about complicativeness (*Nota bene*: i.e., the empirical difficulty of describing a phenomenon gives its degree of complicativeness) and not complexity. The theoretical difficulty of making predictions about a phenomenon gives its degree of complicativeness but, in order not to make the chapter difficult to read, we will adopt the term used (relatively carelessly) by the overwhelming majority of analysts in the field—that of complexity.
70. We specify that societal order is a concept of the greatest generality—in principle, it subsumes economic order, cultural order, political order, religious order, etc. Political order is, of course, of the greatest importance from a sociological and anthropological point of view, but it will not be treated distinctly in this chapter.
71. Niklas Luhmann accepts two categories of environment for the social system: a) the natural system; b) the psychic system. The strange character of the elimination of the psychic from the social system is the logically necessary result of the fact that Luhmann does not accept the individual (in the case discussed, the human individual) as a component element of the social system either—the component elements of the Luhmannian social system are communications, in relation to which individuals (with their psyches) are only...external sensors (belonging to the psychic system) that validate (or not) communications from the perspective of meaning. Luhmann is actually talking here about understanding, not about meaning, but the semantic "distance" between the two concepts is not very great—understanding can be defined as the allocation of meaning.
72. The non-societal system is, obviously, that system that does not verify the non-empty character of the set EC_C.
73. The autonomous societal order (according to the criterion of self-sufficiency) does not overlap with the closed societal order (according to the criterion of subsumption). The autonomous societal order is not closed, but it does not need (it is not imperative/inevitable) to capitalize on its open character.
74. Economic theory (both at the micro and macro-levels) uses the concept of propensity but in a much simpler sense—as a marginal numerical value that expresses, from a causal point of view, the variation of one economic variable in relation to variation of another economic variable—for example, in microeconomics: the marginal propensity to consumption: $c = C'_I$, where c is the

marginal propensity to consumption, C is the Keynesian consumption (or consumption function) ($C = a + c \bullet I$), and I is current income (C'_I is the partial derivative of the consumption function with respect to current income); in macroeconomics: the marginal propensity to import, calculated in a similar way, as the partial derivative of the import function with respect to national income. Therefore, the concept of propensity currently used in economic theory has no probabilistic connotation, but is just a (not very appropriate) name for a marginal calculation.

75. We recall that there is no change without causality, although the causality in question can be either deterministic or statistical (i.e., stochastic) or, at the limit, random.
76. One of the most fierce (and passionate) criticisms of historical materialism is that of Karl Popper (1957).
77. Among the most famous proponents of this causality is the Scottish writer (also, historian and philosopher) Thomas Carlyle (1993).

References

Carlyle, T. (1993). *On heroes, hero-worship, and the heroic in history*. University of California Press.

Dinga, E. (2025). *Economic resilience during overlapped crises—Antifragility, sustainability and Autopoieticity*. Palgrave Macmillan—Springer Nature.

Dinga, E., Oprean-Stan, C., Tănăsescu, C. R., Brătian, V., & Ionescu, G.-M. (2022). *Financial market analysis and behaviour. The adaptive preference hypothesis*. Palgrave Macmillan—Springer Nature.

Dinga, E., Tănăsescu, C. R., & Ionescu, G.-M. (2020). Social entropy and normative network. *Entropy, 22*(9).

Georgescu-Roegen, N. (1976). *The entropy law and the economic process*. Harvard University Press.

Minsky, H. P. (2008). *Stabilizing an unstable economy*. McGraw Hill.

Popper, K. R. (1957). *The poverty of historicism*. Routledge.

Rawls, J. (1999). *A theory of justice* (Revised ed.). Harvard University Press, Belknap Press.

Vaihinger, H. (2021). The philosophy of "as if". Routledge Classics ed.

von Mises, L. (2012). *Human action. A treatise on economics*. Martino Fine Books.

PART II

Conceptual Family of the Evolutionary Approach of Society

CHAPTER 4

The Capillarism

1 Preamble

We know about the concept of capillary as generally referring to tubes, of any nature (substance, size, etc.), so those tubes that are particularly thin, such as the blood vessels. Of course, in present times, with the nanotechnology developments, such thin tubes are increasingly taken into consideration in different fields, with various uses. So, the concept of capillary is a predicate (more exactly, an adjective) that claims a property of a given tube, namely the property of thinness. Although in what follows, we shall extend this concept beyond the originary tubes, for the moment, we remain at the tubes, since I want to discuss also: (a) the property per se linked to the predicate of capillary; (b) the noun linked to the predicate of capillary; (c) the verb linked to the predicate of capillary.

(a) The property *per se* linked to capillary

A capillary tube must be understood as holding the property of *capillarity*. By capillarity, we understand that property (assigned, for the moment, to a capillary tube) that generates by itself a behaviour of that tube which is contrary (most of the time, diametrically opposed) to the expected or anticipated behaviour. If we talk about tubes, this contrary behaviour is necessary, but, as we see next, such a behaviour can also be contingent. It must be mentioned that the contrary behaviour is,

E. Dinga, *The Economics of Social Justice and Societal Evolution*,
https://doi.org/10.1007/978-3-032-24055-2_4

obviously, causal, in turn, and most times, this causality is known and, consequently, predictable.

(b) The noun associated to capillary

Although the distinction between noun and adjective in the issue of capillary could easily result from the (attentively built) context, it is better to establish that a *capillar* is a tube that can be called capillary tube. Therefore, often, we shall use the noun capillar to name such a tube. Somehow, we shall use the term capillar by elliptic expression of the capillary tube.

(c) The verb associated to capillary

A verb assigned to a capillar or to the property of capillarity must express the process of gaining the property of capillarity or the process of becoming a capillar. I propose to use the following expression for such a (constructive) verb: *to capillarize*.[1]

2 The Capillary Action

The most important "function" of the capillar is to act in the (general) opposite direction compared with the usual, standard, expected, and, *prima facie*, predicted direction. For example, in a capillary tube standing vertically, a liquid opposes the gravitational force and, consequently, instead of flowing down, it climbs up. Of course, from a scientific point of view, this behaviour is completely intelligible, based on the surface tension of liquids, namely the force of the surface tension is greater than the force of gravity, just because the thinness of that tube. But we are interested here in the very tendency (or property), called above capillarity, to oppose the expected, that is, usual, or "correct" behaviour, no matter the cause, intelligible or not.

The above explanation is the prose version of the capillarity. Starting from it, I want to introduce a much more extensive concept of capillarity, for my objectives in the present research.

2.1 *The Cryptocause*

I remind you that nothing happens (more generally, nothing changes) in the Universe without a cause. This is the very content of the principle of causality. Of course, in some cases, the cause, as a particular/contextual hypostasis of the causality, is known; in other cases, such a cause is unknown. The fact that a particular cause is unknown does not mean, at any rate, that it does not act and, *a fortiori*, it does not mean that the causality, as a principle, is put under doubt. An intermediate case is that of the statistical cause, or the probabilistic cause, that refers to the punctual (analytical) cause of the average of a population's hypostases of a given phenomenon. I am interested here in the case in which the cause is unknown, no matter it is presumed as either an analytical or a statistical cause. I would call such a cause: *cryptocause*.

Moreover, I would associate the cryptocause to capillarity. Obviously, in some cases (for example, that of blood vessels, or industrial/scientific artefacts) the cause is known, so it is not at all a cryptocause. However, in other cases, either in Nature or (especially) in society, the causes are of cryptocause type.[2]

2.2 *The Constraint and the Cryptocause*

Generally, a phenomenon that is of some interest for a decision-maker (or simple observer) is subsumed, at least partially, to a rationality model which the decision-maker (or observer) holds. As a result, the general causality is known—I say, general causality, in the sense that the observer knows how that phenomenon behaves. The problem arises when some constraints that exceed the rational model interfere with the phenomenon unfolding. Of course, some constraints are known (or even introduced) by the observer, but others could be ignored. The ignored[3] (for any reason) constraints in the rationality model are the source (in fact, the cryptocause) for the capillary behaviour of that phenomenon. To maintain the terminology introduced, we have to do here with *cryptoconstraints*.

The idea that the cryptocause is an effect of cryptoconstraints is very important, since otherwise the capillary movement becomes almost unintelligible or even... mysterious.

At the same time, the list of cryptoconstraints has a historical nature: new cryptoconstraints enter the list and old cryptoconstraints leave that list. The extending of the list is the result of the complicatedness of the reality of interest, while the narrowing of it is caused by the development of knowledge (especially of scientific nature).

2.3 Complicatedness Versus Complexity

The *complicatedness* of an entity (event, phenomenon, system) is that property of the entity so that it is difficult to describe it inside a rational (intelligible) model, generally of logical type. This complicatedness is due to either an "agglomeration" of structural components or functional connections among the structural components (i.e., to the functionality of the entity), or an "agglomerated" interactions between the entity and its environment which could also contain complicated entities (i.e., to the behaviour of the entity).

The *complexity* of an entity addresses, instead, the unpredictability of the unfolding of that system. Of course, the complicatedness could, as well, generate unpredictability, but this unpredictability is subsumed to the knowledge progress—the more knowledge held about that entity, the less unpredictable the entity is. Then, why is the concept of complexity needed? The unpredictability generated by complexity has no relationship with the complicatedness, so it has no historical nature. More exactly, while the complicatedness is changing in time (for example, by the size changing of the list of cryptoconstraints), that is, it has a relative character, the complexity is absolute. This absolute character is generated by free will. Some considerations are required here:

- free will cannot subsist other than in cultural beings, i.e., those beings having the capacity of representation; as this capacity is a function of consciousness, free will is held only by the human being, namely, by each human being;
- consequently, the property of complexity cannot be assigned other than to the social (*Nota bene*: better said, societal system[4]) systems populated with human beings, that is, to the social artefacts as result of social (societal) construction;

- it results from the above that a system can be as non-complicated as possible and yet be complex, and vice versa, a system can be as complicated as possible and be, however, simplex (*Nota bene*: I oppose the simplex to complex);
- in the above conceptual framework, it can be said that the unpredictability is contingent in the complicated systems, but is necessary in the complex systems;
- of course, there can be systems both complicated and complex—in fact, contemporary societies are of such a type. I would call this type of system a *cryptosystem*.

Since I am interested in the present research in society (societal system), I shall work with cryptosystems only. By correlating the concept of cryptosystem with that of symbolic species (see Chap. 1), it is obvious that a cryptosystem is also a symbolic species.

Figure 1 synoptically systematizes the above discussion (*Nota bene*: the complex systems are of two kinds: cryptosystems and simplex systems, while the non-complex systems are of two kinds: complicated systems and simple systems).

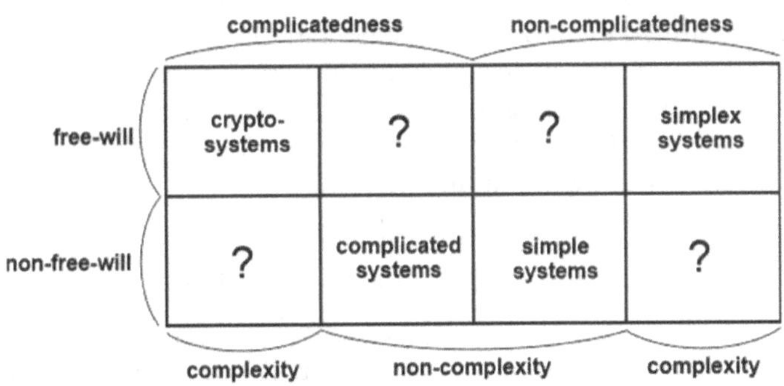

Fig. 1 Complicatedness and complexity in generic systems (*Source* author)

2.4 What About Free Will?

The free will can be defined as the capacity to oppose the social necessity. Well, I must say something about the social necessity. The "standard" concept of necessity is that of natural world (for example, induced by the laws of Physics, or Chemistry, or Biology). So, the natural necessity, so to speak, is a phenomenon which nothing can block to manifest as it is expected—at the time, in the place, and in the mode established by the laws in case. However, there is another kind of necessity, let us call it social necessity, that are characterized as follows:

- it is owned by society (societal system) only, not by Nature;
- it is contingently created, not necessarily—generally, it manifests in the normative framework of the society, that is, what is often called positive law[5];
- it is an artefact, i.e., a social (societal) construction; while the natural necessity is objective, the social necessity is objectified[6];
- as an artefact, the social necessity can be modified or even abolished through the same inter-subjective agreement that created it.

To the social necessity, the subject can oppose, no matter that social necessity was established dictatorially or democratically. This opposition is only possible by the intermediation of free will, in the form of either ignoring, violating, or exploiting to gain (illegal or immoral) advantage. At any rate, I want to say that the opposition to social necessity is based on free will. This conclusion will be useful further.

2.5 Cryptocause and Free Will

When free will opposes the social necessity,[7] it does so since the social necessity in case has become too narrow or, the same, it has introduced some constraints which the individual(s) or group(s) do not accept or consider that their acceptance requires a too high price, of any nature—for example, affecting the standard of life, the democratic standard of society, the freedom, the self-esteem, etc. It is obvious that the state (as representative of the society's members) cannot predict such a reaction, so that, for it, the reaction based on free will is assigned to a cryptocause.

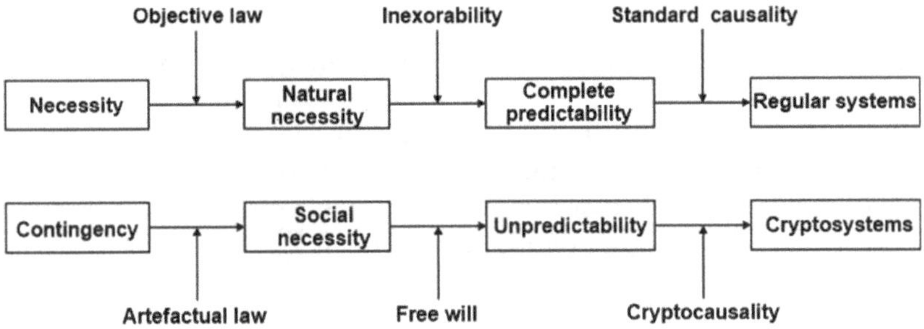

Fig. 2 Causality of cryptocausality (*Source* author)

Even if the cryptocause is put under free will's umbrella, this is only a label, not an explanation, and, as it is known, no prediction is possible without an explanation.[8]

2.6 *Free Will and Capillarity*

Now, it seems clear enough that, in the social field, the property of capillarity, as it was defined above, is generated, as background, by free will, that is, by an unpredictable behavioural factor, since it is perfectly subjective. I would say that the social capillarity (to maintain the discussion inside the societal system, since only inside such a macro-artefact, free will is possible) is a result of the cryptocauses "hosted" by free will. To be repeated, that free will is opaque to the observer.[9] Indeed, if another factor, less opaque to the observer, were involved in the property of capillarity, that transparent factor would be considered and would reject the capillarity concerned.

A synoptic suggestion of the above findings is shown in Fig. 2.

2.7 *A Stylized Model of Capillary Action*

As it was said before, a capillar will unfold a movement (change, action) in the opposite direction related to the expected/anticipated one. We must hold that this opposite direction is not known by the observer (analyst, decision-maker, etc.), so it is not predictable.[10] This ignorance is a direct consequence of ignoring the cryptocause involved, as a result, in turn, of (necessary) ignorance of the free will of individuals/groups.

In this paragraph, I shall provide a (rather stylized) model of the capillary action, that is, of a cryptosystem, in the generic case.

First of all, I must discuss the issue of rationality model of a generic individual. Any individual holds a rationality model, no matter its degree of sophistication[11] and even the degree of consciousness which the individual has about his/her own rationality model concerned. Generally, a rationality model has the following components (pentagonal model of rationality—$\mathcal{R}^p$):

(a) (*C*) *a credence/belief* or a set of beliefs. The credence/belief can be of either a religious kind (faith) or a laic one. The credence/belief is the intellectual foundation of the rationality model that the individual uses in making decisions. This component generates what is called the theoretical rationality or the theoretical rationality model (TRM). The TRM has a primitive nature and its role is the following: to justify, in an inter-personally non-communicable way, the decisions made. The credence/belief is credited as being relatively immutable or, at least, lasting in the very long term (at limit, throughout life);

(b) (*V*) *a set of values*. It is generated by the very credence/belief,[12] and is relatively stable in the long term. *Nota bene*: of course, the set of values is not uniquely generated by a given credence/belief; many sets of values can be "enacted" by the same credence/belief. Consequently, the set of values has less stability than the credence/belief, depending on both the societal context and the idiosyncrasies of the individuals;

(c) (*P*) *a set of principles*. It is generated by the set of values. By a principle must be understood a fundamental rule to guide the reasoning inside the model of rationality concerned. Usually, the set of principles is embedded in a logic, namely the logic of the model of rationality;

(d) (*R*) *a set of reasoning procedures to assign means to goals*. It is generated by the set of principles. It is aimed at finding, generally by optimization, the most appropriate means (of any kind, including, for example, the time) to the proposed goals/purposes, following the "three E", i.e., efficacy/effectiveness, economicity, and efficiency—efficiency is the cost of effectiveness[13];

(e) (B) *a set of biases*.[14] It is generated by four factors: (a) free will (i.e., the voluntarism regarding the opposition to social necessity); (b) psychological idiosyncrasies; (c) experience; (d) contextual contagion by observing the behaviours around.[15]

Formally, a model of rationality is written as a logical conjunction of the five sufficiency predicates:

$$\mathcal{R}^p \leftarrow (C) \bigwedge (V) \bigwedge (P) \bigwedge (R) \bigwedge (B)$$

Comment: except the predicate B, all the predicates are inferable from one another, in the order indicated above.

Secondly, it must be said that the capillarity is caused, essentially, by the predicate B. Some more detailed considerations are needed here:

(i) the issue of biases has been intensively studied for decades, especially within the behavioural approaches, and appeals the psychology (both cognitive and behavioural), sociology, and general anthropology[16];
(ii) there are, already, good systematizations of the biases in the economic behaviour although, in my opinion, needing some reductionist analyses so getting a simpler and more intelligible "map" of the biases concerned (see Cognitive Bias Codex, created by John Manoogian III, and Buster Benson, that contains about 180 biases);
(iii) a question arises here: why free will is considered as a species of biases? My positioning is as follows:

- generally, the biases are accumulated based on experience, education, tradition, and others of the same. We can call this category of biases: biases contingently gained (BCG);
- free will is a (cognitive) property that the generic individual is necessarily endowed with, as a result of being a holder of consciousness and, consequently, as having the potential of representation. We can call this category of biases: biases necessarily gained (BNG);

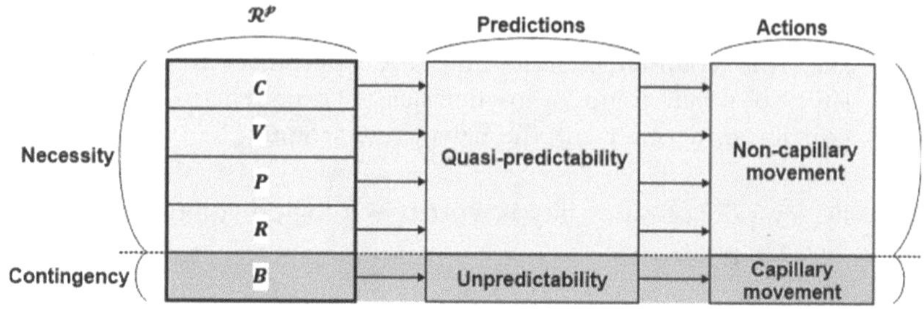

Fig. 3 Capillary action (*Source* author)

- so, both the BCG and BNG act contingently and unpredictably, no matter their origin, either contingent or necessary;
- as a conclusion, I think that free will is a species of biases.

Figure 3 provides a suggestion regarding the way in which a cryptosystem works.

Discussion

- Fig. 3. is just indicative, since the predictions and actions in the "sphere" of necessity are always affected by the component B of $\mathcal{R}^p$;
- there are neither pure action of BCG nor pure action of BNG—always there is a combination (linear or non-linear) between the two species of biases. For example, a linear combination of them to make a prediction (Pre) could have the form:

$$Pre = \alpha \cdot BCG + \beta \cdot BNG$$

where $\alpha, \beta \in \mathbb{R}$, and $\alpha + \beta = 1$.

3 Capillary, Capillarity, to Capillarize—A Conceptual Family

Capillary is the noun, capillarity is the property/attribute, and capillarize is the process/verb in the conceptual family of the capillar.

A capillary always has the property of capillarity, and the capillarity will always capillarize.

I would come back to the previous discussion regarding the predictability in relation to the property of capillarity. Generally, this property of a given (generic) system is known, so the capillarity is one among other properties of that system and, consequently, it is considered both when the predictions are made and the observations are registered—for example, the up movement of blood within the sanguine vessels, although it should move down under the gravity force.

However, in this book, the capillarity will be considered as a property of a cryptosystem (see the above considerations in this matter). Its cause is also a cryptocause and, even if we might be able to assign a label to that cryptocause, in reality, the cause concerned is unknown to us. As we shall see further, generally, such labels were applied in the last decades (especially in the behavioural studies), without which we have acquired knowledge, in this way, about those causes.

A terminological clarification

The question could be put: a predictable capillarity is it still a capillarity? My answer is ambivalent based on the following:

- on the one part
  - once the causality is known, it loses its crypto character and becomes a normal (regular) one[17];
  - the property of capillarity has, clearly, a relative character: indeed, like in the case of the Special Theory of Relativity, we are not sure whether (to recall the example of blood vessels) the narrowed diameter of the vessels induces the adverse effect or, by the contrary, the gravity force is responsible for that[18]—*Nota bene*: of course, I ignore here the fact that the example is associated with a non-capillary phenomenon, since we have not, really, a cryptocausality in the case discussed.

- on the other part
  - if some kind of movement of a system is expected, but we register another movement (either opposed or only deviated from the expectation), and we can identify the cause that generated that deviation, it seems we have, still, a capillary movement, although there is no cryptocause involved.

So, it seems we need here a (general) typology of the property of capillarity. I provide below such a proposal.

(i) Regarding the cause

(a) Regular capillarity (*RC*)

Regular capillarity addresses the cases in which the expected movement of a system/process is modified by a known or (potentially) inferable cause or, often, conditionality.[19] Regular capillarity can be of the following classes:

- *RC* of *direction*[20] (*RCD*): refers to the case in which the direction of movement (of the given system) is different from that expected/hoped. If the deviated direction keeps the sense (vectoral orientation of the direction), we call that capillary effect an *adverse effect*, and if the deviated direction also changes the sense, we call that capillary effect a *perverse effect*;
- *RC* of *speed/acceleration* (*RCS* or *RCA*): refers to the case in which, compared with the expected "version", the movement of the system has a different speed (either greater or smaller) or has a different acceleration (either greater or smaller);
- *RC* of *significance*[21] (*RCS*): refers to the case in which, compared with the expected "version", the movement of the system has a significance for the relevant individuals (or a homogenous group of individuals) which is changed in one manner or another.

(b) Cryptocapillarity (*CC*)

Cryptocapillarity addresses the cases in which, for the modified movement of the system compared with the expected movement, the cause involved is not known, even whether it could be assigned to a label for the comfort of inter-personal communication. Cryptocapillarity can be of the following classes:

- *CC* of *improvement*: refers to the case in which, by the capillary effect, the expected result from the movement of the system is improved, in one manner or another. This means the capillary effect "works" in the same paradigm which is expected from the system concerned—for example: the increase of the tax base when the tax rate increases in the fiscal phenomenology. This capillary effect is an *effect of path*;
- *CC* of *worsening*: refers to the case in which, by the capillary effect, the expected result from the movement of the system is worsened, in one manner or another. This means the capillary effect "works" in a contradictory paradigm compared with that which is expected from the system in the case—for example, if we remain within the fiscal paradigm: the decrease of the tax base when the tax rate increases.[22] This capillary effect is, also, an *effect of path*;
- *CC* of *equivalence*: refers to the case in which, by the capillary effect, the expected result from the movement of the system changes in such a way that the final result is, somewhat, equivalent with the expected one. This means the capillary effect "works" in the same paradigm which is expected from the system in the case. This capillary effect is an *effect of process*.

(ii) Regarding the origin

(a) Capillarity externally induced (*CEI*)

An external factor creates the capillary property at a given moment. For example, the fiscal policy could increase the tax rate. The taxpayer is expected to increase his/her tax base to cover the difference in tax due to the public budget, to preserve their net gain. Instead, he/she might reduce the tax base (at least the observable tax base for the Government), appealing to tax fraud—a version of Laffer's curve. Of course, the external factor might come from the economic process itself or, more rarely, from the natural events (earthquakes, floods, etc.).

- *CEI* by the *economic process*: these capillarities are generated by the economic environment of the system concerned, no matter whether the reasons for such a phenomenon are known or not to that system;
- *CEI* by the *normative authority*: these capillarities are enacted by the state, through its agencies, and they are, generally, of normative types. Some norms could cause deviation from the expected behaviours and, in this way, lead to capillary phenomena.

(b) Capillarity internally generated (*CIG*)

An internal factor creates the capillary property at a given moment. For example, a decrease of supply (in goods and services of a given kind), that is expected to generate an increase of the price,[23] could, instead, cause a decrease of that price, since new suppliers enter the market concerned, by observing the opportunity provided by the decrease of the existent supply, so, in fact, the demand for the first supplier moves down, and the prices moves down too.[24]

- *CIG* by *overcoming the elasticities*: this type of internally generated capillarities arises when, in the relationship between two behavioural variables, one of them varies so that it passes beyond the elasticity with which the correlated variable reacts. When the elasticity (either known or unknown) is overcome, a capillary effect happens. For example, if the price decreases for a good or service that is rigid related to the price (as staple goods or services), the decrease in the price does not lead to an increase in demand, as it is expected;
- *CIG* by *overcoming the complementarities*: this type of internally generated capillarities arises when, in the relationship between two behavioural variables, one of them varies so that the rate of complementarity between them is non-punctual; namely, it is either greater or smaller than it is required. For example, if a worker who can work, at a time, with a single piece of equipment is provided with two or more pieces of such equipment, the productivity not only does not increase, but it will even decrease compared to the initial state.

To conclude, for us, here, the capillarity is an adverse effect of the (known) causality. Moreover, we have no hope of eliminating this non-knowledge, since it is generated by the biases and, especially by free will.

Nota bene: an issue can be highlighted here: if a bias affects our decision (prediction, action, etc.), and free will opposes that bias, this does not mean that the bias concerned was eliminated. In other words, here does not work the negation of negation that leads to the non-negated, to speak so.

4 Capillarism—The Concept

In this paragraph, I would try to increase the population of "isms' world", by introducing the concept of *capillarism*.

4.1 A Narrative Description

Capillarism should be understood as a paradigm of either praxiological or practical order at the societal level. A short description of such a paradigm could hold the following features:

- it regards the individual (rarer, the group or larger communities) behaviour during different kinds of social/societal actions (either acts—to do, or abstentions—not to do);
- it implies some peculiarities of the individual (or group) so that the behaviour deviates or even opposes the expected (because known) behaviour, so to speak, opposes the orthodox behaviour;
- generally, the causality (conditionality) of that deviation/opposition of actual behaviour compared to the expected, "normal" one, can be known or unknown by both the actor and the observer of the action concerned;
- the causality (conditionality) of the deviated behaviour, i.e., of the capillary behaviour, is unpredictable, whether it is known or not;
- although the capillarity is met in both Nature and society, the capillarism, as an actional—either praxiological or practical—paradigm, is proper to society only;
- however, regarding holding the statute of a paradigm, about capillarism must be said the following:

- it is an incomplete paradigm, or, so to speak, a pseudo-paradigm, because some sufficiency predicates of a paradigm[25] are not verified (Dinga et al., 2022), namely:
- regarding the *value*: properly speaking, the capillarism has no founding value, it is not searching for a fundamental such value on which to ground its finality in the individual's behaviour;
- regarding the *nucleus*: the capillarism provides not a primitive principle to guide, let us say, the capillary behaviour. The capillary behaviour is, many times, a short episode of idiosyncratic necessity in a longer chain of non-idiosyncratic contingency;
- regarding the *function*: the capillarism has as its function to locally optimize the result of a behaviour that is constrained by global restrictions;
- regarding the *logic*: the capillarism exhibits an intuitive rationalization of the behaviour concerned.

So, the capillarism lacks two of the sufficiency predicates that institute a (praxiological paradigm), namely the value and the nucleus. For these reasons, I propose the capillarism be considered a pseudo-paradigm or, more exactly, a structureless paradigm—a structureless paradigm continues, of course, to be a functional paradigm.

Some considerations on the two sufficiency predicates of a paradigm that are verified by the capillarism are provided as follows:

- the *function*:

The local optimization of the result of behaviour implies, of course, the operationalization of a model of rationality that could be called a *capillary model of rationality* (*CMR*).

A model or rationality (Dinga et al., 2025) is, generally, an intellectual protocol (a procedure) to assign means to a purpose. In fact, such a definition addresses practical rationality only. There is, also, a theoretical rationality that is more fundamental than the practical one (Mele & Rawling, 2004), and has the following content: the justification of the practical rationality from the axiological perspective. This justification means simply the identification of the belief (or the set of beliefs) based on which the practical rationality is put into reality. Figure 4 synoptically describes the relationships between theoretical rationality and practical one.

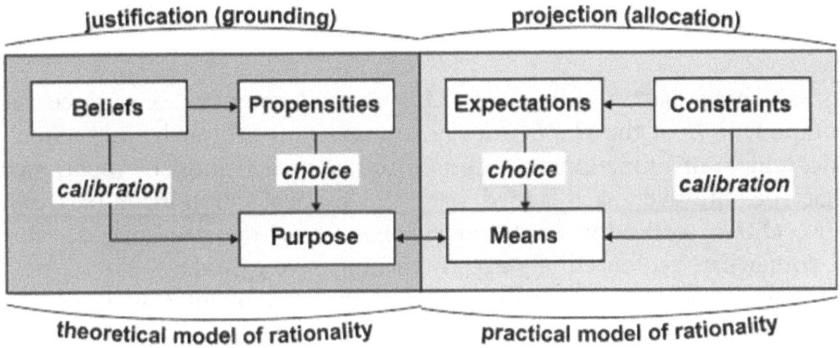

Fig. 4 Relationships between theoretical rationality and practical rationality (*Source* author)

Discussion

- the genuine purpose is always established (chosen) independently from the means required to get it. This choice is the privilege of theoretical rationality, which is grounded on beliefs, which, in turn, generate the propensities;
- operationally, the propensities choose the purpose, which, in turn, simultaneously, calibrates that purpose, to make it harmoniously correspond to the deep beliefs of the involved individual or group or society as a whole;
- from the practical rationality part, the general constraints, of any nature, allow the expectations of the subject, and, based on those expectations, the means to get the purpose are selected; simultaneously, the constraints calibrate the selected means;
- so, from the concomitant action of theoretical and practical rationality, the purpose and its adequate means are put together.

- the *logic*:

As said previously, the logic of *CMR* is an incomplete one, since the component *B* of the *CMR* does not have a rational (analytical, systematic, and so on) functioning, but an intuitive one. It must be mentioned that the intuitiveness is added over the rational component of *CMR* (i.e., *OMR*—orthodox model of rationality), so that the final decision is, somewhat, "coloured" by exactly this intuitive episode.

A short discussion about the nature of the component *B* within *CMR* is required now:

- the component *OMR* of *CMR* is founded necessarily, that is, a decision resulting from operating the *OMR* leaves no room for manoeuvre, and that decision is incompatible with free will (freedom) in making decisions. The necessity, in the logical sense, is, therefore, assigned to *OMR* within *CMR*;
- on the contrary, the *B* component of *CMR* is without the necessity,[26] so that it is entirely a manifestation of voluntarism (free will);
- this relatively abstruse combination between necessity and contingency in making decisions is, in fact, specific to *CMR* (*Nota bene*: for instance, the artificial intelligence could never have the intuition of *B*, but only, and exclusively, the necessity of *OMR*.

4.2 A Stylized Formal Description

The capillary model of rationality (*CMR*) has the following basic "blocks":

(i) (*OMR*) orthodox *MR*, as both a theoretical and practical procedure to make decisions, as discussed above;

- the credence/belief is not miscible with the biases, since, if it was, the biases would enter the *OMR*;

(ii) (*B*) a set of biases, no matter their origin, of idiosyncratic signification and local functioning;

- each individual assigns his/her own significances to his/her biases, either consciously or non-consciously;
- the local and particular functioning of the biases is mandatory, while, on the contrary, the orthodox model of rationality is working globally and generally;

(iii) (I) intuitive integration of OMR and B, without a rational/procedural way or algorithm to do that;

- although (the most) part of the decision-making belongs to OMR, the impact of biases on the final positioning of the individual is introduced in a non-rational way, i.e., intuitively[27];

(iv) (H) non-analytical validation of the final decision as a mix between OMR and CMO;

- enacting of the final decision is not anymore rational (as done in OMR), i.e., analytically validated before it is provided to the environment, but it is holistically assessed (from this, the "H").

Figure 5 suggests a general view on the CMR functioning.

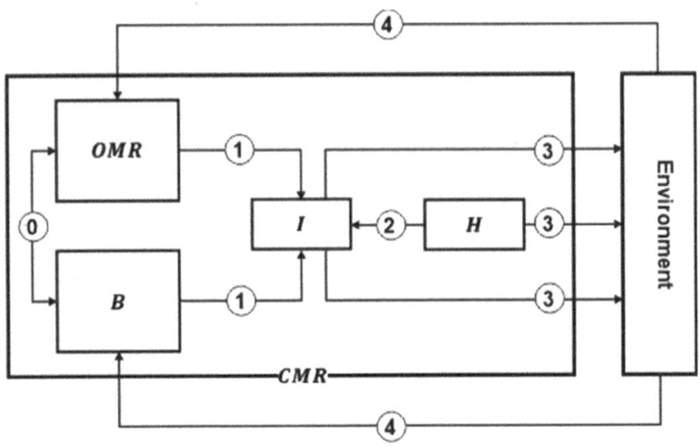

Fig. 5 Functioning of the capillarity model of rationality (*Source* author)

5 Capillarism—A General Typology

From the assertions already made, we can now provide a general typology of capillarism, as a pseudo-paradigm (or, more exactly, quasi-paradigm) in the praxiological/practical field.[28]

(a) (*EC*) *emergent capillarism*: is a potential capillary property held by individuals in their quality of human beings endowed with consciousness and the capacity of representation, as well as benefitting from experience, memory, and own aspirations;
(b) (*IC*) *induced capillarism*: is a potential capillary property held by the societal artefacts (usually, of an institutional kind) to generate capillary behaviours and actions, based on both rational models and possible biases;
(c) (*SC*) *survival capillarism*: is a potential capillary property of generic systems, either natural or social/societal, to search, find, and use those ways to treat the environmental as well as internal challenges in order to survive[29];
(d) (*RE*) *reconstructive capillarism*: is a potential property of generic systems, either natural or social/societal, to change their own structure (and, consequently, their own functions, both as functionality and as behaviour[30]) as a response to external or internal actions liable to destroy or irreversibly damage the systems concerned.

Based on the above classes of capillarism, I shall try further to show that each of the basic approaches in human behaviour, at the individual and societal level, holds a species (a class) of capillarism, which provides a ground and common intelligibility (maybe, an explanation) for those approaches. I strongly think that, in this respect, we should reject the artificial construction of the neoclassical theory in Economics, and, generally, in the social field, and reconstruct the praxiology starting from the irreducible humanity of humans.

6 Capillarism and Other *Isms*

In my opinion, except the neoclassical economic theory,[31] all the (more realistic) other approaches of the economic phenomenology and, by extension, of the social/societal phenomenology, have a kernel, more or less obvious, of capillarity. As I have tried to show above, the real individual is far from a perfect calculus machine (as, for example, the artificial intelligence could be—really?), because it is "inhabited" by a lot of biases of different nature, origins, intensities, and impact, that give the idiosyncratic colour of decisions made, especially by the intermediation of free will.

Although the abstracting, generalization, and logical analysis are indispensable to get a true model of the world, these abstracting, generalization, and logical evaluations must be made on the real world, not on an imaginary one. This "recommendation" is not to ensure the truth of utility, but, on the contrary, to ensure the utility of truth.

I shall consider four of the (in my opinion) most relevant approaches of the economic/societal system—with some benevolence, I would call them theoretical models, hypotheses, or theories—related to which I shall provide some considerations from the perspective of the capillarism: (a) behaviourism; (b) institutionalism; (c) viabilism; (d) autopoieticism. Based on these evaluations, I shall propose, finally, to consider an evolutionary perspective of the societal dynamics, which constitutes, in fact, the very purpose of this book.

6.1 Behaviourism

Generalities

In a narrow sense, behaviourism is an attitude of scientists or decision-makers, so that the realization of the actions (based on corresponding decisions) is explainable by appealing the psychological traits of the generic human being. Although this seems to be a truism, the behaviourism arising is a reaction to the mechanicism of the neoclassical economic theory that totally ignored the "imperfections" of the human being, namely exactly the psychological (causal) determinants.

In a large sense, behaviourism is a doctrine that takes into consideration the impact of psychological traits (both for humans and animals) in the process of decision-making regarding the behaviour (action, attitudes, interpretations, etc.).[32] In fact, as a doctrine, behaviourism aspires to a metaphysic statute regarding the living, in general.

The main subjects of interest that behaviourism is in charge of are (SEP, 2025): (a) psychology as a science of behaviour,[33] but not of the inner mind; (b) the sources (in last resort, the causes, or the determinants) of behaviour are not in the internal psychological processes, but in the environment; (c) all accidental psychological/mental terms appear in explaining the behaviour they must either be eliminated, or translated into behavioural terms.

Generally, three species of behaviourism are the most "visited" by scientists or decision-makers:

- (MB) Methodological behaviourism

Methodological behaviourism keeps the above-mentioned object of study, namely the behaviour, without any appeal to mental states or psychological determining of decision or action.[34] Conceptually, this species of behaviourism holds the initial intentions of such a research.

- (PB) Psychological behaviourism

Psychological behaviourism is a direction of research developed within the psychology itself, so that it uses the findings in the psychology—often called behavioural psychology.[35]

- (LB) Logical behaviourism

Logical (or analytical) behaviourism is a direction of research developed within philosophy. It is a semantic (more extensive, a semiotic) examination of the concepts and terms regarding the functioning of consciousness. The mental state is derived, in fact, from the behaviour itself or by observing the tendencies (propensities) to act or abstain in specified contexts.[36]

Based on the above, *prima facie*, behaviourism can be described as follows: *a doctrine that considers behaviour as a reaction of the individual (either human or animal) to environmental stimuli.*

The problem of stimuli has been deeply examined, starting with the works of Skinner (1938, 2019),[37] but gradually, some psychological traits (i.e., inner or mental phenomena) have been introduced into individual behaviour. Although, generally, the psychological traits are considered idiosyncratic, there are attempts to give them a certain generality, namely for the generic individual (for example, Kahneman, 2011). In this way, in fact, behaviourism becomes a combination (mix) of psychological traits and environmental stimuli, so that, somewhat, a new model of rationality is necessary to explain a behaviour simultaneously (and, possibly, synergically) based on the two factors.

Consequently, I would define behaviourism as follows: *the theory (hypothesis) claiming that behaviour in the animate world is caused/ conditioned by the pair stimuli–reaction in relation with the environment, where reaction is triggered by the stimuli but is caused by the psychological traits*.

Capillarism and Behaviourism—Five Theses

After sketching the content of the concept (theory, doctrine, hypothesis) of behaviourism, I shall examine the possible, either necessary or contingent, relationships between behaviourism and capillarism. I shall do that by formulating a number of theses, with the corresponding comments.

- (*thesis 1*): any behaviour of a given system depends on the structure of that system

As known, being given a generic system, with a structure (i.e., a set of components that have at least one common trait of all components, and at least one different trait when the components are compared two by two[38]), that structure generates the system's behaviour, i.e., the relationships between the system's components, on the one hand, and the system's environment, on the other hand. Consequently, the behaviour of a system necessarily depends on its structure;

- (*thesis* 2) the relationships of a system with its environment are mediated by the functions whose action crosses the system's membrane, both outward and inward

A generic system receives impulses from its environment and, symmetrically, sends impulses to that environment. Both the system and the environment (which must also be considered as a system) design their function of response as reactions to actions. So, each reaction takes into consideration both the characteristics of action and the characteristics of its own structure to form that response-reaction;

- (*thesis 3*): different systems (like, for example, a punctual system or its environmental system) hold different structures and, consequently, are willing to form specific response-reaction functions to the action functions

In forming (designing) the response-reaction function, a system uses its structure. This way, the response-reaction will be influenced by the system's idiosyncrasy. Regarding the humans, this idiosyncrasy is done by the psychological state of the individual, so the response-reaction will take over the psychological peculiarities consisting in: beliefs, experiences, traditions, contagions from other actors/systems, and so on;

- (*thesis* 4): the decision that grounds a response-reaction is neither completely rational nor completely i-rational (or a-rational) but a rather inextricable mix of the two groundings

In decision-making process, there is a permanent causal circulation between OMR and B. However, the causal chain begins with B, then this first impression[39] is passed to OMR, and, finally, the point of view of OMR is again filtered by B. This three-step process of decision-making in behaviourism, depends, however from the context in which the decision is made. If the individual concerned is deciding without any pressure (for example, without the pressure of surviving), then the circular passing between OMR and B could continue iteratively many times, because, after the first "cycle", the individual could feel the need of refinement his/her decision. But, if some pressures exerts on that individual, then the decision is made even based on the first step only, namely the impression. Figure 6 provides a pyramid of pressures (or threatens).

Discussion

- in the inverted pyramid of threats, the meaning of the (Arabian) figures is:
  - 0: degree 0 of threat—regards the most dangerous threat, for example, the imminence of death;

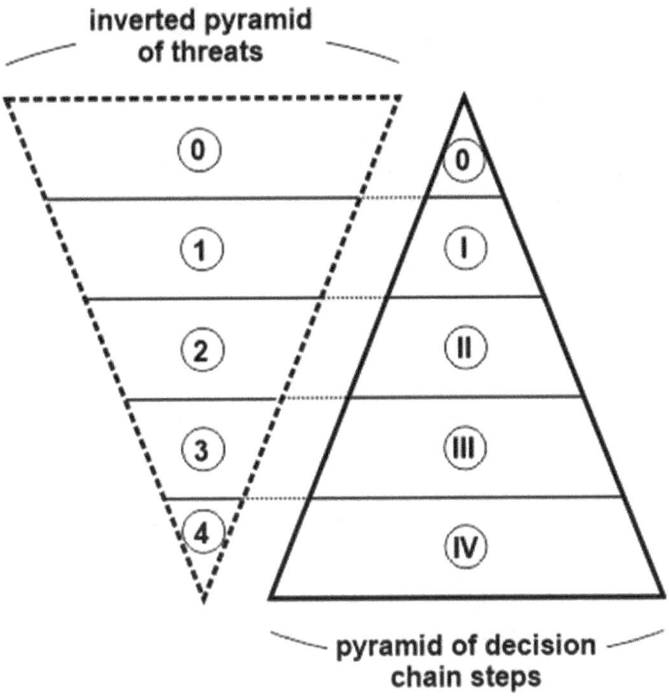

Fig. 6 Pyramid of threatens from the environment (*Source* author)

- 1: degree 1 of threat—regards a dangerous threat, for example, entering the subordinated positioning related to the environment (i.e., to be dominated by the others, like losing freedom and so on);
- 2: degree 2 of threat—regards a little dangerous threat, for example, losing the social position (including the job);
- 3: degree 3 of threat—regards the uncertain, dangerous threat, for example, losing self-esteem;
- 4: degree 4 of threat—regards the least dangerous threat, for example, losing wealth.

- in the pyramid of decisions chain steps, the meaning of the (Roman) figures is:
    - 0: zero steps of decision-making chain—regards the decision-making directly and exclusively inside B[40];
    - I: 1 step of decision-making chain—regards the decision-making that implies the "circulation" of reasoning from B to OMR and from OMR to B;
    - II: 2 steps of decision-making chain—regards the decision-making that implies the path: $B - OMR - B - OMR - B$ or, formally: $B^{(3)}OMR^{(2)}$ (*Nota bene*: as said before, always the decision-making process begins from$B$);
    - III: 3 steps of decision-making chain—regards the decision-making that implies the path $B^{(4)}OMR^{(3)}$
    - IV: 4 steps or more of decision-making chain—regards the decision-making that implies the path $B^{(k)}OMR^{(k-1)}$, where $k \geq 4, k \in \mathbb{N}$.

Nota bene. At the presumptive question: when the decision-making chain experiences $k > 4$? My answer is the following: when the individual develops activities without any danger, for example when he/she writes about the cases in which is activated $k > 4$.

- (*thesis 5*): the capillarity involved in B functionality is not an invariant

The biases an individual holds have not only a personal character, but also an evolutionary one. Despite some traits that are quasi-invariant—for example, the credence-belief shared with the native community—the life path of each individual changes (more precisely, actualizes[41]) the content of B, so that, the unpredictability that characterizes the B-based actions, extends throughout the individual's life span.

What Kind of Capillarism?

Based on the above, I think that behaviourism is compatible, both structurally and functionally, with the *emergent capillarism* (EC).

Some Concluding Remarks
The (relatively) rigid typology of behaviourism, with the three types, should be completed with a fourth one, which I would call: ***evolutionary behaviourism*** (EB). Such a new type of behaviourism has the following basic features:

- the OMR component of CMR is the hard core of the last, and holds a relative invariance, at least in the short and medium term;
- the B component of CMR is the belt around the hard core,[42] and has a relative volatility—we can say it has an invariant volatility;
- between OMR and B subsists an osmotic zone (OZ), in which there is a permanent and automatic (without the conscious control of the individual concerned) exchange of information, reasons, motivations, and so on, from OMR to B and inversely. In time, some biases from B enter OMR, and, symmetrically, some attitudes from OMR enter B;
- the osmotic zone is the melting pot that builds the evolutionary path of the behavioural actions (either acts or abstentions);
- in fact, EB is generated by the (co-evolutive) binomial *ORM* – *B*. This way, Thorndike's theory of learning (including Skinner's reinforcements) is extended from B to CMR, so we have to deal with an evolutionary learning at the binomial *ORM* – *B* level, where each of the binomial's components initiates mutations in the other component.

6.2 Institutionalism

Preamble
Human society functions as a system. From a logical point of view, we are dealing with a symbolic[43] system. Being a system, human society is composed of a leading subsystem (which can be formed by several leading sub-subsystems in a certain relationship of mutual conditioning) and a driven subsystem, also formed by several driven sub-subsystems. Being a symbolic system, it is characterized by the following:

- the membrane that separates it from its environment is an institutional one, specified in positive law, primarily in the Constitution;

- the component elements are: human individuals, institutions, organizations, social (positive) laws, procedures (including customs, traditions, ethical/moral rules), and the like;
- the functionality of the symbolic system called society refers to the interactions between the intra-membrane component elements: between the elements of the driven subsystem, between the elements of the leading subsystem, between the elements of the leading subsystem, on the one hand, and those of the driven subsystem on the other hand;
- the behaviour of the symbolic system called society refers to the interactions between the intra-membrane elements (either of the leading subsystem or of the driven subsystem), on the one hand, and the environment of the symbolic system in question, on the other hand. The state and society are two components that appear in tandem, the appearance of one logically attracting the appearance of the other.

The Concept of Institution

An institution is understood as an artefact, that is, a social construction, intended to order (regulate) social interaction between individuals or groups of individuals. Institutions are classified according to at least three fundamental criteria: (a) by character; (b) by sphere; (c) by nature.

(a) by character

- (C^c) *codified* institutions: institutions that are subject to the normative framework of society (e.g., taxation);
- ($\overline{C}^c$) *non-codified* institutions: institutions that are not subject to the normative framework of societies (e.g., inter-personal greetings);

(b) by sphere

- (S^c) *public* institutions: they concern public "affairs", that is, those interactions in society that are intended to achieve the public interest (generally understood as common interests at the level of the whole society)—see, here, the set IC_C in Chapter 3;

- (S^p) *private* institutions: they concern private "affairs", that is, those interactions in society, carried out between individuals or groups of individuals whose interactions do not concern a general interest of societies, but particular interests of the interacting individuals;

(c) by nature

- (N^o) institutions of the *organization* type: they are those institutions that take the (normative) form of organizations (for example, a minister or a NGO);
- (N^c) institutions of the *concept* type: these are those institutions that do not take the form of an organization but are created and operate, themselves, either within organizations (for example, the state budget, as it is established and operates within the Ministry of Finance), or independently, without belonging to an organization (for example, the ethical principles).

Basic Coordinates of Institutionalism

The institutionalism is a social theory that originated in the theory of the state. Briefly, it supposes that the social contract, based on which the state arose within a given community, is basically built on a set of commonly agreed norms (generally called institutions), integrated by a macro-norm called the Constitution.

The institutionalism was developed mainly as a theory of the social (*Nota bene*: more precisely, it must be said: societal) institutions. As expected, the genealogy of institutionalism goes till Aristotle, but a deep examination is provided by the German Historical School. The institutionalism arose as a reaction to the (Neo)Classical Economics and, basically, it rejected the deductive, i.e., logical inferentiality in modelling the economic (larger: societal) process. The (final) vision of institutionalism is concerned with Political Economics, which combines the history, the sociology, and the empiricism. In the large framework of institutionalism is put into evidence the so-called new institutionalism (which differs from the "old" institutionalism by focusing on individual/collective behaviour under the norms rather than by focusing on the formal/political institutions of the society).

The institutionalism defines its vision exactly as a critique of the classical (and, then, neoclassical) economic theory, especially for the unreasonable presuppositions regarding the perfect rationality, the absence of lags in getting new information, the unlimited capacity of processing information, and other of the same. However, replacing the perfect rational behaviour of individuals with the perfect capacity of the state to enact the behavioural norms does nothing but bring a... collective perfect rationality in the economic (and, generally, social/societal) phenomenology. As we see further in this book, both institutionalism and behaviourism should be integrated into a larger theoretical synthesis called evolutionism.

Like behaviourism, institutionalism is a theoretical construction that paradigmatically embeds human behaviour within the societal system. It focuses on an external factor, namely the norms (more generally, the normative framework). As behaviourism also considers an external factor to which the individual reacts, some distinction between behaviourism's external causal factor and institutionalism's external causal factor is required:

- regarding the behaviourism
  - behaviourism's external causal factor (notedE_B) is a non-deliberative, often random factor, initiated by the individual's environment, either intentionally to the individual concerned or without any directed intention. For example, the famous invisible hand, which acts in the economic field (but, equally, at the societal level, besides), is composed of a myriad of decisions and actions, any of which serve the individual concerned without intending so;
  - the E_B has not a purpose as such, but only a finality; this finality is generated by the mix between cooperation (C^1) and competition (C^2), that is within the $C^{(1)}C^{(2)}$ societal game;
  - at the societal level, like within the economic field, there are some societal structures and forces (partially, I have referred to them in Chapter 2, namely to the societal forces) that cause and guide the societal evolution in its largest sense. Some of them are deliberative, other of them are spontaneous, generally

random,[44] but none is directed to other individual. Since something could remain unclear here, I shall provide the following comments:

of course, there is a purpose/goal in any decision or action (either act or abstention) of each individual within the societal system;

however, that purpose is an one-sided reflexive (or a self-reflexive) one, it concerns the only individual who issued and implemented the action to get the respective purpose, not the other individuals;

it results that, from a logical point of view, in behaviourism, as related to the individual that constitutes the external causeE_B, the other individuals constitute just means to get his/her purpose.

- regarding the institutionalism
  - institutionalism's external causal factor (notedE_I) is a deliberative (never random) factor, initiated by the state (that positions itself in the individual's environment). This environment is, however, a special one, fundamentally different from the individual's environment in the case of behaviourism, namely:

    the enacting of the norms by the state implicitly extends the norms' purpose on all the individuals eligible as recipients of those norms, so, this time, the individuals are viewed as purposes, not exclusively as means to get purposes[45]—the norms not only ensure the public goods for individuals, but also regulate the fair relationship among them in any societal field of social interaction (either cooperation or competition);

    consequently, the institutionalism's purpose is a two-sided reflexive (or, a bivalently reflexive) one; it concerns both the issuer (the state), and the recipients (the ordinary individuals who are eligible for those norms);
  - the institutionalism's impulses, stimuli, or constraints (i.e., normative ISCs) are perfectly predictable, the reaction functions of individuals can be *ex ante* built on, so those ISCs enter as independent variables;

- the institutionalism's ISCs are codified, i.e., endorsed by the public power, which means: (a) opposable to anyone; (b) sanctionable when violated;

Nota bene: to consider only the institutional norms (i.e., the institutions) issued/enacted by the state addresses only a small part (the smallest part) of the societal institutions—in fact the most part of the institutions regulating the society functioning are norms without issuer, that is, uncodified norms. Obviously, the state will do well to consider the uncodified (having a diffuse character) norms in the society to formulate and issue the codified ones. Between codified ISCs (1-ISCs) and non-codified ISCs (0-ISCs) subsists an osmotic area, inside which a permanent circulation happens, so that some 0-ISCs enter the 1-ISCs, or some 1-ISCs either disappear or enter 0-ISCs. Practically, within the osmotic area, testing and corroborating/rejecting of the 1-ISCs are always made.

More recently, Richard Thaler has tried to combine behaviourism and institutionalism in what I would call *behavioural institutionalism* (*BI*). *BI* aims to design the institutional norms in such a way that they are compatible with the psychological reactions of individuals, on the one hand, and synergistic with the biases involved in "standard" behaviourism, on the other hand. In my opinion, with Thaler, the institutionalism passes from a collective target (as in its classical view) to an individual one.

Capillarism and Institutionalism

The relationship between institutionalism and capillarism is not so obvious as in the case of behaviourism, but is not less relevant. To put this into evidence, I shall provide some dedicated considerations:

- a norm is an institutional device that, *expressis verbis*, nominalizes at least (from a logical point of view) the following items:
  - the sufficient conditions for the eligibility of individuals who are required to apply the norm concerned;
  - the behaviour prescribed for the eligible individuals, including the conditionalities, limits, etc.;
  - the sanction that is applicable if the behaviour prescribed is violated[46];

- the narrower the gap between sanction and correlative award, the greater the probability with which the individual will choose to behave capillarily, that is to explore the niches that satisfy both the norm and his/her own interest;
- so, the capillarity does not come from the idiosyncratic biases, but from the anatomy (consequently, the physiology) of the norm/institution.[47]

What Kind of Capillarism?
Based on the above, I think that institutionalism is compatible, both structurally and functionally, with the ***induced capillarism*** (*IC*).

Some Concluding Remarks
The (relatively) subjectivism (*Nota bene*: a kind of... collective subjectivism, located at the level of norm-makers!) of institutionalism should be completed with what I would call: ***evolutionary institutionalism*** (*EI*). Such a new type of institutionalism has the following basic features:

- it combines the four types of the "new" institutionalism (rational, sociological, historical, and discursive), so that the evolutionary institutionalism advances simultaneously on the four "legs";
- evolutionary institutionalism allows the capillarism, this time not based on the idiosyncratic biases, but on collective biases, that are public, transparent, and the object of societal agreement (social contract);
- although the "basic" capillarism of institutionalism is the induced capillarism, some interferences of the reconstructive capillarism can also occur in the institutionalist paradigm;
- in fact, the most closed paradigm to the capillarism is exactly institutionalism, since the strategies/programs institutionally elaborate easily can introduce, in a deliberative (most of cases, predictable) way, capillary "tubes" (i.e., channels of transmission for the public policy impulses) in the societal system functioning.

6.3 Viabilism

Generalities
While both behaviourism and institutionalism are well enough developed theoretically, methodologically, and pragmatically, instead the viabilism is rather an exotic concept, that remains at the stage of academic discussions, most often linked to the biological world.[48] The tropism, again from the biological world, is getting close enough to viabilism, without, however, instituting an articulated theory in the matter.[49] What I want to put into evidence is that, with viabilism, in the societal (chain of) paradigms, enters, for the first time,[50] the ethical (or moral) dimension. Indeed, neither stationarity, optimality, nor sustainability do not require and, in fact, do not allow the ethics (morals), they are functional paradigms that target a pre-established finality, no matter the significance of getting that finality and, especially, without any preoccupations for the path through which the system involved passes from the starting point to the final one. From Fig. 1 (Chapter 2), we remember that only the progress as a form of societal evolution requires and allows the values that are, in turn, generators of ethics (morals).

The Content of Viabilism
As the name suggests, the viabilism is concerned with the preservation of life, of course, both in a biological sense and in a logical sense. I have shown in many places that there are three living species: (a) biological, (b) symbolical, and (c) logical. The viabilism performs a unification, from a conceptual point of view, of the three categories of species, so generalizing the concept of living.[51]

I would remind to the reader the abstract concept of the living entity (LE) that I proposed some years ago (Dinga, 2020):

- (L_1) *entropic exchange with the environment* (EEX)—this means that the entity has input–output relationships with the environment, regarding the entropy; of course, the environment can be considered as being a system as well, so, logically, the entropic exchange occurs between two systems;
- (L_2) *negative entropic gradient with the environment* (NEG)—this means that the entity has always a less level of entropy than its environment does; a logical consequence is, also, it has the potential of maintaining this negativity of the entropic gradient during of a given

(finite[52]) time horizon; increasing of that negativity is not a distinct case of the negativity, but rather a degree of it; often, this sufficiency predicate is called *dissipativity*[53];

- (L_3) *specific self-replicability* (SSR)—this means that the entity has the structural (i.e., inherent and immanent) potential to duplicate itself, within a specific (that is, associated with the species of that individual) pattern, with a given specific frequency and during a given (finite) time horizon[54];
- (L_4) *trans-individual evolution* (TIE)—this means that the entity has the structural (i.e., inherent and immanent) potential to change its own characteristics by chronologically passing to another hypostasis of itself, as a result of the SSR sufficiency predicate working.

So, the logical "birth" of a living entity (LE) occurs if and only if:

$$LE \leftarrow (L_1) \bigwedge (L_2) \bigwedge (L_3) \bigwedge (L_4)$$

It is observed that the definition above applies equally to each of the three species of the living entities, because it does not appeal to carbon as being the last instance (or the "brick") of the living entity construction.

Based on the content of the living entity, I will now propose a definition of the viabilism. I think the following sufficiency predicates should be held by a system/process, etc., to enter the paradigm of viabilism:

- (V_1) a *population of living entities* (PLE)—the system contains a set of living entities, as defined above. Of course, there can be a combination of the three categories of LE s, not a single one. Besides, the real cases are exactly constituted of such combinations (mixes);
- (V_2) a *moral code* (MC) assigned to that system/process—this means that the PLE is forced to behave according set of rules of moral nature. A morale code works outside the utilitarianism (see Chapter 7); in fact, it works inside the symbolism, i.e., according to the symbolic utility[55];
- (V_3) an *evolutionary propensity* (EP)—refers to some principles (i.e., rules of the largest force and applicability) that drive the path (chreod) of that system/process by providing sufficient (generally, structural) capabilities for designing and applying reaction norms

(see Chapter 9) to the actions suffered from both the internal environment and the external one. By the reaction norms, the system/process in the case adapts to its environment and, at the same time (perhaps, in a smaller size) determine the environment to adapt to itself;

- (V_4) *conservative finality* (CF)—the system/process, even if it adapts to the environment (see V_3), does not lose its identity[56]; in fact, it does not aspire to change its identity but only to "navigate" in the environment according to its principles. This implies, perhaps plausibly enough, that this sufficiency predicate ensures that the system does not change, in turn, the environment's identity.

So, the viabilism (V) is generated by the logical conjunction of the four sufficiency predicates:

$$V \leftarrow (V_1) \bigwedge (V_2) \bigwedge (V_3) \bigwedge (V_4)$$

It is interesting to examine if the viabilism, as it was logically defined above, verifies the four conditions of a generic paradigm (see note 25).

- *value* (V): is delivered by the moral code (V_2);
- *nucleus* (N): is delivered by the evolutionary propensity (V_3);
- *function* (F): is delivered by the V_1, more exactly, by the specific replicability (L_3), since $L_3 \subset V_1$);
- *logic* (L): is delivered by the conservative finality (V_4).

So, the viabilism can be considered as being a paradigm (viabilism paradigm), namely a complete paradigm, since it holds the four sufficiency predicates of a generic paradigm (Dinga et al., 2022).

Capillarism and Viabilism

The relationship between capillarity and viabilism can be expressed as follows:

- capillarity can be interpreted as a way to ensure the viability, i.e., viabilism, of the living species involved. Indeed, many times, a lateral, indirect, perhaps insignificant, and unpromising path or action could prove to be a better solution for surviving than the standard, common, direct path or action;

- in turn, viabilism seems to be an inexhaustible basin for getting "tubes", i.e., capillarities on the chreod of the living entities, according to the old precept saying that there is an infallible teacher, namely the need;

Nota bene: the suggestion that capillarity and viabilism form a special co-evolutionary binomial is irrepressible, but, of course, such an objective exits the purpose of this book.[57]

What Kind of Capillarism?

According to the profile of viabilism, it is obvious that the species of capillarism that is the most appropriate to the paradigm of viabilism is the *survival capillarism* (*SC*).

Some Concluding Remarks

Viabilism is, as I think, the next praxiological paradigm that follows the current (but, as it seems, tired enough) optimality (optimalism), and the incoming sustainability (sustainabilism). My opinion is that the sustainabilism will not arrive at being generalized, because the ethical/moral commandments are so strongly put into evidence in the contemporary stage that viabilism will take over the sustainability, to which will graft exactly the ethics (and, as I have shown in Chapter 7, societal æsthetics).

In Fig. 7, I indicate my opinion regarding the succession of the praxiological paradigms in the humankind history (the paradigm on the left is the very cause of the paradigm on the right, in an endless evolutionary process).

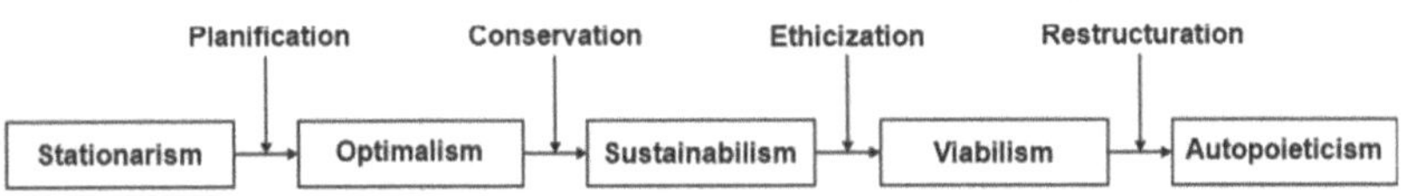

Fig. 7 Evolutionary change of the praxiological paradigm (*Source* author)

6.4 *Autopoieticism*

Autopoiesis is an ancient term (and concept, as well) meaning the capacity of doing, i.e., in terminology used here, to objectify something, of any nature, either substantially, ideally, or institutionally. Since about the concept of autopoiesis as such I discussed elsewhere (Dinga, 2025), here it only will be examined from the perspective of being connected with the concept and process of capillarity.

The Content of Autopoieticism

The autopoieticism is a *modus operandi* of an entity (system/process/phenomenon) related to both itself and its environment, along the path/chreod of that entity. Since the *modus operandi* refers to the functions of the entity involved, it results that the autopoieticism manifests as a structural property, named as a property of autopoieticity. Consequently, what is to be examined is the very concept of autopoieticity as such a structural property.

As shown elsewhere (Dinga, 2025), the autopoieticity enters into action when the previous "defence lines" of the entity against the perturbations (either internal or external) fail. In fact, there is a logical (and, as a result, a chronological) order in which those "defence lines" are activated. Figure 8 suggests this ordering.

Comment: the step "6" is based on the fact that, following the autopoietic restructuration of the entity delivers another entity (since the restructuration means the change of the structure, and the structure gives the very identity of the entity).

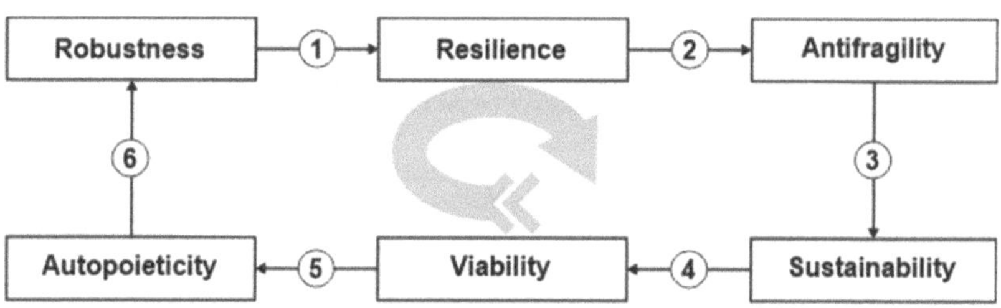

Fig. 8 Logical (and chronological) order of the "defence lines" against perturbations (*Source* author)

Nota bene: the interested reader could examine, *mutatis mutandis*, the connections between capillarity, on the one hand, and robustness, resilience, and antifragility, on the other hand.

Like the viability is its preceding (i.e., sustainability) to which ethics/morals is added, the autopoieticity is its preceding (i.e., viability) to which the ability of restructuration/reconstruction (see Fig. 7) is added. In this framework, I think the sufficiency predicates of the autopoieticity are as follows:

- (AP_1) the property of *viability* (V)—this means all four sufficiency predicates of viabilism (viability) are taken over, so that, like viabilism, autopoieticism refers to the three categories of living entities (biological, symbolical, and logical);
- (AP_2) *capacity* of $NRDS$: *navem repara dum supernatat* (in Latin: repair the ship while it floats)—this means that the restructuring (changing the structure) of the entity in question must be in such a way that the entity continues to function at its basic parameters. A question arises here: as the restructuring means the change of the structure, and, in turn, the change of the structure means the changes of the functions, how must the requirement of maintaining the functioning of that entity be understood? Of course, maintaining the functioning based on a new structure means maintaining the role; namely, the new set of functions, as generated by the new structure, must accomplish the same role[58] as the preceding one, at least until the evolutionary process can change the role as well;
- (AP_3) *potential* of$RRAS$: restoring the new "defence lines" (for the new entity with a new structure), namely robustness, resilience, antifragility, and sustainability.

So, the autopoieticism (AP) is generated by the logical conjunction of the three sufficiency predicates:

$$AP \leftarrow (AP_1) \bigwedge (AP_2) \bigwedge (AP_3)$$

Capillarism and Autopoieticism

Let us examine, based on the above findings, how the autopoieticism connects with capillarism. I think the following considerations could be kept:

Table 1 Capillarism and the four "isms"

	The "ism"			
	Behaviourism	*Institutionalism*	*Viabilism*	*Autopoieticism*
Type of capillarism	Emergent capillarism (EC)	Induced capillarism (IC)	Survival capillarism (SC)	Reconstructive capillarism (RC)

Source author

- the need for changing the entity (its structure, more exactly), i.e., the need for autopoieticism, could come through the very capillary "tubes" involved in the entity's functioning[59];
- the change itself of the old structure of the entity involved can go in the direction of initiating new "tubes" (i.e., capillary functionalities) assigned to the new structure in the case.[60]

What Kind of Capillarism?
As autopoieticism functions, it seems that the most appropriate type of capillarism to be associated with autopoieticism is the *reconstructive capillarism* (RC).

A recapitulation of the assigned type of capillarism to the fours "isms" is provided in Table 1.

7 Other Disparate Remarks

(1) From the perspective of behaviourism, there are three instances of decision:

- the *self*: is characterized by *capillarism* (belief, intuition, desire, will, biases);
- the *ego*: is characterized by *rationalism* (calculus, inference, connection means—purpose);
- the *superego*: is characterized by *normativism* (both natural and social/societal).

(2) The capillarism of the evolutionism consists in both mutation and selection; like the mutation, which (generally) arises from niches, the selection is (generally) performed on particular cases (individuals/phenotypes), not in general cases (species or genera).
(3) The constructal law, the evolutionism, even our proposal regarding the entropic interaction based on the minimal entropic gradient seems to imply the capillarism (capillarity).

Annex 1: Causality and Correlation

1. Briefly on the causality

Do not recall the two-thousand-debate details on the concept of causality, but I should propose some considerations that are indispensable to building the discussion on the economic correlation.

Firstly, I do not say that concept is else than a creation of the mind of the cognitive subject,[61] but I should say, however, that it orders, to a sufficient degree for the knowledge, the accessible phenomenology for the human being. In addition, this order (that is, one of diachronic nature) seems to be, at least by now, of a very good quality.[62]

This means its application to the objective reality (that is, to the sensible experience) generates real effects that are isomorphic, at an acceptable (tolerable) degree, with the anticipated effects generated by the a priori intuition on causality. The general concept of causality is also adequate for the economic and social/societal phenomenology.

Secondly, the causality must be seen as a relationship between two things[63] (objects, events, processes) and not as an attribute of a thing or of another. The two things between which emerges the relationship generated by causality have established denominations: cause, respectively, effect. If one of the two things is noted with C, and R the another, if, in addition, two moments of time are associated, t_i, respectively t_j to C, respectively to R, so we can write $C(t_i)$, respectively $R(t_j)$ (*Nota bene*: t_i and t_j are moments of the clock time[64]), then we will call $C(t_i)$ as cause for $R(t_j)$, and $R(t_j)$ we will call the effect of the $C(t_i)$, if are the following requests are, simultaneously verified:

I. $t_i!L(\mathcal{E}_i)$, $t_j!L(\mathcal{E}_j)$, with $\mathcal{E}_j > \mathcal{E}_i$
II. $(C, R) \in I_p^{(i,j)}(C, R)$
III. $C(t_i) \to R(t_j)$
IV. $\overline{R}(t_j) \to \overline{C}(t_i)$

The signification of the symbols used is:

- !: a logical constant that means "is occurring"
- $\mathcal{E}_i$: a measure for the entropy level in the Universe
- $L(\mathcal{E}_i)$: the Universe version that contains the entropy level $\mathcal{E}_i$
- $t_i!L(\mathcal{E}_i)$: "the t_i moment of time occurred in the Universe version that contains the entropy level $\mathcal{E}_i$"
- $I_p^{(i,j)}(C, R)$: the set of possible interactions,[65] within the interval of time (i, j), between C and R
- $\to$: a logical constant meaning "implies"

The above four conditions must be read as follows:

- *Request I*: t_i occurs in a Universe version with a smaller entropy level, and t_j occurs in a Universe version with a larger entropy level; according to those above mentioned, we can say t_i is earlier than t_j (by a language convention, we say $t_i < t_j$)
  - *request I signification*: the cause is the antecedent, and the effect is the subsequent[66] in our inference
  - *falsification of request I*: the effect can be the antecedent of its own cause[67]
- *Request II*: between the things (objects, events, processes) C and R can exist interactions[68]
  - *request II signification*: the causal relation is a species of the genus called interaction
  - *falsification of request II*: the causal relation is not possible

- *Request III*: the manifestation of the thing C at the moment t_i causes[69] the manifestation of the thing R at the moment t_j
  - *request III signification*: it is impossible to have the manifestation of the thing C at the moment t_i and not to have the manifestation of the thing R at the moment t_j
  - *falsification of request III*: $C(t_i)$ is not a cause for $R(t_j)$, although between C and R could exist interactions (for instance, of non-causal nature)
- *Request IV*: non-manifestation of the thing R at the moment t_j "is causing"[70] the non-manifestation of the thing C at the moment t_i (or, in other words, if we do not observe the manifestation of the thing R at the moment t_j, this logically implies the non-manifestation of the thing C at the moment t_i)
  - *request IV signification*: there is not another cause $C\prime(t_i)$, with $(C\prime(t_i) \neq C(t_i))$, and $(C\prime, R) \in I_p^{(i,j)}(C\prime, R)$ for $R(t_j)$
  - *falsification of request IV*: $C(t_i)$ is not a cause for $R(t_j)$

Thirdly, the problem of multiple causality is arising now. Let's consider a set of things, that we call multiple cause at the moment t_i, symbolized: $\mathcal{C}(t_i) = \{C^1(t_i), C^2(t_i), \ldots, C^n(t_i\}$. To say that $R(t_j)$ is an effect of the multiple cause $\mathcal{C}(t_i)$, we need to verify, simultaneously, the following requests:

I': $t_i!L(\mathcal{E}_i)$, $t_j!L(\mathcal{E}_j)$, with $\mathcal{E}_j > \mathcal{E}_i$

II':$(C^k, R) \in I_p^{(i,j)}(C^k, R)$, for $k = \overline{1, n}$

III': $\left(C^1(t_i) \bigwedge C^2(t_i) \bigwedge \ldots \bigwedge C^n(t_i)\right) \to R(t_j)$

IV':$(C^k, C^q) \notin I_p^{(i,j)}(C^k, C^q)$, for $k = \overline{1, n}$, $q = \overline{1, n}$ and $k \neq q$

V': $\overline{R}(t_j) \to \left(\overline{C}^1(t_i) \bigvee \overline{C}^2(t_i) \bigvee \ldots \bigvee \overline{C}^n(t_i)\right)$

Fourthly, I want to discuss the issue of the conditions in the causal relationship. It is generally accepted that the actualizing[73] of an interaction is dependent, in turn, on the occurrence of some conditions. The notion of "condition" is of great vagueness, but my opinion is that the situation is very easy to clarify if the concept of multiple cause is used. If the cause occurred, but the effect didn't, I have already shown we are facing a false cause. If we have a genuine cause[74] that occurs, but the effect doesn't, that means we are in the case of a multiple cause, and one of the causes in $\mathcal{C}(t_i)$ didn't occur. In fact, the famous condition that didn't... facilitate the effect occurring is nothing else than one of the causes in $\mathcal{C}(t_i)$ which didn't occur (see the request V').

I will introduce here the concept (the heuristic fiction) of the *effector basin*, symbolized$\mathcal{B}_i^E(R_j)$, and defined as the set of possible causes associated with a given effect. It is not necessary to admit the effector basin is composed only by the causes (simple or multiple) associated with a given effect, because it is perfectly admissible to consider that there are also many other causes (simple or multiple) which have the potential to produce the given effect, but which don't do, that is, they don't become actual (an example in the economy could be so: growth of the saving can be generated either by the growth of the disposable current nominal income, or by negative anticipations concerning the future inflation, but only one of the two potentialities becomes actual; the other cause don't become actual, but both the causes are components of the effector basin). As a consequence, in the case of the effector basin, the request III' becomes III'bis: $\left(C^1(t_i) \bigvee C^2(t_i) \bigvee \ldots \bigvee C^n(t_i)\right) \rightarrow R(t_j)$ or, in the case of the multiple cause,$\left(\mathcal{C}^1(t_i) \bigvee \mathcal{C}^2(t_i) \bigvee \ldots \bigvee \mathcal{C}^n(t_i)\right) \rightarrow R(t_j)$, which means that the effector basin is a disjunction of the conjunction of causes.[75] An objection could arise here: the condition is that cause which is initiated (activated, generated) by another cause, so, if the last cause doesn't work properly, the condition is not generated, so the effect is not generated. It is, I hope, very clear that this objection is superfluous, because either (a): we have a distinct causal chain (where an effect of a cause becomes, in its turn, a cause for another effect), so nothing new, or (b): we have a failure in verifying the request III' of a multiple cause.

Therewith, I consider the issue of the condition in the matter of the causal interaction to be a false issue.

Fifthly, the issue of the multiple effect must be approached. Let's consider a set of things, called multiple effect at the moment t_j, and symbolized $\mathcal{R}(t_j) = \left\{R^1(t_j), R^2(t_j), \ldots, R^m(t_j\right\}$. We say that $C(t_i)$ is a cause for the multiple effect $\mathcal{R}(t_j)$ if the following requests are simultaneously verified:

I'': $t_i!L(\mathcal{E}_i)$, $t_j!L(\mathcal{E}_j)$ so $\mathcal{E}_j > \mathcal{E}_i$

II'': $(C, R^k) \in I_p^{(i,j)}(C, R^k)$, for $k = \overline{1, m}$

III'':$C(t_i) \rightarrow \left(R^1(t_j) \bigwedge R^2(t_j) \bigwedge \ldots \bigwedge R^n(t_j)\right)$

IV'':$(R^k, R^q) \notin I_p^{(i,j)}(R^k, R^q)$, for $k = \overline{1, m}$, $q = \overline{1, m}$ and $k \neq q$

$$\text{V'':}\ \left(\overline{R}^1(t_j) \bigvee \overline{R}^2(t_j) \bigvee \ldots \bigvee \overline{R}^m(t_j)\right) \rightarrow \overline{C}(t_i)$$

Sixthly, the question of the consequences must be analysed. It is generally considered that the emergence of an effect is accompanied by the emergence of a type of result called consequences. I think, as well, we have here a needless complication,[77] because if a result of the cause $C(t_i)$ has emerged, it cannot be else than either an effect of the mentioned cause, or an effect of another cause, but which is coexistent (that is, emerges at the same moment of time t_j at which the other effects of the cause $C(t_i)$ emerge). I want to introduce here a symmetric concept (as heuristic fiction) with the concept of effector basin, namely *collector basin*, symbolized$\mathcal{B}_j^C(C_i)$, and defined as the set of the possible effects associated with a given cause. It is not necessary to admit that the collector basin is composed only by the effects (simple or multiple) associated with a given cause, because it is perfectly admissible to consider that there are also many other effects (simple or multiple) which have the potential to be produced by the given cause, but which don't do, that is, they are hampered to become actual (I resume the issue in the context of the concept of the antithetic causality below).

Therewith, I consider the issue of the consequence in the matter of the causal interaction to be a false issue.

Seventhly, I think we have to discuss the question of the *antithetic causality*. Logically, the antithetic causality captures both the issue of the conditions and the issue of the consequences. We have an antithetic causality when two causes of the effector basin neutralize one another, that means the effect generated by one of the causes is the mirrored image of the effect generated by the other cause. If the neutralizing is complete, the effect doesn't arise,[78] and, in the case in which an effect arises, this means the mutual neutralization is incomplete (that is, there is a net resulting cause). To note that the two causes do not affect one another (in such a case, we would have a common causal chain that was already treated), but both causes generate effects, and these effects neutralize one another.[79] Here is arising the question concerning the way in which the two causes neutralize one another. This neutralization is possible in two kinds: a) either an effect becomes cause for the second, in the mirror, or, b) the two effects get being but both vanish by mutual annihilation (a nearly parallel could be made with the matter–anti-matter interaction). My interpretation of all this is the following: if the mutual neutralization is complete, the cognitive subject could do not observe the developed process, but if the neutralization is incomplete, then the net cause of the two initial causes could be called condition (so, the condition is, in the most benevolent case, a causal residue), and the net effect could be called consequence (so, the consequence is, in the most benevolent case, a residual result).[80]

2. Briefly, on the correlation

The causality is, as is resulting from the precedents, a species of the genus called interaction. The interaction can be of a non-causal type (for example, all functional or structural interactions are of a non-causal type[81]). I will discuss below the concept of correlation (beginning from this point, our discussion will be closer to the economic action field).

In my opinion, the correlation needs to be considered as a species of interaction. But what kinds of interaction? What are the specific differences from the genus? In this context, I will deliver the following considerations:

a. the correlation implies an interaction of non-causal type, but of structural type. A structural interaction is simply a coexistence that has two basic attributes:

   - exhibits a structural configuration, that is, a system of relationships[82] among the observed parameters of the two things[83] analysed;
   - this structural configuration exhibits a persistence in time so being significant[84] for the cognitive subject (of course, the scale of such a persistence is very variable: in the Quantum Mechanics could have milliseconds or less, in the economy could be years, in geology could be millions of years, in cosmology could have billions of years).

b. the correlation implies two things[85] of the same nature: the two correlated things are neutral, one faced the other, so, either both are causes (for no matter what effects), or both are effects (from no matter what causes).

Firstly, I will make some comments on the concept of structural configuration. A structural configuration is a frozen image of the relationship system between the two things considered, although it is possible to exist more such relationship systems which can be considered, either successively or simultaneously, depending on the cognitive (or praxiological) interest of the subject, as well as on the cognitive (or praxiological) competence of the mentioned subject.

This means that the two things stay, simply, in those relationships, without any communication between them, of any nature.[86] Of course, as time went on, after reaching the signification threshold, mentioned above, we can have some alterations of the structural configuration, but, during the new period of time, as long as the signification threshold is not yet reached, the structural configuration is frozen again. We could talk, perhaps, about a *structural inertia* (Dinga, 2012). Based on the above comments, I will call the correlation with the term *dead coexistence*.[87]

Secondly, it is needed to highlight the fact that the correlation has a strong feature of stability. The explanation consists in the fact that the correlation stability is not of order 1 (like, for example, the direct relationship between cause and effect, that is, having the constant feature of generating the same effect, with the same descriptive parameters, by the same cause, with the same descriptive parameters), but of order 2 (structural relationships between either causes, or effects[88]).

Thirdly, must be eliminated, from the concept of correlation, any connotation of the process. The correlation is not generated by something; it simply happens. The correlation is observed as an attribute of the version $L(\mathcal{E}_j)$ of the Universe, so it doesn't need an explanation.[89]

Formally, the correlation between two things,$A(t_i)$, respectively$B(t_i)$, where the set of descriptive parameters of the thing A is$P_A^{t_i} = \left(a_1^{t_i}, a_2^{t_i}, \ldots, a_{n_A}^{t_i}\right)$, and the set of descriptive parameters of the thing B is $P_B^{t_i} = \left(b_1^{t_i}, b_2^{t_i}, \ldots, b_{n_B}^{t_i}\right)$ can take an undefined number of structural configurations (that is, of dead coexistences), depending on the knowledge or praxiological interest of the subject. For example, if the interest is focused on the coefficient of intensity$c_k^{t_i} = a_k^{t_i}/b_k^{t_i}$, then will result the following correlation:$[AB]_{t_i}^{a/b} = \left(c_1^{t_i}, c_2^{t_i}, \ldots, c_f^{t_i}\right)$, where$f = min(n_A, n_B)$.

But, if the correlation is simply what happens, without any comprehensive bases, if the correlation only exists and is observed (recorded) as such by the cognitive or actional (praxiological) subject, then what is its signification for knowledge or for action? I think the following comments could be made in the matter of the above question:

a. in the social field (respectively, in the economic field that is a species of the genus social), the prediction based on the causal relationship is compromised from more perspectives: (a) the impossibility to conserve the invariability of the initial conditions, due to the structural presence of the subject within the economic process—the indiscernibility subject-object in the economic field): (b) the vagueness of the concept of truth of the economic propositions (of course, the prediction must be expressed propositionally, as an assertorical statement)—it seems that even the substitution of the veracity based on factual correspondence with the hermeneutical likelihood is not sufficient, we need to go further, probably to the concept of acceptability, so to build a direct bridge between the causal teleology and the axiological assessment of the needed effect: (c) the overwhelming presence of the multiple causality, respectively of the multiple effect, that makes extremely difficult to analytically detect the causality relationships to be recaptured in formulating the prediction;
b. the presence of the intra-contingent necessity (I understand by this syntagma the followings: the economic act is caused by the goal, so by the teleology, but, once the economic act is triggered, in the period of time between its triggering and the goal reaching, could arise (and, in fact, arise) many causal relationships of ontological nature, so based on eutaxiology[90]—I call this situation with the syntagma of intra-contingent necessity; this combination between necessity and contingency in triggering and performing the economic act complicates very much the causal relationship and, consequently, the possibility of the economic prediction.

3. A proposal for a working predictor in the economic field

I believe a satisfactory as well as operational solution in the above-described situation is to renounce the ambition to make causal predictions[91] and to proceed through two subterfuges, in order to trick the economic process:

a. substituting the causal predictions with normative targets (the normative targets will completely renounce the causality and would be based only on desirabilities),[92] mostly often of political order, in the large sense of the notion);
b. using the correlations as a vehicle for structural predictions (non-causal).

Having in mind the current theme of our discussion, I will analyse only the second proposal.

The proposal to use the correlations as a vehicle to make non-causal predictions in the economic field is based on my faith in the economy we have, generally, multiple cause, as well as multiple effect. In other words, a competent cognitive or actional (praxiological) subject will observe (will record) an effector basin, respectively a collector basin, and perhaps, he or she will be capable of making some sharper observations, like a multiple cause associated with a multiple effect. But this is all. It will be almost impossible to identify an individual cause linked to an individual effect.

Starting from here, the cognitive subject will agree to leave the individual causes to handle themselves in forming the multiple cause, and in the same way, he or she will proceed with the effects—they will be left to handle themselves in forming the multiple effect occurrence. All will be of interest for such a subject is to identify patterns (configurations) relatively stable (this relativity leads to the particular interest of the subject, either cognitively, or actionally), both at the level of the effector basin (more restrictive, but more efficacious, would be at the level of the multiple cause) and at the level of the collector basin (more restrictive, but more efficacious would be at the level of the multiple effect). To calculate the correlations aimed at, the subject will choose (based on criteria that can have or not have links to his or her cognitive or actional interest) the parameter or the set of parameters that will be numerically calculated, and will design the dead coexistence both at the level of the multiple cause and at the level of the multiple effect. We remember the correlation is an interaction of order 2, and this ensures it with the relative stability compared with the interaction of order 1. Formally, we have, for the beginning, two correlations (one for the multiple cause and the other for the multiple effect, both of order 2), as follows:

- $[C^1C^2\ldots C^{nc})]_{t_i}^{\cdots} = \left(\alpha_1^{t_i}, \alpha_2^{t_i}, \ldots, \alpha_Q^{t_i}\right)$, where $\alpha_k^{t_i} = h_C(c_{1(k)}^{t_i}, c_{2(k)}^{t_i}, \ldots, c_{n_C(k)}^{t_i})$
- $\left[R^1R^2\ldots R^{n_R}\right]_{t_j}^{\cdots} = \left(\beta_1^{t_j}, \beta_2^{t_j}, \ldots, \beta_P^{t_j}\right)$, where $\beta_k^{t_j} = h_R(r_{1(k)}^{t_j}, r_{2(k)}^{t_j}, \ldots, r_{n_R(k)}^{t_j})$

Now, a correlation between the two correlations can be calculated (that is, a correlation of order 3).

- $[\mathcal{CR})]_{(i,j)}^{\cdots} = \left(\delta_1^{(i,j)}, \delta_2^{(i,j)}, \ldots, \delta_T^{(i,j)}\right)$, where $T = min(n_C, n_R)$, $\gamma_k^{(i,j)} = h_{CR}(\alpha_k^{t_i}, \beta_k^{t_j})$, and

$$\delta_k^{(i,j)} = h_{\mathcal{CR}}(\gamma_{1(k)}^{(i,j)}, \gamma_{2(k)}^{(i,j)}, \ldots, \gamma_{n_T(k)}^{(i,j)})$$

If we write $\widehat{\mathcal{C}}(t_i) = \left\{\widehat{C}^1(t_i), \widehat{C}^2(t_i), \ldots, \widehat{C}^{nc}(t_i)\right\}$ the multiple cause ***known*** at the moment t_i, respectively $\widetilde{\mathcal{R}}(t_j) = \left\{\tilde{R}^1(t_j), \tilde{R}^2(t_j), \ldots, \tilde{R}^{nc}(t_j)\right\}$ the multiple effect ***predicted*** at the moment t_j, then:

- $\left[\widehat{C}^1\widehat{C}^2\ldots\widehat{C}^{nc})\right]_{t_i}^{\cdots} = \left(\widehat{\alpha}_1^{t_i}, \widehat{\alpha}_2^{t_i}, \ldots, \widehat{\alpha}_Q^{t_i}\right)$, that is, the correlation of order 2, at the level of the multiple given (known) cause
- $[\text{CR})]_{(i,j)}^{\cdots} = \left(\delta_1^{(i,j)}, \delta_2^{(i,j)}, \ldots, \delta_T^{(i,j)}\right)$., that is, the correlation of order 3, supposed stable on the time interval (i, j), and extrapolated for the moment j.

Now, we can formulate the structural (non-causal) prediction related to the multiple effect:

- $[\tilde{R}^1\tilde{R}^2\ldots\tilde{R}^{n_R}]_{\tilde{t}_j}^{\cdots} = \left(\tilde{\beta}_1^{t_j}, \tilde{\beta}_2^{t_j}, \ldots, \tilde{\beta}_P^{t_j}\right)$, where: $\tilde{\beta}_k^{t_j} = h_{CR}^{-1}\left(h_{CR}^{-1}\left(\delta_k^{(i,j)}\right), \hat{\alpha}_k^{t_i}\right)$

Finally, we can calculate the numerical quantities $\tilde{r}_k^{t_j} = h_R^{-1}\left(\tilde{\beta}_k^{t_j}\right) = h_R^{-1}\left(h_{CR}^{-1}\left(h_{CR}^{-1}\left(\delta_k^{(i,j)}\right), \hat{\alpha}_k^{t_i}\right)\right)$,

what allow us to formulate the predicted multiple effect.

Some consequences of the proposal:

a. of the advantages nature:

- the problems, principled insurmountable, of the economic predictions, are avoided;
- the solution, too radical, of substituting the causal prediction with establishing normatively the targets of command, is avoided;
- the new kind of predictions performed are based on structures, that is on ontological arrangements, relatively stable;
- any analysis of causality is abandoned, because the correlations, as were introduced above, automatically and impersonally take over all constellations of causes, including the operation of "netting" the contradictory causes between them (in addition, is also solved the complicated issue of the causal conditions, respectively of the final consequences);
- the calculation of scenarios, by varying the multiple cause, is automatized.

b. of the disadvantages nature:

- the ambition of the individual prediction (one cause associated with one effect) must be abandoned; now it is only possible to predict multiple effect,[94] since the economic science does not need more, and it will not be asked for more.

Notes

1. This is similar to other verbs constructed in the dynamics: sustainabilize, stabilize, organize, etc.
2. For example, when econometricians establish their findings, they establish (plausible statistical) correlations, not causes, so they find cryptocauses.
3. Often, the methodological condition *ceteris paribus* is the cause of… cryptocauses.
4. I remind that a societal system is a social system “endowed” with a society, that is, a social system plus the state over it.
5. The positive law should also codify the natural law from the perspective of human behaviour.
6. Something is objective if its ontology does not depend on the subject, while something is objectified if its ontology is an intersubjective agreement (for example, a theory or a public policy). The objective entities enter Popper’s first world, the subjective entities enter Pooper’s second world, and the objectified entities enter Popper’s third world.
7. For example, a social revolution is always illegal, since it opposes the law order of the society involved (of course, it can be—not mandatorily, however—legitimate). The legality/illegality, as well as the legitimacy/illegitimacy of opposing or violating the social necessity, are, as a rule, under the verdict of the historians, namely, it is a *post factum* evaluation.
8. Logically, an explanation is an *ex post* prediction, while a prediction is an *ex ante* explanation—so that, explanation and prediction are, along the time scale, equivalent (Dinga, 2025).
9. As I shall show further, free will is opaque (to a rather high degree) even for the subject involved.
10. Maybe I should say: it is not predictable with a reasonable certitude, since, perhaps, some indices could exist about that opposite direction of movement.
11. There are experiences that show that a prediction done based on Black–Scholes theory (a rather sophisticated model from a mathematical point of view) and one done based on a simplistic rule of thumb are equivalent enough regarding the accuracy of prediction.
12. Some readers could raise the objection that the causal order should be reversed, namely, that the values ground the credence/belief.

I want to reject the objection as follows: (a) the *historical* argument: the credence/belief is gain by the individual still in his/her childhood, under the pressure of education (either inside family or within the school), so before the child acquire the consciousness of the concept (or of a list) of values; (b) the *psychological* argument: the values, viewed as "axioms" of the behaviour need a ground where be anchored in a synergetic way. The basic condition required by that synergy is provided just by the credence/belief, so the credence/belief must be "there" before the values arise.

13. Here, we have to deal with the practical rationality model.
14. Generally, it is speaking about cognitive biases.
15. Here, we are talking about what I named elsewhere with the term *implicit information* (Dinga et al., 2022).
16. A very succinct list of authors (some of them awarded with the Nobel Prize for Economics, exactly for the study of such biases) contains: Kahneman, Tversky, Mlodinow, Thaler, Sunstein.
17. The situation is analogous to that of non-intended unknown consequences of a decision (or action), on which Popper draws attention, especially for economists: if those consequences were known in advance, they would no longer hold the character of non-intentionality.
18. One can formulate here a "theorem": when two causalities (causal forces) act on the same process in opposite directions, any of them might be considered as the capillary causality, depending on either the research interest or the praxiological/practical interest.
19. The logical distinction is not so crisp as desired between cause and conditionality, since above a threshold of impact, the conditionality (the "colour" of the context) could actually become and act as a genuine cause.
20. I draw attention to the (rigorous) difference between direction and the sense of that direction: direction is the family of all curves parallel among them, while the sense of direction is the orientation of the vector describing the direction—a direction has two (opposite) senses. In my text, by direction must be understood both the direction and its sense.
21. As in other interventions, I distinguish between meaning and signification: meaning addresses a common (at least within a given community) signification, i.e., it refers to the same referential for all

the individuals involved, while signification addresses the idiosyncrasy of an individual. Using other words: signification is the subjectified meaning. For example, if the minister of public finance enacts a fiscal norm that obliges the taxpayer to pay some new tax, the meaning of the norm is the same for all taxpayers in the given economic/fiscal system. However, for individuals with a small tax base, it has a different significance compared with that for taxpayers holding a large tax base (see here, the interesting concept of nudge, provided by Richard Thaler).

22. I remind, here, the famous Laffer's curve.
23. According to the standard "law" of supply and demand imposed by the neoclassical economic theory.
24. See, here, the phenomenology of the oil price under the (political) decisions regarding the oil production across the world.
25. I remind the four sufficiency predicates of a general/abstract paradigm (Dinga et al., 2022): (1) *value* (**V**): the value addresses the founding of the paradigm's finality—for example, the complete rationality (or hyper-rationality); (2) *nucleus* (**N**): the nucleus addresses the prime (primitive, fundamental) principle of paradigm—for example, the selfishness. To be noticed that, here, the term *nucleus* does not hold the semantic sense of Lakatos nucleus/hard core, so it is one of the components of research program, alongside hypotheses and negative and positive heuristics (Lakatos, 1999); (3) *function* (**F**): the function addresses the finality of paradigm (in fact, the purpose of actors using that paradigm)—a for example, the minimizing of the opportunity cost in neoclassical economic theory. The finality is more general than the purpose—the purpose is the conscious finality; (4) *logic* (**L**): the logic addresses the principles of rationalization of paradigm—for example, the methodological individualism. Rationalization is a justification based on a model of rationality. Although, principled, rationalization occurs before decision and action (by a valid inferring of that decision from the model of rationality concerned), behavioural psychology has shown that, frequently enough, the rationalization occurs after the decision is taken or the action is performed (see, also, the Pearl Harbour effect).
26. Except the case in which we would be adepts of the fundamentalist determinism, so that free will is explainable, itself, through microscopic neurologic determinants, without any psychology.

27. Of course, there are reasons for that (including cost–benefit evaluation, or some axiological conditionalities, like ethical ones, and even aesthetic reasons!—see, in this matter, my further considerations on the societal aesthetics—Chapter 6), but such reasons are not rationally examined.
28. The typology provided at point 4.3 is a typology of capillarity or the capillary effect. This time, a typology of capillarism is provided as a special positioning of individuals (and even society) in the praxiological and practical actions.
29. I remind you, here, of the point of view that the constructal law provides (or, at least, hopes so) a theory of such general (and abstract) searching for survival and prosperity.
30. I remind that the functionality defines the interactions among the system's components, while the behaviour defines the interactions between the system's components, on the one hand, and the environment, on the other hand.
31. However, the *homo mathematicus* model (wrongly called *homo œconomicus*), so Nobel awarded, proposes, was permanently revised by relaxing the initial axioms, starting with Herbert Simon's bounded rationality aimed at replacing the (alleged) perfect rationality of the individual.
32. In fact, humans have an animal part, for example, the instinct, in their being. The social justice theories (that will be examined in Part III of the book) take into consideration the animal "heritage" of humans.
33. I remind that Husserl repeatedly insisted that psychology is not a science, and, moreover, it cannot be, in principle, a science (Husserl, 2012).
34. Generally acknowledged for research in this direction is John Broadus Watson, who is credited with coining the term behaviourism and founding behaviourism as a school of thought. He considered that behaviourism must study the externally observable behaviour, not the internal one.
35. This type of research began with Pavlov (with his conditioned reflexes), followed by Edward Thorndike, with his theory of learning, and B. F. Skinner, with his schedules of reinforcement as a result of external stimuli.
36. The first scientist on this lane is Gilbert Ryle. Then, other (especially) philosophers approached this species of behaviourism:

Ludwig Wittgenstein, U.T. Place, and Daniel Dennett. This approach was also used by economists in their trying to identify the preferences—see, for example, Paul Samuelson's concept/hypothesis of the revealed preferences, in fact, of extracting the preferences from the very actions (acts or abstentions) of the individual under examination.

37. Skinner said, however, that behaviourism is not a science of human behaviour, but a philosophy of that science.
38. If those components have no common trait, then they cannot form a system, while if the components, taken two by two, have no different trait, then those components are not individualized (the components concerned are identical see Leibniz's maxim: *the identical are indiscernible* but, obviously the reciprocal is true: *the indiscernibles are identical*, because the indiscernibility means the same properties, or sufficiency predicates, so the same entity).
39. The term impression has, here, a meaning very close to that of impressionism in painting, namely, very much like sensation.
40. For example, the well-known practical maxim of behaviour: *fight or flight*.
41. I remind that to actualize something means three alternative acts: (a) deleting; (b) adding; (c) modifying.
42. The analogy (but, of course, from a different perspective) with Imre Lakatos's concept of research program is at hand.
43. There are three categories of systems, according to the cause of their genesis: (a) *natural* systems—the cause is contained in the action of natural laws, characterized by natural necessity (100% predictable necessity), being an internal cause of the *causa sui* type; (b) *symbolic* systems—the cause is human action (usually at a social level), based on social laws (positive laws, i.e., institutions), characterized by social necessity, which is a quasi-necessity, because free will can oppose it; we are talking, in this case, about *causa alterius*; (c) *logical* systems—the cause is also at the level of human action (*causa alterius*), this time dealing with a logical necessity, which is also a quasi-necessity, even "weaker" than social necessity.
44. Do not forget that randomness means unpredictability (both analytically and statistically), not noncausality.
45. It is interesting that, in this case, Kantian maxim/formula for Humanity is fully verified: "People should not be used as a means to an end".

46. Rarer, the norm stipulates, alternatively, the award for respecting the norm concerned.
47. The Nobel laureate Richard Thaler (2009) ingeniously exploits such a possibility and, together with Cass Sunstein, invents the concept/term of *nudge*, that is neither obligation, nor shoving, but just a small touch/suggestion into the "correct" direction of the behaviour. Somewhat, as I have remarked, Thaler performs a *sui generis* synthesis between behaviourism and institutionalism.
48. Some excursions in philosophy are rare enough and veiled in a mysterious and discouraging halo (see, for example, Bergson's vitalism).
49. As I have shown elsewhere, the constructal law proposal seems to extend the concept of tropism to all three Popperian worlds. In this sense, the constructal law proposal has, of course, many affinities with the (paradigm of) viabilism.
50. From now on, any paradigms will require and allow the ethics (morals), as we will see when the autopoieticism is examined next.
51. This concept will be analytically and largely discussed in my next book, entitled: *The Economics of Social Living Systems. A New Research Methodology*, which will be printed in 2027 by Palgrave Macmillan—Springer Nature.
52. Probably, the only entity with an undefined time horizon for the potential to maintain the negativity of the entropic gradient with the environment is God (although some questions can arise here regarding His membership or non-membership to our Universe).
53. Applying this predicate to biological living entities, when that negativity is not verified anymore such an entity exits from its state of being living, and enters the state of being dead. For the concept of dissipativity (in fact, dissipative structures), see Prigogine and Stengers (1984). To be observed that Umberto Maturana's concept of autopoietic system is consistent with Ilya Prigogine's concept of system far from equilibrium.
54. In my opinion, the self-replicability is genus for the Luhmannian species called self-reflexivity.
55. The morals is the common intersection of all individuals' ethics in a given system of *PLE*. This means that morals is usually codified in forma norms, in contrast to individual ethics, which are non-codified at the communitarian level (are, in fact, informal).

56. I remind the reader that keeping the identity means keeping the (basic) structure.
57. Instead, the reader will meet such a development in the announced book (see note 51).
58. As is known, the role means the finality of the functions in their inter-conditioning.
59. Remember that the mutations in the evolutionary paradigm usually are small, random, and, especially, accidental (*Nota bene*: of course, in the societal field, deliberativeness has its acknowledged role). But these features describe the capillarity well enough.
60. I remind the reader that the constructal law invokes exactly such a behaviour of the entities, although non-mentioning, expressly, the property of capillarity (besides, the constructal law includes the capillarity as a particular case of the evolutionary process).
61. That is, an Idea, in the Kantian terminology.
62. By "the best quality" I mean "of the greatest operational utility".
63. Any imaginable thing enters the category of phenomena, that is, the category of the cognoscible reality.
64. I call "clock time" (or an absolute diachronic clock) that time whose frequency (rate of modification) is independently from the things to which it is associated (which it "measures"). Although this absolute character of the clock time has many inconveniences in the economic field (more generally, in the social field), for the moment it is not important to develop more this issue. However, in Dinga (2012) I discuss the concept of... *economic time*, dependent on the economic process measured.
65. The possible (as noun, not as adjective) contains the ontological necessity, as well as the ontological contingency.
66. I insist on the fact that all these considerations must be seen, for the moment, at the subject level, and mustn't be compulsory projected on the reality (that is, on the sensitive phenomenology).
67. It is talking here about the efficient (effective) cause only, since, in the social/societal field, the effect is in the antecedent of the cause (i.e., the final cause—*causa finalis*).
68. I do not limit in any way the nature of these interactions. They could address the substance, the energy, the information.
69. The signification of the expression "causes" is of a logical necessity. If the logical necessity is overlapping the ontological necessity, it is not, for the moment, an issue to be examined here. We see,

further, that the overlapping of the two kinds of necessities means confirmation of the tested hypothesis, and the non-overlapping mean rejection of the hypothesis (generally, this was the rationality by which Karl Popper introduced his falsifiability criterion for the scientific truth).

70. The term "causing" has, here, only a metaphoric value: if an occurrence generates an occurrence, then the non-occurrence work *as if* it generates a non-occurrence.
71. This is a condition of the independence of the individual causes for the given effect, ones faced others, within the multiple cause.
72. For $k = q$ a question arises: the *causa sui* question (a thing is its own cause). This question makes sense only for the God, because for any non-divine thing a self-causation cannot occur instantaneously (given the limitation of any interaction speed by the speed of the light), so $t_j > t_i$, so we re-find the classical causality relationship (because $C(t_i) \not\equiv C(t_j)$, and $C(t_j) \equiv R(t_j)$, that is the two hypostases of C are associated with two different versions of the Universe (because the different entropy level of every version).
73. Here, the notion "actualizing", as derivation from the term "actual", has the Aristotle-ian meaning, that is, the actually manifestation of a potentiality.
74. Here appears a certain circularity, because the question is not if the cause is or is not genuine, but the question is if the cause become or not become genuine, depending on the occurring or on the non-occurring of the effect. For the moment, we will accept this licence of reasoning.
75. If this disjunction is also exclusive it depends on the level of knowledge in the matter.
76. This is a condition of independence of the individual effects of the cause, ones faced others, within the multiple effect.
77. The term "un-useful" has exactly its proper signification: without adding to the utility (although, generally, heuristic fictions creation is not un-useful, in this particular case the introducing of a new concept related to the effect is not justified—among others, because violates the Occam's razor principle).
78. Better said, it is not observed (recorded) by the observer. The question of whether the two mirrored effects emerged, without being observed, and then they have neutralized one another, is an extremely important and difficult question (which I will resume in

another intervention). Here, only the ideational association with the quantum mechanics case can be made, where a quantum particle could be (or even is) in an infinite number of locations, and it "is choosing" to be in a macroscopically determined place just following (or, because?) the observation act.

79. An example at hand could be borrowed from arithmetic: simultaneously adding and subtracting the same value to/from a given value. The given value will remain constant, because two mirrored effects occurred, one by augmenting the given value by the value added, other by reducing the given value by the value subtracted. This example is not totally adequate, because it is a-temporal (mathematics addresses structures, not processes), but it suggests acceptably the idea I want to highlight.
80. One of the most pregnant examples of antithetic causality is offered by the economic counter-cyclically policies: the economic policy (the actional subject) generates a cause of nature to produce a mirrored effect related to the initial effect produced by another cause (is not relevant here the fact that the initial cause is generated by the market, and the response-cause is generated by the state, because, for example, we can use an automatic stabilizer in order to create a mirrored cause).
81. Is it possible, probably, to put some objections against defining the structural relationships (relationships of coexistence, so, of synchronic type) as being, however, interactions. In my opinion, no structure can exist if it is not accepted the fact (of course, as a heuristic fiction) that among the components of the structure a kind of "communication" *sui generis* is acting, that ensures the components maintain the mutual positions or functions, that is the mutual general accommodation for a sufficient period of time so be observed by the cognitive subject and evaluated as forming a diachronic identity (probably, an abbreviated definition of structure could be: a synchrony with diachronic identity). I call this "communication" (which is a concept more general than the concept of interaction) with the term structural interaction (so, another species of interactions, comparable with the causal interaction discussed by now).

82. No matter the nature of these relationships: they could be spatial (geometrical configurations), numerical (identical pairs of quantitative values), kinematical (identical speeds or accelerations of their temporal variations), etc.
83. To consider only two things as correlated has only a generic (methodological) reason, because the concept of multiple correlation is already well built.
84. The signification threshold of temporal persistence depends on the field as well as on the cognitive interest.
85. We will also discuss the multiple correlation, but the generic case is the bi-ple correlation (the correlation between two things). The multiple correlation constitutes a simple extension of the bi-ple correlation (in the same way in which mathematics has extended the three-dimensional space to the n-dimensional space.
86. I cannot fail the occasion to remark the enthusiasm with which so many experts in mathematical statistics and econometrics make confusions between causality and correlation (in a further intervention, we will see another confusion between correlation and contagion, that means the imagination is really unlimited).
87. The proposed term is justified by the fact that the temporal interval inside which the system maintains its structure, against perturbations from the environment, is called the dead time.
88. The economists are familiar with such a successive order of relative stability: rate of variation is more stable than the absolute value of an economic variable, while a marginal value of an economic variable is more stable than its rate of variation, etc.). See also the concept of *differance* (Jacques Derrida), aimed to capture a superior significance compared to the primary difference.
89. The explanations constitute a description of a causality (of a causal relationship), including the logical way (the so-called explanation by covering laws).
90. I think we can call the goal a teleological cause, while the other three Aristotelian causes (material, formal, and efficacious) could be called, together, as an eutaxiological cause. While the teleological cause has a contingent nature, the eutaxiological cause has a necessary nature. Is not the appropriate place here to discuss the important question of the a priori character of the two kinds of causes (I will resume the discussion in another intervention).

91. I think exclusively of the economic matter (in the natural sciences, the situation is very different).
92. Very often, the target creates (or highlights) its own resources to be reached.
93. The technical method to calculate the correlations depends on the competency and the experience of the analyst, as well as on the analysis goal.
94. Some macroeconomic models (or, larger, global models) claim their success in calibrating the final endogenous variables by the immense number of equations that link the individual causes and the individual effects. The undeniable proof of their exaggerations is delivered by the extremely frequent modifications of prognoses, even at the most famous "houses".

References

Dinga, E. (2012). *Rebuilding Economics: A Logical, Epistemological, and Methodological Approach*. Lambert Academic Publishing.

Dinga, E. (2020). *Logically Living System—A Generative Machine for Auto-Poietic Systems*. In M. kowska (Ed.), *Handbook of Research on Autopoiesis and Self-Sustaining Processes for Organizational Success*. IGI Global Publishing Tomorrow's Research Today.

Dinga, E., Oprean-Stan, C., Tănăsescu, R. -C., Brătian, V., & Ionescu, G. -M. (2022). *Financial Market Analysis and Behaviour. The Adaptive Preference Hypothesis*. Routledge—Group Taylor & Francis.

Dinga, E. (2025). *Economic Resilience During Overlapped Crises—Antifragility, Sustainability and Autopoieticity*. Palgrave Macmillan—Springer Nature.

Dinga, E., Tănăsescu, C. -R., & Oprean-Stan, C. (2025). *Sustainability as an Axiological Arrow*. In Cristina Roxana Tănăsescu, Camelia Oprean-Stan, Samuel O. Idowu, & Belén Díaz Díaz (Eds.), Advancements in Sustainable Development. Springer.

Husserl, E. (2012). *Logical Investigations* (Vol. 1). Routledge.

Kahneman, D. (2011). *Thinking, Fast and Slow*. Farrar, Straus and Giroux.

Lakatos, I. (1999). The Methodology of Scientific Research Programmes. In J. Worrall & G. Currie (Eds.), *Philosophical Papers* (vol. I).

Mele, A. R., & Rawling, P. (2004). *The Oxford Handbook of Rationality*. Oxford University Press.

Prigogine, I., & Stengers, I. (1984). *Order Out of Chaos: Man's New Dialogue with Nature*. Flamingo Edition.

SEP—*Stanford Encyclopedia of Philosophy.* (2025). Library of Congress.
Skinner, B. F. (1938, 2019). *The Behaviour of Organism: An Experimental Analysis*. B.F. Skinner Foundation.
Thaler, R., & Sunstein, C. (2009). *Nudge: Improving Decisions About Health, Wealth, and Happiness*. Penguin Books.

PART III

Social Justice—A General View

CHAPTER 5

State and Politics

1 The State

The basic statements on the state arising, including its "pair", called society, so the societal phenomenology, were sketched in Annex 2 in Chapter 1. Consequently, in this chapter, I shall provide some considerations regarding the state functioning after its birth.

1.1 The Public Goods

Generalities

The generic term of public goods refers to those goods and services that are necessary and useful for a given community, that is, for each individual and for the community as a whole, but which goods and services cannot be produced by the individuals themselves, either individually or through voluntary cooperation between them. In this (working) definition, several ideas appear that need to be clarified in order to be able to move forward with the concept of public good:

(a) *firstly*, it is about the expression public goods—although, as has now been shown, this includes both goods and services,[1] the generic name used is that of public goods. We will not pedantically dismantle this already established expression, although, as we

E. Dinga, *The Economics of Social Justice and Societal Evolution*, https://doi.org/10.1007/978-3-032-24055-2_5

will see, the largest part of public goods is constituted by… public services;

(b) *secondly*, it is about the necessary character of public goods—the phrase *necessary character* has, here, its very meaning from logic, that is, it refers to something that cannot be missing, i.e., something essential for a given purpose;

(c) *thirdly*, it is about the usefulness of public goods—the public goods satisfy human needs, no matter the nature of those needs: material/economic, regarding education, wellness, socialization, and, in the largest meaning, the social capital (in the next chapter, I provide a short examination of the concept of social capital);

(d) *fourthly*, it is about the fact that public goods are necessary and useful both for each individual and for the community as a whole[2]—indeed, the double addressability of public goods must be maintained in their conjunction, because a public good necessary for a community but which does not maintain its necessity for each individual component of that community is unlikely to maintain its presence in the long term. On the other hand, a public good necessary for each individual may or may not be necessary for the community as such. We therefore believe that, for the rigorous definition of the concept of public good, the aforementioned conjunction of necessity (both for each individual and for the community as such) must be preserved;

(e) *fifthly*, there is the issue of the utility of public goods—for example, an individual who has a physical impairment that prevents him from travelling on public roads might consider that the public road is not useful to him and might claim not to be involved (from a cost point of view—see further on the issue of the costs of public goods) in the design and production of this type of public good;

(f) *sixthly*, there is the "property" of public goods that they cannot be produced by individuals themselves, either individually or through voluntary cooperation between them (of course, within a given community). The following considerations may be of utility in this point:

- the impossibility of producing public goods at the level of individuals refers to an economic impossibility, not a technological one: the price of such public goods would be exorbitant and, obviously, completely prohibitive—for example, it would mean that each individual would have to produce his/her own army, his/her own police, his/her own gendarmerie unit, his/her own highway, etc.;

- cooperation of individuals in the realization of public goods is also questionable—in a small community the public goods needed could not be produced, no matter how much voluntary cooperation was involved, there simply are not enough resources for this. In addition, in two close communities conflicts would certainly arise, for example, between police forces, or regarding roads/highways, etc.;
- the only possibility of solving the problem is the inter-individual cooperation at the most extensive level of the community—usually the national or state community. Cooperation at the level of the maximum extension of community has some necessary (mandatory) particularities:

  it involves specialization: a certain contingent of individuals, trained precisely in the production and distribution of public goods, will be normatively charged with this activity (this is what we call the public sector[3]);

  it involves the participation, from a cost perspective, of the entire society in the production and distribution of public goods (this is the concept of taxation);

  of course, in this context, the problem of individual agreement to bear the costs of production and distribution of public goods reappears; although the moral issue remains, not yet receiving a generally accepted/acceptable justification, from a constitutional point of view it has received the resolution of the legal (normative) support;

(g) *seventhly*, the production and distribution of public goods imply (as indirectly resulted from the above) a decision, somehow, taken by an elite group, which decision, however, concerns the entire community. Indeed, this elite (we will see that, by this, we mean, ultimately, the state) establishes both the necessity and the utility of public goods and, of course, the structure, quality, and quantity of their production and distribution to the community. This decision is not, however, entirely discretionary—we bring, in support of this assertion, the following arguments:

- the state (which arises together with human society[4]) appears either as a result of a founding act (the choice of first or basic principles, in the original position—see Rawls' theory), or as a result of the action of the invisible hand, through the spontaneous aggregation of an association for the defence of individual rights of any kind, as they are "stipulated" by natural law (see Nozick's theory). Therefore, in both cases (*Nota bene*: Martha C. Nussbaum does not present a mechanism for the emergence, or formation, or institutionalizing of the state, but focuses on the role and functions of the state, which actually interferes, in the most substantial part, with the two theories mentioned), the state represents an objectification of individual options, as they are aggregated in one way or another. Somehow, what the state is going to do—among other things, the establishment, production, and distribution of public goods—is approved, through a founding act, by the very individuals who make up a generic community;
- therefore, it cannot be said that there is a rupture of purpose between the founding individuals of the state (i.e., of society) and the individuals called upon, subsequent to the emergence of the state (in fact, perpetually[5]), to decide and ensure the production and distribution of public goods at the community level. We can accept, of course, that, regarding the means of achieving the goal assumed at the time of the emergence/establishment of the state, there may be "novelties" that were not anticipated at the time in question, but the goal remains untainted in its essence[6];
- goals formulated by that elite (i.e., the state) may also appear, which goals were not considered by the individuals who participated, from a historical point of view (but, especially, from a logical point of view) in the emergence/establishment of the state. This possibility resides in the course of the historical evolution of the community, when new challenges arise and, therefore, there is a need to establish new goals. However, the establishment of new goals cannot depart from the general principle that requires that the goals of the state aim at safeguarding individuals and the community as such, of which the individuals are part. The (possible) deviation from this sacrosanct principle is fined precisely through the electoral

mechanism, when representatives who appear to deviate (or seem intending to deviate) from the respective principle can be withdrawn from state structures (institutions, authorities, agencies).[7]

Methodological Issues

In this paragraph, we will examine, in a more analytical way, the concept of public good and we will establish, based on some criteria,[8] a taxonomy of them, thus obtaining the classes of public goods that can exist in a generic community (more precisely, society).

(a) Criteria for taxonomy of public goods

Two criteria for classifying the public goods seem to be of interest:

(a1) the way in which public goods are distributed at the level of society (it being established, with a sufficiency character, that their production is the prerogative of the state—of course through institutions, authorities, and specialized agencies);

(a12) the nature of the public good, or the type of social need that public goods satisfy.

(b) Classes of public goods

According to the criterion regarding the method of distribution (a1), public goods can be:

- (PG_1^1) distributed by the state through the public sector: for example, national defence;
- (PG_2^1) distributed by the state through the private sector of the state: for example, free or subsidized electricity granted by the state to the private sector;
- (PG_3^1 1) distributed by the private sector, under a subsidy granted by the state: for example, food for students or for people with deficiencies/disabilities/handicap[9];

- (PG_4^1) distributed by the state sector in a complementary manner with similar private goods and services: for example, education or health.

According to the criterion regarding the method of distribution (a2), public goods can be[10]:

- (PG_1^2) public goods aimed at biological survival;
- (PG_2^2) public goods aimed at individual freedom;
- (PG_3^2) public goods aimed at the full integration of the individual into society/community;
- (PG_4^2) public goods aimed at the safety and security of life;
- (PG_5^2) public goods aimed at the intellectual development of the human being;
- (PG_6^2) public goods aimed at the harmony between the individual (community) and the non-anthropic environment;
- (PG_7^2) public goods aimed at the preservation and adaptation[11] of community identity;
- (PG_8^2) public goods aimed at the emotional development of the human being (art, religion);
- (PG_9^2) public goods aimed at the harmony between the human being and artificial intelligence;
- (PG_{10}^2) public goods aimed at the formation and protection of self-esteem.

Of course, the two criteria can be combined, so that they act simultaneously, thus resulting in a number of 40 theoretically possible classes of public goods (Table 1).

Discussion

- *firstly*, let us note the incompatibilities between the two criteria, i.e., the combined classes of public goods that "cannot exist": the incompatibilities refer to the public good PG_2^2 (individual freedom)—this public good is too important (probably, the most important—we say probably, because the public good PG_{10}^2(self-esteem) could also "compete" for this title) to ignore the private sector, whose general behaviour criterion is to obtain profit, if possible, at its maximum

Table 1 Classes of double-classified public goods

Criterion a1 / *Criterion a2*	PG_1^1	PG_2^1	PG_3^1	PG_4^1
PG_1^2		x	x	x
PG_2^2	x	–	–	–
PG_3^2		x	x	x
PG_4^2				x
PG_5^2			x	x
PG_6^2		x	x	x
PG_7^2		x	x	x
PG_8^2			x	
PG_9^2	x	x	x	x
PG_{10}^2		x	x	

Source author

level, manage it, either independently or in cooperation with the public sector;

- *secondly*, let us make the following observations:
  - the public goods provided only by the state aim at freedom and the achievement of harmonious "symbiosis" between the human being and artificial intelligence; the greatest overlap of providers of public goods occurs in the case of public goods offered (not produced, as shown) by the private sector through state subsidies (8 cases out of 10 possible); in second place are goods offered complementary by the state and the private sector (7 cases); and in third place are public goods offered through the private domain of the state (6 cases). In Annex 1, a mutual examination of the capabilities proposed by Nussbaum and the public goods proposed by me (according to criterion 2—the nature of the public good) is carried out.

1.2 State Legitimacy

To introduce the concept of state legitimacy, it is necessary to introduce, in advance, the abstract concept of legitimacy, and, for this latter purpose, the abstract concept of legality will have to be introduced.

Legality

Legality is a property of any entity (*Nota bene*: of the three distinct entities in the world: thing, property, relationship), established from the perspective of a given, external criterion. It must be said that a property is not revealed to the observer unless there is a criterion for extracting the property in question, so that the same entity in question can exhibit different properties in the "light" of different criteria. Returning to the property of legality, this is revealed by a criterion such as the norm (considered in the broadest possible sense). A few examples may be useful:

- a conclusion in a syllogism is legal (it is also said to be valid) if the inference by which it is extracted from the premises respects the (three) principles of logic;
- a behaviour is legal if it does not violate the rules established by the authority entitled to formulate those rules;
- the use of a word (in a verbal sentence) is legal if it verifies the grammatical rules established with regard to it.

Therefore, legality is that property of conformity to the norm, regardless of whether the norm is correct, from various points of view, or is performative, from other points of view. A change in the norm will, of course, lead to changes in the assessment of legality regarding the entities that were conditioned by that norm, so we will have… legalities and illegalities.

There are three generic norms: (1) norm of *obligation*—O; (2) norm of *prohibition*—F; (3) norm of *permission*—P.[12] *Nota bene*: in Annex 2 a short synthesis of the concept of norm is presented. If we denote by N a normative proposition (i.e., which contains a norm), by E_N the action to execute the provision in the proposition N, and by $\overline{E}_N$ the abstention (in-action) to execute the provision in the proposition N, then there can be the following cases of legality/illegality of behaviour (Fig. 1).

<u>Discussion</u>

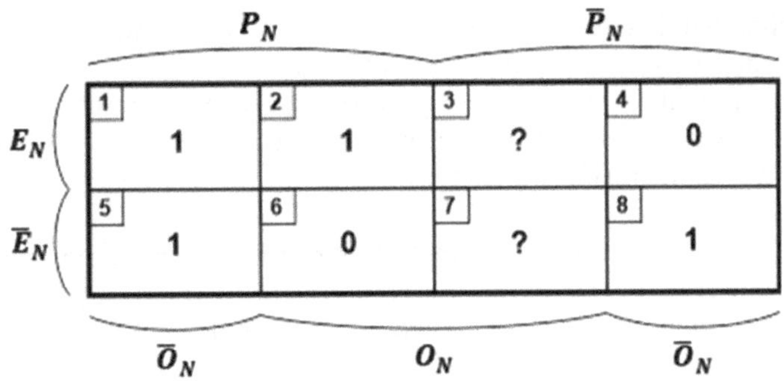

Fig. 1 A Karnaugh diagram for cases of legality/illegality of action/inaction (*Source* author)

- in the eight boxes of Fig. 1, the case of legality was entered with the number "1", and the case of non-legality (illegality) with the number "0". We therefore have four cases of legality (see details below), two cases of non-legality, and two cases of contradiction (the "?" sign);
- box [1]: it is legal to perform the action provided for in the sentence N because the action is permitted (P_N) and not mandatory ($\overline{O}_N$);
- box [2]: it is legal to perform the action provided for in the sentence N because the action is permitted (P_N) and mandatory (O_N);
- box [3]: refers to a normative contradiction: on the one hand, the action performed is not permitted (i.e., it is prohibited), and, on the other hand, the execution of the action is mandatory—so we are dealing with an error of normative logic;
- box [4]: it is illegal to perform the action prescribed by the sentence N, because the action is not permitted and, moreover, it is not obligatory;
- box [5]: it is legal not to perform the action prescribed by the sentence N, because the action is not obligatory, although it is permitted;
- box [6]: it is illegal not to perform the action prescribed by the sentence N, because the action is permitted but, at the same time, it is obligatory;
- box [7]: refers to a normative contradiction: on the one hand, the action performed is not permitted (i.e., it is forbidden), and on the

other hand, the execution of the action is obligatory—so we are dealing with an error of normative logic;
- box [8]: it is legal not to perform the action prescribed by the sentence *N*, because the action in question is both non-obligatory and forbidden (not permitted).

Of course, the above refers to logical, abstract cases regarding legality/illegality which, in particular-concrete situations, may acquire specific meanings and connotations—however, the rules derived from Fig. 1 are of general use.

Legitimacy

We have seen that legality is a property that is identified/validated from the perspective of a referential that we have called norm, in the most general sense of this word. Legitimacy is also a property of an entity (thing, property, relationship). The question arises: what is the referential with respect to which the legitimacy property is identified/validated? Next, we will propose such a referential.

Legitimacy must be related to and inferred from a *value*. The most primitive value and, therefore, with the greatest founding force (including with respect to the other values in the axiological matrix of the individual and society) is *individual freedom*. The qualification of the value we call freedom as individual freedom, therefore of the individual, or which is validated in the individual horizon is crucial, because the freedom assigned to a group or a wider community (ethnic, geographical, linguistic, etc.) allows, within the group[13] or community in question, to exist deprivation of freedom, in the name and on the "altar" of community freedom.[14] In other words, from individual freedom one can infer (in fact, corroborate) group or community freedom, but the inverse relationship is liable to falsification.

Therefore, a decision/action/activity is legitimate if it verifies this criterion or referential of individual freedom. It seems that we have arrived, however, in a kind of vicious circle: in order to verify legitimacy, it is necessary to have defined the referential, that is, freedom, but defining the referential can only be done through a norm, which could induce the idea that legitimacy is always the consequence of legality. The reasoning is correct only on the false assumption that all values are or must be codified. Freedom as such, as a value, cannot be codified, it is assumed by society and by each individual, it is a fundamental value (some would say a fundamental right), it must corroborate not only other values but also all norms (codified or informal, as the case may be). In the best case, what can be codified are the liberties (e.g., the liberty of expression), but not freedom as such.

1.3 *The Relationship Legality–Legitimacy*

We have seen that legality and legitimacy are defined (as properties) by appealing to different referentials—the first to a norm, the second to a value. So, the relationship between legality and legitimacy will result from the analysis of the relationship between the two referentials. It is beyond doubt that value takes precedence, both in the logical order and in the psychological order. As a result, legitimacy is more primitive in these two orders than legality. Moreover, it can be said that the norm should legalize the value, in this case (individual) freedom/liberties. This relationship between legality and legitimacy, in which legality cannot (in the sense that it is prohibited from) violate legitimacy, will be used later. Of course, in a concrete-historical reality, the conditionality of freedom is sometimes (or often, depending on the political regime of a given society) violated, but, in principle, a decision/action is legitimate if and only if it verifies the criterion/referential that we call freedom. In this sense, we can certainly have legitimated but illegal decisions/actions (e.g., the social movement, initially revolutionary, of 1989 in Romania, was illegal because it opposed the constitutional order of that moment, but was legitimate because it claimed the ideal of individual freedom), just as there can be legal but illegitimate decisions/actions (e.g., the case where a norm codifies a behaviour that violates the principle of freedom). It can be noted that, most of the time, the violation of legitimacy occurs not at the moment of deciding and/or carrying out an action (either act or abstention, as the case may be), but at the moment of norming. Through this procedure, illegitimacy is actually masked with a legal measure: the issuance of a norm that violates legitimacy.

Therefore, the final model of normative activity is to obtain free behaviour of the subjects of the norm, respectively of the agents of the action. This implies an internalization of the norms, so that they become an endogenous motivational factor. The efficiency of normative action is all the greater the more the norm is internalized, felt as an inner impulse (therefore it acquires an increasingly pronounced character of an autonomous norm), which makes the corresponding action all the more motivated, therefore more cultural. Because, if discipline is defined as a constraint that suppresses deviation from the norm, it (discipline) must transform itself into a cultural attitude towards the norm. In this sense, culture is defined or definable as *the development of one attitude (or aptitude) without suppressing another*. The cultural stage of normative behaviour is obtained by internalizing the norm.

There are two main ways of receiving the norm:

(1) the *psychological* way: the individual internalization of the norm. In this case, there are six attitudes that can manifest themselves: (a) refractory; (b) conformist; (c) opportunist; (d) amoral; (e) conflictual; (f) moral (authentic);

(2) the *sociological* way: the criterion of internalization is the social influence exerted by the norm. Therefore, the legitimacy (or rather, the legitimation) of the norm is nothing other than its degree of internalization, so legitimacy is a measure of normative internalization. The issue of the model (or process) of legitimation is controversial in the specialized literature. In this sense, several models of legitimation have been outlined, on which we will not insist here:

  (a) legitimation by *belief* (Max Weber): the motivation of legitimation is required;
  (b) legitimation by legitimation of the norming rules themselves, or of the normative activity (Carl Schmidt);
  (c) legitimation through *rational motivation of values* to which the actual legitimation is then related (Johannes Vinckelmann);
  (d) legitimation through *recourse to the basic norms of rational discourse*, therefore to practical discourse (Jürgen Habermas).

The legitimacy of norms is one of the essential sources of the freedom of decision/action of agents.

1.4 State Legality

In this paragraph, we will particularize the results established above, in the case of the state. First of all, it must be specified that, regardless of which of the two ways of the emergence of the state, evoked previously (the social contract, respectively the voluntary formation of associations[15]), the state, therefore the society, or the societal system, is formed, this—i.e., the state—is of the type of artefact, that is, it is the result of a teleology, of a deliberate project. The emergence of the state is consecrated by the appearance/adoption of some basic, fundamental principles regarding the organization and functioning of the state, which are agglutinated in a body of norms, considered primordial/primitive, and this body of norms bears the name: Constitution. Therefore, the state is, from the beginning, founded on the Constitution, which can be considered the macro-norm that constitutes the legal substratum of the state. Social philosophers consider that, through the Constitution, what is called the basic structure of society is identified and consecrated, that is, those primitive, founding principles, which will function as axioms of the organization and functioning of the state/society. In this sense, the state, as an entity of the type of social construction, is liable to be considered to have full legality, just by definition. Let us briefly examine the legality of the state's decisions/ actions.

Based on what has been previously stated regarding legality, we will now be able to say the following, relative to the state:

- the property of legality of the state's decisions/actions is given by the concordance between these decisions/actions and the content of the norm in the macro-norm called Constitution, that regulates the decisions/actions in question;
- the norms of positive law that are inferred from the Constitution constitute, in turn, effective norms for further guiding the decisions/ actions of all members of society;
- Constitution itself is, of course, also of the nature of positive law, and the inference of the "ordinary" norms from the constitutional macro-norm is made by the legislative structure of the state—the Parliament[16]—and, occasionally, by the executive power of the state—the Government. In general, there is a control over the constitutionality of these inferences/derivations, exercised by the Constitutional Court or Supreme Court. From a logical point of view, the Constitutional Court therefore verifies the validity of the inference in question, which refers to the logical correctness of drawing conclusions from the premises.

1.5 State Legitimacy

We have seen, above, what legitimacy is, in general. As in the case of legality, we will particularize the concept of legitimacy in the case of the functioning of the state, the results being established in an abstract manner. Therefore, the decisions and actions of the state must not violate individual freedom—by individual freedom we mean, of course, also the freedom of various forms and modalities of association of individuals in companies, organizations, institutions, NGOs, etc. It is not about a collective freedom, but about the freedom of the individuals who compose those forms of association/cooperation. The question arises of identifying a criterion on the basis of which we can evaluate the legitimate or illegitimate character of the decisions/actions of the state. It should be noted that these decisions/actions concern the society in which the respective state functions, because, with regard to the state itself, more precisely with regard to state institutions/organizations, the question of legitimacy does not arise, but only that of legality, which was discussed previously.

The Criterion of Legitimacy of the State's Decision/Action
We propose the following criterion of legitimacy of state intervention in society[17]: *self-testability*. The significance of this criterion is as follows:

- it concerns the internal capacity of a societal system (other than one belonging to the public sector only) to establish and use a mechanism for testing its own decisions/actions. Testing may refer to (at least) the following aspects: (a) appropriateness; (b) effectiveness; (c) efficiency; (d) sustainability; (e) unintended consequences;

Nota bene: I said above that the public sector is excluded from the application of the legitimacy criterion. Indeed, with regard to the public sector, as previously mentioned, only the issue of legality arises, not that of legitimacy. However, the private domain of the state remains "uncovered" in this respect. In relation to the private domain of the state (public enterprises), we specify the following in the context of the legitimacy criterion:

- as being owned by the state, it follows that the state assumes the decisions/actions of this domain, to the same extent and in the same way as in the case of the public sector;

- however, being of a private nature, this domain has its own responsibility in relation to the decisions/actions taken/undertaken;
- in my opinion, in relation to the private domain of the state, the legitimacy criterion acts in a, let's say, shared way:

    with regard to the strategic decisions of the private domain, by virtue of the property owned by the state, the criterion of legality operates just as in the case of the public sector;
    with regard to the operational/tactical decisions of the private domain, by virtue of the private nature of the patrimony of this domain, the criterion of legitimacy operates exactly as in the case of the rest of society (the private sector, respectively civil society);

- it refers to a potential aspect of testing, namely to testability, not to actual testing. This clarification is very important, so we will make some additional considerations:
    - it is not mandatory that the private sector (respectively the private domain of the state, from the perspective of the operational/tactical decision) actually carries out the test, but there must only be the possibility, the capability (perhaps, the probability) that the sector in question can carry out the test. *Nota bene*: it is worth noting the strong analogy—not exactly the similarity, see below—with the factual testability discussed in the field of scientific knowledge (also known as falsifiability or, simply, scientificity, in Karl Popper's critical rationalism);
    - of course, as we will see below, the state must have its own methodology or procedure through which it can establish (or ensure) that the private sector has this ability—which must have a structural character, in order to ensure a relatively high degree of certainty, respectively of permanence and continuity of the ability in question—to carry out the respective test;
- it targets individual freedom—indeed, if a certain entity in society has the possibility/capacity/potential to test its own decisions/actions (more precisely, the consequences of these decisions/actions), it follows that it has the freedom to redesign these decisions/actions, as it had the freedom to make/execute them. The fact that the

proposed criterion of legitimacy, namely self-testability, ultimately aims to ensure individual freedom, is the best argument in favour of... the legitimacy of the criterion itself;

Nota bene: here comes back an issue intensely discussed in the specialized literature (including from the perspective of state theory, political theory, or social philosophy), namely the order of priority (more precisely, of primitiveness) between two values: life (in the sense of survival), respectively freedom. Social-historical practice has apparently given priority to freedom. There is also intense discussion, in philosophical, sociological, and anthropological debates, about another value that would actually be in an even more primitive position in relation to freedom or life (survival): *self-esteem*. These debates and polemics, however, exceed the limited objective of the present research—see some general considerations on the self-esteem in (Dinga et al., 2020).

- a very important question now arises: what is the nature of the testability (or testing) of the decision or action? My answer in this matter is the following:
  - testability, as an ability/capacity/potentiality, aims at sustainability (*Nota bene*: I recall that the present work has in mind, as the purpose of the research approach, precisely the obtaining of sufficient conditions to ensure sustainability). Sustainability is a kinematic (more precisely, dynamic[18]) property of maintaining stability in a given temporal "tunnel" (time horizon);
  - obtaining sustainability (Dinga, 2025) aims at two complementary aspects: (a) *resilience*—which means the restoration of a state or a position on the trajectory of an entity that has been disturbed from that state or position; (b) *adaptation*—which means moving into a state or placing oneself on a trajectory that anticipates the selective demands of the future environment;
  - resilience is achieved through feedback, either negative or positive:

    the case of *negative feedback*—e.g., if the price of a product increases, the quantity demanded (*Nota bene*: be careful not to confuse the change in the quantity demanded, caused by the inversely proportional change in the price *ceteris paribus*, with the change in demand, caused by the shift in the directly proportional change in income, *ceteris paribus*) will decrease, which will reduce the price, we therefore have self-regulation or, with the term used above for the legitimacy criterion, self-testing; as I said, however, the possibility of self-testing is sufficient, that is, self-testability is sufficient; we say that negative feedback ensures resilience, that is, returning to the initial state/position;

the case of *positive feedback*—e.g., an investment that leads to an increase in demand for the product/service produced by that investment will cause the entrepreneur in question (or the economic system in question, in its entirety) to make new investments, anticipating precisely this increase in demand; we say that positive feedback avoids/eliminates shocks by anticipating (more precisely, by an anticipated adaptation to) the shocks predictable in the rationality model used.

Operationalizing the Legitimacy Criterion

The operationalization of the criterion of legitimacy of state intervention in society (especially in the economy) involves the following actions on the part of state institutions/authorities/agencies, i.e., the public sector:

(i) the creation of a "map" (topology)—by areas of societal activity, by types of societal actions, etc.—so that, for each of the cases in which the state considers to be necessary to intervene to maintain sustainability and to respect the public interest (for which the state itself emerged in society), i.e., for the provision of public goods, self-testability can be established, without equivocation. In this way, the state will be able to ensure that its intervention is always legitimate, and for cases in which legitimacy is not covered by legality, the state will be able to issue the appropriate norms to overlap of legality and legitimacy. We repeat here what was previously mentioned, namely the fact that legality follows legitimacy, not vice versa. Figure 2 suggests a conceptual basis from which to proceed in order to ensure the legal legitimacy or, equivalently, the legitimate legality of state intervention in society.

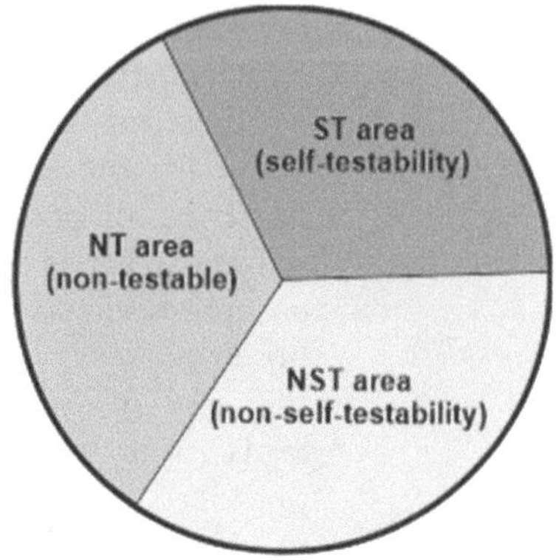

Fig. 2 Generic cases of legitimacy/illegitimacy of state intervention (*Source* author)

Discussion

- *self-testable* area (ST): it is that area of society (domains, actions) that has the capability to test itself based on internal principles of organization and functioning. In this area, state intervention is illegitimate, even if (due to incompetence or intention) there is a norm that makes the intervention legal; obviously, this area, as being self-testable, is, *a fortiori*, testable;

Nota bene: as an example of a typical ST area, the private economic sector is often given. It must be said that the self-testability of the private economic sector is generic, within this sector there may be sub-areas (enclaves) that are not self-testable. For example, it is demonstrated in standard (neoclassical) economic theory that the logic of the private economy (especially if that economy or economic system is relatively close, in organization and functioning, to the type of free competition) leads to the emergence of monopoly (or monopsony or bilateral monopoly, as the case may be) that are characterized by positive feedback, not negative feedback. But, as previously shown, only negative feedback is inherent to self-testability;

- the *non-self-testable* area (NST): it is that area of society (domains, actions) that does not have the capability to test itself based on the internal principles of organization and functioning. In this area, state intervention is optional from the perspective of legitimacy (of course, under the conditions in which legality is already ensured); the NST area remains, obviously, testable, so that the state, based on criteria other than that of legitimacy (which is ensured in this area), can decide whether to intervene or not—both intervention and non-intervention of the state are, therefore, legitimate;

- the *non-testable* area (NT): it is that area of society (domains, actions) in which testability does not exist and, *a fortiori*, self-testability does not exist either. In this area, state intervention is mandatory and, as a result, is considered legitimate, from the perspective of the role and purpose of the existence of the state in general. The question arises, of course: what is the logical and institutional basis for the existence of the non-testable area in society? In this regard, we make the following considerations:
  - the logical basis of non-testable area is the predominance of positive feedback over negative feedback. This leads to the installation and perpetuation of a self-escalating (self-catalytic) process that makes the system in such an area unable to slow down, or stop, or turn from the indefinitely increasing or decreasing trajectory, as the case may be;
  - the institutional basis of non-testable areas is represented by the need, from the perspective of the completeness of the societal structure, to regulate the creation and functioning of artefacts that imply unsustainability—for example, the possibility of concentrating economic production in monopolies (which are non-testable, and therefore, *a fortiori*, are not self-testable) is accepted normatively (institutionally) for reasons of economies of scale.

In conclusion, the societal complex has three significant zones from the perspective of state interventionism: two testable areas—one of which is self-testable and the other that is externally testable—and one non-testable area. State intervention (allegedly legal) is illegitimate in the self-testable area, optional in the non-self-testable area, and mandatory in the non-testable area.

2 Liberty, Responsibility, Authority

2.1 Liberty

Relationship Human Nature–Human Condition

(a) The concept of human nature

Man is a biological being, both in terms of genesis and from the point of view of primary existential conditioning (he/she can only exist through permanent and favourable entropic exchange—consumption of low entropy from the non-anthropic environment and discharge of high entropy into this environment). The human nature of man[19] therefore consists in his/her existence as a biological being, which implies:

- a "hierarchy" of behavioural criteria, i.e., a hierarchy based on relevance for survival:
  - the first criterion: *individual survival* (biological maintenance), having a primordial character[20];
  - the second criterion: *survival of the species* (biological reproduction);
  - the third criterion: *survival of the community* (tribe) (social reproduction).[21]
- the irrelevance of liberty[22]: from the perspective of human nature, liberty has no meaning,[23] because it does not condition survival.

(b) The concept of the human condition

In addition to his/her biological conditioning, human being has also a cultural conditioning. Although other animals are also social animals, that is, they establish and live in social groups, in these cases we can at most speak of a social conditioning, which is added to the biological conditioning, but not of a cultural conditioning. Cultural conditioning is a species of social conditioning, but, as we have shown, not every social conditioning is a cultural conditioning. We can say that the human condition is what culture makes of human nature. Therefore, the fundamental attributes of the human condition could be the following:

- the primacy of liberty in relation to survival
- the hierarchy of survival behaviour becomes:
  - individual survival
  - community survival[24]
  - species survival
- the emergence of values as criteria for choosing behavioural criteria, primarily ethical values,[25] respectively moral values.

(c) The relationship human nature–human condition

Therefore, from a historical (chronological) point of view, human nature is prior to the human condition. The human condition builds on human nature by culturalizing it, so that it can be said that the human condition is human nature seen through a cultural filter. However, just as the brain (the natural basis of consciousness) is not redesigned when moving from nature to culture,[26] neither is human nature abandoned when moving to the human condition.[27] Therefore, although we know what the human condition is in relation to human nature, they coexist in the historical (empirical) individual. In fact, the cultural socialization of man only brackets human nature,[28] without abolishing it. It is very important to remember that human nature and the human condition are not two chronological (historical) stages in the evolution of human consciousness, but two conditionings, determinations that coexist, with the increasing dominance of the human condition over human nature as civilization registers social progress and, especially, axiological progress.

Discussion: a logical problem

The question arises: when does one move from human nature to the human condition, more precisely, when does the human condition begin to predominate over human nature, given that human nature will probably never disappear, as we know it? (see the footnote regarding transhumanism). My opinion in this regard is the following:

- we are dealing with a qualitative leap generated by quantitative accumulations.[29] Quantitative accumulations refer to the increasing dominance of the common interests of individuals, at the level of human society;

- the human condition therefore becomes dominant when the safeguarding of individual interest (regardless of its nature) becomes dependent, to a major extent and, very importantly, inevitable, on the safeguarding of community (social) interest;
- the human condition logically implies the subsumption of individual good by public good.[30]

Primary Values vs. Secondary Values

The concept of primary values is different from that of primordial values, as shown above. About primary values can only be spoken relative to the human condition, not relative to human nature, where we are dealing only with aspects of primordiality of values. In general, primary values mean those values that generate, ensure, defend, and guarantee the self-esteem of the individual. By self-esteem we will understand security (more precisely, securitizing or safeguarding) of the individual in relation to society,[31] from the following disjunctive perspectives:

- the absence of challenge, influence or alteration, from the other private individuals,[32] of the formulation and pursuit, from the individual concerned, of his/her private purpose[33];
- the absence of the exercise of injustice (non-entitlement[34]) from the other private individuals.

All other values facilitated by the manifestation of the human condition must be considered secondary in relation to the primary ones. Secondary values do not necessarily have to be derivable from primary ones (although some are), since they can occur or can be generated autonomously. The most important primary value provided by the human condition is the value called freedom. Freedom is, in fact, defined by the first condition of self-esteem, so by freedom we will understand (in an apophatic definition) *the situation of the private individual who is not disturbed, in no way, by the actions of the other private individuals in formulating and pursuing his/her private purpose*. In connection with this definition, the following details are useful:

- freedom is not defined in relation to nature, but in relation to society. In this sense, a seemingly paradoxical definition of freedom (but which is not contradictory to the already given one) is as follows: freedom is the possibility of the individual to oppose social necessity[35];
- as I have already said, freedom concerns the security of private purpose towards the interference of private individuals. In this sense, an interference of the state regarding the private purpose of an individual is not considered a limitation of freedom (for example, the state prohibits the formation of the purpose of killing another individual).[36] Also, an interference of a private individual regarding the means of reaching the purpose set autonomously does not represent a limitation of freedom;
- freedom, however, involves a self-limitation. Being self-limiting, this is not a limitation of freedom itself, because, as we have already seen in the definition of freedom, its restraint must come from the outside of the individual, more exactly, from another individual. Self-limiting freedom is explained as follows:
  - any private individual who wants to be free expects no other private individual to affect his/her private purpose establishing; by generalizing at the level of society, it turns out that the individual who expects this behaviour from the others must, in turn, refrain, as a private individual, to affect, in any way, the formulation of the private purpose of the other private individuals, that is, to self-limit their own freedom of action;
  - this description of the self-limitation of freedom is the content of the popular expressions "my freedom stretches until you meet your freedom"[37] or "what you do not like, you must do not do to other".

The Pyramid of Values

Within the human condition, the problem of a hierarchy of values can be raised, starting from the primary ones and continuing with the secondary, tertiary values, and so on. Although such an enterprise is theoretically risky,[38] it can be useful, because it gives a logical (or, at least, lexicographic[39]) organization of values. Based on the above, we propose the following pyramid of values in the "world" of the human condition (Fig. 3):

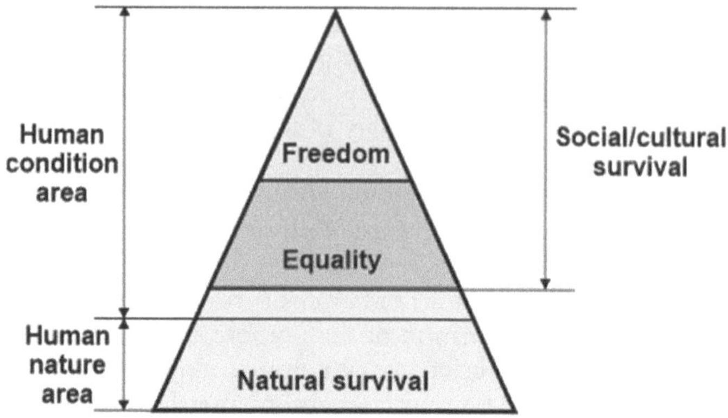

Fig. 3 Pyramid of values from the perspective of the two determinations of human consciousness: human nature, respectively the human condition (*Source* author)

It is observed that the value I called "survival", dominant (in fact, almost exclusive from the perspective of human nature) coexists in the other two values, equality, respectively freedom, which are, in turn, dominant from the perspective of the human condition.

The Survival of... Survival
As it results from Fig. 3, the value of survival represents a reminiscence of the human nature that is kept, in a potential point of view, within the domination of the other two values—freedom, respectively, equality. This is a consequence of both the anatomy and physiology of the brain (maintaining the pre-conscious signalling system), as well as of the psychology developed based on the brain we have.[40] A recent example refers to the society's reaction to the Covid-19 Pandemic (the disease generated by the SARS-COV-2 virus), when some of the freedoms of people were either abolished or restricted for the purpose of (predominance of) survival. It is true that, from a conceptual point of view, there are three issues that should be discussed more detailed:

- the fact that the restrictions or suspensions on freedom were initiated and applied by the public power, not by private individuals (for example, the gendarmes that ensure the respect of the imposed restrictions exercise this function on behalf of the state);

- the fact that the restrictions or suspensions regarding freedom refer mainly to the means, and not to the individual goals/purposes;
- the fact that the restrictions or suspensions on freedom are neither predictable nor definitive, but associated with an unexpected and temporary phenomenon.

Institutional-Normative Issues of Freedom

Freedom, as the most primitive value from the perspective of the human condition, is defined, objectified, guaranteed, and defended (including restored, if applicable) through the normative system of the society, first of all by the Constitution.[41] This means that, in the Constitution, the pyramid of values, mentioned above, as well as the derogations from this pyramid, must be found.[42]

2.2 *Responsibility*

The Concept of Responsibility

Etymologically, the responsibility evokes a property of the individual to have the ability to react or to answer an action, that is, to a cause that produces, for him/her, an effect that affects him/her. In time, the concept of responsibility has gained a connotation of positivity—to be responsible means to have an adequate reaction, according to a system of norms or a community's informal expectations system. Rigorous, the current acceptance is even more restrictive. By trying to highlight the sufficient predicates of this concept, we reach the following such predicates:

- *transcendentality*: the responsibility is originated in ethics, that is, in those precepts of community behaviour that are interior[43] to the individual and which project, from this interiority, the objectified behaviour of that individual;
- *in-reflexivity* (or *self-reflexivity*): the responsibility is always "measured" by reference to the Ethical Code of the individual, regardless of the moral code of the community to which that individual belongs. In this way, there are exceptional individuals, for example,

who manage to impose their own ethical values, thus transforming them into moral values;
- *compliance*: responsibility is, ultimately, a degree of conformity of the manifest behaviour of the individual with his/her Ethical Code. Consequently, responsibility is the result of a comparison between "norm" and its verification in the behavioural exercise;
- *idiosyncrasy*: in principle, it can be said that there are so many kinds of responsibilities as many individuals who experience it exist, because, being transcendental, the responsibility is specific to each individual.[44]

The following definition of responsibility should, perhaps, be accepted: *that behavioural feature of the private (historical) individual, originated transcendentally, inwardly oriented, and idiosyncratically validated.*

Distinction Between Responsibility and Accountability
There is a frenzy to confuse the concept of responsibility with that of accountability. In order to highlight the distinction to be made between the two concepts it is useful to identify the sufficient predicates of accountability:

- *transcendence*: accountability has its origin outside of the individual, namely in the community. The behaviour of accountability is designed by the community and, then, it is projected on the individual (i.e., inversely as it happens in the case of responsibility);
- *ex-reflexivity*: accountability (or accountable behaviour) is always "measured" by reference to the Legal Code[45] of the community[46];
- *compliance*: the predicate of compliance is also maintained in the case of accountability, but, as it has been shown in the previous predicate, the benchmark is no longer the Ethical, but the Legal Code (or, depending on the degree to which the legality overlaps the ethics, the Morale Code);
- *communitarity*: the accountability is established and measured based on the same indicators and procedures for the entire community, without any idiosyncratic "colour".

We notice that the predicate of idiosyncrasy disappears in the case of the concept of accountability. Therefore, the concept of accountability

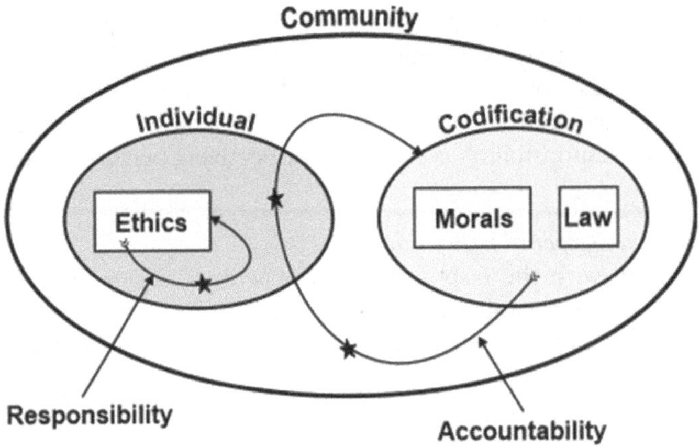

Fig. 4 Conceptual delimitation between responsibility and responsibility (*Source* author)

should, perhaps, be defined as: *that behavioural feature of the private (historical) individual originated transcendently, outwardly oriented, and communitarily validated.*

Figure 4 offers a synoptic image of the distinction between responsibility and accountability.

A Typology of Responsibility

The responsibility can be of several types, depending on the typology of the behaviour of the empirical individual in the community:

- *conceptive* (institutional) responsibility: is that responsibility that refers to the individual's action to propose to the community visions, models (usually political), actions or behaviour schemes, and the like. It is the responsibility of the highest degree and with the highest impact on the community (examples of individuals who have assumed conceptive responsibilities: Plato, Jefferson, Montesquieu, Marx, and, in general, philosophers and social theorists);
- *performative* (executive) responsibility: is that responsibility related to the ethical obligations of the individual regarding the design and execution of his/her actions within the community;

- *resolutive* (regular) responsibility: is that responsibility related to the individual's ethical obligations to evaluate the community in which he/she lives from the perspective of his/her own ethical commands and, consequently, to manifest under the empire of the other two types of responsibility: conceptive, respectively performative.[47]

Maxims of the Responsible Behaviour
In connection with the responsibility (not with freedom, however), the problem of the behaviour's maxims is raised.[48] The behaviour's maxims are of two types: (a) categorical imperative; (b) hypothetical imperative.

- categorical imperative

The categorical imperative is a behaviour's maxim that recommends an action (act or abstention, as the case may be) independent of the consequence of that action. In other words, the recommendation of the action is made from the perspective of the duty, i.e., of the unconditional obligation to carry out that action. In fact, another expression for the categorical imperative is the imperative of the duty, which is an unconditional, absolute imperative. The Kantian proposal for a moral/ethical behaviour was already mentioned. It seems that, in fact, Kantian maxim is not unconditional—indeed, the requirement to agree with the codification (i.e., transforming into positive law) of the maxim in question means to make sure that others will behave related to you as you behave related to them, so the formulation of the maxim of behaviour is considering a consequence, so it is not, in reality, a (clear) categorical imperative.

- hypothetical imperative

The hypothetical imperative is a behaviour's maxim that recommends an action (act or abstention, as the case may be) depending on the consequence (or the consequences) of that action. For example, the Christian behaviour's maxim that recommends actions that do the good of the neighbour shows that the author of the action will get salvation, so he/she has an advantage/gain from the action in question. Rigorously, the hypothetical imperative is a linguistic forcing, because an imperative must be, by definition, unconditional.[49]

2.3 *Correlation Between Liberty and Responsibility*

At this point, the question of the correlation between liberty and responsibility can be examined. The reasons for such an analysis consist at least in the following:

- responsibility can only manifest itself under conditions of liberty. Indeed, if the individual were not free (which means that there would be interference from a private individual regarding the formulation of the private goal of the individual in question), then he/she would no longer have to verify his/her own ethical values when performing an action that affects the community as such or individuals in the community;
- conversely, however, liberty can be objectified (manifested) in the absence of responsibility, but in this case, the liberty of the others would be affected. Moreover, the spontaneous balance of the liberty of interacting individuals can only be achieved in the presence of responsibility;
- the problem that arises here is the following: given that responsibility is addressed to the ethical, and since the ethical is idiosyncratic (unlike moral, which is communitarian), it follows that what is responsibility for one individual can be evaluated as irresponsibility by another individual.[50] Here, the solution can only be the one that calls for the sincerity and honesty of the action in question (which must, however, be proven!).

We therefore believe that liberty is a necessary condition for the manifestation of responsibility, while responsibility is a sufficient condition for freedom.

(a) the right and the obligation go paired

Based on the above, we will conclude that responsible behaviour implies, for the individual who behaves responsibly, a certain obligation, constraint or even, at the limit, duty. Therefore, the right of the other to "suffer", from my part, a responsible action has, as a necessary counterpart, my obligation to behave responsibly. Moreover, even in positive law, the correlative pair right–corresponding obligation is a fundamental principle.

(b) legality and legitimacy

From the way in which the concepts of responsibility and accountability have been defined, somewhat in a mirror image, the distinction between legality and legitimacy also results.

Legality is a property (for example, of an action) that signifies compliance with the legal norm.[51] It is irrelevant whether the legal norm in question is a democratic or dictatorial norm, whether it is appropriate or not, etc., it is sufficient that that norm is in force from a constitutional point of view. On the other hand, legitimacy is a property that signifies compliance with the ethical norm.[52] This means that the legal norm may or may not be legitimate according to how it is in accordance with the ethical constraints. The fact that the legal does not exhaust the legitimate (and, moreover, not vice versa) is very important from a sociological point of view, because the degree of voluntary compliance of the individual to the legal norm is directly proportional to the degree to which the legal is, in turn, legitimate. In fact, the legitimation of a norm is done by internalizing the legal norm in one's own system of values and responsibility. As mentioned earlier, responsibility must be linked to legitimacy, just as accountability must be linked to legality. This means that responsible behaviour can be illegal and, conversely, legal behaviour can be irresponsible.[53]

Nota bene: from an institutional-normative point of view, responsibility is not normed (unless we consider that there is an internal norm, at the level of the individual's subjectivity), while accountability is normed.

2.4 *Authority*

Relationship Power–Authority

The concept of authority is both a deontic[54] concept and a purely philosophical one. In addition, this concept is also used from a more pragmatic perspective, namely from the perspective of management (whether governmental, parental, or organizational). In order to identify and formulate a definition for the concept of authority, some preliminary considerations may be useful, from the perspective of the relationship between authority and power:

- the concept of authority is closely related to the concept of power. By power, in general, is understood a right (it is not important, for now, how this right is earned or conferred) to determine other individuals to perform actions that they would not otherwise perform;
- the immediately preceding idea has an extremely important consequence on the concept of freedom. We recall that freedom was defined as the absence of private interference in the formulation of the individual's private purpose; but, by forcing an individual, based on the power held, to execute an action, that is, to fulfil a purpose that, under other conditions, that individual would not have executed, that is, he/she would not have proposed the purpose to which he/she was forced, it follows that power has the potential to infringe freedom[55];
- between power and authority there may also be a semantic overlap. Thus, when power is conferred through a ritual of empowerment—for example, through democratic elections, or through acclamations,[56] or by establishing the hereditary inheritance of power, etc.—it is confused with authority, or rather, power and authority are acquired "as a package". If, however, power is acquired outside a ritual of empowerment—for example, the acquisition of political power through a coup d'état, or the acquisition of military power through an act of territorial conquest—then power is no longer accompanied by authority;
- the problem of the existence of authority in the absence of the existence of power is more difficult, but not without interest. Here we have the case of moral authority, intellectual authority, artistic authority, and the like (they will be described below, when the typology of authority is treated).

The Concept of Authority

Based on the above, I can now prepare the definition of the concept of authority as follows:

- authority is a pseudo-power, in the sense that it does not confer the right of disposition that power confers, but it nevertheless confers a right of influence. To distinguish the right of disposition[57] associated with power from the right of influence associated with authority,

I will say that power-type influence is an active influence (which emanates from the holder of power), while authority-type influence is a passive influence (the active aspect of authority is located at or emanates from the one who "endures" the authority);

- authority can be transformed into power, but this power is conferred by the one who "endures" the authority, not by the one who holds it[58];
- conversely, power can also be transformed into authority, the conferral of authority being made by the one who "endures" the power, not by the one who holds it[59];
- here, a "novelty" appears regarding the concept of authority, compared to the concept of power: if the concept of authority implies the right to exercise an influence on the environment, the concept of power implies the obligation to exercise an influence on the environment. In this sense, for the "endurer", power is inevitable, while authority is desirable;
- consequently, power is liable to abuse—abuse of power—(exceeding the influence "granted" by the conferment of the power in question[60]), while authority is liable to inaction (i.e., an inactivity in relation to the expectations with which the granting of the authority in question was credited);
- like power, authority is revocable.

The concept of authority can therefore be defined as *the property of a person (or institution, or organization), conferred by the members of the community, either formally or informally (tacitly), to represent the standard in matters of opinion, behaviour, or action in that community.*

A Typology of Authority

The concept of authority can have the following typology:

- from the perspective of the method of conferral:
  - *de jure authority*: it is the authority conferred by a decree of an...authority entitled to confer the authority in question. For example, Parliament is entitled, by the authority of the Constitution, to confer authority on the laws it adopts. Another example: in the judicial field, once a court sentence has been

legally pronounced, it enjoys, from then on, what is called in jargon, the authority of *res judicata*;
- de facto*authority*: it is the authority acquired as a result of the actions carried out and which is simply "conferred" to a certain individual, by the tacit recognition, on the part of the community (or a smaller group, as the case may be) that individual must enjoy (deserves to enjoy) that authority;

- from the perspective of the method of exercise:
  - *permanent authority*: the authority is exercised permanently, sometimes *sine die*[61];
  - ad hoc *authority*: authority is exercised in specific cases, either upon request or on one's own initiative, on particular issues;
- from the perspective of the type of authority:
  - *political authority*[62]: it is the authority that overlaps with political power (the meaning can be ambivalent: the conferral of power entails the formation/conferral of authority or vice versa, the formation/conferral of authority entails the conferral/acquisition of power);
  - *intellectual authority*[63]: it is the authority that addresses knowledge of any type (including artistic, theological, metaphysical, praxiological, and so on);
  - *moral authority*[64]: it is the authority that addresses values (the distinction, already made previously, between ethics and morals immediately results—morals are what the community imposes or recognizes in terms of values).

2.5 Correlation Liberty–Responsibility–Authority

(a) a lexicographic order: liberty–responsibility–authority

From the above, it follows that a lexicographic order of the three concepts discussed can be proposed. Such a lexicographic order is based on the principle of foundation[65]: a concept will be in a superior position to another concept if and only if the first concept needs less foundation than the second (in other words, the position occupied by a concept is all the higher the more primitive that concept is, from the perspective of foundation, than the other concepts considered). In this sense, I consider that a lexicographic order of the three concepts discussed could be:

liberty – responsibility– authority

We have already shown that responsibility is based on liberty, so the concept of liberty seems to be more primitive in relation to the concept of responsibility, that is, we have: liberty–responsibility.

Let us examine the foundational relationship between responsibility and authority. We can say the following:

- authority as power (or derived from power, or associated with power) can only be based on responsibility. Although there is also imposture in the acquisition of power, a power acquired through imposture is never associated, within the community, with authority, because the individuals potentially affected by that authority simply do not confer the authority in the question[66];
- authority that is not derived from or associated with power has all the more need for responsibility, because its exercise cannot be based on the power relationship;
- authority that does not "grow" on the ground of responsibility will be quickly lost (either by explicit revocation, or, most often, but most significantly, by implicit revocation—simply, the respective authority is no longer recognized or summoned by the community.

It therefore results that between responsibility and authority the lexicographical order is:

responsibility– authority

Accepting an order relationship[67] between the three concepts, that is, accepting transitivity, it results that we indeed have the following lexicographical order:

liberty – responsibility– authority

(b) evolutive aspects in the triad liberty–responsibility–authority

An interesting (and important) aspect in the lexicographic order obtained above is that of the co-evolution of the concepts in question. The following considerations may provide arguments in this regard:

- the development of freedom (extensive—as a sphere, respectively intensive—as an impact on the person) necessarily "requires" the development of responsibility. A development of freedom will increase the "risk" of interference with the freedom of the other. As a result, the responsibility in managing freedom is greater. There is a reluctance to accept the development of freedom, quite strange from a psychological and philosophical point of view[68]—which also manifested itself in Romania immediately after the anti-Ceausescu coup in 1989—namely, the reluctance to assume freedom is caused by the inability to assume responsibility that comes "in the package" with assuming freedom.[69] It follows, therefore, that freedom and responsibility are co-evolutionarily linked;
- the development of responsibility (both extensively and intensively) implies authority, namely also in a directly proportional sense: a person who becomes more responsible will be more likely to be granted greater authority (of any of the types mentioned above);
- the development of authority, in turn (extensively and intensively) "requires" more freedom, because both at the level of opinion and at the level of behaviour or action, the person who develops authoritatively needs more manœuvre room to value his/her authority;
- there is, probably, a positive feedback between the three concepts, from a co-evolutionary perspective, but this issue requires a much more detailed logical, psychological, and institutional analysis, which could constitute a further research direction.

Additional comment

A difficult enough issue linked to the concept of responsibility is that of the mandatory vote, or the obligation (instituted normatively) to vote in the process of political elections. In my opinion, this issue is a particular case of the following issue (or a particular application of the answer required by the following question): can freedom/liberty be established by force,[70] that is, in a cataphatic manner?[71] My considerations in this matter are as follows:

- the "sense" of liberty (probably, the... seventh sense[72]) originates in human nature (*Nota bene*: and, obviously, is held vivid in the non-human animals);
- consequently, this "sense", in fact, this primordial aspiration, is complete by exactly the birth of the (generic) individual[73];
- being complete, the freedom/liberty cannot be extended in any way and by any instance, either natural or social;
- so, freedom can (only) be "administered" from the social/societal perspective, and such "administering" cannot be done other than in an apophatic (i.e., negative) key, namely by mutual and sustainable (ethically, and functionally) limitations among the individuals.

Applying this result to the case of the mandatory vote, we think that to introduce such an institution in the democracy functioning is equivalent with extending the unextendible sphere of liberty. Moreover, this would signify the transforming of a right into an obligation.

However, something remains unclear in such a "verdict": how about the correlation between freedom and responsibility? I will comment on this issue as following:

- responsibility is the "other face of medal" in the pair freedom–responsibility;
- no objectifying of the (right of) liberty is possible in the absence of the correlative (obligation of) responsibility;
- the obligation triggering in exerting the freedom is automatically (except, of course, the accidents sanctioned by the rule of law), namely by activating the responsibility assigned to the act of freedom;
- as known from Praxeology, abstention is, like the act, a species of action; not voting means performing an action, as well as voting;
- instituting the obligation to vote would mean introducing an obligation without its (required) correlative in rights (because this "counterpart" already exists through the liberty to vote);

- as a concluding remark, it seems that instituting a mandatory vote does not improve, at least prima facie (namely, from a logical point of view), the functioning of democracy.

2.6 Functions of the State

The Structure of the Generic State

From the perspective of systems theory, the components of the state are the following: (a) the leading subsystem; (b) the driven subsystem; (c) the control and stability subsystem.

- (C1) the *leading/director subsystem*, represented by the three powers in the state[74]: the legislative power (Parliament), the executive power (Government[75]), and the judicial power. The three powers, regulated by means of the fundamental law of the state (Constitution), form what is called the basic structure of society, generated by the very conclusion of the social contract. The leading subsystem transmits, to the driven subsystem, rules and orders (i.e., norms) of an institutional type and receives execution or control reports;
- (C2) the *driven/led subsystem*, represented by all the operational subsystems of society represented by the state: economic, educational, health, defence, public order, cultural, etc. The driven subsystem transmits execution reports to the leading subsystem and receives institutional norms;
- (C3) *the control and stability* subsystem, represented by structures established by the Constitution to monitor, avoid, cancel, or reduce the violation of the basic structure of society. This category includes a public body for constitutional control[76] and one for financial control of public money.[77]

The internal (logical) functioning of the state can be represented as shown in Fig. 5.

The Functions of the Generic State

The functions of a system, and therefore of the state, are generated by its structure. We have seen, above, the three structural components, at an abstract level (Fig. 5) of the state. In my opinion, the generic functions of the generic state are the following[78]:

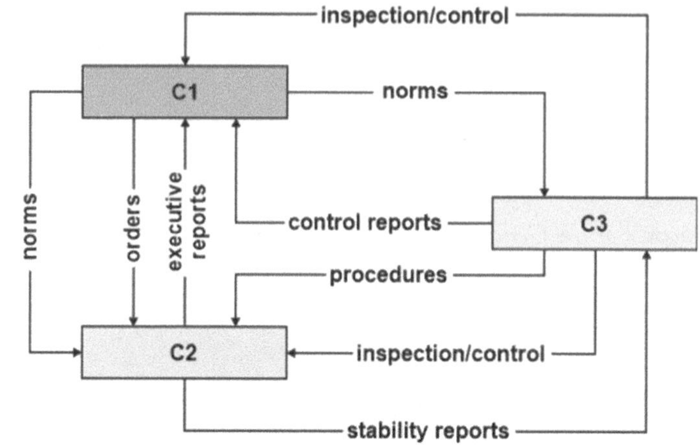

Fig. 5 Functionality of the state system (*Source* author)

- (F_1) *economic administration*: refers to ensuring economic production and distribution for the final consumption of the population, at the standards set as being contextually desirable[79];
- (F_2) *life preservation*: refers to ensuring conditions, considered contextually desirable, for the health of individuals, their defence against dangers to life and physical integrity, and the like;
- (F_3) *cultural-spiritual development*: refers to ensuring conditions, considered contextually desirable, with regard to education, instruction, cultural and/or spiritual manifestation, and the like, regarding the individuals and communities;
- (F_4) *administering of justice*: refers to ensuring the unconditional equality of individuals before the law, by objectifying the moral principle[80] of the rule of law; this function also includes the achievement of social justice (of which, in fact, the administration of justice is a component, namely the judicial component);
- (F_5) *existential defence*: refers to ensuring (from a diplomatic point of view and, if necessary, from the perspective of military force) the preservation of the sovereignty, integrity, and identity of the state.

It is useful to establish, at least in general terms, a hierarchy (of importance/relevance) of the five generic functions of the state system. In my

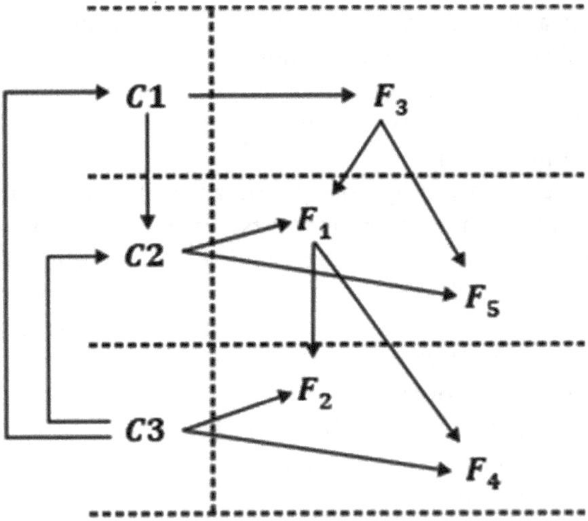

Fig. 6 Order of importance/relevance of state functions (*Source* author)

opinion, such a hierarchy must be established on lexicographic grounds, that is, on the basis of the researcher's intuition, on the one hand, and on the basis of very general justifications derived from the purpose for which the state was "invented",[81] on the other hand. In this sense, the "distribution" of state functions could be as follows (Fig. 6).

3 The Politic

3.1 Preamble

The term *politic* comes from Greek word *polis* (town/city, citadel), meaning "the affairs of the city". By abstracting, it can be said that the term *politic* characterizes, in the most general sense, any interaction between (at least two) individuals concerning any exchange between them of their own interests: resources, survival, life conditions, personal development, and so on. The above-mentioned content of the term *politic* generates the following sufficiency predicates aimed at defining the concept in question:

- (S_1^P) it is a *social concept*: the politic (or the property of the politic) arises only in a social group of individuals, that is, in a community of individuals which cannot live or survive than in such a community. Somewhat, the sociality is a necessary property of those individuals, not a contingent one;
- (S_2^P) it regards a *pooling*: the politic arises if and only if many individuals put together their interests, so generating a pool of such interests that are shared by all individuals involved. How such a pool is formed should be considered the effect of a *sui generis* invisible hand—the best description of this forming is provided by Robert Nozick (1999) in his theory of state emergence outside of a (standard) social contract;
- (S_3^P) it implies a *common* (public) *choice*: the politic provides the possibility that the community concerned to commonly make decision, by using some ways to compare the different positionings/preferences and to harmonize them to a "common nominator". The most known and used such a way is, of course, the democracy;
- (S_4^P) it implies the *authority*: authority means the recognizing and accepting the power of someone from the part of those who are affected by the exertion of that power. Such a recognition can have either an explicit or an implicit character, and, based on this sufficient predicate, the property of the politic is usually described as an authority-based power.

So, if it is noted the concept *politic* with P, then we can write, formally:

$$P \leftarrow \left(S_1^P\right) \bigwedge \left(S_2^P\right) \bigwedge \left(S_3^P\right) \bigwedge \left(S_4^P\right) \equiv \bigwedge\nolimits_{1=1}^{4} S_i^P$$

Nota bene 1: the (social) power can be acquired in many ways, equally performative: heredity (in monarchies), force (coups d'État), elections (democracy), acclamations (totalitarianism), and so on. However, only democracy can "guarantee" the authority, as being directly (or indirectly, after the case) conferred by the voters. It is not prohibited that other ways to be socially empowered to gain authority—in a decreasing order of the possibility (perhaps, even of the probability), these ways are: (a) heredity; (b) acclamations; (c) coup d'État. But what happens if the authority is not gained (more precisely, is not conferred by the driven subsystem)? In this case, logically, the property of the politic is not generated, so, that community, which is, however, a society,[82] remains a non-political society. How could we call a non-political society? Probably: a gregarious society.

Nota bene 2: we can ask now: other individuals than the humans, i.e., the non-human individuals (like bees, ants, lions, etc.) can also gain the property of the politic? My answer is negative, since:

- in the non-human communities, the third sufficient predicate (S_3^P) is violated, because the choice for the community in case is made by the so-called α-individual, not by a deliberation within the community so the final decision be approved, in one way or another by all the individuals of the community;
- in the non-human communities, the fourth sufficient predicate (S_4^P) is violated, because the hierarchy between the leading subsystem and the driven subsystem/s is generated by a force-based power, not by an authority-based power, as in the human communities.

In fact, in the non-human communities (social aggregates of individuals) we have a non-political property ($\overline{P}$) of those communities;

$$\overline{P} \leftarrow \left(S_1^P\right) \wedge \left(S_2^P\right) \wedge \left\{\left(\overline{S}_3^P\right) \vee \left(\overline{S}_4^P\right) \vee \left[\left(\overline{S}_3^P\right) \wedge \left(\overline{S}_4^P\right)\right]\right\}$$

So, in the non-human communities, there are, also, sociality of the individuals (S_1^P), as well as the pooling of mutual interests of any nature (S_2^P).

The violation (negation) of the last two sufficiency predicates (S_3^P and S_4^P) could happen in the human societies as well.

3.2 Politic, State, Democracy

The politic is, of course, a thing,[83] more precisely, an artefactual thing. The politic is a social construction within society, forming a distinct social body alongside other social bodies. In this paragraph, I shall briefly examine the correlations among three artefactual bodies within the society: the politic, the state, and the democracy.

The Politic and the State

Firstly, it must be clarified a sort of "chronology" of the emergence of the state, respectively, of the politic. More exactly, the question is: does the state arise before the politic or inversely? The answer is not too easy to provide; therefore, I shall list some considerations around this question that, I hope, will deliver sufficient reflections to decide between "egg or hen".

- according to both the theories of the state based, respectively, on the social contract (e.g., John Rawls) or on the invisible hand (e.g., Robert Nozick), there is an initial moment/interval at which some actions generate a "seed" of the state[84];
  - in both cases, some agreement arises among the participants (contemporary) individuals regarding a set of principles or of common interests that are considered to be essential and able to provide a good life for those individuals;
  - both the ways establish, de facto (and, logically, *de jure* too) the state—so, it seems that the state arises before the politic;
  - to be observed, however, that we have, here, exactly a pooling regarding either the principles of society functioning or the values considered to be sacrosanct. But this pooling is the very second sufficiency predicate (S_2^P) in the definition of the politic—so, it seems that the state emerging must be grounded on the politic (at least under this sufficiency predicate); in fact, the sufficiency predicates S_1^P and S_3^P are implicitly verified in the event of state emerging—regarding the sufficiency predicate S_4^P of the politic, it seems, also, to be verified (at least, principled), since in the initial moment there is a mutual grant of trust (so, of authority) among the participant individuals;
- based on the above reasoning, I would conclude the question as follows:
  - at the initial moment, both the state and the politic form a tandem (diad); any "tentative" of the state to emerge generates the politic, and reciprocally, any "tentative" of the politic to emerge generates the state;
  - it is true that we have, for now, only rudiments of both the state and the politic, since not all the sufficient predicates of the two artefacts are plenary built and completely in force;
  - so, it seems that the state and the politic are the two faces of the same medal—we could call that medal as being the very society.

This is the logical argument of using the syntagma "societal" instead of "social";

- consequently, the relationship between the state and the politic is one of logical contiguity and causal circularity, so that either of the two artefacts is an existential mark of the other.[85]

Nota bene: we can say, now, that the leading subsystem of the state, above discussed, is (generically speaking) constituted exactly by the politic (or political body of the society).

The Politic and the Democracy

Once the state and the politic enter the Being, and, as a result, form a society, the public choice issue is inevitable and, more than that, crucial (in fact, even critical).

We must remember that both the state and the politic arisen in the presence and agreement of all future members of the emerging society. From a logical point of view, in the initial moment (originary position, as this moment is coined in the theory of the state), we had a democratic choice, since all the interested individuals, who follow to be affected by the decision in the case, voted.[86] At any rate, the problem of public (communitarian) choice concomitantly or, at least, immediately further arises in the presence of the state and the politic.

Obviously, once the politic arose as the leading subsystem of the state/society, it adjudicates the right to decide regarding how the public choice is (more exactly, must be) made. In the periods immediately subsequent to the originary position, the method of making the public decision is, almost certainly, the democracy, that is the vote of all individuals interested in and affected by the decision in question. However, the next stages of the society's functioning could bring changes in the system of public decision-making. Some considerations in this matter could be the following:

- in proportion as the participatory democracy becomes, practically, impossible (for example, because the increase of population), some points of bifurcation[87] could appear in choosing of the public decision-making system; so, this system could pass into a representative democracy,[88] or in different species of non-democracy: authoritarianism, dictature, and others of the same, i.e., systems avoiding the functional[89] vote of the population involved;

- in fact, the more the necessity of political representativeness, the more the risk of hijacking of the popular vote, because the increasing "social distance" between population and the political body. In other words, the alienation of the representatives related to the represented is increasing and the representatives tend to become more and more autonomous related to their voters. This process of autonomization is necessarily accompanied by a decrease in the authority of the political body, that is, the political power becomes more and more based on norms than on individuals' trust;
- so, the democracy, in its representativity hypostasis, is not non-problematic for the politic. Consequently, either the concept of democracy or the concept of representativeness must be revisited in order to preserve the sovereignty in the "hands" of the population involved and, at the same time, ensure the verification of the initial principles of instituting both the state and the politic;
- of course, the state will exist and function no matter the way/system of public decision-making, and the necessary pair between state and democracy is not without polemics. In this regard, I shall make some extra considerations:
- according to the pyramid of values (Fig. 3), equality, which implies the equality of the vote in the public decision-making process, is an intermediate value between natural/biological survival and freedom. Consequently, in contemporary societies, where the natural/biological survival of individuals within the communities is ensured, the equality among individuals becomes the proximal interest to them[90];
- as a result, there will be a permanent pressure from the population towards the democratic organization of the society,[91] but, of course, such a pressure could prove insufficient to move the society in the case to democracy;
- the orientation of the politic to a democratic organization of society depends on the balance between the life realization of individuals, on the one hand, and the (generic) security of them, on the other hand. More exactly, the political body of society could argue in the following ways:
  - choosing of the societal model aimed at providing the plenary (for example, happy) realization of the life could be considered

compatible with the experts only,[92] not with ordinary individuals, by saying that the democracy means that the majority of population vote (in a political competition) a model proposed by experts, since the mass of population has not the expertise to design such a model;
- moreover, another argument could be brought in order to reject democracy: the democratic process of public decision-making is too expensive (the Parliament) and too slow (the democratic procedures), so that the most efficient decision is a non-democratic one;
- the priority of security, of all kinds (including the military one), seems to tip the option towards a unipersonal (either dictatorial or, at least, authoritarian[93]) decision.

To conclude, the pair *the politic–the democracy* is the desirable solution for ordinary/normal times, although in extraordinary times the democracy could be (legally) suspended in order to preserve values of a higher order, for example, freedom, which is placed, in Fig. 3, above the equality.

The State and the Democracy
Of course, the pair *the state–the democracy* will follow the general conclusions extracted from analysing the pair the politic–the democracy, since the politic and the state are mutually inalienable, as shown before. However, some specificities of this pair could be put into evidence, as follows:

- the most natural pair in the society's functioning is that of state–democracy, since the very state arises in a *sui generis* democratic way in the original position of "signing" the social contract;
- the authority of the state (namely, the power based on authority) is at the highest level, exactly by the democratic way of public decision-making.

3.3 Politic, Policy, Politics

As shown above, the politic is a thing, more precisely, an artefact within the general process of social construction. The politic is ontologized into the so-called political body of the society. Principled, the state has two components: (a) the *political* body; (b) the *administrative* body. Both the components constitute the leading subsystem of the society. The political body is just the politic as artefact.

From conceptual perspective, the politic has two outcomes: (i) the policy; (b) the politics. In this paragraph, some considerations will be provided on the two outcomes.

(i) The policy

Like the politic, the policy is a thing. By policy is understood the set of decisions and actions (either as acts—to do, or as abstentions—not to do) aimed at implementing the thing called politic. Generally, the term policy has as its scope the society as a whole, but, occasionally and somewhat by language abuse, policy can also be used for micro-levels or even individual level, to indicate/describe a rational texture of decision/action in achieving a purpose. While the term policy usually addresses the public set of decisions/actions, many times it is also used to refer to private sets of such decisions/actions. It must hold some features of the term policy in the triad politic–policy–politics, namely:

- except the common linguistic root (originating from Greek *polis*), the term policy has no other semantic connections with the term politic and, as we will see, with the term politics. In fact, policy should be understood rather as a coherent description of an actional algorithm based on a rationality model and aimed at achieving a certain goal;
- this rather technical meaning of the term policy allows us to use it in any field of human action and at any level of aggregation of that action;
- the only held connection of the term policy with the term politic refers to the fact that, especially in the case of public policy, the politic is the ground, in a causal meaning, of the policy. In other words, the policy is politically "coloured".

To be mentioned that the policy is connected, generally, with the administrative body of the state.

(ii) The politics

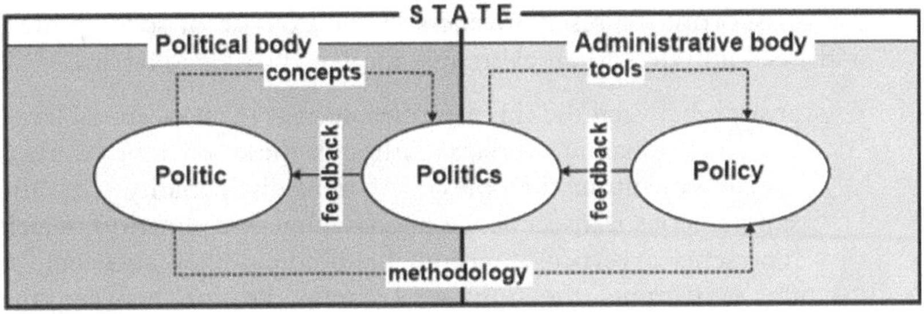

Fig. 7 Topology of triad politic–politics–policy (*Source* author)

Unlike the terms *politic* and *policy*, politics is a property, neither a thing nor a relationship. It is, more exactly, that property characterizing both the politic and the policy. This characterization consists in focusing on the societal affairs or communitarian ones.

Usually, the set of decisions/actions unfolded by the state is subsumed under the term of politics. In this perspective, one could speak of politics as a thing, which is not too far from reality. In fact, this statute of a thing associated with politics is supported by the ways and institutions in which politics is objectified in society: the political parties. So, the politics seems to be a hybrid "animal", that is, half property, half thing.

To be mentioned that the politics is connected, generally, with the political body of the state.

Synoptically, Fig. 7 provides an image of the three concepts above discussed.

4 The Triad *Knowledge–Democracy–Freedom*

4.1 *Preamble*

Regarding the Concepts

The approach of the three issues mentioned in the heading requires, first of all, the clarification of some issues of legitimacy:

a. how is it permissible to join three concepts that claim to come from distinct areas of interest: knowledge refers to the intellectual infrastructure of any human action, democracy refers to a type of vehicle for transporting representativeness in the exercise of social power, and freedom refers to an existential ideal at the individual level?[94]

- answer: between the three entities, seen at the conceptual level, there are semantic overlaps. Although these semantic overlaps usually constitute the sources of trans-disciplinarity (i.e., the simultaneous transcendence of coexisting disciplinarity), which represents a vertical conceptual unfolding, they also fuel, at the same time, the horizontal communication between the concepts involved; therefore, the circle closes around the three concepts;

b. how is it permissible to join three concepts that claim to be of different natures: a necessary concept (knowledge), a contingent concept (democracy), and a normative concept (freedom)?

- answer: knowledge has freedom as its necessary goal, freedom has democracy as its structural matrix, and democracy represents the best way to ensure the indirect representativeness of the desirable models required by knowledge; therefore, the circle closes again around the three concepts;

c. how is it permissible to join three concepts that claim to be of different reasons: a concept that claims to be of pure reason (knowledge), a concept that claims to be of instrumental[95] reason (democracy), and a concept that claims to be of practical reason (freedom)?

- answer: knowledge (the intelligibility of the world) deals with the object-object relationship, democracy deals with the object-subject relationship,[96] and freedom considers the subject-subject relationship; so, for the third time, the circle closes around the three concepts.

Regarding the Grounding

Addressing the three issues mentioned above calls, secondly, for clarification of some motivational issues:

a. why is it relevant to discuss the triad knowledge–democracy–freedom?

- answer: because modern societies are faced with a paradox of democracy: in the absence (or insufficiency) of knowledge, democracy is much more permissive in confiscating legitimacy than other vehicles of representativeness;

b. why is it appropriate to discuss the triad knowledge–democracy–freedom?

- answer: after 36 years of social reconstruction in Romania (but also in other states that started on the same path at the time of 1989), a serious degradation and, unfortunately, with a trend of the same nature, of the values that govern society is observed, which also implies the perversion of freedom;

c. how could the triad knowledge–democracy–freedom (KDF) be developed?

- answer: probably the tetrad knowledge–democracy–freedom–responsibility (KDFR) should be constructed; indeed, freedom without responsibility leads (not necessarily, but there is such a possibility) to inter-individual (possibly also inter-group) domination.

4.2 *Knowledge and Democracy*

Democracy is one of the possible vehicles for "transporting" representativeness. Representativeness is the praxiological aspect of sovereignty, and sovereignty is the repository of legitimate (social) power. Therefore, since, at least in the conditions of modern societies where the population in a legal system such as the state is relatively large, sovereignty cannot be exercised directly (participatively[97]), it is delegated,[98] through an accepted procedure, to representatives of that population: this is the concept of representativeness. Since representativeness is an artefact, it can, of course, be either genuine or falsified. Falsified representativeness is, in my opinion, a necessary result of either a low or inadequate level of knowledge.[99] There are several specific consequences of a low or inadequate level of knowledge regarding the legitimacy of the delegation of sovereignty use (i.e., regarding the authenticity of representativeness):

a. the choosing of representativeness (which is done, of course, by exercising the right of secret, universal, and equal[100] voting) has, in the background, the expectation that the individual (or group, for example, the political party) to whom sovereignty use has been delegated will implement a model of society (in full or in some components considered important, desirable or opportune) that those who delegate sovereignty use propose. If the voter[101] does not have the level of knowledge, for example, the degree of general education, which would allow him/her to consciously and coherently form the model[102] he/she expects from the one he/she voted for, then his/her vote cannot ensure representativeness, that is, as I said above, the authenticity of the act of delegating sovereignty use. Throughout history, some skilful politicians have speculated exactly this channel of manipulation of obtaining the delegation of sovereignty use;

b. the insufficient or inadequate nature of knowledge can also lead to another consequence: it is possible that the politician who is a candidate for receiving the delegation of sovereignty use, who knows that the voter does not have a desirable model to impose on him/her, may himself/herself offer such a model to the voter. This model may be manipulative, in the sense that, although it seems to offer a favourable target to the voter, in reality, it will offer advantages precisely to the politician who is asking for the vote. This false legitimacy is possible precisely as a result of the insufficient or inadequate level of knowledge at the voter's level;
c. the insufficient or inadequate nature of knowledge can also have another of the most serious consequences: the lack of discernment in the allocation of the vote.[103] As is known from the behaviour of the voter,[104] he/she always evaluates the difference between the electoral promises (the model to be implemented) of a politician (or political party) and the actual political action after receiving, in the previous electoral exercise, his/her vote. Based on this assessment, the voter decides whether or not to vote again for that politician (or political party). However, a poor level of knowledge will not allow such an assessment of the voter's political positioning;
d. a political (and moral, in fact) anchor in respecting electoral promises is the political ideology of a politician (or political party) who requests the investiture with the use of sovereignty. This ideology is systematized in the political program. If the level of knowledge does not allow a correct analysis of these ideologies, then

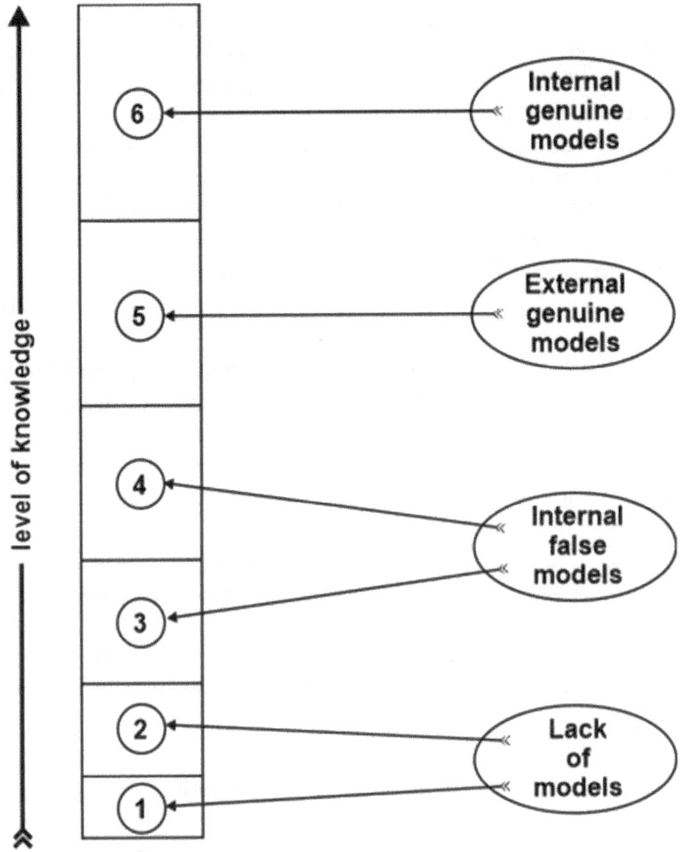

Fig. 8 Diad knowledge–democracy (*Source* author)

the delegation of sovereignty use through voting will lack rationality and, consequently, legitimacy.

Figure 8 provides an image of the diad knowledge–democracy (KD).

4.3 *Knowledge and Freedom*

The connection between knowledge and freedom is probably the most important in the KDF triad. As is known, the most general (and most frequent) framework for defining freedom is that of the relationship between necessity and free will,[105] in other words, freedom begins where necessity ends.[106] However, it is worth noting that this framework defines only individual freedom, without any social context. As the human individual has, by definition, a social nature,[107] we need a definition of freedom in this new framework. In general, we can accept that freedom represents a state of the individual in which he/she can choose (either under conditions of relative constraint,[108] or in the absence of any perceptible constraint[109]) according to his/her own preferences. If he/she cannot choose so, then we are faced with necessity (or absolute constraint).

Well, we can now see the extremely close relationship between knowledge and freedom. Knowledge provides the alternatives of choice, in the sense that the higher the level of knowledge, the more numerous the alternatives of choice, so freedom has a wider area of manifestation. In fact, a true virtuous circle occurs here, because a wider area of manifestation of freedom allows, among the choices, to be found...exactly the knowledge which, in turn, expands the area of manifestation of freedom, and so on. If knowledge is not segmented (for example, if it is not restricted, contingently, to certain individuals or to certain classes of individuals or to certain sectors of knowledge), then the area of manifestation of freedom expands for all individuals. Let us note here some important issues:

a. expanding the area of manifestation of freedom for contemporary individuals is not a zero-sum process (of the win-loss type); the emergence of new alternatives of choice for one individual does not lead to the disappearance of those alternatives for other individuals, because the alternatives in question may not be competing, but independent of each other, for different individuals. As a result, the expansion of the sphere of freedom as an effect of the progress of knowledge is a positive sum (win–win) process. This interstitialization of non-competing alternatives following the progress of knowledge is one of the most important effects of the dynamics of freedom in sophisticated modern societies, and political theory has not yet investigated it in a sufficiently analytical way.[110]
b. both knowledge and freedom are strongly individually contextualized concepts. In fact, only a very small part of knowledge is

communicable inter-personally (this is the knowledge of the scientific type, which communicates causal descriptions with unique meaning for the receptors, in fact, which transmits only denotatively or referentially), while most of the knowledge remains at the level of comprehension, which is completely individualized (idiosyncratic) and almost in-communicable inter-personally. Likewise, the feeling of freedom is an incommunicable one; therefore the freedoms of different individuals can intersect without affecting each other..[111] Moreover, freedom is only contextually dependent to a small extent and, above all, in its superficial determinants.[112]

Figures 9 and 10 provide images of the diad knowledge–freedom (KF).

4.4 Democracy and Freedom

This relationship raises fundamental questions regarding not only the nature of freedom, but even the nature of democracy. We know that democracy is only one of the possible vehicles for "transporting" representativeness. Does democracy have features that make it "preferable" among the (all possible) vehicles for "transporting" representativeness? There are several aspects that I wish to highlight here:

a. the meaning of life is most likely given by the occurrence of freedom.[113] The question that arises is the following: is freedom a matter of result or a matter of procedure? Given what has been stated above, I believe that freedom is of a procedural matter.[114] In other words, if the vehicle for "transporting" representativeness ensures, to a reasonable extent, the procedure (for example, the functioning of the political body) which, logically, has as its effect the non-discriminatory individual freedom, then that vehicle is acceptable from an institutional (and even cultural or axiological) point of view. Let us note that the procedural "version" of freedom does not indicate any criteria for selecting the vehicle.[115] On the other hand, the irrelevance of freedom as a result also stems from the fact that freedom is an exclusively individual "finding", at the level of comprehension. The apperception of freedom is vague, personal, contextual, global (similar to æsthetic or theological apperception),

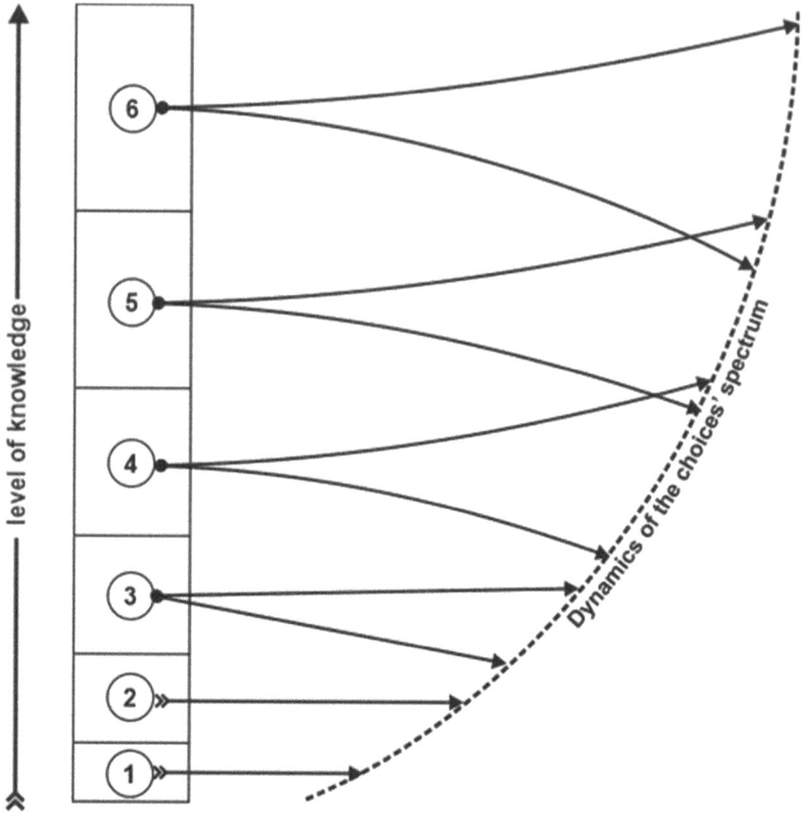

Fig. 9 Diad knowledge–freedom (I) (*Source* author)

all of which are characteristics that elude an analysis of the result, being accessible only to a procedural analysis[116];

b. if freedom is of a procedural matter, but not one of a result, this means that there are, nevertheless, criteria for selecting, *ex ante*,[117] the vehicle of representativeness. It seems that social history indicates a constant propensity (with cessions, but also with persevering resumes) towards a vehicle to "transport" representativeness that verifies the criterion of equality of position. Democracy is a vehicle that verifies this criterion: for example, the vote to delegate the sovereignty use is equal.[118] Although the different institutional

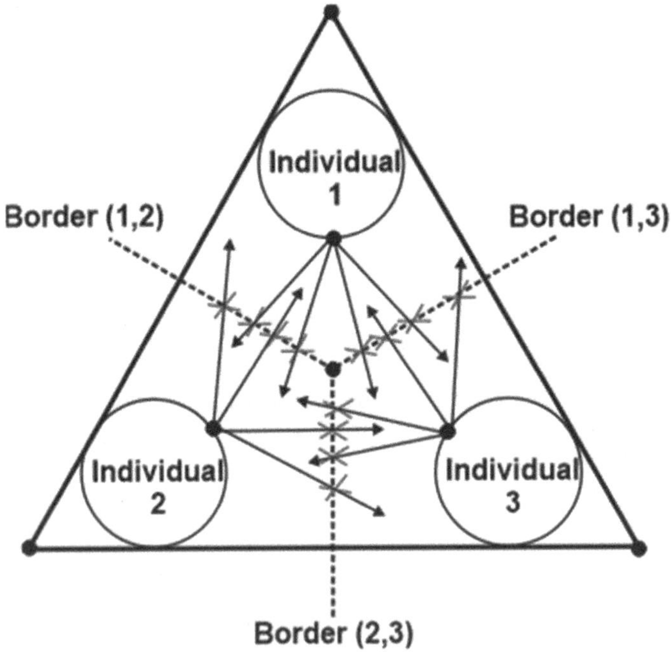

Fig. 10 Diad knowledge–freedom (II) (*Source* author)

ways of "calculating" the result of the vote may introduce nuances (majority vote, proportional vote, etc.), the idea of equality remains as a hard core of this selection of procedure. In this context, the social philosopher has great difficulties in attempting to argue for the substitution of democracy as a vehicle to "transport" representativeness, in order to ensure (procedurally, not as a result) freedom;

c. since democracy represents only a "promise" of the achievement of freedom, it is true that a promise that results from the consistent application of the constitutional principles that "translate" the democratic ideal of society, one can never know whether this promise has de facto been honoured or not. However, de jure (i.e., strictly procedurally), freedom will be considered to be ensured;

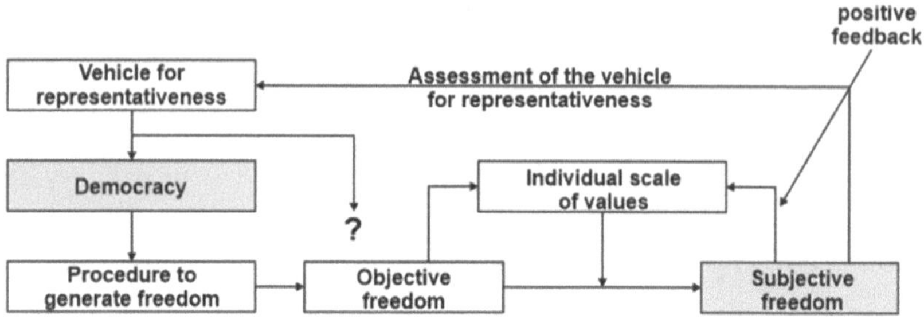

Fig. 11 Diad democracy–freedom (*Source* author)

d. in any vehicle to "transport" representativeness, positive feedback operates, i.e., the vehicle is strengthened (possibly procedurally perfected) by its very use.[119]Democracy is permanently strengthened by its own functioning, because the production of freedom increasingly requires the maintenance of the procedure that "secrets" it.

Figure 11 provides an image of the diad democracy–freedom (DF).

5 Beyond the Triad KDF

Generally, the knowledge–democracy–freedom (KDF) triad functions, even if, for each of the components and for the triad as such, there are still many imperfections, underdevelopments, inconsistencies, or even functional (but not structural) contradictions. Our assessment of these aspects is the following[120]:

- there is a *deficit of responsibility*. In fact, the (possible) KDFR (R stays for responsibility) tetrad is still not built across the world (in Romania, as well), and this should, perhaps, constitute a structural objective for an authentic generical political party. This state of affairs is the effect of a serious deficit in knowledge, both at the level of mandatory education (especially) and at the level of optional education.[121] The absence of the attitude formation component in the competence structure undermines the formation of responsibility. However, in the model of democracy, responsibility is the only negative feedback. This issue is a very delicate one, because the problem of responsibility does not have to do with external instances of control (i.e., of institutional type), as is the case with accountability, but with internal instances (i.e., of ethical/moral type) of verification and control. Therefore, the formation of responsibility is impossible without the formation of attitude. The introduction of attitude formation into the phenomenon of knowledge seems a little unnatural, because attitude is not about intellect, but about character, since the person is a complex entity and constitutes a totality[122];

- there is a *deficit of knowledge*, that is evident in the lack of models of social construction/reconstruction of Romania, an effect of both the narrowness of the information horizon and, above all, the precariousness of philosophical reflection on the progress of Romanian society. The political programs (not to mention the governing programs) of all parties that aspire to make decisions based on their representativeness are rather lists of short-term desirability (pilot programs) than long-term strategies (construction programs). Most politicians who aspire to the sovereignty use delegating to them are far from adequately understanding the deep political, sociological, and axiological issues that must guide, from the background, the dynamics of Romanian society. Their ideal is not to objectify a model of social life, but they have a much more "practical" target[123];
- there is a *deficit of democracy* that is evident in the commercialization of the right to vote (and we are not referring here only to the grotesque, feudal-type aspect of electoral bribery, but to the quasi-general behaviour of parties and parliamentarians who are willing to capitalize on their position on the political stage, namely the vote held in the legislative institution). Of course, a large part of this behaviour of mimicking democracy (in fact, of coercion and diversion on it) is explained by the deficit of knowledge (especially at the level of attitude formation, as shown above), but another part is generated by a process (which is logical, in emerging democracies) of coagulation of a special layer of "elected", respectively of "appointed" by the "elected", namely, a layer that creates (invents) and monopolizes public[124] privileges[125];
- there is a *deficit of freedom* that manifests itself in two ways: (1) one in the responsibility of the state: by reducing or not expanding the sphere of choice at the individual level (for example, insufficient involvement or lack of involvement of the state in creating alternatives of choice, especially in the economic field, but not only);

(2) one in the responsibility of individuals: by expanding their own sphere of choice over the sphere of choice of the other. This kind of manifestation of the freedom deficit is both the effect of the knowledge deficit and the effect of the democracy deficit and, very likely, is the main crucible in which these states of deficit are reproduced. Freedom understood as free will (which means a freedom without limits, broken from any social foundation) is as great a danger as the lack of freedom. Extremes, as we see, are also reached in this area.

In Fig. 12 is described the functioning of the tetrad KDFR.

Nota bene: to go beyond the tetrad KDFR (as I would do) means to introduce sustainability as an embedder of the tetrad, that is the pentad KDFRS. A suggestion for such a further step is provided in Fig. 13.

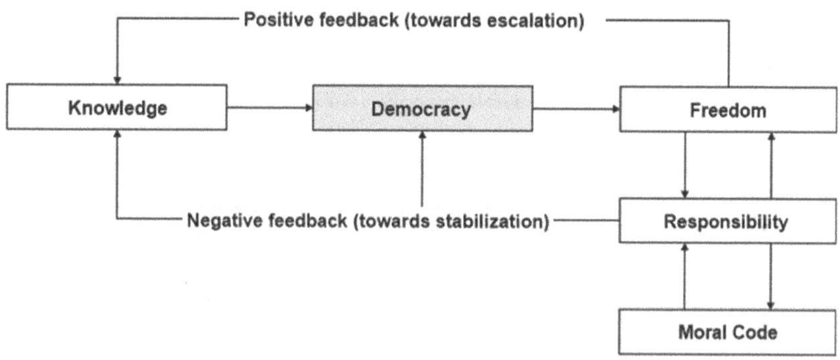

Fig. 12 Tetrad knowledge–democracy–freedom–responsibility (*Source* author)

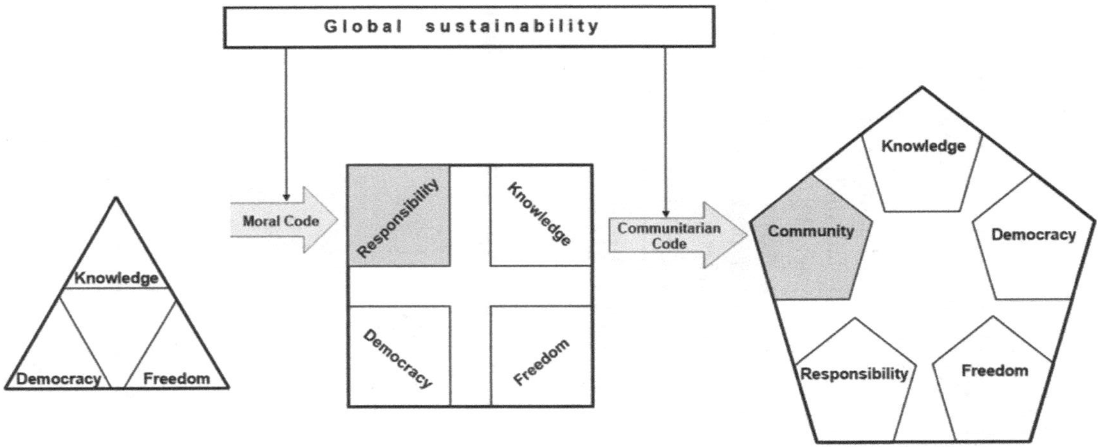

Fig. 13 Pentad knowledge–democracy–freedom–responsibility–sustainability (*Source* author)

Annex i: The Relationship Between Capabilities and Public Goods

Discussion

(i) the capabilities proposed by Nussbaum are not public goods, in the sense in which we define them in this research:

- some of the capabilities proposed by Nussbaum concern opportunities for the functioning of the generic human being that do not necessarily fall under the state's obligation to ensure them—for example, (1) *life*, or (4) *senses, imagination and thought*, or (8) *other species*, are not opportunities that the state can and should offer or, at least, create the institutional conditions for their manifestation;
- other such capabilities, such as: (2) *bodily health*, or (10) *control over one's own environment*, represent mixed obligations of the individual and the state, only in this way can they being fully manifested;

Table 2 Comparative analysis of the capabilities list—C (Nussbaum) and the public goods list—PGs

PG / *C*	PG_1^2	PG_2^2	PG_3^2	PG_4^2	PG_5^2	PG_6^2	PG_7^2	PG_8^2	PG_9^2	PG_{10}^2
1. Life	x			x						
2. Bodily health	x									
3. Bodily integrity	x									
4. Senses, imagination, and thought			x		x		x	x	x	x
5. Emotion						x		x	x	x
6. Practical reason		x	x		x	x	x			
7. Affiliation		x	x			x	x			
8. Other species						x				
9. Play		x	x		x		x	x		
10. Control over one's environment	x			x		x				

Source author

- others, for example, (5) *emotion*, represent capabilities/ opportunities that are exclusively available to the generic human individual, since they are to the highest degree idiosyncratic and over them the state has and can have only, at most, an indirect influence at the level of the status it confers on society as a whole.

(ii) the public goods proposed by us can underlie capabilities, even in a multiplicative way:

- as follows from Table 2, any of the categories of public goods proposed intersects between two (e.g.: PG_4^2) and five (e.g.: PG_6^2) capabilities proposed by Nussbaum, from the perspective of their significance (i.e., of the semantic content or, equivalently, of the referential in question);
- at the same time, no capability proposed by Nussbaum remains "uncovered" by at least one of the public goods proposed by us;
- based on the above, we can conclude that the system of public goods proposed by us is more primitive (more basic) than the list of capabilities proposed by Nussbaum. Of course, this issue is not a goal of the present study, so we will not develop these considerations further, although they may be the subject of a subsequent punctual examination in another context.

Annex 2: Norm: Concept, Genesis, Status

1. *Conceptual issues*

In general, by norm we mean a rule, an abstract prescriptive formula or a concrete indication regarding the way to carry out a theoretical or practical action or activity, respectively of logical thinking, creation, and behaviour.

The norms or rules of human actions—individual or social—are established or formulated in principles, laws, and customs, and are imposed by the very "authority" of the experience accumulated in the actual action process. Science attests that the very genesis of intellectual acts represents a result of an inter-conditioning of two processes of thought:

a. the internalization and generalization of motor acts performed or observed by the subject (Jean Piaget);
b. the improvement of the psychic activity of the human individual under the influence of practical and social acts, of the acquisition of language and culture (H. Wallon).

Thus, Piaget demonstrates that, starting from the object and actions, the child conquers through reconstructions, and constructs the real, based on experience and through actions of internalization of the real from which the operations of logical thinking originate (or what Kant called transcendental apperception).

Norms, therefore, represent rules regarding the conduct of agents of individual and social action, which determine, for distinct classes of circumstances, which conducts are obligatory (O), forbidden/prohibited (F), or permitted (P).

Norms have two points of origin:

- the generalization of practical experience (following the balance of results);
- the rational projection of the desirability of the agent(s).

So, norms are not simple descriptions of fact but also prospects, anticipations, and evaluations of human conduct from the perspective of a system of values. They are, therefore, *projected prototypes of human conduct*.

Generally, in the world, there are several categories of regularities or laws, therefore of pre-established conduct:

- laws of nature;
- laws of the state (projected by the generic action subject)—*Nota bene*: the so-called positive laws;
- laws of logic (thought).

Norms have numerous affinities with the general term of law but they are not laws in the sense of the laws of nature (which are necessarily true and have a purely descriptive character), rather approaching the laws of the state and, partially, the laws of logic (which have a prescriptive character). In this sense, terms such as: model, standard, rule, law, and regulation are frequently used for the concept of norm. Therefore, some norms that come from the laws of nature or that simply describe, in a neutral way, a relationship of consequence (necessarily or only contingently true) are not considered norms themselves. We, therefore, retain as norms only those prescriptions that refer to action. However, there are some so-called ideal rules, that is, norms that do not refer to action but to existence, and which implicitly contain rules of conduct (e.g., "a soldier must be brave") and which, for this reason, are nevertheless considered norms. This type of norm is closely related to the moral concept of good.

The question arises of the primacy of action over norms or of the norm over action. Although, from a formal point of view, when we act, there is already a norm that regulates conduct, from an ontological point of view, the action precedes the norm. Even in the case of the anticipatory, valorizing component of the norm, this also comes from the imperative of a past practical experience. So, the action precedes the norm not only genetically but also ontologically. Moreover, in practice, it is considered/appreciated that a norm is respected only if the prescriptive proposition of the norm coincides with the descriptive proposition of the actual conduct of the subject of the norm. *Nota bene*: I invite the reader to notice the similarity with Popper's falsifiabilist procedure, which takes also into account the factual/empirical.

From the point of view of the genesis of the norm, there are four main determinations of it:

(1) *epistemological* determination: the norm-quality relationship;
(2) *axiological* determination: the norm-legislator relationship;
(3) *actional* determination: the norm-addressee relationship (or the norm-subject relationship);
(4) *formal* determination: the norm-language relationship.

An essential aspect of the norm concept refers to its referential sphere. In this sense, it should be noted that norms do not refer to physical possible states but only to those actionally possible (e.g., the execution of the individual jump from the Earth to the Sun will not be regulated). Norms also do not refer to physically necessary states (e.g., the activity of breathing will not be regulated). We therefore conclude that norms refer to non-necessary and actionally possible states. Graphically, the referential sphere of norms is as follows (Fig. 14):

A norm has a well-determined structure:

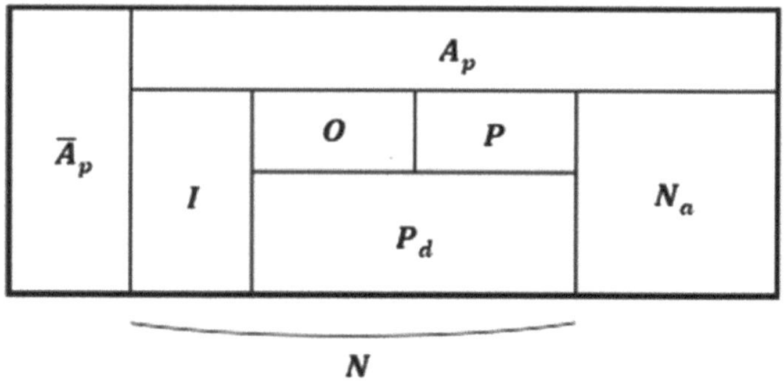

Fig. 14 Norm space (normative space). where A_p = the set of actionally possible states, $\overline{A}_p$ = the set of actionally impossible states, N_a = the actional necessary, N = the space of norms, P_d = the deontically possible, F = forbidden actions, O = obligatory actions, P = permitted actions (*Source* author)

(a) the *general component* (*nucleus*) of the norm, formed by:

(a1) the *character* of the norm (obligation, prohibition, permission);
(a2) the *content* of the norm (the conduct to be followed);
(a3) the *condition of application* (the domain of possibilities for realizing the content of the norm).

(b) the *specific component*, formed by:

(b1) the *normative authority* (the entity from which the norm emanates);
(b2) the *subject of the norm* (the recipient of the content of the norm);
(b3) the *occasion* (the place and time to which the content of the norm refers).

(c) the *functional component* of the norm, consisting of:

(c1) *promulgation* (giving the norm its formal aspect—e.g., publication in the Official Gazette);
(c2) *sanctioning* (penalizing non-compliance with the content of the norm).

2. *On the typology of the norms*

The most important classification of norms is made according to its

(i) *character* of the norm (a_1):

(i1) *obligations* (orders or commands), which refer to what must be done—denoted by O;
(i2) *permissions*, which refer to what can (not in the sense of action ability) be done—denoted by P;
(i3) *prohibitions*, which refer to what cannot (not in the sense of action ability) be done—denoted by F.

It should be noted that F-norms can be assimilated to a point with O-norms, in the sense that what cannot be done can be interpreted as what must not be done (or with the abstention from doing).

Nota bene: we should not absolutize the assimilation of prohibition-norms with obligation-norms or abstention-norms because this is not universally valid. If we exaggerate in considering that the prohibition as a norm has as its exclusive content what cannot be done and we interpret the inability to do as a rule of not having to do or as refraining from doing, we may end up in a situation of inhibiting the creative imagination, the audacity to formulate new hypotheses of knowledge and action that seemed, at a certain reference date, impossible. For example: human flight into space, satellite communications, the transmission of messages or states through telepathy, the search for extra-terrestrial civilizations, artificial intelligence, and many others. Also, the prohibition can be considered, in general terms, as a denial of permission, that is:

$$F = \overline{P} \text{ or } P = \overline{F}$$

(ii) according to the *content* of the norm (a_2):

(ii1) regarding the *scope*:
- norms of *action* (refer to acts or abstentions);
- norms of *activity* (refer to activities[126]);

(ii2) regarding the *practical meaning*:
- *affirmative* norms (the content of the norm is an act);
- *prohibiting* norms (the content of the norm is an abstention);
- *mixed* norms (the content of the norm refers to both acts and abstentions);

(ii3) regarding the complexity:

- *elementary* norms (the content is an elementary act or abstention, e.g., non-aggression);
- *compound* norms (the content is a compound act or abstention).

(iii) according to the *condition of application* of the norm (a_3):

(iii1) *categorical* norms (the condition of application is contained in the content, not being accompanied by any other additional condition);

(iii2) *hypothetical* norms (the condition of application is accompanied by another additional condition), e.g., defence in case of aggression, called legitimate defence.

(iv) according to the *normative authority* (b_1):

(iv1) *autonomous* or self-reflexive norms (they are not given by anyone or are issued by the subject of the norm itself, e.g., helping those in need or exclusively vegetarian nutrition);

(iv2) *heteronomous* norms (the authority is different from the subject of the norm). Heteronomous norms constitute the vast majority of norms, usually legal norms.

(v) according to the *subject of the norm* (b_2):

(v1) *particular* norms in relation to the subject (the norm is addressed to an individual specified in an unambiguous way, e.g., the one who holds the position of prosecutor);

(v2) *general* norms in relation to the subject (the norm is addressed to all those who meet a certain description, e.g., military discipline).

(vi) according to the occasion (b_3):

(vi1) *particular* norms in relation to the *occasion* (the norm refers to a concrete, individual, and unrepeatable occasion, e.g., the norms of international law that protect the right to be born);

(vi2) *general* norms in relation to the *occasion* (the norm refers to a category of occasions that can be repeated, e.g., the norms of law relating to marriages and divorces). In turn, general norms in relation to the occasion are classified into:

- *general conjunctive* norms (refer to all occasions with a certain description that can occur);
- *general disjunctive* norms (refer to at least one of the occasions of a certain description that can occur).

Nota bene: Due to the close functional connection between the subject of the norm and the occasion of the norm, the particular or general character of the norm is established simultaneously according to the two criteria. Thus, we will have particular norms, when they have a particular character both in relation to the subject and in relation to the occasion, or we have general norms when they are general either in relation to the subject or in relation to the occasion. If they are general simultaneously in relation to the subject and in relation to the occasion, then the norms are called *eminently general*, e.g., the legal regulations of monogamy, respectively of the monogamous family.

There is another classification of norms according to the way they act in practice. In this sense, the following categories of norms are circulated:

1. *rules*: norms that are simultaneously descriptive and prescriptive, resembling to a large extent the laws of logic (e.g., the rules of a game, the rules of grammar);
2. *prescriptions* (regulations): represent the most important category of norms. Moreover, the general structure of a norm, as well as the classification made according to the structural components above, expressly refers to prescriptions. The best-known prescriptions are the laws of the state;
3. *customs*: constitute a species of habits (habits represent acquired—not innate—regularities of behaviour, characterized by sociability or socialization. They are imposed by the community and sanctioned in a specific way (e.g., alienation from the rest of the community). Failure to comply with them attracts public opprobrium. It should be noted that customs differ both from regularities in nature (regularities in nature are statistical regularities—that is, they refer to the behaviour of mass phenomena and can present exceptions at the individual level—while customs are nomic regularities—that is, individual and do not allow exceptions) and from prescriptions (customs do not have a normative authority, they do not have a formal, codified character—that is, they are not promulgated, which

is why they are also called implicit prescriptions—and the sanction, as we mentioned, has a special form). It should also be noted that, unlike the laws of nature, but similar to prescriptions or even legal laws, customs have a normative character, that is, they influence behaviour, exerting a normative pressure on the members of the community. Some peoples or ethnic groups respect customary law, which, without being stipulated in legal laws, is not violated by anyone;

4. *instructions* (or technical norms): they refer to the means to be used to achieve a goal. They are neither descriptive nor prescriptive, but only show that a certain condition is necessary for something else. A distinction must be made between technical norms and hypothetical norms (which are, as shown above, prescriptions). Technical norms only show the imminent or necessary possibility if a certain condition is met, while hypothetical norms impose an obligation, a prohibition, or a permission if a certain condition is not met. Often, in the genesis of prescriptive norms, the extraction of these norms from a technical norm is carried out. This process is called practical inference, and many of the autonomous prescriptions are the result of such practical inferences. For example: in order to obtain a good harvest of cereals, it is necessary to observe the optimal sowing period; to ensure the healthy development of the newborn, natural breastfeeding is necessary; repetition is the mother of learning. Here are just a few examples of technical normativity that only indicate the possibility that, if a certain condition is met, we can obtain the expected result. As a rule, hypothetical norms or prescriptions are deduced from these technical norms, in the case of our examples: prescriptions regarding land cultivation (agricultural technology), child care (puericulture), and education-instruction (pedagogy);
5. *moral* norms: they are a special category of norms with a pronounced autonomous character and combining features of all other categories of norms. Very controversial on a theoretical (even philosophical) level, they have a special status. Moral norms, as regulating the principles of human coexistence in relation to their fellow human beings (and even non-human beings), express certain prescriptions, recommendations, and action-behavioural models, which an individual must respect and carry out in order to achieve, through his/her actions, the values of truth, goodness, beauty, values that the community, society and, in general, humanity attest,

respect and above all assume. Moral norms are also learned in a self-imposed manner by each individual, depending on his/her cultural-educational model, the type of civilization in which he/she lives, traditions, customs, cultural heritage, aspirations, etc. At the level of praxis, the application of moral norms is linked to strategies, interests, mentalities, and so on, that condition the success or failure of an action. For example: respecting moral-political norms in a democracy, in a space of rule of law, expressed in a code of ethical–political behaviour, respecting the ethical code in economic relations, etc.

Notes

1. For economists, the difference between a good and a service is clear: a good is a result of human activity (i.e., an artefact) for which the moment of production and the moment of consumption differ between them, while a service is (also) an artefact for which the two mentioned moments coincide. An intermediate position in this taxonomy is occupied by durable goods (which can be called, with equal justification, durable services). In appropriate places, further considerations regarding these concepts will be made.
2. Here, the term community must be considered in its most general sense, that is, it can refer to any dimension or criterion within which a set of individuals coagulate and live together, from certain points of view—for example, it can be a village, a region, a country, or a multi-state integrative system (federal or intergovernmental), or it can be a scientific or professional community or a social category.
3. We make the following conceptual clarifications: economic property is of two broad categories: (a) private property; (b) state property. Private property can be (a1) individual private property; (a2) associative private property—e.g., through shares, stocks, and the like. State property can be: (b1) public property—which, as we will see, produces public goods; (b2) private property of the state—e.g., national companies.
4. Let us recall that, conceptually, the societal is defined as society "applied" to a social group. But the societal is the result of the

emergence of society, and society is the result of the emergence (self-institution) of the state.

5. There are no convincing theories for the "death" of the state, any more than there are (at least relatively convincing) for the death of God—see Nietzsche—or for the death of the subject—see Foucault—or for the death/end of history—see Fukuyama. The Marxist theory of the necessary disappearance of the state has proven inconsistent, and other theories with at least as solid a foundation are not yet developed.
6. This is how things happen in the case of representative democracy that functions today in the vast majority of contemporary societies: individuals freely choose their representatives in state decision-making institutions and authorities, based on the intended purpose, but the means of objectifying those purposes are left (inevitably, from a technical/operational point of view) to the discretion of the elected officials themselves.
7. We recall that not only moments of political elections can play this role of "political hygiene", but there are mechanisms and procedures also between moments of ordinary elections, for example the institution of referendum or, in exceptional cases, the intervention of criminal law, ministerial accountability or, where the state is authentic, the institution of dismissal of persons unworthy of the position and responsibilities of a public servant.
8. Even though it seems pedantic, there is a difference between taxonomy and typology: taxonomy is based on theoretical (generic) criteria, while typology is based on empirical criteria.
9. The three characteristics are conceptually distinct: (a) impairment is the absence of a natural functionality of the person; (b) disability is the inability of the person to perform a function/role required for his/her social integration; (c) handicap is the disability that brings the person in question negative discrimination within society. *Nota bene*: it is not necessary that impairment becomes disability or that disability becomes handicap, but it is contingent that such transitions of meaning occur.
10. There is an interesting proposal of 10 capabilities that the state should ensure for the full functioning of the person, proposed by Nussbaum (2021): (1) life, (2) bodily health, (3) bodily integrity, (4) senses, imagination and thought, (5) emotion, (6) practical reason, (7) affiliation, (8) other species, (9) play, (10) control

over one's own environment—but we consider that they do not exhaust the needs for public goods and, in any case, not on the proposed structure. For example, PG_1^2 targets three of the capabilities proposed by Nussbaum: life, bodily health, and bodily integrity. Freedom is not even provided as a capability (except, partially, in practical reason, respectively in affiliation—possibly also in play), etc. And as for capability no. 10 (control over one's own environment) I find it hard to believe that this should be left to (or required from) the individual/person and should not be assumed by the state.

11. It seems curious to combine the action of preserving community identity (usually national identity) with the action of adapting community identity—in our opinion, we are not dealing with an internal contradiction here, because both socio-historical conditions and inter-community relations (usually international) lead to the need for a reconfiguration of community identity, of course, preserving the background of tradition but not neglecting social evolution.
12. From a logical point of view, prohibition and permission are not independent of each other: thus, we can write $F \equiv \overline{P}$ (prohibition is the logical negation of permission).
13. For example, the family.
14. This is the non-sense of some demands from ethnic or territorial communities for the assignment of freedoms specific to those communities.
15. It is easy to see that both paths are of the nature of the invisible hand. Although this characteristic is more… visible in the case of the formation of voluntary associations of individuals, also in the case of the social contract (i.e., of the "general assembly" of individuals in the original/initial position) is there an individual or a group of individuals who "convene" that position in which the social contract is concluded, that is, here too we have a spontaneous behaviour, of the invisible hand type.
16. Under constitutional conditions, the Government can also issue institutive norms, although in most cases it issues procedural norms. We recall that there are several levels of legislation, which are organized in a "cascade": (1) *primary* legislation—the Constitution and organic laws, which are exclusively institutive; (2) *secondary* legislation—norms that are given in the application

of primary legislation; (3) *tertiary* legislation—norms that are given to establish the procedures (methodologies) for the application of secondary legislation. *Nota bene*: under the conditions of integrative systems (such as, for example, the European Union), the hierarchy of legislation changes with the introduction of the integrative level—treaties, directives, etc.

17. We are talking about intervention in society, not just in the economy, because the economic field, although a very important one (referring to the material means of achieving the social goal) does not exhaust social (societal) phenomenology.
18. Let me recall the difference between kinematics and dynamics: kinematics is interested in the modification of an entity without examining the causes of that modification, while dynamics is interested in the modification of an entity by considering the causes of the modification in question—*Nota bene*: the distinction, which many researchers today neglect, was highlighted by Newton long ago.
19. Transhumanism that "predicts" the transformation of human nature through technology (namely, into cyber-man) is simply an exalted post-modernist fashion, although it is obvious that, to some extent, human nature is indeed modified by technological insertions, but not beyond the threshold at which this nature clearly breaks away from the "old" nature. There will be no inter-natural transition, the only transition is from human nature to the human condition (we do not believe that there is a transhuman nature, although a transhuman condition is possible).
20. The primordial character is different from the primitive character: primordial means prior from a logical point of view, while primitive means prior from an axiological point of view. It should be noted that, from the perspective of human nature, the primordial and the primitive coincide—only with the emergence of the human condition do they "separate" from a criterion point of view.
21. It seems that this criterion historically gains ascendancy over the first two (tribe, city, nation), so that modern states are essentially nothing more than tribes. Hence the visceral (i.e., based on human nature) reluctance to cultural mixing (see the current phenomenon of mass inter-cultural migration), an example being

the resounding failure of multiculturalism promoted by the European Union.

22. The concept of freedom will be defined below.
23. This can be observed in the case of animals (supposed not to be capable of representations, therefore not to have consciousness). The cases in which some animals do not "tolerate" the forced limitation of movement (zoos, cages, etc.)—there have also been reported cases of "suicide", stress, etc., are not caused by the absence of freedom, but are reduced to the violation of the nature of the animals in question (animal nature).
24. Historically, there were many cases in which the community's survival was ensured by individual sacrifice, so the first two levels of the hierarchy can change their places with one another.
25. Ethical values (commandments) originate subjectively, individually, and idiosyncratically (inside the individual, imposing themselves as an internal normativity), while moral values (which may or may not coincide, may or may not overlap with ethical values) originate socially (community-wise), are relatively common (at the level of different spheres of communitarianism) and external to the individual, imposing themselves as external normativity. In this sense, ethical values are always legitimate, while moral values can be legitimate (when they overlap with ethical ones) or can only be "legal", in the opposite case.
26. It contains two signaling systems—a primitive, reptilian one, located in the amygdala and the "floors" at the base of the brain, and a cultural one, located in the cortex and the "floors" at the top of the brain.
27. By "parasitizing" the terminology of the French logician of Romanian origin Ştephane Lupaşco, we can say that the human condition is actualized by potentiating (virtualizing) human nature, but not destroying it. It is worth noting that, in situations where survival is endangered, in most cases (obviously, not in the case of exceptional individuals, namely, of heroes by vocation), human nature is instantaneously actualized, strongly potentiating (virtualizing) the human condition.
28. In a sense very close to the Husserlian *epokhē*.
29. In a sense very close to Hegelian idealist dialectics (with the difference that the reference is made to the historical individual, not to the Absolute Spirit).

30. The good at the family level (and even, to some extent, at the level of a relatively small and socially isolated community) must be considered of the nature of individual good.
31. But not in relation to Nature!
32. The individual is considered private, from the perspective of his/her behaviour, of course, because, otherwise, any individual is private, when that behaviour, which affects another individual, does not represent the fulfillment of an attribution/obligation on behalf of the state (public power).
33. Attention, the following cases are excluded: a) the challenge, influence, or alteration refers to the means of achieving the purpose; b) the challenge, influence, or alteration occurs on the part of the state (public power).
34. The concept of justification is taken here in the sense proposed by Robert Nozick in his work, dedicated to the theory of the state (or social justice), *Anarchy, State and Utopia* (1999).
35. It is, of course, to be noted that social necessity is...contingent, while natural necessity is...necessary. In fact, the so-called social necessity is expressed and implemented through the normative system of society, from which its contingent character results, moreover.
36. This is a relatively difficult question, both from a logical and philosophical point of view. Indeed, why should public power be able to intervene in private purposes and this interference not be considered as affecting freedom? My argument is the following (and it seems to me that it follows quite predictably from the very definition of freedom): the state always intervenes through norms, an authentic norm is an impersonal norm (that is, it is addressed to the generic individual or, in other words, to any individual eligible for the application of that norm), so it does not have in mind the private individual but, somehow, the public... individual (here public has the meaning of the impersonal individual).
37. It is expressed in a somewhat more complicated formulation, but with exactly the same meaning, by Kant: "Act only according to that maxim whereby you can at the same time will that it should become a universal law", in Groundwork of the Metaphysics of Morals (1997).
38. It was also used, for example, by Abraham Maslow, who proposed a pyramid of human needs (not all being economic) in the work *A*

Theory of Human Motivation (2013). The theoretical risk results from the fact that Maslow himself gave at least a fairly substantial rectification of his own pyramid.

39. Logical classification and lexicographic classification differ from the following point of view: logical classification (or hierarchy) is based on previously established and accepted criteria which are independent of the object of classification, while lexicographic classification is based on a principle, accepted as an axiom (therefore, without justification or demonstration); this principle is not autonomous in relation to the object of classification.
40. From an anatomical and physiological point of view, the human brain is a very inefficient construction (which makes it, from a "technological" point of view, easily surpassed by the most basic artificial intelligence structure). Interestingly, however, it is precisely this characteristic of "poorly designed object" that gives rise to the most significant human specificities, which will never be replicated even by the most advanced artificial intelligence: emotion (especially empathy), understanding, and the like (see, here, the work of David J. Linden, 2008).
41. Since any law must be constitutional, it follows that all norms that are constitutional behave towards freedom like the Constitution.
42. As is the case, for example, with the current state of emergency generated by the COVID-19 pandemic. It would be interesting to analyse the Romanian Constitution (and, of course, other states' Constitution) from this point of view.
43. In fact, internalized, because any norms of behaviour are "extracted" from the normative fabric (formal or informal) of the community, so that they acquire idiosyncratic accents, sometimes particularly strong, once they are confronted with the individual's own personality in question.
44. Here the concept of transcendentality does not have the "strong" Husserlian meaning, because a generic individual (subject) is not considered, but historical subjects, that is, empirical subjects, are considered.
45. In the most general (and desirable) sense, the legal framework of a community is the codified moral framework of that community. This is the logically correct sense of the generation (and kinematics) of legality—the codification of the moral norm. In reality, most legal normativity is not the codified expression of

moral normativity, but is somehow autonomous in relation to it and, in some cases, even contradictory to this latter normativity—this is where the fact of applying the law and still doing injustice originates. The Latin phrase *fiat justitia, pereat mundus* has been (correctly) translated as "let justice be done, even if the world perishes", not as "let the law be applied, even if the world perishes". In this sense, there is a problem with the phrase rule of law—although the verbal expression uses the word law, which gives the term justice, the rule of law is understood as the state that ensures the supremacy of the law in society (society is governed by the law, not by people), but the application of the law is not incompatible with injustice.

46. For example, the concept of ministerial accountability refers to compliance (by government representatives) with the law that regulates the executive governmental activity.
47. Following this type of responsibility, social reforms (or sectoral reforms within society—economic, educational, scientific, etc.) or, at the opposite pole, social revolutions, appear.
48. By behavioural maxim is meant a guiding principle of action, which ensures the concordance or harmony (compatibility, consistency) between the action and the accepted ethical values. At this point, the distinction between ethical and moral is not relevant, the two concepts can be considered to be substitutable, so it can be said that the behavioural maxim is a moral principle.
49. In this sense, of course, the phrase *categorical imperative* is a (quasi)pleonasm, while the phrase hypothetical imperative is a *contradictio in adjecto.*
50. The expression *irresponsible behaviour* does not exactly refer to this case: it refers to an action that does not correctly anticipate its (usually, negative, but also positive) consequences. Also, the expression responsible/irresponsible in the judicial field has connotations related to the individual's capacity to exercise, so it does not enter into the present debate.
51. I recall that the legal norm is that norm that has generic recipients (not individualized or personalized), that is, of general applicability regarding the regulated type of behaviour (i.e., it does not introduce arbitrary exceptions, exemptions or exonerations) and, very importantly, it also targets the legislator (*Nota bene*: although

this last characteristic can be extracted, from a logical point of view, from the generality, however).

52. The distinction (which is most often not made) between ethical and moral does not reduce the generality of this characterization. However, if we accept the ethical-moral distinction (already indicated above), legitimacy addresses the ethical, not the moral.
53. Again, in the philosophical sense of the term responsible (or irresponsible), not in its medical or judicial sense.
54. It can be completely formalized based on norms and related logical constants (of course, in bivalent logic).
55. In this description of the relationship between power and freedom lies the difference between democratically exercised power, which refrains from influencing, in a private way, tertiary private goals, and authoritarian (or dictatorial) power, which influences, in a private way, tertiary private goals. Of course, democratic power presupposes the persuasion/convincing (at the limit, manipulation—see the so-called governmental marketing) of the individual that the goal proposed by the power holder is exactly his/her private goal, but this discussion exceeds the objective of this paragraph (perhaps it is worth mentioning here, however, that, in a free democracy—because there are also non-free democracies—social visions must be elaborated by the power holders and only approved by the population).
56. Such as following a military victory or a social revolution.
57. For example, holding an amount of money confers to the holder a power of disposition on some goods and services—in fact, we frequently talk about the *power of purchasing* provided by money.
58. An empirical (historical) case is that of the Czechoslovak (and later Czech) President Václav Havel, who had intellectual (and moral, for that matter) authority and who was also granted, through democratic ritual, political power following the political movements that led to the fall of communism in central and eastern Europe.
59. Another historical example (much older, from almost 2500 years ago) is that of Pericles who, holding political power, also acquired great intellectual and, above all, moral authority, by supporting the spiritual development of his state (ancient Athens).

60. See, for example, the abuse of power by the majority, also manifested in the Romanian Parliament (this abuse of power can only be stopped by the Constitutional Court).
61. For example, the award of the Nobel Prize in Economics confers on the laureate a lifelong and, in a sense, irrevocable intellectual authority in the field of economics. The laureate may express opinions at the level of an economics graduate (as is often the case), but the authority he/she enjoys remains intact. See, here, the so-called "Nobel" syndrome, namely, the curious and, generally, para-scientific opinions (in the most remote areas of their own expertise) which some laureates enact with a mysterious… "authority".
62. This also includes the authority conferred, *eo ipso*, by power.
63. This is where artistic authority comes in (more generally, this includes both *episteme* and *techne* authority, as they were understood in the ancient Greek world).
64. This is where and when the religious, or mythical, or mystical authority manifest.
65. The concept of foundation has the meaning of axiological justification or, at a higher level of subjectivity, of greater ethical acceptability.
66. It is already established above that the authority can never be self-conferred, in contrast to power that can be self-conferred.
67. It can be easily shown that here we have, from an algebraic perspective, a total order relation (comparability, reflexivity, anti-symmetry, and transitivity).
68. See, for example, the work of Erich Fromm (2021).
69. Hence the eternal recourse to paternalism (from which, for example, Richard Thaler's proposal regarding libertarian paternalism in the design of public policies is claimed).
70. A profound discussion about the two "species" of freedom can be found in Isaiah Berlin (1979).
71. I remind you that freedom is defined, by now, in an apophatic way, as the lack of private influence in establishing own purpose.
72. The other six senses are: sight, hearing, touch, smell, taste, and proprioception.
73. In the society, we talk about social freedom, not natural one. Consequently, the social freedom has always (more exactly, necessarily) a narrower extension than the natural freedom.

74. The first suggestion regarding the distinction of the three powers in the state was made by John Locke (following Aristotle's Politics), in his *Two Treatises of Government* (1689; 1988): legislative, executive, and federal. In 1748 (1989), Montesquieu introduced the "tripartite system", in his work *The Spirit of Laws*: legislative, executive, and judicial.
75. In states where the form of government is a presidential republic (or semi-presidential, as is the case in Romania), the head of state (usually called the president) is also part of the executive branch.
76. For example, in Romania, it is called the Constitutional Court.
77. As a rule, this is called the Court of Accounts.
78. Perhaps the structure of the government (the council of ministers or cabinet, as well as government agencies) should be designed exclusively from the perspective of ensuring these functions and not independently of them, as is usually done for partisan reasons.
79. Contextual desirability means a level of assurance of the function in question that is at the maximum level allowed by the context of any kind: normative, cultural, geo-political, etc.
80. This is, moreover (in the case of Romania), also a constitutional principle—see art. 16, (2) of the Romanian Constitution of 2003: '*No one is above the law*'.
81. I recall, in particular, the contractarian/proceduralist theory of the social contract, to explain/justify the emergence of the state, promoted by John Rawls in his *A Theory of Justice*—called the theory of fairness (1971, 1999), in an illustrious line of previous thinkers: Hobbes, Locke, Rousseau, Kant, without mentioning the intuitions in the matter of ancient or medieval philosophers.
82. I remind that a society (i.e., societal system) is the logical, institutional, and axiological mix between the social and the state.
83. I remind that, in the Universe, there are only three categories of entities: things, properties, and relationships.
84. Either the basic structure of the society (theory of social contract) or the association of protection of individuals (theory of invisible hand).
85. This conclusion, based on logical, non-contextual reasoning, is supported, from a factual point of view, by the historical evolution of human society.

86. We have, more exactly, a process of participatory democracy, since initially it was possible to gather in the same "agora" all the interested participants.
87. Partially, exactly as in the Theory of Chaos (the theory of non-linear systems dynamics).
88. Jürgen Habermas proposes a third type of democracy, called *deliberative democracy*, but entering this discussion goes far from my objectives in this book.
89. Using the syntagma "functional vote" is deliberate, since there are so many contemporary cases in which, formally, the population expresses the vote but the politic hijacks it, to announce exactly the result desired by the political body only, not the population.
90. To be observed that equality does not imply freedom, and neither vice versa. Of course, equality is a very strong premise for freedom; this is why equality is placed, in Fig. 3, both logically and (perhaps) chronologically, before freedom.
91. The politicians' intuition has worked perfectly here: maintaining population under the pressure of survival, that population will no longer interrogate the politic about the authenticity of the democracy.
92. See, here, the (failed, besides) proposal of Plato, in antiquity.
93. Here, the term authoritarian has not anymore the meaning introduced above, but simply means a discretionary attitude.
94. In my opinion, the concept of freedom assigned to a social group is meaningless. Like consciousness, affectivity, or experience, freedom is a parameter assignable exclusively to the individual.
95. Following Jürgen Habermas, we could invoke communicative reason here (see his concept of communicative action).
96. Institutions, as objectifications of subjective intentions, are considered objects (because they are perceived as alterities).
97. An *agora* can no longer function, literally.
98. However, the sovereignty is never ceded; it remains as the basic predicate of the population/community/nation, but only its use is entrusted (delegated) to the representatives of the owner.
99. Such an under-development of the knowledge manifests, in this case, as a lack of minimum political discernment.
100. In fact, from a logical point of view, the authentic delegation of sovereignty use requires only the universal and equal nature of the vote, not the secret or, in some states, the mandatory nature.

Although the issue of the mandatory nature of the vote to delegate sovereignty use involves more subtle discussions, we will not develop them for the time being. They will be resumed, however, when, at the end of my report, I address the issue of responsibility.

101. Here we have, of course, in mind the unfortunate concept of the average voter (like any average, the average voter is a mystification, because, for example, if from individuals one can infer the average, from the average one cannot infer the individuals who constituted that average; this epistemological impossibility, applicable, for example, to the calculation of probabilities, makes the average voter an inadequate or even profoundly inadequate sociological and political concept).
102. The model in question does not necessarily have to be created by the voter (not all voters are social philosophers!), but the voter can adhere to a pre-existing model or, as we will see below, can even take over the model proposed by the politician who is asking for his/her vote.
103. The risk of lack of discernment in the allocation of votes has been eliminated, from the point of view of biologically or physiologically conditioned discernment, by establishing a minimum age at which the legal right to vote is activated. The case in which persons who have discernment from a biological or physiological perspective, but do not have the right to vote as a result of prohibitions established by legal norms is somewhat more complicated because, in fact, the restriction does not concern lack of discernment, but signifies a punishment. In my opinion, from a philosophical point of view, it is difficult to support the restriction of the right to vote for reasons other than biological or physiological ones.
104. See, for example, the excellent systematization of this matter in A. Downs, *An Economic Theory of Democracy*, (1957).
105. A famous definition of freedom says that it is understood necessity (in the sense of accepted necessity). Obviously, we are talking about a social necessity, which is a necessity established contingently, therefore reversible through the same mechanism as the institution of.
106. I remind that it is speaking about the social necessity, not about the natural one. As is known, Derrida further expands the area of necessity, saying that freedom begins where calculation ends

(obviously, Derrida removes all rationality from the realm of freedom, and we would can ask what is left of freedom in this context).

107. That is, the nature of the human being is social (which is why the clear distinction that so many analysts make between human nature and human condition is not so clear, because human nature is permeated with the social, which, in their opinion, should be granted only to the human condition). As can be seen, Kant was absolutely right in saying that many books would have been much clearer if it had not been intended to be so very clear.
108. By relative constraint we mean the constraint that allows at least two alternative choices. The case where the choice is unique will be called absolute constraint.
109. The term perceptible used here is crucial: only God is not subject to any constraint (although Hegel believes that He too had a constraint, of a transcendental nature, of course, when He created man, in order to know Himself; from which it can be inferred that the purpose itself is of the nature of constraint, that is, the concept of constraint, is broader than the concept of purpose and, of course, also than the concept of finality).
110. The most famous formula of the interdependence of individual freedoms in the social space was expressed in the manner: my freedom is limited only by your freedom; by generalization, one could say: the extension of my freedom is limited by the extension of your freedom. Both formulas are false if we consider what was said above. The main reason for this falsity lies in the fact that the mentioned formulas assume (namely, by an implicit assumption) that the individual values of different individuals are the same (the assumption of common preferences, which also constitutes the basis of most of the "theorems" of economic behaviour), so that the alternatives accessible to different individuals are the same, so they enter mutual competition. As the preferences (of any kind) are different for different individuals, some extensions of an individual's freedom can penetrate the space of freedom of another individual, without competing with the second individual's freedom space. *Nota bene*: this idea results, somewhat, from Fig. 10.
111. A perfect metaphor for expressing this idea is that of a collision between two galaxies: the component stars of the galaxies are so

far among them that the two galaxies can pass through each other without any star belonging to one of the galaxies colliding with a star belonging to the other galaxy.

112. Let us remember (Romanian) Father Steinhardt, who felt freer in his penitential cell than his guards outside.
113. There are, however, (competent and *bona fide*) analysts who believe that there is a trade-off between freedom and quality of life. Without going into details that exceed the objectives of this report, I will only say that, in my opinion, freedom has no substitute, only complements.
114. Relatively recent detailed discussion of this issue can be found in particular in J. Rawls, R. Nozick, D. Schmidtz, or J. Buchanan.
115. Churchill expressed this aphoristically, saying that democracy is the worst political system, but we have no better one. This idea of the *second best* was also expressed by Einstein (regarding epistemology) who said that our theories should be as simple as possible, but not simpler than that.
116. Here is an unusual example: while preparing for his interview for American citizenship (he had been invited to IAS Princeton by Einstein), the great logician Gödel had to study the US Constitution. After a purely logical examination of it, he concluded that consistent compliance with the constitutional provisions would result in the establishment of a dictatorship in the USA. Obviously, this was a conclusion of a procedural nature, and not one of a result (so far, this procedural conclusion has not come true; it is possible that Gödel's warning worked like the law of expected effect, which works in economic behaviour, see the Oedip's effect). The new Trump administration seems determined to prove Gödel right, working hard in this direction—let's hope it does not succeed.
117. The question of the a priori character of this selection is much more difficult and I will ignore it in this report. However, to express a simple incipient opinion, I will only say that this question is not of a theoretical nature but of a practical one (in Kantian sense of the concept of practice), that is, a purely empirical question. If, indeed, this were the case, then the selection cannot be a priori, but can be *ex ante*, on the basis of social experience (current or historical).

118. A deeper discussion will have to deal with the concept of equality. As it is stipulated in current constitutions, it is about equality of position (once eligible as a voter, each such voter has an equal power to determine the outcome of the vote with any other eligible voter). There have been historical cases in which it was not about equality of position, but about equality of responsibility (for example, census voting, or voting differentiated by educational level, and therefore by potential for discernment). Many of the constructive criticisms of contemporary functional democracy refer precisely to these questions of equality.
119. This is the theoretical reason why emerging democracies (as is the case with Romania) are, for a certain period, until reaching a certain consolidation threshold, in danger of reversibility (democracies that have a certain "age" are, inherently, further from this danger).
120. My statements are focused especially on Romania *statu quo*, so they cannot be generalized without some precautions.
121. As is known, competence is cumulatively constituted by three components: a) *knowledge*; b) *skills*; c) *attitudes*. Although the level of performance of the instructional process (both the initial and the LLL type) is still deficient in the first two components, the third component is quasi-non-existent in the instructional-educational process. However, the formation of attitude is the humus on which responsibility sprouts and grows.
122. Epistemologists will counter that totalities cannot be subject to scientific examination, but I rely on the defence of metaphysicians, who will, of course, argue the opposite.
123. I put the practical term in quotation marks so that the meaning we give it in this paragraph is not confused with its philosophical (especially Kantian) meaning.
124. I call a public privilege a legal but illegitimate right granted to elected persons or those appointed by elected persons (privilege actually means private law or, more precisely, law given in private interest, not in public interest).
125. I give here only the example of the use of parliamentary immunity for matters not related to the exercise of parliamentary function (similar is the case of the need for approval, in Parliament, for the initiation of criminal prosecution of a parliamentarian, or the need for approval by the president of the country for the initiation of

criminal prosecution of a minister or former minister who is not currently a parliamentarian).

126. An activity is a logical and chronological concatenation, both structural and functional, of more actions aimed at performing a common end.

References

Berlin, I. (1979). *Four Essays on Liberty*. Oxford University Press.

Dinga, E., Tănăsescu, C.-R., & Ionescu, G.-M. (2020). Social Entropy and Normative Network. *Entropy, 22*(9).

Dinga, E. (2025). *Economic Resilience During Overlapped Crises—Antifragility, Sustainability and Autopoieticity*. Palgrave Macmillan – Springer Nature.

Downs, A. (1957). *An Economic Theory of Democracy*. Harper and Brothers.

Fromm, E. (2021). *The Fear of Freedom*. Routledge.

Kant, I. (1997). *Groundwork of the Metaphysics of Morals*. Cambridge University Press.

Linden, D. J. (2008). *The Accidental Mind: How the Brain Evolution Has Given Us Love, Memory, Dreams, and God*. Belknap Press.

Locke, J. (1988). *Two Treatises of Government*. Cambridge University Press.

Maslow, A. H. (2013). *A Theory of Human Motivation*. Lulu.com.

Montesquieu, C. (1989). *The Spirit of the Laws*. Cambridge University Press.

Nozick, R. (1999). *Anarchy, State and Utopia*. Blackwell Publisher Ltd.

Nussbaum, M.C. (2007). *Frontiers of Justice: Disability, Nationality, Species Membership*. Belknap Press.

Rawls, J. (1999). *A Theory of Justice*. The Belknap Press of Harvard University Press.

CHAPTER 6

Plenary Life and Capabilities Providing

1 Preamble

First of all, it is needed to introduce some supporting concepts: (a) the consciousness; (b) the subconsciousness; (c) the representation; (d) the imaginary; (e) the instituting.

(a) On the real—from sensation to reasoning

To get the consciousness it is needed to show the cognitive chain of the human being, that is: (a1) sensation; (a2) perception; (a3) conceptualization; (a4); judging; and (a5) reasoning.

(a1) Sensation

The sensation is the first (and an un-substitutable, and, *a fortiori*, a non-avoidable) step of interaction between a human being and its (general, namely, including also other human beings) environment.[1] More exactly, the physical signals or impulses from outside the individual biological body impress their (six) natural senses. These impressions are, in this stage, exclusively of physical nature—e.g., *wavelength*—for the eye; *transverse vibration frequencies* of the air molecules—for the ear; *pressure*—for the tactile sense; *chemical dissolution*—for the sense of taste or the sense of smell; *gravitational attractions*—for the proprioceptive sense.

E. Dinga, *The Economics of Social Justice and Societal Evolution*, https://doi.org/10.1007/978-3-032-24055-2_6

The physical impressions can be "managed" without the intermediation of consciousness, based only on psychism[2] "managed", in turn, by the basic brain, namely by what we call today the subconsciousness. It works automatically, by what is known as tropism.[3] In fact, the tropism is the phenomenon through which the biological individual's (no matter it is speaking about human beings or non-human beings, either plants, animals, or fungi) subconsciousness reacts to the physical sensations. *Nota bene*: regarding the reaction of non-living entities to the variation of the environment, it is not a result of sensations, but is a necessary (namely, in logical terms, obligatory) reaction imperatively required by the very laws of Nature.

The sensations must be considered as *primary qualities* with which a sensible entity (usually, a living entity) takes contact once it is, ontologically, "thrown" in the world, as would say Heidegger.

(a2) Perception

Although the tropism can work directly under the "command" of subconsciousness (or, as mentioned above, of the simple psychism), many reactions have their origin in perceptions which presuppose the consciousness. The consciousness is, for today, more a label than a genuine concept. Indeed, we do not know, as generally accepted by the scientific community, how consciousness emerges from (in this regard, there is no doubt) the brain's functioning.[4] In this context, I will accept that consciousness exist as such and I proceed only to defining it, for my purpose in this chapter. So, it can be said that *consciousness is a property of a living entity to know about itself*. Some considerations are required here:

- to know something is shared by human beings with non-human living entities which are endowed with brain;
- generally, to know implies, primarily, a memory (i.e., a *sui generis* deposit) holding/conserving, in specific ways, either biological or technological—for the latter, see the artificial memory, until the artificial intelligence—past knowledge (acquired by experience or, as in the case of a human being, by reflection) and, secondarily, a procedure to access the stored knowledge, for example, by remembering[5];
- for a given entity, to know does not imply knowing that knows. The consequence of this is that such an entity knows only if the object

of that (past) knowledge is before it, in the flesh and blood[6]; this means, the entity in the case is capable only of perceptions;
- instead, the consciousness implies the capacity of representation, that is, the capacity to have/construct/remembering something (image, sound, pressure, taste, smell, position in space) from the past, without the condition of the presence, in the flesh and blood, of the object in the case before the subject;
- therefore, the representation and the perception have as common property exactly the perception: any representation is a perception, but not any perception is a representation.

(a3) Conceptualization

With the capacity of representation, we enter the territory of consciousness. Inside consciousness, the perceptions[7] or representations, after the case, become concepts. If, for the sensations are required the senses, for conceptualizing is required the intellect. It is to be mentioned that conceptualization of perceptions has a semantic function, that is, it is aimed at correlating the names provided by perceptions to objects, properties, or relationships (either objective or subjective, or objectified) of the world, i.e., it consists in finding the referentials/denotations. The concepts are derived from perceptions or representations by operations of abstracting and generalizing.

To abstract and to generalize are not logically equivalent, because:

- abstracting means to identify the essential predicates of the perception/representation involved, by ignoring the peripheral features; more precisely, abstracting means passing beyond the individual to species or, after the case, beyond the species, to the genus;
- generalizing means to apply the particular[8] features of perception/ representation to all the individuals involved in that particular. Usually, the generalization uses the induction, which is liable of false.[9]

(a4) Judging

In intellect, also happens the judging. By judging is understood an arrangement of the concepts (categorematic terms) and required connecting terms among the concepts (sincategorematic terms) in propositions (sentences/statements), based on pre-established syntactic norms. Obviously, this process unfolds using both the lexical deposit and the grammatical rules of a given natural language.[10] Judging has a syntactic function, so that it constitutes the fundamental way in which the human being integrates the world into him/her and integrates himself/herself into the world.

(a5) Reasoning

The propositions generated in the intellect "go" further and are related to each other by the intermediation of logical vehicles called syllogisms.[11] The syllogisms are the way in which the reason works, and the process of using syllogisms is called reasoning. By reasoning, other propositions can be obtained, using the logical inference, so that, finally, a coherent, consistent, and complete such reasoning can lead to a (cognitive) model of/on the world (for example, a theory).

(a) On the objectification

The world is composed of three ontological regions: (1) the *objective* region, causally independent from the subject[12]; (2) the *subjective* region, causally dependent from the subject; (3) the *objectified* region, which is a transforming into objective of the subjectivity.[13] Usually, the three regions are known as Popper's three worlds—*world 1*: the objective region; *world 2*: the subjective (psychological) region; *world 3*: the objectified region.

(b) On the imaginary

The human being (she or he) has the capacity, provided by consciousness, to represent both the world and himself/herself within the world. This representation is not only about the past (remembering from memory), or the present (current world and individual positioning related to the word) but, also, about the future ("remembering from future"). Of course, the imaginary objects can "populate" both the present, the past, and the future versions of the world.

The problem of imaginary is extremely complicated and, of course, not yet clarified neither in science nor in philosophy (metaphysics). I provide some considerations in that matter, without daring to propose a solution, except a timid suggestion:

- from the origin perspective, the imaginary object is "hosted" by subjectivity (i.e., Popper's world 2), since any vision on reality, whether it is or not objectified, arises in the subject's mind;
- if the imaginary object is objectified in one way or another, then it enters Popper's world 3; if it is not objectified, it remains in Popper's world 2[14];

A synoptic picture of the three regions of the world is provided in Fig. 1.

Discussion

- the world 1 (the objective region of the world) is strictly separated from the society, which contains the world 2 (the subjective world) and world 3 (the objectified world)[15];
- the world 2 receives suggestions from world 1 (for example, the airplanes, suggested by birds);
- the world 2, by intermediation of socialization (i.e., putting together the ideas and the activities to materialize them), causally generates (builds) the world 3;
- from the world 3, suggestions come to world 2, generating, by positive feedback (*Nota bene*: sometimes, however, by negative feedback,

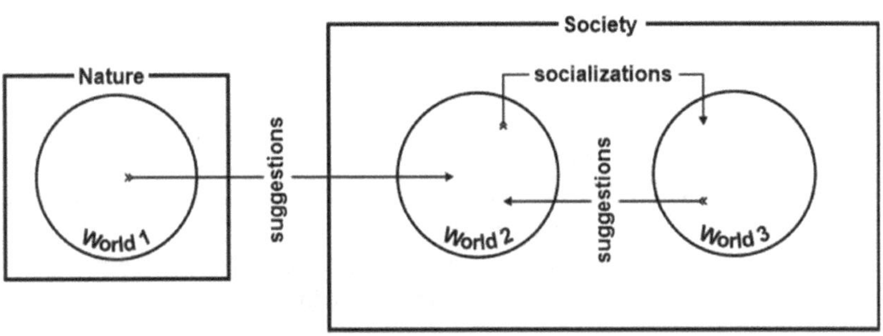

Fig. 1 Phenomenology of the three regions of the world (*Source* author)

for example, linked to the ecological protection of world 1), new socialization processes, and so on.

2 The Vision of Plenary Life

2.1 *Preliminaries*

From a quantitative perspective, the human being's life refers to a time[16] duration in which an individual is living from a biological point of view.[17] But this perspective is shared by all living entities of the world, not only by human beings. Regarding the human being, qualitative determinants of the life are (much more) important, since the human being is capable of representations, that is, of such qualitative determinants of the life.

We can imagine a pyramid of the layers of life,[18] analogously to Maslow's pyramid of needs, as follows:

- ($L0$) layer 0: is the *biological layer*—that layer/level of the life in which the biological indispensable needs are satisfied so that the species in the case survives, that is: (a) individuals survive; (b) individuals reproduce:
- this layer does not imply values
- ($L1$) layer 1: is the *personal layer*—that layer/level of life in which a human being elevates from the condition of an individual to the condition of a person. A person presupposes an individual, of course, but holding some crucial extra attributes, more exactly, holding values[19]:
- leading values regarding own path of life—safety, wellbeing, self-esteem, freedom, purposes, means, etc.
- leading values regarding individual decisions, actions, evaluations, and interpretations—efficacy, adequacy, optimality, sustainability, viability, autopoieticity, etc.
- ($L2$) layer 2: is the *communitarian layer*—that layer/level of life concerned with the local community where the individual is inserted/included, presupposing:
- leading values regarding family and relatives, proximal neighbourhood, proximal future generations, proximal environment, security, ethics, empathy, etc.

- ($L3$) layer 3: is the *social layer*—that layer/level of life focusing the largest possible homogenous[20] community (usually, in contemporary times, national states, or national societies), presupposing:
- leading values regarding the historical and cultural identity (first of all, by language), territorial, economic, and political sovereignty, social capital, and so on.
- ($L4$) layer 4: is the *global layer*—that layer/level of life addressing the planetary space,[21] which contains the largest economic, social, political, and cultural diversity, presupposing:
- leading values regarding the positioning in the global world, and the relationships with the global world, either individually or communitarily (including nationally).

Discussion

(i) as mentioned at endnote 17, $L0$ is *conditio sine qua non* for any other layer of life to come into existence, so it is the possibility condition of the life layers;
(ii) the realization of the layer "k" presupposes the pre-existence of the layer "$k - 1$" (with $k \in \mathbb{N}$, and $k \geq 1$);
(iii) the layers of life follow a process of agglutination (from layer "0" to layer "4") similar to the process of agglutination in the case of brain evolution;
(iv) the non-human living entities stop themselves from constructing the layers of life at layer "0".

2.2 *Building of the Life's Layers—Structural View*

As shown above, each life's layer is added over the immediately preceding layer, so any layer of level "k" structurally (and, of course, functionally) contains all layers of levels "$q < k$", with $q, k \in \mathbb{N}$. Consequently, each subsequent layer is richer than the antecedent/s one/s. This richness has, of course, a qualitative signification, not a quantitative one. From an axiological perspective, the higher the level of life's layer, the more complete is that individual as a person. To mention that the layer "0" is assignable to human nature, while other layers are assignable to human condition. The responsibility of a person for the global world (layer "4") signifies, so, the highest level at which a person can get to.[22]

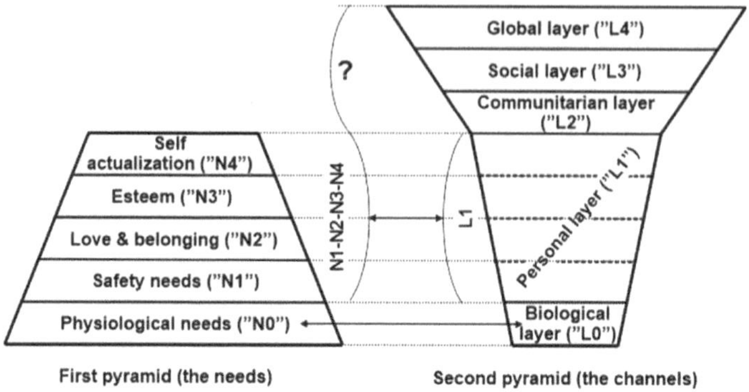

Fig. 2 Logical correspondence between life's layers and human needs (*Source* author)

The life layers pyramid and the human needs pyramid (in Maslow's view) are in a certain logical correspondence, as Fig. 2 tries to synoptically represent.

Discussion

- Maslow's pyramid of needs is focused on the human being viewed as an individual, although it is obvious that the levels 2–5 of the pyramid involve, logically, the community of any scale, while the inverted pyramid of life's layers is concerned of all the hypostases in which the individual could be within the Nature and Society;
- in Maslow's pyramid of needs there is an arrow we could call the *arrow of required needs*, (let us note it with $A1$) from the pyramid's basis to its peak, while in the inverted pyramid of life's layers also there is an arrow that we could call the *arrow of social of stratification*, (let us note it with $A2$) from the peak of pyramid to its basis—the two arrows have inverse directions;
- the "bijective" correspondence between Maslow's pyramid of needs and the inverted pyramid of life's layers happens only at the first items of the two pyramids: physiological needs of the individual in Maslow's pyramid and the biological layer of the inverted pyramid of life's layers;

- all the needs of levels 2–5 in Maslow's pyramid of needs correspond to the second level of the pyramid of life's layers: $(N1 - N2 - N3 - N4) \leftrightarrow (L1)$;
- the levels 3–5 of life's layers have not correspondence to Maslow's pyramid of needs.

The two pyramids are not, however, either contradictory or incommensurable between them—in fact, each of them addresses different coordinate of the individual's life, as put into evidence by the two arrows above mentioned, so they should be considered together.

2.3 *Building of the Life's Layers—Qualitative View*

There is another (possible) pyramid regarding the individual's life, namely the *pyramid of life realization*. Some considerations in this matter are as follows:

- this pyramid provides a hierarchy of the level at which the needs of the individual are satisfied; so, it is not about the needs required by a (generic) individual, as Maslow's pyramid establishes, but about the degree to which those needs are satisfied;
- from the theory of systems, the needs of an individual are inputs, and the degree of satisfying those needs is output in relation to the system called an individual.

Nota bene: regarding the pyramid of life's layers, it is neither possible nor useful to establish a degree of realization, since this pyramid does not establish requirements (as Maslow's pyramid of needs does), but provides the conditionalities or *sui generis* environments in which an individual's life can unfold.

Specifically, such a third pyramid consists in the following levels of satisfying the needs:

(i) $(S0)$ level "I": *material* (economic) satisfaction[23]—addresses the access to basic resources aimed at supporting the biological life and development; usually, this level of satisfying the needs is called *standard of living*[24];

(ii) ($S1$) level "II": *qualitative* satisfaction—addresses the quality of needs satisfying, regarding any item of such a satisfying; usually, this level of satisfying is called *quality of life*;
(iii) ($S2$) level "III": *stylistic* satisfaction—addresses the idiosyncratic way in which an individual satisfies his/her needs, in either quantitative and qualitative dimensions; usually, this level of satisfying is called *style of life*;
(iv) ($S3$) level "IV": *relational* satisfaction—addresses the society functioning in relation with needs satisfying (e.g., employment, social assurance, and so on); I propose to call this level of satisfying *mode of life*;
(v) ($S4$) level "V": *significance* satisfaction—addresses the evaluation that an individual or a group (at limit, the society as a whole) evaluates the needs satisfying (e.g., the freedom space, the social capital, etc.); I propose to call this level of satisfying *significance of life*.[25]

Of course, the pyramid of life realization has its own arrow, that I would call the *arrow of life realization* (let us note it with $A3$).

2.4 The Logical Triads

We can put together the content of the three pyramids and their arrows, as suggested in Figs. 3 and 4.

Based on Fig. 3, we will form the all triads ($N\alpha - L\beta - S\gamma$), from which it will can be extracted the triads of interest for this chapter.

Let us establish the compatible pairs ($N\alpha$ – $L\beta$), in Table 1. *Nota bene*: we note with "C" the cases of compatibility, and with "$\overline{C}$" the cases of incompatibility, and with "$\approx$" the cases of neutrality. I do not consider either incompatibilities or neutralities.

So, are of interest the following dyads:

- ($N0$, $L0$)
- ($N0$, $L1$)
- ($N1$, $L0$)
- ($N1$, $L1$)
- ($N1$, $L2$)
- ($N1$, $L3$)

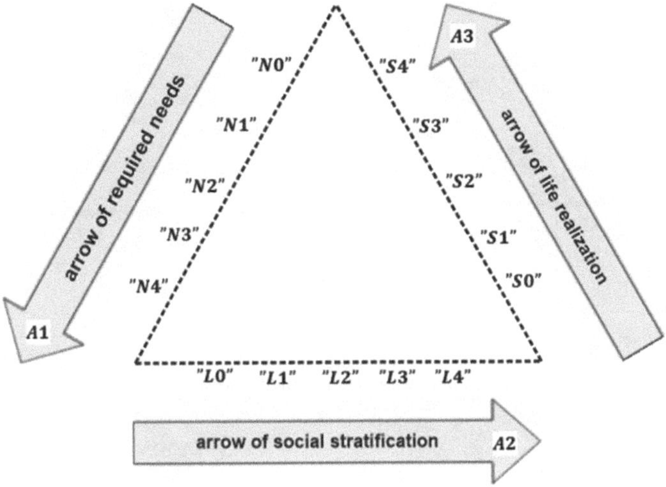

Fig. 3 Three pyramids and their arrows, regarding the individual life (*Source* author)

- $(N1, L4)$
- $(N2, L1)$
- $(N2, L2)$
- $(N2, L3)$
- $(N2, L4)$
- $(N3, L1)$
- $(N3, L2)$
- $(N3, L3)$
- $(N3, L4)$
- $(N4, L2)$
- $(N4, L3)$
- $(N4, L4)$

Analogously, let us establish the compatible pairs $(N\alpha - S\gamma)$—Table 2. So, are of interest the following dyads:

- $(N0, S0)$
- $(N0, S1)$
- $(N1, S0)$

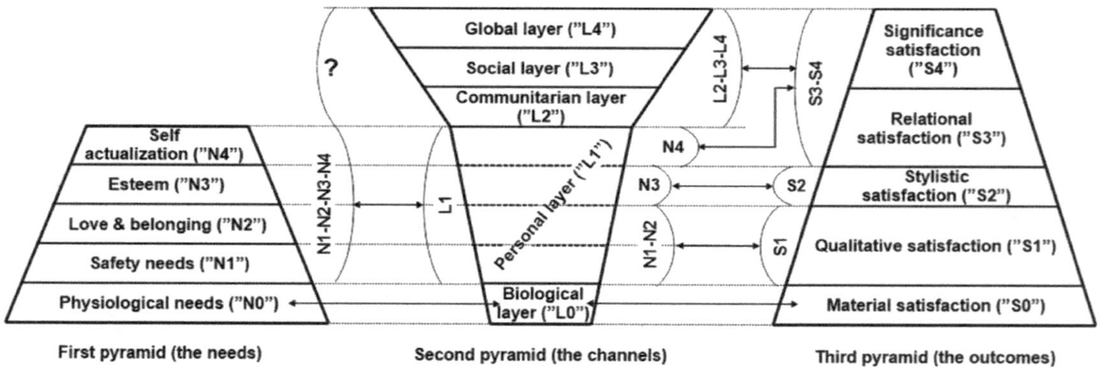

Fig. 4 Three pyramids and their logical correspondence (*Source* author)

Table 1 Compatibilities in dyad ($N\alpha - L\beta$)

		L				
		*L*0	*L*1	*L*2	*L*3	*L*4
N	*N*0	*C*	*C*	$\approx$	$\approx$	$\approx$
	*N*1	*C*	*C*	*C*	*C*	*C*
	*N*2	$\overline{C}$	*C*	*C*	*C*	*C*
	*N*3	$\overline{C}$	*C*	*C*	*C*	*C*
	*N*4	$\overline{C}$	$\approx$	*C*	*C*	*C*

Source author

Table 2 Compatibilities in dyad ($N\alpha - S\gamma$)

		S				
		*S*0	*S*1	*S*2	*S*3	*S*4
N	*N*0	*C*	*C*	$\approx$	$\overline{C}$	$\overline{C}$
	*N*1	*C*	$\approx$	$\overline{C}$	$\overline{C}$	$\overline{C}$
	*N*2	$\overline{C}$	$\overline{C}$	$\approx$	*C*	$\approx$
	*N*3	$\overline{C}$	$\overline{C}$	$\approx$	*C*	*C*
	*N*4	$\overline{C}$	$\overline{C}$	$\overline{C}$	*C*	*C*

Source author

- ($N2$, $S3$)
- ($N3$, $S3$)
- ($N3$, $S4$)
- ($N4$, $S3$)
- ($N4$, $S4$)

Analogously, let us establish the compatible pairs ($L\beta - S\gamma$)—Table 3. So, are of interest the following dyads:

- ($L0$, $S0$)
- ($L0$, $S1$)
- ($L1$, $S0$)
- ($L1$, $S1$)
- ($L1$, $S2$)

Table 3 Compatibilities in dyad $(L\beta - S\gamma)$

		S				
		$S0$	$S1$	$S2$	$S3$	$S4$
L	$L0$	C	C	$\overline{C}$	$\overline{C}$	$\overline{C}$
	$L1$	C	C	C	$\overline{C}$	$\overline{C}$
	$L2$	$\overline{C}$	$\overline{C}$	$\overline{C}$	C	C
	$L3$	$\overline{C}$	$\overline{C}$	$\overline{C}$	C	$\approx$
	$L4$	$\overline{C}$	$\overline{C}$	$\overline{C}$	C	$\approx$

Source author

- $(L2, S3)$
- $(L2, S4)$
- $(L3, S3)$
- $(L4, S3)$

Based on the three sets of dyads, we now can list the triads of interest provided by the three pyramids discussed above by putting them together. I will use the relation of transitivity in relation to the operation of making compatible the dyads to get the triads:

$$\{[(N\alpha)C(L\beta)] \wedge [(L\beta)C(S\gamma)] \rightarrow [(N\alpha)C(S\gamma)]\} \rightarrow (N\alpha, L\beta, S\gamma)$$

or, equivalent:

$$\{[C(N\alpha, L\beta)] \wedge [C(L\beta, S\gamma)] \rightarrow C(N\alpha, S\gamma)\} \rightarrow C(N\alpha, L\beta, S\gamma)$$

The result is the following:

- $(N0, L0, S0)$
- $(N0, L0, S1)$
- $(N0, L1, S0)$
- $(N0, L1, S1)$
- $(N0, L1, S2)$
- $(N1, L0, S0)$
- $(N1, L0, S1)$
- $(N1, L1, S0)$
- $(N1, L1, S1)$

- $(N1, L1, S2)$
- $(N1, L2, S3)$
- $(N1, L2, S4)$
- $(N1, L3, S3)$
- $(N1, L4, S3)$
- $(N2, L1, S0)$
- $(N2, L1, S1)$
- $(N2, L1, S2)$
- $(N2, L2, S3)$
- $(N2, L2, S4)$
- $(N2, L3, S3)$
- $(N2, L4, S3)$
- $(N3, L1, S0)$
- $(N3, L1, S1)$
- $(N3, L1, S2)$
- $(N3, L2, S3)$
- $(N3, L2, S4)$
- $(N3, L3, S3)$
- $(N3, L4, S3)$
- $(N4, L2, S3)$
- $(N4, L2, S4)$
- $(N4, L3, S3)$
- $(N4, L4, S3)$

2.5 *The Life Chains (Paths)*

The question is: what are the viable chains among the three pyramids, in the logical order adopted in Fig. 3?

To proceed to such an examination, the following five "principles" should be operationalized.

(1) a (viable) life path designing must contain the level "0" of each of the three pyramids (i.e., $N0$, $L0$, $S0$).[26] *Nota bene*: from now on, I will note the triad $(N\alpha, L\beta, S\gamma)$ with $T^{\alpha\beta\gamma}$, so the basic triad is T^{000};

(2) a chain "i" containing "x" triads will be noted $P_i(x)$;

(3) the concatenation of two triads, $T^{\alpha\beta\gamma}$ and T^{mnq}, will be written simply:

$$P_i(2) = T^{\alpha\beta\gamma} T^{mnq}$$

(4) in a generic triads concatenation, it must be verified the conditions:

$$m \geq \alpha$$

$$n \geq \beta$$

$$q \geq \gamma$$

with the following possible cases:

- if $m > \alpha$, then it can be accepted $n \geq \beta$; if $m = \alpha$, then it must be $n > \beta$
- if $n > \beta$, then it can be accepted $q \geq \gamma$; if $n = \beta$, then it must be $q > \gamma$
- if some bifurcation arises when verifying the "principle" (4), it will be written

$$P_i[1(2)] = T^{\alpha\beta\gamma}\left(T^{mnq}, T^{abc}\right)$$

This means that the first triad is concatenated with the first triad inside brackets, or also the first triad is concatenated with the second triad inside brackets. Consequently, in fact, we have two distinct chains with a common triad (namely, the first one outside brackets):

$$P_i^1[1(1\cdot)] = T^{\alpha\beta\gamma} T^{mnq}$$

$$P_i^2[1(\cdot 1)] = T^{\alpha\beta\gamma} T^{abc}$$

So that

$$P_i[1(2)] = \left\{P_i^1[1(1\cdot)]\right\} \vee \left\{P_i^2[1(\cdot 1)]\right\}$$

Nota bene: of course, we can have more complicated cases, but all of them can be managed based on the "principles" adopted above. For example, if we have:

$$P_i[2(1(1)1)1] = T^{\alpha_1\beta_1\gamma_1}T^{\alpha_2\beta_2\gamma_2}\left(T^{\alpha_3\beta_3\gamma_3}\left(T^{\alpha_4\beta_4\gamma_4}, T^{\alpha_5\beta_5\gamma_5}\right), T^{\alpha_6\beta_6\gamma_6}\right)T^{\alpha_7\beta_7\gamma_7}$$

Then, the following analytical writing is equivalent:

$$P_i^1[2(1\cdot(1\cdot))1] = T^{\alpha_1\beta_1\gamma_1}T^{\alpha_2\beta_2\gamma_2}T^{\alpha_3\beta_3\gamma_3}T^{\alpha_4\beta_4\gamma_4}T^{\alpha_7\beta_7\gamma_7}$$

$$P_i^1[2(1\cdot(\cdot 1))1] = T^{\alpha_1\beta_1\gamma_1}T^{\alpha_2\beta_2\gamma_2}T^{\alpha_3\beta_3\gamma_3}T^{\alpha_5\beta_5\gamma_5}T^{\alpha_7\beta_7\gamma_7}$$

$$P_i^1[2(\cdot 1)1] = T^{\alpha_1\beta_1\gamma_1}T^{\alpha_2\beta_2\gamma_2}T^{\alpha_6\beta_6\gamma_6}T^{\alpha_7\beta_7\gamma_7}$$

with

$$P_i[2(1(2)1)1] = \left\{P_i^1[2(1\cdot(1\cdot))1]\right\} \vee \left\{P_i^1[2(1\cdot(\cdot 1))1]\right\} \vee \left\{P_i^1[2(\cdot 1)1]\right\}$$

Depending on the final purpose of the life path, different life chains could be built. For the moment, I will select the viable such chains, based on the identified triads. By verifying the "principles" (4) and (5), we have the following possible life chains.

A synoptic image of the triads concatenations in the life chain is provided in Fig. 5.

Based on the proposed procedure, the following (possible) life chains can be identified (Table 4).

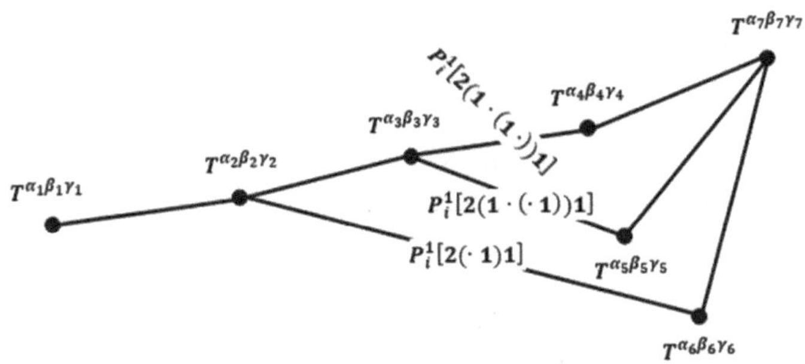

Fig. 5 Three life chains (paths) (*Source* author)

Table 4 "Data base" to identify the viable life chains (paths)

		1–	*2–*	*3–*	*4–*
–1	000	101	x	x	x
–2		x	x	x	x
–3		x	x	x	x
–4		x	x	x	x
–0		110	210	310	x
–1		111	211	311	x
–2		112	212	312	x
–3		x	x	x	x
–4		x	x	x	x
–0		x	x	x	x
–1		x	x	x	x
–2		x	x	x	x
–3		123	223	323	423
–4		124	224	324	424
–0		x	x	x	x
–1		x	x	x	x
–2		x	x	x	x
–3		133	233	333	433
–4		x	x	x	x
–0		x	x	x	x
–1		x	x	x	x
–2		x	x	x	x
–3		143	243	343	443
–4		x	x	x	x

Source author

Based on Table 4, the life chains (paths) can be identified as follows: 000–101

- $P_1(5) = T^{000}T^{101}T^{211}T^{312}T^{423}$
- $P_2(5) = T^{000}T^{101}T^{211}T^{312}T^{424}$
- $P_3(5) = T^{000}T^{101}T^{211}T^{312}T^{433}$
- $P_4(5) = T^{000}T^{101}T^{211}T^{312}T^{443}$
- $P_5(5) = T^{000}T^{101}T^{211}T^{323}T^{424}$
- $P_6(5) = T^{000}T^{101}T^{211}T^{323}T^{433}$
- $P_7(5) = T^{000}T^{101}T^{211}T^{323}T^{443}$
- $P_8(5) = T^{000}T^{101}T^{211}T^{324}T^{433}$
- $P_9(5) = T^{000}T^{101}T^{211}T^{324}T^{443}$

- $P_{10}(5) = T^{000}T^{101}T^{211}T^{333}T^{443}$
- $P_{11}(4) = T^{000}T^{101}T^{211}T^{343}$
- $P_{12}(5) = T^{000}T^{101}T^{212}T^{323}T^{424}$
- $P_{13}(5) = T^{000}T^{101}T^{212}T^{323}T^{433}$
- $P_{14}(5) = T^{000}T^{101}T^{212}T^{323}T^{443}$
- $P_{15}(4) = T^{000}T^{101}T^{212}T^{324}$
- $P_{16}(4) = T^{000}T^{101}T^{223}T^{324}$
- $P_{17}(5) = T^{000}T^{101}T^{224}T^{333}T^{443}$
- $P_{18}(4) = T^{000}T^{101}T^{224}T^{343}$
- $P_{19}(4) = T^{000}T^{101}T^{233}T^{343}$
- $P_{20}(3) = T^{000}T^{101}T^{243}$

000–110

- $P_{21}(5) = T^{000}T^{110}T^{211}T^{312}T^{423}$
- $P_{22}(5) = T^{000}T^{110}T^{211}T^{312}T^{424}$
- $P_{23}(5) = T^{000}T^{110}T^{211}T^{312}T^{433}$
- $P_{24}(5) = T^{000}T^{110}T^{211}T^{312}T^{443}$
- $P_{25}(5) = T^{000}T^{110}T^{211}T^{323}T^{424}$
- $P_{26}(5) = T^{000}T^{110}T^{211}T^{323}T^{433}$
- $P_{27}(5) = T^{000}T^{110}T^{211}T^{323}T^{443}$
- $P_{28}(4) = T^{000}T^{110}T^{211}T^{324}$
- $P_{29}(5) = T^{000}T^{110}T^{211}T^{333}T^{443}$
- $P_{30}(4) = T^{000}T^{110}T^{211}T^{343}$
- $P_{31}(5) = T^{000}T^{110}T^{212}T^{323}T^{424}$
- $P_{32}(4) = T^{000}T^{110}T^{212}T^{324}$
- $P_{33}(5) = T^{000}T^{110}T^{212}T^{333}T^{443}$
- $P_{34}(4) = T^{000}T^{110}T^{223}T^{324}$
- $P_{35}(5) = T^{000}T^{110}T^{223}T^{333}T^{443}$
- $P_{36}(4) = T^{000}T^{110}T^{223}T^{343}$

000–111

- $P_{37}(5) = T^{000}T^{111}T^{212}T^{323}T^{424}$
- $P_{38}(5) = T^{000}T^{111}T^{212}T^{323}T^{433}$
- $P_{39}(4) = T^{000}T^{111}T^{212}T^{324}$
- $P_{40}(5) = T^{000}T^{111}T^{212}T^{333}T^{443}$
- $P_{41}(4) = T^{000}T^{111}T^{212}T^{343}$

- $P_{42}(4) = T^{000}T^{111}T^{223}T^{324}$
- $P_{43}(5) = T^{000}T^{111}T^{223}T^{333}T^{443}$
- $P_{44}(4) = T^{000}T^{111}T^{223}T^{343}$
- $P_{45}(4) = T^{000}T^{111}T^{224}T^{343}$
- $P_{46}(4) = T^{000}T^{111}T^{233}T^{343}$
- $P_{47}(3) = T^{000}T^{111}T^{243}$

000–112

- $P_{48}(5) = T^{000}T^{112}T^{223}T^{333}T^{443}$
- $P_{49}(4) = T^{000}T^{112}T^{223}T^{343}$
- $P_{50}(4) = T^{000}T^{112}T^{224}T^{343}$
- $P_{51}(4) = T^{000}T^{112}T^{233}T^{343}$
- $P_{52}(3) = T^{000}T^{112}T^{243}$

000–123

- $P_{53}(4) = T^{000}T^{123}T^{224}T^{343}$
- $P_{54}(4) = T^{000}T^{123}T^{233}T^{343}$

000–124

- $P_{55}(3) = T^{000}T^{124}T^{243}$

000–133

- $P_{56}(3) = T^{000}T^{133}T^{243}$

000–143

- $P_{57}(2) = T^{000}T^{143}$

Discussion

- there are 57 possible (namely, verifying the principles of concatenation) life chains (paths);
- from them:

- with five links, i.e., a complete cycle—$P(5)$: 30 (52.63%)
- with four links—$P(4)$: 21 (36.84)
- with three links—$P(3)$: 5 (8.77%)
- with two links—$P(2)$: 1 (1.75%)
- with a single link—$P(1)$: 0 (0.00%)

- if the bifurcation points are considered, the life chains (paths) become:

(a) based on $T^{3--}(\overline{P}_i)$

- $\overline{P}_1 = T^{000}T^{101}T^{211}T^{312}(T^{423}, T^{424}, T^{433}T^{443})$
- $\overline{P}_2 = T^{000}T^{101}T^{211}T^{323}(T^{424}, T^{433}, T^{443})$
- $\overline{P}_3 = T^{000}T^{101}T^{211}T^{324}(T^{433}, T^{443})$
- $\overline{P}_4 = T^{000}T^{101}T^{211}T^{333}T^{443}$
- $\overline{P}_5 = T^{000}T^{101}T^{211}T^{443}$
- $\overline{P}_6 = T^{000}T^{101}T^{212}T^{323}(T^{424}, T^{433}, T^{443})$
- $\overline{P}_7 = T^{000}T^{101}T^{212}T^{324}$
- $\overline{P}_8 = T^{000}T^{101}T^{223}T^{324}$
- $\overline{P}_9 = T^{000}T^{101}T^{224}(T^{333}T^{443}, T^{343})$
- $\overline{P}_{10} = T^{000}T^{101}T^{233}T^{343}$
- $\overline{P}_{11} = T^{000}T^{101}T^{243}$
- $\overline{P}_{12} = T^{000}T^{110}T^{211}T^{312}(T^{423}, T^{424}, T^{433}, T^{443})$
- $\overline{P}_{13} = T^{000}T^{110}T^{211}T^{323}(T^{424}, T^{433}, T^{443})$
- $\overline{P}_{14} = T^{000}T^{110}T^{211}T^{324}$
- $\overline{P}_{15} = T^{000}T^{110}T^{211}T^{333}T^{443}$
- $\overline{P}_{16} = T^{000}T^{110}T^{211}T^{343}$
- $\overline{P}_{17} = T^{000}T^{110}T^{212}(T^{323}T^{424}, T^{324}, T^{333}T^{443})$
- $\overline{P}_{18} = T^{000}T^{110}T^{223}(T^{324}, T^{333}T^{443}, T^{343})$
- $\overline{P}_{19} = T^{000}T^{111}T^{212}T^{323}(T^{424}, T^{433})$
- $\overline{P}_{20} = T^{000}T^{111}T^{212}T^{324}$
- $\overline{P}_{21} = T^{000}T^{111}T^{212}T^{333}T^{443}$
- $\overline{P}_{22} = T^{000}T^{111}T^{212}T^{343}$
- $\overline{P}_{23} = T^{000}T^{111}T^{223}(T^{324}, T^{333}T^{443}, T^{343})$
- $\overline{P}_{24} = T^{000}T^{111}T^{224}T^{343}$
- $\overline{P}_{25} = T^{000}T^{111}T^{233}T^{343}$

- $\overline{P}_{26} = T^{000}T^{111}T^{243}$
- $\overline{P}_{27} = T^{000}T^{112}T^{223}T^{333}T^{443}$
- $\overline{P}_{28} = T^{000}T^{112}T^{223}T^{343}$
- $\overline{P}_{29} = T^{000}T^{112}T^{224}T^{343}$
- $\overline{P}_{30} = T^{000}T^{112}T^{233}T^{343}$
- $\overline{P}_{31} = T^{000}T^{112}T^{243}$
- $\overline{P}_{32} = T^{000}T^{123}T^{224}T^{343}$
- $\overline{P}_{33} = T^{000}T^{123}T^{233}T^{343}$
- $\overline{P}_{34} = T^{000}T^{124}T^{243}$
- $\overline{P}_{35} = T^{000}T^{133}T^{243}$
- $\overline{P}_{36} = T^{000}T^{143}$

(b) based on T^{2--} ($\overline{p}_i$)

$$\underset{1}{\overline{\overline{P}}} = T^{000}T^{101}T^{211}$$

- $$\begin{pmatrix} T^{312}\left(T^{423}, T^{424}, T^{433}T^{443}\right), T^{323}\left(T^{424}, T^{433}, T^{443}\right), \\ T^{324}\left(T^{433}, T^{443}\right), T^{333}T^{443}, T^{443} \end{pmatrix}$$
- $\underset{2}{\overline{\overline{P}}} = T^{000}T^{101}T^{212}\left(T^{323}\left(T^{424}, T^{433}, T^{443}\right), T^{324}\right)$
- $\underset{3}{\overline{\overline{P}}} = T^{000}T^{101}T^{223}T^{324}$
- $\underset{4}{\overline{\overline{P}}} = T^{000}T^{101}T^{224}\left(T^{333}T^{443}, T^{343}\right)$
- $\underset{5}{\overline{\overline{P}}} = T^{000}T^{101}T^{233}T^{343}$
- $\underset{6}{\overline{\overline{P}}} = T^{000}T^{101}T^{243}$
- $\underset{7}{\overline{\overline{P}}} = T^{000}T^{110}T^{211}\begin{pmatrix} T^{312}\left(T^{423}, T^{424}, T^{433}, T^{443}\right), \\ T^{323}\left(T^{424}, T^{433}, T^{443}\right), T^{324}, T^{333}T^{443}, T^{343} \end{pmatrix}$
- $\underset{8}{\overline{\overline{P}}} = T^{000}T^{110}T^{212}\left(T^{323}T^{424}, T^{324}, T^{333}T^{443}\right)$
- $\underset{9}{\overline{\overline{P}}} = T^{000}T^{110}T^{223}\left(T^{324}, T^{333}T^{443}, T^{343}\right)$

$$\overline{\overline{P}}_{10} = T^{000}T^{111}$$

– $$\left(\begin{array}{l} T^{212}T^{323}\left(T^{424}, T^{433}\right), T^{212}T^{324}, T^{212}T^{333}T^{443}, T^{212}T^{343}, T^{223} \\ \left(T^{324}, T^{333}T^{443}, T^{343}\right), T^{224}T^{343}, T^{233}T^{343}, T^{243} \end{array}\right)$$

– $$\overline{\overline{P}}_{11} = T^{000}T^{112}\left(T^{223}T^{333}T^{443}, T^{223}T^{343}, T^{224}T^{343}, T^{233}T^{343}, T^{243}\right)$$

– $$\overline{\overline{P}}_{12} = T^{000}T^{123}\left(T^{224}T^{343}, T^{233}T^{343}\right)$$

– $$\overline{\overline{P}}_{13} = T^{000}T^{124}T^{243}$$

– $$\overline{\overline{P}}_{14} = T^{000}T^{133}T^{243}$$

– $$\overline{\overline{P}}_{15} = T^{000}T^{143}$$

(c) based on T^{1--} ($\tilde{P}_i$)

$$\tilde{P}_1 = T^{000}T^{101}(T^{211}$$

– $$\left(\begin{array}{l} T^{312}\left(T^{423}, T^{424}, T^{433}T^{443}\right), T^{323}\left(T^{424}, T^{433}, T^{443}\right), \\ T^{324}\left(T^{433}, T^{443}\right), T^{333}T^{443}, T^{443} \end{array}\right),$$

$$T^{212}\left(T^{323}\left(T^{424}, T^{433}, T^{443}\right), T^{324}\right), T^{223}T^{324},$$

$$T^{224}\left(T^{333}T^{443}, T^{343}\right), T^{233}T^{343}, T^{243})$$

$$\tilde{P}_2 = T^{000}T^{110}$$

– $$\left(\begin{array}{l} T^{211}\left(\begin{array}{l} T^{312}\left(T^{423}, T^{424}, T^{433}, T^{443}\right), \\ T^{323}\left(T^{424}, T^{433}, T^{443}\right), T^{324}, T^{333}T^{443}, T^{343} \end{array}\right), \\ T^{212}\left(T^{323}T^{424}, T^{324}, T^{333}T^{443}\right), T^{223}\left(T^{324}, T^{333}T^{443}, T^{343}\right) \end{array}\right)$$

$$\tilde{P}_3 = T^{000}T^{111}$$

– $$\left(\begin{array}{l} T^{212}T^{323}\left(T^{424}, T^{433}\right), T^{212}T^{324}, T^{212}T^{333}T^{443}, T^{212}T^{343}, T^{223} \\ \left(T^{324}, T^{333}T^{443}, T^{343}\right), T^{224}T^{343}, T^{233}T^{343}, T^{243} \end{array}\right)$$

- $\tilde{P}_4 = T^{000}T^{112}(T^{223}T^{333}T^{443}, T^{223}T^{343}, T^{224}T^{343}, T^{233}T^{343}, T^{243})$
- $\tilde{P}_5 = T^{000}T^{123}(T^{224}T^{343}, T^{233}T^{343})$
- $\tilde{P}_6 = T^{000}T^{124}T^{243}$
- $\tilde{P}_7 = T^{000}T^{133}T^{243}$
- $\tilde{P}_8 = T^{000}T^{143}$

(d) based on T^{000} ($\hat{P}$)

$$\hat{P} = T^{000}(T^{101}(T^{211} \left(\begin{array}{l} T^{312}\left(T^{423}, T^{424}, T^{433}T^{443}\right), T^{323}\left(T^{424}, T^{433}, T^{443}\right), \\ T^{324}\left(T^{433}, T^{443}\right), T^{333}T^{443}, T^{443} \end{array} \right),$$

$$T^{212}\left(T^{323}\left(T^{424}, T^{433}, T^{443}\right), T^{324}\right), T^{223}T^{324}, T^{224}$$

$$\left(T^{333}T^{443}, T^{343}\right), T^{233}T^{343}, T^{243}),$$

$$T^{110}(T^{211} \left(\begin{array}{l} T^{312}\left(T^{423}, T^{424}, T^{433}, T^{443}\right), T^{323} \\ \left(T^{424}, T^{433}, T^{443}\right), T^{324}, T^{333}T^{443}, T^{343} \end{array} \right),$$

$$T^{212}\left(T^{323}T^{424}, T^{324}, T^{333}T^{443}\right), T^{223}\left(T^{324}, T^{333}T^{443}, T^{343}\right)),$$

$$T^{111} \left(\begin{array}{l} T^{212}T^{323}\left(T^{424}, T^{433}\right), T^{212}T^{324}, T^{212}T^{333}T^{443}, T^{212} \\ T^{343}, T^{223} \\ \left(T^{324}, T^{333}T^{443}, T^{343}\right), T^{224}T^{343}, T^{233}T^{343}, T^{243} \end{array} \right),$$

$$T^{112}\left(T^{223}T^{333}T^{443}, T^{223}T^{343}, T^{224}T^{343}, T^{233}T^{343}, T^{243}\right),$$

$$T^{123}\left(T^{224}T^{343}, T^{233}T^{343}\right), T^{124}T^{243}, T^{133}T^{243}, T^{143})$$

- so, the general (canonical) expression of the life chain (path) is formed by 102 triads, that can generate 57 distinct life chains (paths), concatenated in different bifurcation points.

2.6 A Hermeneutic of the Life Chain (Path)

Base on to the third pyramid above discussed (namely, that of the degree in which the needs of first pyramid are satisfied through the "channels" of the second pyramid), it can now be elaborate a hermeneutic of the life chain (path).

What is of the greatest interest, in fact, addresses the most appropriate life chain (path) that meets the concept of plenary life. The content of plenary life integrates the following (cumulative) properties (I use Fig. 4):

- it aspires to match the peak of the third pyramid, namely, to realization of the significance satisfaction of life (level V, i.e., *S4*—see Sect. 2);
- although the significance satisfaction is idiosyncratic, it is based on three trans-personal channels (means), namely: communitarian layer (L2), social layer (L3),[27] and global layer (L4);
- the need for self-actualization (N4) is satisfied by two categories (layers) of satisfaction: relational satisfaction (S3) and significance satisfaction (S4);
- a question arises here: is it "required" that the peak of the third pyramid be reached within a continuous life chain (path) or, if possible, even within a broken such life chain, if, of course, that life chain is logically operational, namely, is in the list of those 57 life chains already identified (see the Sect. 2.5). My considerations in this matter are as follows:
- let me introduce the concept of *link saturability*[28]—I refer to the links of the third pyramid, that is, S0, S1, S2, S3, and S4. A link is non-saturable if and only if the corresponding link in the first pyramid is a need that comes back periodically, that is, it can only be repeatably satisfied, not definitively; for example, N0 can only be periodically satisfied, so S0 can never be saturated;
- the link saturability is that property of the link to be saturable;
- the saturability allows the saturation, not guarantees the saturation in fact[29];

Nota bene: only S0 is an obviously saturable link.

- a continuous life chain (from S0 to S4), without skipping any link, is, most probably, desirable, since any link is based on a saturation of the immediately previous link;
- the saturation of a link before accessing the immediately following link (from bottom to top) provides a great degree of irreversibility from the new link to the former one. This irreversibility is *conditio sine qua non* of the sustainability property of the involved life chain (path)[30];
- an unsustainable life chain presupposes that there are (the probability of) reversions in the layers involved, i.e., in the link "k";
- an incomplete life chain presupposes that not all intermediate links between S0 and S4 are covered, so that the life chain has less than 5 valid links, i.e., links that verify the stipulated relationships among α, β, and γ;
- a complete life chain is that life chain that is both non-incomplete and sustainable;

Nota bene: the *plenary life* chain is selectable from the complete life chains only.

2.7 Towards Plenary Life

To get the plenary life means primarily to find a complete life chain. After verifying the 57 life chains identified, the following complete life chains, i.e., with five links concatenated, can be held—30 cases (with T_j I note the link "j" in the life chain:

- $P_1(5) = T_1^{000}T_2^{101}T_3^{211}T_4^{312}T_5^{423}$
- $P_2(5) = T_1^{000}T_2^{101}T_3^{211}T_4^{312}T_5^{424}$
- $P_3(5) = T_1^{000}T_2^{101}T_3^{211}T_4^{312}T_5^{433}$
- $P_4(5) = T_1^{000}T_2^{101}T_3^{211}T_4^{312}T_5^{443}$
- $P_5(5) = T_1^{000}T_2^{101}T_3^{211}T_4^{323}T_5^{424}$
- $P_6(5) = T_1^{000}T_2^{101}T_3^{211}T_4^{323}T_5^{433}$
- $P_7(5) = T_1^{000}T_2^{101}T_3^{211}T_4^{323}T_5^{443}$
- $P_8(5) = T_1^{000}T_2^{101}T_3^{211}T_4^{324}T_5^{433}$
- $P_9(5) = T_1^{000}T_2^{101}T_3^{211}T_4^{324}T_5^{443}$
- $P_{10}(5) = T_1^{000}T_2^{101}T_3^{211}T_4^{333}T_5^{453}$
- $P_{12}(5) = T_1^{000}T_2^{101}T_3^{212}T_4^{323}T_5^{424}$

- $P_{13}(5) = T_1^{000} T_2^{101} T_3^{212} T_4^{323} T_5^{433}$
- $P_{14}(5) = T_1^{000} T_2^{101} T_3^{212} T_4^{323} T_5^{443}$
- $P_{17}(5) = T_1^{000} T_2^{101} T_3^{224} T_4^{333} T_5^{443}$
- $P_{21}(5) = T_1^{000} T_2^{110} T_3^{211} T_4^{312} T_5^{423}$
- $P_{22}(5) = T_1^{000} T_2^{110} T_3^{211} T_4^{312} T_5^{424}$
- $P_{23}(5) = T_1^{000} T_2^{110} T_3^{211} T_4^{312} T_5^{433}$
- $P_{24}(5) = T_1^{000} T_2^{110} T_3^{211} T_4^{312} T_5^{443}$
- $P_{25}(5) = T_1^{000} T_2^{110} T_3^{211} T_4^{323} T_5^{424}$
- $P_{26}(5) = T_1^{000} T_2^{110} T_3^{211} T_4^{323} T_5^{433}$
- $P_{27}(5) = T_1^{000} T_2^{110} T_3^{211} T_4^{323} T_5^{443}$
- $P_{29}(5) = T_1^{000} T_2^{110} T_3^{211} T_4^{333} T_5^{443}$
- $P_{31}(5) = T_1^{000} T_2^{110} T_3^{212} T_4^{323} T_5^{424}$
- $P_{33}(5) = T_1^{000} T_2^{110} T_3^{212} T_4^{333} T_5^{443}$
- $P_{35}(5) = T_1^{000} T_2^{110} T_3^{223} T_4^{333} T_5^{443}$
- $P_{37}(5) = T_1^{000} T_2^{111} T_3^{212} T_4^{323} T_5^{424}$
- $P_{38}(5) = T_1^{000} T_2^{111} T_3^{212} T_4^{323} T_5^{433}$
- $P_{40}(5) = T_1^{000} T_2^{111} T_3^{212} T_4^{333} T_5^{443}$
- $P_{43}(5) = T_1^{000} T_2^{111} T_3^{223} T_4^{333} T_5^{443}$
- $P_{48}(5) = T_1^{000} T_2^{112} T_3^{223} T_4^{333} T_5^{443}$

From the set of complete life chains, we must now reject those cases where the following conditions are disjunctively violated:

(i) according to Fig. 4, all levels (layers) of the first pyramid are logically connected to either level L0 or level L1 of the second pyramid. Consequently, there are two cases in which $\beta_k = \alpha_k$, namely for $k = 0$ or $k = 1$. All other cases (namely, if $k = 2, 3, 4$) for which $\beta_k \leq \alpha_k$, must be accepted as valid;

(ii) according also to Fig. 4, must be considered acceptable the cases in which $\gamma_k < \alpha_k$ for $k = 2, 3, 4$;

(iii) we cannot have $\beta_3 = 0$, since this would mean that, for example, the safety needs could be satisfied by the biological layer and, further, could reach the material satisfaction—consequently, the cases $P_1 - P_{14}$, and P_{17} must be rejected from the set of what I call *viable life chains* (paths), noted VLCs[31];

(iv) we cannot have $\gamma_2 = 0$, since this would mean that, for example, safety needs (N1), by intermediation of personal layer (L1), will lead to material satisfaction (S0);

(v) we can have $\gamma_1 < \alpha_1$; $\gamma_2 < \alpha_2$; $\gamma_3 < \alpha_3$;

As a result, the following set of life chains is complete and continuous, that is, what I called above VLCs, that is, five VLCs.

(1) $P_{37} = T_1^{000} T_2^{111} T_3^{212} T_4^{323} T_5^{424}$
(2) $P_{38} = T_1^{000} T_2^{111} T_3^{212} T_4^{323} T_5^{433}$
(3) $P_{40} = T_1^{000} T_2^{111} T_3^{212} T_4^{333} T_5^{443}$
(4) $P_{43} = T_1^{000} T_2^{111} T_3^{223} T_4^{333} T_5^{443}$
(5) $P_{48} = T_1^{000} T_2^{112} T_3^{223} T_4^{333} T_5^{443}$

2.8 *Getting a Plenary Life*

(a) Identifying the Plenary Life Chain

From the VLCs we must now to identify the plenary life chain (PLC). The unique criterion is, of course, reaching of the "floor", i.e., "peak" of the third pyramid, namely the significance satisfaction (S4). From the result of Sect. 2.7, this PLC is unique, that is, P_{37}:

$$P_{37} = T_1^{000} T_2^{111} T_3^{212} T_4^{323} T_5^{424}$$

(b) A qualitative analysis of the plenary life chain

To provide the qualitative features of the PLC, the graph in Fig. 6 is useful.

<u>Discussion</u>

- as a quantitative (rather metaphorical) analogy, the five links of the (uniquely possible) PLC have an increasingly "volume" of life (*Nota bene*: it can be considered as if the numerical mark/order exactly quantifies some uniform measure):

$$V_1 = 0 \cdot 0 \cdot 0 = 0$$

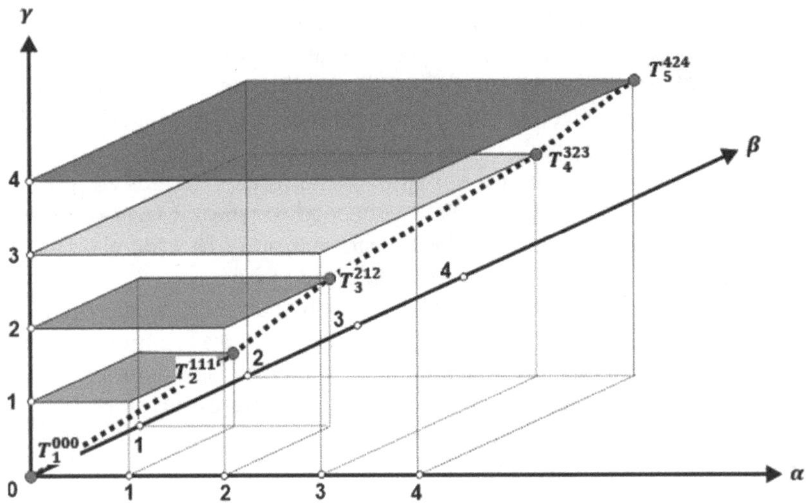

Fig. 6 Topology of the plenary life chain (*Source* author)

$$V_2 = 1 \cdot 1 \cdot 1 = 1 \ (+1)$$

$$V_3 = 2 \cdot 1 \cdot 2 = 4 \ (+3)$$

$$V_4 = 3 \cdot 2 \cdot 3 = 18 \ (+14)$$

$$V_5 = 4 \cdot 2 \cdot 4 = 32 \ (+15)$$

- the links, as logically ordered by the bottom number of triads, imply, also, a chronological order mapped on the logical one: triad T_k^{---} is, chronologically, i.e., on the time axe so that:

$$T_{k-1}^{---} \ltimes T_k^{---} \ltimes T_{k+1}^{---} (k = 1, 2, 3)$$

where the symbol "$\ltimes$" put between variables "x" and "y", that is: $x \ltimes y$, must be read: "x occurs earlier than y", which is, of course, equivalent with "y occurs later than x".

- the triads T_2 and T_3 use the same channel (or transformation operator), namely L1 (personal layer), to satisfy both N1 (safety needs) and N2 (love & belonging) into S1 (qualitative satisfaction); so, in the PLC, we have, at those triads/moments, a stationarity of the layer involved, namely of the personal layer;
- at the triad T_4, all the three marks of the three pyramids are greater than the marks of T_3, that is, it is needed for the L2 layer (communitarian layer) to perform the transformation of the "demand" (the needs manifestation) into offer (the need satisfying);
- a very interesting issue is, in the PLC, the fact that neither the layer L3 (social layer) nor the layer L4 (global layer) are required to "contribute" to satisfy the highest (and, somewhat, ambiguous) need, namely the self-actualization (N4). This is interesting since it leads us to conclude on the following:
- the social layer (L3) and the global layer (L4) seem to be simple extensions (so, purely quantitatively) of the communitarian layer[32];
- for the highest levels in the third pyramid (S3 and S4, respectively), it is necessary, in fact, that all layers of the second pyramid (except the layer S0) participate, which means that S3 and S4 are, by far, the most desirable ends of the people.

Starting from Fig. 6, the PLC can be visualized as shown in Fig. 7.

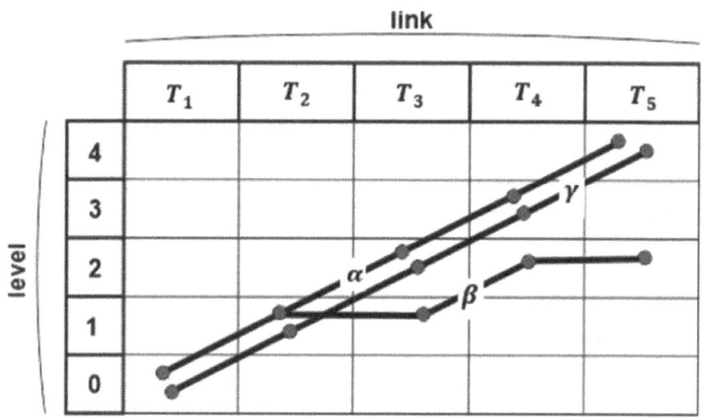

Fig. 7 Topology of the plenary life chain (*Source* author)

3 Providing of Capabilities

3.1 Some Preparative

In Chapter 5 (see, especially, Annex 1 in Chapter 5), I discussed the issue of public goods provided, as an obligation required by the social contract, by the state. Also, I examined a possible (logical) parallelism between public goods, on the one hand, and the capabilities, on the other hand. However, despite that (possible) parallelism, the concept of public good and that of capability have important and relevant, for this chapter, differences.

The current paragraph will provide a definition of the concept of capability, will search the sources (origins) of capabilities, and, finally, will propose a typology of the capabilities. All these will prepare the discussion in which the plenary life chain is put in relation to the capabilities.

3.2 The Concept of Capability

Precursors

Over time, aspects or emphases of the capabilities approach in the theory of social justice (or, more generally, in social theory) have been highlighted by different "generalist" thinkers.[33]

- Aristotle
  - Aristotle did not present a coherent theory on the issue of social justice, but he has references to what can be called distributism[34] or distributional theory (in *Politics* and *Nicomachean Ethics*)[35];
  - the basic idea that Aristotle supports regarding what will later be called the capabilities approach (or capabilities theory) consists of the following requirement: a good political arrangement in society (*Nota bene*: in the city—the Greek *polis*—in his time) must be such that it has in mind or tends to ensure a good life for people, in the permitted or available circumstances[36];
  - by good life, Aristotle understands a good functioning[37] of the human being (of course, in given, historical circumstances, not ideally);

- however, based on his eudaimonism vision, Aristotle sees this functioning of the human being or this good life of the human being as happiness[38];
- Aristotle insists on the fact that it is a tragedy if a human being or even a non-human living creature, which has an innate capacity for a certain functioning, is prevented from operationalizing that functioning or from fulfilling the corresponding functions;
- there are two fundamental ideas regarding economics: (a) the problem of motivation: how should I live; (b) the problem of social significance, which transcends the individual.[39]

- Adam Smith
  - the connecting element between Smith's thinking and the capabilities approach/theory is revealed by Smith's theory of human capital;
  - Smith believes that the behaviour, therefore the functioning of the human individual, depends on his/her morals (habits, culture, traditions, social affiliation) and education, which distinguishes him/her from the behaviours of other individuals. In this sense, Smith believes that human beings are mutilated in their growth and development when various constraints, including the lack of information about educational opportunities, prevent them from completing their education[40];
  - Smith accepts that the manifestation of capability (i.e., the functioning of the human being) differs (or may differ) from one society to another, depending on the general cultural background (axiology) of the societies in question;
  - Smith mitigates his principle of egoism by using the phrase *common prudence*[41] (which also implies group altruism)—see his work *The Theory of Moral Sentiments* (2007)[42];
  - good behaviour means self-discipline and sympathy—each must see himself not as separate from others, but as a citizen of the world, as a member of the community with nature (sometimes, this requires sacrificing individual interest—own little interest).

- Karl Marx

- insists that human beings be treated as ends and not as means[43]; this has as a consequence the creation of conditions for the human being to function according to his/her own ends[44];
- the creation of conditions for treating the human being as an end (*Nota bene*: of society) refers, first of all, to economic conditions but, of course, also to the normative ones[45];
- the human being is defined as the being with "rich human need" (Nussbaum, 2006);
- the human being must live in dignity—the dignity is understood as the availability of true human functioning; moreover, human dignity cannot be defined before and independently of human capabilities, but simultaneously and in interconnection with them;
- the availability of true human functioning refers to the availability for activity, not to the simple availability of resources (e.g., talent);
- Marx believes that the human being needs a plurality of activities in life.

- Hillary Putnam and Vivian Walsh
  - the position of the two researchers in the field of capabilities theory was exposed in the work *The End of Value-Free Economics* (which they coordinated[46]), published in 2011, by Routledge (Taylor & Francis Group);
  - first of all, it is necessary to abandon the strict dichotomy between facts and values, a dichotomy recommended by logical positivism[47] that (still) underlies the mainstream in the field of economic theory (*Nota bene*: see the *homo œconomicus model*); in this sense, there is talk of the disappearance or eclipse (Ostapiuk, 2020) of economic theory that abstracts from values (value-free Economics);
  - secondly (especially Walsh), Sen's position is supported regarding the need for economic theory (the current Economics) to return to its state initially intended by Smith, namely that of political economy (*Nota bene*: it is considered that the first "wave" in this endeavour is represented by Pierro Sraffa, who is joined by Bertram Schefold and Luigi Passineti,[48] and, in the second "wave", by Sen);

- Walsh develops, independently of Sen, a concept equivalent to the concept of the functioning of the individual (associated with capability), which he calls achievement[49];
- morality depends on functioning within the framework of capability, not vice versa. This positioning rejects the a-historical (*Nota bene*: that is, logical) character of Kantian morality and returns to its contingent aspects, supported by Aristotle;
- Putnam rejects the dichotomy between values and norms (supported by Habermas), showing that norms must contain an ethical component (Putnam & Walsh, 2014).[50] At the same time, he considers that the attack on the mainstream is supported by a wider group of economists, among whom he lists Partha Dasgupta, Joseph Stiglitz, Peter Hammond, and John Roemer, all of whom call for the reconnection between facts, values, and theory, in order to increase the relevance of economic theory;
- Walsh shows that Rawls (who is concerned with an ideal society—*Nota bene*: like Kant, one of his mentors in moral philosophy) also admits or claims the entanglement between facts, values, and theory; obviously, this entanglement is carried to its (possible) ultimate consequences by the capabilities approach, registered in Sen's and Nussbaum's "account".

Amartya Sen

The scientist who laid the foundations of the capabilities approach in the field of social justice and, more generally, in social philosophy, is Amartya Sen (1987). The basic work in which this theory/approach is articulated is *On Ethics and Economics*, published in 1988 by Blackwell Publishing (Sen, 1999). Below, we will briefly review the main theoretical coordinates of this work.

(a) General considerations

- the book deals with the relationship between economic theory and moral philosophy;

- the contributions that the theory of general economic equilibrium can bring to moral philosophy are suggested;
- it highlights the damage that the erroneous use of selfish behaviour has brought to the quality of economic analysis;
- it is considered that one of the major deficiencies of economic theory is its distance from ethics;
- it is appreciated that economic logic has influenced welfare theory, but not vice versa (it is also suggested that the opposite path should be followed);
- economic theory should pay more attention to the ethics of economic behaviour, not just its rationality;
- it is necessary to incorporate rights (with intrinsic value, not just instrumental) into economic analysis;
- the mainstream economics reduces rationality to the consistency (non-contradictory) of choice, i.e., to the maximization of self-interest, but, it seems, this is not exactly the real economic behaviour[51];
- Sen distinguishes between wellbeing-type behaviour and agency-type behaviour; he also distinguishes between distributive justice and broader assessments of the individual and the group;
- a broad consequential approach can provide a basis for prescriptive thinking related to rights and freedoms;
- economic analysis must move away from the approach based on individual egoism;
- in economic theory, norm and behaviour must be put together[52];
- Economics has two origins (both related to politics): ethics and engineering—so far the emphasis has been mainly on the "engineering" component (i.e., on positive economics: called exactly Economics), but an emphasis on ethics is needed;
- Sen introduces the concept of commitment, having a meaning close to that of the concept of assumption the principle of behaviour in Nozick; however, while in Nozick, the assumption in question has an inter-subjective character (the assumption is, as a rule, publicly declared, consisting in this publication also a certain "guarantee", for the other members of society regarding the observance of the commitment), in

Sen's case it seems that the respective assumption has an intra-subjective character;

- Sen rejects, in his entire approach, the concept of value-free economics, which is, moreover, *conditio sine qua non* for reconnecting economic theory (and economic action) with ethics;
- in Sen's view, rationality consists rather in the evaluation of goals and values than in the evaluation of the order of preferences[53]; this means that the emphasis should be placed not on the theory of rational choice, but on the theory of social choice (*Nota bene*: it should be noted that social choice is not equivalent to public choice—see, for example, institutionalism—because public choice theory is also developed under the paradigm of rationality, not under that, as one might say, of sociality).[54]

(b) Special considerations

- a gap between positive economics (predictive economics) and welfare economics was created, in the sense that the influence of predictive economics on welfare economics was accepted, but not vice versa;
- welfare economics propositions are combinations of: a) behaviour relative to oneself; b) judging the achievement of goals, at a social level, based on utility[55] (*Nota bene*: that is, considering the total utility, at the level of society);
- wrongly, this inter-personal comparison of utility was considered to have a normative or ethical character—this is false: inter-personal comparison of utility is nonsense from both an ethical and descriptive point of view[56];
- Sen announces what he calls the fundamental theorem of welfare economics:
  - <u>direct theorem</u>: if there are no externalities (i.e., interdependencies outside the market), then the equilibrium of perfect competition is a Pareto economic optimum;
  - <u>converse of the direct theorem</u>: if there are no economies of scale, any social Pareto optimum is an equilibrium of perfect competition[57];

- like Nozick (and, in principle,[58] like Rawls), Sen considers that the only intrinsic value for ethical calculation is individual utility; in this sense, he is a follower of what is called welfarism;
- within the fundamental theorem proposed by Sen there is a logical vulnerability: the concept of Pareto optimum/equilibrium[59] requires the equivalence of advantage with utility (*Nota bene*: I recall that Rawls, in his efforts to detach himself from utilitarianism, had separated the advantage generated by the application of the difference principle from utility in general, and Nozick, although he did not reject utility as a criterion for the application of his third principle—the principle of correction—he considered only or especially symbolic utility valid and acceptable).

- in Sen's view, utilitarianism is a combination of three elements:
  - *welfarism*: the good state of a situation depends only on information about the utility of that state;
  - *additivity*: information about the state can only be evaluated by summing up all the utilities involved;
  - *consequentialism*: any choice is evaluable by its effect on the state (*Nota bene*: Pareto optimality only targets the first component—wellbeing, although, from a logical point of view, consequentialism is also involved);

- one of Sen's most interesting (and productive) positions on the subject of social justice is the one regarding the relationship between wellbeing, agency or action, and freedom:
  - agency (action in order to achieve a goal) is not independent of wellbeing, although the two concepts are distinct;
  - agency is not entirely intended for wellbeing, which it sometimes serves only indirectly[60]; *Nota bene*: so far, in general, research has focused on wellbeing and less on agency;
  - although utility is interpreted in terms of wellbeing, it might be more appropriate to see it in terms of agency;

in any case, utility should not be confused with wellbeing, the essence of wellbeing consisting, rather, in agency/action/diligence which is, in turn, the essence of capability, that is, of the individual's functioning within society;
  - agency (behaviour) can deviate from the criterion of wellbeing when the behaviour in question is not guided by preferences but by external circumstances (for example, by norms);
- Sen proposes five criteria for establishing the capabilities of the individual:
  - the importance of real freedoms in assessing a person's advantage;
  - individual differences in the ability to transform resources[61] into valuable activities;
  - the multi-variable nature of activities that give rise to happiness (*Nota bene*: Aristotelian eudaimonism, not simple hedonism);
  - a balance of material and non-material factors in assessing human wellbeing;
  - concern for the distribution of opportunities within society[62];
- the ethical approach refers to rights and freedoms.[63] Sen shows that to be free means to be free to give up, which implies being free to choose[64];
- freedom must be evaluated in itself, not with reference to the achievement of some goals[65];
- the set of capabilities chosen by someone depends on the way of life chosen by that person (so, the choice of the way of life is logically prior to the choice of the set of capabilities). *Nota bene*: this lexicographical "ordering", proposed by Sen, is equivalent, in my opinion, to the choice of a principle (i.e., to the assumption of a commitment) within the framework of Nozickian theory;
- the perspective of capabilities is necessarily pluralistic[66];
- maximization (e.g., of welfare) is not an extremizing, but has the meaning of Simon's concept of *satisficing*;
- Sen completely abandons utilitarianism on the issue of social justice and even in economic reasoning.

Martha C. Nussbaum

- the capabilities theory/approach aims at the good life of the individual as an effect of the social or political framework or arrangement in the (historical) society in question. Therefore, it is not a matter of a natural state, but of a social (cultural) state;
- the capabilities theory (CT) is an "axiomatic" theory, in the sense that it starts from positional or positioning statements that are not disputable (although, obviously, they can be rejected, but, as long as they are not rejected *ab ovo*, they function as axioms);
- the capabilities theory is like the equity/fairness theory (FT—Rawls) and the entitlement theory (RT—Nozick), respectively, a normative theory, not simply positive one;
- the capabilities theory (as a result, among other things, of the fact that it is sharply distinct from proceduralist theories—such as Rawls's theory) is a *finalist* theory. It claims that the finalities of the application of the theory of social justice be known in advance, by each individual and by the entire society, and guaranteed in terms of their effective accessibility;
- from a distributional point of view, CT *does not claim redistribution*. This conclusion is based, of course, on the fact that, since the list of capabilities that must be ensured/guaranteed through a specific social arrangement (of a normative type, obviously) is given, no deviation from it is possible, in principle, i.e., it is not possible to block any individual's access to any of the listed capabilities;
- the so-called capabilities (which represent the potentialities of the individual's functioning in the direction of his/her wellbeing) are qualitative, not quantitative concepts, i.e., a size (quantum, value, frequency, etc.) that must be objectified in relation to each capability is not established. Moreover, the individual is not required, from a normative point of view, to use the capability in question, he/she still has the latitude/freedom to decide whether or not to use that capability that is guaranteed but not mandatory—it is, in other words, a right, without a correlative obligation;
- Nussbaum takes up and integrates Sen's concept of consequentialism, which she correlates with the concept of finality (finalism) of the capability's theory.

4 The Logical Foundations of Capabilities Theory

4.1 Background Issues

Firstly, the capabilities theory/approach aims at the good life of the individual as an effect of the social or political framework or arrangement in the (historical) society in question. Therefore, it is not a matter of a natural state, but of a social (cultural) state, that is, relating to the human condition, even if the social or political arrangement in question considers, more or less, human nature—the capabilities approach does not infer this arrangement exclusively from human nature nor exclusively from the human condition (as Rawls seems to do through the social contract).

Secondly, the capabilities theory (CT) is an "axiomatic" theory, in the sense that it starts from positional or positioning statements that are not disputable (although, obviously, they can be rejected, but, as long as they are not rejected *ab ovo*, they function as axioms). Thus, it declares that the greatest relevance for the individual is the freedom to achieve wellbeing—this could be considered *the first principle of CT*. The essential difference from the first Rawlsian principle, which also refers to the problem of freedom, is that, in CT, freedom no longer constitutes an abstract distribution, although not lacking in firmness and even imperativeness, but an oriented one, in the sense that this orientation aims at the acquisition of wellbeing.[67] The question can be asked, regarding the concept of (individual) wellbeing, whether it represents, from a referential point of view, the most general and/or appropriate objective (or capability) associable to the generic individual. In my opinion, the answer to this presumptive question[68] can be formulated on the basis of the following considerations, which are inferred, moreover, from the economy of Nussbaum's work:

- the wellbeing of the individual is a property or a state of the human being that aims at its free functioning. By free functioning we obviously mean the freedom of the individual to choose the way in which to function;
- therefore, as in Sen's conception, it is not utility (and, *a fortiori*, not substantive utility[69]) that the individual seeks/pursues/expects, but his/her functioning as a human being;
- the functioning of the human being (of the individual) is equivalent to action (or agency, in the terminology established in social

philosophy, respectively in moral philosophy), therefore wellbeing is associated (again, as in Sen, but also as in Marx, for that matter) with agency.

Thirdly, it must be shown that the capabilities theory is, like the equity theory (FT) of Rawls, and the entitlement theory (RT) of Nozick, respectively, a normative theory, not simply a positive one. The normative aspect of the CT results directly from the fact that the individual's functioning in the direction of his/her wellbeing[70] is possible (possibly maximized or, as the case may be, optimized) by the social arrangement of the society in question. Since social arrangement is always a normative arrangement (whether formal, informal, or a formal-informal mix), it follows that CT implies normativism.[71]

Fourth, CT (explicitly) rejects proceduralism. More precisely, CT, for example, in Martha Nussbaum's approach, builds on the rejection of procedural contractarianism, as proposed by Rawls. In this regard, I wish to show that, although the rejection of proceduralism is clear and unambiguous, there are some vulnerabilities in the rejection of contractarianism.

Fifth, CT (implicitly) rejects resilience. This rejection results from (at least) the following considerations:

- by conceiving the social arrangement as a master principle of ensuring (without risks) the capabilities of the generic individual,[72] there is no longer any question that a certain capability will not be ensured to the individual, that is, it will not allow the individual to function in the direction, virtue, and achievement of that capability[73];
- since it is not possible to deny, in any way whatsoever, the capability inculcated in the (normative) social arrangement, there is obviously no need for either compensation (as Rawls proposes—see the difference principle) or restoration to the initial (*Nota bene*: this time, the possible) state (as Nozick proposes—see the rectification or corrective principle);
- since there is no need for a principle (therefore, for an action/agency of a public type) to rectify a deviation from access to the capability in question (therefore to the associated functioning of the individual), resilientism is useless.

Sixthly, CT (as a result, among other things, of its sharp distinction from proceduralist theories—such as Rawls's theory) is a *finalist* theory. It claims that the ends of the application of the theory of social justice are known in advance, by each individual and by the whole society, and guaranteed in terms of their effective accessibility. Conceptually, it is obvious that the existence of known and guaranteed ends through the social arrangement is equivalent to the formulation and assumption (i.e., the declaration of the associated commitment) of a principle of behaviour—we recall that, as Nozick showed, the formulation of a principle of behaviour and the commitment made publicly to respect it function as a *sui generis* procedure[74]; therefore, the anti-proceduralism claimed by Nussbaum is questionable.

Seventhly, from a distributional point of view, CT *does not claim redistribution*. This conclusion is based, of course, on the fact that, since the list of capabilities that must be ensured/guaranteed by a specific social arrangement (of a normative type, obviously) being given, no deviation from it is possible, in principle, i.e., it is not possible to block any individual's access to any of the listed capabilities.[75] Consequently, there is no need for any reparation, either of a compensatory nature (as in the case of the Rawlsian theory) or of a resilient/restoration nature (as in the case of the Nozickian theory). The absence of redistribution from the implicit mechanism of the CT is relevant, because it brings this approach closer, conceptually, to liberalism which, as is well known, rejects redistribution carried out by the public authority (the state) as illegitimate since it is considered to violate the initial distribution presumed to have been carried out on the basis of the distribution of merit. If the fact that the CT *does not claim* redistribution seems quite obvious from a logical perspective, the question arises whether, nevertheless, the CT *allows* for redistribution. In relation to this aspect, I make the following considerations:

- it must be mentioned that the so-called capabilities (which represent the potentialities or, rather, opportunities of the individual's functioning towards his/her wellbeing) are qualitative, not quantitative concepts, that is, a size (quantum, value, frequency, etc.) that must be objectified in relation to each capability is not established.[76] Moreover, the individual is not required, from a normative point of view, to use the capability in question, he/she still has the latitude/

freedom to decide whether or not to use that capability that is guaranteed but not mandatory—it is, in other words, a right, without there being a correlative obligation;

- then, the question arises whether capabilities are transferable or not between individuals. By transferability of a capability is understood the possibility that a capability that is not used or is incompletely used by an individual can be used (in whole or in part, as the case may be) by another individual in the society in question. In this matter, my opinion is the following:
- an affirmative answer to the question posed would have, as a logical consequence, the necessary consideration of capability as being of the nature of a private good, since only private goods are non-rival, in the sense that they are inter-individual transferable;
- I consider, however, that a capability (and therefore the entire set of capabilities) represents a public good.[77] Consequently, a capability is non-rival, so there is no need for its inter-personal transferability or, equivalently, we can say that there is an inter-personal… infinite transferability of capabilities, a common property, obviously, of any public good;
- we therefore hold that a capability is a public good.[78]

4.2 Basic Concepts

A first (in fact, the most important) concept regarding CT is, without a doubt, the concept of the *functioning of the human being*, which comes, in its basis, from the considerations made by Amartya Sen regarding the relationships that must exist between economic and ethical action. The concept of functioning is a primitive concept in relation to the other concepts within CT, even more important than that of capability, because, from a logical point of view, functioning is of the nature of the end, while capability is of the nature of the means. By the functioning of the human being we must understand the following main determinations:

- the functioning of the individual is of the nature of agency (action, diligence), that is, of the nature of *to do*; of course, agency is the consequence of choice/decision, and choice is of the nature of *to be*—you choose according to your own values, beliefs, desires, motivations, and interests;

- the functioning of the individual is *conditio sine qua non* for achieving individual wellbeing, but it does not exhaust the sufficiency predicates of wellbeing, that is, the functioning of the individual does not, by itself, lead to the achievement of wellbeing. This incompleteness at the level of sufficiency (i.e., at the level of meeting the *ex ante* conditionality) is not discussed in detail in the literature on the subject[79]; therefore I will make a few analytical clarifications:
- the functioning of the individual (of course, as an effect of the free choice regarding this functioning) has, in my opinion, two components—they are found implicitly, but not explicitly, in the works of Sen and Nussbaum, respectively: a) the nominal component; b) the performative component. The nominal component refers to the simple fact that the individual has the ensured capability to function towards achieving his/her wellbeing. The performative component refers to the qualitative aspects of nominal functioning, namely: (1) the degree of use of the capability in question—an individual may not fully use a capability, although this use is guaranteed; (2) the effectiveness, respectively the efficiency of the use of that capability—an individual, although accessing a certain capability (i.e., verifying the nominal functioning within the margin of that capability), may use the capability in a defective way, which leads either to not achieving the potential parameters of the capability, or to achieving them inefficiently, i.e., with net costs for the individual; (3) the synergy generated by the use of the capability in question, as a result of the use of other capabilities made available to the individual's functioning—the way in which a given capability is used can lead to negative synergies (or, equivalently, to cancellations or reductions of possible positive synergies).

A second essential concept in CT is exactly that of *capability*. Capability is understood as what the individual is and/or does, according to his/her own choice. The fact that being and doing are not combined with having is significant from the perspective of the ethical component of CT.[80]

Nota bene: functioning and capability form an irreducible binomial, based on the following arguments:

- functioning *does imply* capability (more precisely, the existence of capability, as an opportunity at the individual disposal, designed, implemented, and guaranteed normatively);
- on the other hand, capability *does not imply* functioning, in the sense that, as we have shown previously, an individual may choose not to access a certain capability, for example, because he/she is not interested (or, in some cases, because it is impossible for him/her—for example, in the case of deficiencies or disabilities) to access that capability[81];
- while capability is a right (ensured by the social arrangement), functioning is not a correlative obligation; it is, in turn, a right at the disposal of free individual choice; based on the above, functioning of human being and capability form a symmetrical binomial.[82]

A third concept in CT is that of *consequentialism*. In general, consequentialism is understood as an intellectual position (theoretical, respectively ethical) that, either in deciding or in carrying out an action, often considers decisively the effect which that decision, respectively that action/agency will have, to the extent that such a prediction is possible.[83] However, CT consequentialism is of a special kind, so I will present some considerations in this regard:

- *first of all*, consequentialism is not associated with the individual, but... the state. Indeed, the state (more precisely, the normative mechanism) is required to ensure all the sufficient conditions for the existence of capabilities that allow the (full, plenary) functioning of the generic individual. Therefore, the consequence—which can be called the possibility[84] of individual wellbeing—must be considered by the state when designing the general normative framework of society; we will call this meaning of CT consequentialism: *normative consequentialism*—it should be noted that this consequentialism is of the *ex ante* type. On the question: on whom does the effect of such consequentialism act? my opinion is the following: on both the generic individual and the state, based on the following arguments:
- although CT considers itself non-contractarian, it is difficult, from a logical point of view, to explain, outside of a contractarianism, however diffuse or implicit, why the state should or would want to project capabilities through the normative framework;

- even ignoring or denying the existence or functioning of a contract between individuals regarding the obligation of the state to ensure capabilities for the functioning of the individual, there must be a common "interest" between individuals and the state or, more precisely, between individuals regarding the state, for the normative assurance of the capabilities in question;
- from this perspective, we consider that CT is situated, somewhat, in the "middle" between the Rawlsian theory— declared contractarianist—and the Nozickian theory—declared non-contractarianist; I could say, based on what has just been exposed, that CT is a *quasi-contractarianist theory*;
- *secondly*, there is, however, so to speak, also a consequentialism directly associated with the individual, namely, a consequentialism that is inferable from the discussion above regarding the components of functioning, both the nominal and the performative. This consequentialism, which can be called *operational consequentialism*, is of the *ex post* type and refers to the alternative effects (possibly opposite from the perspective of meaning) that the decision to use or not to use a certain capability that is available through the normative framework has;
- *thirdly*, it must be noted that, if in the first case, normative consequentialism produces effects for both "parties"—individual and state, respectively—in the second case, operational consequentialism produces effects exclusively on the generic individual.[85]

A fourth concept of CT is that of *agency*. By agency we mean a generic activism of the individual, that is, an activism through which the individual in question seeks, in a persevering and determined manner, solutions to solve the problems he/she faces. In this context, the individual must be seen (and interpreted) as a *resolutive searcher*. From the CT perspective, agency refers to the fact that the generic individual will actively manifest itself for its effective manifestation regarding any capability that the normative (legal) framework puts, so to speak, at his/her disposal. There is an immediate semantic connection between the concept of agency and the problem of the objectification of merit (for example, in Hayek): the fact that a potential capability is not actualized through the action (agency) of the individual eligible for that capability simply signifies a legitimate decision by that individual not to do something, although he/

she had the normative possibility of doing[86] something, which obviously refers to the concept of individual freedom.

A fifth concept of CT is that of the *end/finality*. In fact, this concept is crucial for the delimitation of CT from Rawls's proceduralism and even from Nozick's resilientism. By finality is meant an objective in the sphere of wellbeing, of interest to the generic individual, which is assured and guaranteed in this assurance by the normative (i.e., imperative) framework of society. As we have shown above, finality in CT has a potential character, just like Rawls' proceduralist (or procedural) finality, which also has a potential character. However, between the two types of finalities (*Nota bene*: I propose that the finality within CT be called *hypothetical finality*, and the finality within Rawlsian theory be called *categorical finality*) some delimitations could be of usefulness[87]:

- *hypothetical finality* needs the agency of the generic individual to actualize itself (*Nota bene*: that is why the distinction between functioning and capability, examined above, is so important). If this agency does not manifest itself, finality does not take place—obviously, the non-actualization of finality does not have the significance of any conceptual "defect" of CT, on the contrary, this possibility is organically included in the theoretical framework of CT;
- *categorical finality* does not need the agency of the generic individual to actualize itself—it is actualized in a somewhat abstract way (we could even say, impersonal one) through the simple functioning of the procedure in question, which procedure is ensured, of course, also by the normative framework of the society in question;
- the existence (or the acceptance, from a theoretical point of view) of categorical finality in CT implies, of course, references to proceduralism, that is, to Rawls's contractarian theory. I present some considerations in this regard:
- proceduralism does not imply agency and, obviously, neither does agency imply proceduralism;
- not implying agency, categorical finality implies its necessary actualization (i.e., an inevitable actualization)[88];
- despite the necessary character of its actualization (which rejects the conditioning given by agency in the mechanism of this actualization), categorical finality remains at the status of right, not of obligation, that is, it requires a passive (non-actional) agreement of the individual for the objectification of the actualization in question.

In other words, the individual does not actively seek finality but, at the same time, may not accept this finality that occurs outside of his/her activism. To use a metaphor, each individual is provided with an umbrella, but it is his/her decision whether to use it (take it with him/her) or not when he/she leaves home.

4.3 General Structure

In this paragraph, I will discuss (and, in fact, propose) a general structure of CT. As is known from systems theory, structure generates function, so, once we have the structure, the manifestation/objectification of CT functions takes on a necessary character (obligatory, inevitable, fully predictable). Three preliminary considerations are, however, useful:

- CT has a pronounced historical/contextual character, although (as Nussbaum strives), the list of capabilities should be claimed mainly from human nature, rather than from the human condition. By contrast, Rawlsian theory, respectively Nozickian theory, has, rather, a logical character (therefore, relatively a-historical), so representing much more abstract proposals regarding the theory of social justice and, through this abstract character, much closer to structuralism[89];
- CT has, rather, the character of a Lamarckian process, rather than a Darwinian one. Indeed, the list of capabilities is nothing more than a list of the functions that we expect the CT to perform in society, as subject to the (passive) acceptance of the generic individual targeted by the list in question. Based on the list, and starting from it, the establishment, by normative means, of the imperativeness (subject to the same passivity of choice already mentioned) of the objectification of the capabilities in question follows. Expressed in the language of systems theory, this means that the function generates the structure, which is the very content of Lamarckism;

Nota bene: on the contrary, in the case of Rawls, that is, of proceduralism, the choice of basic principles in the original position in which the social contract between the individuals of the future society is concluded signifies precisely the formation of the structure that, according to expectations, will generate, with necessity, and procedurally, the desirable functions, which is, as can be easily observed, the content of Darwinism[90];

- Unlike both Rawlsian and Nozickian theories, which are based on feedback (more precisely, on negative feedback, of pre-stabilization, in the case of Rawls, and of re-stabilization, in the case of Nozick), CT is based on feedforward, that is, on the primacy (logically and chronologically) of the goal/finality over the means. Indeed, the list of capabilities is nothing more than a list of desirability, that is, of finalities, for the objectification of which, consequently, sufficient means are mobilized—in this case, sufficient norms or normative framework;
- CT is much more flexible than the two "competing" theories. Indeed, both the basic principles, of the contractarian type, chosen in the original position (the case of the Rawlsian theory), and the principles, of the quasi-contractarian type, assumed at the individual level (the case of the Nozickian theory) are strongly rigid. Thus, in the case of Rawls's theory, their modification involves the organization of another original position (which, as we have shown previously—and as Rawls's critics, including Nozick and Nussbaum, have also shown—raises extremely difficult problems from a theoretical and methodological point of view), and in the case of Nozick the problem arises of the cost of not respecting the principle assumed and publicly committed. On the contrary, in the case of CT, the list of capabilities can be updated at any time, followed by the corresponding update of the means of their realization, that is, of the normative framework of sufficiency. Positioning of the three theories of social justice from the perspective of: (a) historicism/contextualism vs. logicality/abstractization; (b) rigidity vs. flexibility; (c) Lamarckism vs. Darwinism; (d) feedback vs. feedforward, is presented in Fig. 8 (we make the following notations: PT—proceduralist theory, Rawls; RT—resilience theory, Nozick; CT—capabilities theory, Nussbaum).

Figure 9 suggests a general structure of the capabilities theory (CT).

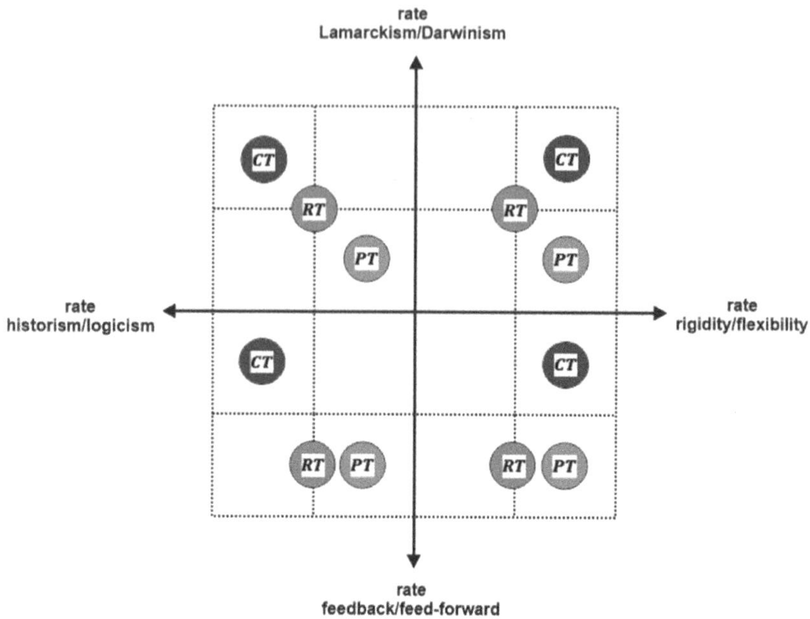

Fig. 8 Theoretical positioning of the three theories of social justice (*Source* Fig. 6 in Chapter 1).

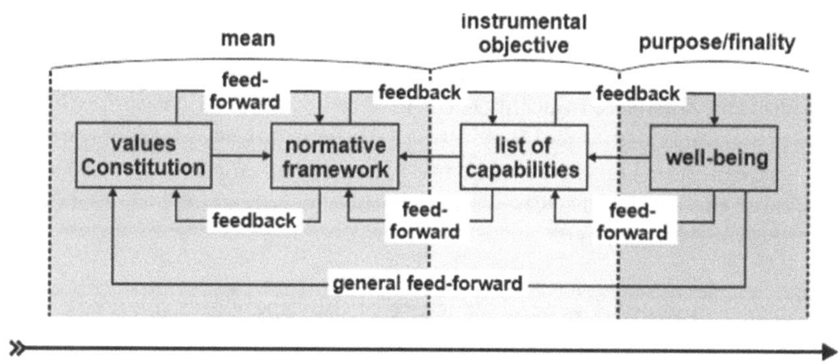

Fig. 9 General structure of capabilities theory (*Source* author)

5 The Functioning of the Capability's Theory/Approach

The functioning of CT refers to the effective realization of the functions that this theory/approach envisages from the perspective of social justice. Therefore, it is necessary, first, to identify the functions that CT is focused on.[91]

5.1 CT Functions

Being completely non-proceduralist (more precisely, anti-proceduralist), CT aims at the direct connection between the end and the means of achieving that end, while the other two "competing" theories need an intermediate link, facilitated by the existence of the principles (as axioms) adopted—the *ex ante* procedure, in the case of Rawls, or the *ex post* quasi-procedure, in the case of Nozick. In this context, we consider that the following functions are targeted by CT:

- (*FI*) the function of ***identifying the opportunity for wellbeing***: refers to the establishment of the list (which should be considered maximal) of capabilities that represent instrumental ways of experiencing opportunities intended leading to or substantiate the achievement of wellbeing at the individual level. This list of capabilities must verify the following attributes:
    - to be ***maximal***: this means that the number of capabilities in the list cannot exceed a threshold considered sufficient for the achievement of individual wellbeing or, in other words, the mutual non-redundancy[92] of the capabilities retained in the list must be ensured[93];
    - to originate in ***natural law***, that is, to consider (predominantly) ***human nature***[94];
    - to aim, as far as possible, at capabilities that are found, as aspirations (*Nota bene*: hence the previous call to anchor capabilities to human nature and not to the human condition), in most generic individuals—in other words, a common (or communicable) core of capabilities associated with the achievement of individual wellbeing. Of course, the list of capabilities must consider not only "normal" people—as Rawls does, for

example, when establishing the "eligibility" of participants in the original position—but, as far as possible, also individuals who need adjusted capabilities (not exclusive capabilities) or calibrated by classes of deficiencies/disabilities/handicaps;
- to contain capabilities that combine the aspiration feature with the possibility feature. Here, the historical (or contextual or a-logical) aspect of CT comes back with force, because, depending on the place a society is on its general chreod,[95] its possibilities, both normative and economic/material, of objectifying capabilities, are different. In our opinion, this attribute of the list of capabilities is the most problematic, because it implies a tension between desirability—the aspiration of the generic individual towards wellbeing—and possibility—the potential of the concrete-historical society to allow the functioning of the generic individual within a given (listed) capability. Moreover, I consider, at this point of the discussion, that the mentioned tension (a tension of a practical nature, in the Kantian sense of the term) is the greatest intellectual vulnerability of CT;

- (FP) the function of *providing the opportunity for wellbeing*: it refers to the fact that the finality of a manifestation of the functioning of the human individual (i.e., precisely the capability) represents an opportunity for the individual, namely an opportunity to achieve the main goal: wellbeing. Compared to the function of identifying the opportunity for wellbeing, which is an "intellectual" function, the function of providing the opportunity for wellbeing is a practical function (*Nota bene*: not praxiological!): it must identify and propose the operationalization of a normative framework—starting with the Constitution—that has the capacity to deliver the capabilities identified by FI, and which will represent the opportunities for wellbeing. The required normative framework must be characterized by the following:
  - *general character*—it must concern the generic individual (or, what is the same thing, all individuals eligible for a certain opportunity);

- *contextual character*—it must be compatible (in causal-conditional agreement) with the context that exists in society over a significant[96] period of time, from all relevant perspectives: economic, political (even geopolitical), axiological, etc.;
- *applied character*—it must specify, in the most precise way possible, the opportunity it legislates, so that there are no possibilities of interpretation or diversion in the practice of access to that opportunity[97];
- *non-principled character*—it must not contain norms of the (strength) level of principles, because this is the only (or most certain) way to avoid proceduralism, which CT declares to repudiate in the matter of social justice, considering that the only (or greatest) certainty regarding access to an opportunity is given by the nominal declaration of that opportunity and the (normative) assurance of the individual's access to the opportunity in question;

- (*FG*) the function of *guaranteeing the opportunity of wellbeing*: the function of guaranteeing the opportunity (more precisely, of guaranteeing access to the opportunity) must be a distinct function from the function of providing the opportunity, discussed previously. However, in my opinion, CT does not yet present (at least, not explicitly) such a function. We believe that CT's reluctance to declare the guarantee function also derives from its effort to avoid proceduralism (*Nota bene*: we recall that both Rawlsian and Nozickian theories have such functions explicitly declared and operationalized—in Rawls through the difference principle, and in Nozick through the rectification/correction principle). Obviously, society has, in its normative framework, levers through which the (total or partial, permanent or temporary) prevention of the access of the eligible individual to a normatively provided opportunity is punished, but this lever is outside CT, belonging to the general normative and functional framework of the society in question. In other words, the "administration" of the norms aimed at guaranteeing opportunities is left outside the CT, namely is left to the norms that regulate compliance with the Constitution and the laws validly derived from it. From a logical point of view, we are obviously also dealing with a procedural aspect that… does not belong to the

CT. Although I will not develop this observation in this research, I consider (and I will take up, to a certain extent, further) that CT seems incomplete from the perspective of this function that has an exogenous status in relation to the CT. Moreover, I appreciate that the analysis I carried out on the CT (especially on Nussbaum's proposal, called the capabilities approach—CA—not the capability theory) led us to the conclusion that this theory or approach does not contain the function of repairing (either *ex ante*, as in Rawls, or *ex post*, as in Nozick) the situation in which a certain function is not operable or operates defectively. This absence (which, in my opinion, as previously stated, is a direct result of the integral rejection, ab initio, of proceduralism) creates a certain vulnerability to the structure of society that must apply this theory of social justice.

5.2 *CT Functioning*

Based, on the one hand, on the structure of CT (Fig. 8) and, on the other hand, on the functions of CT, I will examine, in this paragraph, the (abstract) functioning of this theory of social justice. I will carry out this examination based on the synoptic representation in Fig. 10.

Discussion

- each of the basic concepts of CT is associated, in a biunivocal way, to an element of the CT structure, as follows:
  - the practical aspect of CT is generated by the functioning of the individual;
  - the intellectual aspect resides in the identification of the set of capabilities (i.e., in the formation of the list of capabilities);
  - the psychological aspect refers to the way in which the inalienable consequentialism of CT is identified with individual wellbeing;
  - the normative aspect consists of the normative framework that allows (without imposing, as we have previously stated) the agency/activism of the individual;
  - the axiological aspect aims at describing the finality (i.e., the acquiring of wellbeing) by choosing values and mentioning them in the Constitution—the master norm of a society;

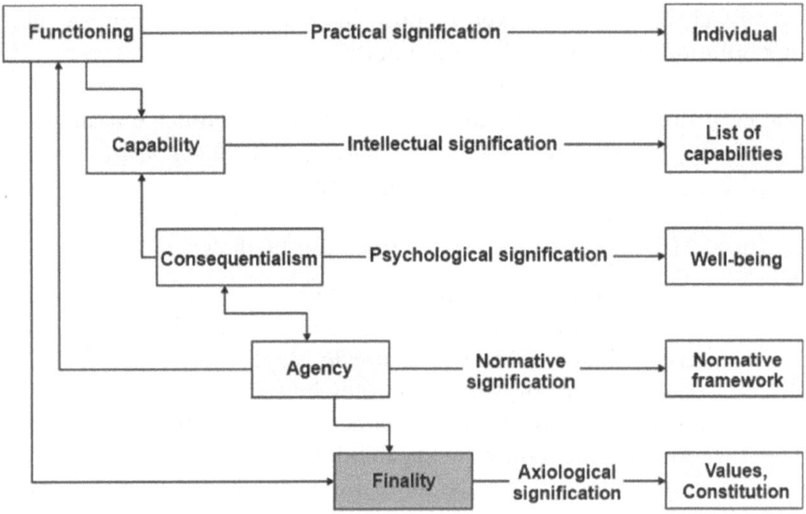

Fig. 10 General/abstract diagram of CT operationalization (*Source* author)

- capability is generated by both the individual's need to function and consequentialism;
- between consequentialism and the individual's agency there is a circular causal relationship (both in the form of negative feedback and in the form of positive feedback, as the case may be);
- finality is caused by both the functioning of the individual and his/her agency.

6 A Brief Critical Assessment of Capabilities Theory

6.1 General Evaluation

First of all, it should be noted that CT rejects contractarianism *ab ovo*, but only from a declarative point of view (*Nota bene*: as did, incidentally, the Nozickian theory). The rejection of contractarianism seems, however, more of an "ideological" positioning than a scientific one, because, at the heart of the problem, the following questions arise that CT not only does not answer, but does not even identify, in order to leave them, possibly, for resolution to the scientific community:

- what does establish the list of capabilities mean other but an agreement between the wills of the participants (*Nota bene*: who are these participants?) regarding the choice and, then, the norming (primarily, through constitutional norms) of the capabilities in question? Here the following conclusions can be drawn:
  - as is known, the contract is defined as an agreement of will of the parties—but, the establishment of a list (finite, even maximal, as we have shown previously) is possible only through an agreement of will, so can only be the result of a contract;
  - such a concrete contract (a concrete list with the verbal expression of the concrete capabilities on which it was agreed) obviously bears a much more accentuated contractarianist mark than even Rawlsian contractarianism, the latter limiting the agreement of will to the two principles that are chosen in the original position. *A fortiori*, the contractarianism in CT is all the more accentuated compared to the Nozickian theory;
  - ironically, although a contract does not imply a written form (more generally, a means of proof), the CT requires that the list of capabilities exist in a form that is opposable to both the initially involved parties and third parties (*Nota bene*: we recall that, in both the Rawlsian and Nozickian theories, the written form is not imperative, which means that the principles chosen, in each of the two theories, are opposable only to the involved parties, not to third parties, that is, they do not constitute means of proof from the perspective of positive law)[98];
- if there is no agreement of will between those interested (which can include, as is understood, the entire society), what is the certainty that those capabilities that lead (or can lead or should lead) to the achievement of individual wellbeing will be available and, in fact, effective in accordance with the finality? For example, Nozick, who also rejects contractarianism, as does CT, ensures some degree of certainty of the achievement of social justice by formulating his three principles (*Nota bene*: the formulation of the principles in question does not have an author, just as the list of capabilities in Nussbaum

does not have an author). Of course, CT requires that, at the level of the normative framework (first of all, in the Constitution), the capabilities in question be written, but here the following question immediately arises: does not the inscription of capabilities in the Constitution represents, *eo ipso*, a contract? The Constitution is elaborated and adopted by a Constituent Assembly which is an elected political forum; therefore it expresses a common will of the individuals who form the society in question. Therefore, it seems that CT, although explicitly declaring the rejection of contractarianism, implicitly allows its existence through all its subsequent theoretical developments.

Secondly, it should be noted CT's (vehement) rejection of proceduralism. According to what has already been said, the reason why CT adopts this position (which the authors—especially Nussbaum—associate with the rejection of contractarianism, which is contradictory, as we will immediately show) is uncertainty. CT's adherents consider that the existence of a procedure does not ensure (at least, not to a sufficient extent[99]) the individual's access to that functioning that the principles foresee as potentiality and, instead, they simply propose the enumeration of the capabilities that can ensure the functioning in question.[100] My comment in this regard refers to the fact that the choice to use a capability, even ensured by the normative framework, implies a choice made by the individual, namely whether or not to use the capability in question—as we have previously stated, the individual's functioning through (using) the capability is a right, not an obligation but, being a right, implies an option of the type of free will. But, as is known, the individual's free will is, probably, the most important and powerful source of unpredictability, and therefore of uncertainty. It seems that proceduralism ensures much greater predictability (and therefore much less uncertainty) than optionalism (*Nota bene*: I use the term *optionalism*, which is not common in scientific literature, to highlight the crucial role of free will in the functioning of the individual through capability).[101]

Thirdly, CT does not have the reparative function (which we have called, above, the function of guaranteeing capability). In my opinion, such… disability, which constitutes, in fact, the rejection of resilience as we have in Nozickian theory (be noted that resilience functions precisely in a reparative sense), has extremely serious consequences from the perspective of a theory of social justice. I list a few considerations in this regard:

- any norm (therefore including the norms required by CT to provide capabilities) can be violated—either by the state or by private individuals—therefore the certainty claimed by CT regarding the functioning of individuals according to the normed capabilities is illusory (*Nota bene*: we have previously shown that this uncertainty is or may be even greater than in the case of proceduralism or resilientism);
- CT has no… procedures, neither *ex ante* (as contractarianism has) nor *ex post* (as resilientism has) to manage cases of violation of norms regarding the functioning of individuals through capabilities. This lack of… capability of CT is, of course, known to those involved in the functioning of such a type of social justice, so the moral hazard related to this situation has a high probability of occurring in society;
- the absence of a reparative function (or vocation) within a theory of social justice is, in my opinion, an unacceptable vulnerability of CT, being, at the same time, an occasion for surprise that researchers in this field have not (yet) completed the standard CT with such a function. Of course, the introduction of the reparative function in question should avoid both contractarianism and resilientism (*Nota bene*: in the above, I have shown, I hope to a sufficient extent, that the aforementioned characteristics cannot, in fact, truly and entirely be avoided).

Fourthly, it seems that at least two elements of the functioning of the CT, as it is present in the specialized literature, must be established in an unambiguous manner: (a) who draws up the list of capabilities? (b) what criteria underlie the concrete capabilities included in the list?

(a) Authors of the list of capabilities

The problem of the authors of the list of capabilities is ignored by the standard CT. Somehow, it turns out that the authors in question are the very researchers of the problem (for example, Nussbaum) who establish, through their own methodologies, these capabilities—in Nussbaum's case, ten capabilities. The grounding idea here is that the list of capabilities must be established by an elite, for example, by social philosophers. Obviously, such an assumption is unacceptable, because the capabilities must be chosen by those who need them, that is, by individuals who aspire to a functioning of the capabilities that will lead them to the achievement of wellbeing. In my opinion, CT is in dire need (at least from this point of view) of a "dose" of contractarianism, even if it could resist (for the moment) proceduralism.

(b) The criteria for selecting/choosing capabilities

The problem of the criteria that could generate the (minimal) list of capabilities is, of course, closely related to the previous problem, namely of the authors of the list of capabilities. From a logical point of view, here arises the difficult problem of the individual (or group) interest of the one who establishes these criteria, a problem that is analogous to the one that Rawls faced in organizing the original position (*Nota bene*: Rawls found the solution to the veil of ignorance, a solution that was so powerful that it simultaneously solved also the question of the morality of choosing basic principles). More precisely, the problem of these criteria faces the following distinct sub-problems:

- those who propose the criteria for establishing/choosing capabilities must be different (independent) from those who apply these criteria for the purpose of concretely identifying, in verbal expression, the respective capabilities. The explanation lies in the general argument of avoiding ante-pronunciation: if this independence is not ensured, the criteria could be chosen with regard to the capabilities, instead of the causal relationship being exactly the opposite[102];
- the list of criteria must be inferred from a model of rationality or, at least, from a principle (or set of principles) that exists previously. In other words, from a logical point of view, the criteria in question must represent theorems inferred, validly, from pre-existing axioms. As I have shown, CT does not accept such pre-existing models of rationality[103];
- the absence of criteria for choosing capabilities raises, of course, the question of the representativeness or significance of these capabilities. It is true that CT claims that the list of capabilities takes up the generic elements of natural law (without appealing to anarchy,

as Nozick does), but how is this origin (logically) ensured? From another perspective, one could accept the idea that natural law represents the very model of rationality to which I referred above, but from such a supposed model of rationality, the criteria on the basis of which to choose (and formulate in verbal expression) the capabilities were not explicitly extracted.

6.2 Sources of Capabilities

As I said before, a capability is an opportunity to which the generic individual has access to achieve his/her wellbeing or, according to the concept used above, to enter the plenary life chain (path)—PLC. In contrast to the public goods, the capabilities are not only publicly (i.e., being provided by the state), but they can also be privately originated. In this context, I will now discuss some issues regarding the sources of capabilities.

Preliminaries

A capability must be understood neither (or neither only) as a resource, i.e., a thing, nor (or nor only) as a property, but as a *relationship*. Such a suggestion can be "defended" as follows:

- if the capability would be considered as a resource, this means that we need a distributional procedure (based, of course, on a specialized normative framework) for allocation of that resource—namely, eligibility of individuals to benefit from the respective resource, share of the resources that each individual deserves, etc.[104];
- a capability is activated if and only if an individual claims it and, as a consequence, use it for improve, in one way or another, his/her wellbeing or, equivalently, his/her position on the plenary life chain (path) trajectory—or, as I called before: chreod, i.e., plenary life chreod. If this is the case, it results that a capability exists only if it enters a relationship with the generic individual;
- so, the capability is a potentiality (in contrast to an ordinary public good, which is an effectivity or, better, an actuality)[105];
- moreover, I would say that a capability is, sometimes, created by the very need for it (I will return to this issue)[106];
- as a relationship between the individual's need to improve his/her wellbeing and the opportunity to do that, the capability will define

itself starting from this relationship towards its property or to its ontology (as a third world's thing);
- the capability must be considered as being at a sufficient level—quantitative, structural, and qualitative. From a logical point of view, we must say that the capability is a sufficient[107] predicate (or sufficient condition) for the individual to get the wellbeing or the plenary life chain.

Figure 11 indicates the way in which, logically, a capability arises.

Discussion

- the primitive cause of the arising of the capability as opportunity is the need of the generic individual to get his/her wellbeing, i.e., to place on the chreod called plenary life chain (path)—PLC;
- the primitive cause presses on the individual as an existential constraint (*Nota bene*: not in a simple surviving mode, but regarding the plenary existence, as will be detailed below);
- the first, both logically and chronologically, hypostasis of the capability is the opportunity as a relationship between the individual's purpose and the sufficient means to achieve the purpose;
- the opportunity as relationship generates the opportunity as property, and, in turn, the opportunity as property generates the opportunity as thing (as shown, an "inhabitant" of Popper's third world).

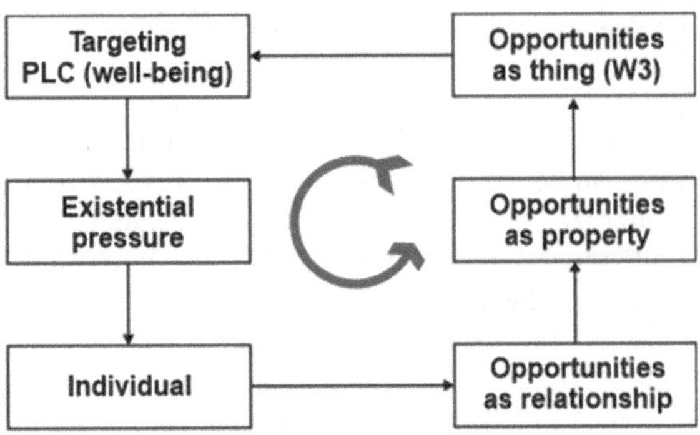

Fig. 11 Generic way of capability arising (*Source* author)

Nota bene: this scheme is indefinitely replicated, so the set of opportunities (as relationship, property, and thing) changes together with the individual's purpose and, consequently, the existential pressure over the generic individual.

On a Typology of the Sources of Capabilities

Starting from the above preliminaries, I think the following sources (origins, causes) of the capabilities could be held (I denote: with *S*—source, with *P*—public, with *Pr*—private, with *e*—external, with *d*—domestic, with *p*— personal, with *o*—organizational).

- (*PS*) *public source*: the source of capability is the state (more exactly, the social normative framework), based on the social contract or on a presumptive (implicit) social contract.[108] The public source addresses all individuals within a political organization (usually, a nation) having a vocation similar to the positive public externalities. The public source of capability can be, in turn, of two kinds:
- (*PS/e*) *public external source*: the capabilities are created under the influence of external organizations/institutions, either integrative (for example, in the Romanian case, the European Union suprastatal normative framework) or regulative (for example, the IMF, WHO, UN, and so on). Regularly, such influences are taken over in the internal normative framework and, in many cases, the external origin is forgotten. Such a component of the public source is, however, a minority;
- (*PS/d*) *public domestic source*: the capabilities are created within the national borders, forming the majority of capabilities provided by the social normative framework;
- (*PrS*) *private source*: the source of capability is the individual himself/herself (more exactly, the private normative framework[109]). The private source of capability can be, in turn, of two kinds:
- (*PrS/p*) *private source of personal type*: the capabilities are created by the individual himself/herself who are interested in have on his/her disposal the capabilities in question. Such capabilities are strongly idiosyncratic, (usually) temporary and, of course, local. Such self-providing of capabilities are, in fact, extremely rare but, from scientific point of view, it must be mentioned;
- (*PrS/o*) *private source of organizational type*: the capabilities are created by the private sector in the society[110] (by organizations

that can be either lucrative or non-lucrative). The vast majority of non-lucrative organizations (so-called non-governmental organizations—NGOs) constitute what the political theory call civil society.[111]

6.3 A Typology of Capabilities

Now, it is time to examine the possible typologies of capabilities, by avoiding a discretionary proposal (as, generally, current literature provides) which is based on intuition or is, simply, a bet with the scientific community.

Some Preparative

I remind that a capability, as described above (and, besides, the specialty literature holds), is a means for a purpose, where the purpose is achieving the wellbeing or, as proposed to be denominated from a logical perspective, plenary life chain (path).

As a means, the capability must be mapped on the second pyramid (the pyramid of channels), see Fig. 4. Consequently, we have found a logical criterion of grounding the capabilities typology, avoiding the simple intuition or a discretionary lexicographical proposal.

Although the second pyramid offers a "guide" to identify the classes (or genus) of the capability, such classes are to be specified, i.e., to be particularized as species or, even, individuals of the respective classes, but the last operation is not a theoretical issue but an empirical one.

Without the basic typology, that mapped on the second pyramid, some dichotomies regarding the capabilities can be made:

(a) Existent capabilities vs. created capabilities

This dichotomy has rather a historical signification, from the perspective of a given (generic) individual. Indeed, an individual finds a set of capabilities at his/her birth, which will be (or not) accessed by that individual. However, the individual himself/herself could act, during his/her life, to create new capabilities—for example, if that individual is a political activist or an opinion driver, either practical/praxiological or theoretical.

(b) Hidden capabilities vs. visible capabilities

Such two opposite classes can be either intended or non-intended. For example, in dictatorial (or just authoritarian) societies, some rights of individuals could be hidden from political reasons, in order to maintain the population under obeying. The polar case is that of visible (transparentized) capabilities, no matter they are or not accessed by those entitled.

(c) Public capabilities vs. private capabilities

This dichotomy was already discussed at the section "Preliminaries".

(d) Exogeneous capabilities vs. endogenous capabilities

This dichotomy was also already discussed at the section "Preliminaries".

It can be identified even a trichotomy of the capabilities, as it is suggested in Fig. 10, namely: (i) capability as opportunity of relationship type; (ii) capability as opportunity of property type; (iii) capability as opportunity of thing (ontological) type.

The Basic Typology

As said, in proposing the basic typology of the capabilities, I will follow the structure of the second pyramid—the pyramid of channels of transmitting the needs impulse to the outcomes response. In fact, the three mentioned pyramids (from which the first one is proposed by Maslow) function as a cybernetic system of order four.[112] Figure 12 offers a synoptic picture of this idea.

Discussion

- the needs (pyramid 1) act as inputs in a transformation operator, called a black-box,[113] while the outcomes (pyramid 3) act as outputs provided by that transformation;
- the needs are quantified considering also anticipations (feedforward) about the outcomes—for example, no needs whose satisfying is impossible, either principled or historically, will be actualized, i.e., objectified, i.e., introduced into the black-box;

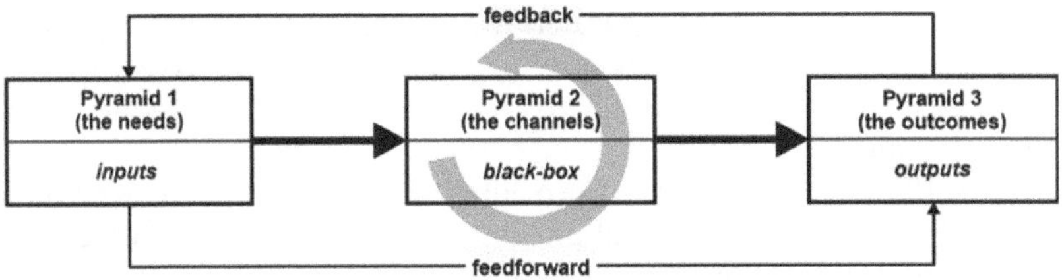

Fig. 12 Cybernetic system of order 4 regarding the three pyramids (*Source* author)

- from pyramid 3 a feedback operate on pyramid 1, in order to correct the future inputs (both quantitatively and qualitatively), so the cybernetic system of order 4 formed by the three pyramids will function indefinitely.

The basic typology of the capabilities will, therefore, be built based on the pyramid 2. In the first instance, the following classes of capability can exist:

(1) (*C*0) capability aimed at providing the *individual's survival*: this capability, which is operated by layer L0, provides sufficient opportunities[114] to ensure the biological survival of each individual and the biological replication of the human species. C0 can be operated by the intermediation of three "individuals" of this class:
(a) (C01) capability aimed at providing the *self-ensuring of the standard of living* by the individuals (primarily jobs)
(b) (C02) capability aimed at providing *health* (both physical and mental) of individuals
(c) (C03) capability aimed at providing a compatible and synergic *physical environment*
(2) (*C*1) capability aimed at providing the *personal development*: this capability, which is operated by layer L1, provides sufficient opportunities to ensure the personal development of the individual, in its idiosyncrasy. C1 can be operated by the intermediation of three "individuals" of this class:
(a) (C11) capability aimed at providing sufficient access to *instruction*,[115] generally according to the opportunities of jobs in a predictable time horizon regarding the labour market. To mention

that C11 is strongly correlated with C01; in fact, between the two sub-classes of capabilities, a *sui generis* co-evolution process occurs. This capability contributes to form the *intellectual capital* of the individual

(b) (C12) capability aimed at providing *axiological education*—ethical values, political values, cultural values, and others of the same. This capability contributes to form the *cultural capital* of the individual

(c) (C13) capability aimed at providing *affective education*—arts, humanities, religion, and philosophy. This capability contributes to form the *emotional capital* of the individual

(3) (*C*2) capability aimed at providing the *proximal inclusion*: this capability, which is operated by layer L2, provides sufficient opportunities to ensure the common life within small communities—families, villages, small towns, and so on, based more or less on direct knowledge among the individuals, many times (especially in the case of family or small villages) based on kinship.[116] In any case, this capability addresses the proximity in geographical and kinship meaning. It has three individuals:

(a) (C21) capability aimed at providing *inter-personal communication*: this capability provides sufficient stimuli/facilities so that the individuals exchange among them, without constraints, ideas, positioning, visions, and so on, regarding the wellbeing of everybody within the proximal community

(b) (C22) capability aimed at providing *general empathy*: this capability provides sufficient practical[117] occasions in which the individuals in small communities experience empathy both among them and about non-human animals and, generally, with the non-anthropic (non-artefactual) environment

(c) (C23) capability aimed at providing *conservative identity*: this capability provides sufficient (generally, institutional) conditions and devices to design, project in time, defend, and promote the identity of the small community concerned as well as the individuals living in those communities

(4) (*C*3) capability aimed at providing the *political inclusion*: this capability, which is operated by layer L3, provides sufficient guarantees and institutions/norms so that a political life can exist, where political life is concerned with both individual interest and the general interest of the society as a whole, providing a positive

synergy between the two categories of interest. In turn, this class of capabilities has three components:

(a) (C31) capability aimed at providing *social capital*: this capability provides the social capital (Dinga, 2014) aimed at "governing" the social level (the extended community) within the national territory, where the national sovereignty is exerted. The social capital refers to the national community, i.e., that level of community associated with a political state that administers the sovereignty owned by the population within the national borders (in Annex 1 in this chapter I present a short examination of the concept of social capital)

(b) (C32) capability aimed at providing *freedom*: as shown before, individual freedom is ensured when it is not the case that establishing their purpose, individuals are disturbed by an external private unsolicited influence,[118] so the normative framework must deliver such conditionalities that to be verified with certainty, permanently, and continuously, within the borders of the national state concerned

(c) (C33) capability aimed at providing *democracy*: as also shown before, democracy means the public decisions (choices) are made based on the majority's options (votes) of the population concerned by the national state in question

(5) (*C*4) capability aimed at providing the *global synergy*: this capability, which is operated by layer L4, provides sufficient conditionalities/opportunities so that the transnational (i.e., global/planetary) issues to be sustainably and equitably treated and solved. This class has, also, three components:

(a) (C41) capability aimed at providing *global communication*: the global communication is essential to account for the emergence, kinematics, chreod, and impact of global issues (for example, global heating, global pollution, global political/religious/cultural/ military conflicts) so that there is a global awareness and implication related to resources mobilized and behaviours redesigned

(b) (C42) capability aimed at providing *global empathy*: the global empathy is the projection, at the global level, of both C12 and C13, including the non-living Nature (including Cosmos), living Nature, and human society, as the latter is populated with individuals belonging to the same and unique species, *homo sapiens sapiens*

(c) (C43) capability aimed at providing *global sustainability*: this capability is required considering the relatively recent phenomena of economic, social, political, environmental, etc., kinds, that undermine the probability that the global/planetary civilization can continue and progress. The capability must ensure a replicable path of human civilization in an indefinite time horizon.

So, we have obtained a matrix of the capabilities ($\mathcal{M}(C)$), with five columns and three lines, that is, of 15 classes of capabilities:

$$\mathcal{M}(C) = \left(C0\ C1\ C2\ C3\ C4 \right)$$

i.e.,

$$\mathcal{M}(C) = \begin{pmatrix} C01\ C11\ C21\ C31\ C41 \\ C02\ C12\ C22\ C32\ C42 \\ C03\ C13\ C23\ C33\ C43 \end{pmatrix}$$

The Correspondence Between the Present List of Capabilities and Nussbaum's List

Table 5 offers a possible (logical) correspondence between my proposal regarding the (maximal) list of capabilities and Nussbaum's list of such capabilities (Nussbaum's list of capabilities is "borrowed" from Annex 1 of Chapter 5). *Nota bene*: Nussbaum's capabilities are noted Nx.

Comments

- the greatest number of compatibilities of Nussbaum's capabilities with the proposed capabilities is held by N6 (Practical reason)—seven capabilities are compatible with N6;
- the greatest number of compatibilities of proposed capabilities with Nussbaum's capabilities is held by C31 (Social capital) and C43 (Global sustainability—three capabilities are compatible with C31 and with C43, respectively.

Table 5 Logical correspondence between the proposed capabilities and Nussbaum's capabilities

		N1	*N2*	*N3*	*N4*	*N5*	*N6*	*N7*	*N8*	*N9*	*N10*	*Total*
C0	C01	x										1
	C02		x	x								2
	C03										x	1
C1	C11				x							1
	C12						x					1
	C13					x						1
C2	C21						x					1
	C22					x			x			2
	C23							x				1
C3	C31						x	x		x		3
	C32						x				x	2
	C33						x			x		2
C4	C41	x									x	2
	C42						x		x			2
	C43	x					x				x	3
Total		3	1	1	1	2	7	2	2	2	4	25

Source author

7 Connecting Plenary Life Chain with Provision of Capabilities

In my opinion, the second pyramid is "responsible" for the general means aimed at achieving the plenary life chain (path)—PLC. In this last paragraph of the chapter, I will try to connect the findings on PLC with those on capabilities.

7.1 Preliminaries

Connecting the PLC with capabilities set, as I have proposed here, means examining the capability (or the mix of capabilities, after the case) that seems to contribute, to a relevant degree, to achieving the points (of three coordinates) on the trajectory (path, chreod) of PLC. For the case in which more than one capability seems to be required to ensure the functioning of a given triad in PLC, it is necessary to see if there are (logically) incompatibilities among the 15 capabilities identified with the five classes/categories.

Table 6 Compatibilities among the capabilities

		C0			*C1*			*C2*			*C3*			*C4*		
		C01	*C02*	*C03*	*C11*	*C12*	*C13*	*C21*	*C22*	*C23*	*C31*	*C32*	*C33*	*C41*	*C42*	*C43*
C0	C01	–	0	1	1	0	0	0	0	0	0	1	1	0	1	1
	C02	0	–	1	1	1	1	1	1	1	1	1	1	0	1	1
	C03	1	1	–	0	0	1	0	1	1	1	1	0	0	1	1
C1	C11	1	1	0	–	2	2	2	2	2	2	2	2	2	1	1
	C12	0	1	0	2	–	2	1	2	2	2	2	2	1	2	2
	C13	0	1	1	2	2	–	2	2	2	2	1	1	1	2	1
C2	C21	0	1	0	2	1	2	–	2	2	2	2	2	2	2	2
	C22	0	1	1	2	2	2	2	–	2	2	1	1	1	2	2
	C23	0	1	1	2	2	2	2	2	–	2	2	0	0	0	1
C3	C31	0	1	1	2	2	2	2	2	2	–	2	2	2	2	2
	C32	1	1	1	2	2	1	2	1	2	2	–	0	0	0	0
	C33	1	1	0	2	2	1	2	1	0	2	0	–	0	0	0
C4	C41	0	0	0	2	1	1	2	1	0	2	0	0	–	1	1
	C42	1	1	1	1	2	2	2	2	0	2	0	0	1	–	1
	C43	1	1	1	1	2	1	2	2	1	2	0	0	1	1	–

Source author

Such a compatibility analysis is provided in Table 6, below. The notations used are: "2" full compatible, "1" reasonably compatible, "0" indifferent, and "−1" incompatible.

Nota bene: as expected, no case of incompatibility occurs, which makes the proposed list of capabilities form a complete, consistent, and convergent set in that matter. This means that, if needed, any two or more capabilities could be invoked to "feed" a given triad in the PLC.

7.2 *A Simple Allocation Model*

Let me remind you the logical formalization of the PLC (see Sect. 2.8):

$$PLC = T_1^{000} T_2^{111} T_3^{212} T_4^{323} T_5^{424}$$

Now, the capabilities must be associated with the triads in PLC, paying attention to the following:

- position "α" is allocated to pyramid 1, position "β" is allocated to pyramid 2 (i.e., to the pyramid "responsible" for the capabilities), and position "γ" is allocated to pyramid 3;
- to position "β" can be allocated one of many capabilities so that they be compatible among them;
- if is the case that among the capabilities allocable to a triad in PLC there is an indifference relationship (i.e., the number "0" in Table 6), the decision must be taken based on extra criteria.

So, the allocation of capabilities to PLC seems to be, in an abstract/ general way, as follows (Fig. 13).

Discussion

- at least two capabilities seem to be needed to "feed" each triad in the PLC;
- two of triads claim for two capabilities each (T_1 and T_3), two of triads claim for three capabilities each (T_2 and T_4), and a triad (T_5) claims five capabilities;
- so, it seems the outcome S_4 is the most "costly" outcome in the society, that is, providing the significance satisfaction[119];
- based on Fig. 12, the PLC can be written in a more suggestive logical form, as:

$$\begin{aligned} PLC =&(N0; C01, C02; S0) - (N1; C03, C11, C12; S1) \\ &- (N2; C13, C21; S2) - (N3; C22, C23, C31; S3) \\ &- (N4; C32, C33, C41, C42, C43; S4) \end{aligned}$$

- the fact that layers "3" and "4" of pyramid 2 (the pyramid of capabilities, as it can be called now) are not used to host capabilities aimed at achieving the plenary life (PLC) leads us to the following (general) conclusions:
- both social layer ("L3") and global layer ("L4") are only extended layers of the basic (fundamental) layer, namely, the communitarian one ("L2"), so the focus in providing the PLF must be concentrated on the layer "L2";
- the (practical, in Kantian sense) test of the PLC must be made on the layer "L2", so a presumptive falsifiability of the conjectures in

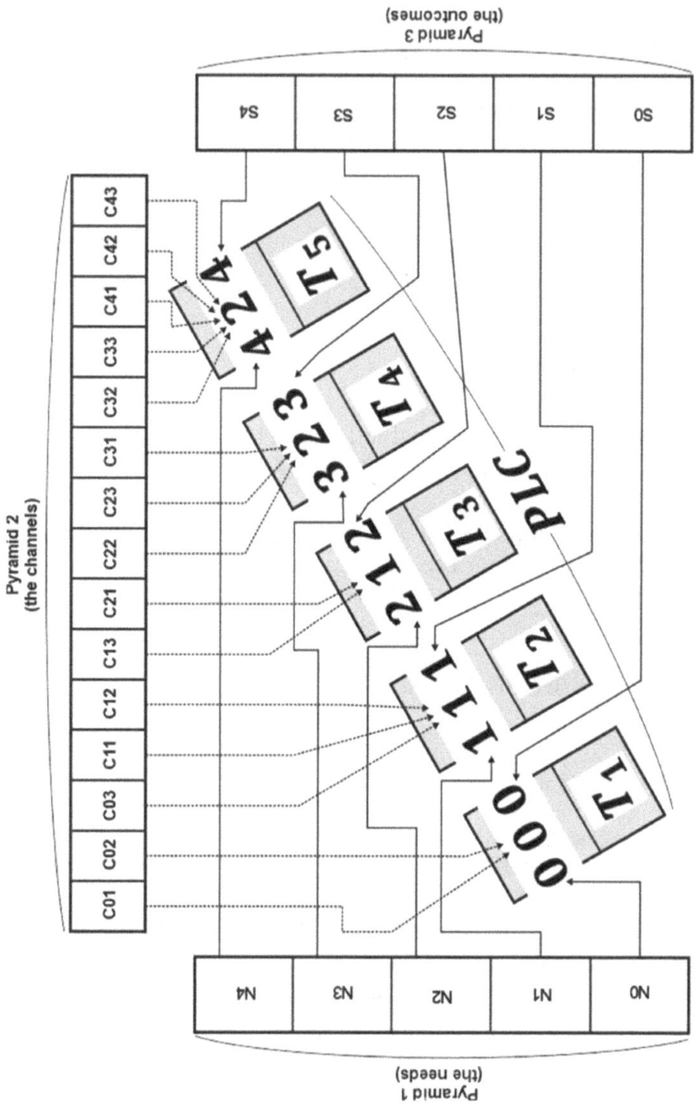

Fig. 13 Allocating of capabilities to PLC's triads (*Source* author)

the matter of social justice must be operated on the layer ("L2"), the only layer credited with relevance of that test.

Annex I

If we can imagine our planet (that is limited from any point of views) as a circle, then a model of its sustainability could be imagined as an equilateral triangle inside, as is shown in Fig. 14:

It is clear that a restraint of any triangle sides through an extending of others means a bias from the sustainability paradigm. The sustainability paradigm is an artefact, and it was not been invented by the Nature (the Nature has invented only the surviving).

In fact, the history of the human society is only the history of the dominance of one or other of capital category. Every category of the dominant capital has imposed its own logic principle of movement, has built its own actional paradigm, and has generated its own social establishment, as it is shown in Table 7:

So, the necessity (under the extinction penalty) for the human society to access the sustainability paradigm by removing the optimality paradigm seems to be without alternative.

1. What is the social capital (SC)?

Generally, we call capital anything entity (either substantial or informational) that brings an advantage of any kind for the owner of it. This advantage can be of current or of future type, this doesn't matter. According to Fig. 2, there are six fundamental distinct categories of capital: (a) *natural* (example: a river); (b) *substantial or tangible* (example: a house); (c) *financial* (example: a monetary income); (d) *biological* (example: the individual health); (e) *intellectual* (example: knowledge); (f) *social* (example: human rights).

These types of capital can be also associated with the quality of life categories, as Fig. 15 shows:

The social capital has as necessary framework and primary roots the social networks of any kinds. This network can be formal (the set of formal institutions) or informal (the set of traditions or moral principles).

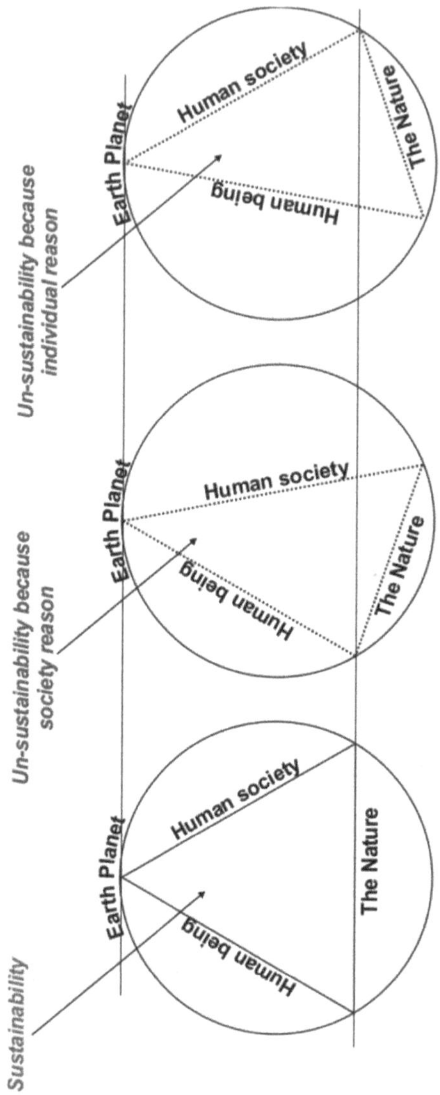

Fig. 14 Sustainability paradigm (*Source* From Emil Dinga [2014])

Table 7 General scheme of capital types and the associated societal paradigms

	Type of capital (Fundamental or crucial resource)						
	Natural	*Cultural (Artefactual)*					
		Physical		*Non-physical*			
		Substantial (tangible)	*Financial (intangible)*	*Individual*			*Social*
				Biological	*Intellectual*	*Moral*	
The logic principle	Methodological collectivism	Methodological individualism				Methodological holism	
The actional paradigm	Stationarity	Optimality				Sustainability	
The societal establishment	Naturalism	Capitalism[120]				Viabilism	

Source From Emil Dinga (2014)

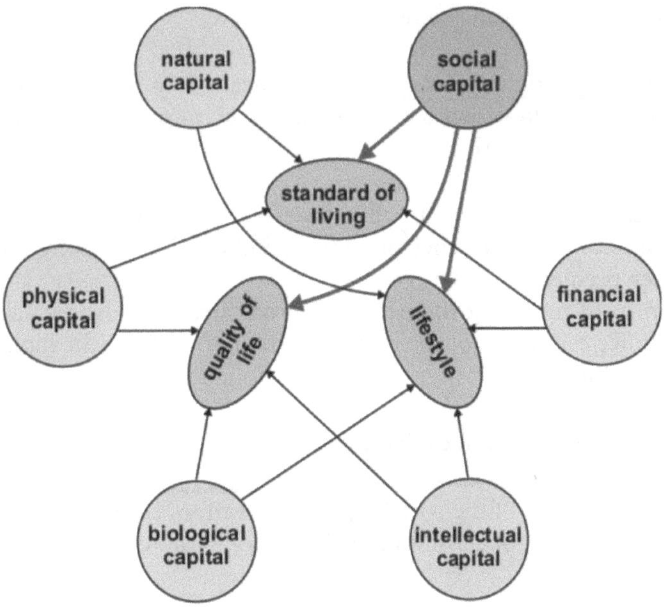

Fig. 15 Causal relationships among the capital types and the life qualifications (*Source* From Emil Dinga [2014])

To get the definition of the SC we need to identify and systematize the sufficiency predicates[121] of the concept of social capital. We believe these sufficiency predicates are the followings:

a. (SP1) internal pro-cyclical: *the social capital has a permanent positive feedback; this is equivalent with a law of increasing returns*[122];
b. (SP2) horizontal non-rivalry: *the social capital can be used by any contemporaries without its "quantity" being reduced as consequence of using*;
c. (SP3) vertical non-rivalry: *the social capital can be used by any non-contemporaries*[123] *without its "quantity" being reduced as consequence of using*;
d. (SP4) formal institutionality: *the social capital is only generated and used in a formal*[124] *institutional way*.

Once an entity has verified the above-mentioned predicates, the entity will become social capital. Once an entity became social capital, it will generate a new predicate—a necessary predicate:

e. (NP1) axiological assigning: this means *the social capital will generate up in, a necessary way, a list of values that constitutes its base (its reasoning)*.

So, in fact, the social capital will expose five necessary predicates, from which four are also sufficiency predicates, and one is a necessity but not a sufficiency predicate.

The map of matching the necessary predicates of the social capital by the other five categories of capital is presented in Table 8 (the highlighted cells mean matching):

2. What kinds of social capital there are?

To get the typology of the social capital we need, of course, a criterion[125] (or a set of criteria) of classification. In our opinion, can be retained two such criteria:

Table 8 Matching the necessary predicates by the capital categories

	SP1	*SP2*	*SP3*	*SP4*	*NP1*
Natural capital (NC)					
Physical capital (PC)	x			x	x
Biological capital (BC)		x	x		
Intellectual capital (IC)	x	x	x		x
Moral capital (MC)		x	x		x
Social capital (SC)	x	x	x	x	x

Source From Emil Dinga (2014)

a. (**I-S**) the socialization criterion: by socialization phenomenon we understand the process of insertion of the individuals into the society (i.e., of building of the society by the individuals);
b. (**S-I**) the individualization criterion: by individualization[126] we understand the process of autonomization of the individual inside the society (i.e., of building of the individuals by the society).

Every mentioned criterion can deliver a classification of the social capital, as follows:

(a) based on the (I-S) criterion, there are:

- (**C**) communication: the degree and the quality in which the individuals can freely communicate, live, and work with other individuals; this type of social capital is especially "responsible" for the communitization process (building up of such communities as: families, teams, clubs, organizations, countries, integrated regions, all types of social networks, etc.);
- (**P**) participation[127]: the degree and the quality in which the individuals have the possibility to take part of the public decision-making[128]; this type of social capital is especially "responsible" for building up of the political[129] structure of the society;
- (**M**) mutualisation: the degree and the quality in which common goals and common means can be built from the inter-individual harmonization or competition[130]; this type of social capital is "responsible" for all contractual[131] associations among individuals (including the nation, or the state).

(b) based on the (S-I) criterion, there are:

- (**F**) freedom: the degree in which the individuals can use their own free will[132];
- (**T**) trust: the degree in which the individuals freely agree to pass some of their rights or interests to the state (the Government);
- (**S**) symmetry[133]: the degree in which the individuals have the same access to the societal positive externalities (education, justice, health, other public goods, or chances).

To be observed that the socialization kinds of social capital are of process nature, while the individualization kinds of social capital are of phenomenon nature. This observation could lead us to a very interesting conclusion: the individualization social capital is a result of the socialization social capital. As consequence, we must accept a kind of aprioriness of the socialization social capital related to the individualization social capital. In other words, we could consider the individualization social capital as a specification[134] of the socialization social capital.

We believe all the proposals in the dedicated literature concerning the typology of the social capital can be introduced in the six pieces scheme delivered above, so our proposition could be considered of a largest generality and abstractness.

3. *The pairs of the social capital*

In fact, we can pair the three types of the socialization social capital with the three types of the individualization social capital, based on the above remark concerning the specification nature of the individualization social capital related to the socialization social capital. So, we have the following pairs of social capital types:

- (**C-F**), i.e., (Communication-Freedom): we can denominate this pair as the "cultural binomial" of the social capital;
- (**P–T**), i.e., (Participation-Trust): we can denominate this pair as the "axiological binomial" of the social capital;
- (**M-S**), i.e., (Mutualization-Symmetry): we can denominate this pair as the "praxiological binominal" of the social capital.

The reasons for proposals of the binomials consist in the causality relations between the pair's members, the causality arrow having the origin in the socialization type of social capital, and the destination in the individualization type of social capital. Indeed, the communication process will generate the freedom for the individuals, that is, will allow them to experience the free will. Similarly, the participation process will generate the trust, and the mutualization process will generate the symmetry.

Notes

1. To be noting that internally, i.e., from own biological body, sensations are working, as well.
2. The question of whether plants or fungi are endowed with psychism is still under discussion. For the sake of (a unitary) discussion, we can accept a sort of such psychism for any living entity, without perturbing the logic of reasoning.
3. We must be attentive do not confuse the *trop*, from where we have *tropism* (in Biology), with *trope*, from where we have *tropoiesis* (in literature)—the latter means the use of figures of speech, e.g., metaphors.
4. The biologists (and even the metaphysicians) could say something similar to what cosmologists say. The latter affirm that they can explain any physical phenomenon/event/process since the Big Bang, with the condition that the Big Bang emergence be accepted without discussion. Similarly, the biologists/metaphysicians could say they can explain any phenomenon/event/process involved by consciousness, with the condition that no question regarding its emergence is put.
5. It is not yet clarified whether the non-human entities which are endowed with "sufficient" brain, have or not rememberings. If we do not consider the human being as a special creation of Nature (or God, after preferences), we should accept the hypothesis that they can remember. However, at a prudent level, I would accept for the non-human entities only a remembering of perceptions, not of representations (see further discussion in the main text).
6. For example, in the case of human being, the new born child is capable only of such remembering, that is, when the object involved (e.g., his/her mother) is before him/her in the flesh

and blood, else he/she completely forget the mother. This means incapacity of representations, as I will show below.

7. There is a "moment zero" of acquiring perception, namely the first time when perception is experienced. Before the "moment zero" for a given perception, no representation of the object of that perception is possible. *Nota bene*: however, Phenomenology believes somewhat differently.
8. Those particular features could be either peripheral or essential.
9. See, for example, the famous examples called "Russell's hen" or "Hempel's raven".
10. Even in the case of formal language (logical, mathematical, symbolical, etc.), that language is introduced and controlled by a natural language.
11. I do not detail more on the concept of syllogism, since the common understanding of it is sufficient for my objective in this chapter. Essentially, by syllogism is understood a logical procedure (i.e., a procedure based on the three logical principles—*Nota bene*: we have in view the bivalent logic, that is, of *tertium non datur*) through which, from true premises, true conclusions are obtained.
12. Any subject (*Nota bene*: from now further, by subject I do understand only the human being, that is, only the subject capable of representations) is, in turn, a component element of the real, of course.
13. Usually, but not mandatorily, the subjectivity in the case is objectified as an inter-subjectivity, that is, a cooperation of different subjects to objectify the same subjective construct (for example, a theory).
14. So, the human being has not access into Popper's world 1, although it is a world's thing (so, belonging to the world 1), and its consciousness cognitively scrutinizes the world 1.
15. It is to be mentioned that the human being, as a biological entity, belongs to world 1, since it is an objective entity. The birth in vitro raises, however, the question of the new-born's belonging. The question is complicated enough, since, on the one hand, the new-born remains a biological entity (so, it should belong to world 1), but, on the other hand, it implies the socialization of the respective process (so, it should belong to world 3). Belonging to world 3 implies the predicate called artefact,

but the process in the case is partially biological, so it is not an artefact properly said. For this chapter (and book, besides), I will consider this case, which is placed at the border between world 1 and world 3, to be solved by considering the new-born in vitro as a component of world 1.

16. I have in mind, here, the clock time, namely, an impersonal time, equal with itself, with an invariant "speed", which is not influenced by the measured entity/process/phenomenon, and does not influence that entity/process/phenomenon. The most well-known example of clock time is the time variable used in Newtonian Mechanics equations.
17. A generic individual can simultaneously have many categories of lives: biological, social, political, professional, affective, and so on. Of course, biological life is the logically necessary condition to experience any other category of life, so having not only primacy in chronological order, but primordiality in a logical one.
18. This typology is not linked to the values; the latter generates another typology, which I will discuss below.
19. I ignore the attribute of self-awareness, since, from now on, I have in attention the human being only, who is presumed to hold such an attribute as a result of his/her capacity of representation.
20. The homogeneity involved regards: territory (together with the associated political sovereignty), history, language, traditions, and so on, that is, sufficient homogeneity liable to confer a non-ambiguous identity of that large community.
21. Even the extra-planetary space—Cosmos—if considering the global problems arisen on Earth regarding the natural resources, pollution, climate change, competition among countries (and individuals) aimed at the economic property on other celestial bodies (i.e., the cosmic law), etc.
22. So, the person in the case is not only a world's citizen, but also a Universe's citizen.
23. This level implies the quantitative and structural satisfaction of needs.
24. I think this is a rather inappropriate denomination.
25. I remind that the concept/term *meaning* addresses the denotation of something (which is common for a large community of individuals), while the concept/term *significance* addresses the connotation of something (which is completely idiosyncratic). In

this context, the levels L0–L3 refer to meaning, and the level L4 refers to significance.

26. According to the ancient principle: ***primum vivere, deinde philosophari***.
27. Between the communitarian layer (L2), the social layer (L3), and the global layer (L4) are not vertical (i.e., qualitative or categorial) differences, but only a horizontal (i.e., quantitative or of sphere) difference. In a notation imported from set theory, it can be written as: $(L2) \subset (L3) \subset (L4)$.
28. I remind that the concept of saturation, even not as term, which is replaced by the term satisfied, there already is in relation with the first pyramid (Maslow's pyramid of needs)—a need does not enter the individual's behaviour just if the immediately precedent need in the first pyramid is satisfied (*Nota bene*: I would use the expression is saturated). So, the need satisfaction is not sufficient to pass to the urgency of the immediately successive need; it must be saturated, namely, it must not mobilize further the attention and the interest of that individual. For example, I can satisfy my need to eat, but tomorrow, that need will manifest again. The conclusion is that a saturation of a need means (or, should mean) that need become passive, what is logically equivalent with this statement: the saturation of a need means that need is "ensured" from the perspective of its satisfying—to continue the example of the need of eating, that need is associated with a permanent income based on which its satisfying exits from the pression of the individual involved. It results that periodically needs, i.e., needs of which satisfying requires repeatable episodes, cannot be at all saturation, but only satisfaction, instead the needs of which satisfying is of one-off type can be saturated. The needs that cannot be saturated, as shown above, should be denominated as renewable needs (RNs), while the needs that can be saturated should be denominated as saturable needs (SNs).
29. The logical equivalence of the relationship between saturability and saturation with the relationship between (factual) testability and (factual) testing is irresistible.
30. The concept of link saturation is one of great difficulty, since it cannot be viewed as either completely objective, completely subjective, or completely objectified. Of course, a dedicated model of rationality should be developed in this matter, so that

the saturation of the link can be given at least a qualitative evaluation, if not a quantitative one.

31. A complete and continuous life chain (path) will be called a *viable life chain* (VLC) and will constitute, as we will see further, a fundamental concept in the economy of the book.
32. A sociologist or a social philosopher could conclude that nations are the largest communities that have relevance from the point of view of realizing the plenary life cycle. Since the fundamental objective of this book does not cover issues of political theory, I leave the theme for more qualified colleagues in this matter.
33. In this review of precursors, I follow quite closely Nussbaum's work (2006).
34. In fact, Aristotle was a follower of what is called eudaimonism.
35. However, Martha C. Nussbaum (see below) considers that what can be called, in Aristotle, distributism, is a genus that also includes the species introduced by Rawls, namely distributism as equity.
36. Otherwise, Aristotle argues, catastrophes may occur (Nussbaum, 1987).
37. We will see that the idea of (potential) functioning is central to the approach of capabilities that Nussbaum proposes.
38. The concept of happiness is what is called a 3rd order goal. Thus, there is: (1) 1st order goal/finality—that goal that is dependent on means; (2) 2nd order goal/finality—that goal that is intended for itself; (3) 3rd order goal/finality—happiness (Crespo, 2012).
39. See, here, my vision regarding the third pyramid, that of satisfying the need of the first pyramid—in the third pyramid, the highest level is exactly the satisfaction from the signification perspective.
40. By education, here I also mean instruction.
41. By common prudence, Smith understands the unity between motivation and understanding (*Nota bene*: it is not difficult to make the connection, in this matter, with the concept of freedom defined as the understanding of necessity).
42. It is very interesting that Smith also uses other terms—*self-command*; *self-love*—but he does not use the term egoism.
43. In fact, that maxim belongs to Kant.
44. I recall that individual freedom is defined as the absence of private constraint on the formulation/choice of one's own goals.

45. In Marx's terminology, the normative framework is called society's suprastructure.
46. I note that among the contributors to this handbook-type work are Martha C. Nussbaum (who, in her intervention, responds to Walsh) and Amartya Sen who, in his intervention, also responds to Walsh.
47. Taken up, it seems without a full and correct understanding, by Lionel Robbins and widely disseminated in the foundations of economic theory known as economic positivism (or as positive economic theory). *Nota bene*: Robbins is one of those who proposed the (unfortunate) definition of economic theory as a theory that deals with the allocation of scarce resources with alternative uses, a definition that transformed economic theory into a kind of... management.
48. I consider, at this point in the discussion, that omitting Marx's contributions to the return of economic theory to the status of political economy is unjustified.
49. The concept of (full) realization of the human being is, moreover, also at the centre of Marxist economic theory. Also, I remind that, in the first pyramid (of needs) above discussed, Maslow use, for the highest level of needs the expression *self-realization*.
50. Although I will not develop it further here, my opinion is that the presence of ethics in norms does not in any way equate norms with values—values can also exist outside norms and independently of norms, so I consider that Habermas's position can be supported (probably, Putnam was looking for as many dichotomies as possible to reject under the aegis of necessary entanglement, but, obviously, entanglement, even necessary, does not imply indistinction or indiscernibility—a simple logical analysis leads us to the following result: an entanglement that leads to indiscernibility is *contradictio in terminis*, it being denied/cancelled precisely by accepting the indistinction as a conclusion validly inferred from the premises). In the same context, I would argue that Quine's attempt to annul the Kantian analytical/synthetic dichotomy is susceptible to the same interpretation: an epistemological suicide.
51. However, Sen shows that considering actual behaviour as rational (for example, *homo œconomicus* model) leads to fewer difficulties than considering it as irrational. In the same vein, it should

be noted that Stigler demands the separation of egoism from ethics, which makes it more difficult to join ethics to economic behaviour—in this sense, he deduces the concept of egoism from Smith's concept of *common prudence*.

52. A direct link to institutionalism (see Chapter 4).
53. In this sense, Sen even develops a theory of maximization under conditions of an incomplete set of preferences (*Nota bene*: thus, something analogous to Herbert Simon's well-known proposal regarding bounded rationality).
54. I recall that the absence of rationality in social choice is illustrated, peremptorily, by Arrow's famous theorem on the impossibility of (rational) ordering of preferences (*Nota bene*: what is a generalized development of the Condorcet paradox). See, here, my opinion regarding the second pyramid.
55. Robbins introduces, in 1930, the inter-personal comparison of utility (i.e., utility seen at the level of the individual). *Nota bene*: of course, it is not about comparing preferences but about comparing the effects of expressing preferences.
56. It seems, says Sen, that economists tend to call all ethical propositions meaningless propositions (*Nota bene*: it is easy to see here the connection between this fundamentalist positivism and the precepts of the Vienna Circle regarding metaphysical propositions, considered to be, also, meaningless—more precisely, without significance, having no factual referential).
57. The converse is more applicable to welfare economics than the direct theorem (although it does raise a number of issues regarding access to information). However, it can only be applied (even if the issues related to access to information are overcome) if there are political possibilities for *resources redistributing*.
58. I say *in principle* because, as Nozick (and Nussbaum in particular) shows, the difference principle is of macroeconomic applicability, so it concerns (and "regulates") social justice at the group level, not the individual, although the first Rawlsian principle—from which the difference principle is inferred—concerns the microeconomic (the individual).
59. In the specialized literature, both terms are encountered—optimum and equilibrium, respectively. In my opinion, it is about equilibrium, because the optimum implies a set of constraints that must be verified. However, in the Paretian problem, the

only "constraint" is the preservation of the state/position of the rest of the system when the state/position of an element of the system improves; it is obvious that such a "constraint" is specific to equilibrium problems (see, for example, the invisible hand mechanism). *Nota bene*: as Edgeworth shows, the utilitarian optimum implies the Paretian optimum, but, on the other hand, the Paretian optimum does not imply the utilitarian optimum.

60. For example, the welfare aspect seeks one's own advantage (without being, by this, selfishness, since it does not consider substantive utility), while the agency aspect seeks (also) the advantage of others, therefore including altruism.
61. I recall that egalitarianism applied to resources or resource egalitarianism constitutes the essence of liberalism (*Nota bene*: it is wrongly considered that liberalism refers to the egalitarianism of opportunities/chances). In the matter of evaluating advantage, from the perspective of egalitarianism, the works of the American philosopher Ronald Dworkin are interesting.
62. It is obvious that Sen is trying to use, simultaneously, both the idea of balance (egalitarianism) regarding resources and that of balance (egalitarianism) regarding opportunities. Moreover, the term *balance* is relatively frequently used by the social economist in question. I recall that Rawls also felt the need to use the concept (and term) of balance—see the phrase *reflective balance* recommended to the participants in the original/initial position. The concept of balance represents one of the pillars of connection between the three distinct theories of social justice (equity/fairness theory, entitlement theory, capabilities theory) between which, in our opinion, it is necessary to build a *sui generis* synthesis.
63. This is a new connecting element between the three theories of social justice.
64. The proximity of this position to Sartre's vision of freedom is obvious.
65. Here a series of polemical aspects arise regarding the capabilities approach proposed by Nussbaum (which, in our opinion, deviates on this point from the position expressed by Sen—in fact, she deviates, from the same perspective, from the positions of Rawls and Nozick, respectively).

66. This is not a methodological pluralism, but rather an ontological one, in my opinion.
67. It should be noted that, in CT, the concept of wellbeing is assigned (without being "arrested") to the individual, not the community—we therefore have a clear delimitation from utilitarianism which (also) considers non-individual utility, i.e., either average utility or global/societal utility.
68. I would like to point out that the author does not develop an analytical, logical discussion in this regard, although, obviously, such a discussion is required by the very place and role given to the concept in question, even at the level of the guiding principles.
69. By substantive utility, I understand the (usual) economic utility.
70. It is particularly important to note that the pursuit of wellbeing, which involves agency, will make each person's wellbeing dependent on the wellbeing of others, because, as shown above (see note 60), agency involves altruism.
71. Again, it is suggested a close communication between CT and institutionalism.
72. As we have seen (see Chapter 2), Nussbaum proposes a list of 10 capabilities (*Nota bene*: a kind of decalogue of the individual capabilities).
73. A situation that is perfectly possible in both the case of equity/fairness theory and the case of entitlement theory.
74. In fact, it is a predictor for the other individuals regarding the behaviour of the involved individual.
75. Of course, the possibility of such a blockage exists as an accident—for example, a deliberate blockage, for various reasons—but such an accident is punishable simply by positive law, as a reaction to the violation of legal rules. The accident in question is not a possible consequence, much less a necessary consequence, of the social arrangement in question.
76. Obviously, as in the case of the other two competing theories of social justice, capabilities refer to capabilities regarding rights, not capabilities regarding resources—here, again, we have a certain "separation" from liberalism in the case of CT, despite the proximity identified from the perspective of the lack of an explicit generic call for redistribution..
77. This qualification results immediately, moreover, from the fact that all capabilities are ensured and accessible on a normative

basis, through the appropriate social arrangement required for this. It should be noted that accessing a public good represents a personal choice of the individual, a property that is also found in the case of capabilities approach.

78. This quality is common to both the two Rawlsian principles and the three Nozickian principles—all of which are of the nature of the public good: non-rival, inexhaustible, and free. As a public good, it falls to the state to provide the set of capabilities considered historically and culturally appropriate in a given society.
79. Such a discussion should be conducted, in my opinion, exclusively from a logical, abstract, non-historical perspective.
80. I specify that the state of having is not completely and unequivocally eliminated by either the Rawlsian or the Nozickian theory—since the former, through the principle of difference, ensures, *ex ante*, the absence of loss or advantage, and the latter, through the principle of rectification, ensures, *ex post*, the correction of loss, that is, the restoration of advantage.
81. Of course, the particular (and concrete) forms of accessibility of the capabilities should prevent cases in which the use of a capability is blocked, although the individual concerned wants to use that capability.
82. If one of the components of the binomial were the counterpart of the other (i.e., an obligation would correspond to a right and vice versa), then between functioning and capability we would have an anti-symmetric (or mirror) relationship, with all the ingredients of the nature of necessity involved.
83. We recall that, for example, Kantian morality is non-consequentialist (the imperative of duty is categorical), while Christian morality is consequentialist (behaviour is guided by reward/punishment linked to salvation).
84. The use of the term *possibility* expresses the potential, rather than actual, character of the "valorization" of the capability in question in order to achieve wellbeing through the functioning of the individual (a potential aspect evoked several times previously).
85. The meaning of the phrase *generic individual* is the following: it is not about a representative (or average) individual as economists, and even sociologists, usually consider, but about an "individual"

individual, concrete, but whose particular character is not, for the moment, of interest, so it remains a generic individual.

86. Of course, there is also the case where an individual's deficiency or disability is transformed, on occasion (in a praxiological sense, here) into a handicap, that is, into an effective (quasi-objective) impossibility of using, for one's own benefit or, at least, in the exercise of the associated right, the respective capability. Of course, here the question arises of the adequacy of the capability (in terms of accessibility) to a-normal situations of deficiency, disability, or handicap, either from a physical or from an intellectual perspective.
87. The informed reader has already noted that the categorical nature of Rawls' proceduralist finality stems from the Kantian concept of the categorical imperative within the Königsberg philosopher's theory of practical reason.
88. I recall that the *categorical* predicate is semantically equivalent to the *unconditional* predicate.
89. Although Nozick criticizes, in particular, the structured character of Rawlsian theory (a character that he extracts, as I have shown in the appropriate place, from the proceduralist nature of that theory).
90. Of course, these categorical "labels" should not be considered absolutely but, rather, as semantic marks of some utility in the somewhat dichotomous characterization of the theories of social justice discussed in this study.
91. Although the most references in literature are for the syntagma "capabilities theory/approach", in my opinion the more appropriate such syntagma should be "capability's theory/approach" or even "capability theory/approach", since a theory must treat the generic concept, not a list of species belonging to that concept. However, in the book, I do not exaggerate with such pedantry.
92. For example, Nussbaum proposes 10 such capabilities, (the number 10 probably has a biblical significance!—the Decalogue of the commandments/capabilities—because the author does not offer a criterion, qualitative or quantitative, for this limit (as, for that matter, neither for identifying each capability in particular). Of course, this ignoring of the criteria is in line with the author's "care" not to offer any element that could be interpreted as a concession made to proceduralism.

93. The problem of the absence of mutual redundancy of capabilities is a difficult one: it is possible that redundancy (or a certain degree of redundancy) ensures a higher degree of effectiveness of CT from the perspective of the fundamental goal—achieving individual wellbeing, but this issue will not be developed in the present study.
94. The effectiveness of the capabilities obeys human condition (e.g., the normative framework), but the potentiality of them must obey human nature. It should not be understood, from the retention of this attribute, that a reference is made to the state of anarchy (as the Nozickian theory does). Although in the state of anarchy natural law is dominant, it is not necessary that the consideration of natural law implies an appeal to the state of anarchy.
95. The chreod is a concept introduced by the English biologist C.H. Waddington, with regard to the living cell, meaning a path or trajectory of development/evolution of the cell. Of course, in the present study, the meaning of the concept of the chreod is relative to the social domain.
96. Establishing the size of the significant period is, of course, a problem per se (which I will not refer to in the present study).
97. The reader is asked to note the distinction I make (or rather, which must be made) between the general character of the constitutional normative framework and its applied character (the two attributes seem to be contradictory or, at least, divergent): thus, the general character refers to the subject (addressee) of the norm in question, while the applied character refers to the object to which the subject must have access in the exercise of his/her functioning as an individual..
98. So, no matter how we look at things, it seems that CT is more contractarian than the contractarian theories of social justice. As said many times, Nozick's resilientist theory also has clear contractarian marks.
99. Unfortunately, the concept of *sufficient measure* is not clarified either logically or semantically.
100. It is very important here to emphasize that neither the Rawlsian nor the Nozickian theory discusses a specific finality of the application of the principles of social justice they propose—this is a clear sign, from a logical perspective, of the fact that both of these theories are proceduralist (proceduralism does not need

to "aim" at finality, since this is a necessary consequence, i.e., logically obligatory, of the principles).

101. It can easily be seen that, logically, Nozick's resilientism lies in the "middle ground", between Rawls' proceduralism and Nussbaum's optionalism.
102. A variant of ante-pronunciation avoidance (which can also be called conflict of interest avoidance) operates in the field of public policy: the design of public policy must be done independently of the administration (application) of that policy.
103. By contrast, both Rawls and Nozick accept such models of rationality, more or less explicitly.
104. I note that neither the public goods should be considered as resources, because they are non-rival, non-exhaustible, and non-price acquiring.
105. For example, the public good called national defence/security is a thing (belonging to Popper's third world, i.e., to the objectified world) that exists no matter if an individual (or many, or all) needs it or claims it.
106. To make a link with a principle from the economic process, this is a case in which the demand creates its supply, which economists call Keynesianism.
107. The sufficiency (viewed quantitatively, structurally, and qualitatively) implies adequacy.
108. As I have shown before, Nozick's theory and Nussbaum's one implicitly hold, in the (invisible) background, the mark of contractarianism (explicitly declared by Rawls's theory), despite the vehement rejection of it. This is not logically necessary that a social contract comes before the society's birth, but it can occur any time after the society in the case is instituted/constituted.
109. It could seem quite curious to one to speak about personal normative framework, but it is obvious that any person or organization (for example, a corporation) has his/her or its own principles of functioning, based on instruction, education, tradition, values, etc. (for persons) and on statute, role, etc. (for organizations). To get a unitary terminology and some symmetry of discussion, I would ask the reader to accept such a concept.
110. I remind you that there are also private positive externalities, similar to the public positive externalities. By the way, the concept of corporate social responsibility is closely related to the origin of

private positive externalities. It is to be mentioned that the private positive externalities cannot be considered as public goods.

111. In the civil society, for example, the political party—a political party that has access to the state power (government) exits, of course, from the civil society.
112. The cybernetic systems (i.e., systems with self-regulation, namely with a predominance of negative feedback) are of four orders: (1) cybernetic systems of order 1—non-artefactual (i.e., natural, non-anthropomorphic) systems with exogenous human subjects; (2) cybernetic systems of order 2—non-artefactual systems with endogenous human subjects; (3) cybernetic systems of order 3—artefactual systems with exogenous human subjects; (4) cybernetic systems of order 4—artefactual systems with endogenous human subjects.
113. By black-box is understood an operator/device, of any nature (technological, intellectual, ethical, etc.) that transforms an input (a cause) into an output (an effect), without us being concerned for the particular way in which such a transformation occurs. From the concept of black-box, Mario Bunge coined the term black-box-ism to generalize the description provided above.
114. Probably, it should distinguish, however, between capability and opportunity, namely, establishing that a capability is a set (convergent, consistent, and complete) of opportunities aimed at sufficiently actualizing that capability.
115. The consecrated term in literature is education, but here, this term intends to mean instruction, that is, of acquiring, in formal or informal ways, some degree of general information, professional background, and instrumental ability, either from a general or specialized perspective. Consequently, I prefer to call it instruction, not education. It is to be noted that C01 provides aptitudes in the most general meaning of this term.
116. I remind you about Dunbar's number: affectively and stably, an individual can "manage", directly, relationships with only 150 other individuals.
117. The qualification of occasions as being of a practical type considers the meaning of the practical action in Kant's philosophy, where the practical relationships are understood as those relationships that occur among subjects (for example, the religious relationships).

118. So, we have four conditionalities (sufficiency predicates) that must be cumulatively verified: (a) *external* influence; (b) *unsolicited* influence; (c) *public* influence; (d) influence *exerted on purpose* (not on the means aimed at getting that purpose).
119. This justifies the presumption that the human being is, in the last instance, a *homo significans*.
120. The communist episode hasn't a genuine optimality, so it couldn't be registered in the societal history else than an accident (i.e., a contingent phenomenon but not a necessary one).
121. Sufficiency predicates for the social capital are those characteristics or attributes that by their simultaneous verification will qualify certain entity as social capital. Any sufficiency predicate are also a necessary predicate, but the inversely is not true.
122. To be mentioned that this implies a principle of increasing marginal utility.
123. Here, non-contemporaneity means at least a temporal duration of a generation, i.e., about 21–25 years.
124. The formal institutions are the institutions which were codified (i.e., they are opposable to all). Of course, in the society there are also many informal (i.e., un-codified) institutions, which are opposable only to individuals or to local groups.
125. A criterion of classification is a parameter, of any nature, that simultaneous verifies two conditions: (1) is assignable to the entity concerned; (2) has the property to exhaust the entity (i.e., to ensure a complete topological covering of the entity concerned).
126. The exactly meaning, here, is that of individuation, that is, of passing from species to individual; however, we continue to use the word individualization, but inside the concept of individuation as it was now explained.
127. Notions as engagement or implication can be considered as equivalent.
128. This includes the formal construction of institutions themselves that follow to host the participation of the individuals.
129. Here the notion of political has the widest possible signification.
130. See here also the concepts of *bonding social capital* (for homogenous individuals), or of *bridging social capital* (for heterogeneous individuals), introduced by Robert D. Putnam.

131. Generally, by contract must be understood simply a free agreement, without any compulsory written or other witness prove (for example, the J.J. Rousseau-ian social contract).
132. Shortly, the free will signifies the possibility, capacity, and willingness of the individuals to oppose or reject external decisions or acts (more precisely, to forbear or refuse them).
133. Probably, a more appropriate denomination for this concept could be homogeneity.
134. Here the concept of specification has the Kantian signification.

References

Crespo, R. F. (2012). The Capabilities Approaches and Aristototelian Reason. *Revista De Instituciones, 57*, 57–86.

Dinga, E. (2014). *Social Capital and Social Justice*. Procedia Economics and Finance, 8/2014.

Nussbaum, M. C., & Sen, A. K. (1987). *Internal Criticism and Indian Rationalist Traditions/Martha Nussbaum and Amartya Sen*. World Institute for Development Economic Research.

Nussbaum, M. C. (2006). *Frontiers of Justice. Disability, Nationality, Species Membership*. The Belknap Press of Harvard University Press.

Ostapiuk, A. (2020) *The Eclipse of Value-Free Economics. The Concept of Multiple Self versus Homo Economicus*. Publishing House of Wroclaw University of Economics and Business.

Putnam, H., & Walsh, V. (2014). *The End of Value-Free Economics*. Routledge.

Sen, A. (1987). *Freedom of Choice: Concept and Content*. World Institute for Development Economic Research (UNU-WIDER).

Sen, A. (1999). *On Ethics & Economics*. New Delhi.

Smith A. (2007). *The Theory of Moral Sentiments*. Book Jungle.

CHAPTER 7

Ethics and Æsthetics in Societal Dynamics

1 Preamble

The human being, as a being with consciousness, that is, holding the capacity of representation, both of world and self, has the status of a being capable of giving significance, again, to both world and himself/herself. In Chapter 6, otherwise, I have shown that the highest outcome of the plenary life chain (path) is exactly the satisfaction of the significance. In this preamble, I propose to briefly discuss only the concept of significance. The clarification of this concept will support me in approaching the important issues of ethics, morals, and æsthetics in society.

1.1 Three States of the Individual

The individual can experience, in his/her whole being, three categorial states of affairs, more precisely, three states of his/her sensibility and rationality: (a) satisfaction/utility; (b) joy/pleasure; (c) happiness/eudaimonia.

The *satisfaction* (S) is a feeling, i.e., an idiosyncratic perception on a *relationship* between an expectation (desire, dream, and so on) and a state of affairs, as that relationship is perceived, either emotionally or rationally, by the individual. So, the satisfaction is neither a thing, nor a property, for it needs two entities (which can be either things, properties, or relationships, or a paired combination between them[1] to be perceived as such), it is a relationship.

E. Dinga, *The Economics of Social Justice and Societal Evolution*,
https://doi.org/10.1007/978-3-032-24055-2_7

The *joy/pleasure/delight* (J) is also an idiosyncratic perception on a *property* (i.e., on neither a relationship nor a thing). Being a property, it is assignable either to a thing or to a relationship, or even to another property (to get a property of order 2, namely property of property). This state must also exist for the individual (i.e., for the subject).

The *happiness/eudaimonia* (H), is, again, an idiosyncratic perception on a *property*, but, this time, without any assignment to a thing, or relationship, or property. To the presumptive question: what is happiness assigned/related to, the answer is: exclusively to the individual himself/herself.

So, it can be identified the representatives for the following states experienced by a generic individual:

- states related to two entities simultaneously, that is, relationships–*satisfaction* (S);
- states related to one entity, that is, properties–*joy/pleasure* (J);
- states non-related to any entity,[2] but also property–*happiness/eudaimonia* (H).

Table 1 indicates a synoptic picture of the above conclusions—T means thing, P means property, R means relationship, $K(y)$ means K is applied to y, where $y \in \{T, P, R\}$ and $K \in \{P, R\}$. With E is noted the pure existence (of course, of the individual).

As I said, the satisfaction, joy, or happiness have as their final referential the individual state, no matter the entities involved from the individual's

Table 1 States of perceptions and their representatives

	Satisfaction (S)	*Joy* (J)	*Happiness* (H)
$E(T)$			x
$E(P)$			x
$E(R)$			x
$P(T)$		x	
$P(P)$		x	
$P(R)$		x	
$R(T - T)$	x		
$R(P - P)$	x		
$R(R - R)$	x		

(*Source* author)

environment in causing that state. However, among the three categories there are differences regarding the degree of dependence on the environment.

- *satisfaction* depends on two external entities, so it can be presumed as having the degree 2 of dependence;
- *joy* depends on one external entity, so it can be presumed as having the degree 1 of dependence;
- *happiness* does not depend on any external entity,[3] so it can be presumed as having the degree 0 of dependence.[4]

1.2 Satisfaction (S)

I think we have, in fact, three species of satisfaction: (a) economic (or substantive) utility; (b) evidential utility; and (c) symbolic utility. Fundamentally, I follow here the suggestion provided by Nozick (1993), but filtered through the systemic approach of Table 1.

Before characterizing each of the three species of satisfaction, put under the concept of utility, some considerations regarding rationality are useful.

- rationality is a *property* assigned to a reasoning, so that reasoning verifies a set of pre-accepted principles. So, the principles are primitive in relation to rationality; this means that the property of rationality must be judged within and only within that set of principles. This means the property of rationality is principled closed, namely, closed related to the involved principles[5];
- being a property, rationality is assigned to a model of rationality. It must be said that a given rationality (that is, a given set of principles) can generate many models of rationality, equally valid from the perspective of the rationality concerned; obviously, while the rationality is a property, the associated model of that rationality is a *thing*;
- the (property of) rationality may be defined as the way in which conclusions are inferred from premises or, equivalently, as the type of syllogism involved in reasoning;
- the rationality is of two categories (a) theoretical rationality; (b) practical rationality

- theoretical rationality: that rationality whose the (primitive) principles are of belief type. The belief is somewhat, a kind of axiom, based on which the involved reasoning is unfolded. The theoretical rationality is unjustifiable, it is a kind of intellectual "taste";
- practical[6] rationality: that rationality aimed at correlating, based on a pre-established criterion, the means with the intended purpose/goal. The practical (or, as I would prefer, praxiological) rationality is, in turn, of two kinds: (b1) instrumental rationality; (b2) justificatory rationality.[7]

(a) Economic utility

The economic utility (U_I) is a relationship between the need of an individual and the covering of that need. Such a covering can be provided by an acquisition of a good or service, by a donation, subsidy from the state, etc. More exactly, however, the economic utility is a relationship between two properties, namely: the need (of any nature), which is a property of the state of the individual, and the coverer of that need, which is a property of the good or service aimed at covering that need. So, according to Fig. 1, the utility is an "object" of type $R(P - P)$, that is, it represents one of the three possible species of satisfaction.

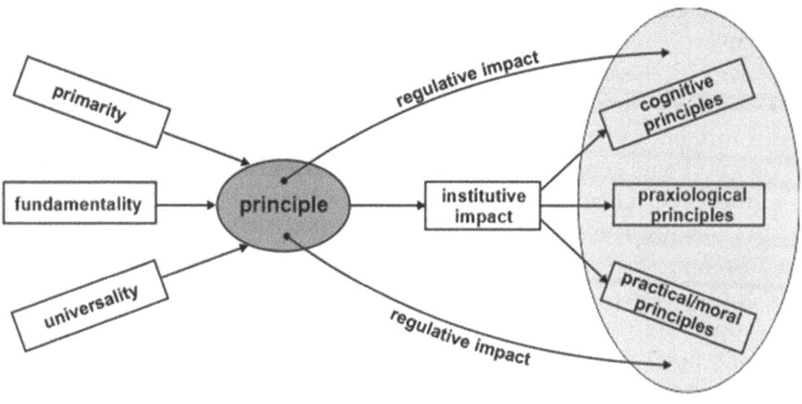

Fig. 1 Role of principles in constructing cognitive devices (I) (*Source* author)

The most known utility is the economic (equivalent: substantive) utility, that is, provided within the generic economic system/process. About the economic/substantive utility, the following features can be held:

- it is evaluated in a psychological way, by each individual[8];
- generally, it cannot be (completely and relevantly) "translated" into money or a common measure inter-subjectively exchangeable, but in empirical cases, such a "translation" is both possible and used;
- the best proxy of it is the price,[9] which allows the commensurability between individuals' utilities;
- the perception of utility follows an increasing and concave curve related to the quantity of goods or services "mobilized" to cover the corresponding need, or, equivalently, a decreasing curve of the marginal utility.[10]

The economic utility is of a substantive type (for example, it can be expressed in money or something equivalent), more precisely, of a *causal substantive* type. This means that one of the properties is cause for the other property in the relationship concerned. It belongs to an *instrumental rationality*, as a species of practical rationality, and is assignable to *meaning* (not signification).

(b) Evidential utility

Evidential utility (U_E) addresses the issue of the probation regarding an outcome/effect of an action (either act or abstention). Consequently, the evidential utility is described by the species $R(T - T)$. Evidential utility is not causal, but correlational, since it describes the relationship between two properties (analogously with the causal/economic utility)—a property of an action and a property of an outcome. So the evidential utility is a *correlational substantive* type. It belongs to a *justificatory rationality* as another species of practical rationality. Like the economic utility, the evidential utility is assignable to *meaning*.

(c) Symbolic utility

The symbolic utility (U_S) is that species of satisfaction expressing the relationship between relationships—denoted in Fig. 1, with $R(R - R)$. The symbolic utility is not too much "visited" and debated in the literature. To my knowledge, an abstract and general approach in a sufficient degree is delivered by Robert Nozick (1993). Nozick's theory of the symbolic utility can be systematized as follows:

- symbolic utility is focused on (and, so, assignable to) signification[11];
- symbolic utility is generated by the behaviour's principles, as they are not only formulated and assumed but also made public, for example, by announcements;
- as a result of how symbolic utility is caused, it plays the role of a predictor (more or less credible) for the other societal agents/actors.

The symbolic utility is of a *credential* type, so it belongs to a *theoretical rationality*.

Table 2 tries to put together the features of the three species of satisfaction, i.e., utilities.

1.3 Joy

As shown, joy ($\mathcal{J}$) is assigned to a property, no matter what (of a thing, a property, or a relationship), which has relevance of any kind for the involved subject. If satisfaction comes to solve a need, joy comes to solve an expectation/hope/desirability, which is assumed to be incorporated by the property concerned. Another difference between joy and satisfaction is the following: while satisfaction has degrees of satisfaction, joy has no degrees, that is, joy is of a dichotomic type—either it exists or does not. Of course, joy can refer even to the subject in the case, namely to a property that the subject holds or gains.

If satisfaction is "regionalized" within the economic and social interactions, joy, on the other hand, leaves the societal sphere, entering the spiritual sphere (e.g., religious, metaphysical, and the like). Of course, joy can (not mandatorily) be generated, either causally or conditionally, by satisfaction itself, but joy's causality is much more extensive than the societal one. For example, the joy of being in love, or the joy of praying to God, is not generated by satisfaction; they are *causa sui*.

Table 2 Species of satisfaction (the three utilities)

			Practical rationality		
		Theoretical rationality	Instrumental rationality	Justificatory rationality	
Substantive	Causal		Economic utility		$R(P - P)$
	Correlational			Evidential utility	$R(T - T)$
	Credential	Symbolic utility			$R(R - R)$
		Signification	Meaning		

(*Source* author)

1.4 Happiness

Happiness ($\mathcal{H}$) does not need either a relationship between properties (satisfaction—solving a need) or a property as such (joy—solving an expectation), but it is free of any "anchoring" outside the subject. Otherwise, it is said that one is happy when he/she does not expect anything.[12] If satisfaction and joy are states of mind that are perceived synchronically, happiness is always perceived a-synchronically—that is, we are aware regarding the state of happiness (much time) after that state occurred, not concomitantly with the time/duration within it happens.[13]

If satisfaction and joy could be considered as "regional" states of the mind, happiness should be thought as "general" such a state. Moreover, if satisfaction and joy are states of conscious mind, happiness is, rather, a state of the unconscious mind. Of course, the individual is always aware of its happiness, but the "initiation" of that state happens, usually, in the unconsciousness.

Comment

A problem arises: is there (or could be conceived) a hierarchy among the three concepts (in fact, states of the mind), and if so, based on which criterion and with which signification/relevance? My opinion on this matter is as follows:

- yes, a hierarchy is not only possible, but it seems it should be mandatorily designed, since the human being functions based, generally, on hierarchies, which constitutes the grounding for relevance, decision, and action (either act or abstention) within the societal system;
- the criterion for such a hierarchy should be, I think, the number of degrees of constraint. In such a context, I recall that satisfaction has two degrees of constraints (it can be said that satisfaction is bi-anchored), joy has one degree of constraint (it can be said that joy is mono-anchored), and happiness has no degrees of constraints (it can be said that happiness is null-anchored or, equivalently, non-anchored at all);
- consequently, based on the criterion accepted, we have the following hierarchy of the basic states of mind, in a decreasing order of the number of constraints:
- happiness ($\mathcal{H}$)
- joy ($\mathcal{J}$)

- satisfaction ($\mathcal{S}$)
- symbolic utility (U_S)
- evidential utility (U_E)
- economic utility (U_I)
- the relevance (and... utility) of such a hierarchy consists in the following:
  - it indicates a continue humanization of the human being, that is, an increasingly freedom related to the external factors;
  - it seems to verify the whole field of historical reflexions in which the individual's purposes were established based on what could be called human realization arrow, that is, from economic utility to happiness.[14]

2 Ethics and Morals within Society

Based on the above (brief) considerations, I pass now to examine the concepts of ethics and morale within the society, i.e., inside the societal system.

2.1 Ethics

Preliminaries

Ethics constitutes a way of life, in what could be called the latter's foundations of life. The foundations of the way of life, generically speaking, reside in the principles of that way of life, and, consequently, in the abstract scheme on which the way of life is designed, engaged, and objectified. I do a short characterization of this idea below:

- the principles themselves of general behaviour (i.e., no matter the "region" of the societal system involved), are exactly the commitment of the individual in question about both himself/herself and the others (his/her societal alterity[15]);
- it is not mandatory for the principles to form a complete, convergent, and consistent system of principles—rather, such principles are empirical enough, for example, acquired through education, tradition, or other means without a deep deliberation from the part of the individual involved[16];

- the principles grounding the way of life—that I would call ethical principles or, simpler, ethics—are completely subjective and idiosyncratic; they are the exclusive "intellectual property" of the individual involved. Consequently, generally, the ethics, that is, the ethical principles, are not commensurable among historical/empirical individuals;
- the principles in question are theoretical, neither praxiological nor practical. This means they are established/selected/chosen based on reasons that are not rationally justifiable or sustainable face to the other individuals in the society concerned. Generally, they must be considered as anchoring themselves in belief or credence, no matter how and when this belief/credence has been acquired;
- it is non-mandatory for the principles to generate a (re)cognoscible model of rationality.[17]

About the Construction of a Theory of Ethics

Ethics cannot be less than a solid theory, so, it needs a logical construction based on principles (axioms), theorems, lemmas, and, of course, procedures of testing.

In this paragraph, I do not develop an own proposal of an ethical theory according to the above mentions (such a suggestion will be provided in a next book concerned of economic order and ethical order[18]), but only some considerations on the basics (logics) of such a construction.

The logical basis of my further statements resides in the originary qualification of Ethics as a practical/moral theory/discipline.[19] In this light, I will develop the following issues on the theory of Ethics: (a) the principles; (b) the finality; (c) the methodology; (d) the outcomes; (e) the testability.

(a) On the principles

The principles (or, the same, axioms) constitute the background, i.e., the backbone, of any cognitive construction. The principles incorporate, rather implicitly, the finality designed, the methodology operable, the outcomes expected, and the testability possible.

Figures 1 and 2 provide a general view on the role of principles in constructing a theory of ethics.

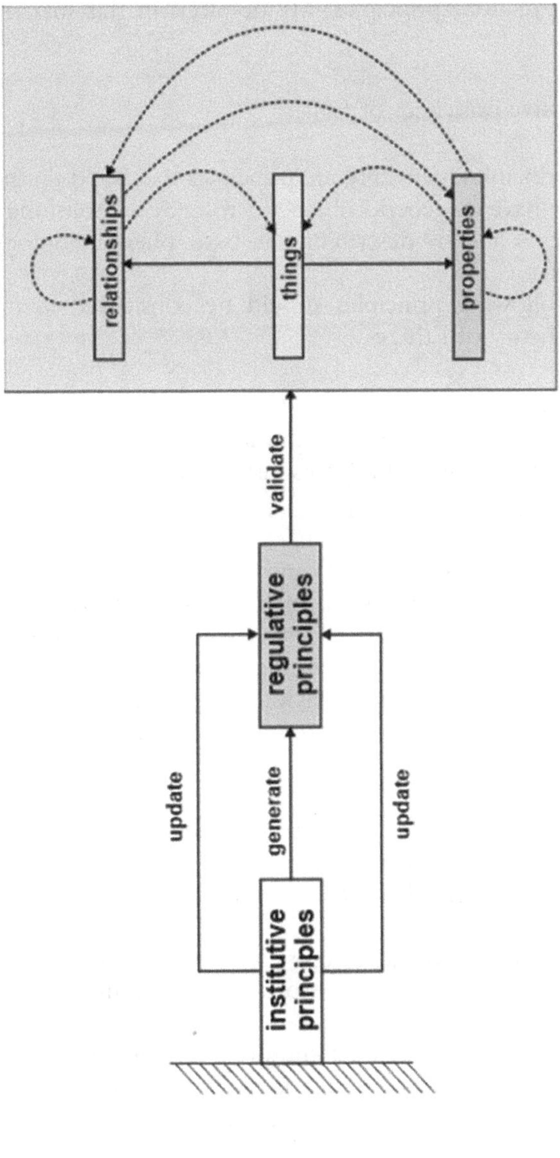

Fig. 2 Role of principles in constructing cognitive devices (II) (*Source* author)

According to Figs. 1 and 2, there are (or must be) two categories/classes of principles which should ground Ethics, namely: (i) institutive principles; (ii) regulatory principles. My opinions in this matter are the following:

(i) The institutive principles of Ethics

The institutive principles, generally, are principles that build up the theory of Ethics. They have a generical/genetic role by establishing the set of needed concepts and by describing the basic phenomenology of the theory concerned.

I think the following principles should be considered as institutive principles for a theory of Ethics:

- ($P_I^E/1$) any behaviour (decision and/or action) is acceptable[20] if and only if it is a valid inference[21] from a belief/credence of the individual concerned. I would call this institutive principle: the *principle of origin*.

The principle asserts that the only and supreme justification, so the "right" to objectify a certain behaviour is provided by the theoretical rationality of the individual, which is based, as is known, on the belief/credence. This grounding of the behaviour guarantees exactly the genuineness (authenticity) of the behaviour considered.

Nota bene: about the sincerity, evoked in note 21 above, the following considerations could be of usefulness:

- sincerity is not related to the pair true—false, in the bivalent logic—so, it is not related to knowledge, but to the conscious behaviour of the individual in his/her manifestations using words/statements/narratives, etc.;
- more exactly, the sincerity ensures, if it exists, that what the individual concerned knows is also expressed in communication, of any form, to others;
- again, if the involved individual knows something and expresses that knowledge to others, no matter if his/her knowledge is true or false, the basic condition is that the individual expresses what he/she knows or believes they know.

- ($P_I^E/2$) any acceptable behaviour plays as a self-commitment of the individual concerned, related both to self and the others. I would call this institutive principle: the *principle of guarantee*.

According to Nozick (1993), the principle is, in its essence, a commitment of the "owner" related to both self and the others. Consequently, the principle issues, in the "ether", a message according to which the individual will respect what he/she says[22] that will respect—somewhat, the principle acts as a predictor in the benefit of the other societal agents/ actors.

Nota bene: the commitment related to self deserves some extra comments, as follows:

- the commitment to self implies a sincerity of second order, let us to say (if the sincerity to others would be considered as sincerity of first order);
- the sincerity of second order is much opaque to others than the sincerity of first order, since it is not expressed publicly, so it cannot be tested by others;
- of course, by intermediation of the revealed preference (Samuelson, 1938), other individuals will finally "guess" if the individual concerned respected or not his/her own principles, that is, if he/ she is or is not sincere to himself/herself[23];
- if the sincerity to self is violated, this could compromise the next principle of the theory of Ethics (the principle of symmetry), since the individual can be viewed as an alterity (another) faced to self.
- ($P_I^E/3$) any acceptable behaviour must have symmetrical acceptability, namely, it must be not rejected from an individual if other individuals objectify it on that individual. I would call this institutive principle: the *principle of symmetry*.

This principle is a transformed form of the well-known Kantian maxim, saying, essentially, that a generic individual who operates (objectifies) a given behaviour must be prepared to suffer the impact of the same behaviour when it is operated (objectified) by another individual.

- ($P_I^E/4$) any acceptable behaviour must be activated by empathy,[24] namely by the emotional implication (either visible or, most often, invisible, for the "recipient" of the involved behaviour) of the individual concerned into another human being, either an individual or a group. I would call this institutive principle: the *principle of empathy*.

(ii) The regulatory principles of Ethics

The regulatory principles, generally, ensure the autopoieticity of the whole body of the theory concerned (primarily, of the set of institutive principles and, of course, on the set of concepts derived from the institutive principles), following the outcomes delivered by that theory or, as the case may be, the results of testing the predictions based on the theory, either corroborations or refutations. Shortly, the regulatory principles ensure the dynamic invariance of the theory, by valuing its functioning—e.g., by feedback, feedforward, restructuring, and so on.

I think the following principles should be considered as regulatory principles for a theory of Ethics:

- ($P_R^E/1$) the institutive principles can be updated only in the direction of strengthening the commitment involved by them. I would call this regulatory principle: the *principle of supra-committing*.

This regulatory principle is analogous to the "principle" required by Popper regarding the ad hoc hypotheses when a (scientific) prediction is made, either it is corroborated or refuted—Popper requires that the ad hoc hypotheses should reduce the probability of corroboration (implicitly, to increase the probability of refutation). In our case, by strengthening the commitment assigned to a given principle, the individual increases his/her exposure to others regarding the predictability of the behaviour engaged. The principle of supra-committing monitors the changes in the institutive principles, so that their force of commitment does, at least, not weaken.[25]

- ($P_R^E/2$) the concepts, procedures, and testing of ethical behaviour must be free of any utilitarian meaning and connotation. It must be specified a very important detail: it is about the economic and evidential utility, not about the symbolic utility. In other words the principle prevents the behaviour from the substantive utility. I would call this regulatory principle: the *principle of anti-utilitarianism.*

Ethics is not a theory of decision (it is not even a cognitive theory, as stated before); consequently, within the ethical "region", the evaluation of the behaviour from the perspective of cost–benefit analysis is completely forbidden. This principle of anti-utilitarianism monitors that the theoretical construction of theory of Ethics do not contain (or do not maintain if, accidentally, contains) elements assignable to substantive, i.e., economic or evidential, utility.[26]

- ($P_R^E/3$) the ethical behaviour must keep an interdependent autonomy[27] face to other individuals and the society as a whole. I would call this regulatory principle: the *principle of autonomy.*

The ethics allows individual/s some freedom in their behaviour, face to both other individuals and the society (more exactly, the state). Essentially, by autonomy[28] (according to its etymology—from Greek αυτονομία, with αυτο, that means self, and νόμος, that means law/rule/norm) is understood that state of affairs in which an individual is free to design and implement his/her rules/norms based on which he/she takes decisions and performs actions (either acts or abstentions). Between freedom and autonomy subsist the following general relationships:

- Autonomy is, like freedom, a relationship (neither a thing, nor a property);
- like, again, freedom, autonomy means not independency from other individuals and the state, but an interdependency regulated exactly by the autonomy[29];
- it can be said, abstractly, that autonomy is the historical/empirical objectification of freedom[30];
- a crisp difference between autonomy and freedom is the following: freedom is a relationship similarly evaluated by a given community, while autonomy has a strong idiosyncratic character, namely, the same normative and general cultural framework could signify different scale and quality of autonomy at the individual level.
- ($P_R^E/4$) the ethical behaviour does not optimize the behaviour. I would call this regulatory principle: the *principle of viability.*

To note that Nature never optimizes,[31] it only ensures the replication and, as a finality, the viability of the natural systems. The eventual best solutions that we observe in Nature are only the current state of numerous essays (trial and error), from which most were dead ends. There is no evidence that an improvement of a given natural state was chosen as such from the first step, i.e., by optimizing.[32] In fact, historically/empirically, human behaviour is, overwhelmingly, a non-optimizing behaviour (despite the claims of the *homo mathematicus*, wrongly called *homo œconomicus*), but rather a viable one or, temporarily and locally, sustainable.

Nota bene: according to Fig. 5 (below) the optimizing societal paradigm is necessarily followed (i.e., causally generated by the optimizing paradigm itself[33]) by the sustainability paradigm (Dinga, 2025). Since the sustainability paradigm does not imply, logically, ethics, I think the sustainability paradigm will be only a transitory paradigm from the optimality paradigm to the viability paradigm (see Sect. 6.3 in Chapter 4). Consequently, one of the regulatory principles of Ethics must be the principle of viability.

- ($P_R^E/5$) the ethical behaviour produces, continuously and permanently, social capital. I would call this regulatory principle: the *principle of social capital.*

Essentially, the ethical (re)construction of a human being is finalized in the human capital, understood as the humanity *eidos* of the individual. On the other hand, the ethical individual interacts with another ethical individual, and this interaction is finalized with the generation of social capital (Dinga, 2014). A brief presentation of the concept and typology of social capital is provided in Chapter 6, Annex 1 in Chapter 6. As I will show at Sect. 2.2, morality is built up from the ethics by the intermediation of social capital.

(b) On the general methodology

A theory of Ethics must follow a general (and abstract) procedure, in order to provide not only the performative role of that theory but, also, its outcomes and, especially, testability. Figure 3 suggests such a procedure.

The basic methodological "rules" of elaborating a theory of Ethics, I think are the following:

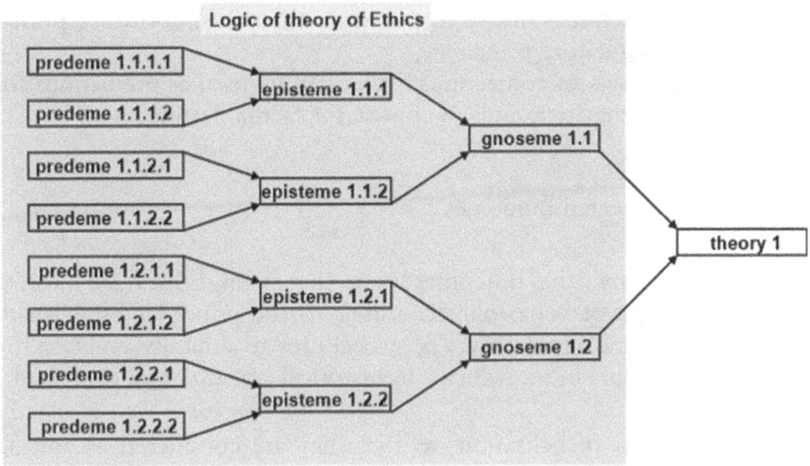

Fig. 3 Abstract logical procedure to elaborate a theory of Ethics (*Source* author)

- elaborating the logic of the theory of Ethics (see Fig. 3)
  - *predeme* is a presupposition which is exogenous related to the theory concerned, for example is based on belief/credence;
  - *episteme* is a concept formed by concatenation, in one way or another, of some predemes;
  - *gnoseme* is a meta-concept formed by concatenation, in one way or another, of some epistemes;
  - *theory* is, consequently, a concatenation, in one way or another, of gnosemes;
- elaborating the institutive principles of the theory of Ethics (at section "About the Construction of a Theory of Ethics", I have suggested four such institutive principles);
- elaborating the regulatory principles of the theory of Ethics (at section "About the Construction of a Theory of Ethics", I have suggested four such regulatory principles);
- elaborating the theorems of Ethics, based on the institutive principles;
- proposing proofs for the theorems, based on logic, institutive principles, and regulatory principles;

- elaborating lemmas of Ethics, based on theorems, institutive principles, and regulatory principles;
- elaborating sets of conjectures[34] that can be used as predictions for an ethical behaviour, and, of course, for factual testing.

(c) On the expected outcomes

Abstractly speaking, the outcomes of a theory of Ethics are of two kinds: (i) maxima of behaviour according to the principles established, both institutive and regulatory; (ii) procedures to ethically evaluate the empirical behaviours of individuals, in historical contexts well described.

(i) the maxima of behaviour, as that they are considered as ethical, have the well-known Kantian maxim meaning (*Nota bene*: I remind you that this category of outcomes of a theory of Ethics is firmly required by the third institutive principle, $P_I^E/3$, namely the principle of symmetry). Somewhat, the outcomes in question form, essentially, a *sui generis* library of maxima, so that the adepts of that theory may find advice for an ethical behaviour. The library of maxima (*LM*) will be permanently enriched with new maxima which are formulated by the researchers in the theory of Ethics. Symmetrically, from the library are rejected those maxima which, as predictions on the ethical behaviour (by intermediations of conjectures or hypotheses), have been refuted (see, below, the issue of testability of ethical truth). Logically, the maxima of ethical behaviour are not, principled, different from conjectures (or hypotheses) about the ethical behaviour;

(ii) the procedures to ethically evaluate the empirical behaviours of individuals are consistent, convergent, and complete batteries of filters aimed at verifying the ethical principles, both institutive and regulatory, in the case of empirical/historical behaviours that occurred. These analyses are, also, held in a dedicated library (let us call it library of cases—*LC*).

Nota bene: like in the judiciary field, the two libraries above-mentioned act as "source of law" for the theory of Ethics, i.e.: *LM* generates the "ethical laws" from a theoretical reflection, while *LC* generates "ethical laws" from an empirical observation.[35]

(d) On the testability

Regarding the testability, it must start, again, from the fact that Ethics is not a cognitive theory, nor a praxiological one, but a practical theory. In this context, I will examine the following issues: (d1) the ethical truth; (d2) the factuality of prediction in the ethical area; (d3) the testability of the ethical truth; (d4) the (actual) testing of ethical truth.

(d1) the ethical truth.

We are "programmed" to understand the truth as a cognitive concept. Indeed, still from Aristotle, the truth is assigned to knowledge. Such an assignment, generally, requires that an opinion about reality (objective, subjective, or objectified), usually expressed verbally, be true.[36] This is the so-called correspondence-truth. I want to put under doubt the correspondence-truth from the ethical perspective. To this end, I will examine several issues: (i) do we need an ethical truth? (ii) is there such an ethical truth? (iii) how could we define the ethical truth?

(i) why an ethical truth?

Any human action (be it theoretical/cognitive, praxiological, or practical) needs a criterion of validation from the perspective of its finality, more exactly, from the perspective of achieving the purpose expected/hoped/dreamed. Usually, we call this criterion *truth*. Of course, the truth cannot be than a relationship, namely a relationship between the description of the purpose (for example, in the form of a prediction[37]) and the description of the state of affairs after the action aimed at achieving that purpose is performed.

In the societal field, which I am interested in, the *ethical ethos*[38] is interstitially present in any decision, action, and evaluation. Consequently, a criterion of validation (or invalidation, as the case may be) of an action is required, with the same intensity and necessity as in the natural field (for example, in Physics).

Once the necessity of the truth in the societal (ethicized) field is outside doubt, we are entitled to speak about an ethical truth (*ET*).

(ii) what is the ethical truth?

In the context of the above considerations related to Ethics, I will now proceed to characterize the (required) ethical truth, as follows:

- the ethical truth (*ET*) cannot be a correspondence-truth, since it does not focus on the knowledge as such (which must be factually irrefutable), but on the *behaviour* (which must be ethically corroborated);
- so, to introduce a denomination, the ethical truth should be a *compliance-truth*, not a correspondence-truth;
- the compliance-truth does not have a general signification, as the correspondence-truth has, but an idiosyncratic one, i.e., particularized to each individual[39];
- somewhat, the compliance-truth is a "personal" truth, which is not possible (or, is very difficult) to be communicated in a common language[40] to other individuals within the society;
- in this context, I would conjecture that a minimal agreement among the individuals (either contemporary or non-contemporary) on the commonly shared ethics (see the Sect. 2.2) is analogous to the commonly shared agreement among individuals (either contemporary or non-contemporary) on the social contract—see, here, the Rawlsian theory of justice[41];
- the compliance-truth is not an epistemological truth, but an axiological one.

(iii) defining the ethical truth

Defining the ethical truth, i.e., as said, the compliance-truth, means to put together the features of this truth, as they were identified at the point (ii). I propose the following definition: *the ethical truth (compliance-truth) is a quasi-idiosyncratic truth applied to human behaviour, either one's own or that of others, based on the theory of Ethics, and evaluated from the perspective of the relationship between the desirable/expected behaviour and the actual/observed behaviour.*

(d2) the factuality of the ethical prediction.

Although the compliance-truth is aimed at human behaviour, it is established factually, like the correspondence-truth (in the last case, the "behaviour" is assigned to objects, not to the subjects, as in the case of compliance-truth). This means that the behaviour observing and assessing must be operated on the objectification of the behaviour concerned, not on a virtual version of the behaviour in question (*Nota bene*: however, like in the case of correspondence-truth, mental experiments can be useful, although not decisive—rather, the mental experiments can provide suggestions, intuitions, and so on).

Consequently, the predictions (or, better, presdictions,[42] as I proposed) on the behaviours must have as object the real behaviours, that is, the manifestations[43] of those behaviours in the societal practice. In other words, the predictions/presdiction in the ethical field must be focused on factual/empirical[44] events.

(d3) the testability of ethical truth.

The testability of the ethical truth does not require a predictive statement, respectively, a descriptive statement (between which a semantical comparison must be operated), like in the case of correspondence-truth, but two descriptive statements:

- (*EAS*) *ex ante* descriptive statement about the behaviour of an individual with whom the individual concerned interacts. *EAS* is a statement formulated based on the ethical theory, more exactly, on the institutive principles;
- (*EPS*) *ex post* descriptive statement about that behaviour. *EPS* is a statement formulated based on observation of the actual behaviour of the individual with whom the interaction is performed;
- the compliance-truth is not inter-personally testable, while the correspondence-truth is so;
- the testability of the compliance-truth is not based on prediction, but on expectation[45];
- both correspondence-truth and compliance-truth are normatively formulated, but bound to very different normative plans, as follows:
  - the correspondence-truth is testable based on a theoretical normativity—the theoretical normativity is a normativity of theoretical rationality type;

- the compliance-truth is testable based on a practical normativity—the practical normativity is a normativity of practical rationality type (Mele & Rawling, 2004);

- like in the case of correspondence-truth, the testability of the compliance-truth is logically equivalent to falsifiability.[46]

(d4) testing the ethical truth.

If the ethical truth is testable, then it can be tested. Before examining the (valid) procedure of testing, it is important to mention that, in the compliance-truth case, the experiments are rather irrelevant, because the involved subjects, who are informed regarding the experiment organization, could design and implement behaviours that meet the ethical principles, so that the results of the experiments are biased. Consequently, in this field, it is recommended to approach the natural experiments, i.e., experiments in vivo, not in vitro, as in the organized experiments.

To test the ethical truth means the following steps:

- step 1: describing the behaviour of interest to be evaluated. The selection of the particular behaviour is at the discretion of the analyst/observer/researcher—let us name this behaviour: *empirical behaviour* (E_B);
- step 2: designing the expected behaviour, by anchoring the empirical behaviour in the theory of Ethics (i.e., institutive principles and regulatory principles, respectively)—let us name this behaviour: *canonical behaviour* (C_B);
- step 3: describing the observed behaviour as it is objectified by the individual/s involved in the appropriate natural experiment—let us name this behaviour: *actual behaviour* (A_B);
- step 4: designing the analysable behaviour, by anchoring the actual behaviour in the theory of Ethics (i.e., institutive principles, and regulatory principles, respectively)—let us name this behaviour: *factual behaviour* (F_B);
- step 5: comparing the canonical behaviour with the factual behaviour.[47]

(d5) the result of testing the ethical truth.

Like in the case of the correspondence-truth, the testing of the compliance-truth can have two exclusive results (the testing's result is dichotomic): (i) corroboration; (ii) refutation.

(i) Corroboration

Corroboration ($\mathbb{C}$) of the presdiction in the ethical testing means that the factual behaviour is similar, from the perspective of involved theory of Ethics, to the canonical behaviour, that is:

$$\mathbb{C} : F_B \bowtie C_B$$

where with " $\bowtie$" is denoted the logical constant called *similarity*, so the above formula will be read: "the factual behaviour is similar to the canonical behaviour".[48]

Nota bene: an extremely important issue occurs here, namely, the significance of corroboration. As is known, in the case of correspondence-truth, the corroboration (as indicated by the term itself) means yet non-refutation, that is, the corroboration is not definitive/decisive, but provisory—from this, the epistemologically recommended positioning for agnosticism. This understanding of the corroboration in the case of correspondence-truth is explainable by the fact that that type of truth is a common one (at least inside a given cognitive paradigm—Kuhn, 2012), so inter-personally communicable. Instead, in the case of the compliance-truth, this communality is violated; each individual involved has its own values and understanding of the Ethics principles, which leads to the incommunicability of the result obtained in testing. In other words, as being so local (in fact, idiosyncratic), the corroboration is definitive/decisive for the involved individual, which no longer requires the agnosticism. It is very interesting that we (probably) should be agnostic in the cognitive field, but gnostic in the ethical field.

(ii) Refutation

Refutation ($\mathbb{R}$) of a presdiction in the ethical testing means that the factual behaviour is different enough from the canonical behaviour. The difference is enough to mean, simply, the non-similarity between the two compared behaviours. Like corroboration, refutation is established by semantical comparison between the two propositional descriptions—on the canonical behaviour and on the factual behaviour, respectively. Formally, the refutation will be written as follows:

$$\mathbb{R} : F_B \overline{\bowtie} C_B$$

Refutation, as well, has a different consequence from the case of correspondence-truth. A refutation of a presdiction in the ethical field is not equivalent to the definitive rejection (falsification) of the hypothesis (e.g., principle) involved in formulating the given presdiction, as happens related to correspondence-truth (where we talk about prediction, not presdiction, however). In other words, refutation is no longer an *experimentum crucis* that rejects without appeal the presdiction and its grounding hypothesis/conjecture. Like corroboration, refutation is local and temporary.

So, the result of testing the compliance-truth of a presdiction in the ethical field is:

$$\mathbb{C} \bigvee \mathbb{R}$$

The eventual equivocal regarding the result of testing can be discussed only after the concept and the measurability of similarity will be clarified. Based also on those clarifications, the issue of probability assignable to testing the compliance-truth will become possible to examine.

The Content

Some positionings provide a too narrow sphere of ethicality. For example, there are "definitions" of ethics saying that ethics refers to what is correct or wrong (Wight, 2015). Besides the unacceptable narrowness of proposal, such a definition lacks any usefulness, since it needs the criterion on which the correctness or wrongness is qualified as such.

Other positionings enact formulations so extensive as they are, in fact, erroneous. For example, Kenneth E. Boulding (1969) states that "No science of any kind can be divorced from ethical considerations". Leaving aside the risky assumption that Economics is a science,[49] it remains that the proposal admits ethical evaluations of the theoretical (even, scientific[50]) activity. The last consequence is enormously problematic. So, the game of manufacturing definitions at random is dangerous and counter-productive.

Generally, there are three accepted ethical frameworks: (a) the utilitarianism/consequentialism—it is an ethics based on results; (b) the deontologism/Kantianism—it is an ethics based on procedures; (c) the virtuism/inneism—it is an ethics based on virtues. Utilitarianism/consequentialism is outside of ethical interest (Rawls, 1971; Nozick, 1993), because it is, simply, a calculus based on cost–benefit analysis, which rejects it from the axiological field. Deontologism means rather a learnt ethics—through either education or instruction,[51] formal or informal—but it does not exit the axiological field, however. The virtuism is the one closest to my "preference" for the origin of ethics, being the most suitable because of its maximum autonomy (see the regulatory principle $P_E^R/3$ above). *Nota bene*: the acquisition of the ethical posture of the individual implies, also, the forming of an *ethical sensibility*, analogous to the artistic sensibility.[52] Forming the ethical sensibility is strongly required by the institutive principle $P_I^E/4$ above,[53] and, somewhat, institutes a social alert as a special feature of the individual. It is worth mentioning that the utility is not commensurable between individuals (because of the non-commensurability of preferences), while both deontologies and virtues are commensurable.

Starting from this general (and, of course, "stylized") picture of the concept of ethics, I think that a more fundamental (primitive) approach to the concept of ethics is required, so that, as possible, no more primitive fundamentals can exist. In what follows, I will provide certain considerations in this line.

1. A first question is: *why have we need for ethics?*

    - the deepest need of people is the justification of life (some call this finding the meaning of life);
    - justification of life can be done with respect to two instances:
        - the external (social) instance—social rule—which requires accountability;
        - the internal (individual) instance—moral rule—which requires responsibility;
        - while accountability is governed by positive laws, responsibility is governed by moral laws;
        - the legitimacy of legality can transform legal laws into moral laws, that is, it can replace accountability with responsibility;

- finally, ethics is needed to legitimize (more precisely, to justify) our actions (acts or omissions) that affect (or could affect) ourselves or others (regardless of the good or bad meaning);
- the meaning of our actions must be evaluated only from the perspective of the actors, not from the perspective of those who bear the effects of the actors' actions.[54]

The (logical) way in which the ethics is born is suggested in Fig. 4.

2. A second question is: *what significance does ethics have?*

- some preliminaries
- about the existence of the ethical sense, the following can be said:

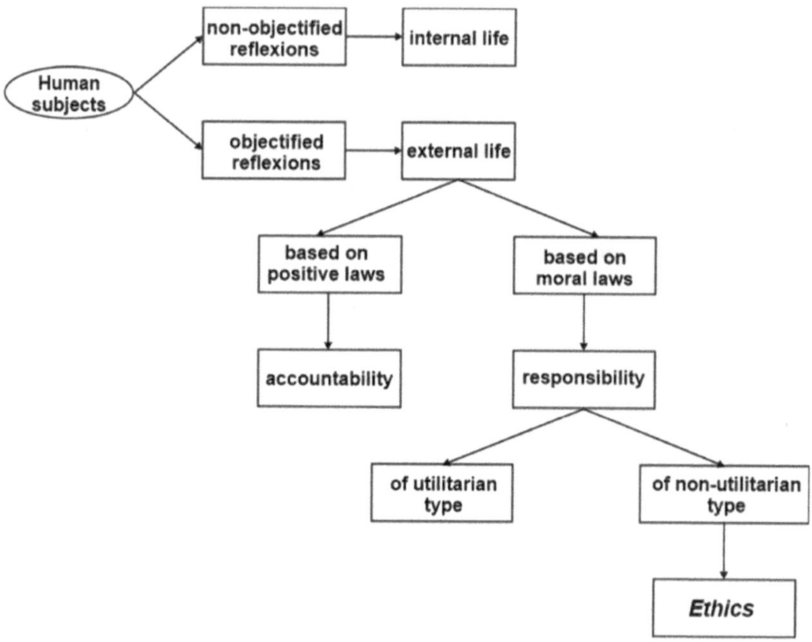

Fig. 4 Logical derivation of the concept of ethics (*Source* author)

- the ethical significance is necessarily acquired within the framework of social interactions;
- the ethical significance is attributed only to the individual, never to groups; no individual who has passed beyond his/her instinctual age lacks the ethical sense;
- like general instruction, the ethical significance is the result of the life of social groups, whether deliberative or non-deliberative;
- but ethics belongs to education, not instruction.

The (abstract) phenomenology of ethical significance is suggested in Fig. 5.

3. A third question is: *which is relationship between ethics and economy*?

- some preliminaries
  - any social interaction necessarily requires two types of filters designed to distribute the social costs of these interactions between individuals (not between groups):
    - the utilitarian filter (including both the "invisible hand"and legal laws);
    - the ethical filter (which seems to include/generate the justice filter);
- there are levels of ethical urgency, which are "assigned" to actions, based on the potential self-defence capacities of the recipients against the effects of the actions, through an inverse proportionality;
- so, it seems that there is a special character of ethics in the economic field: economic interaction is characterized by a high degree of impersonality (no other praxiological or practical activity has a comparable degree of impersonality, neither political, nor religious, nor æsthetic); therefore, economic interaction possesses the lowest degree of potential self-defence capacity against the negative effects of social interactions;
- the economic field (which brings together the economy, economic activity, economic policies, economic impact, economic theory, etc.) seems to be, by far, the most sensitive and the greatest "applicant" for an ethical dimension—that is, economic ethics is indeed special (or, at least, with the greatest impact on individuals and society as a whole);

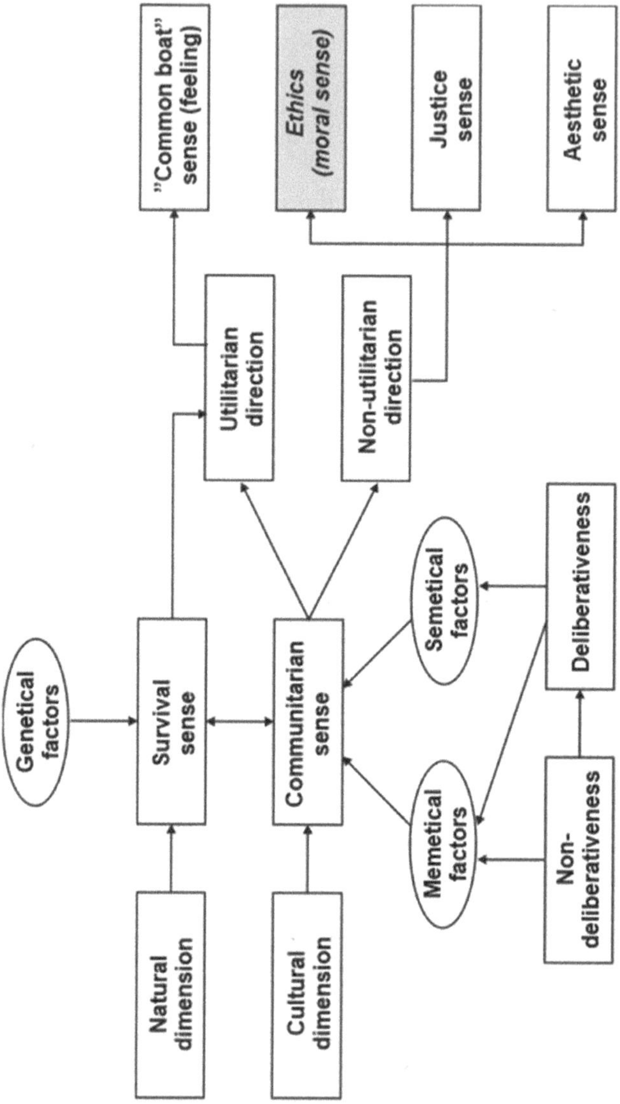

Fig. 5 Arising of the ethical significance/sense (*Source* author)

The (abstract) topology of ethical significance distribution on societal fields is suggested in Fig. 6.

4. A fourth question is: *is there difference between* ex ante *ethics and* ex post *ethics*?

   - some preliminaries
     - being a non-utilitarian concept, ethics is, essentially, an *ex ante* concept;
     - more precisely, ethics is a concept driven by two imperatives:

       by intentionality (not in Husserl's sense, but simply based on an intention);

       by non-contextual values (i.e., by principles);
   - authentic ethics is always *ex ante*, and it can never be *ex post*;
   - considering an "ethics" to be/act *ex post* is similar to Popperian falsifiability (*ex ante* ethics is the hypothesis/prediction, while

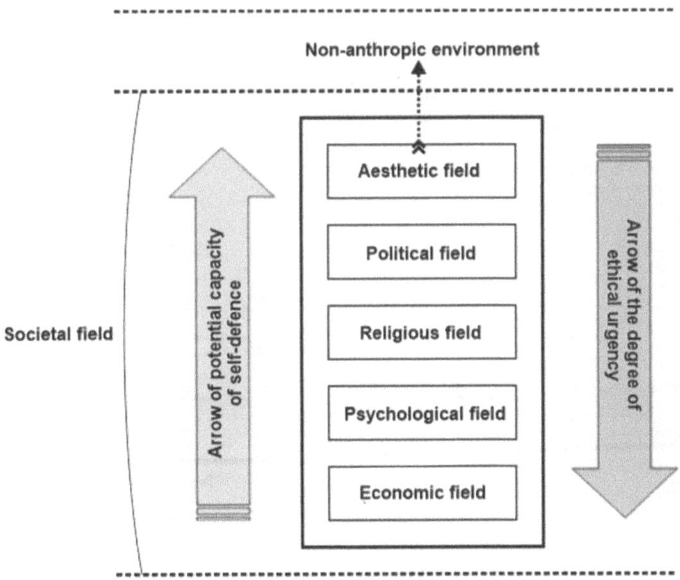

Fig. 6 Opposite dynamics between the potential of self-defence and the urgency of ethics (*Source* author)

ex post ethics is the factual that can corroborate or refute the hypothesis)
   - we could have here a practical (more precisely, a praxiological) version of cognitive factual testing of scientific theories;
- since ethics has no relation to truth,[55] *ex post* ethics is a meaningless concept;
- any consideration of *ex post* ethics leads us directly to utilitarianism.

Figure 7 shows the double relation *economic–cognitive* fields, respectively *ex ante–ex post* ethics.

5. A fifth question: *can ethics be learned*?

- being a cultural outcome, ethics cannot be acquired other than through learning, regardless of whether learning is deliberative or non-deliberative, accidental or systematic;

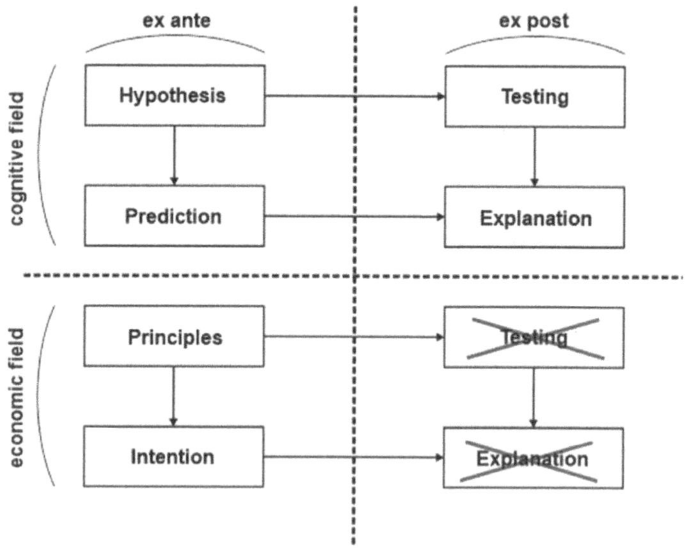

Fig. 7 Economic–cognitive fields in relation with *ex ante–ex post* ethics (*Source* author)

- awareness of the binding character of ethics in the economic field could provide the institutional framework for learning ethics with a deliberate and systematic profile;
- education and instruction in learning ethics should be combined to rationalize (through instruction) the ethical principles learned (through education);
- when it comes to learning ethics, two crucial directions must be followed:
  - maintaining an ethical educational environment for the "student" in ethics:

    any theoretical learning about ethics can be distorted by ethical memes with adverse meaning (the maxim "do as the priest says, not as the priest does" does not work);

    social law should be inspired and based on ethical principles and values;
  - creating an instructive device (institutional and/or non-institutional) to provide models of rationality for ethical principles, values, and behaviour

    including: through school (at all levels), through research, public debates, natural experiments, and the like.

Figure 8 suggests the logic of ethical learning.

6. A sixth question: *what about ethics and bioeconomy*?

Ethics is very closely related to praxiology and practical activity. By now, I have referred to ethics especially from the practical (relationships subject–subject) perspective, but at least of the same relevance is ethics from a praxiological perspective (relationships subject–object), as, for example, the economic phenomenology. Since the overall relationships between economy/economics and ethics will be examined in an upcoming book (see note 18), here I briefly approach some issues that connect ethics with a special economic "region", namely, bioeconomy/bioeconomics.

Figure 9 shows the place of bioeconomy/bioeconomics from the perspective of the paradigm.

Discussion

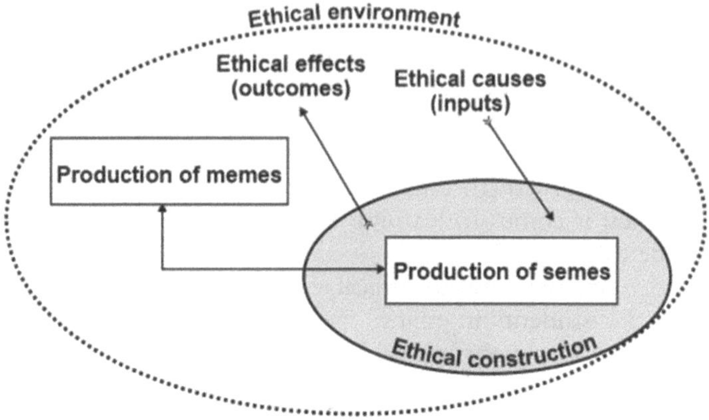

Fig. 8 General scheme of ethics learning (*Source* author)

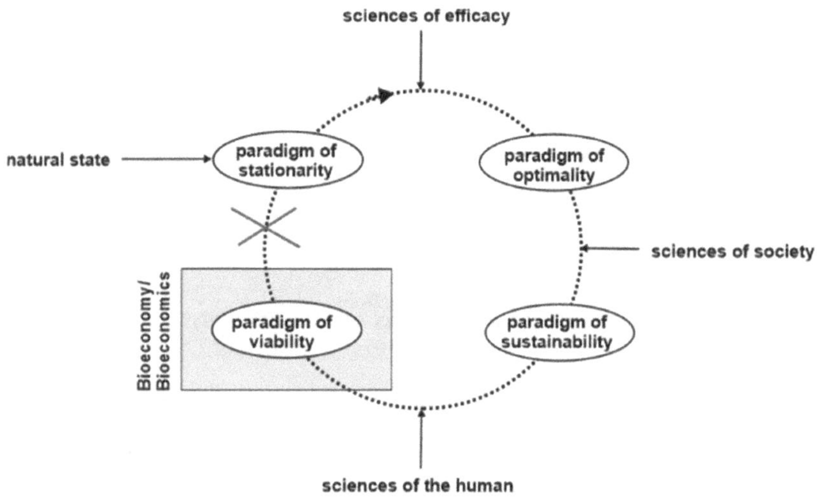

Fig. 9 Bioeconomy/bioeconomics and the theory of paradigm (*Source* author)

- the natural state (Rousseau's historical preference) generates the paradigm of stationarity, that is, a state without kinematics, conservative, invariant;

- the development of the sciences of efficacy generates the paradigm of optimality (which searches the best solution within a given system of constraints), which is the today in force paradigm (the capitalist societal order);
- the development of the sciences of society generates the paradigm of sustainability (that abandons the first-best solution and adopt the so-called second-best solution, able to provide the replication of the system/process of interest);
- the development of the sciences of the human (humanities sciences) generates the paradigm of viability, which is the paradigm of sustainability to which is added the (generic) ethical code. In fact, the paradigm of viability is the paradigm within which bioeconomy/bioeconomics unfolds.

Nota bene: the paradigm of viability is not equivalent to the paradigm of stationarity; it has kinematics, but within a tunnel of viability, so it is no longer pure conservative or invariant.

(a) Generic relationships between ethics and bioeconomy

I will discuss six topics in the relationships between ethics and bioeconomy.

(i) the permeability of the bioeconomy to ethics

- arguments in favour of permeability
  - bioeconomics remains a social discipline, although much more sensitive to the biological component of the social, without exaggerating Wilson's socio-biology (1975), than to neoclassical economics;

    as the ethical is a product of the social (although on an inevitable biological basis), bioeconomy and bioeconomics "expose" a decisive channel for the penetration of the ethical;
  - within the social in which bioeconomy is immersed, the rapport between socialization and solidarization shifts decisively in favour of solidarization—see José Ortega y Gasset (1960);

solidarization, more than socialization, allows the massive penetration of the ethical into the bioeconomic phenomenon;
    - bioeconomy/bioeconomics does not pursue the maximum good, but the adequate good (however, the category of the good is the key category of the ethical).
- eventualities against permeability
    - attempts (such as those within neoclassical economics) to develop quantitative equational modelling in which ethics is almost impossible to formalize;
    - the resurrection of positivism, in the absence of the development of a solid theory of normativism.

(ii) ethics: middle term in the *bioeconomy–social justice* "syllogism"

- in the current (still "in power") neoclassical economics, social justice is relegated to a simplified and impersonal theory of expected utility, i.e., to a theory of the final state as Pareto optimum, Kaldor-Hicks criterion, and the like;
- bioeconomy, concerned with the *well* rather than the *good*, emphasizes not the final state in the distribution of the good, but the procedure for obtaining the good;
    - this means that obtaining the good is significant from the perspective of the procedure for obtaining it, not from that of the quantity obtained
- this shift in significant emphasis pleads, from an ethical perspective, for a social justice of a procedural type
    - the well/good pursued by bioeconomy/bioeconomics is validated procedurally, i.e., ethically. *Nota bene*: a procedure is ethical even if it violates the Pareto criterion;
- the incorporation of ethics into bioeconomy is very well exemplified, as a possibility, by two theories of justice that are different in conceptual basis but equivalent in result:
    - Rawls' theory: the difference principle is a pure ethical principle;
    - Nozick's theory: the three principles (acquisition, transfer, correction) are of an ethical type.

(iii) locality: middle term in the *ethics–bioeconomy* "syllogism"

- bioeconomy (like biodiversity) has no authentic meaning except the local;
  - locality is required by both natural and cultural particularity;
- ethics, as an uncodified institutional ensemble, is also exclusively local in significance;
  - ethics is a cultural niche efflorescence, it is a culture within culture;
- it follows that locality is the logical (from the perspective of bioeconomy) and axiological (from the perspective of ethics) element which is common to ethics and bioeconomy;
  - as a result, locality is the vector of integration of ethics into bioeconomy;
- ethics has a strongly *allopatric*, and almost insignificantly *sympatric* evolution;
- there is a certain *cultural autism* of ethics, as a result of its locality;
- bioeconomy, in turn, manifests (by definition) a certain *social autism* (solidarity, specific to bioeconomy, cannot be socialized on a trans-local scale).

(iv) ethics and institutive/constitutive principles of the bioeconomy

Bioeconomy (respectively, bioeconomics as the founding theory of bioeconomy) has or must have its own institutive principles. I think the following four institutive principles are fundamental for bioeconomy (respectively, bioeconomics).

- ($P_I^{BE}/1$) *principle of living–non-living mix*: bioeconomy combines the biological principles with the thermodynamic principles so that the bioeconomic process is a mix between living entities and non-living entities. This is by far the most important institutive principle of bioeconomy (and, of course, of bioeconomics). To support this principle, ethics provides, through specific means, *social protection*, as either social justice or social rightness;

- ($P_I^{BE}/2$) *principle of normativism*: although the economic process (no matter whether it is of neoclassical, i.e., mechanical type) is always based on normativity, in the case of bioeconomy, the normativity is extended towards the ethical norms. To support this principle, ethics provides, through specific means, *norms*, i.e., the required normative framework;
- ($P_I^{BE}/3$) *principle of personalism*: the principle of personalism refers to the fact that bioeconomy has, in its conceptual hard core, the person, not only as the economic individual (*homo œconomicus*) but, primarily, the person, i.e., the individual driven by values, including, of course, the ethical ones. To support this principle, ethics provides, through specific means, the prevalence of *purposes* in organizing the bioeconomic activity;
- ($P_I^{BE}/4$) *principle of desiderative rationality*: the desiderative rationality is a rationality that is not pure inferential, but is, especially, aimed at considering the own values of individuals, more exactly, the aspirations of individuals to a plenary life (see Chapter 6). Consequently, to support this principle, ethics provides, through specific means, the prevalence of *values* in the decision-making process.[56]

Figure 10 exposes the relationships between ethics and the institutive/constitutive principles of bioeconomy.

(v) ethics and regulatory principles of the bioeconomy

Bioeconomy (respectively, bioeconomics as its founding theory) has or must have, also, its own regulatory principles. I think the following five regulatory principles are fundamental for bioeconomy (respectively, bioeconomics).

- ($P_R^{BE}/1$) *principle of circularity*: this principle ensures the sufficient and necessary procedures (institutional, methodological, instrumental) so that any outputs of the economic systems becoming an input to other economic systems (or, as the case may be, in the same economic systems). To support this principle, ethics imposes, through specific means, verification of the *acceptability* of those systems/processes, from the perspective of circularity;

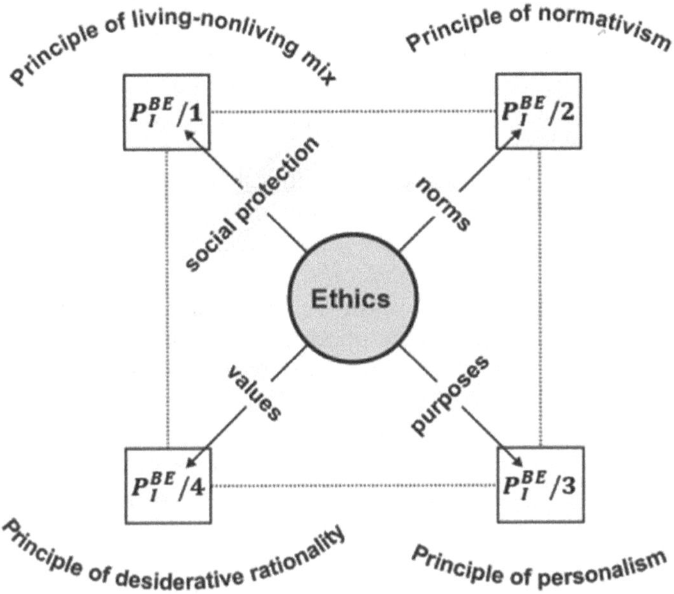

Fig. 10 Ethics and the institutive/constitutive principles of bioeconomy (*Source* author)

- ($P_R^{BE}/2$) *principle of co-evolution*: this principle provides the sufficient and necessary conditions so that the two categories of components of bioeconomy (living systems and non-living systems, respectively) adapt reciprocally to one another, and, this way, co-evolve. To support this principle, ethics imposes, through specific means, the *coherence* (consistency and convergence) of the living systems, and non-living ones, taken together;
- ($P_R^{BE}/3$) *principle of locality*: bioeconomy is a species of economy much more fragile and sensitive to context (resources, culture, normativity, etc.) than other such species (as, for example, a multinational company). Consequently, a bioeconomic system is extremely finely harmonized with the local region, in its geographical and economic understanding, which leads us to the conclusion that a bioeconomic process is designable and implementable locally only. To support this principle, ethics imposes, through specific means, the *niching*, both referring to inputs and outputs;

- ($P_R^{BE}/4$) *principle of a-legal responsibility*: firstly, this principle exits from the accountability (*Nota bene*: as known, accountability plays under the legality, that is, based on compliance with the legal norms); secondly, responsibility is, in turn, susceptible to play under norms but, this time, it is speaking about a-legal norms, as, for example, ethical ones (or, if the ethical norms are codified, moral norms—see Sect. 2.2). To support this principle, ethics imposes, through specific means, the *responsabilization*[57];
- ($P_R^{BE}/5$) *principle of an-alethical testability*: this principle reminds us that ethics is not a cognitive theory, but a behavioural one, namely, it is interested not in the correspondence-truth, but in the compliance-truth. Consequently, the testability of the ethical conjectures must be made outside the alethical "region", being accepted that the term alethic is assigned to cognition and, especially to the communitarian truth (i.e., correspondence-truth). To support this principle, ethics imposes, through specific means, the *fitness*, that is, the matching between (as said before) the canonical behaviour and the factual one.

Figure 11 exposes the relationships between ethics and the regulatory principles of bioeconomy.

(vi) ethics and the genesis of social rightness within the bioeconomy

- the bioeconomy escapes two praxeological tyrannies:
  - the tyranny of maximizing substantive expected utility (the utility given by the possession of goods);
  - the tyranny of methodological (atomic) individualism;
- as a result, bioeconomy is more interested in social rightness than in social justice:
  - i.e., the preference for the *right procedure* is dominated by the preference for the good (results);
- ethics, in turn, has a "preference" for the procedure, rather than for the final state
  - this is because the procedure aims at the well, while the final state aims at the good
- consequently, the (inevitable) integration of ethics into bioeconomy will generate, causally and conditionally, the prevalence of social rightness in the economic process. *Nota bene*: Sen's "dream" of fully integrating ethics into economic

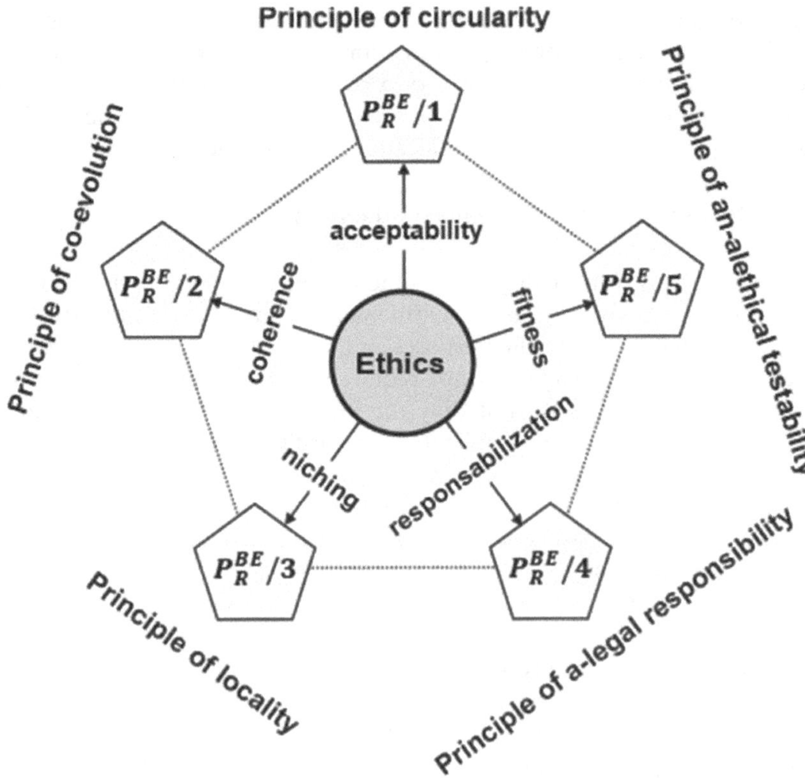

Fig. 11 Ethics and the regulatory principles of bioeconomy (*Source* author)

theory has no chance of success within neoclassical economics (which is "ossified" at the level of the mechanical rationality model of *homo œconomicus*[58]), but only within bioeconomy

– thus, bioeconomy is a simultaneous vehicle for ethics and for social rightness.

2.2 *Morals*

The Concept of Morals

Morals is a set of constraints about the behaviour of individuals in a given society or, more generally, in a certain societal system. It addresses not the autonomous individual, but a community of individuals, as aggregated based on an accepted criterion—for example, a nation, a union of nations (as the European Union), or a region characterized by a shared ethos. Three of those mentioned (or implicitly suggested) in describing the concept of morale require clarification, which is delivered below.

(i) Morals is a set of constraints on the behaviour

Morals is an institution of society functioning that acts in the context of freedom.[59] As freedom is the entitlement of the generic individual to establish on his/her right the purposes and, then, to choose the allowed[60] means in achieving them, it is not required to grant, by intermediation of morals, the permission, but only the interdictions. Also, morals does not establish or recommend obligations regarding the behaviour. Useless to remind that the moral norms are not positive norms (although they remain norms, which confer on the concept of morals its status as an institution). So, the basic relationships between positive norms and moral norms are as follows:

(i1) similitudes

- both categories of norms refer to the generic individual, that is, the norm is applicable to any individual who verifies the criterion of eligibility for the norm concerned;
- both categories of norms have as a criterion of eligibility for the applicability the behaviour of the generic individual;

(i2) differences

- positive norms are codified, so that they are formal norms, while moral norms are uncodified, so that they are informal or non-formal norms;
- positive norms are complete norms (see Chapter 5, Annex 2 in Chapter 5), while moral norms are incomplete ones—especially they lack the mandatory sanction[61];
- the positive norms are learned by formal institutional education (for example, by school), while the moral norms are learned by informal institutional education (for example, by family).

(ii) Morals addresses the community

Morals is constituted by the common ethical "provisions" of the individuals in a given community. This ethical hard core, which is shared by the individuals concerned, is the moral chain that links the individuals in question. As a result, what community knows, can monitor, and, if the case, could sanction,[62] is exactly this moral chain. Consequently, if ethics has an idiosyncratic signification, morals has a communitarian signification.

Based on the above, there can exist both a theory of ethics[63] and a theory of morale. While the theoretical philosophy could be interested rather in a theory of ethics (for example, Phenomenology, especially in Heidegger's understanding), the social philosophy could be interested rather in a theory of morals (for example, the theories of social justice).

(iii) Morals is a predictor for ethics

As described, morals constitutes, at the level of the community concerned, a predictor for the individual's behaviour. Indeed, the community knows, although in an informal and, often, non-systematic way, the moral norms tacitly accepted and valued in that community. Like Nozickian principles, the moral norms pre-announce to the members of the community about which behaviour of a given individual will be objectified. So, together with the positive law (which is a predictor of behaviour, as well), morals can act as such a predictor of behaviour. As morals is an "intersection" of the ethics of all individuals in that community, the expected behaviour predicted by the morals says something about the ethical ethos of the individual concerned.[64]

The Logical Genealogy of the Morals

As said many times (and the reader already expects), my approach in this book is logical and epistemological, not historical nor empirical. Consequently, the genealogy of the morals will be examined in an abstract way, to identify the logical causality that links ethics, morase, and positive law. Figure 12 proposes such a logic of genealogy of morale.

<u>Discussion</u>

- any community develops, within its general context (including geographical one), a culture, together with a civilization[65];

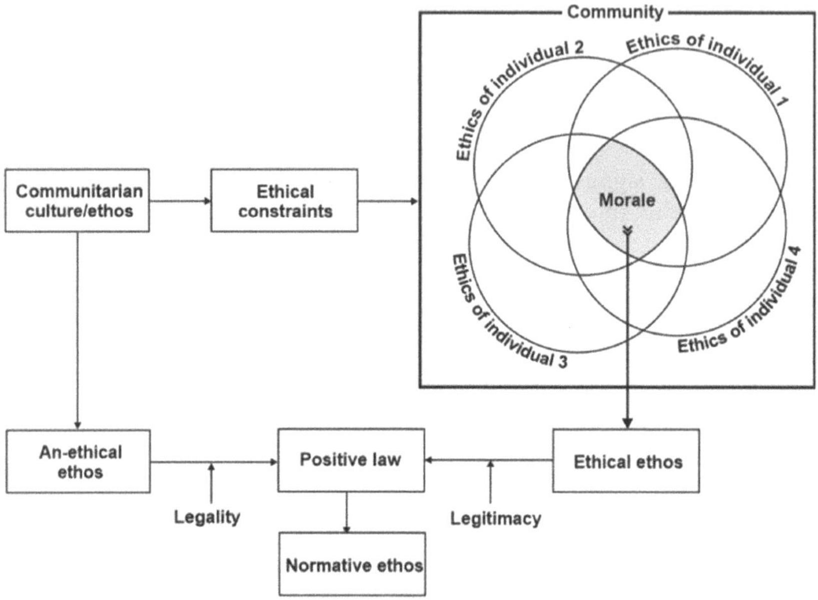

Fig. 12 Abstract genealogy of the morale (I) (*Source* author)

- inevitably, the question of the good and the bad arises within that community, which generates ethical constraints; these ethical constraints are, more or less, an object of awareness;
- the ethical constraints are unique to each individual (are strongly idiosyncratic) and, as a result, they are, reciprocally, not too visible;
- however, after a while, by the process of adaptation, cooperation, and competition, the individuals of community tacitly establish a "list" of ethical constraints that seem to be common to all individuals (i.e., all individuals share that constraints); the constraints in that "list" form the morals (*Nota bene*: morals is not required to be officially codified);
- the morals, so generated, generates, in turn, the ethical ethos of the community; this ethical ethos, if publicly codified, generates the legitimate component of the positive law (another component is the legal one, generated by the an-ethical ethos);

- the two components entering the positive law constitute, in their inter-conditioning (including synergy effects), the normative ethos of the community concerned.

Nota bene: most often, we are not sure about the (genuine) ethics of an individual; instead, by intermediation of the morals, we can approximate that ethics, at least in its principles, both institutive and regulatory.

Figure 13 offers a synoptic scheme regarding the relation between the natural law, and positive law, in the context of birth of ethics and morals.

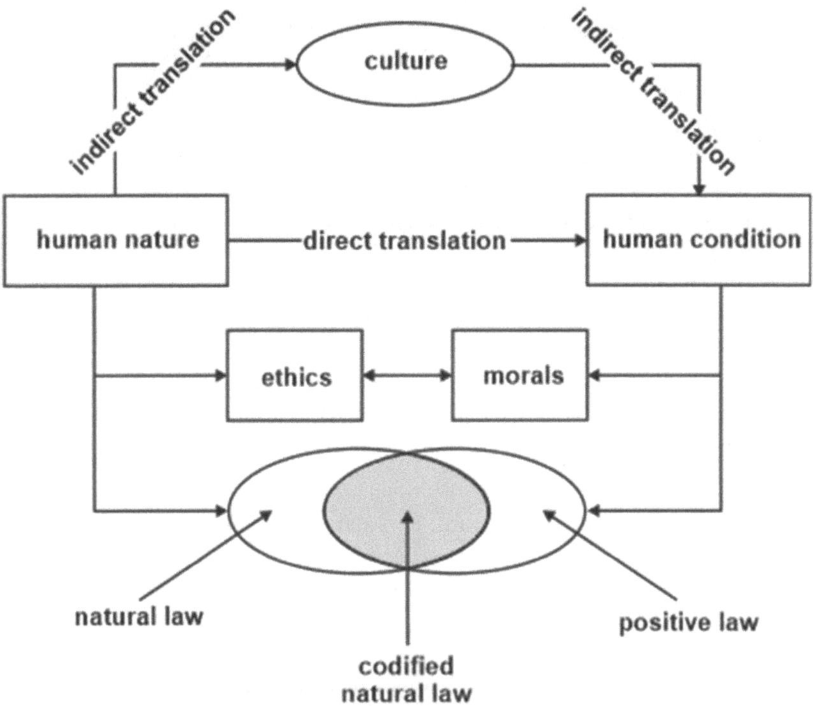

Fig. 13 Abstract genealogy of the morale (II) (*Source* author)

3 Societal Æsthetics

3.1 Preliminaries

The issue of æsthetics from the social/societal perspective seems, from the beginning, to be strange and puts the question of its utility and productivity in the discussion hosted by this book. However, some considerations could justify, at least partially, such an intention.

- Nature itself is characterized by harmony expressed by symmetry, not only from the cosmological perspective (day–night alternance, as symmetry in time; stellar systems integrated in galaxies, as symmetry in space; expansion–contraction of the Universe, as symmetry in both space and time; matter–anti-matter, as symmetry in quality), but also from the sub-lunar perspective, as happens on our Earth;
- scientific cognition has, in its deep background, the intuition of the symmetry as a criterion of the truth—see the conservative laws in the sciences of dynamics, or the laws of algebraic structures, or the invariants searched by any science which aspires to a high statute of knowledge;
- the art is, *par excellence*, the prototype of harmony/symmetry; in fact, primarily, the concept of æsthetics arose within art (poetry, architecture, sculpture, and so on)[66];
- the society, as based on either social contract (Rawls) or minimal state emerging (Nozick), edifies structural symmetries in order to provide functional, i.e., procedural, even symmetries as results' symmetries:
  - the principle of freedom, as a symmetrical right of an individual related to the rights of other individuals;
  - the Constitution, within the national entities, and the international law, among those national entities, as symmetrical norms of interaction;
  - the (of increasingly relevance) need for the harmony/symmetry between humans and the non-anthropogenic environment, including the cosmic space, as a basic constraint of survival and flourishing of humankind;
  - the social capital (so important, from the ethical perspective, as shown before), which is based exactly on the reciprocity, i.e., on the harmony/symmetry of individuals' interactions.

In this context, I will develop, further, briefly, some discussion on the general concept of æsthetics, then the results will be, mutatis mutandis, particularized/specified to the case of society.

3.2 The General Concept of Æsthetics

The intractable baroque of the debates on the concept of æsthetics forces me to treat this issue in a succinct key and from a logical perspective, which will allow me (at least, I hope so) to obtain a description, as they say in semiotics, sufficient for its use in achieving the purpose of this section.

I will do this by formulating a number of theses that verify, to the highest degree, the condition set by Leibniz's principle of sufficient reason.

- *Thesis 1. The æsthetic is a perceptual, not intellectual property*

The concept of æsthetics (which comes from the Greek αεστέζια) refers to sensation, and sensation is a physiological, not intellectual phenomenon, generated by the interaction of external stimuli with the natural senses (the six natural senses[67]). In other words, the æsthetic stops at the "gate" of the concept, a gate through which it does not cross.

- *Thesis 2. The æsthetic does not aim at perceptual beauty, but at perceptual harmony*

Although in common language and in common belief, the æsthetic has beauty as its sole referential, a more general approach can show that the æsthetic must refer to something other than beauty or, more precisely, to more than beauty. First of all, it should be noted that, as far as the category of beauty is concerned, this is not a primitive category (although the history of philosophy considers it in the famous triad *beautiful–true–good*, in which all three concepts are equivalent and substitutable for each other), but a derived one. I believe that the æsthetic property should be considered to have the harmonious or the harmony as its referential.[68] *Nota bene*: of course, thesis 2 should not be contradictory to thesis 1, that is, why I refer to perceptual harmony, not to a harmony identified or identifiable from an intellectual, comprehensive, hermeneutic, discursive perspective.

- *Thesis 3. Perceptual harmony, as the basis of æsthetics, manifests itself through symmetry/asymmetry*

Harmony is perceived through symmetry, respectively asymmetry.[69] Symmetry is a similarity of perception from the perspective of an axis of symmetry or a point of symmetry or a plane of symmetry, and so on. These axes or points or planes can be either in space, in time, or from both perspectives. From a perceptual point of view, an asymmetry is observable as a deliberately de-symmetrized symmetry; therefore asymmetries that have a certain, let us say, symmetry are species of harmony. This clarification is particularly important: just as the ugly (un-beautiful) is integrable in harmony, so asymmetry is integrable in symmetry if it verifies the following structural condition: an asymmetry must be found within a symmetry, that is, there must be a symmetry of asymmetries. A very useful idea at this point (but which I will not develop for now) is that of the fractality,[70] that is, of the self-similarity, in space and time.

- *Thesis 4. Asymmetrical asymmetry is non-æsthetic*

This thesis is, in fact, a logical consequence of thesis 3 and refers to the fact that the lack of control over the harmony can generate or tolerate asymmetries that are not subsumed under an integrative symmetry. This means that the asymmetry thus perceived is not the effect of deliberate construction, but an accident caused by the lack of the mentioned control. It must be said that, from a technical point of view, it is much more difficult to obtain a symmetrical asymmetry than a simple symmetry.

- *Thesis 5. The æsthetic is both a natural and an intentional property*

Harmony, i.e., symmetry, including symmetries of asymmetries, can be either natural, that is, non-intentional (from the human subject perspective) or, as we are interested in, intentional. The non-intentional harmony/symmetry exists, of course, for self, not in self, since Nature cannot perceive its own harmony.[71] Instead, the intentional harmony is both in self and for self, since it is an artefact, that is, a human (social) deliberative construction. In this section, the interest is focused on the intentionally built harmony but it is obvious that, in fact, the societal harmony includes both the non-intentional (non-artefactual) and intentional (artefactual) harmony. As a result, at the societal level, there is an integrative harmony, so we can speak about a general (societal) æsthetics, as I will do further.

3.3 The Social/Societal Æsthetics

Extracting the Concept of Socional

The societal æsthetics must be examined in relation to a species of artefacts which I would call ***socional*** (from societal and relational) ***artefacts***. To clarify the concept of socional artefacts, I will examine a (possible) general map of social/societal artefacts generation (Fig. 14).

Discussion

- within the society (societal system), there are three categories of interactions/relationships: (a) theoretical (interactions object–object); (b) praxiological (interactions subject–object); (c) practical (interactions subject–subject);
- all the three categories of interactions are artefacts, that is, objectification of the inter-subjectivities[72];
- from artefacts, the intellectual ones are of interest, which contains the three categories interactions above mentioned;
- from the three categories of interactions, the practical ones are the best "qualified" to express the relational artefacts in the society;
- finally, from the four practical artefactuals, two are the most closed to the relational type of artefacts: politics and ethics;
- consequently, I consider that the two practical artefacts form the proposed concept of socional.

Nota bene: For symmetry of terminology reasons, I will discuss the (theoretical/logical) justification of introducing a special "sense", at the social level, which could be called *social sense*.[73] Some supports for the proposal are as follows.

- the social sense is, essentially, a *non-sensitive* sense[74] (as, for example, the justice sense, or the ethical sense, as discussed above). It can be said, even, that the social sense (or, equivalent, societal sense) is an

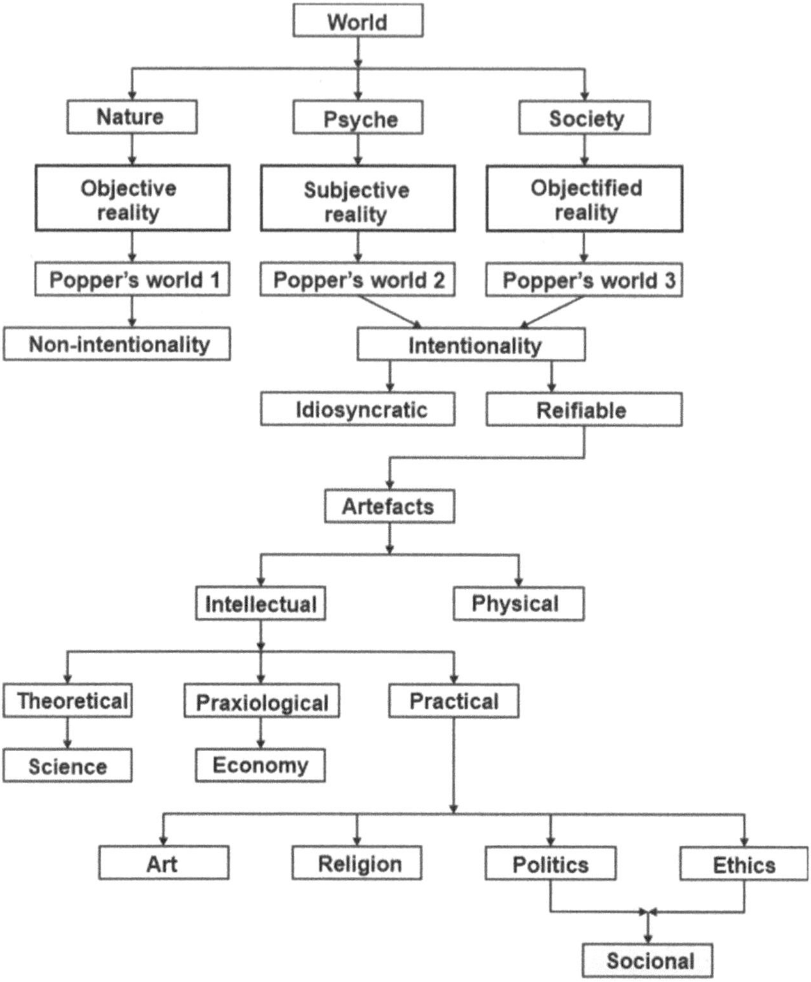

Fig. 14 Logically extracting of the concept of socional (*Source* author)

intellectual sense. This means that this sense must be "processed" by intellect or, in most cases, by rationality;

- however, it is hazardous to state that the social sense is entirely deliberative; rather, I would say that there is an inextricable combination (mix) of intuition and comprehension in this case;
- the intuition is required by the fact that the observer of societal structure and functioning is himself/herself inside the society concerned[75]; on the other hand, the comprehension is required by the fact that the observer could predict the events in whose sphere of impact is submersed;
  - the social sense is focused on the *relationships*, not on things or properties found within the society;
  - the social sense is a *cultural* one, and is acquired as consequence of interactions, of different nature, within the societal system;
  - essentially, the social/societal sense is the *genus* for many species: justice sense, ethical sense, social æsthetical sense, and so on; it is another, different, genus of sense than the individual (or individual's) genus of sense, i.e., sense of self, sense of time, sense of rightness, etc.

The Content of Social Æsthetics

Based on the above, the content of the social/societal æsthetics can be described as follows: *a harmonious network of socionals aimed at and able to viably maintain the individuals on the chreod of achieving the plenary life*. Some detailed clarifications of this definition are provided below.

(i) not all the interactions among individuals are socionals, but only those interactions (relationships) which are aimed at and able to conduct the involved individuals to their plenary life, as each of them understands and assesses the concept of plenary life;

(ii) not all the interactions among individuals are socionals, but only those that are subsumed under either political or ethical interactions. The reason for these delimitations consists in the fact that the other two practical interactions (artistic and religious) are not aimed at and able to conduct the individuals to their plenary life—of course, art and religion have the potential to do that, but for any individual in his/her solitude, not as a result of interactions;

(iii) not all the interactions among individuals are socionals, but only those that are harmonious. To be harmonious, the interactions must be symmetrical. Let us comment a little bit on the harmonious/symmetrical interactions:

- the symmetry refers to the results, not to the means in achieving the results—for example, in the interaction called gifting, the gift received must not be identical to the gift offered[76];
- in line with the above, probably, the symmetry does not require the identity between the procedures—for example, I leave you to enter the first in the room, instead you thank me for that;
- also, the symmetry does not require the contemporaneity (simultaneity) between the actions (either acts or abstentions) of the two individuals who interact—for example, I leave you to enter the first in the room, instead you leave me to exit the first from that room, later;

(iv) the term network, introduced in the definition of social/societal æsthetics, means that this æsthetics doesn't need to be exclusively designed and controlled by the leading component of a system (for example, the statal system), but it can function as a network[77] as well;

(v) the social/societal æsthetics must aim at the plenary life of the individuals involved in the social/societal entity (see the concept of plenary life, which has been introduced in Chapter 6). Obviously, not all societal interactions have as their finality the achieving of the plenary life of individuals, although they could be beneficial for those individuals, in different degrees and different ways;

(vi) finally, the social/societal æsthetics must be able to conduct the individuals involved in those interactions to the plenary life. This ability of interactions must be carefully analysed and assessed, so not to introduce into the social/societal æsthetics irrelevant interactions.

On the Principles of Societal Æsthetics

In this context of the content of social/societal æsthetics, the question of the principles by (or on) which a theory of social/societal æsthetics could be edified is arising. In what follows, I will make some proposals in this matter. I will discuss two issues: (a) the institutive principles of the social/societal (*Nota bene*: from here, I will use only the syntagma societal æsthetics, which is a species of social[78] æsthetics, in which I am interested in this book).

(a) Institutive principles

- the symmetry refers to the results, not to the means in achieving the results—for example, in the interaction called gifting, the gift received must not be identical to the gift offered[76];
- in line with the above, probably, the symmetry does not require the identity between the procedures—for example, I leave you to enter the first in the room, instead you thank me for that;
- also, the symmetry does not require the contemporaneity (simultaneity) between the actions (either acts or abstentions) of the two individuals who interact—for example, I leave you to enter the first in the room, instead you leave me to exit the first from that room, later;

xAs mentioned before, the symmetry assigned to the societal æsthetics does not focus on the means or procedures, but on the final results of the interactions involved. This can be expressed by the syntagma symmetry of the final states. But three questions occur here: (i) what about the intermediary states, till the final states? (ii) how can it be assessed that the course (for example, the intermediary states concatenation) will maintain the chance to achieve the final state (presupposing that the final states are known by the individuals involved); (iii) what exactly does the symmetry of states mean? I provide some considerations in this matter:

(i) almost never is a final state achieved without passing through intermediate states[80]; consequently, it is not required that the symmetry of the individuals' states be verified for each intermediate state, but, of course, in particular circumstances, such symmetry can either occur or be asked;

(ii) it is necessary to make some evaluations, complicated enough, since they presuppose some models of rationality accessible to the individuals involved, so that they can appreciate the probability[81] with which a given intermediate state maintains the "system" on the track towards the final state expected. In real life, such an evaluation is, of course, intuitive, i.e., what is often called naïve evaluation or decision-making (Körner, 2010), but, principled, there can be models of rationality that calculate the tree of probabilities leading to the final state;

(iii) symmetry of states, where the states belong to different individuals who interact, is incommensurable between them. So, those states are assessed separately, and incommunicably, by each individual involved, so it is an idiosyncratic evaluation. In fact, the evaluation is analogous to the procedure discussed in relation to the ethical truth (the compliance-truth), that is, each of the individuals compares, based on his/her internal (non-public) model, the expected state before the interaction, with the actual state after the interaction, and decides consequently. The evaluation that the individuals in question make is always correct and undisputable, no matter which it is.

- ($P_I^{AE}/2$) societal æsthetics implies a *symmetry between entitlements and duties* (which belong to the natural law—coming from the natural state of the individual or human nature), respectively between rights and obligations (which belong to the positive law—coming from the cultural state of the individual, or human condition).

The principle $P_I^{AE}/2$ is not redundant with the principle $P_I^{AE}/1$, since while the principle $P_I^{AE}/1$ is focused on the symmetry of final states (no matter the ways in which that symmetry is objectified), the principle $P_I^{AE}/2$ is focused on the ways of obtaining that symmetry of the final states. Figure 15 provided a synoptic scheme of these reasons.

Nota bene: the term *society* includes the other individuals, as well, not only the states as such.

- ($P_I^{AE}/3$) in the societal interactions, the socionals must have a *symmetry of asymmetries*.

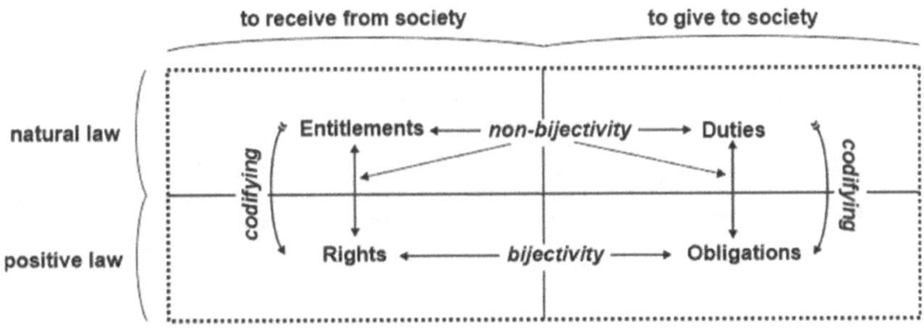

Fig. 15 Symmetry of ways to get the societal æsthetics (*Source* author)

The symmetry of asymmetries refers to the fact that the procedures/ways used in the accomplishment of the principle $P_I^{AE}/1$ are not required to be symmetrical from any point of view. As a result, they could be (very) different, that is, asymmetrical. The condition is, according to this principle, that the possible asymmetry be integrated into a symmetry. To take an example: in the interactions on the labour market, the wage is proportional to the contribution brought to realizing the economic product in the case.[82] The contribution could be different for two individuals, because their qualifications, diligence, responsibility, and so on are different as well. Consequently, the wage will differ according to those differences in contribution. This means we have a symmetry of asymmetries: the symmetry is the proportionality of wage with the actual contribution, and the asymmetry is that of the wages.

- ($P_I^{AE}/4$) the *socionals* must be *subsumed* under the *social capital.*

The socionals, i.e., the interactions that occur in politics and ethics within the practical activity (see Fig. 16), must have (dominantly) as inputs the social capital, and as output, the same social capital. According to the general concept of sustainability, the recovering (or, even, increasing) of inputs through the corresponding outputs signifies, at least, the perpetual replicability of the system (in our case, the societal æsthetics), and at most, the positive feedback towards augmenting the social capital, which constitutes both inputs and outputs in the phenomenology of societal æsthetics.

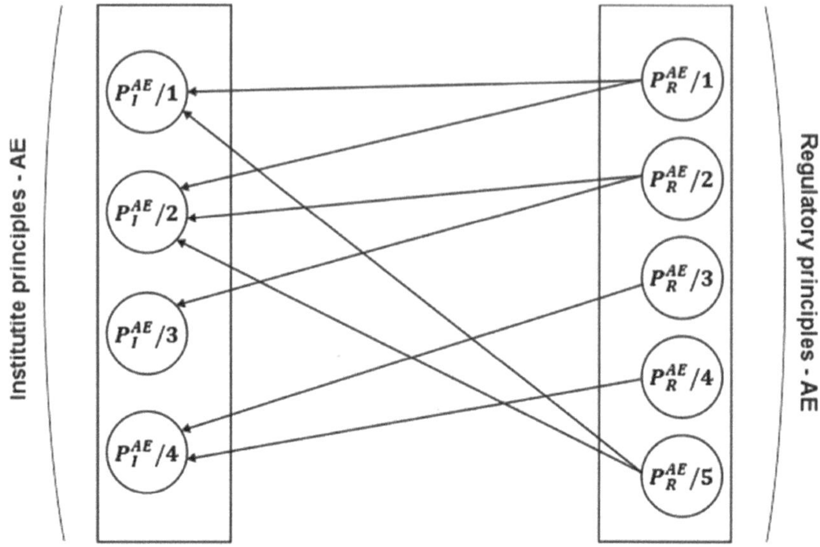

Fig. 16 Societal æsthetics—relationships between institutive and regulatory principles (*Source* author)

(b) Regulatory principles

- ($P_R^{AE}/1$) the institutive principles can be updated only in the direction in which the *social capital increases* or, at least, maintains, never in the direction (or with the presumed impact) that implies the social capital decreases. I would call this regulatory principle: the *principle of self-sustaining*.

The social capital is the most significant "product" of the interactions of individuals in the form of socionals. More exactly, the social capital is the only capital that deserves to be produced, since it is of a symbolic utility type, that is, it contributes in the highest degree to the realization of the plenary life.

- ($P_R^{AE}/2$) the *rate* of socionals of symmetric type over the socionals of proportion type is either *increasing* or *stationary*. I would call this regulatory principle: the *principle of symmetrisation*.

As said, the harmony of the socionals can be either of a symmetry type or of a proportion type. However, since the proportion can be subsumed under the idea of symmetry of asymmetries, I think that symmetry should be preferred to proportion in the set of socionals. Of course, there can be oscillations in the rapport between symmetry and proportion, but the trend should be towards the more rapid increase of the symmetrical socionals, compared with the increase of proportion socionals.

- ($P_R^{AE}/3$) the socionals work towards *contamination* of the *praxiological activity* in the society. I would call this regulatory principle: the *principle of trans-regional expansion.*

The praxiological activity within the society is, par excellence, the economic activity. In the economic activity, the economic (substantive) utility, as discussed previously, prevails. The economic utility is a calculus, not a value in an axiological meaning. The societal æsthetics implies, as a consequence, a penetration of the symbolic utility in the economic phenomenology—in this way, the æsthetism of the society gains much more quantity and more significant relevance for the individuals.

- ($P_R^{AE}/4$) the socionals must be anchored exclusively into the *symbolic utility*. I would call this regulatory principle: the *principle of societal symbolism.*

If the regulatory principle $P_R^{AE}/3$ expresses the means to extend the socionals to the praxiological (economic) component of the society, this regulatory principle ($P_R^{AE}/4$) expresses the finality of that extension, namely, the (if possible) generalization of the symbolic utility at the society as a whole. So, in fact, the two evoked regulatory principles will lead to an increase of the societal symbolism, which is much more compatible with the concept of plenary life than the economic utility (and even than the evidential utility).

- ($P_R^{AE}/5$) the rate of socionals propensity to communitarianism over the propensity to individualism is supra-unit. I would call this regulatory principle: the *principle of communitarization.*

As discussed regarding the social capital, there are two processes which unfold concomitantly and inter-conditionally: individualization[83] (particularizing the social capital to individuals), respectively socializing (generalizing the social capital from individuals to the society level). *Nota bene*: I call the socializing flow of the social capital as communitarization of it. This regulatory principle requires that the flow of socializing (communitarization) of social capital be more intensive than the flow of individualization of the social capital. The reason for such a choice is the following: the human being is increasingly a cultural being, and, as a consequence, is less and less a natural being. In this dynamics, the socialization/communitarization regarding the social capital is necessarily more and more significant for a plenary life realization.

Nota bene: in fact, there is a dynamic balance between the propensity to socialization (communitarization) of the social capital and that of individualization of social capital. As Fig. 16 suggests, two of the practical actions in society are aimed at individualizing the social capital, namely art and religion, and two of them are aimed at socializing (communitarizing) the social capital, namely politics and ethics (these last two actions deliver exactly the socionals). The idea of the principle $P_R^{AE}/5$ is that the socializing/communitarizing propensity of the social capital is, on average, predominant.

The general relationships between institutive principles and regulatory principles of the societal æsthetics can be suggested as shown in Fig. 16.

Discussion

- the most regulatory actions seem to be exerted on the $P_I^{AE}/2$ (symmetry between entitlements and duties), namely, from the regulatory principles $P_R^{AE}/1$, $P_R^{AE}/2$ and $P_R^{AE}/5$;
- the less regulatory actions are exerted on the $P_I^{AE}/3$ (symmetry of asymmetries), namely, only by the regulatory principle $P_R^{AE}/2$;
- in total, eight regulatory actions are exerted by the regulatory principles on the institutive principles (the average of actions: two per institutive principle).

4 The Binomial Æsthetics–Ethics

4.1 Generalities

In my opinion, the social/societal ethics is an æsthetics, and reciprocally, the social/societal æsthetics is an ethics. This does not mean either that ethics automatically generates societal æsthetics, or that societal æsthetics automatically generates ethics, but only indicates that the two macro-institutions go shoulder to shoulder. Further (see Sect. 4.2), this mention will be illustrated by a (stylized) model of co-evolution æsthetics—ethics, which I would propose to be called the ***æsthics model*** (from ***æsthetic***s and e***thics***) of the society.

Based on the sets of institutive principles, for both ethics and æsthetics, the following conclusions could be drawn regarding the relationships between the two macro-marks of the societal system:

- there is an obvious logical communication between the institutive principles of ethics (P_I^E/x) and the institutive principles of æsthetics (P_I^{AE}/x), where $x \in \{1, 2, 3, 4\}$, namely:
  - $P_I^E/1$ indicates the origin of ethics, while $P_I^{AE}/1$ indicates the destination of æsthetics;
  - $P_I^E/2$ indicates the guarantee of ethics, while $P_I^{AE}/2$ indicates the modality of æsthetics;
  - $P_I^E/3$ indicates the expression of ethics, while $P_I^{AE}/3$ indicates the generalization of that expression by æsthetics;
  - $P_I^E/4$ indicates the channel of ethics, while $P_I^{AE}/4$ indicates the expression of that channel by æsthetics;
- there is one (almost) overlap between ethics and æsthetics, regarding the fourth institutive principle:
  - $P_I^E/4$ targets the empathy as a vehicle to objectify ethics, while $P_I^{AE}/4$ targets the socionals as expressions of objectifying the social capital;
  - it is obvious that empathy is of the nature of social capital, and vice versa, the social capital is an expression of empathy;
  - so, at least at the level of the fourth institutive principle, ethics and æsthetics are, somewhat, the same "animal";

Based on the sets of regulatory principles, for both ethics and æsthetics, the following conclusions could be drawn regarding the relationships between the two macro-marks of the societal system:

- there is an obvious logical communication between the regulatory principles of ethics (P_R^E/y) and the regulatory principles of æsthetics (P_R^{AE}/y), where $y \in \{1, 2, 3, 4, 5\}$, namely:
  - $P_R^E/1$ indicates the way of regulating ethics, while $P_R^{AE}/1$ indicates the result of regulating æsthetics;
  - $P_R^E/2$ indicates the sphere inside ethics will be regulated, while $P_R^{AE}/2$ indicates the modality of regulating æsthetics;
  - $P_R^E/3$ indicates the conditionality regulating ethics, while $P_R^{AE}/3$ indicates the direction of regulating æsthetics;
  - $P_R^E/4$ indicates the limits/borders of regulating ethics, while $P_R^{AE}/4$ indicates the aspiration of regulating æsthetics;
  - $P_R^E/5$ indicates the target of regulating ethics, while $P_R^{AE}/5$ indicates the conditionality of regulating æsthetics in objectifying the ethics mentioned target;
- there is one (almost) overlap between ethics and æsthetics, regarding the fifth regulatory principle:
  - $P_R^E/5$ targets the social capital as regulating ethics, while $P_R^{AE}/5$ favours the communitarization as regulating æsthetics;
  - it is obvious that social capital (re)producing implies the process of communitarization of socionals, and vice versa, the communitarization of socionals implies (re)producing of social capital;
  - so, at least at the level of the fifth regulatory principle, ethics and æsthetics are, somewhat, the same "animal".

4.2 A Binomial Co-Evolution

From all the above, it seems we have, in fact, a reciprocal conditioning between ethics and æsthetics within society. The complete and analytic model of this state of facts will be done in my pre-announced book (see note 16), but in this section, some stylized and basic features will be provided.

The Æsthics

Based on a so strong interrelations between ethics and æsthetics (causal, structural, functional, and finalist), provided by now, I think can be introduced a hybrid concept, evoked above (see Sect. 4.1) that tries to put, logically, together the ethics and the æsthetics within the society—it is what I have called *æsthics* (as shown, from ***æs****thetics* and *e****thics***). Regarding this concept, I will provide some considerations, as follows.

- both ethics and æsthetics have their own stabilization mechanisms; such a mechanism is provided by the regulatory principles, as they were mentioned previously;
  - as being cybernetic systems, both ethics and æsthetics ground their stabilization mechanisms on negative feedback—I would call these mechanisms: stabilizers of first order (S_1^E, for ethics, respectively S_1^{AE}, for æsthetics);
  - at the level of æsthics (the hybrid æsthetics–ethics), as a supra-system composed of the two systems, must work a stabilizer of second order (S_2^{EAE}); such a stabilizer stabilizes ethics based on æsthetics' feedback, and reciprocal stabilizes æsthetics based on ethics' actions/reactions. This means that feedback must be of a foetal[84] kind from the perspective of their recipients;
  - consequently, at the level of a hybrid called æsthics, work two mechanisms of stabilization, namely the two types of stabilizers: of order 1 within ethics, respectively æsthetics, and of order 2 between ethics and æsthetics;
- so, æsthics could function as the logical model, at the society level, aimed at providing individuals with the path of achieving the plenary life.

About the Evolution "Ingredients"

Of course, a hybrid such æsthics functions within another binomial: society–non-anthropogenic environment,[85] so, in reality, we have a binomial into another binomial.[86] As said, for the moment, I am interested only in identifying the basic (co)evolutive "ingredients" in the case of the binomial coined æsthics. My considerations in this matter are as follows (Table 3). It must be mentioned that mutation is always born inside the regulatory principles, not in the institutive ones.

Table 3 Basic concepts of co-evolutive model of æsthics

	Æsthics			
	Æsthetics		*Ethics*	
	Denomination	*Location*	*Denomination*	*Location*
Phenotype	Final state	$P_I^{AE}/1$	Empathyness	$P_I^E/4$
Genotype	Social capital	$P_I^{AE}/4$	Belief	$P_I^E/1$
Mutation	...	$P_R^{AE}/4$	...	$P_R^E/4$

(*Source* author)

(a) autonomous evolution

The autonomous evolution occurs inside each component of æsthics.

(a1) *inside æsthetics*: the mutation occurs in the social capital structure. It can be generated either internally or externally (for example, from the ethics side, somewhat). Internally, mutations arise in the social symbolism structure of behaviour. The mutation is translated into a change in the phenotype (final state of individuals), and the new phenotype, or the new version of phenotype, is (or not) selected by the society, including the influence of ethics in the process of fitness validation;

(a2) *inside ethics*: the mutation occurs in the belief structure. It can be generated either internally or externally (for example, from the æsthetics side, somewhat). Internally, mutation arises in the viability structure of interactions. The mutation is translated into a change in the phenotype (the empathyness of individuals), and the new phenotype, or the new version of that phenotype, is (or not) selected by the society, including the influence of æsthetics in the process of fitness validation.

(b) bound evolution (co-evolution)

The bound evolution (co-evolution) occurs inside æsthics. Consequently, it must be identified the corresponding elements of Table 1, but this time related to the hybrid called æsthics. Some considerations are required to establish the three elements of (co)evolution in the case of æsthics.

- although æsthics functions is an integrated entity, the two components (æsthetics and ethics, respectively) do not lose their identity by melting into a whole. They remain distinct but strongly entangled between them;
- as acting as a whole, æsthics must have its own phenotype, genotype, and mutation;
- in my opinion, the genotype of æsthics must be located in ethics, and the phenotype in æsthetics. My arguments are as follows:
    - the societal relationships (more precisely, the socionals) must be the objectification of ethics; in other words, the ethical behaviour is the purpose, while socionals are the means for that purpose. Consequently, the "genetic program" must be located within the ethics;
    - on the other hand, what materializes the ethics into objectified behaviour are the socionals, that is, the phenotype of æsthics belongs to æsthetics. Consequently, the fitness of socionals will be assessed and selected (or rejected, as the case may be) by the ethics, that is, by the "environment" of the æsthetics;
- the mutation that affects the genotype of æsthics comes, as I believe, from the æsthetics. The explanation is the following:
    - the ethics is, by definition and content, much more stable on long term compared with æsthetics. Indeed, on the one hand, the socionals are more volatile than the ethical behaviours, and, on the other hand, for the same pattern of ethics could exist and implemented many patterns of æsthetics;
    - according to $P_R^{AE}/1$, the regulating is assigned to a (self)sustainable path of æsthetics, but, as known, a sustainable path allows oscillations, small destabilizations, and other of the same, with the condition of maintaining that path inside a pre-established tunnel[87];
    - such oscillations inside the mentioned tunnel (which is the so-called tunnel of sustainability) could institute, as was said previously, new patterns of æsthetics, while the pattern of ethics remains invariant;

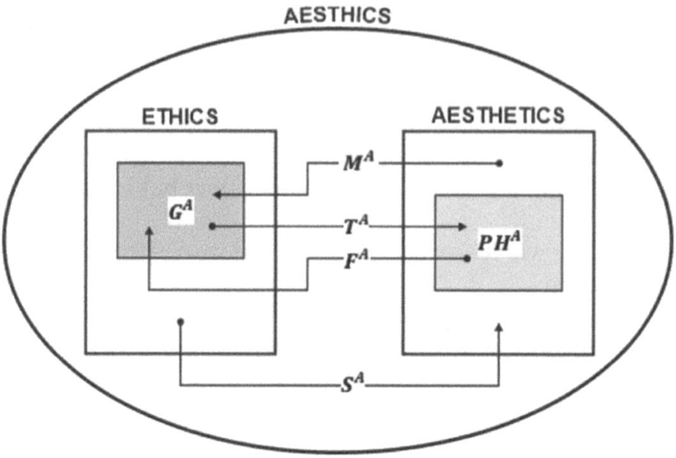

Fig. 17 Co-evolutive logic of the binomial æsthetics–ethics (*Source* author)

- conclusion is that the impulses for mutations will appear rather in the æsthetical component of æsthics and will affect the genotype located in ethics;

- after the mutation is transcribed and translated into the phenotype, the fitness of the phenotype is selected/validated or rejected/invalidated by ethics, which constitutes, as said above, the environment for æsthetics.

A general scheme of co-evolution of the binomial æsthetics–ethics (that is, the evolution of æsthics) is provided in Fig. 17—it is de: æsthics genotype with G^A, æsthics phenotype with PH^A, æsthics mutation with M^A, translation of mutation with T^A, æsthics fitness with F^A, æsthics selection with S^A.

5 Notes

1. Somewhat prosaically, satisfaction is the genus for many species, as, for example, the empirical falsifiability in knowledge theory: the empirical falsifiability will compare the predictive statement with the descriptive statement, both on a given factual context

(where the predictive statement is enounced, both logically and chronologically, before the descriptive one).

2. As understood from the previous, happiness is related (only) to the individual in his/her quality of subject. A subject is a special thing of the world endowed with cognitive capacity—the cognitive capacity is the sensitive capacity to which rationality is added.
3. Of course, any historical/empirical individual is by definition inserted into an environment (both natural and social), but no entity of that environment is punctually involved in the state of happiness, although, essentially, all entities in the environment are involved in a diffuse, non-punctual way, in such a state.
4. For example, for a Christian, the simple existence of God is sufficient to cause a state of happiness. But God cannot be considered something from the individual's environment, because it would be considered as a thing of the world, although it created the world from outside of the (yet inexistent) world.
5. I.e., the rationality is axiomatically closed.
6. Although the literature generally holds the syntagma practical rationality (Mele; Rawling, 2004), I think that a more appropriate denomination should be that of praxiological rationality, since in Kant's sense of the practical qualificative, theoretical rationality has (rather) the property of the practical (i.e., relationship between subjects).
7. These conceptual distinctions will be extra explained below, when the species of satisfaction will be examined.
8. See, here, the marginal calculus introduced in Economics by the neoclassical Economics.
9. In fact, the utility is related to the economic value. Still, for the objective of this chapter, I do not develop the relationship between the economic price and the economic value. It is worth mentioning that, in the neoclassical economic theory, the economic value is determined by the economic equilibrium price, as the free market delivers it.
10. The suggestion of such a descending curve comes from the history of thinking, more exactly from Daniel Bernoulli, in his attempt to solve the St. Petersburg Paradox.

11. I recall to you that signification is very different from meaning. So, while meaning is a denotation that leads to the referential (that is, it is relatively common to a given community), signification is a connotation assigned to denotation, but which is strongly idiosyncratic and, consequently, incommunicable inter-subjectively.
12. This does not mean that the involved subject (individual) solved all needs and expectations, but simply that there are no external or internal states/properties desired. See, for example, Buddhism and other religions that suggest such states of mind.
13. Occasionally, the state of happiness manifests as an anticipation of it, i.e., also de-synchronized related to the real occurring of that state.
14. I remind here only Epicur's maxim according to which: *Non quae habemus, sed quae fruimur abundantiam nostram constituit*, which means: *It is not what we have, but what we enjoy that constitutes our abundance*.
15. There are, also, of course, non-societal alterities related to a generic individual—for example, the non-anthropic environment.
16. Of course, it is not excluded that the case may arise when an individual elaborates a sophisticated system of such principles, but, realistically speaking, it seems this is not the common case.
17. But, of course, equally, it is not prohibited to get such a model of rationality.
18. This book will be entitled *Economic Order and Ethical Order. A New Logic and Paradigm of the Society*.
19. From prudence, I remind to the reader that there are three categories of human activities: (a) theoretical/cognitive activities: regard the relationships object–object (e.g., Physics); (b) praxiological activities: regard the relationships subject–object (e.g., Economics); (c) practical activities: regard the relationships subject–subject (e.g., Politics).
20. The acceptability means lack of objections of any nature, no matter the impact of that behaviour on other individuals or the society as a whole (including the non-anthropogenic environment).
21. That inference does not mandatorily be of a rational type; it could also be based on intuition. If the inference is rational/intellectual, its acceptability has a logical nature, while if it is intuitionistic, its acceptability has a credential nature. In both cases, the sincerity is presumed.

22. The complete commitment is ensured by the publicity of the principle involved, so the other individuals to know about that principle but, in my opinion, this is rather a "methodological" issue not theoretical one. At most, it could be considered as a regulatory principle (or, at least, sub-principle).
23. To note that revealing the sincerity itself is also a predictor for others regarding the future (or, as the case may be, the past) behaviours of the individual concerned.
24. The empathy is the emotional (namely, unconscious) (pre)disposition to put yourself into the general (or specific, after the case) position/state of another and, consequently, to somewhat experience that position/state so that your behaviour is designed and objectified according to that virtual experience.
25. A parallel (perhaps, a little bit exaggerated) with the entropy law is at hand: like the entropy, the strength of the institutive principles of Ethics always increases, namely in a spontaneous way (caused by this regulatory principle).
26. Needless to say that the symbolic utility is not forbidden by this principle.
27. The concept of interdependent autonomy is not so evident as it seems prima facie—essentially, it means an autonomy (i.e., the potential to edify one's own norms of behaviour) by considering the behaviour of others. *Nota bene*: this description is an alter ego of the description of the (general) evolutionism.
28. It is not the case here to develop a historical excursion on the phenomenology of the concept of autonomy. It is considered the best "anchor" for freedom, esteem, and a full life. Systematic approaches to the individual's autonomy begin with John Stuart Mill (the concept of utilitarian liberalism) and gain their abstract and universal expression with Kant's moral philosophy. Generally, ethics (and, more generally, morals) are viewed as autonomous, i.e., being involved in relationships that provide autonomy. Logically, many kinds of autonomy can exist, but here I am interested in the ethical/moral autonomy. *Nota bene*: perhaps, the syntagma ethical/moral autonomy could be "guilty" of some pleonasmism.
29. It can be paraphrased, from the well-known phrase about freedom, as: my autonomy spreads until it rapes your autonomy.

30. I would draw attention to the following issue: autonomy is not a species of the genus called freedom. Rather, as stated in the main text, autonomy is the manifestation, in the "region" of the contingent, of freedom.
31. One of the most relevant examples here is the human brain evolution—the new components/layers of the brain were added without any sign of optimization, rather coincidentally, so that many old functions (as the animal's instinctual ones—see the reptilian actions/reactions) coexist with the new and specific to human beings functions, as is the frontal cortex.
32. *En passant*, let me say that capitalism, as a societal order, is dominantly based on an optimizing paradigm (e.g., in the economic field—within the neoclassical economic theory—and in the social/political field—within the libertarianism).
33. Here, there is neither suggestion regarding the existence and action of historical laws, i.e., regarding the existence of a historical necessity (as claimed, for example, by Marxism), but simply I want to speak about a logical causality, so not a determinism (i.e., necessity) at all.
34. However, in this stage (of elaborating the main body of the theory of Ethics), this step—elaborating of the conjectures—is not mandatory, since the conjectures concerned could be formulated when the question of predictions arises.
35. As we see further, there is a third library, generated by the tests applied to the maxima of the first library.
36. The way in which the opinion is proved as true (or false, as the case may be) will be explained at point (d3) below.
37. I do not complicate the discussion here by saying that, in the societal field, we do not have pure predictions, but an inextricable mix between prediction and prescription (that I called, elsewhere, presdiction).
38. The ethical ethos is, of course, a component of the ethos. in general. Regarding a given community.
39. However, I will consider a hard core of ethics which is common to, at least, small communities in the world (for example, nations) so that, on the hard core, it can be edified exactly the morals.
40. Instead, of course, it can be communicated using the "behavioural language", in an analogous way in which we often enough use the "corporal language".

41. In fact, a similar agreement (although, as it seems, only among contemporary individuals) takes place in Nozick's theory of the state and social justice.
42. I remind the reader that a presdiction is a logical combination between a prescription and a prediction.
43. Again, here the similarity with the concept of revealed preferences of Samuelson is obvious.
44. There is confusion between the concepts of empirical and factual. Generally, the empirical is a non-repeatable factual (as known, the singular events are not predictable), so the correct term is factual/factuality.
45. I want to mention that, logically, a prediction is not an expectation, but an anticipation—while the expectation is subjective/idiosyncratic, an anticipation is relatively objective (or, at least, inter-subjectively objectified).
46. Obvious, the concept of ethically false must be conceived "mirrored" with the concept of ethically true, that is, from the subjective perspective, not inter-subjective one, as the concept of false is in the case of correspondence truth.
47. As I said, a proposal much more extensive and analytical on Ethics I will provide in another upcoming book. In that book, the procedure of testing the compliance-truth will receive the deserved attention.
48. Again, the development of the concept of similarity in testing the compliance truth (i.e., the ethical truth) will be analytically done in the announced upcoming book (see note 18).
49. Since the economic process is constituted by singular (unrepeatable) events, it cannot be associated with predictions, so that the factual falsifiability is compromised or even impossible, which rejects the economic from the "region" of sciences.
50. It is worth mentioning that any science is (or has) a theory, while not any theory is a science—for example, the theological theory is not a science, since it is factually non-testable (see the logical positivism of the Vienna Circle—I remind the fundamental verificationist principle of the logical positivism: any statement is either tautologic or factually verifiable).
51. The ethical preparation of the individual implies two inter-related components: (a) the intellectual component; (b) the attitudinal component. Sometimes, in special contexts, an inconsistency

(contradiction) could appear between the two components, analogous to the cognitive dissonance—we can name such dissonance: *ethical dissonance*.

52. Only the perceptive or sensation sensibility is innate (natural), the other possible or required types of sensibility are culturally generated.
53. A very interesting direction of research here (which I will approach in the announced upcoming book) is the following: could it be accepted that the worth of an individual is directly proportional to its ethical sensibility? Of course, as ethics is a relationship, that individual's worth has significance for humankind, not (only) for the individual involved.
54. Indeed, the values scale (axiological matrix) can be and, in fact, is, most probably, different from one individual to another, whether they are contemporary or not.
55. More precisely, with the correspondence truth.
56. It is worth remembering that the change driven by values is called (social) progress, so ethics is directly connected with the (social) progress, not with a simple transformation or, even less, with development (for these categories, see Figure 1, in Chapter 1).
57. Do not include here the corporate social responsibility, since any corporation, as a lucrative organization, does not respect ethical/moral prescriptions, but only legal norms.
58. *Homo œconomicus* (despite the repeated relaxations from psychological or methodological perspectives) is, in fact, as I said many times, in many places, a *homo mathematicus*, both unrealistic and futile.
59. As shown elsewhere, freedom does not logically imply democracy, although, in the contemporary age, it is considered that the pair *freedom–democracy* provides the strongest and most relevant institutional combination towards the plenary life of individuals and society as a whole.
60. The choice of means is allowed by the positive law of the society concerned.
61. It is worth mentioning that the moral norms bear sanctions, as well, but such a sanction is not applied by a public institution (state or a statal agency), so that that sanction takes the form of community's opprobrium, more or less directly manifested—in fact, usually operating tacitly through a unfavoured and respectless

behaviour of the community regarding the individual who violated a moral norm. At any rate, the sanction regarding the moral norms is non-mandatory; it could be either applied or not applied.

62. In the case of a moral norm, the sanction is not contained in the structure of the norm, but it is external. Also, the punisher is not the state (as for positive norms) but the community as a whole, and/or any individual of that community.
63. It must distinguish between a theory of ethics and an ethical theory. Generally, a theory is not required to be ethical, because it is pure cognitive, addressing the knowledge, not the behaviour (I remind you that Ethics addresses the behaviour, but the theory of Ethics is interested in the knowledge of the behaviour). On the other hand, a certain theory could be ethical if its goal is to provide a set of ethical rules for acquiring knowledge in a given field, for example, in the field of human cloning. Of course, such an issue is outside the basic objectives of the book. The same can be said about the distinction between a theory of morals and a moral theory.
64. Similarly to Samuelson's concept of revealed preference in the economic field (*Nota bene*: but that concept can be extended to any behaviour in the societal system), it can be spoken about something as *revealed ethics*, with the meaning that such a revealing is provided by morals. If the revealed ethics is a species of the genus called revealed preference is a good question that could be examined—I think the answer must be affirmative.
65. I adhere to the point of view according to which civilization is the artefactual objectification of culture. In other words, the culture "lives" in Popper's world 2, while the civilization "lives" in Popper's world 3.
66. One could examine whether exist (or should exist) the golden number (1.618, which is contained even in Fibonacci's sequence) in the societal construction, organization, and functioning, of course, by "translating" the numerical rate into a more appropriate expression (perhaps, quantifiable and commensurable in time and space) from the social/societal perspective.
67. In addition to the five well-known senses, a sixth sense is also accepted: the proprioceptive sense or proprioception, which refers to the perception of the position of the receiver's physical body in space (see the considerations, in a phenomenological key, of

Maurice Merleau-Ponty, following in the footsteps of Husserl). The process (usually visual, but can also be thought in relation to the other "classical" senses) called anamorphosis aims, to a significant extent, precisely at this sixth natural sense.

68. Obviously, in this framework, the beautiful (like the ugly, the grotesque, etc.) represents a species of the genus called harmony.
69. Harmony, as a genus, has two basic species: (a) symmetry; (b) proportion. Symmetry implies proportion, but proportion does not imply symmetry (for example, the proportion expressed by the golden number—1.618—is, obviously, asymmetrical, but still harmonious.
70. Fractality refers to a property (either spatial or temporal, or both) that relates to self-similarity. Fractality was introduced and developed as a mathematical property but, given its structural, spatiotemporal dimension, it is evident that it can be very productive in social/societal theory.
71. I want to make, here, some additional comments: (1) harmony is involved in the general evolution, so, even though Nature is not awareness of its harmony, it "uses" harmony for its general "purpose"—survival/perpetuation; (2) cooperation and competition (the two processes of the living entities (both biological and logical) are based on nothing else than on symmetry, i.e., harmony. Some scientists intuited that, for example, starting from the fact that the second law of Thermodynamics (the law of entropy) is asymmetric, that it must exist a more primitive law, based on symmetry, which includes the law of entropy—for example, the constructal law, of Professor Adrian Bejan, or the minimal entropic gradient of interaction, of myself—but, in this matter, it is still much to be done.
72. Accidentally, objectifications can arise from a single subjectivity (for example, Robinson Crusoe made artefacts without interactions with other subjectivities), but, following Aristotle, science is interested in the genus, not in the species or individuals.
73. As is known, there are many other such (in fact, metaphorical enough) concepts—I recall some of them: artistic sense, justice sense, measure/proportion sense, ethical sense (at the individual level, not a societal one), time sense, etc.
74. Instead, some senses are sensitive, as artistic sense or time sense.

75. As said before, the society is a cybernetic system of order 4 (an artefact which includes the observer).
76. I ignore, here, the subtle issue of the (required, from cultural reasons) dis-equilibrium between the gift received and the gift given (Mauss, 2002). It seems that, at least in this example, there is a symmetry of asymmetries, but I do not develop this line of analysis. However, a more developed analysis on the socionals could gain a new and interesting perspective on the special harmony in the societal system, perhaps by amending (even, diminishing) the symmetry as the expression of harmony and replacing it (or combining, as the case may be) with another concept (which one?).
77. I remind the reader of the distinction between system and network: the system has two basic components: (a) the leading component; (b) the driven component, while in a network, all components are "equal" as position, signification, and role/function. Of course, the real entities are combinations of systems and networks.
78. The social is composed of: (1) human social, which can be called societal; (2) non-human social. The non-human social refers to the social groups (structure, functions) formed by non-human living individuals: ants, bees, lions, and so on.
79. This is not referring to the interactions between individuals and the non-anthropogenic environment, but the interactions that occur among individuals, even if those interactions are focused on the non-anthropogenic environment. This mention is important in order to keep the societal æsthetics inside the practical relationships, since the relationships between individuals and the non-anthropogenic environment belong to praxiological relationships, not to practical ones.
80. Usually (and smartly) an intermediate state, once achieved, becomes a resource, of any nature, for the consecutive intermediate state, and so on, till to the final state.
81. Rigorously speaking, it is not about probability (which requires archives of the same events occurring in the past, with the actual probabilities, what is called Kolmogorov probability, or Kolmogorov field of probability), but about propensity. The propensity is assigned to the singular (unrepeatable) events, which is exactly the case with the societal æsthetics. I remind you that the concept of propensity (initiated by Aristotle, in his Physics) was popularized in the philosophy of science by Karl Popper.

82. More exactly, the wage is the monetary expression of the marginal productivity of labour.
83. I remind you that by individualization must be meant individuation (see note 126 in Chapter 6).
84. The issue of fetality (fetal property) of action/reaction was examined in my (and others) book (2023).
85. This crucial analysis will, however, be postponed.
86. Here is a beautiful example of fractality.
87. Theoretically, such a tunnel is represented by an ideal path of ethics.

References

Boulding, K. E. (1969). Economics as a moral science. *The American Economic Review, 59, no. 1.*

Dinga, E. (2014). Social capital and social justice. *Procedia Economics and Finance, no. 8/2014.*

Dinga, E. (2025). *Economic resilience during overlapped crises—Antifragility, sustainability and Autopoieticity*. Palgrave Macmillan—Springer Nature.

Gasset, J.O.y. (1960). *The revolt of the masses*. Norton.

Körner, T. W. (2010). *Naïve decision making*. Cambridge University Press.

Kuhn, T. (2012). *The structure of scientific revolutions*. The University of Chicago Press.

Mauss, M. (2002). *The gift. The form and reason for exchange in archaic societies*. Routledge.

Mele, A. R., & Rawling, P. (2004). *The Oxford handbook of rationality*. Oxford University Press.

Nozick, R. (1993). *The nature of rationality*. Princeton University Press.

Rawls, J. (1971). *A theory of justice*. Belknap Press.

Samuelson, P. (1938). A note on the pure theory of consumers' behaviour. *Economica, new series.,* 5(17).

Wight, J. B. (2015). *Ethics in economics*. Stanford University Press.

CHAPTER 8

Social Justice, Social Capital, and Wellbeing

1 The Concept of Rightness

1.1 A Definition

In the specialized literature and, in general, in the public debate on the quality of life, one of the omnipresent issues is that of rightness.

Rightness has as its etymological root the idea of right which, in turn, has a series of connotations such as those of correct, proper, in accordance with a norm/prescription or in accordance with a common belief (philosophical or just at the level of common sense), etc. The scientific concept of rightness is contaminated, like any other concept, by its meanings in common language; therefore it will have to be defined rigorously, so that the analyses and interpretations based on it are free from ambiguity or equivocation.

To define the concept of rightness, we will first have to establish its sufficiency predicates.[1] We believe that the following five sufficiency predicates should be retained, in this case:

- (R_S^1) refers to a *social relationship*: the concept of rightness refers to human being and the interdependent relationships that the individual[2] has with the rest of society (contemporary or not). In other words, the concept of rightness is not a concept that concerns the whole of reality, but only social reality;

E. Dinga, *The Economics of Social Justice and Societal Evolution*,
https://doi.org/10.1007/978-3-032-24055-2_8

- (R_S^2) a *value* is *attached* to the social relationship: not all social relationships have values attached (i.e., axiological marks), many of them are purely functional in nature and even possess automatic, routine characteristics. The concept of rightness refers to those social relationships that have significance for the individual and for society, and, in order to have significance, they must have a value attached. Therefore, to define the concept of rightness, we must operate a selection in the set of social relationships, so as to retain only the subset that has values attached;
- (R_S^3) is of a *practical* nature: given that we have already introduced the predicate of sufficiency relative to the social relationship, it seems that the predicate requiring a practical nature for the concept of justice is superfluous (redundant). The objection is unfounded, however, because social relations are of three types: a) cognitive type (for example, the development of knowledge); b) praxiological type (for example, economic activities); c) practical type (for example, political or religious activities). Through this latter predicate we want to exclude the first two types of social relations and select only practical-type social relations[3];
- (R_S^4) the attached value is of a *moral* type: among the social relations that have attached values, we will have to select, further, those social relations that have attached moral values. We consider the concept of moral value to be known for the needs of the present study—in principle, a value is of a moral type if it aims at or has a signification related, in one way or another, to the dignity/esteem of the human being[4];
- (R_S^5) morality is of the *non-utilitarian* type: we want to exclude utilitarian aspects from the concept of rightness, although there are approaches in the specialized literature (for example, the Pareto optimality principle) which, although seem to "protect" those at risk of having their situation worsened (therefore, of registering a decrease in the wellbeing) actually aim at a final state, that is, a category of utility. In this sense, I ask the concept of rightness to also verify this predicate of sufficiency, that is, non-utilitarianism.

So, from a formal point of view, the concept of rightness (R) can be described as follows:

$$R = \left\{R_S^1, R_S^2, R_S^3, R_S^4, R_S^5\right\}$$

or equivalently:

$$R \leftarrow \left[\left(R_S^1\right) \bigwedge \left(R_S^2\right) \bigwedge \left(R_S^3\right) \bigwedge \left(R_S^4\right) \bigwedge \left(R_S^5\right)\right]$$

Figure 1 provides a synoptic view of how the concept of rightness is obtained based on sufficiency predicates.

Based on the sufficiency predicates established above, we can formulate the following definition of the concept of rightness: *rightness is that social relation of a practical and non-utilitarian type, which objectifies human dignity/esteem.*

A brief qualitative analysis of the concept of rightness, thus defined, would consist of the following:

- rightness is a *social relation*. This means that rightness is a relational concept, but not a property of something, of a choice for example. This remark is important because it prevents the equating of rightness with a state (for example, a desirable final state, as required by the Pareto optimality principle);
- rightness *does not have utilitarian significance*. This means that rightness is not related to wellbeing, happiness, and other similar concepts that are generated by the concept, or through the concept of utility;

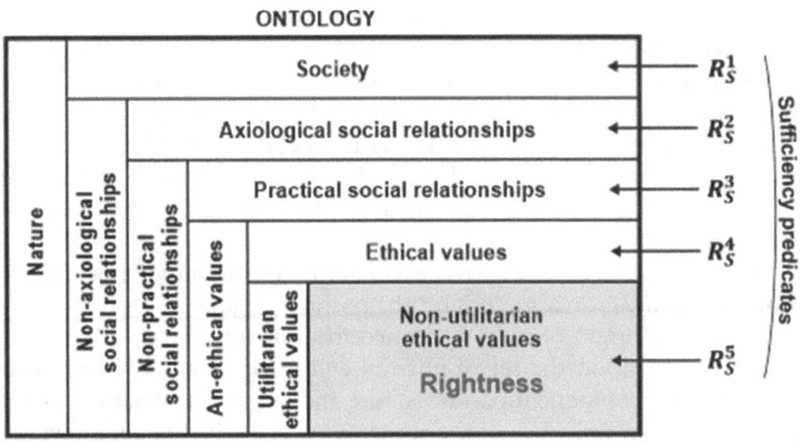

Fig. 1 Logical derivation of the concept of rightness (*Source* author)

- rightness is a *practical social relation*. Considering the other two characteristics (sufficiency predicates) mentioned above, this means that rightness is closer to the procedural[5] aspect.

1.2 Natural Law Versus Positive Law

Based on the concept of rightness, I will define, in the following, the concept of *right*.

First, let us note that the term right is of a predicative nature (adjective, from a grammatical point of view), which means that it expresses a property. This property is of the social relationship of a practical nature, a relationship that generates rightness, as it was defined above.

Second, the concept of rightness and that of right are in the following logical relationship: rightness is accomplished when the associated social relationship is right. In other words, the vehicle for the accomplishment of rightness is the right character of the choice, decision, action, or behaviour that objectifies the social relationship associated with rightness.

Third, rightness is a cumulative concept, that is, it is accomplished only if all the events (choices, decisions, actions, behaviours, and so on) associated with the social relationship that aims at rightness are right.

Based on the above considerations, the predicate of right can be defined as follows: *is right that act (or abstention, as the case may be) that objectifies the self-esteem of the individual.*[6]

A very important result of what has been discussed so far is the following: right is a state, and right character (i.e., rightness) is a procedure. In other words, the state of right is achieved if the procedures that lead to that state are right—so, the right procedure must be considered as an operational predicate, and the right, to which the right procedure leads, must be considered as a desiderative noun (state). Figure 2 suggests these conceptual distinctions.

The predicate *right* can have two alternative (although not entirely distinct) origins: (a) natural origin; (b) positive origin.

The natural origin of right is claimed from *human nature*. By human nature is understood the set of physical and mental traits of the human individual, as a component part of Nature and as a result of natural evolution, without any influence of the social. Of course, the human individual has never been a-social, but it can be assumed that, from the evolutionary

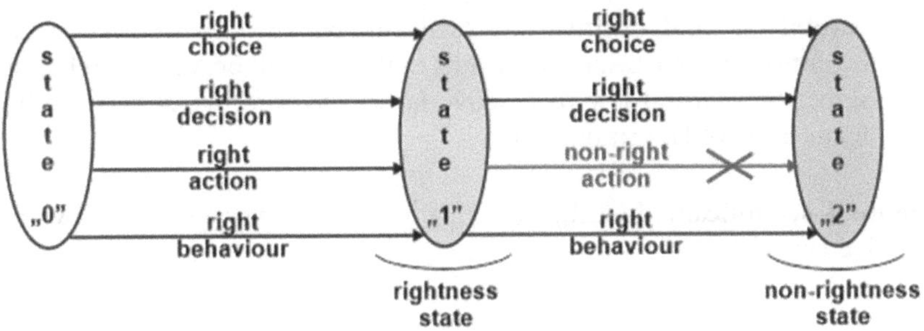

Fig. 2 Rightness as a cumulative state of a right procedure (*Source* author)

biological perspective, we can isolate the set of physical and mental traits that are exclusively naturally conditioned.

The positive origin of right is claimed from the *human condition*. By the human condition is understood human nature adjusted by culture. In other words, the human condition, although it has human nature as its "backbone", is "contaminated" by values, institutions, traditions, etc. If human nature can be considered, in general, invariant, the human condition has a preponderantly historical and contextual character, it is relative not only from the perspective of time, but also from that of space.

A few additional considerations may prove useful in the conceptual dissociation of natural law from positive law:

- *natural law* can only be objectified through the mediation of positive law—natural law is an inalienable foundation of human being, but which, in principle, can never manifest itself as a right per se, but only as positive law;
  - it is desirable that positive law does not interfere in a contradictory way with natural law. This means that positive law must, as far as possible, represent public codifications of natural law;
- *positive law* is much richer, from the point of view of the denotative sphere, than natural law, in the sense that the same natural law can be codified in different positive law norms (of course, all being convergent with the natural law in question);
- natural law is what we might call legitimate law, while positive law could be called legal law;

- natural law and positive law establish, between themselves, a co-evolutionary process.[7] This means that there will be a causal relationship from natural law to positive law,[8] and a feedback relationship from positive law to natural law.[9]

Figure 3 synoptically describes the relationship between natural law and positive law.

1.3 Rightness Versus Justice

Based on the distinction made above between natural law and positive law, we can now move on to examining a more general distinction (and more important for the subject of the present study), namely the distinction between rightness and justice. The concepts of rightness and justice are often used as interchangeable. Although in common language there are no serious consequences of this indistinction, when it comes to scientific examinations (or when it comes to their practical application), much more attention and rigour are required with regard to these concepts, because unpredictable adverse effects can occur. In the following, we will draw some obvious conceptual distinctions between rightness and justice.

Rightness–Reflection of Natural Law
Rightness is the state of a social system in which natural law is verified. This means that the rights in question do not need to be publicly codified,[10] but that they are considered by the population in question (or its majority) as legitimate, inalienable, and definitory for the generic human being. Thus, an essential role in preserving the state of rightness of a society (community) is played by tradition, collective memory, as well as what is called popular wisdom. Therefore, in the establishment, constitution, and functioning of rightness, moral norms[11] are fundamental. The assessment of the state of rightness is always made by verifying the morality of decisions, actions, and behaviours. Rightness is generally subjectively evaluable, but, especially in small communities, an inter-subjective assessment can also function, although at the level of society as a whole, the inter-subjective assessment of the state of rightness is difficult, if not impossible. Essentially, it can be said that rightness (or the state of rightness of a social system) is established when natural law is put into practice. The state contrary to rightness is called unrightness/unfairness (or state of unrightness/unfairness).

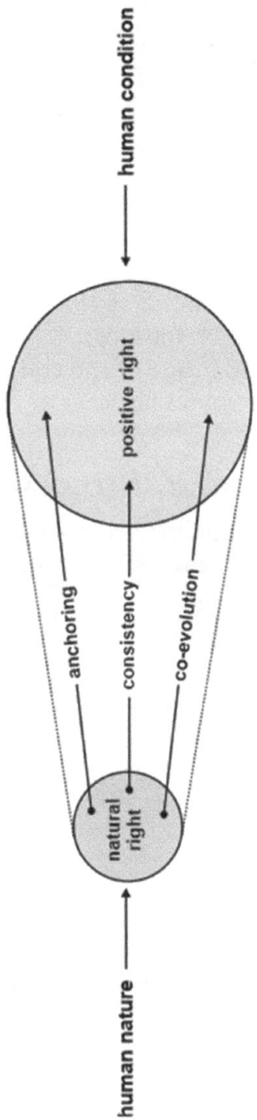

Fig. 3 Logical relationships between natural law and positive law. (*Source* author)

Justice—Reflection of Positive Law
Justice is the state of a social system in which positive law is verified. This means that the rights in question need to be codified publicly (through legal norms with different legal forces[12])). Codification and ensuring publicity (public transparency) are *conditio sine qua non* of positive law. The assessment of the state of justice is done, simply, by verifying the non-violation of positive norms. It follows, therefore, that if a natural right is not codified in the form of positive law, even if the positive right is fulfilled, so the state of justice is verified, it is possible that, by doing so, a natural right is violated, that is, the state of rightness is not verified. In this context, the common phrase—*rule of law*—refers to the verification of the state of justice, not the state of rightness. The state contrary to justice we call injustice (or state of injustice).

Figure 4 provides a synthetic image of the conceptual distinction that must be made between rightness and justice.

1.4 The Concept of Theory of Rightness

The concept of a theory of rightness refers to a logical, epistemological, and methodological foundation of the state of rightness in society.

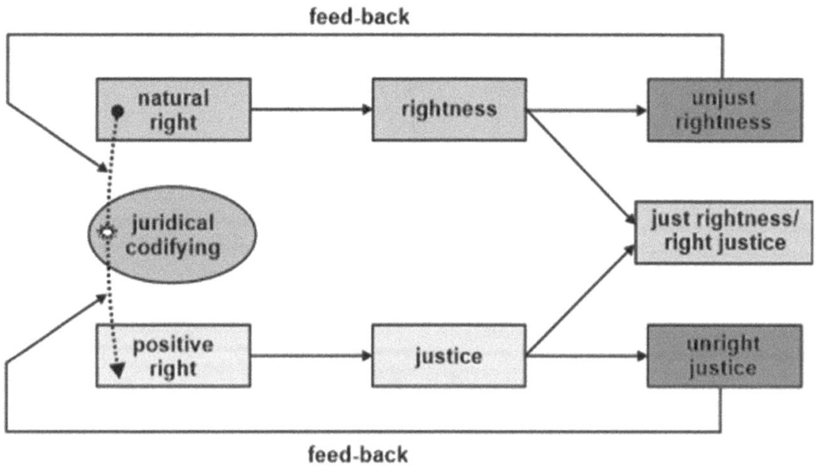

Fig. 4 Logical relationships between rightness and justice (*Source* author)

From a *logical point of view*, the concept of a theory of rightness must specify the basic principles ("axioms") of the establishment of this concept and examine these principles from at least the following five perspectives:

- the *primitive character* of the principles: the principles must be self-founded, they are not allowed to be logically derivable (which would "degrade" them to the state of theorems) from other principles, more primitive than them;
- the *sufficient character* of the principles[13]:: the principles must allow the derivation of all the theorems, lemmas, and propositions of interest for that theory, in a consistent and decidable manner from an alethic perspective[14];
- the *consistent character* of the principles: the principles must be non-contradictory among themselves (taken two by two), that is, the verification of one principle must not undermine the verification of another principle;
- the *independent character* of the principles: the principles must not be derivable from each other, that is, they must not be redundant at the level of the entire set of principles.[15] Although redundancy is a feature of great importance and significance in the functioning of any system (including a social system, such as the system inside which states state of rightness or a state of unrightness can occur), at the level of the set of principles of a theory, it is inadmissible;
- the *convergent character* of the principles: the verification of all the principles, simultaneously, must lead the phenomenon/process to which the theory in question is associated, towards achieving the specific objectives. The convergence of the principles is often ignored in the logical analyses of theories, although, in our opinion, it is of the same "strength" as the other four characteristics of the theory, mentioned above.

From an *epistemological* point of view, the concept of a theory of rightness must specify what are the chances that rightness will be implemented, what are the institutions, procedures, and mechanisms for testing the achievement of rightness. In other words, this aspect must indicate both testability, as a property of the institutions, procedures, and mechanisms involved, and the ways of effective testing. The testability of the achievement of rightness does not, of course, refer to correspondence-truth,[16]

Table 1 Comparative aspects of a theory of rightness

	Logical aspect	*Epistemological aspect*	*Methodological aspect*
Grounding	axioms	purpose	way
Functioning	deductively	normatively	assessly
Evolution	to the middle included	to pragmatic truth	to self-control
Reason	justification	belief	preference

Source author

it does not concern the cognitive aspect of the matter, but refers to the achievement of a goal—the achievement of rightness. This means that testability (and effective testing) in the matter of rightness concerns the semantic coincidence between the verbal formulation of the goal before it is achieved, and the verbal formulation of the goal already achieved. We could also say that testability in the matter of rightness refers to the semantic coincidence between the normative statement and the descriptive statement regarding a given factual. The epistemological aspect of the theory of rightness highlights the *significance* of the action (either act or abstention) of doing rightness.

From a *methodological* point of view, the concept of the theory of rightness must specify which institutions (including norms), procedures, and mechanisms ensure the doing of rightness. It should be noted that the methodological aspect of the theory of rightness focuses, first of all, on the potential nature of the doing of rightness and, secondly, on the actual nature of this doing. The methodological aspect of the theory of rightness highlights the *possibility*[17] of the action (either act or abstention) of doing rightness.

Some comparative delimitations between the three aspects of a theory of rightness could be systematized as given in Table 1.

2 The Concept of Social Justice

2.1 *Social Wellbeing and Social Capital*

Preamble

The concept of social wellbeing is seen, in the specialized literature (and in all empirical studies, in any case), as a multidimensional concept. In the present chapter, I will start directly with some of my own considerations regarding this concept and, where appropriate, I will position myself, either critically or adheringly, to the significant positions in the specialized literature, instead of carrying out, in a distinct and autonomous way, a neutral review of this literature.

a. a distinction must be made between wellbeing and utility. While (the orthodox) utility[18] has a narrow material (or substantive) meaning, wellbeing has a broader referential, also involving non-substantive components of the life of the individual (or community). There are authors who even consider that wellbeing and quality of life are perfectly interchangeable concepts[19];
b. wellbeing is associable (and, most of the time, is associated) with the so-called welfare state, reaching the point where wellbeing is considered, in the welfare state (Pestieau, 2006), as a fundamental human right. However, given the multidimensionality of the concept of wellbeing, as will result from what follows, considering that wellbeing is a fundamental right is, at least from a theoretical and philosophical point of view, quite risky. This line of thinking would probably have more to gain if it followed a procedural scheme of "guaranteeing" wellbeing, and not one of the final result types[20];
c. wellbeing is generally considered as a subjective, global (therefore, rather synthetic than analytical) and, to some extent, intuitive (not rational) perception. This way of considering wellbeing leads to the concept of individual wellbeing (more precisely, of the wellbeing of the individual). As is quite obvious, subjective wellbeing is incommensurable between individuals, therefore the need to conceive wellbeing at the level of the collective (or at the level of the entire society) led to the introduction of the concept of social wellbeing (Dean, 2020). To a large extent, social wellbeing should be considered an objective[21] concept;
d. both individual and social wellbeing can be measured (with the necessary precautions and approximations), with the caveat that individual wellbeing will be quantified, at best, in very narrow socio-professional and cultural categories—based on the self-assessment statements of the subjects involved—while social wellbeing will have to resort to aggregated, macro-social indicators that will be measured without resorting to the subjectivity of those involved in the research;

e. the concept of wellbeing (seen at both the individual and social levels Land & Spilerman, 1975) is specifically positioned in relation to other concepts used (especially in works on moral philosophy or in works on ethics) by two "old" concepts: happiness and eudaimonia.[22] In what follows, I will not make distinctions regarding the three "competing" concepts—because such a discussion shifts the focus of the research in a direction that I do not intend to follow in this chapter—but I will limit myself to specifying, to a degree and in a manner that is as appropriate as possible, the concept of wellbeing as such.

Social Wellbeing and Individual Wellbeing

As the term suggests, wellbeing is a concept that refers to a *state*. Being an axiological category, the concept of wellbeing refers to the person (or the individual, in a crude economic terminology). Therefore, wellbeing has the following semantic features:

- refers to the *person* (individual): this targeting is, from a scientific point of view, generic, that is, it refers to the individual himself/herself, not to a specific individual framed socially and historically[23]; here we have a *subjective "dating" of the analysis*—the subject in question is chosen as a pre-condition for carrying out that analysis (Nussbaum, 2006);

Nota bene: however, within the framework of social wellbeing, the "individual" will be represented by the *entire society*, or the nation.[24]

- refers to the *state* (static profile): the targeting in question represents a "photograph" of the components[25] of a state vector considered adequate, representative, relevant, and practicable for the research in question; here we have an *objective "dating" of the analysis*—the research is carried out exclusively within the framework indicated (allowed) by the respective state vector;
- it targets a *moment*: the targeting in question (more precisely, the establishment of the empirical values of the state vector that refers to the individual) still refers to a certain moment (or, as the case may be, a period of time); here we have a *calendar (temporal) "dating"*[26] *of the analysis*.

Therefore, the concept of wellbeing (denoted B) is a function of two characteristics:

$$B = f\left(P_i^j, V_i^k\right)$$

where P_i^j is the person j examined at moment i; V_i^k is the state vector k, calculated for moment i. The algebraic expression can be written, more simply, as:

$$B = f\left(V_i^{jk}\right)$$

by associating the targeted person with the state vector used.

From a theoretical point of view, several aspects should be highlighted:

- the function f is not a mathematical operator in the known/ standard sense of the term, but only indicates that wellbeing is dependent (quantitatively) on the values that the components of the state vector k associated with person j have at time i;
- of course, the (rather, logical) function f can be transformed into an algebraic function, through certain external assumptions; for example, in most cases, such an algebraic function is constructed as a score function, associating with the different numerical values of the components of the state vector, certain numerical values that enter the "level" of wellbeing;
- the components of the state vector are not substitutable[27]; this is an extremely important issue in the matter of social justice (which is the counterpart of the concept of social wellbeing in this study) and, therefore, it will be the object of a brief methodological development. Generally, two causal (or conditional, or correlational) factors are substitutable if the substitution of one (totally or partially) with the other quantitatively (or, in more subtle cases, even qualitatively) leaves the aggregate result to which the two factors contribute or are presumed to contribute, invariant. Substitutability therefore means at least the following:
  - the two factors are not contradictory in their impact, but are compatible with each other;
  - in addition to compatibility, the two factors are convergent in their impact, that is, they "pursue" the same aggregate result;

– neither of them is redundant, to any extent, in relation to the other.[28]

These considerations can be detailed in a synoptic image such as the one in Fig. 5 (the two factors are denoted by x, y, respectively, and the aggregate result to which they lead is denoted by R). It is worth noting that the range of substitutability between the two factors is very narrow (as I said, in most cases and to the greatest extent, this range is quasi-non-existent).[29]

Discussion

- on the substitutability range one can calculate, of course, according to known mathematical methods (cancellation of the 1st order differential of the welfare/wellbeing function), the marginal rate of substitution ($mr_s^{x/y}$) between the two causal factors of welfare/wellbeing:

$$dR = 0$$

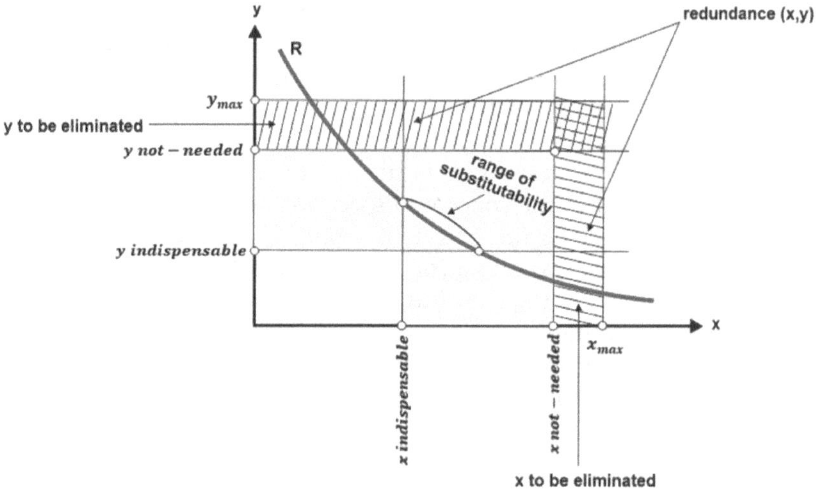

Fig. 5 Range of substitutability between wellbeing factors (*Source* author)

$$df(x, y) = 0$$

$$f_{x'}dx + f_{y'}dy = 0$$

$$mr_s^{x/y} = \frac{dy}{dx} = -\frac{f_{x'}}{f_{y'}} < 0, \text{ since } f_{x'} > 0 \; f_{y'} > 0$$

- with great caution, the mentioned function f could possibly be used only as a transformation operator, not as a calculation one—for example, a variation above a certain threshold of one of the factors may indicate either an increase or a decrease in a so-called indicator (or index) of welfare/wellbeing;
- in Fig. 6, which exemplified the issue of substitutability between welfare/wellbeing factors, the presumed indifference curve for an outcome (level) R of welfare/wellbeing has been given a decreasing-convex shape over the entire domain of definition. This means that welfare/wellbeing is a non-linear function of its causal (or determining) factors. The decreasing-convex shape of the welfare/wellbeing indifference curve reveals an important property of the substitutability between the two factors taken, exemplarily, in the analysis here: namely, that the more "abundant" a factor is in causing welfare relative to the other factor, the greater the amount by which it must change when the other factor changes by one unit (obviously, inverse proportionally), and vice versa. Such a property can be exemplified visually as shown in Fig. 6.

Discussion

The non-linearity of the welfare/wellbeing function can be assumed to lead to a certain graphical form, likely to suggest the dynamics of welfare[30] in relation to the kinematics of the causal factors. If we aggregate all the welfare factors (which, for now, we have not referred to) into a single factor, considering, in addition, that the individual factors have the same impact on the dynamics of welfare as the aggregate factor, in our opinion, the graphical form of the function f is the following (Fig. 7). Such a non-linear form should constitute the main methodological suggestion for constructing an algebraic welfare function. The introduction of the *ratchet effect*[31] not only illustrates (and theoretically

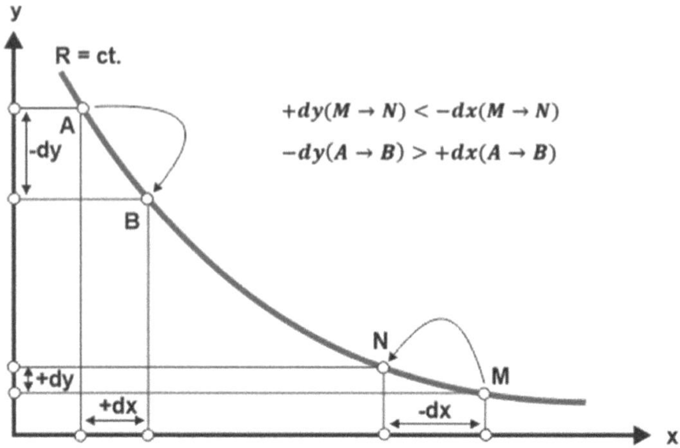

Fig. 6 Variation in the marginal rate of substitution of welfare/wellbeing factors. (*Source* author)

justifies) the non-linearity of the welfare function but also introduces a suggestion (which, however, will not be developed in the present chapter, although we consider that it has a certain broader significance for macroeconomic variables in general) regarding the *quantum* (i.e., discrete) character of these variables.

As said, the non-linear form of the welfare function can be suggested as shown in Fig. 7.

Discussion

- from a subjective point of view, wellbeing is an individual perception, therefore an idiosyncratic assessment of welfare.[32] The rational component of wellbeing, as perceived by a generic individual, is very low (generally, it is non-existent). An individual who declares himself/herself satisfied with his/her wellbeing will not be able to explain why he/she believes he/she enjoys wellbeing, he/she will only be able to declare that he/she feels good or is in a good general human condition;
- from an objective point of view, however, the assessment of wellbeing (i.e., the perception of welfare) will have to receive a more

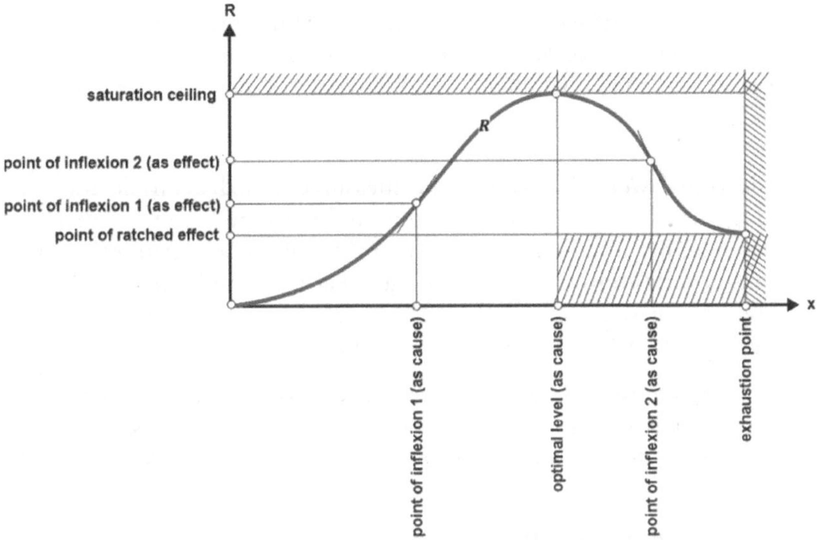

Fig. 7 Non-linear form of welfare function. (*Source* author)

extensive rational component (regardless of whether we refer to individual wellbeing or social wellbeing). This rational component will translate into the selection of objective indicators that have the same meaning–or are proposed to have the same meaning–for each individual and for all individuals (respectively for society, in the case of social wellbeing).

In this chapter, we will be interested in wellbeing from an objective perspective, in terms of both the generic individual and society as a whole, so in a, somewhat mix between wellbeing and welfare. To this end, some extra considerations on the social/societal wellbeing (or welfare) and the individual wellbeing could be of usefulness.

(a) Individual wellbeing

Individual wellbeing, as it will be considered in this chapter, refers to the generic individual, considered by what all empirical individuals have in common (or are assumed to have in common), from the perspective of the perception of wellbeing, on the one hand, and to what is objectively observable, recordable, and inter-personally communicable in this perception, on the other hand. In this regard, I develop the following clarifications:

- individual wellbeing cannot be measured based on indicators that target substantive/economic utility in its narrow sense, of wealth or income, because it is assumed (and this will be my assumption) that the generic individual has more general goals and closer to human dignity (or self-esteem) than the simple relative positioning on the social scale from the perspective of the economic assets held;
  - based on the above, I will use another category of assets, which I consider closer to the evaluations and aspirations of individuals, namely *social assets* or, as it is also known, *social capital*[33];
- the choice of indicators that refer to social capital is, of course, a choice external to the concept of individual wellbeing itself (which, as we have shown, is an idiosyncratic expression of a perception regarding the plenitude[34] of the life. i.e., plenary life of a particular individual), but this is the theoretical price that must be paid in order to obtain a concept (and an associated measure) of generic individual wellbeing. In order to reduce the arbitrariness (which cannot, of course, be entirely eliminated) of such a procedure, I have based, in the choice of the indicators in question, on ethical considerations and social justice ones, which, to some extent, also proceed on the basis of criteria external to the areas of interest;
- from a methodological point of view, the verification of the conditions/indicators of individual wellbeing at their level considered as a standard will lead to the establishment of a benchmark in the matter of individual wellbeing; somehow, such a benchmark will represent the "normal" level of individual wellbeing. The most difficult methodological problem will be the contextualization of such a benchmark from a socio-historical point of view—here the study will try to make a proposal for methodological equivalence,[35] based on equivalence scales (Collins, 2019);

- from an empirical point of view, the level of individual wellbeing must be determined by interpreting the deviation (absolute or relative, as the case may be) of the particular empirical case from the established benchmark (and brought to its equivalent value).
- Social/societal wellbeing

Social wellbeing/welfare refers to the concept of wellbeing applied at the level of a given community (usually the national community, constituted within a state). As in the case of individual wellbeing, social wellbeing will be examined (and even to a much greater extent) from an objective perspective. This perspective is not, however, without vulnerabilities, both conceptual and methodological. I recall some of them:

- social wellbeing (regardless of whether it is seen as aiming at symbolic utility or substantive/economic utility) can be determined either as an aggregate quantity—the wellbeing of the society or community in question—or as an average quantity (for example, if we consider substantive utility measured by income, GDP per capita);
- it is not at all certain which of the two possibilities for calculating social welfare—as an aggregate or as an average—is the most appropriate, since both can be misleading, primarily from a distributional perspective: a large inequality in the level of the considered utility can lead, from the point of view of individual perception, to a considerable gap, either positive or negative, compared to the "objective" measurement of social welfare;
- methodologically, social welfare is not a macro size obtained by adding micro sizes, but rather, the opposite is done: having the macro size, the micro size is obtained, in this case, from the aggregate size of social welfare its average size is obtained;
- the theory of symbolic utility, which captures the significance of social capital, is poorly developed in the literature, with the specialized literature offering only sporadic flashes, usually in contexts that target other research objectives (Nozick, 1993) but which, tangentially, also touch on the issue of symbolic utility. In my opinion, symbolic utility must function as the ultimate "carrier" of substantive

utility (currently, things are exactly the opposite, that is, substantive utility—for example, income or wealth—are carriers of symbolic utility—for example, social position);
- the measurement of social wellbeing has a degree of autonomy, in relation to the effective perception (at the individual level) of the state of wellbeing, much higher than in the case of individual wellbeing. If at the individual level (or, in a slightly more aggregated way, at the level of social or professional communities) the individual in question could be "asked" which indicators he/she considers to describe his/her state of wellbeing, on the contrary, in the case of social wellbeing, this set of indicators (possibly with inflection points or thresholds) will be established by "experts", completely external to individuals as such. In my opinion, there is no other solution that would provide a higher degree of scientificity in this matter.

Therefore, the concept of social welfare will aspire to measure (evaluate and interpret) the state of wellbeing at the level of society, for example, in the most common case in our era, at the level of the national community (organized in national states). If I would have to decide, right now, on the choice between aggregate social welfare and average social welfare, I will opt for aggregate social welfare, based on the following considerations:

- both indicators are, as shown above, almost equally vulnerable to the distribution effect, that is, they can be misleading regarding social inequality within the respective society (Collins, 2019), so, according to this criterion, the choice lies on the indifference curve;
- aggregate social welfare, however, gives a more meaningful assessment, in our opinion, of the potential of the society in question to produce social capital (Bhandari & Yasunobu, 2009) (for the moment, I ignore, again, the issue of distribution, or rather, the issue of social justice involved in the distribution of social capital and, as a result, in the distribution of the economic capital);
- average social welfare is, in any case, a purely statistical result of aggregate social welfare; in this context, determining median social welfare would be more meaningful, but this implies achieving a structure of the population by socio-professional categories relevant from the perspective of social welfare seen through the "filter" of social capital, not economic capital;

- aggregate social welfare captures the synergy effect present in any system (especially in a large system, such as the social system viewed at the national level). This effect cannot be highlighted if one starts from average social welfare towards aggregate welfare, but only by proceeding in reverse.
- Relationship individual wellbeing–social wellbeing

The relationship between individual wellbeing and social wellbeing is complicated, from both a causal and a methodological perspective.

(i) from a causal perspective:

  - it cannot be said either that individual wellbeing is the cause for the formation of social wellbeing, or that social wellbeing causally generates individual wellbeing; there are no logical and, possibly, empirical[36] arguments to establish, with sufficient certainty and justification, the causal arrow between the two concepts[37];
  - however, one cannot deny, neither logically nor empirically, the interdependence between the two categories of wellbeing; it is, of course, a matter of co-evolution: a certain level of social wellbeing generates a certain level of individual wellbeing which, in turn, transmits an impulse for the variation of social wellbeing, and so on;
  - the concept of co-evolution that inter-relates social wellbeing and individual wellbeing no longer presupposes the unilateral identification of cause and effect, but accepts an iterative cause-effect correlation, which is, as known, the very content of the concept of co-evolution[38];

(ii) from a methodological perspective:

  - given the above considerations, social wellbeing will be correlated exclusively with social capital, while individual wellbeing can be correlated with both social capital and economic capital (usually, current income or wealth);
  - given the fact that the (causal and methodological) relationships between social capital and economic capital can also be reduced to a co-evolution relationship, it follows that,

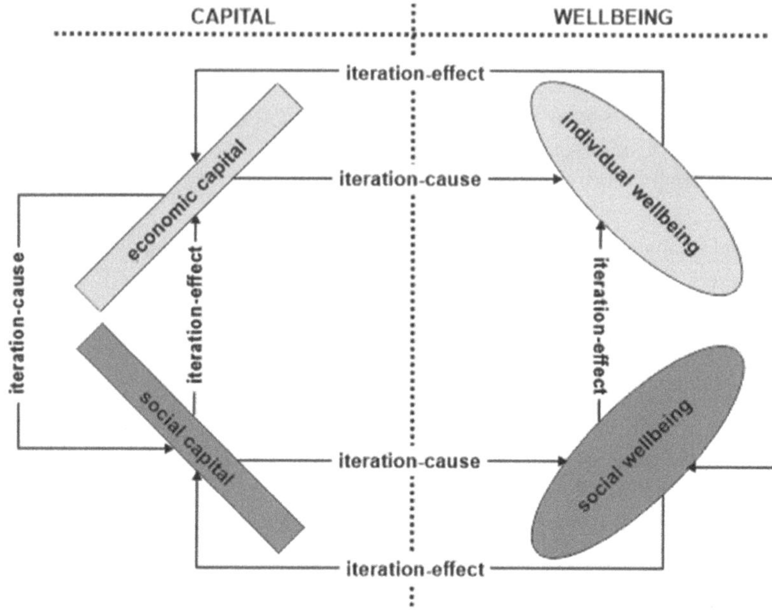

Fig. 8 Co-evolutionary correlations between capital and welfare. *Source* author

from a methodological perspective, the pair *social capital–economic capital* is a very good proxy for the pair *social wellbeing–economic wellbeing*[39] (Garrett, 2018).

Figure 8 systematizes the general and abstract relationships between social wellbeing and individual wellbeing.

2.2 *Logical Correlations Social Wellbeing—Social Capital*

(a) Direct and inverse reaction social capital–social wellbeing

The co-evolutionary relationship *social capital–social wellbeing* does not exclude the claiming of a beginning in this relationship. In my opinion, the greatest logical justification is the direct relationship (i.e., a direct, constitutive causality) from social capital to social wellbeing. The existence and variation of social capital necessarily (although non-linearly) have the effect of the existence and variation (directly proportional) of social wellbeing.

I will resume Fig. 15, from Chapter 6, Annex 1, to which I will add a logical mechanism by which the social capital could causally condition the wellbeing, at both individual and social level[40] (the denotations are: C for communication; P for participation; M for mutualization; F for freedom; T for trust; S for symmetry)—Fig. 9.

The social wellbeing (welfare or social progress) is generated by the categories of social capital established according to the criterion of socialization, that is, according to the criterion that "transfers" social capital from individual/idiosyncratic perception to the objective/communitarian level,[41] i.e., communication, participation, and mutualization. As can be seen, all six categories of social capital involve human interaction.

In this context, I consider that, from social welfare to social capital, a reverse reaction (feedback) is formed, which constitutes a kind of *sui generis* validation of the social capital involved in the direct (causal) reaction. Of course, the concatenation in time of these direct and reverse, linked reactions produces a co-evolutionary result of social capital, respectively of social welfare.

(b) Stability in the social capital–social welfare relationship

How stable is the *social capital–social welfare* relationship? First of all, we must accept the fact that none of the categories of social capital can grow indefinitely, as is the case (hypothetically, however) of economic capital. It can be assumed with sufficient reason that, at the community level, a "saturation" with social capital will occur which, thus, will reach its functional growth limits.[42] Does this mean that social welfare will stop growing, once the growth of social capital stops? The answer is both affirmative and negative. It is affirmative in the sense that, from the point of view of direct causality, there is indeed a cessation of the exercise of an impulse to increase social welfare, and it is negative in the sense that the increase in social welfare is also a synergistic effect, which leads to its increase as a result of the structural and functional combination of the categories of social capital. We could make an analogy here with the theory of utility (total and marginal), but without, of course, understanding by this that social welfare is a kind of substantive utility (an aspect previously discussed

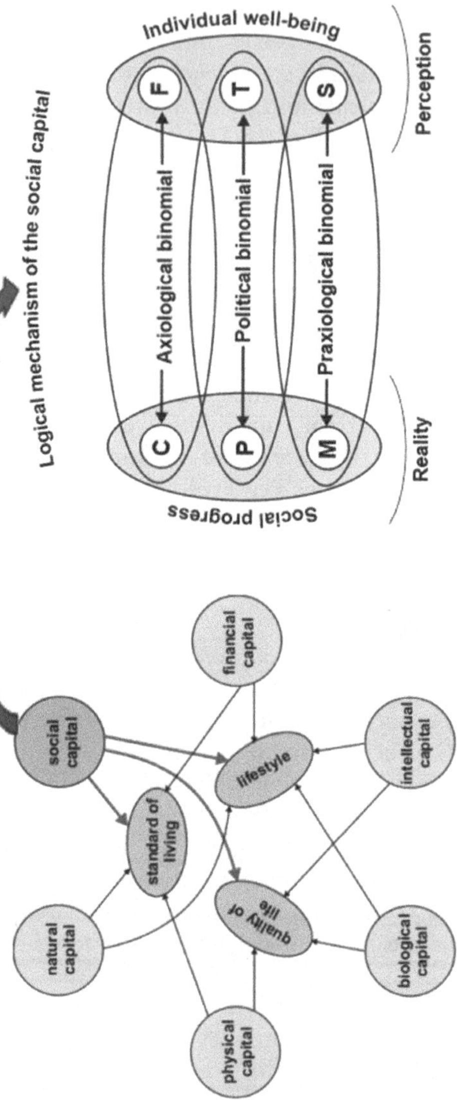

Fig. 9 Co-evolutionary correlations between capital and welfare (*Source* author)

in detail). Based on this analogy, we can synoptically represent the stability aspect of the *social capital–social welfare* relationship as shown in Fig. 10.

Discussion

- the "closest" asymptotic threshold occurs in the case of the category of social capital called *participation*. Indeed, participation is the most restrictive type of social capital because it cannot be expanded arbitrarily. For example, participation in democratic political life is restricted from the perspective of direct participation (direct democracy) given the growth of the population or the universalization of the citizen's right to vote and to be elected in the process of political leadership of society. As for the alternative to the difficulty of direct democracy, namely representative democracy, it is obvious that, in this case too, participation is restricted to the delegation of the exercise of sovereignty to those elected as representatives (for example, members of Parliament);
- the next asymptotic threshold that is reached is that of *mutualization*. Indeed, it can be accepted that mutualization (either of advantage or even of participation—for example, the mandate) "goes" further than participation, the restrictions acting on it being reduced (or fewer) than those acting on participation;
- finally, at the latest, the asymptotic threshold of *communication* is reached. Again, it seems obvious that, compared to mutualization, communication is much more "relaxed", being able to grow more. In fact, communication is the basis of the two types of social capital previously evoked but it has reserves of expansion beyond them, being able to refer simply to community life that is anchored neither in participation nor in mutualization (for example, communication relationships from the perspective of empathy, altruism, benevolence).

The graphical representation in Fig. 11 identifies the allure of total (aggregate) social welfare. Based on it, as I have announced above, a curve of marginal social welfare[43]can be deduced (for now only graphically).

(c) Axiological implications in the *social capital–social wellbeing* relationship

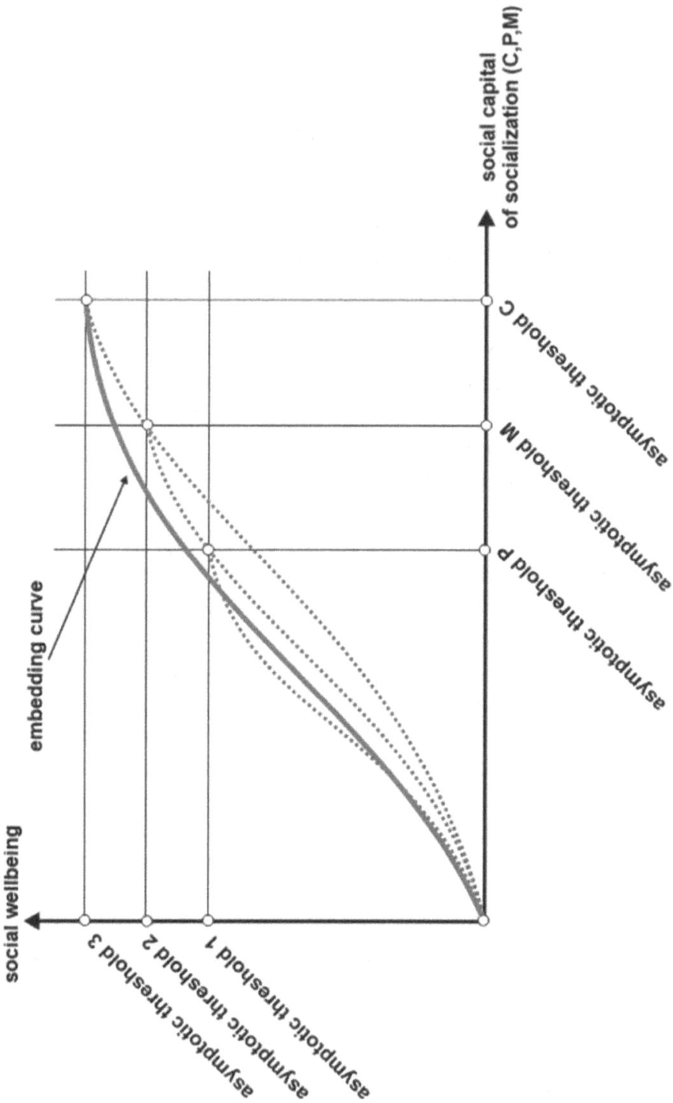

Fig. 10 Involving social capital in achieving social wellbeing. (*Source* author)

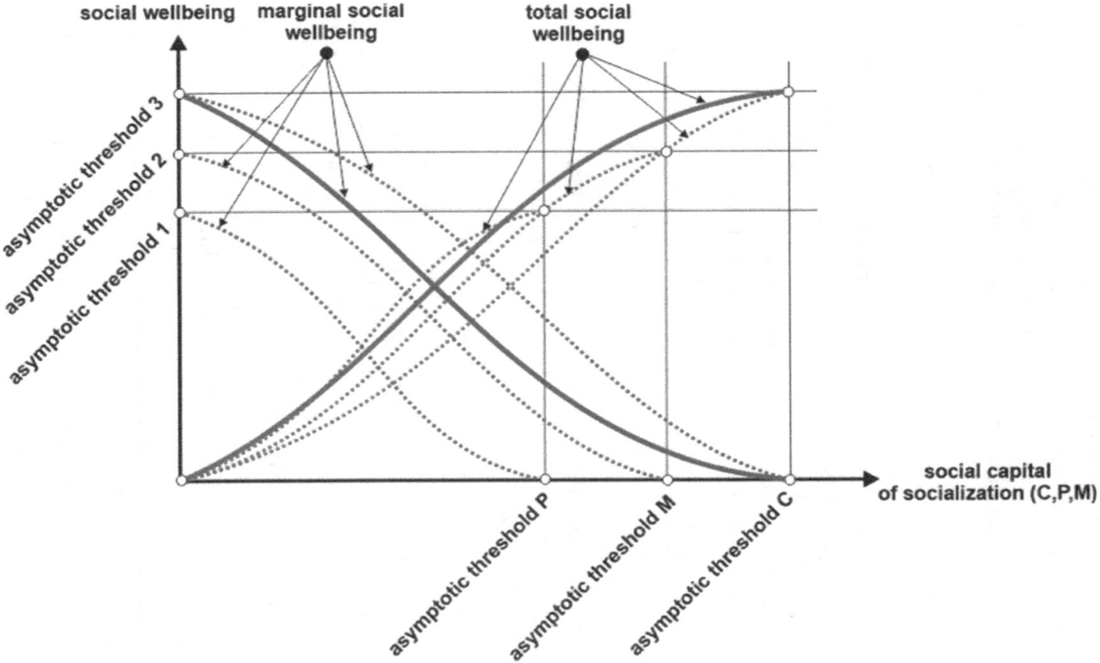

Fig. 11 Generic curves of total and marginal social wellbeing. (*Source* author)

In my opinion, *prima facie*, social capital is cause and social wellbeing is effect (even if we accept a general co-evolutionary relationship between the two variables), but it is not certain that this is also the perception of individuals (or the global opinion at the level of society). This perception depends on the scale of values of each individual. In this sense, the following comments can be formulated on this perspective:

- "establishing" social capital as cause and social wellbeing as effect has a *procedural* significance—society/state ensures the cause that will produce the effect,[44] while reversing the causal relationship, from social wellbeing to social capital has a *final result* significance[45]—society/state directly ensures the final result, subsequently leaving the co-evolutionary relationships to unfold by themselves;
- it is not a question, here, of ordering (even lexicographically) between social capital and social welfare, but of establishing (as far as possible) whether one or the other, or both, constitute values in themselves, that is, goals of individuals (and society) or, on the contrary, means;
- in the hypothesis in which social welfare is the goal and social capital represents the means, the following logical and axiological consequences can be drawn:

  - the state (level, structure, dynamics) of social welfare can only be established by each individual for himself/herself, because freedom means exactly this (apophatic definition): the absence of private constraint on the establishment of the individual goal;
  - since social capital is to be the means, and, as we have shown above, one of the categories of social capital (based on the criterion of individuation) is freedom itself, it means that freedom, being a means, can be the object of private constraint;
  - a contradiction therefore results, which means that, from a logical point of view, wellbeing cannot be an end, which entails the consequence that social capital (for example, freedom) is a means;

- in the hypothesis in which social capital is the end and social wellbeing represents the means, the following logical and axiological consequences can be drawn:

- the state (level, structure, dynamics) of social capital (in fact, of all six types of social capital, or, if we refer to the pairs proposed above (see Fig. 9), of the three pairs of social capital) is established by the individual;
- this time, no contradiction arises between the fact that freedom is "established" by the individual, since, *eo ipso*, the definition of freedom is respected;
- since social wellbeing is a means, it can also be the object of private constraints.[46]

• Social justice implications in the *social capital–social welfare* relationship

The social justice implications of the relationship between social capital and social wellbeing seem the most obvious and will, in fact, form the very core of the present chapter. My opinion on this matter can be summarized, after the above discussion, as follows: *the purpose of social justice is the formation, maintenance, and improvement of social capital.* The main, although not the only, means for this is the formation, maintenance, and improvement of social wellbeing. From these results a very important aspect of a moral nature: decreases or worsening of social wellbeing can be accepted if, by doing so, social capital is preserved or even, if possible, social capital increases. We intuit, here, and in fact propose, the formulation of a *principle of difference* applicable to social capital, analogous to the one proposed and instrumented by Rawls (1999), but he does this with respect to economic capital–income and wealth, in the following terms: *the decrease in social welfare is acceptable if the endowment of society with social capital increases more than in any feasible other alternative* (for example, by avoiding the decrease in social welfare). The basic features of this difference principle, which we propose to call the *social principle of difference*,[47] are the following:

- the Rawlsian principle of difference applies, as we have already said, to economic capital, while the social principle of difference applies to social capital;
- the application (functioning) of the economic (Rawlsian) principle of difference is measurable in a cardinal way (through the difference between the *ex ante* and *ex post* distribution of income/wealth, respectively, following an increase in economic inequality in society,

measured at the level of these two macroeconomic indicators), while the application (functioning) of the social principle of difference will have to be measured ordinally (for example, by measuring the deviation of society's endowment with social capital before and after a decrease in social wellbeing) (Field, 2008);

- if the economic (Rawlsian) principle of difference targets an economic category—the most disadvantaged category/class in terms of holding economic capital, income or/and wealth—the social principle of difference targets society as a whole. The justification for this perspective consists of the following:
  - the variation of social capital, in any of the forms considered in this chapter, does not apply differentially, precisely because it is *social* capital: for example, an increase in the degree of individual freedom applies, in accordance with positive law, to any member of society and to all of them; likewise, an increase in communication at the level of society does not apply differentially to different social groups, but to all social groups, or to the communitarian level[48];
  - social capital is not produced by each individual autonomously, as is the case with economic capital,[49] but only as a global result, at the level of society; logically, social cooperation is a condition of sufficiency for the production of economic capital, while, in the case of social capital, social cooperation is a condition of necessity;
- although it is not a difference in relevance of the first two previous differences, there is still a difference between the two principles: while the economic (Rawlsian) principle of difference applies to an *increase*[50] in the command variable (in this case, economic inequality), the social principle of difference applies to a *decrease* in the associated command variable (in this case, social welfare).

Of course, it is expected that the two principles of difference, one economic, the other social, can be integrated into a unitary theory of social justice, which is still incoming.

3 Modelling of the Triad: Social Wellbeing, Social Justice, and Social Capital

3.1 The Function of Social Wellbeing

In order to extract the function of social welfare, in its meaning discussed above, that is, removed from the imperative of substantive utility (either total or average) at the level of society, it is necessary to clarify whether it is a procedural concept or a final result concept. In fact, I will opt from the beginning for a procedural vision of social welfare, that is, a vision that I will argue in the following:

- social wellbeing cannot be a concept of the finality or final result type,[51] because this means that the different hypostases of this concept are comparable to each other[52]; the comparability of two hypostases of social wellbeing is, of course, much more accessible than the comparability of individual preferences or utilities, due to a much higher "objective" character that removes the concept of social wellbeing from the idiosyncrasy of individual subjects, but, nevertheless, the association of social wellbeing with social capital brings back the imponderable aspects that we have just escaped;
- the entire logic, above exposed, which causally and functionally links economic capital, economic wellbeing, social capital, and social wellbeing in an iterative (and, possibly, self-sustaining, i.e., autopoietic) mechanism "recommends" the option of the procedural character of the social welfare function, rather than the finality (final result) one;
- the option for the procedural character of the social wellbeing function also avoids considering social wellbeing as a Pareto-type variable (or indicator); the significance of such avoidance consists, at least, in the following:
  - the Pareto model implies the idea of optimum (or optimization)[53]; however, social wellbeing is not presumed to be subject to optimization criteria (either minimization or maximization);
  - it is extremely difficult to identify a criterion for improving a component of the system called social wellbeing, since it is not a system that exhibits (possibly final) states, but rather propensities;

- but, the propensity properties refer immediately, from a methodological point of view, to processes or procedures and not to "frozen" final states.

Based on the above, the social welfare function, which we can denote by SW_i^j—social wellbeing at time i in society j—can be formalized as follows:

$$SW_i^j = f\left(C_i^j, P_i^j, M_i^j\right)$$

with the already known notations for the basic components of social capital of socialization.

3.2 The Function of Social Justice

If social wellbeing is a direct function of social capital of socialization (hence a function of three independent variables[54]), social justice is a direct function of the components of social capital of individualization/individuation—denoting social justice at time i in society j, with SJ_i^j (i.e., also a function of three independent variables), we can write:

$$SJ_i^j = g\left(F_i^j, T_i^j, S_i^j\right)$$

with the already known notations for the basic components of social capital of individualization. The justification for this theoretical proposal consists in the following:

- social justice, by definition, concerns the individual, not society as a set of individuals, no matter how homogenized that society may be from various perspectives; as a result, the components of social capital of individualization, not those of social capital of socialization, are relevant;
- it is true, at the same time, that social justice concerns the individual as a *sui generis* individual, not as a particularized individual; however, it is not about the so-called representative individual (operated, in particular, by economists, but, in some cases, also by sociologists), or about the average individual.[55] The solution is the construction of a relatively abstract individual, which does not hypostasize in socio-historical individuals but which takes on the basic, common, and

relatively invariant characteristics of all possible socio-historical individuals in the context of a given society, at a given time; it is, if I can express myself in this way, a *concrete non-particular individual*,[56] but not yet a general individual;
- indexing by society (the upper index j) is not superfluous, since it is obvious that both social wellbeing and social justice are strongly contextualized historically (and therefore also geographically, culturally, etc.). Therefore, when comparative analyses of two societies are made, at a given time, their spatial indexing is needed;
- indexing by time (bottom index i) is also useful because any society evolves, and this evolution leads to changes in both social wellbeing and social justice. Therefore, in order to distinguish temporally, when analysing the same society at two different points in time, this temporal indexing is needed.

3.3 The Functional of Social Wellbeing

We recall that, from the point of view of mathematical methodology, a functional is a function whose independent variables are, in turn, functions of another independent variable. In our case, writing such a functional should consider the following:

- social wellbeing is the dependent variable in the logical model we propose;
- social wellbeing, as the dependent variable, is, in turn, a function of the three independent variables mentioned;
- on the other hand, social wellbeing is a dependent variable that depends on an independent variable, namely social justice;
- at the same time, the independent variable of social wellbeing is, again, a dependent variable on three other independent variables, as mentioned;
- from all of the above, it follows that, for a complete description of the model of social wellbeing as depending on social justice, a series of developments for reasoning analytics are still necessary.

Our hypothesis in this research is the following: *social justice is a vehicle for implementing social wellbeing*. For the moment, we make some very general clarifications regarding this hypothesis:

- social justice "controls" categories of social capital of individualization/individuation. How can we justify that, by operationalizing them, we reach the "control" of the categories of social capital of socialization, that is, the implementation of social welfare? I believe that the following arguments can be retained:
  - *first*, such a relationship between the two categories of social capital occurs through norms, interactions, contracts, and perceptions;
  - *second*, as we have seen, the categories of social capital of individualization/individuation can only manifest (and therefore be implemented) through the interaction of individuals; but, through this interaction that establishes the limits of the social capital of individualization, the categories of social capital of socialization are produced, which constitute the seeds of social wellbeing;
- social justice functions as an institutional device for *validating* social wellbeing although it has also an important role (precisely through the categories of social capital of individualization/individuation that it promotes) in *generating* social wellbeing. Through these two roles—contribution to the generation of social wellbeing, especially by creating the seed of it, and respectively contribution to the validation (or invalidation, as the case may be) of social wellbeing in its version of substance, as we will show immediately—social justice is constituted and functions as a vehicle "carrying" social wellbeing;
- as a vehicle of social wellbeing, social justice has co-evolutionary relations with social wellbeing (in both hypostases of the latter: as germs/seeds, respectively as substance), exactly as co-evolutionary relations exist between individuals of each of the two categories of social capital.

On these bases, social wellbeing is presented, for the moment, in the following three conceptual perspectives:

(a) as a *direct function* of categories of social capital of socialization;
(b) as a *structural and functional integrator* of two own phases of genesis and evolution: 1) as *germs/seeds*, which is a phase generated

by functions performed by categories of social capital of socialization, respectively (2) as *substance*, which is a phase generated by the impact on the functions of realization of categories of social capital of socialization in forming the substantive utilities (or economic utilities);

(c) as a *functional*: its direct function (of categories of social capital of socialization) is, indirectly, dependent on social justice, which is, in turn, a direct function of categories of social capital of individualization/individuation.

From a formal point of view, I will develop the third perspective mentioned above, by an analytical examination. It can be written successively:

$$F_i^j = \beta_1\left(P_i^j, M_i^j\right) \rightarrow \begin{cases} P_i^j = \beta_{1P}^{-1}(F_i^j) \\ M_i^j = \beta_{1M}^{-1}(F_i^j) \end{cases}$$

$$T_i^j = \beta_2\left(C_i^j, P_i^j\right) \rightarrow \begin{cases} C_i^j = \beta_{2C}^{-1}(T_i^j) \\ P_i^j = \beta_{2P}^{-1}(T_i^j) \end{cases}$$

$$S_i^j = \beta_3(C_i^j, M_i^j) \rightarrow \begin{cases} C_i^j = \beta_{3C}^{-1}(S_i^j) \\ M_i^j = \beta_{3M}^{-1}(S_i^j) \end{cases}$$

To be mentioning that each of the categories of individualizing social capital is derivable as two distinct functions of two of the categories of socializing social capital.

Thus:
$C_i^j = \beta_{2C}^{-1}(T_i^j)$ and $C_i^j = \beta_{3C}^{-1}(S_i^j)$
$P_i^j = \beta_{1P}^{-1}(F_i^j)$ and $P_i^j = \beta_{2P}^{-1}(T_i^j)$
$M_i^j = \beta_{1M}^{-1}(F_i^j)$ and $M_i^j = \beta_{3M}^{-1}(S_i^j)$

This can have the following interpretation:

- the (simultaneous) functioning of two causal "channels" for the formation of each of the categories of social capital of socialization:
  - *participation*: can be generated either by the existence of freedom or by the existence of trust;

- *mutualization*: can be generated either by the existence of freedom or by the existence of symmetry;
- *communication*: can be generated either by the existence of trust or by the existence of symmetry;

- the functioning of a single causal "channel" for the formation of each category of social capital of socialization, but which presents equivalent effects depending on the social capital of individualization/individuation from which it is claimed; this equivalence of effect implies the following algebraic equalities:

$$\beta_{1P}^{-1}\left(F_i^j\right) = \beta_{2P}^{-1}(T_i^j)$$

$$\beta_{1M}^{-1}\left(F_i^j\right) = \beta_{3M}^{-1}(S_i^j)$$

$$\beta_{2C}^{-1}\left(T_i^j\right) = \beta_{3C}^{-1}(S_i^j)$$

- the existence of a redundancy, at the level of society, in terms of the formation of social capital categories of socialization based on the social capital of individualization/individuation. In other words, the existence of a redundancy, at the level of society, in terms of the generation of social wellbeing through the functioning of social justice (Barry, 2015).

Therefore, returning to the problem of the functional that characterizes the working of social wellbeing, it can be now written:

$$JS_i^j = g(\beta_1, \beta_2, \beta_3)$$

$$BS_i^j(I) = f\left(C_i^j, P_i^j, M_i^j\right) = f\left[\beta_{2C}^{-1}\left(T_i^j\right), \beta_{1P}^{-1}\left(F_i^j\right), \beta_{1M}^{-1}(F_i^j)\right], \text{ or.}$$
$$BS_i^j(II) = f\left(C_i^j, P_i^j, M_i^j\right) = f\left[\beta_{2C}^{-1}\left(T_i^j\right), \beta_{1P}^{-1}\left(F_i^j\right), \beta_{3M}^{-1}(S_i^j)\right], \text{ or.}$$
$$BS_i^j(III) = f\left(C_i^j, P_i^j, M_i^j\right) = f\left[\beta_{2C}^{-1}(T_i^j), \beta_{2P}^{-1}(T_i^j), \beta_{1M}^{-1}(F_i^j)\right], \text{ or.}$$
$$BS_i^j(V) = f\left(C_i^j, P_i^j, M_i^j\right) = f\left[\beta_{2C}^{-1}(T_i^j), \beta_{2P}^{-1}(T), \beta_{3M}^{-1}(S_i^j)\right], \text{ or.}$$
$$BS_i^j(VI) = f\left(C_i^j, P_i^j, M_i^j\right) = f\left[\beta_{3C}^{-1}(S_i^j), \beta_{1P}^{-1}(F_i^j), \beta_{1M}^{-1}(F_i^j)\right], \text{ or.}$$

$$BS_i^j(VII) = f\left(C_i^j, P_i^j, M_i^j\right) = f\left[\beta_{3C}^{-1}(S_i^j), \beta_{1P}^{-1}(F_i^j), \beta_{3M}^{-1}(S_i^j)\right], \text{ or.}$$
$$BS_i^j(VII) = f\left(C_i^j, P_i^j, M_i^j\right) = f\left[\beta_{3C}^{-1}(S_i^j), \beta_{2P}^{-1}(T_i^j), \beta_{1M}^{-1}(F_i^j)\right], \text{ or}$$

$$BS_i^j(VIII) = f\left(C_i^j, P_i^j, M_i^j\right) = f\left[\beta_{3C}^{-1}(S_i^j), \beta_{2P}^{-1}(T_i^j), \beta_{3M}^{-1}(S_i^j)\right]$$

3.4 Sketching a Co-evolutionary Model: Social Wellbeing–Social Justice–Social Capital

Integrating social wellbeing and social justice into a single model obviously means integrating into a supersystem two systems that "obey" different logics: social wellbeing is based on a finalist logic (a logic of result, or final state), while social justice is based on a proceduralist logic. To make two analogies with some significance, we can say: a) while social justice is claimed from the process, social wellbeing is claimed from the state; b) from a logical perspective, it can be said that, framing the discussion into the structure of a syllogism, social justice constitutes the two premises of the syllogism,[57] while social wellbeing constitutes the conclusion of the syllogism in question.

It is obvious that a co-evolutionary model of the social wellbeing–social justice "package" exactly implements the hypothesis of the chapter, namely the fact that social wellbeing, as a result, is (also) generated by social justice, as a process. Therefore, based on the results and conclusions obtained so far, here I will design a logical co-evolutionary model of this institutional "package".

The essence of a co-evolutionary model[58] consists in the functional correlation (therefore, implicitly structurally one) of the reciprocal reaction norms. A reaction norm is a quantitative measure[59] of the response of a system to the impulse (action norm) received from another system with which the first system is in interaction. In the same sense, the first system will have a reaction to the reaction of the second system, and so on. The correlation of these reaction norms gives the interactional evolution of the two systems involved, i.e., the property of co-evolution.[60] The co-evolutionary logical model of *social wellbeing–social justice* is based on the following:

- Notations:
- J: social justice system

- W: social wellbeing system
- N_i^J: reaction norm of the social justice system, at time i, to the action (or reaction, as the case may be[61]) of the social welfare system
- N_i^W: reaction norm of the social wellbeing system, at time i, to the action (or reaction, as the case may be) of the social justice system
- F_i^J: fetality range of the social justice system[62]
- F_i^W: fetality range of the social wellbeing system
- Functional conditions
- $\{N_i^J\} \in \{F_i^W\}$
- $\{N_i^W\} \in \{F_i^J\}$

To describe and analyse the social wellbeing–social justice co-evolutionary model, we will use the graphic representation in Fig. 12, which takes over the entire verbal description above, and synthesizes the procedural role of social justice as an institutional vehicle for achieving final social wellbeing, integrating the social capital (notations: I is for income, A is for assets/wealth).

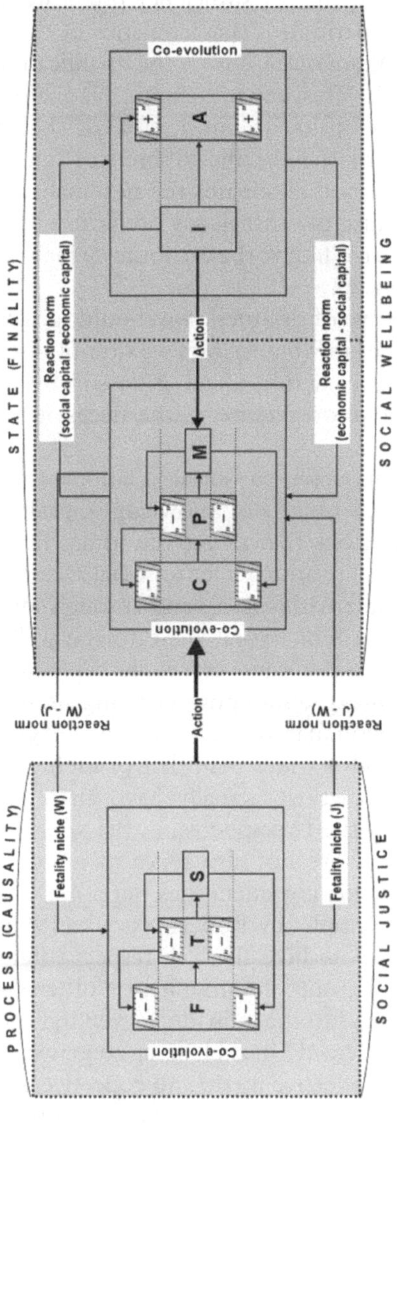

Fig. 12 Meanings that positional relative social wellbeing can have (*Source* author)

Notes

1. I remind the reader, that by sufficiency predicates of a concept we understand those attributes/characteristics of that concept which, once verified simultaneously, ensure the qualification of the concept in question as such. This way of definition is analogous to the Aristotelian way of definition (identification of the proximate genus and introduction of the specific difference) but is more general. Moreover, this method eliminates the nominalization of the proximate genus, because the sufficiency predicates list, in a "cascade", as through successive filters, the attributes which ultimately specify the respective concept.
2. From the perspective of rightness, we should speak of person rather than individual, but in what follows we do not distinguish between the two terms, considering them inter-substitutable. When the needs of argumentation require it, the necessary specification will be made.
3. Cognitive relations refer to social relations that target objects (including people as objects of knowledge), praxiological relations refer to social relations that target the interaction of people with nature, and practical relations refer to social relations that target the interaction of people with society and among individual humans.
4. We do not want to limit moral value to the well-known concept of the good, because it can very easily slip into the concept of useful. In this context, although everything useful can be a good, not everything good has to be useful. So, logically, the significant sphere of good is wider than that of useful (some researchers believe, however, that we actually have an intersection, not an inclusion, between the two spheres, in the sense that there can be types of useful that are not also types of good), but we do not develop such semantic considerations here.
5. Summoned, for example, by Robert Nozick (1999).
6. It is important to note here that self-respect (dignity) never refers to the collectivity, group, community, or other social aggregative structures, but always to the individual, even if, inevitably, he/she is sociologically "immersed" in such an aggregative structure. Therefore, there are no collective merits, no collective guilt, no collective obligations, no collective responsibilities, but only individual ones.

7. Although the human nature is, principled (at least from the time horizon accessible to the human being), invariant, the term co-evolution for the pair natural law—positive law is not inconsistently used, because the natural law constitutes the acceptance, at the societal level, of the normative consequences of the human nature—so, the sphere of the acknowledged consequences of the human nature within the natural law is not invariant, so it can be subject to evolution. In fact, the natural law (by contrast to the human nature) is also an artefact, like the positive law.
8. From a logical point of view, this causal relationship signifies a legalization (or public codification) of legitimacy.
9. Obviously, not in the sense of establishing new natural rights, because natural law is invariant, but in the sense of additionally specifying the set of natural rights, as well as the ways in which natural rights are found in positive rights.
10. Public codification must be understood to mean, simultaneously, two properties: a) the codification is carried out by the public power (the state); b) the codification is, from an informational point of view, publicly accessible (in practice, such public informational accessibility—or transparency—is ensured by the publication of the norms in a consecrated document—in Romania this is the Monitorul Oficial/The Official Monitor).
11. We specify that moral norms are not codified, but this aspect does not affect their quality as norms. When a moral norm is publicly codified, it becomes a positive (legal) norm.
12. Thus, the norm with the greatest legal force is the Constitution. Then come organic laws, ordinary laws, government decisions, and the like, which together form primary legislation. Based on primary legislation, secondary legislation is developed/codified (methodologies, procedures, institutional mechanisms that serve to implement primary legislation). Government ordinances (adopted during the parliamentary recess) and government emergency ordinances (adopted during the parliamentary activity period) are considered laws, subject to their ratification in Parliament.
13. Often, in the specialized literature, the sufficiency of a set of principles (or predicates, as the case may be) is also called completeness. From a semantic point of view, the two terms—sufficiency, respectively completeness—are obviously equivalent.

14. There is, of course, the problem of Gödel's two theorems. but, as is known, the theorems in question have a relatively limited "validity": they refer only to axiomatized theories and, within them, only to those theories that include arithmetic (since the theorems in question are "dependent", from the point of view of demonstration, on the natural numbers). In this sense, theories of rightness could "escape" from Gödel's constraint (*Nota bene*: Wittgenstein doubted the relevance of Gödel's theorems, given precisely the extremely limited scope of their validity for the very wide spectrum of human reason and action).
15. It should be noted that this characteristic is not, in turn, redundant with respect to the one requiring the primitive character of the principles. Indeed, all principles can be primitive and, nevertheless, at least two of them may not be independent of each other.
16. Correspondence truth is the concept of truth proposed by Aristotle and refers to the semantic coincidence between the statement that describes a factual without verifying/inspecting that factual and the statement that describes the same factual by verifying/inspecting the factual in question. A version of correspondence truth (especially targeted by the empirical sciences) is the semantic coincidence between a predictive statement about a factual and a descriptive statement about that factual.
17. Here we could refer to efficacy instead of possibility, but we consider that what is truly relevant, from a methodological point of view, is the possibility of rightness being done and not the actual degree of doing. The degree of doing is, of course, important, although we could hardly accept degrees of rightness. However, just as degrees of truth are accepted in the theory of science (with the necessary semantic clarifications), it would perhaps not be an exaggeration to accept, in the theory of rightness, degrees of doing it (but these analytical developments will not be pursued further in this chapter).
18. We refer here to the most common acceptance of utility, namely to the utility of the economic type or, as it is known, to the substantive utility.
19. See Veenhoven, R. (1991) *Questions on happiness: classical topics, modern answers, blind spots*, in Strack, F., Argyle, M. and Schwarz, N. (Eds) *Subjective Wellbeing: An Interdisciplinary Approach*, Pergamon Press: Great Britain (apud Daniel Teghe and Kathryn

Rendell: *Social Wellbeing: A Literature Review*, Central Queensland University, August, 2005).

20. An example of a procedural scheme is the theory of justice as equity/fairness, proposed by John Rawls, and an example of the final result scheme is the approach of capabilities, proposed by Martha C. Nussbaum.
21. According to the terminology used in this book, we have to do rather with an objectified, not an objective, concept. (*Nota bene*: in this case, the concept is understood as a cognitive artefact, of course).
22. See my considerations in the matter, provided in Chapter 7.
23. Although, of course, applied empirical analyzes will have to specify this frame in a more detailed way.
24. The distinctions operated in the specialized literature between *society–state–nation–people* (e.g., Grotius, Rawls, Nussbaum) are not relevant to the objectives of the present chapter, although, from the perspective of social justice, certain considerations will be made, at the appropriate time.
25. These components are established autonomously, before the applied study. Their choice is based on a theory (or principles) self-standing which, for the case applied, is constituted by an external methodological framework (i.e., exogenously).
26. This time, according to common language, quotes are no longer justified.
27. This is the crucial reason why the logical function *F* cannot, in general, be transformed into (or interpreted as) a score—like algebraic function, because the weights allocated to the components of the state vector—they being, themselves, subjective and, possibly, arbitrary, because they are "expert opinions"—involves the substitutability of these components.
28. Obviously, if there was such a redundancy, the amount that falls under redundancy could be eliminated (if there is an "order" to eliminate redundancy, that is, if a certain factor qualifies the first for elimination—totally or partially—is a separate problem, which will be ignored here, being too special for the chapter goals). This elimination would act, *mutatis mutandis*, like an Occam's razor.
29. For example, one can imagine a substitutability between freedom (or some concrete liberties) and security (as is the case in the context of Covid-19 pandemic) but, of course, it has a very narrow

margin of manœuvre, some citizens (namely, those who demonstrate against the restrictions imposed by authorities) believe that the two elements are completely non-substitutable.

30. I will choose, from now on, to use the term welfare for the social wellbeing, and the term wellbeing for the individual wellbeing. This choice is (partially) based on the standard use of the syntagma welfare state—it is obvious that, in this syntagma, the state provides wellbeing at the social level, so it provides welfare.
31. Proposed, in the economic theory, by James Duesenberry (in 1949), regarding the consumption as a function of the current income (such a function of consumption is proposed by Keynes). There is also a ratchet effect on investment (proposed by Arthur Smithies). Both proposals aimed to improve the realism of the Hicks model on economic growth (a consumption-investment model), by endogenizing the model. It is, however, obviously, that such a ratchet effect can also be extended in the field of wellbeing (for example, minimal income—social assistance—or even the minimum wage is designed from the perspective of such a ratchet effect that prevents the standard of living from decreasing below a certain level considered incompatible with human dignity or a right society.
32. Etymologically, wellbeing means good condition, that is, a well state, without a concretization (substantive, symbolic, institutional, etc.) punctual, rational, or calculable as score-function.
33. I remind the reader that the concept of social capital has been extensively discussed in Chapter 6 (Annex 1). Of course, *mutatis mutandis*, social capital will also form the basis for examining the concept of social wellbeing (welfare).
34. In a way, the vagueness of a term as plenarity is necessary to carry out qualitative reasoning, although the difficulties that it puts under the empirical aspect will have to receive, at the right time, less vague solutions.
35. The problem of methodological equivalence is particularly difficult and problematic, because a "normal" social–historical context will have to be chosen.
36. I have not performed such analyzes (involving huge methodological precautions); it is, rather, an assumption.

37. Of course, we can play with modeling and econometrically estimations, for the sake of publishing articles, but scientificity (as a factual testability) of these superfluous exercises is almost null.
38. Obviously, a more applied study (which will not be carried out in this chapter, which has another fundamental objective) will have to reach the logical and quantitative formalization of the co-evolution process (and, from a statistical point of view, between the two indicators assigned). As it is known, Lotka-Volterra equations describe exactly the co-evolution phenomenon within the *prey–predator* pattern.
39. Of course, such a correspondence is neither absolute nor linear; it is, rather, a conceptual correspondence.
40. The wellbeing or welfare at the social/societal level could also be named social/societal progress if some (validating) axiology is considered.
41. This process is analogous to the process of objectification of intersubjectivity, which underlies Popper's constitution of the third world.
42. For example, the COVID-19 pandemic has drastically reduced the possibilities of communication within the community. However, this is a situation of external (autonomous) shock on the category of social capital called communication, and not a phenomenon of its own, intrinsic (endogenous) of the respective category of social capital. Of course, positive law—in the case discussed, emergency ordinances and military ordinances—has established endogenous prohibitions on communication (travel, gatherings, etc.) but only as a legal reflex of the external, autonomous shock.
43. Marginal social wellbeing can be determined either for each category of social capital, i.e., separately, or (if there is a formal way of aggregating the cumulative effect of the variation of each category of social capital) for the entire social capital of socialization. The formula for calculating marginal social welfare is: $SW_i^m = \frac{\Delta SW_i}{\Delta_i^{SC_k}}$, where ΔSW_i denotes social wellbeing at time i, and SC_i^k denotes social capital of type k at time i (obviously, $k \in \{1,2,3\}$, where $k = 1$ means social capital of the communication type, $k = 2$ means social capital of the participation type, $k = 3$ means social capital of the mutualization type.

44. For example, this is the essence of Rawls's theory of social justice, which requires that, at the moment of concluding the social contract, the basic political principles be configured so that will give what he calls the basic structure of society (in particular, and from the perspective of positive law, exactly the Constitution of that society).
45. For example, this is the essence of the outcome theory of social justice, called the capabilities approach as proposed by Martha C. Nussbaum.
46. It should be noted that public constraints (of course, within the constitutional framework, i.e., respecting the basic political structure of society) are legitimate, in terms of both goals and means.
47. Correlatively, Rawls's difference principle regarding economic capital should be called the *economic* difference principle.
48. The fact that there may be accidents, at the individual level, or at the group level, due to external causes and independent of the variation of social capital itself, is not relevant for the principled discussion carried out here. It can be stated that there are no favored social groups, respectively disadvantaged social groups from the perspective of social capital (as is the case with the economic capital).
49. Of course, we do not ignore the fact that no economic activity can take place other than by social cooperation (the social division of labour), but, nevertheless, income is awarded at the individual level based on the marginal productivity of labour (in the form of wages or other types of economic income), while social capital is produced by all members of society without individual "contributions" to its creation being able to be allocated.
50. Rawls does not systematically discuss anywhere the mirror case of decreasing economic inequality and, therefore, how his (economic, as we have called it here) principle of difference should be applied in this case, although the problem is interesting and even, as it seems to me, more complicated than the application of the respective principle to the case of increasing economic inequality.
51. I draw attention to the following risk of confusion: not being of a final result nature does not mean not being an effect. In fact, as shown above, the social wellbeing is a means for the social capital (which is a goal), but this is not contradictory with the fact that

the social wellbeing is of a procedural nature, not of a final result nature.

52. Of course, since we are talking about a concept that has significance only at the level of society as a whole, we are not faced here with the already known problem of the incommensurability of individual preferences (or utilities) at a given moment, but with two "values" of social wellbeing at two moments in time or, possibly, at the same moment, but between two different social spaces (societies).
53. Let us recall the concept of Pareto optimum (or equilibrium): in a given system, an improvement (under any admissible criterion) of the state (position, size, etc.) of a component of the system is acceptable if and only if, by doing so, the state of at most one other component of the system in question does not worsen (under the same criterion). (It should be noted that, to my knowledge, worsening under a different criterion in the Pareto problem is not discussed or resolved in the specialized literature.) At the moment when no improvement, under the mentioned condition, is any longer acceptable, the system is considered to be Pareto optimal (we also recall that the Pareto optimum is a particular case of the Kaldor-Hicks problem). In order to settle the issue related to the qualification of the Pareto model as an optimal or an equilibrium problem, we bring into discussion the fact that the modification of the structure/state of a system from the Pareto perspective is done outside a proper system of restrictions (although the condition is that the state of any component of the system in question does not worsen), therefore I believe that, in the strict sense of the terms, the Pareto model is an equilibrium model, not an optimal one. This conceptual clarification (distinction) does not, however, affect the substance of the discussion in the present chapter.
54. The relative non-independence (between them) of the three components of social capital is not likely to introduce methodological vulnerabilities, since, as shown above, they are not substitutable with each other or, in a more pretentious terminology, they are not mutually fungible.
55. If this were the case, then, logically, one could easily return to the concepts of average and aggregation (additivity and substitutability, respectively), which I just rejected when I criticized substantive utilitarianism.

56. The distinction between concrete and particular is obvious: while concrete is a term in the binomial concrete-abstract, particular is a term in the binomial particular-general. Thus, an entity can be concrete and particular (or general), just as an entity can be particular and concrete (or abstract). Of course, from a logical point of view, all valid pairs of properties can be identified on the basis of these dichotomous classes.
57. Let us recall the two premises of a standard syllogism: (1) the major premise, or the statement of a universal or at least general law (also called the covering law of the syllogism); (2) the minor premise, or the statement of a particular case of the major premise.
58. The definition of the co-evolutionary model is, of course, also valid for more than two interacting systems (in our case, we have, however, only two systems) but, as is known, for the case of more than two systems the difficult three-body problem arises (with a terminology established by cosmology) which, it seems, is still not solved (*Nota bene*: it seems, however, that, numerically, not analytically, and locally, solutions have been delivered) although there are numerous claims to solve it (Poincaré himself was wrong in this regard).
59. However, in a generalization that may prove useful, not only the quantity but also the timing of the exercise of that reaction norm may be significant.
60. For example, the entire evolutionary conception (Darwinian and neo-Darwinian) of biological life (not of symbolic or logical life) is subsumed under the co-evolution of the *organism–environment* pair of systems.
61. Since the first impulse is the only action in this interaction, we will consider, through some abuse of language, that we have only reactions. However, from a logical point of view, identifying the "originating" action implies a process of regression ad infinitum.
62. By fetality range is meant an interval (e.g., numerical range) within which impulses coming from another system (actions or reactions) are functionally integrable in the target system of those impulses. In other words, in the terminology of Humberto Maturana (credited with introducing the concept of autopoiesis in biology), by ensuring the fetality of the reaction norm, a system creates, in the target system, its own niche.

References

Collins, P. H. (2019). *Intersectionality as Critical Social Theory*. Duke University Press. https://doi.org/10.1215/9781478007098

Dean, H. (2020). A radical humanist approach to social welfare. *Ethics and Social Welfare,* 1–16. https://doi.org/10.1080/17496535.2020.1777454

Land, K. C., & Spilerman, S. (1975). *Social Indicator Models*. Russell Sage Foundation.

Nozick, R. (1993). *The Nature of Rationality*. Princeton University Press.

Nozick, R. (1999). *Anarchy*. Blackwell Publisher Ltd.

Nussbaum, M. C. (2006). *Frontiers of Justice*. The Belknap Press of Harvard University Press.

Pestieau, P. (2006). *The Welfare State in the European Union: Economic and Social Perspective*. Oxford University Press. https://www.questia.com/library/118829194/the-welfare-state-in-the-european-union-economic

PART IV

Evolutionism and Justice—A Co-Evolutive Model

CHAPTER 9

Interactions, Reactions Norms, and Stabilizers

1 Preamble

The concept of evolution is a concept assigned (or assignable) to a system, like the concept of state, with the difference that the state is a picture (state picture) of the system at a given time/moment, while the evolution is a set of (concatenated) state pictures during a time interval (range). Some additional commentaries are of usefulness at this point.

(a) The state

Be a system $\mathbb{S}$, to which is associated a set of parameters that sufficiently characterize it so it can be non-ambiguously "extracted" from its environment. If we note the characterizing parameters with $\int_i^j$ (state parameters), where i counts the parameters, and j counts the time, and the state of the system with $\mathcal{S}$, then the system $\mathbb{S}$ is cognitively done at the moment j by constructing the state vector $\mathcal{S}$:

$$\mathbb{S}^j \leftarrow \mathcal{S}^j = \left(\int_1^j, \int_2^j, \ldots \int_n^j\right)'$$

So, the system $\mathbb{S}$ is donated to the observer/analyst, at any (punctual) moment of time, by its state vector at that time. Of course, the parameters considered must be, to each other, independent and consistent (non-contradictory). Also, the set of parameters must be complete, that is,

E. Dinga, *The Economics of Social Justice and Societal Evolution*,
https://doi.org/10.1007/978-3-032-24055-2_9

it must have the potential to "extract", as said, non-ambiguously, that system from its environment at the given time (*Nota bene*: this "extraction" is of a cognitive nature, although it can also be of a physical one if appropriate[1]).

Since two or more systems could be taken into analysis, the notations must be adjusted as follows (the index k counts the system):

$$\mathbb{S}_k^j \leftarrow \mathcal{S}_k^j\left(\int_{k1}^j, \int_{k2}^j, \ldots, \int_{kn_k}^j\right)'$$

(b) The process

I resume Fig. 1 (Chapter 2), as Fig. 1, regarding the (abstract) typology of the change.

So, there are two categories of change: (a) changes of order 1, namely modification, which means a quantitative change, with two species: movement and growing, respectively; (b) changes of order 2, namely evolution, which means a qualitative change, with three species: development, transformation, and progress.

A change is a different "animal" from the state, it is a process. By process must be understood a passing from a state (a state vector) to another state (another state vector).

Any change occurs and can be measured only between two moments of time. The measurement means a comparison between the two state

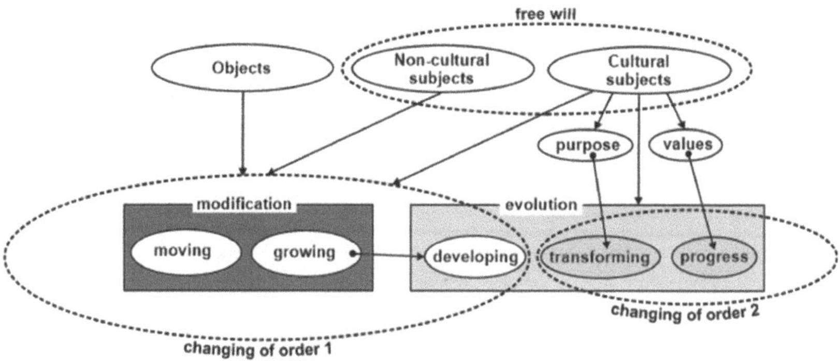

Fig. 1 General (abstract) scheme of changes in the world (*Source* Chapter 2 (Fig. 1))

vectors at the two moments of time. How to make such a comparison is another issue and will be specified, for the objective of this book at the appropriate place and time.

We note the process assigned (or assignable) to the system $\mathbb{S}_k^{j,\tau}$ with $\mathcal{P}_k^{j,\tau}$, where the two moments of time between which the process unfolds are noted with j and τ, so that $\tau > j$, the results of comparison between the state vector components with $\delta_i^{j,\tau}$ so that $\delta_i^{j,\tau} = \int_{k1}^{\tau} \ominus \int_{k1}^{j}$, where $\ominus$ describes the operator of comparison (either quantitative or qualitative, after the case) of the two state vector components, then we can write:

$$\mathbb{S}_k^{j,\tau} \leftarrow \mathcal{P}_k^{j,\tau}\left(\delta_{k1}^{j,\tau}, \delta_{k2}^{j,\tau}, \ldots, \delta_{kn_k}^{j,\tau}\right),$$

A string of concatenated such processes will describe a map of (continuous[2]) change of the system in the case. If that map is reversible, we will call it *trajectory*, while if it is irreversible,[3] we will call it chreod.[4] Consequently, if a string of moments of time is given, let us say:$\mathcal{T}(\sqcup_1, \sqcup_2, \ldots, \sqcup_m)$, a chreod ($\mathbb{C}_k^{\mathcal{T}}$) of the system $\mathbb{S}_k^{\mathcal{T}}$ can be expressed as:

$$\mathbb{S}_k^{\mathcal{T}} \leftarrow \mathbb{C}_k^{\mathcal{T}}\left(\mathcal{P}_k^{\sqcup_1,\sqcup_2}, \mathcal{P}_k^{\sqcup_2,\sqcup_3}, \ldots, \mathcal{P}_k^{\sqcup_{m-1},\sqcup_m}\right),$$

If we note $\sqcup_q, \sqcup_w$ with $\sqcup_{qw}$, then:

$$\mathbb{S}_k^{\mathcal{T}} \leftarrow \mathbb{C}_k^{\mathcal{T}}\left(\mathcal{P}_k^{\sqcup_{12}}, \mathcal{P}_k^{\sqcup_{23}}, \ldots, \mathcal{P}_k^{\sqcup_{(m-1)m}}\right),$$

Analytically, the chreod is a matrix:

$$\mathbb{C}_k^{\mathcal{T}} = \begin{pmatrix} \delta_{k1}^{1,2} & \delta_{k1}^{2,3} & \ldots & \delta_{k1}^{m-1,m} \\ \delta_{k2}^{1,2} & \delta_{k2}^{2,3} & \ldots & \delta_{k2}^{m-1,m} \\ \ldots & \ldots & \ldots & \ldots \\ \delta_{kn_k}^{1,2} & \delta_{kn_k}^{2,3} & \ldots & \delta_{kn_k}^{m-1,m} \end{pmatrix}$$

Nota bene: obviously, the assignment of a string of time moments does not depend on the system, so the index k is no longer necessary.

Based on the above conceptualization of the state and the process, the following debate within the chapter will be built.

2 The Concept of Reaction Norm—Generalities

The reality is formed by systems.[5] Those systems are ontological in status, but often, cognitive systems are "cropped" from reality (either objective, subjective, or objectified), which do not necessarily have an ontological correspondent. In fact, this is one of the crucial vulnerabilities of (scientific[6]) knowledge—if the cognitive system does not have an ontological corresponding system, when the knowledge acquired by studying the cognitive system is applied to an ontological system (cropped arbitrarily), the results could not meet the expectations[7] formed based on that knowledge.[8]

2.1 *Inputs, Outputs, and Reaction*

The systems, either ontological or (only) cognitive, are characterized, abstractly, by: (a) inputs, of any nature (substance, energy, information, competence); (b) outputs, of any nature, too; (c) a transforming operator (called black-box) which transforms the inputs into outputs. The inputs come either from outside of the system (the system's environment) or from inside of it (the system itself—e.g., self-consumption). Analogously, the outputs go towards either outside of the system or inside of it.[9]

The concept of reaction means an action generated by another action, either from outside or inside. Consequently, a reaction is not independent, while the action is so, or, in other words, the reaction is a function of an action. The overwhelming number of actions that *prima facie* appear to us as actions are, in fact, reactions. However, some cautions must be highlighted:

- an output is not a reaction to an input, although the output occurs as an effect of an input. Since a reaction is a direct response to an action, and the output is an indirect effect of an input, namely an effect intermediated by the transforming operator (black-box), it results in the above conclusion: the output is not a reaction;
- there is no bijectivity between action and reaction; so, many actions could cause a single reaction, as well as a single action could cause many reactions. Anyway, this is not a theoretical issue, but a practical/praxiological one;
- a question arises now: cannot an action, however, generate indirectly a reaction? My opinion in this matter is as follows:

- an action can cause a reaction even if it exerts an indirect influence of the latter, namely, exerting, first, an influence on an action which, in turn, exerts influence on the given effect-reaction, if the action considered does not lose its identity by exerting that influence—is it clear that the input "dissolves" its identity being transformed by the transforming operator (black-box), so it violates this condition;
- how about the pair action–reaction (noted A-R) if there is an indirect influence of an action on the reaction?
  - the intermediate system on which the considered action exerts its influence will respond, of course, with a reaction, but we have here a direct relationship A-R;
  - consequently, we must consider that reaction as an action on a third entity/system—obviously, it is a reaction from the perspective of the first action/system, but an action (since it is not provoked) from the perspective of the third system, and so on;
  - of course, a stop criterion problem occurs here: we must establish which is the entity/system whose reaction is the "searched" one. This establishment is, however, an external problem, and I do not develop it here.

Figure 2 illustrates the discussion above.

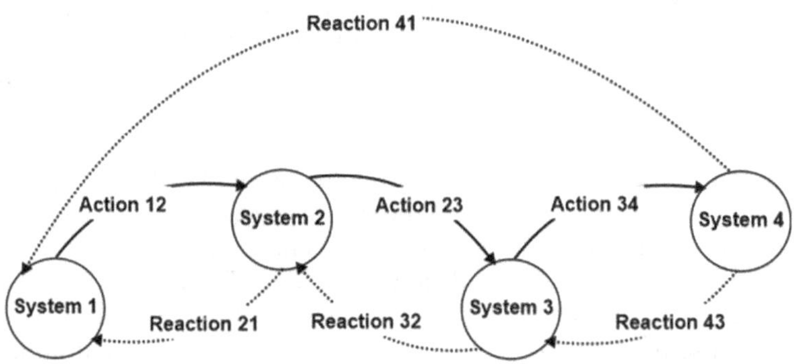

Fig. 2 Reaction to indirect action (*Source* author)

Logically, we have the following pairs A-Rs:

$$P_{12} : A_{12} - R_{21}$$

$$P_{23} : A_{23} - R_{32}$$

$$P_{34} : A_{34} - R_{43}$$

$$P_{14} : (A_{12} \oplus A_{23} \oplus A_{34}) - R_{21}$$

2.2 The Concept of Reaction Norm

Input vs. Action

Principled, there is no proportionality between action and reaction, from any point of view: intensity, duration, nature, and so on. Reaction depends on the characteristics of the target system of the action, on the one hand, and on the effects of the action on the target system, on the other hand.

As said above, the inputs cannot be considered as an action that claims a reaction, because the input does not conserve its identity. A conceptual issue that occurs here is the following: could be the action considered as an input for the target system? I think that:

- an action exists if and only if it produces a (principled, measurable) change, of any nature, in the identity of the target system[10];
- the identity of the target system is expressed by its structure, which, generally, is constituted by its black-box;
- the inputs do not produce a change in the black-box, since the target system must function predictably, and the predictability is provided by the invariance of the black-box;
- to cause a reaction, an action must behave very different from an input, that is, it must produce a change in the target system black-box; this is the only case in which the target system will generate a response to the action, i.e., a reaction (from **re**sponse and **action**);
- in conclusion, an action is “another animal” compared with an input.

What a Norm Is It?

About the norm, I analytically discussed in Chapter 5, Annex 2, so here I do not resume those findings. However, some abstract/general considerations regarding the purpose of introducing the concept of reaction norm will be provided below.

Generally, by norm is understood a benchmark face to which a given set of concepts, actions, results, behaviours, etc., are assessed, in order to establish if such concepts, actions, results, and behaviours verify (or not) that benchmark, that is, the norm in question.

The concept of norm is universal in our world, whether objective, subjective, or objectified. From surviving to self-esteem, all our signalizations as living (biologically) systems, and socially integrated individuals, either for self and for others, are exclusively conducted by norms of any nature and type.

Principled, it seems to be the following typology of the abstract norm:

(i) (N_S) *structural* norms: those norms that require some mandatory relationships between structural components of an entity in order that entity exist or be viable[11]; the relationships in question could be quantitative and/or qualitative; for example: a system must have a leading component and a driven component (or some driven components);

(ii) (N_P) *performative* norms: those norms that ensure on a behaviour or action/reaction to be achieved; for example: to read must know the alphabet;

(iii) (N_F) *functional* norms: those norms that require some mandatory rapports between action and reaction; for example: the wage must be proportional with the marginal labour productivity;

(iv) (N_A) *assessing* norms: those norms that establish patterns of evaluation for anything; for example: the economic value of goods and services must be evaluated based on the monetary price;

(v) (N_M) *signification* norms: those norms that address the idiosyncratic meaning of the world's facts/events.[12]

The Reaction Norm
First of all, it must be said that a reaction norm is a pentadic norms, i.e., a norm that possesses characteristics of the above five categories of norms. Formally, a reaction norm (norm of reaction) can be written as follows:
$N_R = N(N_S, N_P, N_F, N_A, N_M)$, or, simpler:

$$N_R = N_{SPFAM}$$

Discussion

- the reaction norm is a function of five variables—S, P, F, A, M—that represent weights with which each category of norms contributes to "1";
- if are denoted with s, p, f, a, m, the respective weights, so: $s + p + f + a + m = 1$;
- it can be drawn a synoptic image of a reaction norm (Fig. 3).

Nota bene: Fig. 3 represents the reaction norm of the following parameters:

$$N_R(0.375, 0.25, 0.125, 0.25, 0)$$

A reaction norm must verify two categories of conditionalities: (a) conditionalities of the source of reaction; (b) conditionalities of the destination of reaction.

Let us presuppose we have two systems, k and q, where the system k is the source of action, and the system q is the destination of the action of system k.

(a) conditionalities of the source of reaction

The conditionalities of the source of reaction are somewhat pre-established. This means that a given system cannot generate any imaginable reaction, but only those reactions that are possible in the structure and functionality of that system. For example, a mechanical system cannot react ethically. By knowing the identity of a system, we implicitly know the range of reactions that system can generate—analogously with the case of syllogism: knowing the premises, we will know the conclusion.

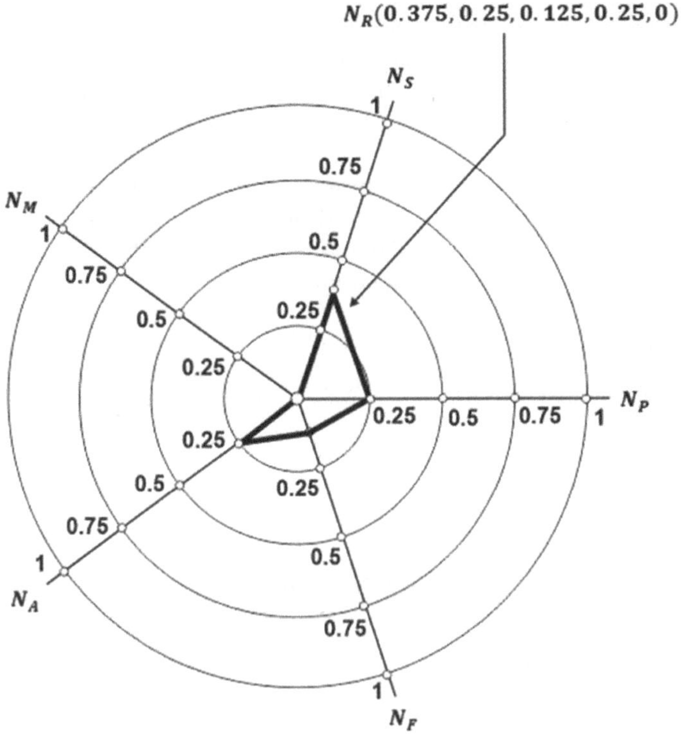

Fig. 3 "Form" of the reaction norm (*Source* author)

Nota bene: the conditionalities of the source of reaction also function as the conditionalities of the source of action.

We will denote with $\mathcal{A}_k^P$ the actionally possible world of a system k, and with $\mathcal{A}_k^O$ the set of objectified (or objectifiable) actions (or, equally, reactions) of that system. Then, it must be verified the belonging condition:

$$\mathcal{A}_k^O \in \mathcal{A}_k^P$$

(b) conditionalities of the destination of reaction

The conditionalities of the destination of reaction (equally, of action) are pre-established too, but they must be in some correspondence with the conditionalities of the source of reaction (action). We can say the following in this matter. If we denote with q the system of destination, with $\mathcal{A}_q^A$ the allowed[13] reactions world of the system q, and with $\mathcal{A}_q^O$ the set of objectified (or objectifiable) reactions towards the system q, then, it must be verified the belonging condition:

$$\mathcal{A}_k^O \in \mathcal{A}_q^A$$

As $\mathcal{A}_k^O \in \mathcal{A}_k^P$, we can have:

$$\left(\mathcal{A}_k^O \in \mathcal{A}_k^P\right) \bigwedge \left(\mathcal{A}_k^O \in \mathcal{A}_q^A\right)$$

or, the same:

$$\mathcal{A}_k^O \in \left(\mathcal{A}_k^P\right) \bigcap \left(\mathcal{A}_q^A\right)$$

Can exist the following cases:

- $\left(\mathcal{A}_k^P\right) \bigcap \left(\mathcal{A}_q^A\right) = \varnothing$: no action/reaction is possible between systems k and q (more exactly, from k to q);
- $\left(\mathcal{A}_k^P\right) \bigcap \left(\mathcal{A}_q^A\right) = \mathcal{A}_k^P$: all actions/reactions from system k to system q are working;
- $\left(\mathcal{A}_k^P\right) \bigcap \left(\mathcal{A}_q^A\right) = \mathcal{A}_q^A$: all actions/reactions perceptible by the system q are available to the system k;
- $\left(\mathcal{A}_k^P\right) \bigcap \left(\mathcal{A}_q^A\right) = \mathcal{C}$: a subset of actions/reactions (namely $\mathcal{C}$), contained by both system k and system q, is full working between the two systems.

Based on the above, the concept of reaction norm will now be introduced. The following issues will be examined: (1) what is the reaction norm; (2)

why a reaction norm is required; (3) the evolutionary potential of the reaction norm.

1. What is the reaction norm?

The reaction norm is, generally, *causa formalis* based on which the reaction (or, equivalent, the action) of a system forms from all the perspectives of that forming: quantitative, temporal, qualitative, directional, etc. The reaction norm differs from one to another, depending on the class that the reaction belongs to (see the typology of reaction norm, below). This means the reaction is always modelled by its norm. The reaction norm (or norm of reaction) is a self-building principle—either implicitly or explicitly, see letter (g) below—and it has a crucial importance, relevance, and significance for the most evolutionary processes: robustness, resilience, antifragility, sustainability, and autopoieticity (Dinga, 2025).

2. The reason of reaction norm

As an action is defined, fundamentally, by its potential/capacity to cause an (any) change in the target system of that action, it is obvious that such a change will modify (in an identitary[14] tunnel, however) the target system. As a result, the target system will react for different "reasons"—no matter whether those "reasons" are mechanical or originate in consciousness: surviving, robustness, resilience, antifragility, optimality, sustainability, autopoieticity, viability, and so on.[15] Besides, the issue of the reason for the reaction norm will be developed at point (h) below.

3. Evolutionary reaction norm

Just by its definition, the reaction norm must create, maintain, and (if possible) improve the potential of the target system to at least survive and, once surviving, to strengthen its mentioned potential.[16] It is obvious that such "objectives" can be achieved only (or best) by an evolutionary property of the reaction norm. The basic idea, here, is the following: the reaction evolution is simply the necessary effect of the reaction norm evolution, since the reaction is already contained in its own norm—the reader is once again invited to make the analogy with the syllogism, namely: the conclusion *on evolution* is the necessary effect of the premises *of evolution*.

3 A Qualitative Analysis of Reaction Norm

3.1 *Lab of Norming the Reaction*

In this paragraph, I will examine the mechanism through which the reaction norm is "manufactured". Producing the reaction norm is an evolutionary process, generally based on the trial-and-error mechanism. Even in the case of humans, who deliberatively establish the changes that interest them, the (any) knowledge is never sufficient to ensure the lack of errors in shaping the (reaction) norms of behaviour—in fact, in this case, we have a mix between prediction and fortune, so the trial-and-error phenomenon subsists. In fact, to design the reaction norms, humans (and societies) proceed through a process of general falsifiability, i.e., starting with an abduction, testing hypotheses based on the abduction, and correcting and correcting the reaction norm after the reaction is performed. Figure 4 sketches a stylized synopsis of the lab of norming the reaction (*Nota bene*: the case of non-human systems is a particular case of the latter; namely, they lack the conscious component of abduction and hypothesis formulation).

The trial-and-error procedure is the general mechanism through which Nature (especially the living Nature) evolves. No pre-established plan of

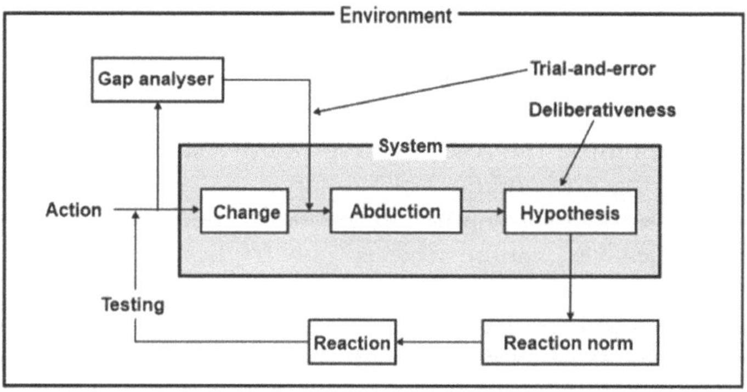

Fig. 4 Generic lab of norming the reaction (*Source* author)

the evolution (can) exist, the mutations randomly occurring are "examined" by the environment of the bearer of that mutation, and the least is selected (accepted) or not, depending on the fitness in the case. The trial-and-error procedure gains a considerable part of deliberativeness in the case of society, where the mutations, generally, belong to strategies, programs, and simply desiderability (see the concept of the desiderative thought) but, even in this case, which is (can be) never completely deliberative, errors in the mutations performed can appear and must be, subsequently, corrected/adjusted. Moreover, the agnosticism in principle required by scientific knowledge implies the same trial-and-error mechanism of gaining knowledge. As the fallibility in knowledge and action is (wisdomly) accepted, the trial-and-error mechanism is inalienable in the societal path.

3.2 A Typology of Reaction Norm

To establish a typology of the reaction norm, the criteria of typology is required. I think the following criteria are appropriate for such an issue: (a) the multiplier/divisor of the reaction; (b) the nature of reaction; (c) the similitude/di-similitude of reaction; (d) the structure of reaction; (e) the species of reaction; (f) the arrow of reaction; (g) implicit vs. explicit norms of reaction; (h) the reason of reaction; (i) the objective of reaction.

(a) Multiplier/divisor of reaction

The multiplier/divisor of reaction refers to the proportionality factor between action and reaction, in a *sui generis* chain that can indefinitely continue. The proportionality factor can be: (a) sub-unitary—reaction is less than action; (b) unitary—reaction is like action; (c) supra-unitary—reaction is more than action. The qualifiers *less*, *like*, *more* address any features of action/reaction: nature, intensity, duration, etc. The qualifier *less* means that reaction is a divisor of action, the qualifier *more* means that reaction is a multiplier of action, and the qualifier *like* means that reaction is neither a divisor nor a multiplier of action. From a temporal perspective, depending on the context, the pairs *action–reaction* can be, regarding the proportionality factor, either increasing, decreasing, or stationary. The increasing case means that either the divisor or multiplier becomes higher and higher, the decreasing case means that the two factors become lower

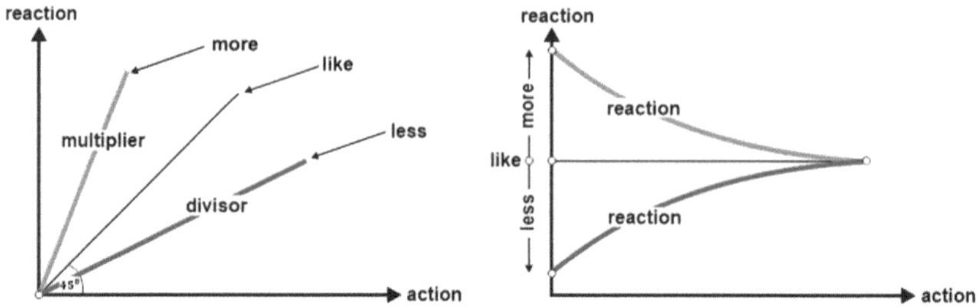

Fig. 5 Multiplying and dividing of reaction related to action (*Source* author)

and lower, while the stationary case means that the factors are invariants. A synoptic image of the described cases is provided in Fig. 5.

So, based on this criterion, the reaction norms can be:

(1) multiplying norm: reaction is *more* than action
(2) dividing norm: reaction is *less* than action
(3) conservative norm: reaction is *like* action

(b) nature of reaction

Principled, the actions could be of any (possible) nature, and the same can be said about the reactions. Consequently, according to this criterion, the reaction norm can address (1) the same nature of reaction as the nature of action, or (2) a different nature of the reaction in response to the nature of action.

(1) the same nature of reaction

Let us take an example: presuppose a worker attends a course of re-qualification, during which he/she receives new information about a given specialization. After attending the course, the worker will apply at his/her job more information about that specialization. We have the same nature of reaction with the nature of action.

(2) a different nature of reaction

Let us take an example: presuppose that happens an increase of demand for a given good in the market. As result, the supply of that good will increase, since the increase of demand has increased the price, so more sales brings more profit. We have another nature of reaction compared with the nature of action.

(c) similitude/di-similitude of reaction

The similitude/di-similitude of reaction face to action refers to the coincidence/non-coincidence of the area of reaction with the aria of action. So, according to this criterion, can exist two categories of reaction norm: (a) similar reaction with action; (b) di-similar reaction with action.

(1) similar reaction with action

Let us take an example: presuppose that Trump administration increases the import taxes for the European Union goods. In order to preserve its commercial balance, European Union increase, in turn (in a multiplying or dividing manner), the import taxes for United State goods. The reaction is similar with action.

(2) di-similar reaction with action

Let us take an example: presuppose that the fiscal authority in a country increases the personal income tax rate. In order to evade the diminishing of net income, the individuals will accept to work in the underground economy, so to hide the (taxable) gross income. The reaction is di-similar with action.

(d) structure of reaction

The structure of reaction is based on the five-factor definition of a norm (see section "What a Norm Is It?"). So, any reaction is composed by a fraction (from unity) of each of those five factors. According to this criterion can exist the following classes of reaction norm:

(1) *pure norms*: norms that exhaust the structural unity with one factor only, so there are: (i) structural norms—N_S; (ii) performative norms—N_P; (iii) functional norms—N_F; (iv) assessing norms—N_A; (v) signification norms—N_M. These norms are, in fact, non-structured norms, and they action unilaterally;

(2) *structured norms*: norms contain at least two of five structural factors/determinants in their construction. These norms action multilaterally (at least, bi-laterally).

(e) arrow of reaction

The arrow of reaction refers to the time arrow according to which the reaction occurs. Generally, there are two species of reaction: (a) reaction caused by a past action, namely the so-called feedback; (b) reaction caused by a future action, namely the so-called feedforward. Each of the two species has two subspecies:

(1) the feedback

The feedback is a reaction past-oriented, that is, it occurs if and only if a past action is not calibrated so to lead to the expected result. If we note with E_R the expected result, with A_R the actual result, with $\overline{T}$ a normed threshold above which the correction operated by feedback is required, and with T the actual such threshold, where the index j counts the time, then:

$$T^j = \left| E_R - A_R^j \right|$$

The feedback is generated if the following condition is verified:

$$G_T^j = T^j - \overline{T} > 0$$

where with G is noted the gap between expectations and actualizations.

Nota bene: here $\overline{T}$ is considered as invariant. This assumption is realistic enough but, on long term, the threshold /benchmark $\overline{T}$ could change.

Depending on the objective of the feedback, there can exist two subspecies of it: (1.1) negative feedback; (1.2) positive feedback.

(1.1) negative feedback: is that reaction aimed at reducing T towards $\overline{T}$. It is a stabilizing reaction, namely, the next action will be calibrated so that:

$$G_T^{j+1} < G_T^j$$

(1.2) positive feedback: is that reaction aimed at increasing T face to $\overline{T}$. It is an escalating reaction,[17] namely, the next action will be calibrated so that:

$$G_T^{j+1} > G_T^j$$

Nota bene: of course, in particular contexts, we can have negative feedbacks inside (i.e., embedded by) a positive one, or vice versa. In complicated contexts, a single feedback, either negative or positive, is a *rara avis*. In fact, in reality, networks function through feedbacks, with complicated entanglement between negative and positive feedbacks—obviously, to (logically and quantitatively) modelling such complications does not constitute an insurmountable problem.

(2) the feedforward

The feedforward is a reaction future-oriented, that is, it occurs if and only if a future action seems be not calibrated so to lead to the expected result. Some extra considerations are required here:

- that future action is, of course, a prediction, no matter the methodology through which it has been formulated;
- being a prediction and, at the same time, being considered for the current reaction, it results we are in the context of Oedipus effect;
- so, the current reaction to a future (predicted) action could change exactly the future action which, as consequence, could differ from the predicted action;
- this requires an iterative, *ex ante*, grounding of the reaction to the future action, to consider the very implied Oedipus effect;

- these complications (of methodological/operational nature) identified will be, of course, ignored here, since my objective is only to introduce the concept of feedforward.

The feedforward, in turn, has two subspecies, as follows:

(2.1) negative feedforward with the same meaning, *mutatis mutandis*, as of the negative feedback;
(2.2) positive feedforward, with the same meaning, *mutatis mutandis*, as of the negative feedback.

(f) implicit vs. explicit norms

To discuss this criterion, it is useful to introduce the dichotomy discretionary—automatic. An action is discretionary[18] if it is explicitly and (usually) formally triggered—for example, a fiscal norm is an explicit and formal action of the fiscal authority in a fiscal space. An action is automatic if it is implicitly and (possibly) formally triggered—for example, a clock alarm is of such a type. *Nota bene*: below, the issue of such a distinction will be detailed and formally examined, from the perspective of automatic stabilizers. Consequently, based on this criterion, we have:

(1) discretionary reaction norm—applied in an explicit and (often) formal way;
(2) automatic reaction norm—applied in an implicit and (possible) formal way.

(g) reason of reaction

The criterion of reason in the reaction norm topic addresses the justification that "legitimates" the reaction in question and, correlatively, the reaction norm used in the context. The main classes of reaction (norm) according to this criterion are:

(1) reaction for surviving—is aimed at ensuring the sufficient conditions, of any nature, that guarantee the survival of a given system;

this reaction provides the functionality of the system, i.e., the relationships among its own components;

(2) reaction for signalizing—is aimed at occupying the appropriate niche, so that the pair cooperation–competition (or, the same, alliance–fight) between contemporary systems by preserved; this reaction provides the behaviour of the system, i.e., the relationships between its own components, on the one hand, and the environment, on the other hand.

(h) objective of reaction

The criterion of the objective/purpose in the reaction norm topic addresses the objective/s intended to be achieved through the intermediation of the reaction (norm). In an abstract horizon, it can be considered the following classes of objectives/purposes in relation to the concept of reaction norm:

(1) *conservative* reaction[19]—is aimed at preserving the structure of a given system, as considering that the structure generates functions:

  (1.1) conservation reaction by robustness—is aimed to ensure the conservation by resistance against perturbations (either internal or external)[20];

  (2.1) conservation reaction by resilience—is aimed to ensure the conservation by recovering the system from the perturbed state as a result of the perturbation impact;

(2) *sustainable* reaction—is aimed to ensure the "movement" of a given system inside a pre-established tunnel of variations for the basic system's parameters;

(3) *antifragile* reaction—is aimed to ensure the acquisition of advantages (of any nature) for the given system, exactly as a result of the perturbation's impact;

(4) *viability* reaction—is aimed to ensure the harmony (the æsthetics—see Chapter 7) between the system and the environment related to a that system;

(5) *autopoietic* reaction—is aimed at reconstructing, reconfiguring, restructuring, repairing, and so on, the given system after the perturbation's impact has been produced.

3.3 Fetality of Reaction Norm

Preliminaries

The concept of fetality comes from biology (and, subsequently, medicine) and, generally, means: something is in accordance or harmony with another thing from the perspective of survival or, sometimes, from other perspectives: understanding, functionality, etc. Some examples: a statement in Romanian that is transmitted to an English native who does not understand Romanian is non-foetal; a book of poetry that is medically grafted to replace one's damaged heart is non-foetal; a tax rate on the personal income that is greater than 100% is non-foetal, etc.

The fetality (F) is a property of a relationship[21] that must verify the following sufficiency predicates:

- (F_1) the relationship considered is of the nature of action/reaction, so, as shown before, it is a relationship that produces (or has the potential to produce) some change in the target system;
- (F_2) the change caused in the target system by that relationship does not exceed (not exit from) the tolerance tunnel of the target system (*Nota bene*: some considerations on the syntagma *tolerance tunnel* are useful):
- the tolerance tunnel (TT) is the range between a minimum (floor) threshold of significance, let us denote it with T_m, and a maximum (ceiling) threshold of significance, let us denote it with T_M, that is:

$$TT = T_M - T_m$$

  - T_m is established so that the target system can perceive the (be sensible to) action (or reaction) exerted on it. Ontologically, an action/reaction does exist for the target system if and only if that system can perceive[22] the action/reaction in the case;
  - the perception of the action/reaction is "validated" by causing a change in the target system as a result of that action/reaction.

It should be mentioned that such a change can be of the basic kinds: (a) structural change; (b) functional change;

- T_m is established so that the target system's identity (*Nota bene*: the identity of a system is exactly its structure[23]) is preserved after the action/reaction occurred;
- so, the TT is, in fact, a surface, since it depends on both structural changes and functional changes. However, the functional TT (let us note it with TT_F) is larger[24] than the structural TT (let us note it with TT_S).

So, formally, the fetality on an action/reaction is defined by the logical conjunctions of F_1 and F_2:

$$F = (F_1) \bigwedge (F_2)$$

Conditionalities of the Fetal Reaction

Similarly with the (basic) formalizing of the conditionalities (or, the possibility space) of the reaction (see section "The Reaction Norm"), now, we can discuss about the conditionalities of the fetal reaction. To be observed that such an issue is put only for the target system (i.e., the destination of the reaction). This way, we will extract some basic conclusions regarding the norm of reaction (reaction norm) from the perspective of reaction fetality.

Let us consider two systems that interact between them (i.e., "change" actions and reactions between them[25]), namely, a system k that generates a reaction (this could be called source system), and a system q that receives that reaction (this could be called target system).

We will denote with $\mathcal{F}_q^F$ the space of fetality of the target system q. Obviously, we have the structural condition:

$$\mathcal{F}_q^F \subset \mathcal{A}_k^O \subset \mathcal{A}_k^P$$

3.4 Feasibility of the Reaction: Possibility and Fetality

By the feasibility of a reaction, I understand a logical conjunction between the possibility of that reaction and the fetality of it. Of course, the possibility addresses the source system, while the fetality addresses the target system. Since the concept of feasibility has significant semantic overlapping with the concept of viability, the feasibility will be noted with $\mathcal{V}$. If with $\mathcal{P}$ is noted the possibility space, then the feasibility is provided by the logical conjunction of $\mathcal{P}$ and $\mathcal{F}$ (R indicates reaction):

$$\mathcal{V}_{k,q}^{R} = (\mathcal{P}_k) \bigwedge (\mathcal{F}_q)$$

3.5 A Stylized Evolutionary Model of the Reaction Norm

This paragraph is aimed at sketching an evolutionary model of the reaction norm, based on the above considerations. As already said, the evolution of the reaction is a result of the evolution of the norm of reaction (reaction norm). This means that, basically, from a scientific perspective, the evolutionary character of the reaction norm is of the first and fundamental interest.

Generalities

What does evolutionary mean? While the concept of evolution is a second-order change, and has three species: based on growth (i.e., development), on purposes (i.e., transformation), and on values (i.e., progress), as Fig. 1 suggests, and being a process, the evolutionarity is a property of that process. I will provide some logical characteristics of the property of evolutionarity and evolutionary, respectively.

(a) evolutionarity

The evolutionarity is a property of the process of evolution, namely, that property characterized by the following:

- any non-fetal in-reaction (*Nota bene*: by in-reaction is understood a reaction or action, as the case may be, that is received by the target system from the environment, i.e., from a source system contained in the environment) is either blocked through robustness, or neutralized through resilience;
    - *reason*: the target system performs, this way, a *sui generis* selection of the environment, more exactly of the out-reaction (*Nota bene*: by out-reaction is understood a reaction or action, as

the case may be, that is oriented from the target system to the environment, i.e., to the source system contained in the environment)[26];

- any fetal in-reaction is structurally integrated according to the finality of the target system;
    - *reason*: if the in-reaction is fetal for the target system, this means that the environment (including the source system that generated the in-reaction in the case) requires the integration of that in-reaction in the target system functioning, so that the structural integration of the in-reaction is needed.

(b) evolutionary

The evolutionary is the essential way in which evolutionarity occurs. In other words, a way/mode of functioning of a system is evolutionary if and only if it is characterized by evolutionarity, as this has been introduced above.

The "Ingredients" of the Reaction Norm Evolution
The object whose evolutionarity property and evolutionary unfold are under examination is the reaction norm—hereafter, noted *RN*. Any system has a set of *RNs* through which it is inserted into the environment and functions in its niche.[27] For the necessities of this paragraph, the following premises are accepted:

- the *RN* (i.e., the *causa formalis* of reaction) is not an independent system that functions as such in a given environment, but it is a component, of cognitive nature, of a system, for example, a component of decisional type, and regards both functionality and behaviour of that integrative system;
- as consequence, *RN* cannot be else, from evolution perspective, than the *genotype* of the integrative system;
- as the integrative system is, obviously, according to the above discussion, a source system,[28] from now on I will appeal the integrative system as the source system (abbreviated *SS*);

- it is, also, peremptory that the SS will generate the phenotype of the evolutive process in which the RN is implied—the phenotype is exactly the reaction, denoted with R.

In this theoretical context, the list of evolutionary "ingredients" related to the RN is the following:

(1) ($\mathcal{G}$) genotype: RN—reaction norm;
(2) ($\mathcal{P}$) phenotype: R—reaction;
(3) ($\mathcal{M}$) mutation: any pressure, of any nature, intensity, etc., either internal to SS or external to it, that has the potential to change the genotype;
(4) ($\mathcal{T}$) transcription: refers to the taking over of the mutation into a change inRN;
(5) ($\mathcal{D}$) translation: refers to the effective modification of$R$;
(6) ($\mathcal{F}$) fitness: F—fetality of R;
(7) ($\mathcal{S}$) selection: integration of the reaction norm (RN) into reaction (R).

The Model
As shown at the Sect. 3.5, we can imagine an evolutionary model of the reaction norm. Of course, the elaboration of such a model must be grounded on the implicit assumption according to which the reaction norm has an evolutionary potential. Next, I will examine the sufficiency predicates to be held by a reaction norm so that it can "experience" an evolutive chreod.

The (abstract) evolutionary model of the reaction norm can be represented as shown in Fig. 6.

Discussion

- (7) the phenotype (reaction) is evaluated by the target system and, as a result, the target system "suggests" a change (mutation) in that phenotype;
- (1) the mutation is examined in the view of transcription;
- (2) the affirmative decision is followed by the transcription of the mutation;

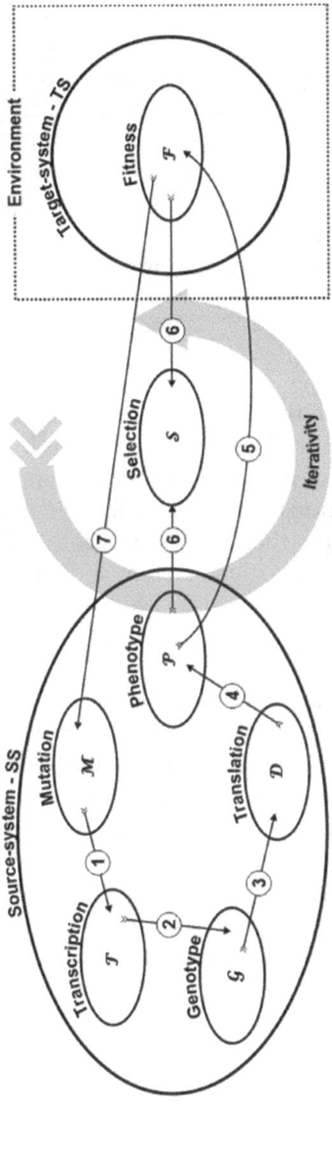

Fig. 6 (Abstract) model of the evolutionary chreod of the reaction norm (*Source* author)

- (3) the transcribed mutation is followed by the translation of transcription into genotype (reaction norm);
- (4) the mutation of the genotype is introduced into the phenotype (reaction);
- (5) the new phenotype is tested by transmitting the new reaction (new phenotype) to the environment (i.e., to the target system), to be evaluated by the last system from the point of view of the fitness, namely, from the point of view of its fetality for the target system;
- (6) the new phenotype, based on fitness evaluation, is selected (or not) by the environment;
- (7) a new mutation occurs regarding the new phenotype (the new reaction), in an iterative circle.

Short Conclusion

An evolutionary model of the reaction, respectively reaction norm, is perfectly conceivable, and its logic is comprehensible. Considering the norm of reaction (reaction norm) as genotype, and the reaction itself as phenotype in an evolutionary process is feasible and, as I think, relevant enough to be used for the (final) purpose of this book, namely a co-evolutionary model of the societal system and social justice system.

4 Two Regional Reaction Norms

The above discussion was aimed at deciphering the grounds of a possible evolutionary model of the reaction norm in an abstract approach. Next, I want to apply the obtained results to my basic purpose of the book, namely, to the two systems I will put in a (co)evolutionary process: the societal system and the social justice system. *Nota bene*: the syntagma regional reaction norms refer to the fact that, this time, the general concept of the reaction norm will be particularized to the two mentioned specific systems of interest.

4.1 Some Generalities

The two systems will be considered in the framework that was described in the previous chapters of the book. Some extra mentions are the following:

- the societal system ($\mathbb{SS}$) will be considered as the target system (TS), since it embeds the second system, namely the social justice system, this one denoted ($\mathbb{SJS}$), which will be considered as the source system (SS);
- topologically, we have the condition: $\mathbb{SJS} \subset \mathbb{SS}$;
- so, the environment for the social justice system is exactly the societal system;
- the "roles" of source system, $\mathbb{SJS}$, respectively of target system, $\mathbb{SS}$ play only for the first action/reaction between them, since, after this moment, each of the two systems plays, alternatively, the roles of source system, and target system, respectively;
- the pattern of the co-evolutionary process of the pair $\mathbb{SJS} - \mathbb{SS}$ is that described in Fig. 6.

The societal system will be credited as following the "law" of the *æsthetics*, while the social justice system is credited as following the "law" of the *ethics*, so that the pair $\mathbb{SJS} - \mathbb{SS}$ forms the system called *æsthics* (see Chapter 7).

4.2 Societal Reaction Norms

The societal system is an entangled pair composed of the social system and the state system. In fact, the social system and the state system co-evolve to form the societal system, but, in this research, the societal system will be considered "in block", namely the internal, so to speak, co-evolution of the societal system will be viewed as a black-box, which means we are interested only of inputs into the societal system, and of outputs from that system.[29]

The reactions of the societal system to the social justice system is governed by a law,[30] which I would call the *law of societal æsthetics* ($LÆ$). This law[31] has two inter-related finalities: (a) to justify, and, based on justification, to explain, the reactions (including the reaction norms) of the societal system to the actions/reactions of the social justice system;

(b) to introduce/indicate the internal arrow that drives the very kinematics of the societal system in relation to the kinematics of the social justice.

(a) justification/explanation

The law/principle of societal æsthetics (*LÆ*) is a regulative law. This means that the respective law is concerned with verifying the societal æsthetics mark in the individuals' relationships (interactions). The societal æsthetics mark refers to the viable functionality of the society (societal system) or, in a more operational perspective, to the sustainability of the society, namely, we can express this law as: ***do not reduce the sustainability property of the societal system as an effect of interactions.***[32] Consequently, the reactions and reaction norms, respectively, of the societal system will be designed, adjusted, and implemented so that the interactions at the society level preserve their sustainability. It is worth noting that we do not, yet, speak about the ethical features of those interactions, since, from the societal perspective, we are primarily and fundamentally interested in the viability/sustainability of the societal interactions of any nature, from economic to political ones.

(b) internal arrow

The law/principle of societal æsthetics (*LÆ*) must, by definition, introduce and, consequently, indicate the direction in which the societal system goes. So, like the justification/explanation finality, the internal law is a regulative principle, by ensuring on the fact that the kinematics of the societal system follows the fundamental arrow of that system. As I will show further, such an arrow addresses the fitness of the mutation occurred in the social justice system (see Fig. 6).

In this context, the societal system will design, adjust, and implement its own reactions based on those norms (reaction norms) that simultaneously verify the two above-mentioned roles permanently played by the law of æsthetics. Technically, the two roles of the law of æsthetics function as filters in cascade. If we note with $E_{Æ}$ the explanatory role of the law of æsthetics, as the first filter, and with $A_{Æ}$ the directing (tied to the arrow) role of the law of æsthetics, as the second filter, then any reaction of the societal system, as response to the social justice system, will be double filtered in the order: $E_{Æ} - A_{Æ}$. It results that the (first) filter $E_{Æ}$ addresses the source system (in this case, the societal system), while the (second) filter $A_{Æ}$ addresses the target system (in this case, the social justice system).

4.3 Social Justice Reaction Norms

The reactions of the social justice system to the societal system is governed also by a law, which I would call the *law of ethics* (*LE*). This law has two inter-related finalities, too: (a) to justify and, based on justification, to explain, the reactions (including the reaction norms) of the social justice system to the actions/reactions of the societal system; (b) to introduce/indicate the internal arrow that drives the very kinematics of the social justice system.

(a) justification/explanation

The law/principle of ethics (*LE*) is a regulative law, like in the case of the societal system. This means that the respective law is concerned with verifying the ethical mark in the individuals' relationships (interactions). The ethical mark of the individuals' interactions can be expressed as follows: *do not reduce the social capital as an effect of the interactions occurred.*[33] Consequently, the reactions and reaction norms, respectively, of the social justice system will be designed, adjusted, and implemented so that the interactions at the society level preserve the social capital, in their two species: social capital of socialization and social capital of individualization/individuation, respectively. It is worth noting that we do not, yet, speak about the ethical features of those interactions, since, from the societal perspective, we are primarily and fundamentally interested in the viability/sustainability of the societal interactions of any nature, from economic to political ones.

(b) internal arrow

The law/principle of social justice (*LE*) must, by definition, introduce and, consequently, indicate the direction in which the social justice system goes. So, like the justification/explanation finality, the internal arrow works as a regulative principle, by ensuring on the fact that the kinematics of the social justice system follows the fundamental arrow of that system. As I will show further, such an arrow addresses the fitness of the mutation occurred in the social justice system.

In this context, the social justice system will design, adjust, and implement its own reactions based on those norms (reaction norms) that simultaneously verify the two above-mentioned roles permanently played by the law of ethics. Technically, like in the case of societal system, the two roles of the law of ethics function as filters in cascade. If we note with E_E the explanatory role of the law of ethics, as the first filter, and with A_E the directing (tied to the arrow) role of the law of ethics, as the second filter, then any reaction of the social justice system, as response to the societal system, will be double filtered in the order:$E_E - A_E$. It results that the (first) filter E_E addresses the source system (in this case, the social justice system), while the (second) filter A_E addresses the target system (in this case, the societal system).

5 The Laws of Regional Reaction Norms

In this section, I will bring some extra comments on the laws introduced at Sects. 4.2 and 4.3 above.

5.1 *The Framework*

The fundamental law/principle always was a siren song, for scientists, philosophers, theologians, and even artists, in the entire history of mankind. This aspiration is, of course, a kind of reductionism but, as I belief, no knowledge is possible without an (implicit or explicit) reductionist assumption. The gravitation law, the second Thermodynamic law, the countless number of conservation laws (especially in Physics[34]), the recent aspirant constructal law,[35] etc., to list only a few examples, each of them pretends to provide a fundamental explanation and, as just suggested above, a basic arrow of the regions to which it is applicable. Of course, some of them claim a universal character (and, so, applicability), as the constructal law, and my own proposal called the *minimal entropic gradient of interaction*.

This section is focused on the issue of finding a basic principle of evolution, where evolution is understood in its widest meaning, that is, regarding any entity of the reality, either objective (things) or subjective (ideas). To be mentioned that Darwinism, as theory of evolution, has three key features: a) addresses the biologically living entities only; b) presents, in fact, a mechanism only, but not a principle of evolution; c) favours the structure over the function, meaning that structure generates function, never inversely.

5.2 *Briefly, on the Interaction*

Generally, by interaction is understood an exchange between (at least) two entities, usually things,[36] of three kinds: (a) substance; (b) energy; (c) information, so that that exchange leaves a mark/trace in the two entities implied. It results these remarkable features of interaction, in its abstract meaning:

- it does not matter the cause/conditionality that triggers or allow such an exchange;
- it must be produced a double impression (if we focus on the standard exchange, which implies two entities) after the exchange;
- it is difficult to establish an active entity vs. a passive one of the exchange, since, for example, the cause of exchange could be located in the very "passive" entity (see the relationship between flowers—the passive—and the butterfly—the active);

In the matter of interaction, the basic question is that regarding the principle (if exist) that drives the interaction (*Nota bene*: or a minimal set of such principles, after the case). It seems there are four such alternative principles[37] that have been proposed:

- the structure of physical mass in the Universe,[38] which we can call: the *ontological geodesic*. This principle of interaction acts, dominantly, in the physical world (*Nota bene*: the biologically living entities are natural ones too);
- the entropy law, which we can call: the *interactive geodesic*. This principle (known also as the second law of Thermodynamics) requires the interaction to follow the pattern which always increases the (Thermodynamic) entropy of the Universe as a whole. Although there are entities/systems that maintain or even decrease their entropy, the dissipative dynamical systems (Nicolis & Prigogine,

1987), this case will lead, finally, also to the heat death of the Universe. This principle acts universally;

- the constructal law (Bejan, 2014), which we can call: the *optimizing geodesic* (Dinga et al., 2023).
- the axiology or the belief or the theoretical rationality (minimal set of common values of the society), which we can call *cultural geodesic* (Dinga et al., 2023).

5.3 General Background

Knowledge, Principles, and Mechanisms

Knowledge (in its meaning of Greek ἐπιστήμη, transliterated *epistēmē*) is not else than generalization, that is, unifying of the particulars, either inside a given territory or (as desirable) putting together as many as possible territories (*Nota bene*: to be mentioned that the knowledge is seen here in the Santiago School of cognition, that is in the simplest sense of sensitivity, of any kind, to the environment action/reaction[39]). Generalization is possible only based on principles, which are, by definition, unifying.[40] A principle (or a law) answers the question "why",[41] by evoking the basic causality involved in some real kinematics (moving on space, growing, (re)shaping, flowing, etc.). So, the relationships between knowledge, principles, and mechanisms could be synoptically presented as shown in Fig. 7.

Criteria of Behaviour

It can be put the question about the existence of a criterion according to which the things work. To answer this question, I shall consider every one of the three possibilities to behave: (i) maximization; (ii) minimization; (iii) surviving. Firstly, some general considerations are useful.

- based on the reason of intelligibility, it must be accepted that any system in the world (that is, in the Universe) is driven by causality (no matter whether that causality is deterministic, or stochastic, or random);
- causality introduces an arrow (that can be called causality arrow[42]) which generates the finality[43];

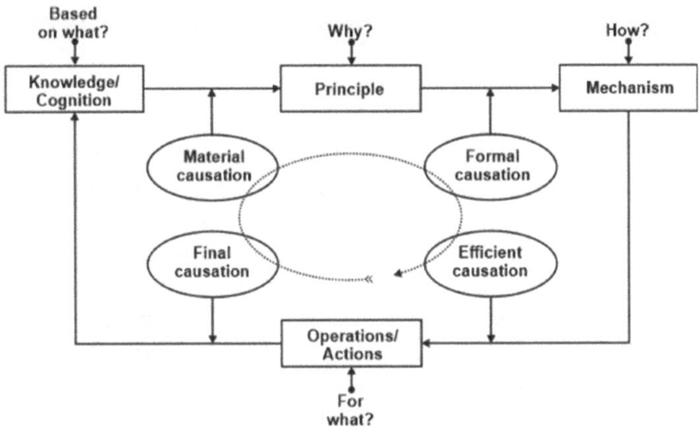

Fig. 7 Tetrad: causality, knowledge, principle, and mechanism (*Source* author)

- generally, to find a criterion of behaviour (that is, of relationships between a system and its environment) means to find a principle that brings the system to its finality.

Let us examine the three ("choice"-based) possible finalities of a generic system.

(i) *maximizing* (of an outcome). It is needed to reach the highest value of a given variable or parameter associated with a system, which verifies a set of constraints. The problem here is how is it known such "best" value? If we must look at the entire Universe, it is obvious that most part of it lacks psychism and, *a fortiori*, lacks consciousness (that is the judgement). Consequently, generally, the world does not maximize.[44] *Nota bene*: in fact, even the (ordinary) humans cannot maximize anything, because of their bounded rationality (but, of course, the mathematical models "can" that). This means the maximizing as criterion of behaviour is not at all general, but rather local, temporary, and contingent[45];

(ii) *minimizing* (of the outcome, also). As known, the criterion of minimizing was coined in 1744 by Maupertuis (the principle of least/stationary action), based on Fermat's principle of least time, and has been formalized in 1834 in the Hamiltonian system. I shall use Maupertuis's principle to discuss the minimizing criterion of behaviour (or of finality). This time, it seems that it is not needed to "know" in advance, as in the case of maximizing, which is the minimum value of the outcome (that is, of finality), due to the action of the first law of Thermodynamics. This means the minimizing as a criterion of behaviour has a necessary character, so being of general application in the world;

(iii) *survival* (as integral entity). To survive means, generally, to ensure a kind of persistence in time of the individual (limited, of course, by internal peculiarities of the system in case), either by replication, including reproduction, or by simple durability (*Nota bene*: the survival of the species is a result of individuals' survival). Of course, the property of survival is applicable to any system, not to living ones only. From logical perspective, it is required, for the analyst, to position the survival in relation to maximizing and minimizing. My opinion is the following:

- essentially, the survival has two thresholds: (a) a floor threshold—that is coincident with the minimizing level; this means getting the minimizing still provides the survival; (b) a ceiling threshold—that is, coincident with the maximizing level (but, as seen, this level is unreachable, it is functioning just like an asymptote);
- consequently, perhaps, it should be concluded as follows:
  - minimizing, as lowest level of survival, is necessarily functioning for the non-living systems, based exclusively on the cognition in Santiago School interpretation—for example: light always traverses space along the mass/gravitational geodesic, which I called above ontological geodesic, so minimizing the road (and, given a constant speed, the time); consequently, for the non-living systems/entities, the functioning is necessarily regulated by the natural laws, and the natural laws always constraint the non-living systems/entities towards minimizing[46];
  - the functioning over the minimizing level and under the maximizing one is only possible for living systems/entities—more general, for the dissipative ones.[47] These entities can "oppose" natural laws (that is, can avoid

the minimizing) by paying a price, namely by accelerating the entropy in their proximal environment. The possibility for this "opposition" is called free will, which requires at least psychism, not necessarily the reasonism.

5.4 *Mechanics of Evolution*

To discuss the issue of evolution in the mechanic world (by which I understand the non-living systems), it is necessary to provide a typology of changing. Figure 8 resumes, for the current necessities, Fig. 1.

The mechanic world addresses only the objects[48] (that is, the non-living entities). In such a world can exist: (a) moving—simple travel of space, that is, modification of the spatial position; (b) growing—simple modification in size, that is, modification in dimension, both being changes of order 1, that is, independently from either purposes or values implied by cultural subjects, although the living entities are also apt by modification.[49] In the mechanic world, only the minimizing criterion of functioning is working, because there is not free will. Another conclusion is that in the mechanic world there is no evolution at all because evolution means, as necessary and prime step, the mutation, which, in turn, implies the structure changing. This conclusion is especially important for the claim of the constructal law (see later) to consider its own causality in the light or towards of evolution.

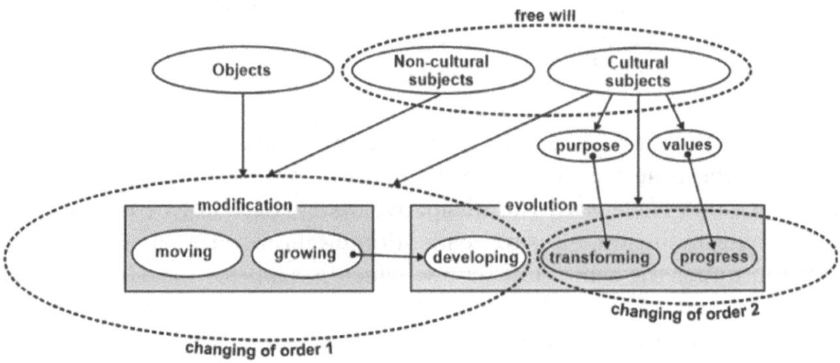

Fig. 8 General typology of changing in the world (*Source* Fig. 1)

Thermodynamics and Evolution

The position of Thermodynamics regarding the evolution is grounded in its second law, called entropy law.[50] Some predicates of the entropy are provided below (Dinga et al., 2021). The term entropy (from Greek: εντροπια, formed from "εν"—to, and "τροπη΄"—turning) means to go to, to turn into the direction. The meaning is that of a necessary propensity of a system/process/phenomenon in an unambiguous direction. That direction is of a permanent spontaneous increase of the entropy at the level of the Universe as a whole. The entropy of a system means the degree to which the energy is bound (is not free, which means unavailable), that is, is available to be used.

The main (orthodox) predicates of the concept of entropy seem to be:

- it is a state-function, not a process-function. Consequently, the value of the entropy variation does not depend on the intermediate stages (path), but only on the initial and final points (*Nota bene*: dependence on intermediate stages leads to process-functions);
- it is a macroscopic value (see Boltzmann's relation for entropy): more precisely, it signifies a macroscopic irreversibility derived from a microscopic possible reversibility (see, here, also the problem of Maxwell's demon);
- it is a statistical quantity (based on the statistical formulation of Thermodynamics); this justifies the occurrence of probability in the analytical formula of entropy in statistical Thermodynamics (because probabilities can only model the average of a population)[51];
- it is an additive (numerical) value.

In a sense, the entropy signifies a *sui generis* time arrow, so that we are sure that the time passes from a world with lower entropy to one with high entropy (*Nota bene*: the dissipative systems are not of relevance in the current discussion—it is to be mentioning, however, that such systems function under the same time arrow, which is valid for the Universe as a whole only; so, even if a dissipative system reduces or, at least, maintains, its level of entropy, exactly by this fact it not only increases but accelerates the global entropy).[52]

Constructal Law and Evolution

The concept of constructal law was introduced into the literature by a Romanian-American researcher—Adrian Bejan (2007). Constructal law aspires to be more primitive than the laws of Thermodynamics[53] (especially than the second law of Thermodynamics—the so-called law of entropy or the law of irreversibility of exergy).[54]

The constructal law has the following wording: "for an open system, of finite dimensions, to persist over time (to survive) it must evolve in such a way as to provide easier and easier access to the flows that pass through it".[55] *Nota bene*: in the constructal theory, any finite system is considered thermodynamically imperfect.

The key features of the constructal law are the following:

- it is placed in the position of principle of evolution[56];
- it targets both non-living and living nature[57];
- it restricts its scope to systems that are characterized by flows, more exactly, by flows that have a physical objectification[58]—both within the membrane of the system and in relation to its environment; moreover, another reduction in scope refers to the fact that the systems in question must move or live generating physical/materials supports for flows,[59] the so-called dendritic tubes[60];
- constructal evolution involves choice (either non-deliberative or deliberative, as the case may be);
- in constructal evolution, choice involves cognition[61];
- the application of the constructal law to evolution (at least in the case of living nature) provides quantitative regularities from an allometric perspective[62];
- constructal law rejects optimization in systems configuration[63];
- the constructal law is considered a law of physics but it is claimed as applicable everywhere, including in the social field, engineering, innovation, or psychology;
- the constructal law acts completely holistically—the evolutionary solution is formed at the level of the system which, thus, may contain subsystems that have not been regulated by the constructal law (Bejan, 2007).

Like the entropy law, the constructal law offers an arrow of time, compared to that provided by the second law of Thermodynamics: time passes in the direction in which the flows (of any nature: substantial, energetic, informational) sustaining the system's life maximize the intersections of those flows with the system's physical configuration.[64] *Nota bene*: again, the idea of maximization occurs, although, probably, it is not needed (or it is even dis-functional, as we will try to show elsewhere).

Revisiting the Concept of Interaction

The criterion of interaction is crucial in my paper, in order to introduce my proposal for an, as I believe, general (maybe universal) law of interaction.

The reality (objective, subjective, and objectified)[65] exists if and only if its components, at all levels of reality, interact, in a way or another, among them—substantially, energetically, and informationally. Indeed, the gravity, entropy, and constructalness[66] are based, in their explanations, on claiming the interaction. So, what is, generally and abstractly, the interaction? I would try to identify the sufficient (SPs) and new[67] necessary predicates (NNPs) that qualify a relationship as being an interaction. *Nota bene*: will be examined the interaction between two entities but, of course, the result is valid for any number of interacting entities, as well.

(i) ($SP1$) has a *double arrow*: the two entities must develop actions/reactions, no matter of what kind, in a double sense (in other words, it must there is a reciprocal activism); this means, simply, that any action is necessarily followed by a reaction. I would formulate this by adopting the assumption that any trace requires a trace—a way to say that any trace delivers a catalyst for a counter-trace. Really, could we take this to infinity? My answer is:

- a trace coming from a paired trace is necessarily smaller as intensity than the first one. Somewhat happens an amortization of the trace's intensity, by its circulating, alternatively, between two systems. As this "principle" is general, it can be written (S_i is the system i, t_{ij}^{τ} is the trace engraved at moment τ by S_i on S_j): $t_{ij}^{\tau} < t_{ji}^{\tau-1}$, for $\tau \in \mathbb{N}$;
- so, we have, in fact, two (logical) necessities here: (1) the necessity of reaction to any action[68]; (2) the necessity of non-perpetuity of action/reaction process (or, equivalently, the necessity of the trace's intensity amortization).

(ii) ($SP2$) leaves a *trace*: any action/reaction must leave a trace on the entity on which it is focused.[69] Leaving a trace means, mainly:

- makes a structural change—this is mandatory, since if the trace is only at functional level, it is either temporary (after a while it disappears) or reversible (the initial functioning is recovered). *Nota bene*: no matter the nature of that change—substantial, energetical, informational;
- the trace must have significance for the structure of the recipient entity—namely, it must have an amount/quantity of impact over the significance threshold of the focused entity.

Nota bene: one could object here that $SP1$ and $SP2$ are not independent of each other, arguing that, once there is a double arrow of the relationship, it results that each arrow leaves a trace in the "partner" of the relationship (so, $SP1 \rightarrow SP2$), and, reciprocally, one both the entities implied leave traces in the "partner" of relationship, it results that a double arrow works (so, $SP2 \rightarrow SP1$). In fact, such reasoning is fallacious. Our reasons are as follows:

- in order of existing a double arrow means that both the entities involved exhibit, concomitantly, the propensity to objectify the relationship in the case. It does not result at all that this contemporaneity of the propensities must leave a trace in both entities engaged[70];
- it is, obviously, possible to leave traces in both the entities engaged in a relationship between them, although the relationship is generated by a single arrow—simply, once the relationship is objectified, each entity involved leaves its trace in/on the other entity.

(iii) ($SP3$) is based on a *rationality* (a reason grounding): any action/reaction must be grounded on a reason—natural laws (for the necessary case), positive laws or even free will (for the social/societal field). The evoked reason is required by at least the following subjacent (of substrate) reasons:

- a logical principle: the principle of sufficient reason—any change arises if and only if there is a sufficient justification (of any nature) for that arising (the fourth "principle" of logic, introduced by Leibniz)[71];

- an ontological principle: the general principle of causality[72]—any change arises if and only if a cause (singular or multiple, as such or in a conditioning way) manifests, either in an objective or subjective manner.

Nota bene: any reason has the potential/capability to deliver a criterion of triggering/stopping the action/reaction phenomenon in case. To be mentioned that: (a) the interactional criterion is not redundant with the reason. The reason is a general justification/motivation, having a grounding meaning, while the interactional criterion has an operational sense, that is, induces the very mechanism of the action/reaction relationship in the case; (b) the interactional criterion can be objective, subjective, or objectified, depending on the world in which it is operated. Perhaps, it must be close related, however, to the reason of action/reaction phenomenon.

(iv) (*SP*4) there is a *criterion of choice grounding*. The criterion of choice must be understood as an indication (of cognitive nature[73]) based on which an entity mandatorily and uniquely establishes with which entity will exchange the actions/reactions. Some additional considerations:

- such predicate requires the interaction to have not only an impact arrow (in fact, a double arrow) but, also, a choice arrow. It is to be mentioned that the choice arrow (which is equivalent to the criterion of choice) is double, too.
- being double, the choice arrow must verify the (instantaneous) coincidence of the two choices of the entities entering an interaction. However, such a coincidence requires some comments:
  - in the case of entities which are not endowed with free will (so, which behave completely necessarily), the coincidence of the two choices is, in turn, necessary—in other words, the instantaneousness of the coincidence of the two choices is unproblematic, better said, is, somewhat, automatic.
  - a problem arises in the case of the entities endowed with free will,[74] where it is possible that the non-coincidence of the two choices to occur (e.g., in the economic field,

in a non-monetary economy, the exchange of goods happens if and only if the coincidence of the traders for the two goods involved happens[75]).

(v) $(SP5)$ is ***universally acting***. In my opinion, such a sufficiency predicate has and has not, equally, the logical "right" to be retained. In this context, the distinction between generality and universality must be done:

- the generality is that property (of a thing, property, or relationship) to be held by all species of a genus (in the logical meaning of the terms species and genus), while the universality extends that property to all genera;
- based on this operational distinction, I would be inclined to accept the universality of action as a sufficiency predicate for the concept of interaction.

Nota bene: so, an interaction (IA) does exist if and only if is valid the following formalization:

$$IA \leftarrow (SP1) \bigwedge (SP2) \bigwedge (SP3) \bigwedge (SP4) \bigwedge (SP5) = \bigwedge_{i=1}^{5} (SPi)$$

(vi) $(NNP1)$ is ***not singular*** (or, equivalently, is inherently repeatable/replicable): an interaction, once arisen in the world as result of conjunction of sufficiency predicates, is necessarily born with internal principles for replicating itself. Why is important this new necessary predicate? I think, for the following reasons:

- a trace produces an effect at the structural level, as $(SP2)$ claims, but such an effect will generate an impact (a second-order trace, more exactly, a trace's trace) to the causality in force of the entity which recorded that trace;
- a change in the causality architecture will necessarily generate a reaction towards the entity that produced that trace's trace, and so on (*Nota bene*: of course, this self-resuming of the interaction is subjected to $(SP1)$, namely to an inherent dynamic amortization of the action/reaction sizing; it can be said that there is here too an (unique) arrow–the arrow of diminishing of the quantity (size) of action/reaction[76];
- the logical generating of the $(NNP1)$ is:

$$(NNP1) \leftarrow (SP1) \bigwedge (SP2)$$

(vii) $(NNP2)$ is at least of *objectifying* signification: interaction cannot be only subjective, that is, narrowed to an individual consciousness—for example, a fantasy, a desire, etc. It must be either objective or objectified in one way or another. The logical generating of this predicate is:

$$(NNP2) \leftarrow (SP2)$$

Discussion

- regarding (*SP1*), if one of the entities involved is, in fact, passive, this means it does not need to react to the action exerted on it, because, for example, the action maintains in the dead zone of the passive entity or because other causes, like the insensitivity. Moreover, in some cases, we could be in a state of a false action[77];
- the action (and reaction, as well) must be understood in their largest meaning: substantive, energetic, informational/communicative;
- the trace required by $(SP2)$ can be of any nature, any size, and with any impact which is not null;
- at $(SP3)$, it is not required that interactors be aware of the reason of interaction, instead, for example, an external observer could be aware of it; $(SP3)$ is not superfluous, although the necessity drives many interactions, since, in the social field, contingency and free will dominate over interactions of any kind, and so contingency leads many decisions/interactions to fall under unconscious driving;
- $(NNP2)$ is the necessary result of $(SP2)$: indeed, if a decision/action remains inside subjectivity, it cannot leave a trace in any other entity[78] (although it leaves a trace in the entity in the case). So, the interactions, as defined here, have existence in Popper's worlds 1 or 3 only.

5.5 *Short Analysis of the Three Claimed Laws of Interaction*

From my perspective on the (universal) concept of interaction, I will provide below a short principled examination of the three well-known and so-called laws of interaction: a) gravity law; b) entropy law; c) constructal law, then I will provide my own proposal regarding such a law of interaction.

Gravity Law

The gravity law has been introduced by Newton in his *Philosophiae Naturalis Principia Mathematica*. Its content is: two masses attract between them directly proportional with corresponding masses and inversely proportional with the square of the (physical) distance between them. Let us verify if the gravity law is a law (principle) of interaction.

- ($SP1$) is *verified*, since the two entities (masses) exert a reciprocal attraction, so there is a double arrow of actions/reactions implied;
- ($SP2$) seems *not* to be *verified*. Indeed, between the two masses, the attraction force does not leave traces, so, if any of the two masses enter further into gravity relationships with different other masses, the gravity law will act as if the two initial masses would not have been in a gravitational relation ever;
- ($SP3$) is *verified*, since the gravitational attraction is a universal necessary principle of natural causality;
- ($SP4$) is *not verified*, since the gravitational attraction occurs instantaneously and non-intermediated by other phenomenon/event—simply, the two masses seat in the places where the space curvature obliges them (*Nota bene*: there is no liberty here, all is necessity only);
- ($SP5$) is *verified* since the gravitational attraction occurs among any entities in the Universe. Indeed, it is no needed those entities have mass, since the gravitation is not a force, but a necessary configuration of the space generated by the masses positioning.

Consequently, since two of the sufficiency predicates of sufficiency ($SP2$) and ($SP4$) are violated, the gravity law cannot be held as an interaction base (principle, law), neither in the natural world so, much less in the world in general. Regarding the gravity law, perhaps we should say that it is a natural *positioning law*, not an interaction law.[79] Considering that gravity is, in fact, a necessary property of the physical world provided by the distribution of mass (i.e., space curvature), then any mass positions itself related to that curvature, and this positioning is made by any mass—so, the physical equilibrium of masses in space is the result of general positioning, not of interactions between masses. That is, the attraction formula of Newton is a consequence, not a cause of such general positioning. Additionally, the gravity law is a non-evolutive law—indeed, the global positioning is got simultaneously by all masses in the Universe, based on initial conditions (the space curvature) and the moving law. If, no matter the causes—for example, a supernova explosion, or a black-hole implosion—the initial conditions change (i.e., the space curvature distribution changes), then instantaneously,[80] the mass distribution/positioning changes, without any evolutive signification. So, the gravity law, as positioning law, is, at the same time, an optimizing law,[81] which means that the redistribution of masses as the effect of change of the initial conditions (space curvature) is the best one (the so-called first best). It must be mentioned also that the gravity law acts instantaneously and globally (IG).[82]

Nota bene: it can be said that gravity law is a non-evolutive, universal, optimizing,[83] and a (IG) positioning law, but not an interaction law.

Entropy Law

The concept of entropy has been introduced by Rudolf Clausius in his work *A Contribution to the History of the Mechanical Theory of Heat*. Principled, the entropy of a system can be defined as a measure of the degree of (molecular) disorder existing in the system.[84] The basic concept of entropy has acquired many other equivalent meanings, including that of the available/bound energy. Here I do not discuss than the entropy law under its (possible) potential to ground the interactions. So, I will verify the sufficiency predicates of the concept of interaction in the case of entropy law.

- ($SP1$) is *verified*. Indeed, when two entities come into action/reaction relationships, the entropic state of each acquires some cognition on the entropic state of the other, in order to "establish" which will be the direction of the entropy flow—namely from the entity with high entropy to the entity with low entropy[85];

- ($SP2$) is *verified*. Indeed, the necessary transfer of entropy from the entity with high entropy to the entity with low entropy changes the entropy in both entities: the entity with high entropy reduces its entropy, while the entity with low entropy increases its entropy—in other words, the relationships leave traces in both entities involved;
- ($SP3$) is *verified*. Indeed, the relationships between entities, under the entropic perspective, are driven exactly by the entropic gradient of the entities involved. This reason is of necessity, like in the case of the gravity law;
- ($SP4$) seems *not* to be *verified*. Two questions arise here (i) whether the entropy law acts instantaneously and globally (IG), like, for example, the gravity law; (ii) whether the localness can offer, by itself, a criterion of choice for the entropic relationship. My opinion is the following:

  (i) entropy law acts sequentially and locally (SL). The sequentialness of entropic relationships denies the instantaneity (I), while the localness of these relationships denies the globality (G);
    - the sequentialness of entropy law action is generated by the fact that, in contrast to gravity law, entropy law implies something like a force, namely, the entropic gradient will necessarily cause the transfer of entropy between the entities involved (*Nota bene*: the new entropic gradient will repeat the phenomenon, until the entropic equalization between those entities)[86];
    - the localness of entropy relationships is based on their sequentialness: the entities involved must be somewhat... neighbours, in order to "know", one about the other, the respective entropy level.[87] Consequently, the entropy law is not a positioning law (as gravity law), but it is, so to speak, an *exchange law*[88];

  (ii) since entropy law is not a positioning law, the entities are contingently positioned one to another (or, in other words, we have a contingent neighbourhood[89]), from the perspective of entropy. Such a state leads to the following outcomes:
    - an entropic exchange occurs between entities exclusively based on spatial proximity;

- such a kind of entropic exchange does not need a criterion of choice regarding the entity with which a given entity will perform that entropic exchange;
- so, it has been shown that $(SP4)$ sufficiency predicate to exist an interaction is violated. In addition, entropy law is an exchange law;

• $(SP5)$ is *verified*. Indeed, the entropy law acts universally, since each real entity permanently increases its entropy, and this increasing occurs, at a last resort, in a relationship between each conceivable entity and the universal environment.

Nota bene: it can be said that entropy law is an evolutive law, non-optimizing one, and a (SL) positioning law, but not an interaction law. It can be qualified as a (universal) *exchange law*.

Constructal Law

The constructal law, as briefly explained at section "Constructal Law and Evolution", aspires as well (like gravity law, and entropy law) to be a law of (universal) interaction. To be a law of universal interaction, this law should, of course, to be, primarily, an interaction law. Let us verify if the constructal law verifies the four sufficiency predicates of the concept of interaction.

• $(SP1)$ it seems *not be verified*. The constructal law is, indeed, uni-directioned: the physical configuration of the system involved (more exactly, the system's dendrites) distributes spatially so that the constructal law principle, above mentioned, to be verified. It is obvious that such a change in that spatially distribution affects the system in the case only, but not at all the environment whose useful flows will intersect the dendrites in (an eventual) maximum mode. In other words, the constructal law exhibit a single arrow of the relationship between system and its environment—from system to environment.[90]

Additional discussion

It can be thought the (symmetrical) case, in which the maximization of the intersections between the environment's useful flows for the system living, and the system's dendritic configuration addresses not the spatial distribution of dendrites but the temporal such a distribution. It is easy to observe that the reasoning is *mutatis mutandis* and respecting the basic principle of the constructal law, basically the same, in the sense that we have not, here, a double arrow of influence.

- ($SP2$) *is verified*. Indeed, the intersection between the environment's needed flows and the dendrites of the system influences both of the two "actors": the environment consumes some of its resources (as they are used by the system), so changing its initial endowment with resources, and the system changes its "standard of life" by consuming those resources;
- ($SP3$) *is verified*. The constructal law is governed by the principle of (spontaneous) distribution of spatial (and temporal as well)[91] of the physical configuration of a generic system[92] so that the contact (intersection) between the system's dendrites and the environment's flows, which are useful (for the system) to ensure its living/survival be maximized;
- ($SP4$) *is verified*. Principled, it is not necessary that both the system involved in a possible interaction have their own (possible different) criteria of choice within the relationship in the case.[93] So, the system in the case has such a criterion to choose, namely the maximization of environment's useful flows intersection with the system's dendrites[94];
- ($SP5$) *is verified*. This issue is difficult enough, consequently I will provide some analytical considerations aimed to clarify the aspects involved:

    (i) some could bring the objection that the constructal law focuses on the spatialized entities. However, it is easy to show that this particularity is not necessary, so, entities that do not exhibit objective spatialized configuration could also fall under this law. It results that such a grounding of the non-universality of the constructal law can be justifiably rejected;

    (ii) some could bring the objection that the constructal law addresses only those entities that are endowed with dendrites (tubes), so the intersection between such dendrites and the environment's useful (for the entity in the case) flows, of any nature, be maximized. However, the dendrites are only particular cases that fall under the principle of constructal law—we can easily imagine entities that maximize that intersection without using dendrites but its body as such. It results that such a grounding of the non-universality of the constructal law can be justifiably rejected;

(iii) some could object that the entities targeted by constructal law are of spatial signification only. I already showed that a spatial configuration is logically equivalent to a temporal configuration (spatialization is substitutable with temporalization). It results that such a grounding of the non-universality of the constructal law can be justifiably rejected;

(iv) some could object that under the constructal law fall only objective entities. However, it can be easily shown that the other two categories of entities in the world (objectified and subjective, respectively) also fall (or can fall) under this law, this time either in a publicly quasi-deliberative way (as in the objectified reality) or in a singular idiosyncratic way (as in the subjective reality). Some details will bright clarifications:
   - the quasi-deliberative way refers to the fact that the objectified reality (the so-called social reality—namely, Popper's third world) is the result of deliberative actions (acts or abstentions) of myriad individuals which follows their interests (in the invisible hand's mechanism), without any common intentionality;
   - the idiosyncratic way refers to three possible cases: (a) unconscious actions (*Nota bene*: which have, however, their... rationality); (b) deliberative (even programmatic) actions, based on an assumed model of rationality; (c) inextricable mix between conscious and unconscious actions, based on propensity.[95]

Nota bene: it can be said that constructal law is an evolutive law, optimizing one, and a (CL) constructive law, but not an interaction law. It can be qualified as a (universal) *structuring law*.

A synthesis of the analytical examinations of the three laws regarding the concept of interaction is provided in Table 1.

So, according to our set of sufficiency predicates, no one of the three laws aspiring to ground the relationships is a law of interaction, because no one does simultaneously verify the sufficiency predicates. The "closest" law to the statute of an interaction law seems to be the constructal

Table 1 Comparative synoptic of the three alleged laws of interaction

	SPs					*Type of law*		
	$SP1$	$SP2$	$SP3$	$SP4$	$SP5$	*Positioning*	*Structuring*	*Exchanging*
Gravity law (GL)	x	?	x	?	x	x		
Entropy law (EL)	x	x	x	?	x			x
Constructal law (CL)	?	x	x	x	x		x	

Source author

law (it verifies four of the five sufficiency predicates, except the double arrow predicate. Of course, one could reject the$SP1$, so the constructal law becomes an interaction law, but such a rejection must be seriously argued. Supposing the $SP1$ is rejected as a sufficiency predicate, then, according to the formal logic, it means that we pass from species to genus. But which is that genus? In our opinion, the largest genus in the matter of relationships is the interaction, so the sphere of interaction cannot be framed into a larger semantical (and ontological, as well) concept).

5.6 *My Proposal*

(a) Preliminaries

Two sufficiency predicates ($SP3$—a grounding reason—and $SP5$ a universal character) are verified by all the three laws examined. On the other part, in two of the three cases, $SP4$ (a choice criterion) is violated, so that predicate seems to be the rarest verified of the five predicates proposed. Gravity law violates two of the five predicates ($SP2$—leaving a trace—and $SP4$—a choice criterion). In such a context, we think that a (genuine) interaction law could start from one of the two laws which violate a single predicate each, that is, either entropy law or constructal law. Since we do not see how to introduce a double arrow ($SP1$) into the general philosophy of constructal law (*Nota bene*: as it is today formulated and accepted, of course), the only possibility to get a (hoped genuine) interaction law seems to us to start from the entropy law. So, in what follows, we try to build up a hypothesis (better said, a conjecture) which will "help" the entropy law to verify the *SP*4 sufficiency predicate, namely a criterion of choice the relationship in which a given entity engages—of course, the result, if our trying succeeds, will not be longer the entropy law, but another law.

(b) The concept

I would call my proposal the *law of minimal entropic gradient*, abbreviated, from now on, as *LMEG*.

LMEG can be expressed as follows: *any entity will interact with that entity with respect to which it has the minimal*[96] *entropic gradient*. Some explanations must be done, briefly: (b1) what is an entropic order? (b2) what is understood by entropic gradient? (b3) which are the problems that arise around the "calculation" of the minimal entropic gradient? (b4) what signifies the concept of minimal entropic gradient? (b5) what about the locality of *LMEG* action?

(b1) entropic order (*EO*)

By entropy we understand, in the most general sense, and relative to some (generic) entity/system, the order which that entity/system holds form an entropic perspective. The concept of order is free-based—an order exists whenever the observer (generally, a cultural subject) can associate that entity/system with no matter what kind of intelligibility. The free character of order refers to the very fact that the intelligibility in the case can be of any kind. Generally, the observer has a list (usually internalized, that could be called *list of known orders—LKO*) of ontological orders and he/she simply compares the intelligibility seized in the entity/system concerned with the items in the list—if a coincidence is found, then he/she assigns the item in the case to that entity/system, while, in the opposite case, either decide the entity/system is un-ordered or (the most frequent case) write in the list the observed state as a new item of intelligibility (a new order).

Additional comments

Any intelligibility is an effect of causality (although can exist causality whose intelligibility is not yet seized). An entity/system can simultaneously hold many orders, some of them not yet registered into the

LKO. In fact, the observer will see the orders according to three distinct criteria (which can work concomitantly as well): a) orders already known, registered in LKO; b) orders he/she can, epistemologically, observe—generally conditioned by the theories accepted; c) orders he/she has an interest of any kind to see and consider.

Among the possible (i.e., actual, and potential) orders that the causality principle enacts is the entropic order (EO). An entropic order (EO) is an order that addresses the internal capacity of an entity/system to generate energy of any kind.[97] The possibility to produce energy is provided by the degree of internal *heterogeneity* of that entity/system—the higher heterogeneity, the lower entropy, and the higher exergy. Of course, the term heterogeneity is applicable from the perspective of any criterion which is observable under the three lenses above mentioned. Consequently, it can exist Thermodynamic entropy, epistemological entropy, behavioural entropy, social entropy (Dinga et al., 2020), and so on.

(b2) entropic gradient (EG)

By entropic gradient, it must be understood the difference between the entropic orders of two given systems/entities. The problem, here, is the commensurability of two entropic orders, belonging to two different systems, between them, since, once they are commensurable, in the matter of measure/measurability/measurement of the entropic gradient, we can presuppose that exists or can be somewhat found such a way of determination. We provide the following considerations on the issue of entropic order commensurability:

- it is not required that the compared systems be of the same category/class/species since the entropic order has a common element for any system in the Universe: the exergy. Of course, the exergy manifests differently in different systems but, no matter the way of quantifying the exergy, any system has a measure of its exergy, which is the entropic order measure;
- the entropic order must be expressed as a real coefficient belonging to the closed real interval [0,1], to easily allow relevant comparison of the entropic order in two systems.

So, after the entropic orders are measured in two systems, as EO_1 and EO_2, respectively, then the entropic gradient will be: $EG = \left|m^{EO_1} - m^{EO_2}\right|$, where with m^{EO_i} is denoted the measure (in an approapriate way) of the entropic order in the system i. If $m^{EO_i} \equiv \varepsilon_i$, where ε is the coefficient of exergy, $EG = |\varepsilon_1 - \varepsilon_2|$. The module is necessary since, by now, we are interested of the magnitude of that difference (the algebraic sign of EG will be considered further).

Nota bene: two fundamental questions arise here: (1) what exactly means exergy for different kinds of entropy conceivable (Thermodynamic entropy, epistemological entropy, behavioural entropy, social entropy); (2) how could calculate the two given systems, themselves, the entropic gradient between them? My opinions are as follows:

(1) the signification of the term exergy

Generally, the exergy is a potential to provide/deliver useful principles for observer/analyst/user, related to a generic given system. For the four classes of entropy, I think the content of the term exergy is the following:

(1.1) *Thermodynamic entropy*: the (absolute or relative) bound energy of different kinds that can be extracted from that system—the "quantity" of such exergy is inversely proportional to the entropy; e.g., coal has a lower entropy than ash;

(2.1) *epistemological entropy*: the (absolute or relative) bound knowledge of different kinds that can be extracted from that system—the "quantity" of such exergy is inversely proportional to the entropy; e.g., an axiomatic theory has a lower entropy than a (pure) narrative one. Something else can be said here: this epistemological exergy could be called exformation, so that an axiomaric theory provides a higher exformation than a (pure) narrative one;

(3.1) *behavioural entropy*: the (absolute or relative) predictions/pre-announcements regarding the future decisions/actions that can be extracted from that system—the "quantity" of such exergy is inverse proportional to the entropy; e.g., a behaviour based on announced/committed principles has lower entropy than a behaviour based on the way called seeing and making;

(4.1) *social/societal entropy*: the (absolute or relative) degree of certainty regarding the achievement of personal purposes related to wellbeing and self-esteem—the "quantity" of such exergy is inverse proportional to the entropy; e.g., a societal system with a Constitution that ensures the free and democratic functioning has a lower entropy than a societal system with an authoritarian leader.

(2) the entropic gradient calculation

There exist three cases, equally possible:

(i) only one of the two systems is "endowed" with intelligence[98]—then (only) that system can calculate EG. For a (presumable) interaction, such a condition is, however, sufficient, so it is not needed that both systems can do the calculus of EG; this case is belonging to the class of systems-observers—this class must contain at least a system "endowed" with adequate intelligence to calculate EG (from now on, I note the cognition based on intelligence with *I-cognition*) and the cognition based on rationality with *R-cognition*;

(ii) none of the two given systems is liable to calculate the EG. In this case, a much more general issue must be examined. As known, between two generic systems, in Thermodynamic terms, the heat from the warmer system is spontaneously transferred to the colder system. The question is whether such a transfer of order (i.e., of high entropy) is, as spontaneously, possible no matter the order involved (namely, not exclusively regarding the Thermodynamic order). Regarding this question, my conjecture focuses on the following points:

- the only order in our Universe, before the life enters the existence, was the Thermodynamic one;
- regarding the Thermodynamic order, the Universe "established" the natural laws, namely, that order spontaneously degraded, either inside a closed system or by, also spontaneously, transfer of that degradation to other systems, in the case of open systems;

- by theoretical induction, it can be accepted (as conjecture) that any kind of order holds the spontaneous propensity to transfer itself from less ordered systems to more ordered ones, if such a transfer is, generally, possible[99];
- such a transfer of order does not need to be observed by an intelligent entity, as a condition to occur[100];
- so, I think we should accept the assumption that any lower order, of any kind, spontaneously transfers itself to (systems of) higher level of that order;
- since the above discussion has presupposed the Thermodynamic order (i.e., entropy), some considerations are required for the other three categories of order (entropies):
  - regarding the epistemological order/entropy: the higher order is spontaneously transferred to lower order (namely, between the systems concerned)—justification: the better cognitive performance of the axiomatic theories;
  - regarding the behavioural order/entropy: the direction of transfers of the order is ambiguous, in some cases the own predictability is desirable, in other cases it is not;—justification: the responsibility assigned to strong, announced, and committed principles of behaviour is accompanied by big costs for violating them;
  - regarding the societal order/entropy: the direction of transfers of the order is also ambiguous, depending on affinities or contradictions from a cultural perspective: values, history, geopolitical placement, political ideologies, religions, etc.

Nota bene: let us presuppose that a system holds a high level of order of kind α, and enters relationships with another system that holds a low level of order of kind β (where $\alpha \nmid \beta$, and the logical constant $\nmid$ means "ontologically incompatible"). No transfer of order α happens from the first system to the second one, and, of course, no transfer of order β happens from the second system to the first one. So, the identity of the orders in the two systems involved in interaction is the sufficient and necessary condition for the spontaneous transfer of the order (either in a direction or another).

Concluding on point (ii), I would say that no matter whether the systems related can or cannot calculate the *EG*, the transfer of the order occurs spontaneously if, as said before, such a transfer is, generally, possible ontologically.[101]

(iii) both the systems in interactions are "endowed" with the sufficient intelligence capable to calculate*EG*, for example contains human beings or, alternatively, artificial intelligence. Ignoring the lack of honesty (*Nota bene*: which lack is largely present in the economic interactions, for example), both systems will calculate the same*EG*.

Consequently, in the cases (i) and (iii) the *EG* can be correctly (and, fairly, if the case) calculated. Regarding the case (ii) some additional considerations are needed, as follows:

- either one or both of the systems involved must hold the unconscious potential of cognition (namely, a cognition capacity in the Santiago School meaning of cognition)—from now on, *S-cognition*[102];
- like in the case of (iii), if both systems have the potential of S-cognition (that is, if both systems are S-observers), the *EG* can be established and, necessarily, its value is the same for each system;

Nota bene: to be observed that, in all cases (i)–(iii), by determining the value of *EG*, the involved systems find, in fact, their environmental niche, as Maturana and Varela stipulated. Of course, we have here an exploring action, not an optimizing one, that is, we have a feature of evolutionism (see the argument of locality at point (e) below).

(b3) *MEG* calculation

The concept of ***minimal entropic gradient*** (*MEG*) addresses the fact that a given system will search the minimal value of *EG* among all such values it can calculate. But this means the system must operate a selection or a sorting out among all the *EG* values it can know by either I-cognition or S-cognition. How does this happen? We have here a cost-problem, namely, by choosing the *MEG*, the system which makes that choice minimizes the cost of entropic interaction—it is working, so, an application of the well-known principle of least action. To find an explanation pattern in this topic, it is needed to introduce a third type of cognition, called *V-cognition*. So, generally, there are four types of cognition:

- *S-cognition* (or ontological cognition): that cognition which does not imply the consciousness—for example, the choice that enzymes make when they catalize a chemical reaction; S-cognition is, as said before, the cognition in Santiago School meaning; S-cognition identifies the *niches*;
- *I-cognition* (or gnoseological cognition): that cognition which does imply the consciousness—for example, the choice of a fiscal normativity; I-cognition presupposes the operational intelligence or intellect (*Nota bene*: in a larger sense, it presupposes the practical rationality[103]); I-cognition identifies the *explanations*;
- *R-cognition* (or rational cognition): that cognition that implies, by the intermediation of the consciousness, a model of rationality, which means that it is accessible to cultural beings (as humans) only. R-cognition is based on both theoretical rationality (belief) and practical rationality (allocating, perhaps optimally, the appropriate means for achieving the assumed purpose; R-cognition identifies *reasons)*;
- *V-cognition* (or axiological cognition): that cognition which does imply also the consciousness, by addressing not only the operational intelligence, not only the rational assessment (both theoretically and practically), but a choice based on values (Audi, 2004). *Nota bene*: here are contained the beliefs or the deep propensities; V-cognition identifies the justifications or *foundations*.

Any type of cognition provides its own type of entropic order (EO), namely there are: (a) ontological entropic order (OEO)—generated by S-cognition; (b) gnoseological entropic order (GEO)—generated by I-cognition; (c) rational entropic order (REO)—generated by R-cognition; axiological entropic order (AEO)—generated by V-cognition. This way, it can be presupposed there are different qualitative costs[104] of entropic interaction related to different types of entropic order.

A brief systematization of the four types of entropic order, based on the four categories of cognition, is provided in Table 2.

Figure 9 synoptically suggests these intuitions (Notations:SC: *standard cost*, i.e., cost generated by quantitative gap between the two entropic

Table 2 Logical correlation *entropic order–cost of entropic interaction*

	S-cognition	*I-cognition*	*R-cognition*	*V-cognition*
Requirement	observational intelligence	operational intelligence	rational intelligence	axiological intelligence
Type or entropic order	OEO	GEO	REO	AEO
Finality	niche	explanation	reason	foundation

Source author

orders of the same type; TC: *transition cost*, i.e., cost generated by importing/exporting low/high different entropic orders); FC: *final cost*, i.e., the sum between SC and TC, namely, $FC = SC + TC$. *Nota bene*: the costs are indicated in a relative (structural) manner, i.e., in all cases,$SC + TC = 1$.

(b4) $LMEG$ meaning

Based on MEG allegations, I propose to take into consideration the ontological status of a law of minimal entropic gradient ($LMEG$) as a fundamental law of the world (both natural and cultural, non-living and living). It is based, of course, on the well-known entropy law (as the second law of Thermodynamics) but, in addition to that law, it is endowed with an entropic interaction arrow—this arrow is exactly theMEG. By

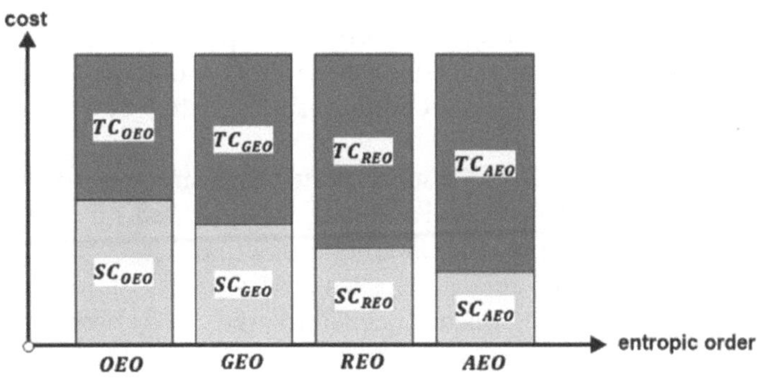

Fig. 9 Logical correlation *entropic order–cost of entropic interaction* (*Source* author)

adding this arrow, the LMEG gains the statute of interaction law (see the analysis at section "Entropy Law"). Of course, as shown above, the Thermodynamic entropic order is only one of the four entropic orders, but essential is the fact that LMEG verifies, this time, in its fundamental bases, the sufficiency predicate of a law of intersection, namely$SP4$.

(b5) locality of $LMEG$

This is a crucial issue in my proposal. Indeed, to search for the MEG, means, principled, calculating all the possible EGs and choosing the lowest among them. But how is it possible such a calculus?[105] Consequently, I will introduce here the concept of $LMEG$ locality. By locality of the $LMEG$ must be understood the spatial limitation of the systems to perform MEG calculus and the required comparisons among them. The limitation is generated by the practicability of the entropic interaction (exchange) between the given system and the other available systems for that interaction. This practicability is a kind of sufficiency from the survival perspective—the more spatially distant a system is, the less relevant it is to the entropic exchange in question. I will call this distance limit as the *entropic interaction horizon* (EIH).[106] The main features of EIH are:

- it is directly proportional with the spatial mobility (ability to move spatially—e.g., the speed) of the calculator system; so, an animal has an EIH much more extensive than a plant. Nota bene: to be mentioned that also the constructal law exhibits such a locality although it does not claim this property explicitly;
- the spatial limit, as such, is established (either spontaneously or deliberatively) based on survival conditionalities. I shall develop this idea a little bit:
- the space in which a system performs searching for partners regarding the entropic interaction is chosen based on a sufficiency (or enough) principle, not on an optimizing one;
- so, it is not needed to scan the entire space available or the entire space accessible; also, it is not needed to establish a criterion for such searching, which is predominantly instinctive[107];
- the space accessibility is assessed by the system in question within the practical rationality,[108] not by theoretical rationality;

- ontologically, EIH is formed by fringes, that is, the limit in question is a fringed limit, because different systems in searching partners for entropic interaction scan more or less space, and even the same system can scan more or less space in different moments or in different locations where it is.[109] To be observed that, somewhat, the constructal law suggests something of this type when it speaks about the spatial dendrites of the systems involved in self-construction: the dendrites act by fringing the space accessibility.

On the contrary, it is even the condition of such universality.

A conclusion with a great theoretical and methodological (maybe metaphysical, too) potential of the present chapter is the following: an interaction law is neither an optimizing, nor a maximizing principle, but a minimizing one. Besides, as well known, the principle of least action (as either Hamilton action or Maupertuis action) and the principle of minimum entropy production (Prigogine) have long entered basic research in all fields, from Newtonian Mechanics to Social Dynamics.

5.7 MEG and the Law of Societal Æsthetics

The societal æsthetics refers to the network of harmonious relationships, of any nature, occurring among free individuals in a societal system (social system "assisted" by the state). As already shown (see Chapter 7), by harmonious relationships are understood those relationships that conserve or increase the social capital. In this paragraph, I will examine the way in which the proposed law of interactions, called MEG (minimal entropic gradient), functions in relation to the societal æsthetics.

Preliminaries

The basic concept of societal æsthetics is the *symmetry*. The symmetry (see Chapter 6, Annex 1) is a category/species of social capital that ensures the individualization/individuation of the sociality, and can be, generally, defined as: the degree in which the individuals have the same access to the societal positive externalities (education, justice, health, other public goods or chances).[110]

The symmetry must address both the results and the means used to get those results. So, we can have a symmetry of finalities (or, with some precautions, of purposes), on the one hand, and a symmetry of the procedures, on the other hand. In other words, there are an *end-symmetry* (ES) and a *mode-symmetry* (MS).

The MEG criterion should act both for the ES and for MS, as well as (what will be shown) for the mixed cases, that is, regarding the symmetry (or asymmetry) between ES and MS—let us call this mixed case EMS. The following considerations examine the issue of interest here:

(I) Regarding the ES

Let us consider an interaction between two free individuals, I_1 andI_2, in a societal system. Presuppose that the interaction is aimed to get two ends for each of the two participants, respectively:R_1^1, and R_2^1 forI_1, andR_1^2, and R_2^2 forI_2. Let us suppose, in addition, that the entropic gradient, $EG_1^{1,2}$ between R_1^1 and R_1^2 isε_1, while the entropic gradient, $EG_2^{1,2}$ between R_2^1 and R_2^2 isε_2. *Nota bene*: the entropic gradient is the difference between the corresponding entropies, and by entropy (E) is understood the difference between actual result ($R_\cdot^\cdot$) and the expected one ($\overline{R}_\cdot^\cdot$), namely:

$$E_\cdot^\cdot = \left|R_\cdot^\cdot - \overline{R}_\cdot^\cdot\right|$$

Let us now hypothesize that $\varepsilon_1 < \varepsilon_2$, that is, the entropic gradient between the results of the two individuals is less for the result of type "1" than for the result of type "2". According to the criterion of interaction called MEG, the two individuals will interact rather concerned by the results of type "1" than by the results of type "2". Let us examine this choice:

– the cases in which $\varepsilon_1 < \varepsilon_2$ are the following:

$$(\varepsilon_1 < \varepsilon_2) \leftrightarrow \left(EG_1^{1,2} < EG_2^{1,2}\right)$$

$$\left(EG_1^{1,2} < EG_2^{1,2}\right) \leftrightarrow \left(E_1^1 - E_1^2\right) < \left(E_2^1 - E_2^2\right)$$

$$\left(E_1^1 - E_1^2\right) = \left|R_1^1 - \overline{R}_1^1\right| - \left|R_1^2 - \overline{R}_1^2\right|$$

$$\left(E_2^1 - E_2^2\right) = \left|R_2^1 - \overline{R}_2^1\right| - \left|R_2^2 - \overline{R}_2^2\right|$$

$$\left[\left(E_1^1 - E_1^2\right) < \left(E_2^1 - E_2^2\right)\right] \leftrightarrow \left(\left|R_1^1 - \overline{R}_1^1\right| - \left|R_1^2 - \overline{R}_1^2\right|\right) < \left(\left|R_2^1 - \overline{R}_2^1\right| - \left|R_2^2 - \overline{R}_2^2\right|\right)$$

We can have the following two distinct and exclusively disjunctive cases: $\left(\left|R_1^1 - \overline{R}_1^1\right| \leq \left|R_2^1 - \overline{R}_2^1\right|\right) \wedge \left(\left|R_1^2 - \overline{R}_1^2\right| \geq \left|R_2^2 - \overline{R}_2^2\right|\right)$, or

$$\left(\left|R_1^1 - \overline{R}_1^1\right| > \left|R_2^1 - \overline{R}_2^1\right|\right) \bigwedge \left(\left|R_1^2 - \overline{R}_1^2\right| > \left|R_2^2 - \overline{R}_2^2\right|\right) \bigwedge$$
$$\bigwedge \left[\left(\left|R_1^1 - \overline{R}_1^1\right| - \left|R_2^1 - \overline{R}_2^1\right|\right) > \left(\left|R_1^2 - \overline{R}_1^2\right| - \left|R_2^2 - \overline{R}_2^2\right|\right)\right]$$

Discussion

- the entropy of the first end for the first individual must be at most equal to the entropy of the second end of the first individual, so that the first individual would choose, from his/her (rational) perspective, the end 1;
- the entropy of the first end of the second individual must be at least equal to the second end of the second individual, so that the second individual would choose, from his/her (rational) perspective, the end 2;
- a question arises here: how do each of the two individuals mutually know what is the end preferred by the other individual? The answer is a single one: each individual can formulate predictions on the other individual's behaviour. Of course, such a supposition is a complicated one per se, but, for the moment, I will consider it as being feasible and performable.[111]

Nota bene: do not forget that the announced and committed principles of behaviour by the two individuals provide for each other a sufficient base to make prediction about the reciprocal behaviour related to each other.

What must be explained is the following: does the MEG criterion of interaction lead to an end-symmetry? My arguments in this matter are as follows:

- the MEG interaction selects, among all possible interactions, that one exhibiting the smallest entropic gap between them. How such an evaluation (or calculus) is performed is another issue that is not of interest here; we can simply presuppose that the selection mentioned is made;

- it is obvious that, whatever the effect of this selected interaction would be, the ends of the two interacting individuals will be either the same or will exhibit the smallest gap between them compared with any other interactions from those possible;
- the above assertion is, of course, true (valid) if the change in the previous states of the two interacting individuals is the same (namely, equal based on a common quantification);
- however, how about the case in which the impact of the interaction selected through the MEG criterion is different for the two individuals involved? My comment is the following:

  - is not impossible that the two impacts are different for each of the individuals involved, but the MEG criterion remains valid if the new entropic difference (after the impacts of interaction act) between the two ends remains, however, the smallest;
  - this condition of invariance of the gap involved allows some differences between the two impacts, but, of course, within a "tunnel" of invariance of the hierarchy among all the entropic gaps from the list of possible interaction;
  - this statement could be interpreted as a species of Pareto condition or, from a more sophisticated perspective, as a species of topological equivalence—both suggestions could be approached by scientists to develop further my allegations. To be mentioning that the Pareto condition is a species of the genus called Kaldor-Hicks test (in Annex 1, I give a basic description of the Kaldor-Hicks test, which is very useful in social justice examination).

Nota bene: from the social justice perspective, the *ES* topic is defended by scientists like Amartya Sen and Martha C. Nussbaum.

(II) Regarding the *MS*

The case of mode-symmetry is considerably more complicated than the end-symmetry one. Indeed, if the changes in the ends/goals of the two individuals are relatively manageable from a quantification point of view, the solution for quantifying or evaluating, even qualitatively, two procedures compared with each other seems to be impossible and, at any rate, without much significance. For this reason, applying the MEG criterion in the case of mode-symmetry presupposes the following:

- it is not needed to quantify or measure in some way the two procedures/modes;
- instead, we must ensure that the applying the two different procedures has as effect the same result for the two individuals involved;
- consequently, it is not important the MEG criterion that selects the interaction so that the effect caused is (approximately, namely, in an acceptable "tunnel") the same for the two individuals, but it is important to select that interaction which generates two procedures credited/liable to produce the same effect for the two individuals.[112]

Nota bene: from the social justice perspective, the MS topic is defended by scientists like John Rawls and Robert Nozick.

The ES and MS work in tandem, but it seems there is no way to choose the particular interaction concomitantly based on the two categories of symmetry. So, depending on the societal context, the MEG criterion of interaction selection will choose either ES orMS.

The MEG-Law of Societal Æsthetics

Based on the above preliminaries, it is possible, now, to verbally express the MEG-law of the societal æsthetics, as follows: *the æsthetical property of the societal system emerges and maintains if and only if either the end-symmetry interactions or the mode-symmetry interactions are selected based on the minimal entropic gradient of the actual ends or, respectively, of the available procedures.*

5.8 MEG and the Law of Ethics

Preliminaries

I think that the basic concept of (societal) ethics is the *mutualization* of interactions among individuals,[113] so a species of social capital that ensures the *socialization of the individual interactions*, namely: the degree and the quality in which common goals and common means can be built from the inter-individual harmonization or competition[114]; this type of social capital is "responsible" for all contractual[115] associations among individuals (including the nation, or the state).

The mutualization implies two sides: (a) the performance of the two goals/expectations (namely, the goals of the two interacting individuals), or *ends-mutualization*—*EM*; (b) the use of equivalent[116] means in order to get the respective goals, or *means-mutualization*—*MM*.

I. Regarding the *EM*

This time, we do not have to compare two ends (of the two interacting individuals), but the expected end and the actual end, respectively, for the same individual. If we note with G_i^e the expected end (goal) of the *i* individual, and with G_i^a the actual end (goal) of the *i* individual, then the MEG criterion has to be applied to compare G_i^e with G_i^a, so the entropic gradient will be calculated, for each of the two individuals, regarding the end (both expected and actual), namely:

$$EG_1^{EM} = \left|G_1^e - G_1^a\right|$$

$$EG_2^{EM} = \left|G_2^e - G_2^a\right|$$

In such a way, the two individuals will choose that interaction between them that ensures the minimal entropic gradient, as above calculated. Some concerns must be examined now:

- the potential interacting individual must make predictions regarding their own goals related to a set of interactions possible with a given other individual, so that, based on those predictions, they can calculate the associated MEG;
- in a sense, a *sui generis* market arises so that the "demand" and the "supply" of interactions compete towards an "equilibrium" point, that is at that interaction that simultaneously minimizes the entropic gradient for the two involved individuals;
- the theme can be (logically equivalently) reconfigured so that, instead of a list of interactions belonging to a given individual, it uses a list of individuals for a given interaction. So, the entropic gradient for the searched interaction of an individual will be chosen so that, for an established (desired) interaction, the most appropriate

individual will be chosen. Of course, the list of such individuals will contain those individuals who hold in their portfolio the interaction of interest.

Figure 10 suggests the functioning of such a *market of interactions*[117] from EM perspective (with P^d is noted the individual who searches the "optimal" individual for a given interaction (or, the "demand"), with P_i^s are noted the individuals who have in their portfolio the given interaction (or, the "supply"), where $i = \overline{1, n}$, with $\overline{I}$ is noted the given interaction, with P_*^s is noted the individual chosen for performing the interaction, with $EG_d^s(i)$ the entropic gradient between P^d and P_i^s (or, the "price") regarding $\overline{I}$, and with $MEG_d^s(k)$ the minimal entropic gradient that has chosen the individual k).

Discussion

- the P^d individual will perform the analysis done in Fig. 10 for each of the interactions he/she wants to objectify, so that he/she holds a "map" of such potential decisions;
- generally, each of interaction of P^d will select another individual P^s, but it is possible that more interactions of interest will select the same P^s; here, one could develop a deeper analysis which I ignore for the moment[118];

II. Regarding the MM

As in the case of mode-symmetry of the societal æsthetics, the means-mutualization in the ethics topic is considerably more complicated than that of end-mutualization because:

- the means have different significations for different individuals, so that the efficacy of the means could not be associated with their desirability from an ethical perspective, so that they can become non-eligible (non-selectable);
- even in the case in which the means are ethically acceptable, they could not perform the required mutualization for the involved individuals.

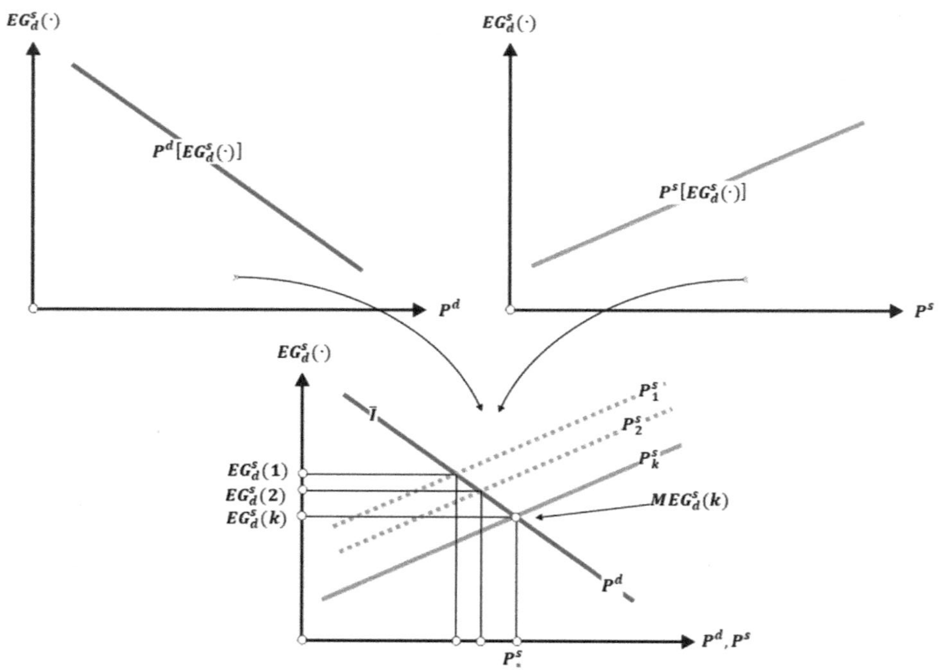

Fig. 10 Market of interactions—the EM case (*Source* author)

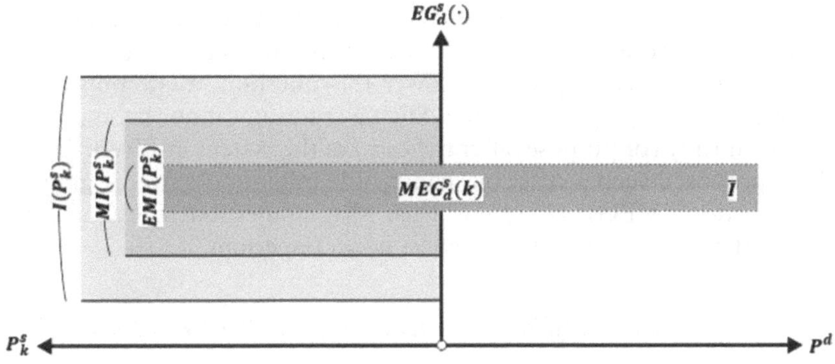

Fig. 11 Market of interactions—the MM case (*Source* author)

Figure 11 suggests the functioning of such a *market of interactions* from MM perspective (with $I(P_k^s)$ we note the complete portfolio of interactions held by P_k^s, with $MI(P_k^s)$ we note the mutually performing interactions held by P_k^s, with $EMI(P_k^s)$ we note the ethically mutual interaction held by P_k^s related to the $\overline{I}$ of interest for P^d).

The MEG-Law of Ethics

Based on the above preliminaries, it is possible, now, to verbally express the MEG-law of the ethics, as follows: *the ethical property of the societal system emerges and maintains if and only if either the end-mutualization interactions or the mode-mutualization interactions are selected based on the minimal entropic gradient of the actual ends or, respectively, of the available procedures.*

6 Reaction Norms and Stabilizers

In the issue of the dynamics of systems, no matter their nature, the crucial idea is that of the *chreod*. A chreod is a complete phenomenology of the change of a generic system, from one state to another state. The concatenation in time of those states exactly constitutes the chreod. A chreod obeys, of course, the general principle of causality, no matter whether the system is deterministic, stochastic, or random.[119] The causality, as principle, is objectified by particular and concrete causes (causal factors).

In turn, the causes are shaped by the reaction norms. The problem is, now, how, more exactly, those norms of reactions are shaped and, as the case may be, re-shaped. To answer this question, a criterion of the shaping (or re-shaping) is required. Such a criterion cannot be, rationally, than the finality (or purpose, after the case) of the system involved. Above, I have proposed such a criterion, namely the minimum entropic gradient of interaction (MEG). Now, I will use that suggestion to examine the issue of the chreod under the reaction norm imperium.

6.1 *On the (Stylized) Phenomenology of Reaction Norm*

As shown previously, the reaction obeys, from a selection perspective, to the MEG. However, the MEG provides only a criterion to choose the interaction—for example, for the societal case, to choose the individual able to perform the interaction desired by the individual in the case. This says nothing about the configuration of the reaction: nature,[120] duration of performing, intensity of performing, etc. In fact, there is a cascade of selections (or, equivalently, filters) that leads to the shaping of the reaction norm. A synoptic suggestion of the process of shaping the reaction norm is presented in Fig. 12.

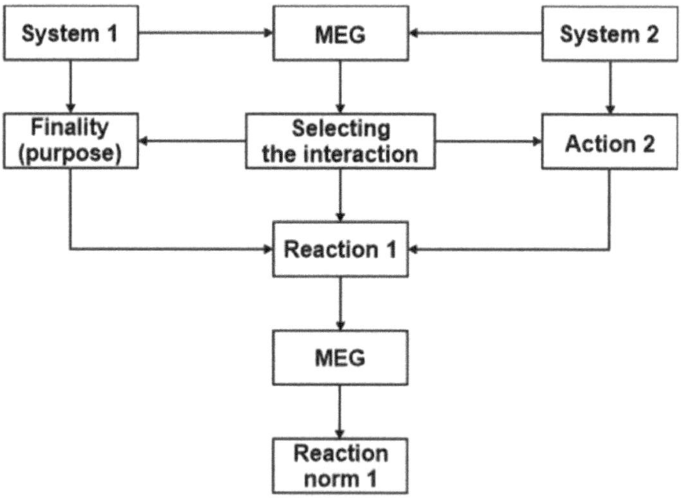

Fig. 12 Filtering process in shaping the reaction norm (*Source* author)

Discussion

- firstly, the interaction between system 1 and system 2 is selected, based on the MEG criterion;
- then, the reaction of the system 1 (the system concerned) is shaped based, on the one hand, on the action 2 (of the system 2), and, on the other hand, on its own finality/purpose. The reaction chosen is contained, of course, in a list of feasible performing reactions of the system 1;
- after the reaction selection, system 1 will establish the norm of that reaction. I think that the reaction norm should be established by a new application of the MEG criterion, this time among the possible norms (in the portfolio of such norms of system 1). Since this second application of the MEG criterion is not obvious prima facie, I will provide some considerations:

  - system 1 (as any other system, besides) holds three portfolio lists: (a) a list of interactions of its own interest; (b) a list of reactions assigned to each interaction from the first list; (c) a list of feasible norms associated with each of the reactions from the second list;
  - the first list (the interactions of interest) is used to select the system (individual) that system 1 will interact with;
  - the second list (of reactions) is used to select the reaction associated with the selected interaction;
  - the third list (norms of reactions) is used to select the norm associated with the already selected reaction. Since I think it must use the MEG criterion a second time to select the reaction norm, I will "defend" such an option as follows:
    - the action 2 (or reaction 2, as the case may be) has already associated with, so known,[121] its own norm;
    - consequently, the second application of MEG will proceed inversely from the first application—while, in the first application, namely, in selecting the interaction, a given interaction of system 1 is the benchmark to select the appropriate interaction of system 2, this time, a given reaction norm of system 2 is used as a benchmark to select a reaction norm of system 1;

· the reason to apply the MEG criterion in selecting the reaction norm of system 1 is analogous to that of selecting the interaction of system 2 through the first application of the MEG criterion.

6.2 Some General Formalizations

Let us make the following notations:

- P_i: the finality/purpose of the system i
- L_i^I: list of interactions in the portfolio of the system (individual) i
- L_{ij}^R: list of reactions of system i associated with the interaction j $(j = \overline{1, n}))$
- L_{ijk}^N: list of norms of reaction of system i, associated with the interaction j and the reaction k $(k = \overline{1, m}))$
- $\overline{\overline{I}}$: the interaction selected from the list of interactions of the partner system of system i
- $\overline{\overline{R}}$: the action/reaction of the partner system of system i, assigned to $\overline{\overline{I}}$
- $\overline{\overline{N}}$: reaction norm of the partner system of system i, assigned to $\overline{\overline{R}}$ of $\overline{\overline{I}}$
- $\overline{I}_i$: the selected interaction of system i, after applying the MEG for the first time
- $\overline{R}_{ij}$: the selected reaction of system i, associated with the selected interaction $\overline{I}_i$
- $\overline{N}_{ijk}$; the selected reaction norm of system i, regarding the interaction $\overline{I}_i$, and the reaction $\overline{R}_{ij}$

General conditionalities to be verified:

- L_i^I, L_{ij}^R, and L_{ijk}^N are finite sets
- $\overline{I}_i \in L_i^I$
- $\overline{R}_{ij} \in L_{ij}^R$
- $\overline{N}_{ijk} \in L_{ijk}^N$
- $\left(L_{ij}^R\right) \cap \left(L_{iq}^R\right) = \varnothing$, for any $j, q = \overline{1, n}$

- $\left(L_{ijk}^{N}\right) \bigcap \left(L_{ijp}^{N}\right) = \varnothing$, for any $k, p = \overline{1, m}$

Nota bene: it is considered that all reactions involved are foetal for the partner system.

Figure 13 visualizes the establishment of the "optimal" reaction norm for the system i.

Additionally comment

- the second application of MEG–MEG(2)—to select the norm of reaction for $\overline{R}_{ij}$ will calculate the entropic gap between all the reaction norms associated with the selected reaction and the norm of reaction $\overline{\overline{N}}$;
- to be observed that, by applying of the MEG(2) in selecting the reaction norm for $\overline{R}_{ij}$, the system i increases the probability that the found reaction norm be foetal for the partner system;
- if the nature of reaction norm is implicitly selected by selecting the nature of reaction (see Fig. 12), instead, by calculating MEG(2), are selected other two parameters of the norm in question: (a) the duration; (b) the intensity. It is obvious that, by selecting the two parameters, in fact, is selected the very quantity of reaction[122];
- however, the duration and the intensity related to the reaction norm are not indefinitely substitutable, but this issue is not theoretical; it is solvable in particular contexts.

6.3 *Discretionarity vs. Automaticity*

Conceptual Delimitations

Discretionarity[123] and automaticity, respectively, are properties that address the decision-making and, by some extension, the action triggered as a result of the decision made. For the necessities of this chapter, I will expose the two concepts from a logical perspective. Three issues are of interest in this matter: (a) the sufficiency predicates of the two concepts; (b) the new necessary predicates of them; (c) their definitions or descriptions. Next, I will consider that the decision-making and the triggering of the action associated with the decision made are the same (logical) "animal".

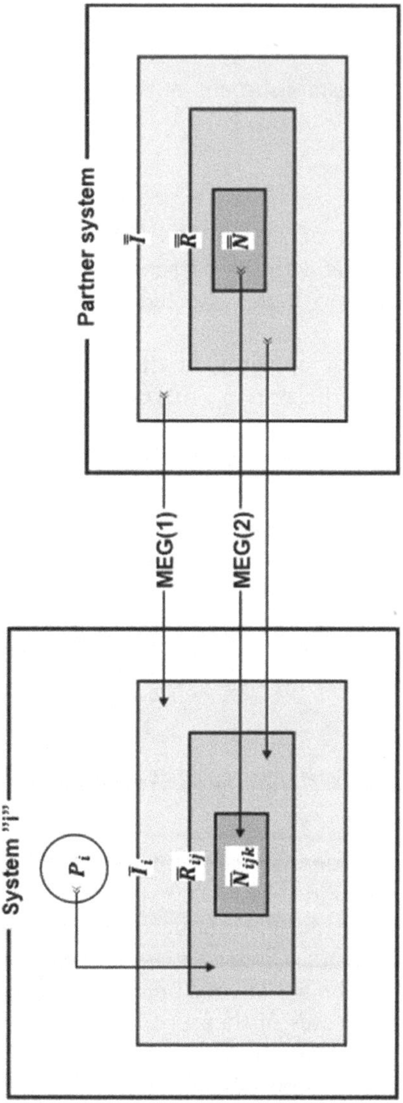

Fig. 13 Establishing the reaction norm based on MEG criterion (*Source* author)

The Discretionarity

(a) the sufficiency predicates

As shown elsewhere in this book, the sufficiency predicates are features/attributes of an entity, so that the simultaneous verifying of them qualifies that entity as such. The number of the sufficiency predicates must verify, in turn, Ockham's razor principle.

I think the sufficiency predicates of the discretionarity are as follows:

- (S_1^D) the decision is made *explicitly*—this means that the decisional "device" (no matter its nature, for example, a committee of decision-making) has elaborated, formulated, and expressed in an explicit and accessible way for others that decision;
- (S_2^D) the decision is made *at the moment*—this means that the decision is "manufactured" exactly at the moment at which it enters into force[124];
- (S_3^D) the decision and the action triggering are *simultaneous*—this means that the decision causes the associated action (either act, i.e., *to do*, or abstention, i.e., *not to do*) concomitantly. *Nota bene*: with the same comment as in the note immediately preceding.

If we denote the discretionarity (which is, of course, a property) with$D$, then it can be logically generated by the conjunction of its sufficiency predicates:

$$D \leftarrow \left(S_1^D\right) \bigwedge \left(S_2^D\right) \bigwedge \left(S_3^D\right)$$

(b) the necessary predicates

Once the discretionarity, as property, is "born", it generates a necessary predicate which I call a *new* necessary predicate.[125] I think there exists a new necessary predicate called (N^D) *adhocness*, which means the mobilization of dedicated resources (information, experts, time) to make the required decision.

Consequently, the complete logical formula of discretionarity is the following:

$(S_1^D) \wedge (S_2^D) \wedge (S_3^D) \to D \to (N^D)$, or

$$D = \left\{ S_1^D, S_2^D, S_3^D, N^D \right\}$$

The Automaticity

(a) the sufficiency predicates

I think the sufficiency predicates of the automaticity are as follows:

- (S_1^A) the decision is made *implicitly*—this means that the decisional "device" already contains the required decision, which is selected based on a pre-existent algorithm, also contained in that decision "device";
- (S_2^A) the decision is made *in advance*—this means that the decision is taken before the requirements for it becoming actual (for example, the decision is "written" in a list that the mentioned decisional algorithm will use to select that decision);
- (S_3^A) the decision and the action triggering are *time-shifted*—this means that the decision's moment and the associated triggered action's moment are different (non-coincident); more exactly, the decision regarding the action implied is made (usually, a long time) before the corresponding action is triggered.

If we denote the automaticity (which is, also, a property) with$A$, then it can be logically generated by the conjunction of its sufficiency predicates:

$$A \leftarrow \left(S_1^A\right) \wedge \left(S_2^A\right) \wedge \left(S_3^A\right)$$

(b) the necessary predicates

I think the sufficiency predicates of automaticity will generate a new necessary predicate, which I would call (N^A) *premeditateness*, which means that the "premeditated" decisions are already programmed in the mentioned algorithm, so it is not needed to made the decision in a discretionary way.

Consequently, the complete logical formula of automaticity is the following:

$(S_1^A) \wedge (S_2^A) \wedge (S_3^A) \rightarrow A \rightarrow (N^A)$, or

$$A = \left\{S_1^A, S_2^A, S_3^A, N^A\right\}$$

6.4 *Functioning*

The two properties of the dynamics systems, namely, discretionarity and automaticity, respectively, work differently, based on their sufficiency predicates. I will list some shared attributes and some different attributes of them.

(b) shared attributes of discretionarity and automaticity

- both are *formal* institutions, that is, they are codified in the normative framework,[126] and, usually, are publicly known;
- both are *procedural*, that is, they follow a scheme to decide, and that scheme is previously established and, usually, publicly known;
- both are *implemented discretionarily*. If this attribute is obvious in the case of the discretionarity, it must be said that the automaticity is also, discretionarily implemented, although after implementation, its functioning is automatic;
- both imply the deliberativeness, i.e., rational foundation.

(c) different attributes of discretionarity and automaticity

- first of all, the sufficiency predicates of the two properties are correspondingly opposed, namely:

$$\left(S_1^D\right) \leftrightarrow \left(\overline{S}_1^A\right);\ \left(S_2^D\right) \leftrightarrow \left(\overline{S}_2^A\right);\ \left(S_3^D\right) \leftrightarrow \left(\overline{S}_3^A\right);$$

- automaticity has a limited number of solutions (decisions), as they are programmed in the algorithm, while deliberativeness has a larger sphere of creativity (novelty);

- automaticity needs, periodically, new episodes of discretionarity, to actualize the portfolio of solutions (decisions)[127];
- while in the case of discretionarity, the very step of initiating the decision-making process is one of discretionarity type, in the case of automaticity, this step is completely automatic, depending only on the reaching of the specified threshold (early warning);
- generally, the result of discretionarity is not predicable, while the result of automaticity is completely predictable—in other words, the discretionarity implies the contingent, while the automaticity implies the necessary.

6.5 *The Structure*

Both discretionarity and automaticity are properties of the decision-making process. They share a general structure, although the features of the structural components give a very logical difference between them. The structural (common) components are as follows: the *ECTAP* model:

(a) ($E^{(\cdot)}$) the (cumulative) conditions/factuals/events to be fulfilled so that the decision-making becomes mandatory; this component is a (minimal) list of those conditions that require a decision (and, possibly, a following action);
(b) ($C^{(\cdot)}$) the criterion based on which the early warning signal is triggered; the criterion could be, usually, a score function that has, as independent variables, the condition of the component E;
(c) ($T^{(\cdot)}$) the threshold to be reached by C; this component signals an imminent perturbation to impact the system in question (an early warning point); this component means simply the verification, from a quantitative perspective, of the component C;
(d) ($A^{(\cdot)}$) the algorithm aimed at making the required decision;
(e) ($P^{(\cdot)}$) the action that is performed as a result of applying the algorithm of decision-making.

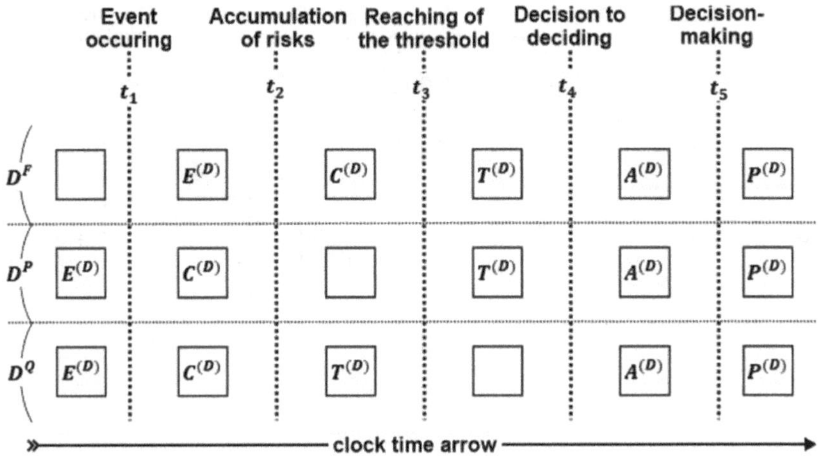

Fig. 14 Logical establishment of the species of discretionarity (*Source* author)

6.6 *Possible Abstract Typologies*

Based on the Structural Configuration

The (common) structure of both discretionarity and automaticity is the key to finding the possible typologies of these properties. The way to find the typologies is to particularize the mentioned structural components.

Regarding the Discretionarity

Probably, three species of discretionarity are of theoretical interest: (a) the full discretionarity—D^F; (b) the partial discretionarity—D^P; (c) the quasi-discretionarity—D^Q. The identification of the discretionarity species is suggested by Fig. 14, based on $ECTAP$ model.

Regarding the Automaticity

Probably, three species of automaticity are of theoretical interest: (a) (A^F) the full automaticity; (b) (A^P) the partial automaticity; (c) (A^Q) the quasi-automaticity. The identification of the automaticity species is suggested by Fig. 15, based on $ECTAP$ model.

Nota bene: if we imagine an arrow of increasing discretionarity and automaticity, respectively, then the "correspondence" between the species of discretionarity and the species of automaticity can be represented as shown in Fig. 16.

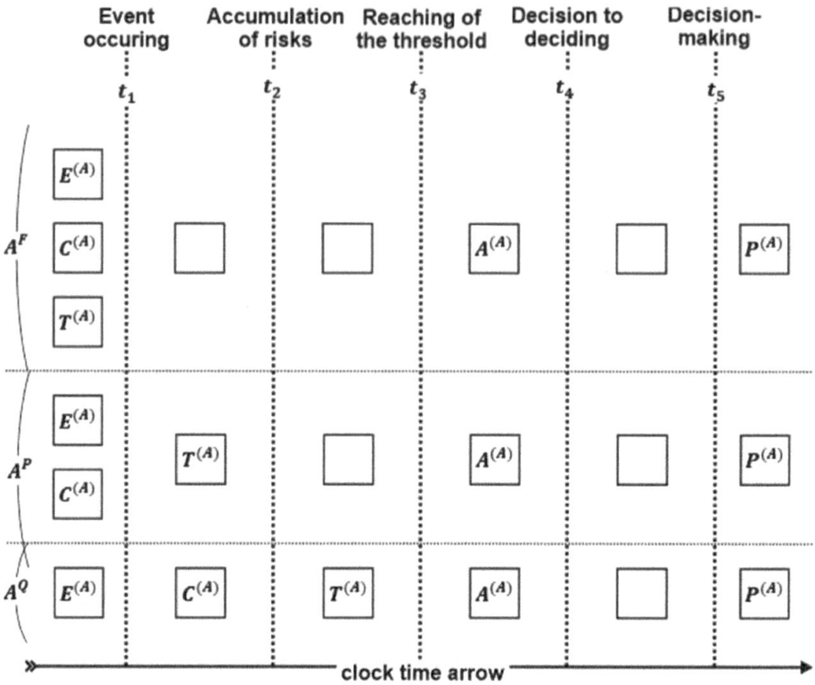

Fig. 15 Logical establishment of the species of automaticity (*Source* author)

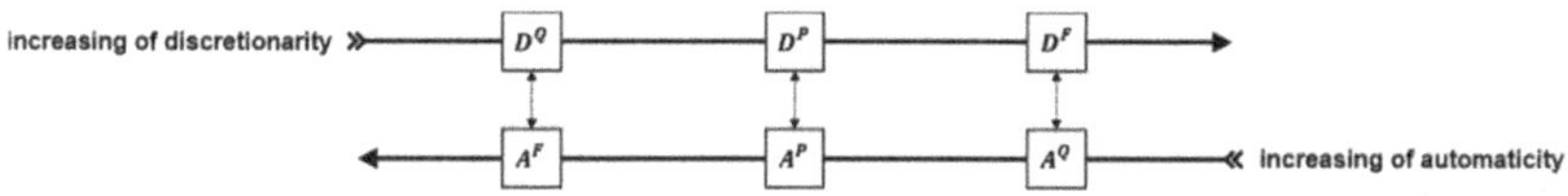

Fig. 16 "Correspondence" between discretionarity and automaticity (*Source*: author)

Based on the Purposes Aimed At

The purpose is a very strong criteria to typologize the discretionarity and automaticity, respectively. I offer a proposal below.

Regarding the Discretionarity

It seems that five categories of purposes are of interest in identifying the classes of discretionarity:

(a) (D^I) discretionarity aimed at obtaining/increasing *robustness*—the discretionary decisions of this type strengthen the resistance potential of a given system against identified perturbations; this passive resistance is known as the property of robustness, and it is built up in a "personalized" way, that is, focused on expected known perturbations, either from the external environment or from the internal one. The strengthening of the robustness increases the threshold at which the system becomes plastic;
(b) (D^R) discretionarity aimed at obtaining/increasing *resilience*—the discretionary decisions of this type provide the capacity of the system to recover the state or kinematic position on chreod, after they are perturbed; this capacity has an active nature, as a reaction (as discussed above). Of course, it is talking about the reactions of restoration;
(c) (D^{AF}) discretionarity aimed at obtaining/increasing *antifragility*—the discretionary decisions of this type provide the capacity of the system to gain (something, somehow) from the very perturbation, either internal or external. The concept of antifragility was popularized by Nassim Nicholas Taleb (2012), and, as I show elsewhere (Dinga, 2025), it differs significantly from the concept of a non-fragile system, as opposed to a fragile one. Rather, a fragile system is a non-robust one, while a non-fragile system is a robust one. So, the conceptual pair of fragile vs. non-fragile is very different from the conceptual pair antifragile vs. non-antifragile;
(d) (D^V) discretionarity aimed at obtaining/increasing *sustainability*—the discretionary decisions of this type provide the capacity of the system to verify the two fundamental sufficiency predicates of the sustainability: (1) inputting any output, that is, any output must become an input, no matter the chain of such becoming; (2) recovering the input through its own output;
(e) (D^{AP}) discretionarity aimed at obtaining/increasing *autopoieticity*—the discretionary decisions of this type provide the capacity of the system to restructure itself so that establishing a new "moment 0" in its interactions with the external environment, as well as with its own internal environment.

Regarding the Automaticity

It seems that four categories of purposes are of interest in identifying the classes of automaticity:

(a) (A^{WP}) automaticity aimed at *avoiding the politics interference*—many decisions at the society level are politically based, which mitigates their efficacy and, sometimes, even their efficiency. The automatization of the decisions avoids such distortions brought by political considerations (Dinga et al., 2022a, 2022b);

(b) (A^{WG}) automaticity aimed at *eliminating the time gaps*—the discretionarity implies many preparative and procedural activities before deciding, which means large time gaps between the optimal moment of decision and the actual moment of decision; these gaps (especially when they are sufficiently large) can compromise the effectiveness of the implied decision. The automaticity has the potential to avoid such ineffectiveness;

(c) (A^{U}) automaticity aimed at *standardization of decisions*—discretionarity can introduce modifications in the decision-making in the same conditions of perturbation (because of different perceptions, competences, and interests), while the automaticity makes the same decision answering the same context and, so, providing some uniformity of reactions;

(d) (A^{MF}) automaticity aimed at *mitigating the fluctuations*—the fluctuations of a system's parameters cannot, principled, be eliminated, since any dynamic system necessarily implies such fluctuations, but they can be mitigated exactly by the intermediation of automatic stabilizers.

Based on the Functioning

This criterion addresses the general way of functioning of the two polar devices of decision-making: discretionarity and automaticity, respectively.

Regarding the Discretionarity

Three classes of discretionarity are of interest:

(a) (D^{S}) *spot* discretionarity—addresses those discretionary decisions triggered by random (principled, unpredictable) perturbations, which are managed case by case, without a historical memory; this type of discretionarity has a *resolutive* function;

(b) (D^C) *periodical* discretionarity—addresses those discretionary decisions that are made, no matter whether a perturbation has occurred or not; this type of discretionarity has a *preventive* function;

(c) (D^N) *follow up* discretionarity—addresses those discretionary decisions that are required by previous discretionary ones in order either to correct them or to augment their favourable impact; this type of discretionarity has an *improving* function.

Regarding the Automaticity

Three classes of automaticity are of interest:

(a) (A^S) *singular* automaticity—refers to a single automatic device of decision-making, implemented in a given context;

(b) (A^C) *concatenated* automaticity—refers to more automatic devices of decision-making, so that they are integrated into a functional chain of automaticity;

(c) (A^I) *integrated* automaticity—refers to some automatic devices that are integrated in mixed chains of discretionarity and automaticity (see Sect. 6.7).

6.7 *Mixing Discretionarity and Automaticity*

Either the discretionarity or automaticity, as species of decision-making genus, actions as decision-discourse. So, if it is denoted with d_i^D the decision made in a discretionary way at the moment i, then a discretionary discourse can be expressed as follows:

(i) monotonic serial discretionarity

$$d_i^{D_1} - d_{i+1}^{D_2} - d_{i+2}^{D_3} - \ldots - d_{i+k}^{k+1} \ldots$$

(ii) monotonic parallel discretionarity

$$\begin{matrix} d_i^{D_1} \\ d_i^{D_2} \\ \ldots \\ d_i^{D_k} \end{matrix} \ldots$$

Similarly, an automatic discourse can be expressed (denoting with d_i^A the decision made in an automatic way at the moment i) as follows:

(i) monotonic serial automaticity

$$d_i^{A_1} - d_{i+1}^{A_2} - d_{i+2}^{A_3} - \ldots - d_{i+k}^{k+1} - \ldots$$

(ii) monotonic parallel discretionarity

$$\begin{matrix} d_i^{A_1} \\ d_i^{A_2} \\ \ldots \\ d_i^{A_k} \end{matrix} \ldots$$

The most realistic case is, of course, that of a mixed discourse, when discretionarity is combined with the automaticity, in different mixtures, depending on the particular contexts.

(i) serial discretionarity and parallel automaticity

$$d_i^{D_1} - \left\{ \begin{matrix} d_{i+1}^{A_1} \\ d_{i+1}^{A_2} \\ \ldots \\ d_{i+1}^{A_k} \end{matrix} \right. - d_{i+2}^{D_2} - \left\{ \begin{matrix} d_{i+3}^{A_1} \\ d_{i+3}^{A_2} \\ \ldots \\ d_{i+3}^{A_q} \end{matrix} \right. - \ldots$$

(ii) serial automaticity and parallel discretionarity

$$d_i^{A_1} - \begin{cases} d_{i+1}^{D_1} \\ d_{i+1}^{D_2} \\ \cdots \\ d_{i+1}^{D_k} \end{cases} - d_{i+2}^{A_2} - \begin{cases} d_{i+3}^{D_1} \\ d_{i+3}^{D_2} \\ \cdots \\ d_{i+3}^{D_q} \end{cases} - \ldots$$

Of course, în the real phenomenology, the combinations between discretionary decisions and the automatic ones are more complicated and, generally, asymmetric. The most important issue here is that such combinations form decisional chains. According to what was said above, the decisional mixed chains are characterized by the following:

- the discretionary decisions are not mandatorily the same for the same challenges, because the components of the decision committee, and, of course, because the conditionalities that exceed the very context in which the decision must be made;
- instead, the automatic decisions in those decisional chains are expected to be, at least in short (perhaps, even medium) term, invariant, since the algorithm is working in a stable manner;
- the particular mixed decisional chains are, as a result, variable enough, since, for example, the very combinations of the discretionarity and automaticity are decided in a discretionary way.

6.8 *Compatibilizing of the Four Criteria of Stabilization Devices*

In fact, the four criteria based on which the above typologies have been obtained are: (1) the type of stabilization (discretionarity vs. automaticity); (2) the species of stabilization, for each of the two types; (3) the purpose of stabilization, for each of the two types; (4) the standard functioning. Table 3 suggests the compatibilities (denoted with either D, or A or DA), incompatibilities, denoted with NO, and indeterminacy, denoted with "?".s

Table 3 Map of compatibility in the stabilization matter

			(D) Discretionarity			(A) Automaticity		
			(D^F)	(D^P)	(D^Q)	(A^F)	(A^P)	(A^Q)
Purpose	(D)	(D^I)	x			–	–	–
		(D^R)		x		–	–	–
		(D^{AF})		x		–	–	–
		(D^V)		x		–	–	–
		(D^{AP})			x	–	–	–
	(A)	(A^{WP})	–	–	–		x	
		(A^{WG})	–	–	–		x	
		(A^U)	–	–	–			x
		(A^{MF})	–	–	–	x		
Functioning	(D)	(D^S)	x			–	–	–
		(D^C)		x		–	–	–
		(D^N)			x	–	–	–
	(A)	(A^S)	–	–	–	x		
		(A^C)	–	–	–		x	
		(A^I)	–	–	–			x

Source author

7 The Stabilizers

7.1 Preliminaries

Generally, the processes (including the artefactual ones, like the economic processes) are either of escalating/amplifying type, or of stabilizing/mitigating type.[128] The escalating processes have the propensity to increase their definitional parameters, while the stabilizing processes have the propensity to decrease their definitional parameters. Such a propensity can be either internal or external to the involved processes—if the propensity is internal, we speak about self-escalating propensity or self-stabilizing propensity, and, if the propensity is externally induced, we speak about induced escalating propensity or induced stabilizing propensity.[129]

Logically, a stabilizer is a negation of escalating (and vice versa), of course, as a tendency (i.e., qualitatively), not quantitatively. However, the impact of an escalation is very different from the impact of stabilization, so I will make extra considerations where required.

As discussed above, both amplifiers and stabilizers can be either discretionary, automatic, or linked in chains that contain both devices. All these delimitations will be examined in what follows.

7.2 *Stabilizers vs. Amplifiers*

A stabilizer is a device, either natural or artefactual/artificial, so no matter if it is discretionary or automatic, is aimed at reducing the volatility of the parameter(s) which it is designed to monitor/control in a given system or process. This means that a stabilizer must "know" at any moment the point at which the given system is on its trajectory/chreod, to compare this actual position with the desired (perhaps, normed) position. If the gap between the actual position and the desired or expected position exceeds a certain pre-established (usually) numerical value, then the stabilizer will make the required decision and trigger the appropriate action, so that the gap comes back under the threshold of warning.

The Structure of a Stabilizer

According to the role of a stabilizer, its structure is required to be established. I consider the following general structure, which is shared by both discretionary and automatic stabilizers—the $PLTSCDA$ model.

- (P) a variable/parameter, of any nature, according to the role of stabilizer, whose volatility must be mitigated or, at limit, avoided or neutralized, after the case;
- (L) a threshold of signification beyond which the value of P is considered undesirable. In many cases, we need for two some thresholds/limits, so that P must unfold between them or, equivalently, inside the tunnel the two thresholds establish[130]; in this last case, we have a lowest limit/threshold (floor threshold), denoted by L_l, and

a highest limit/threshold (ceiling threshold), denoted by L_h—the tunnel of conformity for the P unfolding is, so: $[L_l, L_h]$;

- (T) a variable, of any nature, according to the role of stabilizer, which must be monitored in order to take the appropriate decision of stabilizing$P$,generally, T is different from$P$, but their coincidence is not prohibited, according to the nature of the system/process of interest;
- (S) a device, of any nature, aimed at recording the values (or, equivalently, the states) of P and T, respectively (of course, in separate memories), with a pre-established frequency;
- (C) an analyser, of any nature, capable to calculate the difference between the actual value of P ($\overline{P}$) and L_l or L_h, after the case; let us denote that difference the gap of P, denoted with $G(\overline{P})$, so that: $G_l(\overline{P}) = L_l - \overline{P}$, or, after the case $G_h(\overline{P}) = L_h - \overline{P}$. The warning occurs if $G_l(\overline{P}) < 0$, or, alternatively, if $G_h(\overline{P}) < 0$;
- (D) a decision-making device, aimed at deciding about the action to be triggered as a result of the gap value;
- (A) an action (perhaps, from a pre-existent list of feasible actions) to be implemented in order to objectify the role of stabilizer.

The Functioning of a Stabilizer

To get the mechanism of functioning of a generic stabilizer, Fig. 17 can be useful as suggestion.

Discussion

- *first step*: the memory of the stabilizer is loaded with the identity of the parameter of interest (P), and with the proxy-variable for controlling the parameter P, namely T;

Nota bene: it is supposed that the value/s of L (respectively, L_l and L_h) are constant on at least medium term and stored in the S device. Of course, on long term, perhaps, both limits/thresholds will vary and are stored as such.

- *second step*: the identity of P and T is actualized (if the case) in S;
- *third step*: the values for T and L are sent to the calculator C, to determine the gap of T;

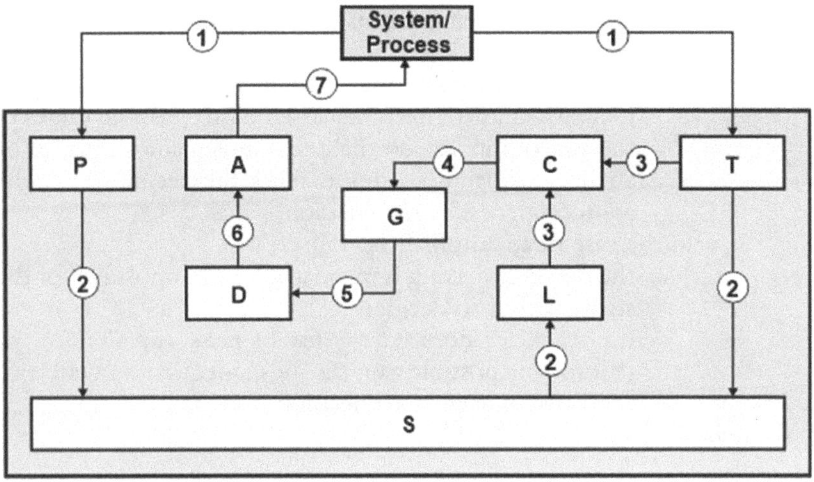

Fig. 17 Functioning of a generic stabilizer (*Source* author)

- *fourth step*: the calculated gap is sent to the device that records the gaps (*G*);
- *fifth step*: the calculated gap is sent to the decision-making device *D*;
- *sixth step*: the *D* device makes the decision and sends it to the actions portfolio, to trigger the appropriate action (*A*)
- *seventh step*: the action (*A*) is exerted on the system/process, that is, on the re-configuration of *P*.

Additional comment

From the generic functioning of a stabilizer, one can particularize the functioning for the discretionary stabilizer, respectively, for the automatic stabilizer. The basic difference resides at the level of the devices *D* and*A*, respectively, as follows:

(a) regarding the device *D*:

- in the case of a discretionary stabilizer:
  - the decision is made within a decisional committee, which can make or not decide concerning the calculated

gap, or can even not organize a meeting concerning that gap occurring;
  - the decisional committee, usually, does not have a pre-established list of decisions assigned to possible values of the gap of interest, so the decision is made (if made) by ad hoc deliberation; this reduces the accuracy and the appropriateness of the decision;
- in the case of an automatic stabilizer:
  - the decision-making is mandatory; it is impossible for the stabilizer not to decide;
  - the stabilizer does have a list of pairs *gap–decision*, so that for any possible gap, the most adequate and effective (perhaps, efficient too) decision is made;

(b) regarding the device *A*:

- in the case of a discretionary stabilizer:
  - the action associated with the decision made is designed and approved also in the decision committee, in a deliberative way;
  - like in the case of decision-making process, the action is not selected from a pre-established list that links the decisions and the adequate/appropriate actions aimed at implementing the decision in question, but is designed and approved in the dedicated meeting of the decisional committee;
  - although, after the decision is made, the action is usually implemented, in some circumstances, the decisional committee can postpone the action for different reasons (for example, political reasons);
- in the case of an automatic stabilizer:
  - the corresponding action that is appropriate to the decision made is already established in a dedicated list of the stabilizer, so that its selection is, in fact, automatic, that is, it was made a long time ago, when the stabilizer was designed and (discretionarily, as shown) introduced in the system concerned;
  - the adequacy of the action for a given decision is, so, established in advance, within a praxiological analysis or even based on presumptive scenarios.

7.3 Functioning of the Stabilizer

The stabilizers are of two kinds: (a) (FB) feedback stabilizer; (b) (FF) feedforward stabilizer.

Preamble

- notations:
  - S: a generic system (that is, without any particular determinations)
  - P: the definitional parameter of the system S, i.e., the parameter whose volatility must be monitored
  - x_t: the input in the system S at the moment t
  - y_t: the output of the system S at the moment t
  - B_t: an operator of transformation from input to output. This operator is not needed to be precisely described; it will be considered as a general (mathematical) function. Moreover, in the short and medium term, the operator of transformation is, generally, invariant, so that we can denote it with B
  - P_t^a: the actual value of parameter P at the moment t, measured adequately, and stored (as shown above) in a memory device; P_t^a is a measured value of y_t
  - P_t^e: the expected value of parameter P at the moment t, measured adequately, and stored (as shown above) in a memory device; P_t^e is a pre-established value of y_t
  - g_t: the gap between the actual value and the expected one of the parameter P, measured adequately, and also stored (as shown above) in a memory device

Comment: the gap is considered in the algebraic module (see definitions below), since the stabilization is required both if $P_t^a > P_t^e$, and if $P_t^a < P_t^e$. Of course, the direction of stabilization depends on the algebraic sign of g_t

- T_t: the threshold of the gap above which the FBstabilizer decides to perform the adequate action aimed at re-bringing the gap under the threshold. The threshold is established previously and introduced in the algorithm (either discretionary or automatic), based on which the stabilizer in question functions. In the short and medium term, generally, the threshold is invariant, so that we can denote it with$T$.

The establishment of the T value considers the past (with success or failure, after the case) of the stabilizer working, or some scenarios, or models of rationality, or even intuitions, and so on

- d_t: the decision taking at the moment t, which is working on the system at the moment $(t + 1)$

- definitions:
  - $g_t = \left|P_t^a - P_t^e\right|$
  - $y_t = B(x_t)$
- decision taking
  - $(g_t > T) \rightarrow D \rightarrow \begin{cases} if g_t > 0 : D^{(1)} \\ if g_t < 0 : D^{(2)} \end{cases}$

.

where $D^{(1)}$ and $D^{(2)}$, respectively, actions in opposite directions regarding the adjustment of the parameter P of the system S, according to the algebraic sign of g_t.

Nota bene: of course, $D^{(1)}$ and $D^{(2)}$ are not actions with "inverse algebraic sign", because an increase of the input is not a mirrored image of a decrease of that input; essentially, we can say only that the two types of actions work in opposite directions, or, better said, with opposite finalities.

The FB Stabilizer

The FBstabilizer performs its role of stabilizing the system/process to which it is assigned (in fact, the parameter P above introduced) by using the information from the past of the system/process phenomenology. This means that the FBstabilizer uses what logically must be denoted as an explanation. The logical scheme of the FBstabilizer functioning is shown in Fig. 18.

Discussion

- at the moment t, an input x_t enters the system;
- through the intermediation of the operator B, the input x_t is transformed into the output y_t at the moment t (*Nota bene*: logically, it is not important that it is needed for a duration—called technological duration—to transform the input into the output);

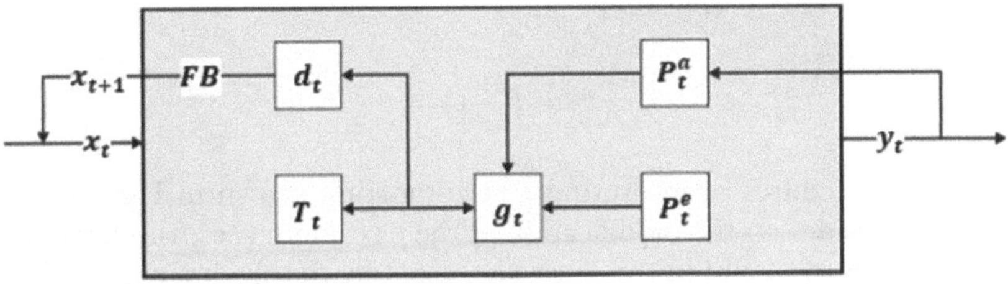

Fig. 18 Functioning of a *FB*stabilizer (*Source* author)

- once y_t is obtained, it is measured, in a specific way, so that the value P_t^a of the definitional parameter of the output is established;
- a gap analyser compares the P_t^a values with the P_t^e (which is pre-established and stored into the system's memory), and the gap (g_t) is calculated;
- the gap value is compared with the T value (memorized, too, by the system) and, if g_t is greater than T, an appropriate change of the input for the immediately next cycle of system functioning is operated, depending on two variables: (a) the quantity with which the gap exceeds the threshold; (b) the algebraic sign of the gap;
- that change is introduced in the new input, at the moment $(t + 1)$.

A (simple) formalization of *FB*stabilizer functioning is as follows. Some extra notation is required:

- $\Delta x_t = \alpha \cdot g_t$: perhaps, not the entire gap will be considered to change the next input, but only a fraction $(0 \leq \alpha \leq 1)$, for example, in the case of a discretionary stabilizer, the decisional committee can decide to not apply any correction. *Nota bene*: of course, it is possible that$\alpha > 1$, that is, the correction will exceed the "indication" brought by the calculated gap. Both values for the coefficient α are based on particular contexts and evaluations.

We know that

$$y_t = B(x_t)$$

So

$$x_t = B^{-1}(y_t)$$

After all procedures of measuring and comparing shown in Fig. 18, the stabilizer decides on the modification of the next input (i.e., x_{t+1}), namely with quantity Δx_t, and in the sense suggested by the algebraic sign of the gap. So:

$$x_t^{fb} = B^{-1}(y_t) + \Delta x_t$$

$$x_{t+1}^{fb} = B^{-1}(y_t) + \alpha^{fb} \cdot g_t$$

from which,

$$y_{t+1}^{fb} = B\left(x_{t+1}^{fb}\right)$$

$$y_{t+1}^{fb} = B\left[B^{-1}(y_t) + \alpha^{fb} \cdot g_t\right]$$

The FF Stabilizer

The FFstabilizer performs its role of stabilizing the system/process to which it is assigned (in fact, the parameter P above introduced) by using the information from the future of the system/process phenomenology. This means that the FF stabilizer uses what logically must be denoted as a prediction.[131] The logical scheme of the FFstabilizer functioning is shown in Fig. 19.

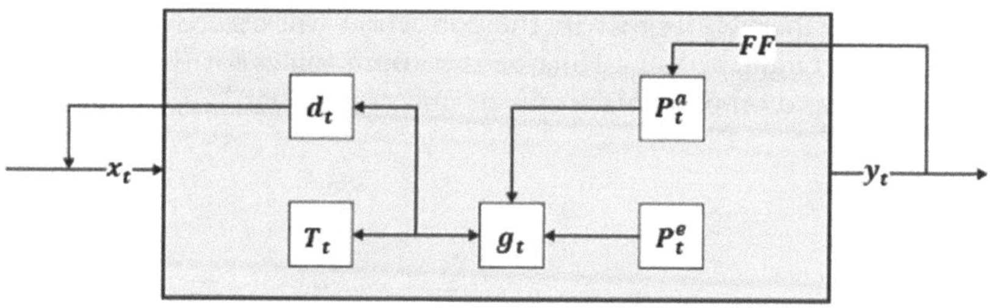

Fig. 19 Functioning of a FFstabilizer (*Source* author)

Discussion

- this time, the correction (adjustment) of the input is made in advance, based on some information, or presuppositions, or even predictions, as said before;
- to calculate the correction of the input (i.e., the input gap), the "mechanism" of the system must function, and, finally, that gap corrects the current input.

A (simple) formalization of FFstabilizer functioning could be the following:

$$y_t = B(x_t + \alpha \cdot \Delta x_t)$$

$$x_t + \alpha \cdot \Delta x_t = B^{-1}(y_t)$$

$$x_t^{ff} = B^{-1}(y_t) - \alpha \cdot \Delta x_t$$

The $FB - FF$ Stabilizer

When a stabilizer uses both the feedback and feedforward, we have to do with a stabilizer of $FB - FF$ type or $F(BF)$ type. This implies a (parallel) combination of feedback and feedforward in the functioning of a single stabilizer, either discretionary or automatic. Figure 20 suggests such a type of the stabilizer.

Discussion

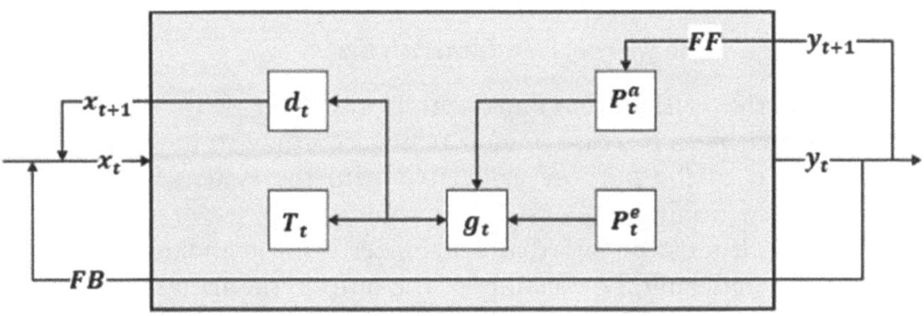

Fig. 20 Functioning of a $F(BF)$stabilizer (*Source* author)

- the combination between feedback and feedforward implies to consider the two types of reactions, either concomitantly, or successively, after the case, but concerned with the same phenomenological cycle of the system;
- however, logically, firstly, the adjustment required by the feedforward is determined, and then, to that adjustment is added, in a specific way, depending on the context and the nature of the system concerned, the adjustment required by the feedback.

A (simple) formalization of $F(BF)$stabilizer functioning could be the following:

In a simple algebraic additionality of the two required adjustments, we have:

$$x_t^{ff} = B^{-1}(y_{t+1}) - \alpha^{ff} \cdot \Delta x_t$$

$$x_{t+1} = B^{-1}(y_t) + \alpha \cdot g_t$$

8 Reactions Norms as Stabilizers

I have discussed, on the one hand, the concept of reaction (and, correlatively, the concept of reaction norm), and, on the other hand, the concept of stabilizer, either discretionary or automatic. In what follows, I will try to provide a link between the reaction norm and the stabilizer, so as to get the conclusion that the reaction norm is, in fact, a stabilizer for a generic system.

8.1 Generalities

As shown above, a stabilizer must correct the input with a quantity[132] amount, either by an increase or a decrease, according to the given expectations related to the purpose associated with the system in which the stabilizer is functioning.

First of all, it must be said that a stabilizer is not mandatorily a device aimed at only reducing the volatility of the output, no matter whether the threshold of that volatility is established rationally, i.e., based on a model of rationality, or is an expectation. Consequently, a stabilizer can use both the negative feedback and the positive feedback to get the stabilization, after the case.

(a) the case of stabilizing through negative feedback

In this case (although, for simplicity, I consider the quantitative correction/adjustment only, since the generality of the conclusion is not logically affected by this particularization), the stabilizer will either increase or reduce the input in the next cycle of the system's functioning, depending on the algebraic sign of the gap between actual value of output and the programmed value of it. Such a process will continue until the gap is null or maintains within an accepted "tunnel" of variation.[133] The crucial predicate of the stabilization through negative feedback consists in the fact that the increase or the decrease can alternate between them, according to the algebraic sign of the mentioned gap.

(b) the case of stabilizing through positive feedback

In this case (considered, also, quantitatively), the stabilizer will either increase or decrease the input but, unlike in the case of negative feedback, the increase or decrease of the input follows a monotonic path, i.e., if the first correction/adjustment is an increase of the input, this increasing will continue until the objective of the output is reached, and the same will happen if the first correction/adjustment is a decrease of the input, this decreasing will continue until the objective of the output is reached.

Nota bene: of course, in a given system, could action both the negative feedback and the positive feedback, so, generally, we can talk only about the dominance of either negative feedback or positive feedback.

8.2 The Logic of Reaction Norm as Stabilizer

Preliminaries

The crucial difference between the stabilizer and the reaction norm consists in their invariance on a reasonable term, regularly, medium term, but, in some cases, long term.[134] A reaction norm is an invariant quantifier (to restrain the discussion to the quantitative perspective), while the stabilizer is not so. Let me develop some considerations here.

- we saw that a stabilizer designs its reaction on the (next) input depending on the gap between the actual output and the expected/desired/anticipated one;
- as the prediction regarding the systems' functioning is not possible in a necessary way (excepting some physical or chemical interactions with very well controlled contexts), but with large enough approximations, it is always possible that the above-discussed gap occurs;
- consequently, the gap analyser in the given system will establish different adjustments to be applied to the (next) input, which means that the generic stabilizer (at least in the economic/social field, which is of my interest in this research) acts non-invariantly.

On the contrary, a reaction norm is quantified structurally,[135] i.e., its functioning is not under the context (environment, accidents, and so on). The structural quantification of the reaction norm means that the reaction norm is "hardified", not "softified", as the latter is the case of a stabilizer.

Nota bene: of course, from a unitary terminology perspective, we can introduce the following considerations:

(i) there are reaction norms associable to any system, in an abstract way;
(ii) the reaction norms which are invariant will be called ***rigid reaction norms*** (RRN s), while the reaction norms which are non-invariant will be called ***plastic reaction norms*** (PRN s);
(iii) so, the reaction norms, as they are developed above, are called RRN s, while the stabilizer's reactions are called PRN s;
(iv) formally, if the reaction norms are denoted with RN s, we have:

$$RNs = (RRNs) \bigcup (PRNs)$$

under the crisp condition:

$$(RRNs) \bigcap (PRNs) = (\varnothing)$$

The Reaction Norm and the Stabilizer

We learned about the difference between the reaction norm and the stabilizer; more precisely, we have seen that the reaction norm is "hardified", while the stabilizer is "softified". The question can be put here: are there analogies (or, after the case, similarities) between the two concepts and mechanisms? My positioning in this matter is as follows:

(a) firstly, a stabilizing proportion could be a multiple of the reaction norm, when one reaction norm in the case is smaller than the output-gap concerned; this possibility is valid, of course, in the (rare) case when a finite number of reaction norms exactly covers the output-gap;
(b) if the mentioned covering does not occur, then the stabilizer could act either less or more than necessary (i.e., than the output-gap punctually requires), so that the regulations of stabilization will come in the next cycles of the system functioning;
(c) so, if the stabilizer cannot use an integer number of reaction norms to complete the output-gap, the stabilization will be oscillatory, that is, will increase or decrease, alternatively, the input concerned;
(d) to go far with the denominations in the matter discussed, a reaction norm with a relatively long duration of invariancy could be called as *quantum of reaction* (QR)—let us note the quantum of reaction with q_r. According to the common understanding of the concept of quantum, the reaction norm that exactly overlaps its own quantum cannot be reduced more.[136]

I think this approach of the reaction norm as a quantum of reaction could be useful enough in modelling, both logically and mathematically, the mechanisms in the economic/social/societal systems functioning, including the public policies involved.

The Reaction Norm as a Stabilizer

Now, based on the propositions regarding the relationship between the reaction norm and the stabilizer, it is time to examine the possibility (and the presumptive value added brought by such a possibility) that the reaction norm acts as a stabilizer.

(a) a generic stabilizer can use either a reaction norm (more exactly, a quantum of reaction), adequate to the phenomenon in the case, or a (non-normed) reaction according to the output-gap;
(b) so, in the case when the stabilizer device uses a reaction norm (or, after the case, a multiple of the reaction norm, i.e., of the quanta of reaction), that reaction norm used acts as a stabilizer;
(c) so, not all reaction norms act as stabilizer and, symmetrically, not all stabilizers are reaction norms (although they are, obviously, reactions).

The question arises here: can a reaction norm act outside a stabilizing device? My position is the following:

- a reaction is a specific response/reply of a system to a preceding suffered action (either from the environment or from the interior) by that system;
- consequently, a reaction is a concept more extensive than a reaction norm or a stabilizer;
- this means that a reaction norm can happen both inside a stabilizer (according to the above considerations) and outside it.

So, a reaction, respectively, a reaction norm can act independently of a stabilizing device. Generally, a reaction norm is associated with a stabilizing device in cases in which the reaction is aimed to provide means of surviving through avoiding the escalation of different phenomena that could endanger the very structure of the system concerned.

Annex 1: About Kaldor-Hicks Test in the Social Justice

The Kaldor-Hicks test (from now on: KHT) concerns distributive social justice;therefore, it is intended for social policies (more generally, economic policies) and is based on utility, which it considers interpersonally comparable and, above all, considers it from a cardinal perspective (quantitative commensurability). The KHT represents a generalization of the Pareto condition.

The TKH accepts that some individuals will be in a worse situation, after the test is verified, while the Pareto condition/test does not accept this; the Pareto condition/test has a firm stopping criterion (that of improving the state), which coincides with the validation criterion, while the KHT does not have such a stopping criterion (it only has a validation criterion), but, like the Pareto condition/test, it refers to the efficiency of the final state, by improving it. KHT ignores the possible efficiency-ethics trade-off (in principle, it only targets efficiency), so it is not a procedural test, but end-state also called the compensation principle. Essentially, the KHT is, in turn, a species of cost–benefit analysis (see welfare economics), so that it refers to an allocation/reallocation of resources that produces more benefits than costs (*Nota bene*: the majority of analysts refer to resource allocation, but it seems that it is actually about the allocation of results).

The KHT is constituted of two tests, in "mirror": (a) the Kaldor test (KT), proposed by Nicholas Kaldor; (b) the Hicks test (HT), proposed by John Hicks.

(a) Kaldor test (KT)

Let there be a state change of a system from state A to state B. The KT is passed if the amount with which the winners of the state change compensate the losers, in order for the last to accept that change, is greater than the losers expect to receive for their acceptance. The KT is a test from the perspective of the winners.

(b) Hicks test (HT)

Let there be a state change of a system from state A to state B. The HT is passed if the losers of the state change compensate the winners, so that they do not accept the change, with an amount less than the winners expect to receive for their non-acceptance. The HT is a test from the perspective of the losers.

Of course, the KHT is a combination of the KT and HT. This combination was performed by Tibor Scitovsky, so that the KHT is, sometimes, called the Scitovsky test (ST). The hypotheses of the ST are as follows:

- the individual preferences are stable and there are no externalities;
- the inter-personal comparisons of welfare are inadmissible;
- the individuals can assess their own welfare.

There are three known critics on the KHT: (a) Scitovsky's critic; (b) Little's critic; (c) Sen's critic.

(a) Scitovsky's critic

- the appeal to the state for compensation refers to a socialist position;
- the KHT test generates a paradox (the Scitovsky paradox or the resilience paradox):
  - (*content*) if, according to the KHT, one moves from state A to state B (so state B is desirable compared to state A), once state B is established, the KHT will establish that it is desirable to move from state B to state A (so state A is desirable compared to state B);
  - (*Scitovsky's solution*) Scitovsky's double criterion: verification of the KHT when moving from A to B and non-verification of the KHT test when moving from B to A.

(b) Little's critic

- (*content*) although it seems that the KHT refers to distribution, in fact it refers to production (but not referring to distribution can neither address nor solve the welfare problem). The KHT is not really a test, but more of a definition;
- (*Little's solution*) also a compensation criterion, but rejects both the KHT and the Scitovsky paradox.

(c) Sen's critic (*Nota bene*: in fact, rather a logical systematization)

- welfare is assessed at the level of individuals;
- essentially, it is used the Pareto criterion (i.e., a species of KHT);
- the KHT does not explain judgements regarding the assessment of welfare.

Notes

1. I remind you that there are three categories of membranes for the (general) systems: (a) physical; (b) cognitive; (c) institutional. A given system must be characterized by at least one membrane; however, it can have two or even all three membranes, without the condition that the membranes (exactly) overlap among them.
2. Obviously, here, the term continuous does not mean the continuous character of change (the successive state vectors remain always discrete), but the smooth concatenation of the state vectors in question.
3. The irreversibility could be "replaced" by hysteresis (which is a quasi-reversibility, as well as a quasi-irreversibility), since both signify different arrows of the kinematics of the system facing the initial arrow.
4. In the social/societal field, there are chreods only.
5. This statement is useful for our discussion, but, in fact, the reality contains both systems and networks, often as systems of systems and networks, or networks of systems and networks, or systems of systems, or networks of networks, etc.
6. Other types of knowledge are equally available: theological, metaphysical, artistic, praxiological/teleological, etc.
7. This vulnerability/risk cannot be totally avoided, for two reasons: (a) we do not know non-ambiguously a "map" of the ontological systems; (b) we could be interested cognitively in a system that does not exactly overlap with some ontological system. Here we have, in fact, the problem of the non-coincidence of membranes of systems: the cognitive membrane and the physical membrane (see note 1).

8. I invite the reader to observe an analogy (of functional type) of this "thesis" with the Quine-Duhem thesis regarding the factual testability of hypotheses within Popper's falsifiability.
9. For the moment, "personality" of the transforming/transformation operator is not of interest.
10. This is the basic reason, for example, for rejecting the quasi-infinite speed of the thought focused on the Big Bang in the Universe—the thought does not produce any change in the Big Bang phenomenon, so we can say that the thought does not really arrive at the Big Bang moment, so the assertion regarding its infinite speed is false.
11. I remind that about viability/viabilism I have discussed in Chapter 4.
12. It is easy to observe that the signification norm is not redundant with the assessing norm—the assessing norm (i.e., the meaning) has a public relevance (at the community level), while the signification/significance norm has a private relevance (at the individual level). It is not "forbidden" that a norm of assessing type overlaps on a norm of signification type, but, at the same time, such overlapping is not mandatory.
13. The term allowed has, equally, the meaning of perceived, that is, the reactions must be perceived by the destination system. For example, an ethical norm is not perceptible for an electrical power system.
14. It is obvious that, if the action moves the target system from its identity, that is, takes the system out of its identity tunnel, that system can no longer react—an eventual reaction belongs to… another system.
15. In the economy of the book, I will provide a principle (or a basic reason, or master reason) for reaction (including for the reaction norm), considering the current accepted proposals in the literature: entropy law, constructal law, gravity law, and so on. By anticipating, I will propose an embedding "law" called the minimum entropic gradient of interaction.
16. Here it is about the *hormesis* (Taleb, 2014), see for this concept and its phenomenology, my book (Dinga, 2025). Let us remind the aphorism of Nietzsche in this context: *What doesn't kill you, makes you stronger*.

17. It is easy to observe that the positive feedback describes a vicious circle, while the negative feedback describes a virtuous circle.
18. The discretionary property of an action (or decision) does not mean an arbitrary property—discretionarity and arbitrariness do not have the same referential at all.
19. I draw attention to the fact that the reason for surviving is not redundant to (respectively, does not overlap with) the objective of surviving, since to survive does not imply conservation, just as the conservation does not (necessarily) imply surviving.
20. An analytical examination of the concept of robustness is offered in Dinga (2025).
21. The three entities in the world are: (a) things; (b) properties; (c) relationships. So, we have properties of things, properties of properties, properties of relationships, as well as relationships between things, relationships between properties, relationships between relationships, etc. Here, we have the case of a property of a relationship.
22. The term perception is used here in its universal signification; for example, a child perceives the mother's frown, and a railway track "perceives" the increase in environmental temperature.
23. It is a separate (and interesting) issue if the structure is logically dependent on the nature of that structure, more exactly, the nature of the structural components. For example, I think that the structure of a mechanical system can be replicated in the form of a system of equations, and I would say that the initial structure has been preserved. The reason for such a statement is the following: the functions of that system are the same, so the structure is the same, no matter the nature (substance) in which the structure is designed. Moreover, we can say that the structure causes the function, and from the function, the structure can be inferred.
24. This assessment comes from the fact that functions (functionality) can change, to some degree, inside the same structure.
25. A more enthusiastic (than me) analyst could examine the action/reaction relationship from the (known) perspective of demand–supply relationship, by observing that the initial action is the supply, while the first reaction is the demand. Further, any reaction that is performed is, concomitantly, a supply–demand pair.

26. The reader is invited to read carefully these statements: the target system from the action perspective becomes the source system from the reaction perspective, and vice versa.
27. Here, the concept of niche is that proposed by Maturana and Varela (1991), from a cognitive perspective (see, also, Santiago School of Cognition).
28. Of course, it is a source system from the point of view of reaction (norm), since it is a target system from the point of view of the action (from the environment) that triggered that reaction.
29. Undoubtedly, a separate model of the co-evolution of the pair *social system–state*, is of great interest and significance, but such a task exceeds my objectives in this book.
30. In this context, the term *law* means principle, i.e., movement law; this is why I do not write the term law in brackets.
31. The concept of law, which drives the societal system, will be further developed at the Sect. 5.
32. This formulation can work as a maxim of behaviour.
33. I want to mention that the formulations of the two laws (both for the societal system and for the social justice system) mean, logically, that both sustainability/viability (in the societal system case) and the social capital (in the social justice case) can either increase or (at least) remain constant.
34. But, also, in Biology (ex.: Darwin's law of evolution), Mathematics (ex.: Noether's conservation theorems), Economics (ex.: public deficit invariance), or Sociology (ex.: Marx's historical materialism).
35. My own proposal in this matter will be approached further.
36. I remind that in the world there are three and only three distinct entities: (i) things (which contain, of course, both non-living and living entities); (ii) properties; (iii) relationships.
37. As will be shown later, this alternativeness is not at all imperative, so two or more principles can be convoked to support some classes of interactions (especially in more complex worlds, such as the social/societal one).
38. Or the gravity—but, since Einstein, gravity is not considered anymore a force (as Newton thought it), but a spatial curvature that provides the cosmological geodesic which "indicates" the path to be (imperatively) followed.

39. This concept was introduced in 1991 by Chilian biologists Humberto Maturana & Francisco Varela, in their book *Autopoiesis and Cognition. The Realization of Living*, Springer Science & Business Media.
40. It seems the only tools of unifying is the logical one since it is completely formal.
41. However, Adrian Bejan (2014), who coined, in 1997, the syntagma *constructal law*, believes that a principle answers (or should answer) the question "how".
42. Causality arrow is not (like that) a time arrow (as the entropy arrow, for example), because of its reversibility in time.
43. For the living systems endowed with psychism (*Nota bene*: someone could require more, namely rationality), the finality is called purpose.
44. The world does not maximize as a whole, since regionally occurring finalities could be (and, in fact, often are), of course, maximized.
45. The contingent means, from a logical point of view, the conjunction of the possible and the non-necessary.
46. This positioning is contrary to the basic assumption of the contructal law regarding the criterion of maximizing, even in the case of natural entities.
47. The dissipative systems include, besides the biologically living systems, the *logically* living systems too (Dinga, 2020).
48. From a phenomenological point of view, for a given observer subject, all the other subjects are objects, but such a philosophical development is not necessary for this communication.
49. For example, the object called a crystal can grow, but cannot develop (to develop means to change the own structure).
50. There are three distinct meanings of the concept of entropy: a) *Phenomenological entropy*—a measure of the macroscopic entropy based on Thermodynamics, that is, anchored in macroscopic properties as heat and temperature (initiated by Clausius, 1865); b) *Statistical entropy*—based on a measure of macroscopic aggregation of microscopic states (initiated by Boltzmann, 1870); c) *Informational entropy*—a measure of entropy based on the probability of states (initiated by Shannon, 1948).
51. In reality, Boltzmann does not consider probabilities in their usual sense, i.e., inductive derivatives, as is the case, for example, of

objective probabilities (or Kolmogorov probabilities), but rather as possibilities; by possibilities we mean states or events, necessary or contingent, unrelated to a previous state archive—in such a context, the concept of propensity, initiated by Karl Popper following Aristotle's Physics, seems to us much more adequate.

52. However, for reasons of consistency, the time arrow in the dissipative systems is not provided by either entropy increasing or entropy decreasing—simply, the entropy ceases to indicate a time arrow inside the dissipative systems.
53. As it is known, the laws of thermodynamics (*Nota bene*: so far, it seems that four laws of thermodynamics have been formulated) do not give any answer about the way or the rule according to which the systems are configured (i.e., acquire their shape and structure).
54. Exergy is the name for useful, available, or bound energy.
55. If the syntagma "easier and easier" is interpreted, as I believe it must be, as meaning more and more efficient, that criterion leads to a maximizing significance, not a minimizing one.
56. In our opinion, the constructal law is not of the power of a principle (or a ... law of nature), as it is presented by the author, but it has the features of a mechanism (like the Darwinian theory of the evolution of life, which is a mechanism, not a principle—for example, Darwinism cannot explain the origin of life, but only its evolution after it appeared; *Nota bene*: neither Physics can explain the singularity at the moment of the Big Bang, but only everything that happened later). The difference between principle/law and mechanism is as follows: principle/law answers the question "why", i.e., "based on which cause", while the mechanism answers the question "how".
57. Probably, a unifying concept could be here our proposal of *logically living system*, which includes the (biologically living systems as a subsystem) (Dinga, 2020). See, also my upcoming book, *The Economics of Social Living Systems. A New Research Methodology* (to be printed by Palgrave Macmillan – Springer in 2027), which examines exactly the phenomenology of the logically living systems (LLS).
58. Which, obviously, detracts from the justification of its universal character.

59. But there are cases in which either there are no such material supports for configuring the shape and structure to allow flows (e.g., cactus), or the movement of the systems in question is very slow (e.g., turtle).
60. Although the emphasis (of the examples given) refers to physical flows, it is obvious that, from a conceptual point of view, any type of flows can be accepted: informational, entropic, ideational, axiological, etc. However, such a generalization is not yet achieved, constituting, in our opinion, a challenge for researchers who consider that the constructal law is a productive direction in epistemology (*Nota bene*: we are not among these researchers, since we have our own fundamental "law" on behaviour, i.e., in a more general sense, interaction, namely the *law of the minimum entropic gradient*—which will be developed later).
61. It is a cognition that has an even wider scope than the one proposed by the Santiago School, because it also includes non-living (non-animated) nature.
62. Allometry (or allometrics) studies the relationships of determination between the body dimensions of living entities and the shape and dimensions of their somatic organs (either internal or external), their internal structure, functions, and behaviour.
63. In this respect, Bejan and other adepts of constructal law are not consequent: for example, when constructal law is proposed as such (i.e., as a law), it is instead described as a law of evolution. But it is obvious that evolution has nothing to do with optimization than, as it could be thought, as a result of infinitely long-time evolution.
64. In addition to these two arrows of time (which are logically consistent with each other), there is also the psychological arrow of time: time increases from the point where the feelings (or lived events) in memory are less numerous to the point where those feelings (or lived events) are more numerous.
65. Namely, the three Popper's worlds.
66. Be not confused with constructivism–constructalness addresses the property of an entity to interact with its environment based on the constructal law. With some pedantry, we could talk about entropyness (interactions based on the entropy law) or gravityness (interactions based on the gravity law).

67. Logically, any sufficient predicate is also a necessary predicate, once the entity generated by the sufficient predicates comes into existence. But, coming into existence generates (or not, after the case) other necessary predicates which, this time, are *new*, for not to be confused with the "old" necessary predicates which are the same as the sufficient ones.
68. Of course, except the first action (which can be either necessary or contingent), any of the next actions are, rigorously, reactions and are necessary. However, about the necessity of reaction to action should perhaps be discussed more, but this issue is lateral enough from my thread of reasoning, so it will be postponed. For example, can there be cases in which (at least in the societal field) an individual who is offended does not offend in turn, so he/she has no reaction.
69. For example, the claim that, by a though experiment, I arrived exactly now on a star which is placed at 100 million light-years, triggering the simple question: show me the trace your eyes left on the star.
70. However, it is necessary that at least a trace be objectified, as logical "witness" that the relationship had place. The question "*Is it possible that a double arrow does exhibit no trace due to objectifying the corresponding relationship?*" is very interesting. Still, it will be, in this paper, ignored.
71. It is to be observed that the very use of sufficiency predicates to formulate the definition of a concept (present in this paper) is an application of Leibniz-ian principle (which, it seems, is not exactly a new principle of logic, besides the three known principles: of identity, of non-contradiction, and of the middle excluded).
72. For conscious entities (like human beings) the causality occurs as intelligibility.
73. The concept of cognition here has the meaning of Santiago School (Maturana; Varela, 1991), that is, a cognition accessible to any (living or non-living entity) which chooses the niche of the entity in case into its environment (*Nota bene*: the environment contains, of course, the entity relatively to which that cognition has been acquired).
74. Briefly, free will is the capacity (no matter its nature) to oppose to contingent constraints/laws (as, for example, the positive laws in the social field of humanity).

75. This is the very reason why money has been (socially) invented.
76. The quantity (size) of an action/reaction is given by multiplying the intensity of the action/reaction with the duration of exerting that action/reaction. Of course, the substitutability between intensity and duration must have clear thresholds, which I do not discuss here.
77. See, for example, the use of decoy drones in the strange army aggression of the Russian Federation against Ukraine.
78. From an evolutive perspective, a subjective trace (which is a non-genuine interaction) will condition the next genuine interactions on a qualitative level, but I will ignore here such a complication.
79. For example, in the social field, an economic agent does obey or does not a fiscal behaviour norm, but never he/she modifies something in that norm—so, the agent positions towards the norm, not interactions with it. Moreover, both positive law and divine law have a positioning nature, not an interaction nature.
80. The issue of entanglement (of non-locality), highlighted by Quantum Mechanics, among all masses in the Universe (a necessary property coming from the Big Bang), gets its head out here, but I do not insist on it.
81. Honestly, this my own statement seems to me to be somewhat disputable. Indeed, an optimization requires a set of constraints within which the best spatial position (i.e., the finality) can be reached. Such a condition subsists only if the space curvature is considered as a… constraint. Obviously, this is possible enough. If the mentioned constraint is unacceptable, then the process of gravitational positioning is a question of equilibrium (more precisely, of static equilibrium), not of positional optimization.
82. As gravity is not a force exerted between/among masses, the question of the speed of transmitting the influence is without sense—no influence is transmitted at all, simply, the entanglement of all masses in the Universe leads to positioning those masses in the places according to their "reservation" by the space curvature (*Nota bene*: a metaphysical reminiscence of Aristotle's Physics is not difficult to be observed here, with the difference that things go towards their places based not on their nature but on their masses).
83. In my opinion, the non-evolutive attribute is equivalent (in a consequentialist view) to the optimizing attribute. In this

view, sustainability, which implies evolution (or co-evolution, more exactly) cannot be of an optimizing type of praxiological paradigm.

84. An order could be (abstractly) defined as follows (Dinga, 2022a): an order is that state of a system which verifies the following sufficiency predicates: (1) (SPO1) *sensory observability*: the phenomenon that will be the basis of the finding (or non-finding) of an ordered configuration must be observable at the sensory level, even if, of course, after the sensory sensation, perception, conceptualization, and judgement (reasoning) occur which ultimately leads to the formulation, through universalization, of the order in question; (2) (SPO2) *intellectual observability*: if SPO1 involves the natural senses of the cognitive subject, instead SPO2 involves the intellect of that subject. As is known, perception represents the form that consciousness gives to sensation. The formation of concepts and the preparation of judgements requires the subject's intellect, which transforms perception into concept. Conceptualization is the crucial step in the deductive identification of order; (3) (SPO3) *catalogue registration*: the application of the first two sufficiency predicates leads only to the possibility of registering an order. The effective sensing of the order occurs only if the result of the application of SPO2 is found in the already existing catalogue of possible orders; the catalogue is, of course, accessible to the cognitive subject in question.
85. The special case (*Nota bene*: that does not violate, however, the entropy law) of the dissipative system will be ignored here, to not complicate the discussion.
86. It remains, of course, to verify if there is, also, in this case, an amortization of the interaction (*Nota bene*: more exactly, a decrease of the reaction norms involved).
87. How this "knowledge" is acquired is another question, which I do not provide comments about in this study.
88. In my opinion, this statute of the entropy law (an exchange law) would have an extraordinary destiny if applied, systematically and precautionarily in the economic/financial (more extended, in the social) field.

89. It is to be mentioned that the neighbourhood (either necessary, in the gravity case, or contingent, in the entropy case) is not incompatible with the movement. A change in the mass distribution in the Universe (no matter the cause implied) will change/move the placement of the masses according to the new spatial curvature. In the same way, the entities involved in the entropic exchange can change their spatial placement, but such a change is external and autonomous on the entropic exchange (*Nota bene*: but that is going to change in the proposal we are going to make).
90. The arrow has its origin in the system which generates changes in the corresponding system, and its destination in the system which suffers those changes—so, in the case of constructal law, the system is determined by its environment to change, according to the principle of the respective law, while the environment is not changed by the re-configuration of the system. Somewhat, the environment "accepts" to be passively exploited by the system.
91. The way in which the combination of spatial action of the constructal law with its temporal action takes place remains, in my opinion, to be further examined. In such cases, the static structure of dendrites' distribution and the kinematic/dynamic structure of their distribution must provide an optimal (or, at least, surviving) spatial–temporal distribution in the case. Of course, the next idea here is that of constructing an indifference curve (or, in fact, an indifference surface), which allows new analytical developments in the matter of this law. Probably, at this point, a connection between the gravity law and the entropy law could lead to the unification of the two "forces". Further, one could try to unify, besides the two mentioned forces, also the entropy "force", in an essay to get a "unified theory", similar to the endeavour unfolding in Physics.
92. Nothing does prevent to be thought also a non-physical configuration (as happens in psychology, including in cognitive psychology, or sociology—as the sociology of science, for example in Kuhn's paradigm).
93. Of course, if the two criteria of choice would coincide, then we would talk about a greater propensity to interaction (under the condition that all the sufficiency predicates would be verified). So, I would say that there are two cases related to this sufficiency predicates (generally valid, not only in the case of constructal law),

namely: (a) *simple propensity* to relationship—when only one of the systems has a choice criterion; (b) *augmented propensity*—when both systems have their own choice criterion.

94. It must be made the following observation here: the maximization of such an intersection is somewhat imprecise enough because it addresses only one of the two factors of what could be called the *quantity of interaction.* If we note with QI the quantity of interaction between the system's dendrites and the useful flows of the environment, with VI the volume of intersection (*Nota bene*: in particular cases, the volume may be reduced to the surface, so we have thenSI, i.e., the surface of interaction), and with EI the quality of intersection (where E comes from the Greek *eidos*), then:$QI = VI \cdot EI$. The maximization of the intersection addresses only the factorVI, but the same VI can be modified (upward or downward) according to EI (e.g., the angle of incidence of solar flows on plants' leaves (namely, exactly theEI), is very important here. *Nota bene*: of course, one more analytical researcher could draw an indifference curve between VI and EI to extract new consequences in the constructal law matter.
95. See my coined concept of *proference* (formed from **pro**pensity and pre**ference**) (Dinga, 2022b).
96. Using the term *minimal* instead of the term *minimum* has the following reason: to get the minimum entropic gradient means to "calculate" all the entropic gradients for all entities in the Universe, given a fixed entity. On the contrary, the minimal entropic gradient addresses the "calculation" of the entropic gradient only in the vicinity of the given fixed entity, which can be called *operational proximity* (*Nota bene*: from here, arises further suggestions for topological modelling of the interaction based on MEG law). Operational proximity is that vicinity where the given fixed entity can operate for interaction without risking its life (here, the term life is taken in the large sense of Bejan or Maturana&Varela), that is, the searching for the minimal entropic gradient will continue until the moment when the life of the searcher is put into threat. From here, it results the local character of the MEG law operating, although the validity of the law is universal. The distinction between validity (which is universal) and operationality (which is local) is consistent with the real way in which the world is functioning—more exactly, it can be said

that the world functions as it can, not as it is best to do that—here we have a new formulation of the sustainability vs. optimality.

97. So, the entropic order does not address the concept of *exergy*, because it does not take into consideration the relationship between the entity/system and its environment.
98. By intelligence, I understand a (structural and functional) property of an entity to elaborate a cognitive model on the objective reality (not on the subjective or objectified ones). This cognitive model will be used by that entity to behave in the reality concerned (*Nota bene*: it is obvious that I consider here exclusively the concept of cognition coined by the Santiago School). If a new property, that of representationality (which involves awareness/consciousness), is added, then we have rationality. So an entity can be intelligent without being rational (for example, a fox).
99. Here it must be solved the issue of locality, see below in the principal text.
100. I remind that the Quantum Theory seems to require, as a sufficiency (namely, mandatory) condition, the observation in triggering and shaping up the quantum events. However, this situation does not infringe our supposition on the (general) non-necessity of an observer for the spontaneous transfer of (high) order.
101. It is not needed to consider the concept of cognition proposed by Santiago School, because it is not needed, generally, for any cognition in the phenomenon examined, although, however, the cognition is not prohibited, as shown at point (iii).
102. Of course, $(S - cognition) \subset (I - cognition)$.
103. Namely, the allocation of the means to the purpose.
104. By qualitative cost of entropic interaction, I understand the cost needed to "translate" a type of order in other type of order, not the cost needed to integrate a lower entropy into a system with a higher entropy (the last cost should be called quantitative cost of entropic interaction). As we shall view next, both types of cost are paid through increasing of the entropy itself.
105. I invite the reader to observe the similarity between this impossibility (more exactly, impracticability—even in the natural world) and the impossibility (or impracticability) of the verificationism proposed by Vienna Circle.

106. A...relative analogy of EIH can be made with the Schwarzschild limit in the General Theory of Relativity.
107. Even in the case of entropic orders which are not of the Thermodynamic entropy type, there are prohibitive costs of searching and calculating the EGs, i.e., there is an ending-criterion of such searching and calculation. *Nota bene*: here could be something analogous to the optimality at the microeconomic level: equality between marginal cost and marginal price/income.
108. The practical rationality is also working in non-living entities cases or in living non-conscious entities cases, because it signifies, generally, adequacy of the means to the finality (or to the purpose, in the conscious living case).
109. Scientists with more imagination (remember Einstein's aphorism: *imagination is more important than knowledge*) could establish a kind of entropic dimension, similarly with fractal dimension (for example, only illustratively, if the plant has an entropic dimension 1, and the animal has an entropic dimension 2, then, the carnivore plant should have an entropic dimension 1.5). Such a way, the MEG could be directly linked to the entropic dimension and a specific theory could be developed in this direction.
110. Generally, to capabilities, as shown in the theory (approach) of capabilities in the matter of social justice.
111. The supposition could be treated in the hypothesis of a duopoly formed between the two individuals, so that each of them knows the reaction norm of the other; as seen, we come again to the crucial concept of reaction norm.
112. I invite the reader to observe that the end-symmetry can be associated with the falsifiability testing, while the mode-symmetry can be associated with the falsifiability testability (not actual testing). From another perspective, the mode-symmetry can be framed into the Vienna Circle theory of confirmability (as opposed to that of verifiability).
113. The mutualization is one of the six categories/species of the social capital—see Chapter 6, Annex 1. I remind here the species of the social capital: (a) as socialization arrow: (a1) communication; (a2) participation; (a3) mutualization; (b) as individualization/individuation arrow: (b1) freedom; (b2) trust; (b3) symmetry.

114. See here also the concepts of ***bonding social capital*** (for homogenous individuals), or of ***bridging social capital*** (for heterogeneous individuals), introduced by Robert D. Putnam.
115. Generally, by contract must be understood simply a free agreement, without any compulsory written or other witness prove (for example, the J.J. Rousseau-ian social contract, or the Rawlsian concept of the social contract agreed in the initial/originary position).
116. Like in the case of the (societal) æsthetics, the means (analogous to the procedures in the case of æsthetics) do not need to be the same or similar, but only to have the same potential to lead to the goals expected.
117. Of course, the discussion is developed in the context of a free society, that is, a society where the liberty to choose is guaranteed.
118. For example, different structures of the market of interactions, like monopoly, monopsony, oligopoly, oligospony, and bilateral monopoly. In the same key, the entropic gradient, as "price" of that market, could be examined in the cobweb model to get the equilibrium "price". Perhaps, even, a concept of the "natural price" (i.e., the "natural entropic gradient") in the market of interactions can also be developed through deeper analyses.
119. In the case of a deterministic system, we have an analytical causality (i.e., invariantly applicable to each individual of a given population of individuals), while in the case of a random system, we have a statistical causality (i.e., invariably applicable only to the mean of the involved individuals, not to each individual as such).
120. Of course, some framing of the nature of the reaction is provided by the very choice of the interaction, since a given interaction admits only some categories of reactions.
121. The knowledge of the reaction and its norm regarding the system 2 is presumed as an indispensable premise of the proposed model of MEG. Although some unrealism is contained (similarly to that of the neoclassical economic theory), for the moment, I would keep it.
122. The quantity of reaction is the product of the intensity of reaction and the duration of reaction.
123. Discretionarity has no connection with any meaning as: at one's discretion, or at one's latitude, or with arbitrariness.

124. The administrative (bureaucratic) lag involved between the moment of decision-making and that of entering into force is not relevant here.
125. As I explained elsewhere, any sufficiency predicate is also a necessary predicate, but there can exist necessary predicates that are caused by the very sufficiency predicates; those necessary predicates are not, however, sufficiency predicates, but, being necessary, they must be called *new* necessary predicates.
126. If we talk about the individual persons, then the discretionarity and automaticity are more difficult to discern; however, as I think, the automaticity has a small enough weight in the total decisions in this case—the automatic decisions (and, perhaps, actions) are "decided" at the subconscious level, while the discretionary decisions are enacted at the conscious level. *Nota bene*: I ignore, here, the complications put into evidence by empirical research, according to which the conscious only "approves" the decision made by the unconscious.
127. Or, equally, to be eliminate some items.
128. Of course, the two episodes could unfold alternatively, in an oscillant way, or, in some contexts, in a cyclical way, especially in the economic component of the societal system.
129. About the general concept of propensity, see my works (Dinga, 2022a, 2022b), and (Dinga et al., 2022).
130. Combining the two limits with the time arrow, in fact, a chreod of the system/process described by P is established.
131. It is easy to show that there is a logical circularity between explanation and prediction—in fact, an explanation is a post-prediction and, in turn, a prediction is a pre-explanation. This is the very hard core of Popper's factual falsifiability, since by testing the prediction is tested an… explanation, that is, a truth (*Nota bene*: an explanation is a description of the causality).
132. The usual case in a stabilizer functioning is the quantitative adjustment, but it can be also needed for other types of corrections/adjustments: (a) qualitative; (b) structural, when the input is a vector of more components; (c) temporal, when the rhythm of inputs are important; (d) ordering, when the order in which the inputs enter the system is important. Of course, in the real world, all five criteria of stabilizing could be of relevance at the same time.

133. Generally, in the economic (or, more general, social/societal) field, the numerical values are not so rigid like in the natural field, so that are of interest rather vicinities of an established number than the number itself. *Nota bene*: the same can be said on the biological field, psychological field, or sociological field, that is, on the social sciences/theories or on the humanistic sciences/theories (humanities).
134. Theoretically it cannot be excluded the cases in which the reaction norm ise established for ever—for example, in biological field or in some axiomatic theories. In mathematics, a function is, logically, a device that works based on invariant reaction norm. By a (little bit) extension, the syllogism is, qualitatively, a device that is working based on invariant reaction norms, which are exactly the principles of logic.
135. Symmetrically, we can say that the stabilizer is designed functionally.
136. Obviously, the quantum of reaction is not a theoretical concept (as are, instead, the quantum of mass, length, energy, space, time, etc., in Physics—the so-called Planck's constants).

References

Audi, R. (2004). Theoretical Rationality: Its Sources, Structure, and Scope. In A. R. Mele & P. Rawling (Eds.), *The Oxford Handbook of Rationality*. Oxford University Press.

Bejan, A. (2007). *Constructal Theory of Social Dynamics*. Springer.

Bejan, A. (2014). *Constructal Law: Optimization as Design Evolution. Journal of Heat Transfer, 137*(6).

Dinga, E. (2020). Logically Living System—A Generative Machine for Auto-Poietic Systems. In *Handbook of Research on Autopoiesis and Self-Sustaining Processes for Organizational Success*. IGI Global Publisher of Timely Knowledge.

Dinga, E. (2022a). *The Economic Order*. In E. Dinga (Ed.), *Economy and Society*. Economica Publishing House (in Romanian).

Dinga, E. (2022b). Proference: Behavioural Mix Between Propensity and Preference on Financial Market. *European Journal of Interdisciplinary Studies, 14*(2).

Dinga, E. (2025). *Economic Resilience During Overlapped Crises—Antifragility, Sustainability and Autopoieticity*. Palgrave Macmillan; Springer Nature.

Dinga, E., Oprean-Stan, C., Tănăsescu, C.-R., Brătian, V., & Ionescu, G.-M. (2021). Entropy-Based Behavioural Efficiency of the Financial Market. *Entropy, 23* (1396).

Dinga, E., Oprean-Stan, C., Tănăsescu, C.-R., Brătian, V., & Ionescu, G.-M. (2022). *Financial Market Analysis and Behaviour. The Adaptive Preference Hypothesis*. Routledge; Taylor & Francis Group.

Dinga, E., Oprean-Stan, C., Tănăsescu, C.R., Brătian, V., & Ionescu, G.-M. (2023). *Economic and Financial Market Behaviour. The Autopoietic Market Hypothesis*. Palgrave Macmillan; Springer Nature.

Dinga, E., Tănăsescu, C.-R., & Ionescu, G.-M. (2020). *Social Entropy and Normative Network. Entropy, 22*(9).

Dinga, E., Tănăsescu, C.-R., & Ionescu, G.-M. (2022). *An Automatic Anchoring of the Reference Social Index*. Social Indicators Research.

Maturana, H. R., & Varela, F. J. (1991). *Autopoiesis and Cognition. The Realization of the Living*. Springer Science & Business Media.

Nicolis, G., & Prigogine, I. (1987). *Exploring Complexity. An Introduction*. Piper.

Taleb, N. N. (2012). *Antifragile: Things That Gain from Disorder*. Random House Publishing.

CHAPTER 10

An Evolutionary Model: Social Justice–Societal System

1 Some Preparative

This chapter aims to put together the findings of the precedent chapters, especially Chapters 2 (*The evolutive change of the society*), 8 (*Social justice, social capital, and wellbeing*), and 10 (*Reaction norms and stabilizers*). This integration aspires to deliver an evolutionary model of social justice within the societal chreod, under the "imperium" of the four forces of the society, as they are identified in Chapter 2.

The basic lanes of reasoning in building up such an evolutionary model are as follows:

- the society/societal chreod obeys not finality (even less, necessity), but purposiveness (i.e., contingency);
- the societal path, in both time and space, is governed by a two-handed mechanism, that is, by a complicated combination of the visible hand (the state intervention in, to be hoped, its legitimate areas—see Chapter 5, especially Sect. 1.2) and the invisible hand[1]; the (ultimate[2]) purpose, in fact, a driving cause, in the sense of Aristotle's *causa finalis*, is the individual's wellbeing;
- the individual wellbeing is obtainable through the production and reproduction of the social capital—this production/reproduction of the social capital is a social/societal process, not an individual one;

E. Dinga, *The Economics of Social Justice and Societal Evolution*,
https://doi.org/10.1007/978-3-032-24055-2_10

- so, the general (efficient) cause of wellbeing is of a social/societal nature, while the purpose (final cause) of it is of the individual nature[3];
- the kinematic of the society (societal system) on its chreod is based on the interactions among the four (binomial) forces identified previously, through their basic functions.

1.1 An Additional Examination of the Societal Forces

I remind you, shortly (from Chapter 2), of the four societal forces that drive the societal dynamics:

1. (F_1) the binomial force "population–resources"—*PR*
   - logical signification: *causa materialis*
   - level of action: societal structure
   - (F_1^R) role: ensuring the biological survival
   - (F_1^f) functions: (F_1^{f1}) demographic sustainability; (F_1^{f2}) ecological sustainability; (F_1^{f3}) cosmic and non-human life sustainability; (F_1^{f4}) economic sustainability.
2. (F_2) the binomial force "science–social construction"—*SC*
   - logical signification: *causa efficiens*
   - level of action: societal infrastructure
   - (F_2^R) role: providing the needed knowledge on the world
   - (F_2^f) functions: (F_2^{f1}) knowing the objective world; (F_2^{f2}) grounding the social construction; (F_2^{f3}) modelling the co-habitation between objective and objectified worlds; (F_2^{f4}) ensuring the self-sustainability of the social construction.
3. (F_3) the binomial "humanities–art"—*HA*
   - logical signification: *causa formalis*
   - level of action: societal suprastructure
   - (F_3^R) role: providing the needed knowledge on the human being (person)
   - (F_3^f) functions: (F_3^{f1}) construction of the ethical profile; (F_3^{f2}) construction of the aesthetical profile; (F_3^{f3}) construction of

the communitarian profile; (F_3^{f4}) construction of the axiological profile.

4. (F_4) the binomial "realization of human being–social justice"—*RJ*
   - logical signification: *causa finalis*
   - level of action: societal structure
   - (F_4^R) role: putting in place, fully functional and accessible, all the capabilities allowed by the other three forces;
   - (F_4^f) functions: (F_4^{f1}) fully providing of the freedom of individual choice; (F_4^{f2}) defending of the life, health, and guaranteeing of completely flourishing, for individuals and community; (F_4^{f3}) providing the equality of individuals before positive law and societal's opportunities; (F_4^{f4}) defending society against monopolization of power (economic, political, cultural).

1.2 A (Seemingly) Hierarchy of the Societal Forces' Functions

For each of the four societal forces, the functions performed can be hierarchized, from a logical point of view, according to their significance provided by the working of the given societal force.

The hierarchy will be established based on the so-called importance/relevance matrix, as follows (Tables 1, 2, 3, 4, respectively). All the functions are compared, two by two, to each other, from the point of view of the importance/relevance for the societal force in question: if first function is more important/relevant than the second, then the number "2" is written in the corresponding cell; in the contrary case, the number "0" is written in the corresponding cell; if the importance/relevance seems to be the same, then the number "1" is written in the corresponding cell. *Nota bene*: the evaluation is made based on what is called the expert's opinion; in two cases (the societal force F_2, and the societal force F_4, respectively, the equality of the numbers was decided based on the expert's opinion, as well).

So, in my opinion, the following (logical) hierarchy could be accepted (Table 5).

Table 1 Functions' logical hierarchy for the societal force F_1

–	F_1^{f1}	F_1^{f2}	F_1^{f3}	F_1^{f4}	*Total*	*Rank*
F_1^{f1}	1	2	2	0	5	II
F_1^{f2}	0	1	2	0	3	III
F_1^{f3}	0	0	1	0	1	IV
F_1^{f4}	2	2	2	1	7	I

Source author

Table 2 Functions' logical hierarchy for the societal force F_2

–	F_2^{f1}	F_2^{f2}	F_2^{f3}	F_2^{f4}	*Total*	*Rank*
F_2^{f1}	1	1	0	1	3	IV
F_2^{f2}	1	1	1	1	4	III
F_2^{f3}	2	1	1	0	4	II
F_2^{f4}	1	1	2	1	5	I

Source author

Table 3 Functions' logical hierarchy for the societal force F_3

–	F_3^{f1}	F_3^{f2}	F_3^{f3}	F_3^{f4}	*Total*	*Rank*
F_3^{f1}	1	1	1	0	3	III
F_3^{f2}	1	1	0	0	2	IV
F_3^{f3}	1	2	1	1	5	II
F_3^{f4}	2	2	1	1	6	I

Source author

Table 4 Functions' logical hierarchy for the societal force F_4

–	F_4^{f1}	F_4^{f2}	F_4^{f3}	F_4^{f4}	*Total*	*Rank*
F_4^{f1}	1	1	2	2	6	I
F_4^{f2}	1	1	2	2	6	II
F_4^{f3}	0	0	1	2	3	III
F_4^{f4}	0	0	1	1	2	IV

Source author

Table 5 A logical hierarchizing of the societal forces' functions

F_1	F_2	F_3	F_4
F_1^{f4}	F_2^{f4}	F_3^{f4}	F_4^{f1}
F_1^{f1}	F_2^{f3}	F_3^{f3}	F_4^{f2}
F_1^{f2}	F_2^{f2}	F_3^{f1}	F_4^{f3}
F_1^{f3}	F_2^{f1}	F_3^{f2}	F_4^{f4}

Source author

2 Two Layers of Evolution within the Society

From the above, one is required not to understand that the (generic) individual is passive in waiting for society to produce and reproduce the social capital needed for achieving his/her wellbeing. In fact, society functions based on the interactions among individuals, exactly in their aspirations for wellbeing. As shown previously, the society, in its entirety and structural components, is an artefact, that is, an objectification of the individuals' cooperative (or non-cooperative, as the case may be) interactions. In fact, the society kinematics is the (principled) unpredictable chreod to which all individuals, groups, and, especially, the state, contribute in a specific order, which I called social (or, better) societal order.

The society construction is simultaneously an intellectual project implementation, and an inextricable set of divergent actions or effects which not mandatorily obey that intellectual project. Generally, such an intellectual project is designed and driven by the elite of the society in case, as the elite is empowered to do that based on democratic and free procedures.[4]

Since a social/societal intellectual project cannot be literally experimented with, it can only be experienced.[5] This means there are never verified solutions to objectify the structure and functions required by the intellectual project in the best way. As a consequence, the path of the societal system on its chreod is, generally, non-linear, and combines the purposes with the accidents (the so-called road accidents). More than that, the effects of synergy, capillarity, self-catalysis, network, pre-announcements, etc., generate not only, as said before, a principled unpredictability of the societal system course, but also unintended[6] consequences. A very interesting thing, here, is that the lateral propensities of the society, as effects[7] of the mentioned phenomena, often indicate the "correct" path of the chreod.[8]

All these phenomena in the society kinematics are integrated and "conducted" by a mechanism, both simple as a concept and complicated as a fact, namely by evolutionism, of course, a social/societal evolutionism. Before beginning the presentation and examination of my own proposal for such an evolutionary model of the societal system in relation to social justice (the very aspiration of this book), some considerations are of use.

As shown previously (see Fig. 1, in Chapter 2), the evolution, that is, the changing of order 2, can be of three types: (a) development, driven by growth; (b) transformation, driven by purposes; (c) progress, driven by values. In this chapter, I will use evolution as a transformation, that is, evolution driven by purposes. The reasons for such a choice are as follows:

- the development is too much obeying the invisible hand, so it generally escapes from the rigorous programming of evolution;
- in turn, the progress implies criteria of evaluation of the change in the case, which introduce polemics and disputes about the significance of the progress;
- it remains that the only (relatively) commonly agreed societal change is the transformation, which presupposes establishing the purposes of that change and evaluating the occurrence of those purposes.

Choosing the transformation as the proxy for the societal evolution has, in addition, a much more significant advantage: the transformation is factually testable. Indeed, as the purposes are known, and the results of transformation are quantifiable, the comparison between the prediction and the factual involved is not difficult, and, more than that, it is inter-subjective communicable and knowable.

The factual testability in the social/societal (including economic) field requires the replacement of the correspondence-truth with the teleological truth[9] (a large presentation of my opinion regarding the teleological truth and the factual testing associated with it can be found in Annex 1).

As the societal forces driving the society's evolution are, in turn, binomial forces, it results that the evolutionary chreod of the societal system unfolds at two layers: (a) (*L*1) the societal individual forces—the binomial evolution; (b) (*L*2) the societal integrated forces—the quadrinomial evolution. Of course, the general/abstract evolution of the society is the quadrinomial (quadrilateral) one.

Nota bene: of course, a question arises here, namely, why it is not appropriate to consider, also, monomial evolution, at the level of each component of the binomial societal forces? My opinion here is as follows:

- principled, a monomial force can, of course, be considered from an evolutionary perspective. In this case, we also have a binomial process, but the second component of that binomial is just the environment of the monomial force in this case. *Nota bene*: to be noted that, conceptually, there is no monomial evolution as such, because it is needed a selector of the mutation that occurred in the system considered;
- so, if a monomial evolutionary process is considered, then it is, in fact, (at least) a… binomial one;
- consequently, any n-nomial evolutionary process is, in fact, a (n+1)-nomial process, because it is needed an external selector of the mutations (and fitness) that occur in the n-nomial process is needed—the selector is placed in the n-nomial process's environment (for example, another n-nomial process).[10]

Figure 1 offers a synoptic picture of the two layers of the societal evolutionary process.

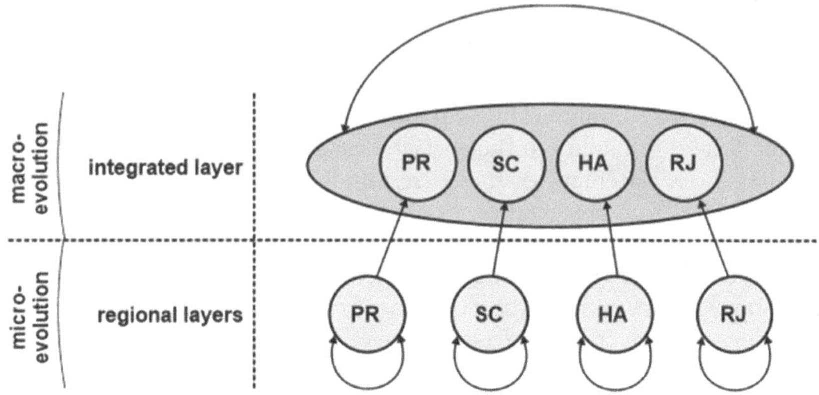

Fig. 1 Two layers of the societal evolutionary process (*Source* author)

3 The Regional Layers of Societal Evolution

In Chapter 2 was presented and interpreted the general evolutionary model of the societal system, based on the four societal forces (engines). This chapter will try to extract the main evolutionary lines of social justice from that general/integrated model.

Each societal force must reach its equilibrium (in the dynamic sense, i.e., inside a "tunnel equilibrium". Being a binomial, such an equilibrium originates in the co-evolution process between the two components of the binomial. So, the first step in building up an integrated evolutionary model at the societal level is to examine the ways in which every regional equilibrium is achieved. *Nota bene*: as mentioned above, this equilibrium is of a dynamical type, so we can call it a sustainable state, i.e., an equilibrium that, despite accidental (or even systematic) deviations from the "equilibrium point", necessarily comes back (Dinga, 2024).[11] In fact, the returning never occurs towards the same "equilibrium point", but to another one—the condition is that the returning does not leave the chreod of the phenomenon in the case, which is the very "picture" of an evolutionary/evolutionist process.

In this framework, each of the four societal forces will be modelled from an evolutionary perspective.

3.1 *The PR Binomial Layer*

The PR binomial layer addresses the societal force F_1 "resources – population". It constitutes the ***causa materialis*** of the societal evolution, actions on the societal structure, and has the role (in fact, the finality/purpose) of ensuring the biological survival of the individuals.[12]

The Evolutionary Variables
The evolutionary variables of the societal force F_1 are as follows:

- (G_{F_1}) *genotype*: F_1^{f4} (economic sustainability)–hosted by the "resources"
    - justification: in PR binomial, the most susceptible to change is the economic component of the society, since most perturbations manifest their impact on this component; so, the probability of mutation occurring is at the highest level related to the economic sustainability as a property of the societal system;
- (P_{F_1}) *phenotype*: F_1^{f1} (demographic sustainability)–hosted by the "population"
    - justification: the achieving of the role of the societal force F_1, namely the biological survival of the individuals, is best assessed by the demographic quality of the society;
- (M_{F_1}) ***mutation***: any perturbation, of any nature, internal or external to the society in question, that changes (not necessarily in a worsening direction)[13] the ***statu quo*** of the economic system;
    - justification: a mutation must represent, according to its general definition, a change sufficiently significant (namely, beyond an established threshold regarding the size, the intensity, or the duration—*Nota bene*: but no matter its nature!) to be considered as such;
- (W_{F_1}) ***transcription***: the mutation is described, in a clear way in programs/strategies and other of the same, in order to be considered for translation into the phenotype;

- justification: transcription is needed to ensure the rationality of the future translation into the phenotype; on the one hand, and to constitute a "memory" regarding the mutations that occurred during a time horizon of interest. Also, the transcription is a good occasion to provide the reasons and, if possible, the adverse effects that could be brought by the eventual translation of that mutation. *Nota bene*: the transcription can have either a normative nature or a non-normative one;

- (T_{F_1}) *translation*: the (normative) introducing into the phenotype, this time exclusively by normative procedures, based on its transcription;
  - justification: the effectivity of the phenotype change by the mutation can only be ensured by the normative way of modifying the phenotype. In addition, the normative modification of the phenotype brings with it the associated/assignable responsibility for the norms implied;
- (F_{F_1}) *fitness*: the concrete modification in/of the phenotype—as nature, size/dimension, and other characteristics that can be of interest, e.g., rhythms, structures, order of implementation, etc. Somewhat, it is formed, a concrete profile of the change in the fitness of the phenotype as a result of operating the mutation into that phenotype. Here, the relevance of the reaction norms, detailed discussed in Chapter 9, strongly appears, as well as the concept that we could verbalize with the syntagma *fetal fitness*. In the case of the societal force F_1, the foetal fitness addresses the configuration of the demographic component of the society so that such (new) configuration is "accepted" (namely, selected) by the selector (see below);
  - justification: the mutation is only a nominal change that is required to be implemented (or not to be implemented, after the case) into the phenotype. In addition to the nominal state of the mutation, the latter possesses a set of features that "measure" the success vs. failure of the phenotype changing, and these features form exactly the fetality (or non-fetality) of the mutation in question;

- (S_{F_1}) *selector*: the issue of the selector for the societal force F_1 (so, for the phenotype represented by the demographic sustainability) is complicated enough, because the following reasons: (a) there is a lag (often relatively large) between the mutation occurred in the economic sustainability and its translation into the demographic sustainability; (b) the normativity regarding the demographic sustainability—population dynamic, structure urban—rural of inhabitants, birth rate, death rate, internal and external migration, and so on. At any rate, the demographic sustainability could not be the selector for itself, since the phenotype is exactly the demographic sustainability. I think we have here an interesting case when the genotype (the economic sustainability) is, at the same time, the selector of the phenotype, which is built up based on its mutation;
  - justification: there are two reasons for which the economic sustainability is, concomitantly (*Nota bene*: however, this concomitancy is only at logical level, not at chronological one, since the selection intervenes after the mutation is integrated into the phenotype) the selector of the mutation: (a) we are obliged to remain within the binomial "resources–population", so that the equilibrium takes place here, without outside involvement; as consequence, as a system cannot be (logically) its own selector, it remains that the economic sustainability must be the selector; (b) in the last instance (as happens, besides, in the non-human animal world), the population (the demographic sustainability) is the very outcome of the economic possibilities to sustain it.[14]

The Evolutionary Binomial

Based on the section "The Evolutionary Variables", we can now draw the evolutionary binomial "resources–population". Figure 2 provides a stylized mechanism in this topic.

Discussion

- *step 1*: a mutation occurs, no matter its nature, intensity, duration, and so on; it could be either from the internal environment (the society), or from the external environment (e.g., from the non-anthropogenic environment);

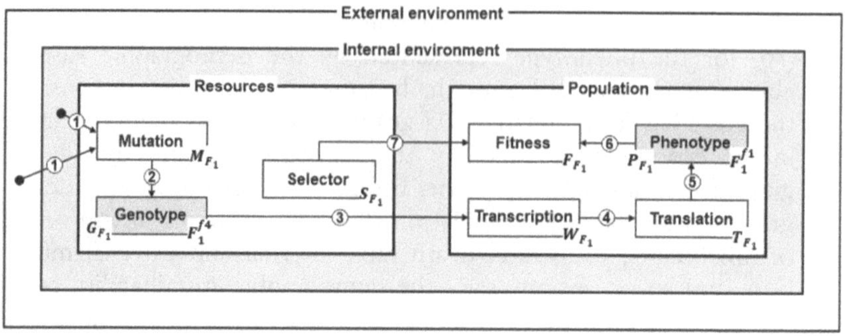

Fig. 2 Mechanism of the evolutionary binomial "resources–population" (F_1) (*Source* author)

- *step 2*: the mutation induces changes into the genotype (the function F_1^{f4});
- *step 3*: the changes into the genotype are included, in a deliberative way, into programs/strategies which will ground the future translation of the mutation;
- *step 4*: the transcribed mutation is used to design the changes into the phenotype, by the intermediation of the norms (normative framework);
- *step 5*: the norms are effectively implemented into the phenotype (the function F_1^{f1});
- *step 6*: following the changes induced by the translated norm/s, the phenotype will acquire a new fitness (that is, a new profile related to its companion, namely, the economic sustainability);
- *step 7*: the "resources" component of the binomial will select (or not, after the case) the new fitness of the phenotype, more precisely, will select (or not) the mutation occurred.

Nota bene: for all the four forces of the societal system, the mutation is, predominantly, of a deliberative nature, perhaps based on dedicated strategies/programs of transformation or progress, as contained into the governmental political programs. However, this nature of the mutations does not modify the above reasoning regarding the mechanism of the evolutionary path (chreod) of the binomial F_1.

3.2 The SC Binomial Layer

The SC binomial layer addresses the societal force F_2 "science–social construction". It constitutes the *causa efficiens* of the societal evolution, actions on the societal infrastructure, and has the role (in fact, the finality/purpose) of providing the needed knowledge on the world.

The Evolutionary Variables
The evolutionary variables of the societal force F_2 are as follows:

- (G_{F_2}) *genotype*: F_2^{f2} (co-habitation between objective and objectified worlds)—hosted by the "science"
  - justification: the societal functioning continuously and permanently introduces tensions between the objective world (Popper's world 1) and the objectified world (Popper's world 3). In fact, science[15] must accommodate the two worlds to each other exactly by the scientific results obtained and implemented;
- (P_{F_2}) *phenotype*: F_2^{f4} (self-sustainability of the social construction)—hosted by the "social construction"
  - justification: what is "tested" in the process of selecting the mutation that occurred in the genotype is the very sustainability of the society (societal model), but that sustainability is, in fact, the self-sustainability of the social construction. It seems, therefore, that the latter is appropriate to be considered for the phenotype of the second binomial;
- (M_{F_2}) *mutation*: in this binomial, mutation occurs when between, world 1 and world 3, some tensions, contradictions, blockages, and other of the same happen;
- (W_{F_2}) *transcription*: the transcription of the mutation means, also, to deposit it in the system of strategies/programs/visions (at least, in the medium term), to be used further;
- (T_{F_2}) *translation*: the translation means that the transcribed mutation is effectively introduced into the phenotype, based on the previous transcription;

- (F_{F_2}) *fitness*: refers to the degree to which the mutation occurred in the genotype is fetal to the phenotype—besides, this fetality is the object of the very selection;
- (S_{F_2}) *selector*: as in the case of the first binomial, the selection will be made by, so to speak, the …genotype;
  - justification: since this second binomial must be closed to itself,[16] the changes into the phenotype cannot be assessed by anything other than the genotype, i.e., the factor that generated the change in the case. Like the first binomial, the genotype exerts, somewhat, a function of internal audit!

The Evolutionary Binomial

Based on the section "The Evolutionary Variables", we can now draw the evolutionary binomial "resources–population". Figure 3 provide a stylized mechanism in this topic.

Discussion

- *step 1*: a mutation occurs, no matter its nature, intensity, duration, and so on; it could be either from the internal environment (the society), or from the external environment (e.g., from the non-anthropogenic environment);
- *step 2*: the mutation induces changes into the genotype (the function F_2^{f2});
- *step 3*: the changes into the genotype are included, in a deliberative way, into programs/strategies which will ground the future translation of the mutation;
- *step 4*: the transcribed mutation is used to design the changes into the phenotype, by the intermediation of the norms (normative framework);
- *step 5*: the norms are effectively implemented into the phenotype (the function F_2^{f4});
- *step 6*: following the changes induced by the translated norm/s, the phenotype will acquire a new fitness (that is, a new profile related to its companion, namely, the economic sustainability);
- *step 7*: the "science" component of the binomial will select (or not, after the case) the new fitness of the phenotype, more precisely, will select (or not) the mutation occurred.

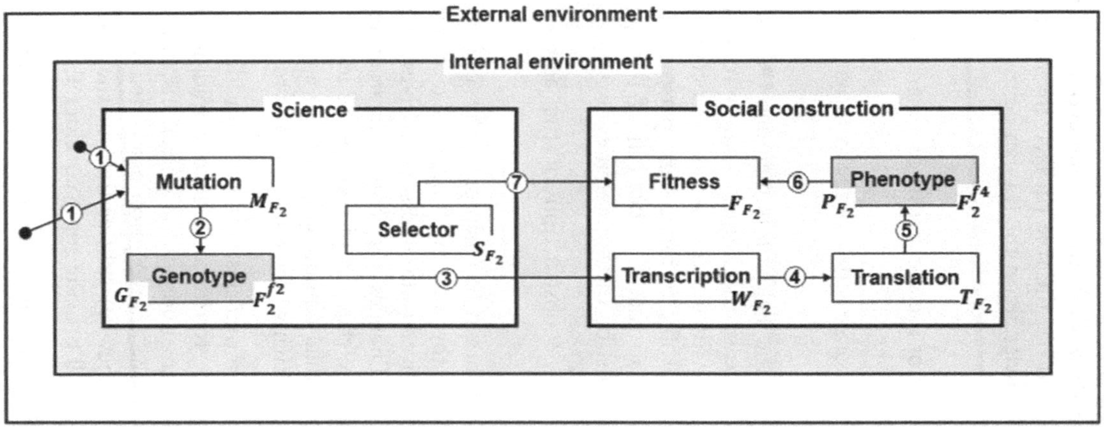

Fig. 3 Mechanism of the evolutionary binomial "resources–population" (F_1) (*Source* author)

3.3 The HA Binomial Layer

The HA binomial layer addresses the societal force $F3$ "humanities–art". It constitutes the *causa formalis* of the societal evolution, actions on the societal suprastructure, and has the role (in fact, the finality/purpose) of providing the needed knowledge on the human being (person).

The Evolutionary Variables
The evolutionary variables of the societal force $F3$ are as follows:

- (G_{F_3}) *genotype*: F_3^{f4} (construction of the axiological profile)—hosted by the "humanities"
  - justification: in the field of humanities ("science" interested in the knowledge of the human being's totality, as a person, not a simple individual), discoveries can occur that change the communitarian profile of the generic person, from an axiological perspective, so that the location of the genotype of this societal force must be the "humanities";
- (P_{F_3}) *phenotype*: F_3^{f2} (construction of the aesthetical profile)—hosted by the "art"
  - justification: as shown in Chapter 7, the æsthetics is a harmonious order of the society functioning. Since this societal æsthetics is perceived (and, in essence, drives the societal system path) and it influences the communitarian environment, it seems appropriate that the phenotype be located in the "art", i.e., in the binomial component that can appreciate (especially by memetic perceiving) the change in the results of humanities;
- (M_{F_3}) *mutation*: the mutations that occur inside the "humanities" can originate in many "territories": history, traditions, inter-cultural contacts, theoretical or philosophical reflections, and so on;
- (W_{F_3}) *transcription*: the transcription associated with this binomial (societal force) is somewhat subtler than in the cases of the other binomials so that I will provide some considerations here:
  - although, of course, there can exist strategies/programs dedicated to the cultural field (generally included in the governing political strategies/programs), many of the mutations will not

yet be expressly included in such "memories", they remain an are circulate, many times, in an informal way;
- even if the mutations are not expressly included (transcribed) into dedicated strategies/programs, they have the potential to form a critical mass of opinions which, in time (generally, in the medium term), exerts some tensions/pressures to be implemented formally, i.e., in a normative way;

- (T_{F_3}) *translation*: like the transcription, the translation is somewhat less formal and even less rigorous in this binomial. Without a "standard" transcription, the translation is not always mandatory, so the phenotype change does not follow automatically the genotype changes;
- (F_{F_3}) *fitness*: the fitness addresses the accuracy with which the mutations occurred in the genotype "moved" into the phenotype, that is, the changes within the humanities meet the changes in the æsthetical behaviour of the members of the community;
- (S_{F_3}) *selector*: like in the preceding binomials, the selector is located at the "address" as the genotype, that is, the selection of the fitness reached by the phenotype (the societal æsthetics) is made by the "humanities");
  - justification: indeed, the "humanities" proposed a change into the phenotype and, consequently, this component of the binomials is the most competent agent to evaluate if (or not) the proposal was been integrated into the phenotype.

The Evolutionary Binomial

Based on the section "The Evolutionary Variables", we can now draw the evolutionary binomial "resources–population". Figure 4 provides a stylized mechanism in this topic.

Discussion

- *step 1*: a mutation occurs, no matter its nature, intensity, duration, and so on; it could be either from the internal environment (the society), or from the external environment (e.g., from the non-anthropogenic environment);
- *step 2*: the mutation induces changes into the genotype (the function F_3^{f4});

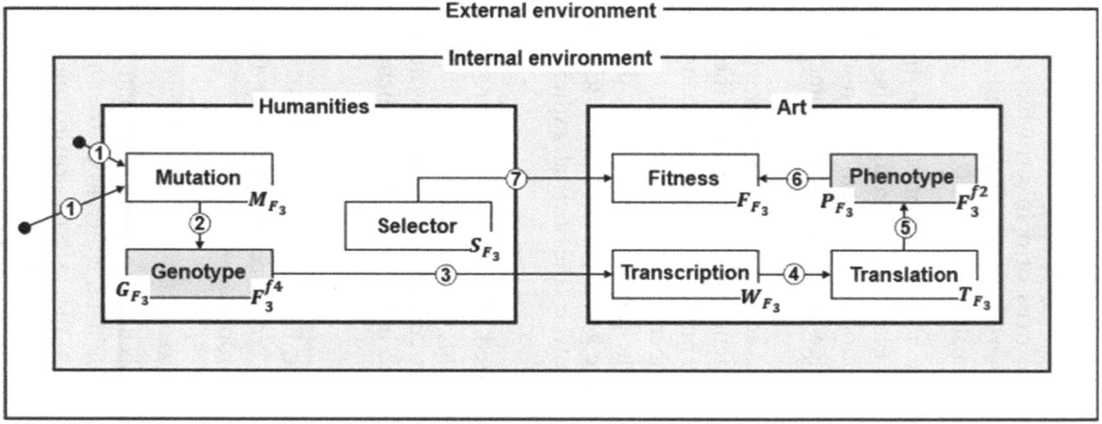

Fig. 4 Mechanism of the evolutionary binomial "resources–population" (F_1) (*Source* author)

- *step 3*: the changes into the genotype are included, probably to a partial enough degree, in a deliberative way, into programs/ strategies which will ground the future translation of the mutation;
- *step 4*: both the transcribed mutation and the mutations remained "in air" are used to design the changes into the phenotype, by the intermediation of the norms (normative framework);
- *step 5*: the norms are effectively implemented into the phenotype (the function F_3^{f2});
- *step 6*: following the changes induced by the translated norm/s, the phenotype will acquire a new fitness (that is, a new profile related to its companion, namely, the æsthetical behaviour within the community);
- *step 7*: the "humanities" component of the binomial will select (or not, after the case) the new fitness of the phenotype, more precisely, will select (or not) the mutation occurred.

3.4 The RJ Binomial Layer

The RJ binomial layer addresses the societal force F_4 "realization of human being—social justice". It constitutes the *causa finalis* of the societal evolution, actions on the societal structure, and has the role (in fact, the finality/purpose) of putting in place, fully functional and accessible, all the capabilities allowed by the other three forces.

The Evolutionary Variables

The evolutionary variables of the societal force F_4 are as follows:

- (G_{F_4}) *genotype*: F_4^{f3} (providing the equality of individuals before positive law and societal's opportunities)—hosted by "realization of human being"
  - justification: among the functions of the societal force F_4, this one is the most susceptible to record changes, from the generic perturbations, on the one hand, and is most "visible" for the individuals themselves (as direct perceptions), on the other hand;
- (P_{F_4}) *phenotype*: F_4^{f1} (fully providing of the freedom of individual choice)—hosted by "social justice"

– justification: in fact, all the insufficiencies in the real life of the individuals, of any nature, are perceived as a reduction, limitation, or blockage in enjoying the freedom, so that this function of the societal force F_4 seems to be the most adequate for the "adult" position;

Nota bene: it is to be observed that both genotype and the phenotype of the societal force F_4 meet, almost punctually, the positions expressed both by Rawls and Nussbaum (somewhat, indirectly, by Nozick as well).

- (M_{F_4}) *mutation*: mutation can occur, mainly, at the level of the opportunities/capabilities, either existing or accessible for the individuals, in their life chain;
- (W_{F_4}) *transcription*: the transcription means, like in the other three cases, registering into strategies/programs or simple societal visions, after the case, of the mutations that occurred;
- (T_{F_4}) *translation*: by translation, the existing transcriptions are transformed, usually, formally, into norms, rules, procedures, and so on, that modify the phenotype;
- (F_{F_4}) *fitness*: the fitness will measure the new profile of the phenotype after the translation is performed;
- (S_{F_4}) *selector*: like in the preceding cases, the selector is located in the first component of the binomial, namely "realization of human being", and will perform the function of selection on the new phenotype;

  – justification: the freedom is, however we see things, a means (the most important, relevant, and efficacy one) for the purpose, namely, the realization of human being. This is why the selector must be, as previously, exactly the genotype of this societal force.

The Evolutionary Binomial

Based on the section "The Evolutionary Variables", we can now draw the evolutionary binomial "resources – population". Figure 5 provides a stylized mechanism in this issue.

Discussion

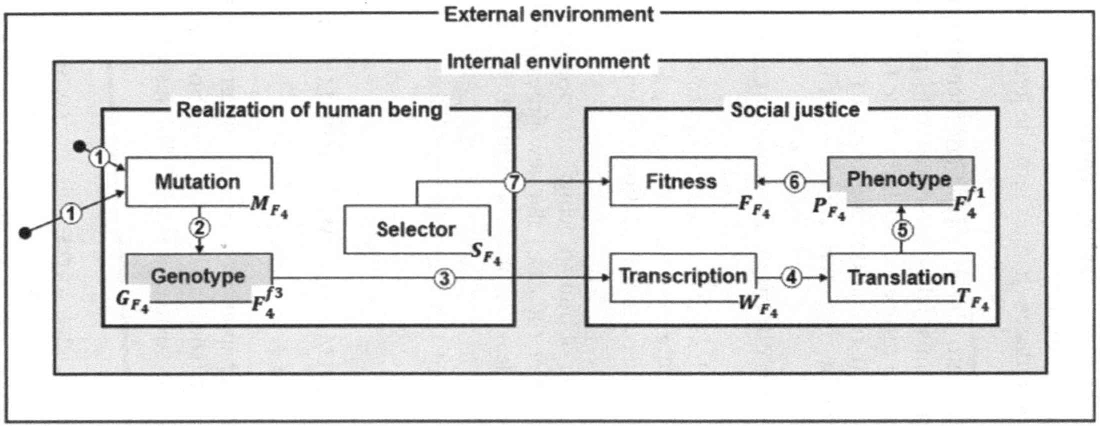

Fig. 5 Mechanism of the evolutionary binomial "resources–population" (F_1) (*Source* author)

- *step 1*: a mutation occurs, no matter its nature, intensity, duration, and so on; it could be either from the internal environment (the society), or from the external environment (e.g., from the non-anthropogenic environment);
- *step 2*: the mutation induces changes into the genotype (the function F_4^{f3});
- *step 3*: the changes into the genotype are included, probably to a large enough degree, in a deliberative way, into programs/strategies which will ground the future translation of the mutation;
- *step 4*: the transcribed mutations are used to design the changes into the phenotype, by the intermediation of the norms (normative framework);
- *step 5*: the norms are effectively implemented into the phenotype (the function F_4^{f1});
- *step 6*: following the changes induced by the translated norm/s, the phenotype will acquire a new fitness (that is, a new profile related to its companion, namely, the realization of human being within the community);
- *step 7*: the "realization of human being" component of the binomial will select (or not, after the case) the new fitness of the phenotype, more precisely, will select (or not) the mutation occurred.

A synoptic recapitulation of the four binomials' features is provided in Table 6.

4 The Quadrinomial Evolution

4.1 Preliminaries

The last section of this chapter is aimed at integrating the reasoning made above into a global (societal) level of evolutionary type regarding the tandem "social justice–societal system". To this end, the following premises will be held:

- each of the four societal forces will be considered as balanced regarding the two components of the respective binomials, as shown above; indeed, any perturbation/mutations are, primarily, handed in the regional layers (those four, horizontally arranged, layers);

Table 6 Conceptual profile of the four regional binomials (layers) in the societal evolution

		F_1	F_2	F_3	F_4
Genotype	Function	F_1^{f4}	F_2^{f2}	F_3^{f4}	F_4^{f3}
	Location	"Resources"	"Science"	"Humanities"	"Realization of human being"
Phenotype	Function	F_1^{f1}	F_2^{f4}	F_3^{f2}	F_4^{f1}
	Location	"Population"	"Social construction"	"Art"	"Social justice"
Mutation	Location	"Resources"	"Science"	"Humanities"	"Realization of human being"
Fitness	Location	"Population"	"Social construction"	"Art"	"Social justice"
Selector	Location	"Resources"	"Science"	"Humanities"	"Realization of human being"

Source author

- the "ingredients" of the integrated (global) evolutionary process will be established at the societal forces level—for example, a mutation will be considered as a (selected) new fitness of a societal force, the genotype will be viewed at the societal force level, and so on;
- for the integrated evolutionary model, the societal forces will be considered "atoms", that is, un-decomposable entities;
- so, conceptually, our model of the evolutionary paradigm of the societal justice within the societal system could be considered as a structural evolutionary model (SEM).

4.2 *The Links*

In this paragraph, we must establish and ground the links required by the elaboration of the integrated model of the co-evolutionary process "societal justice–societal system". To indicate on the societal layer (by contrast with the regional layers by now), we will add, as a prefix, the letter "s" to the concepts discussed above—e.g., the genotype will be denoted as *s-genotype*, etc.

- (G_S) *s-genotype*: F_4 (the binomial "realization of human being–social justice")
  - justification: the F_4 binomial constitutes, obviously, the fundamental purpose of the society functioning (the reason of last instance), so the mutations that occur in this societal force are critical for that purpose. Consequently, we consider this binomial to be the most adequate to be considered as s-genotype;
- (P_S) *s-phenotype*: F_3 (the binomial "humanities–art")
  - justification: despite the denomination of this binomial, their (four) functions—see the Sect. 10.1—are aimed exactly at providing the means, i.e., the channels through which the realization of human being and the social justice is both possible and predictable. To be observed that, in this binomial are contained the two basic coordinates of a humanistic society, namely the ethics and the æsthetics (see Chapter 7);
- (M_S) *s-mutation*: the s-mutations will exert their (distorting) effects on the s-genotype. To be mentioned, here, the following topic: the distorting effect is, in fact, a balanced one that is produced at the (regional) layer of the binomial F_3. So, the issue of the sources/origins of the mutations, as they manifest on the s-genotype level. The following considerations could be useful:
  - the impact of the external (e.g., the non-anthropogenic environment) and internal perturbations (Dinga, 2025) was already integrated by all four societal forces in their process of balancing between their paired components;
  - in this context, we can consider that the proximal sources of mutations for the societal layer are exactly the other two societal forces, namely, F_1, and F_2;
- (W_S) *s-transcription*: the s-transcription follows the same logic as the (regional) transcriptions, namely, the mutations are systematized into strategies/programs/visions, etc., so that they will (perhaps) be translated into the phenotype. *Nota bene*: the transcriptions are made, generally, only for those mutations that are or seem to be desirable for the next profile of the phenotype, so a pre-selection is made even before the mutations are transcribed. This issue is very important, since it is specific to the society chreod (it is not present in

the biological chreod). This is possible based on the deliberativeness of the society's functioning;

- (T_S) *s-translation*: the s-translation means to objectify (implement), in adequate ways, usually normatively, the transcriptions into a new profile of the phenotype;
- (F_S) *s-fitness*: the s-fitness constitutes, as in the regional cases, the degree in which the new profile of the phenotype is "in line" with the expectations of the genotype.
- (S_S) *s-selector*: symmetrically with the regional cases (the four societal forces), the s-selector is located in the s-genotype, so that the desired change can be evaluated by comparison with the actual change in the phenotype. I remind the reader that, logically, this reasoning can be interpreted in Popper's falsifiability, i.e., the s-genotype "makes" a prediction (namely, the normed mutation, and after the mutation is operated (objectified), the one who formulated the prediction verifies if that prediction is corroborated or, after the case, rejected;
  - justification: the s-selector must be closed connected to the purpose of the societal functioning (chreod), since it the only entitled to appreciate the changes in the phenotype (that is, the ethical and æsthetical profile of the society) as being compatible, consistent, and convergent with that purpose, namely, the realization of human being—more exactly, with the placement of the society chreod on the PLC, i.e., the plenary life chain (see Chapter 6).

4.3 The Model

To discuss the model of the evolutionary path of the social justice within the societal system, it is of usefulness to draw a synoptic picture of the mechanism in question (Fig. 6).

The steps in that mechanism have the following signification:

- *step 1*: mutations occur, no matter its nature, intensity, duration, and so on, from three sources: the external environment, the societal force F_1, and the societal force F_2;
- *step 2*: the mutation induces changes into the genotype (the societal force F_4);

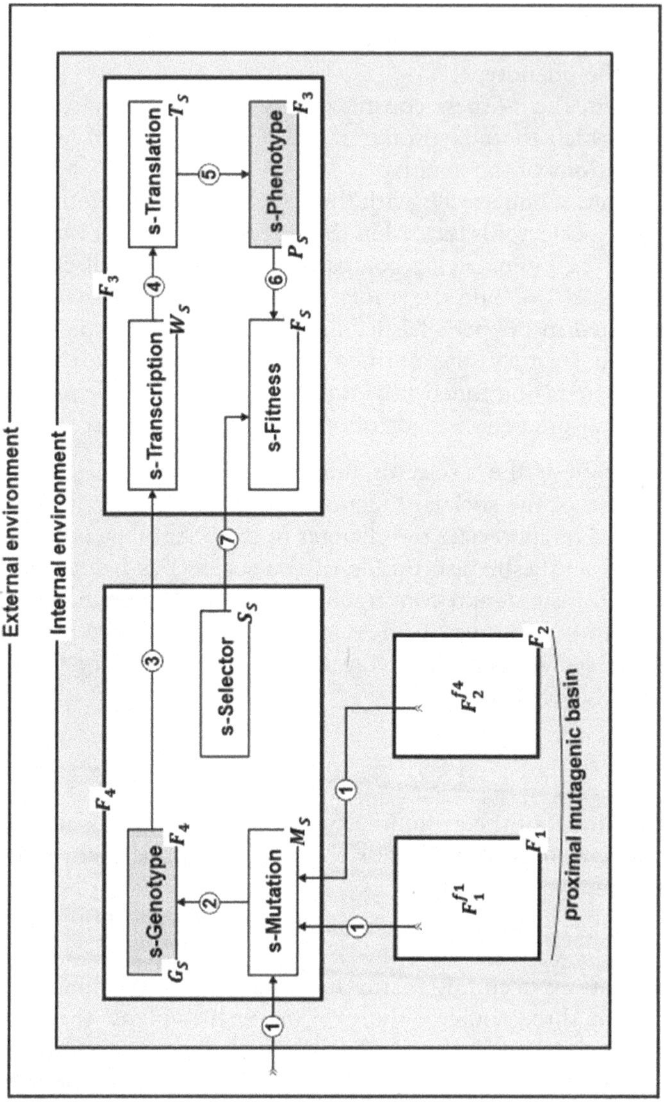

Fig. 6 Mechanism of the evolutionary quadrinomial (*Source* author)

- *step 3*: the changes into the genotype are included, probably to a large enough degree, in a deliberative way, into programs/strategies which will ground the future translation of the mutation;
- *step 4*: the transcribed mutations are used to design the changes into the phenotype, by the intermediation of the norms (normative framework);
- *step 5*: the norms are effectively implemented into the phenotype (the societal force F_3);
- *step 6*: following the changes induced by the translated norm/s, the phenotype (i.e., F_3) will acquire a new fitness (that is, a new profile related to its companion, namely, the societal force F_4);
- *step 7*: the societal force F_4 will select (or not, after the case) the new fitness of the F_3, more precisely, will select (or not) the mutation occurred.

Discussion

About the *s-mutation*

There are three sources of mutations: (1) directly, from the external environment; (b) indirectly, from the societal force F_1; (c) indirectly, from the societal force F_2. Obviously, the two indirect sources, in turn, take over the pressure from the external environment, but it is possible (and, even, probably) that some pressures of the external environment remain un-taken over, so they act as such on the s-genotype.

Another important issue is the following: the indirect mutations (both from F_1 and F_2) are constituted by the new profiles of the corresponding phenotypes of the two binomials. This is because the old profiles of those phenotypes had already contributed to the previous cycle of evolution at the macro-level, and a change in that profile manifests as a perturbation/ mutation occurring currently. The conclusion is the following: exactly by the new balance inside the regional binomials (as discussed at Sect. 10.3), the regional binomials play the role of perturbation/mutation.

About the *s-transcription*

The internally balancing of F_1 and F_2, respectively, has already inscribed the mutations selected at the respective regional layers into the dedicated "memories", namely, strategies/programs, so the selected mutations are, in fact, transcribed. Since the new profile of the F_4 is, this time, a mutation for the quadrinomial system, this new profile will be inscribed in the adequate "memories".

About *s-translation*

Remember that the transcribed mutation is, in fact, the current (i.e., new) profile of the phenotype of the societal force F_4, namely of the social justice. So what must be translated into a norm regarding the social justice functioning is causal factor to improve the social justice which, as seen in the previous chapters constitutes the impulse to realization of human being towards the PLC (plenary life chain).

An important issue arises here: what precisely the translation (i.e., the norm) change into the societal force F_3? Here I think must be accepted something as the *epigenetic* evolution in the quadrinomial evolutionary process, namely, the change indicated by the mutation changes directly the phenotype of the societal force F_3, without the intermediation of the genotype of the last societal force, namely, F_3^{f2} ("art").

About *s-fitness*

The fitness registered by the phenotype of the quadrinomial system is focused on the societal force F_3. In other words, the modification that occurred in social justice must be validated (or invalidated, as the case may be) through the filters involved in the societal force F_3—more exactly, there are four such filters, for each of the four functions of this societal force, namely: (F_3^{f1}) construction of the ethical profile; (F_3^{f2}) construction of the aesthetical profile; (F_3^{f3}) construction of the communitarian profile; (F_3^{f4}) construction of the axiological profile (see the Sect. 10.1).

About *s-selection*

It is strange enough to say that a societal force must select another societal force in the macro system evolutionary process. In fact, the selection is, this time, one that could be called *structural selection.*

Such a structural selection is based on the (logical) hierarchy of the societal forces' functions, as established at section "A (Seemingly) Hierarchy of the Societal Forces' Functions". Now, will provide a brief examination of the possible reasons for which a structural selection can be grounded. Let us remind the functions' hierarchies of the societal forces F_4 (the selector) and F_3 (the fitness), respectively (Table 7):

I will examine what could be called the maximal propensity to selection (MPS), that is, the maximal probability[17] that a function of the societal force F_4 to select one function of the societal forces F_3. We can use, again, the method of the importance/relevance matrix (i.e., an expert's opinion), this time using the propensity matrix, as follows (Table 8).

Table 7 Resuming the functions' hierarchies for the societal forces F_3 and F_4

F_3	F_4
F_3^{f4}	F_4^{f1}
F_3^{f3}	F_4^{f2}
F_3^{f1}	F_4^{f3}
F_3^{f2}	F_4^{f4}

Source Table 5

Table 8 Propensity matrix for the societal forces F_3 and F_4

–	F_3^{f4}	F_3^{f3}	F_3^{f1}	F_3^{f2}
F_4^{f1}	(4)	1	2	3
F_4^{f2}	2	(4)	1	3
F_4^{f3}	2	3	1	(4)
F_4^{f4}	3	2	(4)	1

Source author

The figures in brackets mean the maximal propensity of the function belonging to societal force F_4 to select the corresponding function belonging to the societal force F_3. This means that, the function F_3^{f4} seems to be selected rather by the function F_4^{f1}, the function F_3^{f3} by the function F_4^{f2}, the function F_3^{f1} by the function F_3^{f1} by the function F_4^{f4}, and the function F_3^{f2} by the function F_4^{f3}.

A question arises here: is there a logical order (and, from this, a chronological one) in which the structural selection is performed? My opinion on this matter is as follows:

- the hierarchy of importance/relevance has a larger role, namely, it also establishes a hierarchy of urgency;
- the hierarchy must be established by considering simultaneously the hierarchical position of the selector, and that of the selected (fitness);

- the hierarchy of the urgency should be simply determined by adding the two ranks involved, as follows (*Nota bene*: so, the *pair rank* is the sum of the two ranks involved):
  - for (F_4^{f1}, F_3^{f4}): 1 + 1 = 2
  - for (F_4^{f2}, F_3^{f3}): 2 + 2 = 4
  - for (F_4^{f3}, F_3^{f2}): 3 + 4 = 7
  - for (F_4^{f4}, F_3^{f1}): 4 + 3 = 7
- the urgency is inversely proportional with the value of the pair rank. Since the last two pair ranks are the same, a qualitative examination is extra required, based on the "principle" that the selector dominates the fitness. Consequently, the fourth pair (F_4^{f4}, F_3^{f1}) must be considered as having a smaller pair rank than the pair (F_4^{f3}, F_3^{f2});
- eventually, the logical (and, also, the chronological order) in which the structural selection works is the following:

$$\left(F_4^{f1}, F_3^{f4}\right) - \left(F_4^{f2}, F_3^{f3}\right) - \left(F_4^{f4}, F_3^{f1}\right) - \left(F_4^{f3}, F_3^{f2}\right)$$

Based on the above mentioned, and considering also the provisions in Chapter 7 on the æsthics (the pair æsthetics–ethics), a general scheme of the selection in the quadrinomial case can be drawn as shown in Fig. 7.

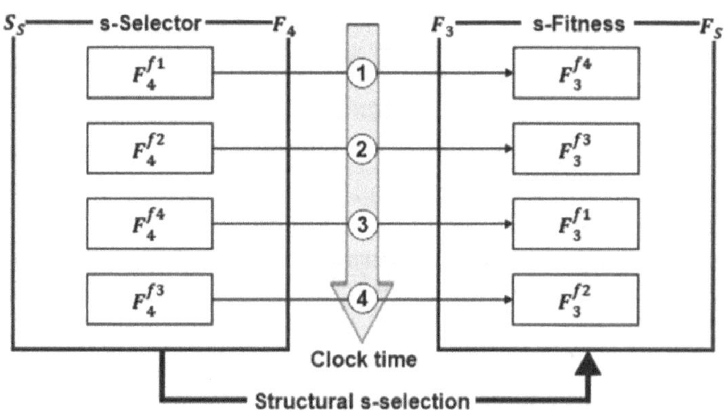

Fig. 7 Synoptic picture of the structural s-selection (*Source* author)

4.4 Some Evaluations

The "happy" case is that when all functions of the s-selector select all functions of the s-fitness. But what about the case/s in which one of more functions of s-fitness are not selected by the corresponding functions of the s-selector? It seems to me that the following issue should be commented here: if there are degrees in the process of s-selection.

To put the question of the degrees of s-selection seems strange enough—a s-selection should probably be a dichotomic evaluation, namely, whether s-fitness was selected or not. However, the following considerations could be made in this matter[18]:

- the translation of mutation, i.e., the designing of the norm aimed at putting into functioning the new phenotype, could be imperfect enough, or even could be planned to be implemented in more stages than in a single one—this is a case in which, in fact, although the s-selection is "legally" performed, that s-selection has a sub-unitary degree of realization;
- the above consideration could be viewed in a structural way, that is, in the case in which not all $F_3^{(\bullet)}$ are s-selected. In such a context, I would say the following:
  - the reducing of the degree of s-selection is depending on the rank (see Table 9) of the pair $(F_4^{(\bullet)}, F_3^{(\bullet)})$ unselected; the degree of s-selection is, so, inversely related with the pair's rank non-selected;
  - so, for example, if of all four pairs of $(F_4^{(\bullet)}, F_3^{(\bullet)})$ are s-selected, then we will say that the s-selection degree is 1. To determine the distinct ranks for the pairs (F_4^{f3}, F_3^{f2}), and (F_4^{f4}, F_3^{f1}), we can consider, conventionally, that the pair (F_4^{f4}, F_3^{f1}) has the rank 6.5, and the pair (F_4^{f3}, F_3^{f2}), = has the rank 7.5. This way, a relative rank of the pair i ($i = \overline{1, 4}$), (R_i^r), can be determined for each pairs, as follows (with: R_i^a is denotate the absolute rank of the pair i):

$$R_i^r = \frac{R_i^a}{\sum_{j=1}^{4} R_j^a}$$

that is:

- for $i = 1$ (pair (F_4^{f1}, F_3^{f4}): $R_1^r = \frac{R_1^a}{\sum_{j=1}^4 R_j^a} = \frac{2}{20} = 0.1$
- for $i = 2$ (pair (F_4^{f2}, F_3^{f3}): $R_2^r = \frac{R_2^a}{\sum_{j=1}^4 R_j^a} = \frac{4}{20} = 0.2$
- for $i = 3$ (pair (F_4^{f1}, F_3^{f4}): $R_3^r = \frac{R_3^a}{\sum_{j=1}^4 R_j^a} = \frac{6.5}{20} = 0.325$
- for $i = 4$ (pair (F_4^{f1}, F_3^{f4}): $R_4^r = \frac{R_4^a}{\sum_{j=1}^4 R_j^a} = \frac{7.5}{20} = 0.375$

Obviously, $\sum_{i=1}^4 R_i^r = 1$.

Table 9 Indicates the degree of s-selection, in all (possible) cases of non s-selection. *Nota bene*: simply, the relative ranks of the s-selected pairs are summed

	"1"	"2"	"3"	"4"	Total
no one is non s-selected	0.1	0.2	0.325	0.375	1
"1" is non s-selected	~~0.1~~	0.2	0.325	0.375	0.9
"2" is non s-selected	0.1	~~0.2~~	0.325	0.375	0.8
"3" is non s-selected	0.1	0.2	~~0.325~~	0.375	0.675
"4" is non s-selected	0.1	0.2	0.325	~~0.375~~	0.625
"1" and "2" are non s-selected	~~0.1~~	~~0.2~~	0.325	0.375	0.7
"1" and "3" are non s-selected	~~0.1~~	0.2	~~0.325~~	0.375	0.575
"1" and "4" are non s-selected	~~0.1~~	0.2	0.325	~~0.375~~	0.525
"2" and "3" are non s-selected	0.1	~~0.2~~	~~0.325~~	0.375	0.475
"2" and "4" are non s-selected	0.1	~~0.2~~	0.325	~~0.375~~	0.425
"3" and "4" are non s-selected	0.1	0.2	~~0.325~~	~~0.375~~	0.3
"1" and "2" and "3"are non s-selected	~~0.1~~	~~0.2~~	~~0.325~~	0.375	0.375
"1" and "2" and "4"are non s-selected	~~0.1~~	~~0.2~~	0.325	~~0.375~~	0.325
"1" and "3" and "4"are non s-selected	~~0.1~~	0.2	~~0.325~~	~~0.375~~	0.2
"2" and "3" and "4"are non s-selected	0.1	~~0.2~~	~~0.325~~	~~0.375~~	0.1
no one is s-selected	~~0.1~~	~~0.2~~	~~0.325~~	~~0.375~~	0.0

Source author

Annex 1: The Teleological Truth

Preamble

Statement, Sense, and Truth

Because the social nature of humans, although our most primary relationships with the world (in which we are sunken) could be pure praxiological, very soon such relationships became linguistic and, from this point forward, they remained essentially linguistic (any non-linguistic relationships between humans and the world are originated and can be translated, in the last instance, into linguistic ones).[19] This means that about the world we cannot speak other than through linguistic statements.[20] Generally, any statement is credited with two attributes: a) sense value; b) truth value. By sense is understood the possibility of the state of affairs (facts) evoked by that statement,[21] in the world. Once a statement has sense (but only after its sense is proved), it is liable to be assigned truth values. While the sense has an a priori (that is, necessary,[22] internal) character, the truth values have an a posteriori (that is, contingent, external) character. Consequently, a statement with sense could be true or false.[23] To be mentioned again, the question of truth can be put only if the question of sense is already affirmatively solved (Wittgenstein, 2010). We have here both a logical conditionality and a chronological one.

Three Categories of Truth

Searching for the truth seems to be required from two human instances: a *cognitive* instance—which is rather an intrinsic curiosity about existence (for example, our theories), and a *praxiological* one—which is an evolutionary process "responsible" simply for our own existence. Since we necessarily must *primum vivere deinde philosophari*, the first (chronologically and logically) category of the truth taken into consideration was, of course, that viewed from the praxiological perspective. It is known as the *correspondence-truth*. By correspondence-truth is understood as the semantic coincidence between a statement about a factual which is not yet inspected (or which is coming in the future)—we can name such a statement as a prediction—and a statement about the same factual that is inspected (or is already actualized)—we can name such a statement as a description. The semantic coincidence between prediction and description means the same factual referential (or factual denotation) is observable for the two statements involved. This kind of truth (first kind) is externally anchored and validated. Formally, the correspondence-truth can be

Table 10 Three categories of truth

	(1) *Correspondence-truth*	*Coherence-truth* (2) *Internal coherence-truth*	(3) *External coherence-truth*
Perspective	Praxiological	Cognitive	
Nature	Experienced	Validated	Demonstrated
Way of testing	Falsifiability	Non-contradictoriality	Inferentiality

Source author

expressed as follows: $R(P_i) \equiv R(D_j)$, where R stays for the referential, P_i is a prediction about a given factual (that is, about the referential involved) at the moment i, D_j is a description about the same given factual at the moment j, with $j > i$. As we will see below, this kind of truth is involved in Popper's proposal for the falsifiability of scientific knowledge. The correspondence-truth must be understood as an experienced truth. The second kind of truth, that is, the cognitive truth, could be named as *coherence-truth*. It exhibits, in its turn, two species: (a) internal coherence-truth[24]; (b) external coherence-truth. The *internal coherence-truth* is understood rather as a validated truth through verifying the grammatical and logical rules which govern the verbal formulation of a given statement, of any kind (not mandatorily addressing the ontological factuals). The *external coherence-truth* is understood rather as a demonstrated truth through verifying the inferential (i.e., syllogistic) rules which govern the verbal formulation of a given statement (e.g., a theorem inferred from an axiomatic system). Table 10 synthesizes the above considerations on the three categories of truth.

Testability

Discussion about *testability* or testing is qualified for the truth value of the statement only. Of course, as it has resulted previously, are testable only the statements that have also and already sense. Consequently, the testability implies an external inspection regarding a given statement endowed with sense. So, the sufficiency predicates based on which a given statement is testable are the following:

- (*T1*) the statement has sense, that is, it is addressing a possible state[25] of the world;
- (*T2*) the statement is contingent, that is, it has an empirical hypostasising of its necessity required by the sense;
- (*T3*) there are external (independent from the given statement) criteria to assess the statement from any of interest purpose;
- (*T4*) applying the external criteria in assessing the statement, the procedure involved necessarily gives an unambiguous result.[26]

If a statement verifies cumulatively the four sufficiency predicates, then it can be qualified as testable. So, the testability (T) of a given statement (S) could be formalized as (S_T):

$$(S_T) \leftarrow (S_{T1}) \bigwedge (S_{T2}) \bigwedge (S_{T3}) \bigwedge (S_{T4})$$

where S_x means that the statement S verifies the sufficiency predicate x.

Scientificity

The *scientificity* is an attribute that is also assignable to statements only. Although scientificity is not considered semantically equivalent to testability, it is viewed, however, as strongly related to it. In our opinion, the extension of the concept of scientificity is not rigorously the same as the extension of the concept of testability. Consequently, we'll formulate, like in the case of testability, the sufficiency predicates that deliver the concept of scientificity of a statement:

- (*S1*) the statement has a public (social) character,[27] that is, at least another individual, except the enunciator, is informed, in a language he/she knows, about the content of the statement in case;
- (*S2*) the statement is comprehensible (understandable) for at least one person, other than the enunciator of the statement in case; again, remember the comprehensibility for others is not required for testability[28];
- (*S3*) the statement is testable.

So, formally, the scientificity of a statement can be expressed as:

$$S_S \leftarrow (S_{S1}) \bigwedge (S_{S2}) \bigwedge (S_3)$$

or, developed, by considering that $S_3 \equiv S_T$

$$S_S \leftarrow (S_{S1}) \bigwedge (S_{S2}) \bigwedge (S_{T1}) \bigwedge (S_{T2}) \bigwedge (S_{T3}) \bigwedge (S_{T4})$$

Relationship between testability and Scientificity
Based on the sufficiency predicates established for the testability and scientificity, respectively, we can now discuss the relationships between testability and scientificity, as follows:

- any scientific[29] statement is testable.[30] Indeed, based on the above logical descriptions,
  $S_T \subset S_S$, so $S_S \rightarrow S_T$;
- there are statements which are testable but are not scientific. Indeed, any statement that only verifies the testability lacks the sufficiency predicates $S1$ and $S2$, so being eliminated from the scientificity;
- testable non-scientific statements can be of three kinds:
  - absolute testable non-scientific statements, defined as verifying the logical expression S_T;
  - publicly testable non-scientific statements, defined as $(S_T) \bigwedge (S_{S1})$;
  - comprehensible testable non-scientific statements, defined as $(S_T) \bigwedge (S_{S2})$.

Synoptically, relationships between the extensions of testability and scientificity, respectively, are shown in Fig. 8.

Popper's Falsifiability

Further we'll narrow our discussion within Popper's worlds, that is, inside the scientificity, as it was defined above. Let's shortly remember the main features of Popper's falsifiability.

- based on the sufficiency predicates of the scientificity, Popper declared no science can be other than empirical, so factually testable;
- by testability, Popper understands the possibility (either for an entire theory or for a theorem of it) to formulate a conjecture[31] about a still unknown factual, under the condition that factual is observable or experienceable after the formulation of the conjecture;

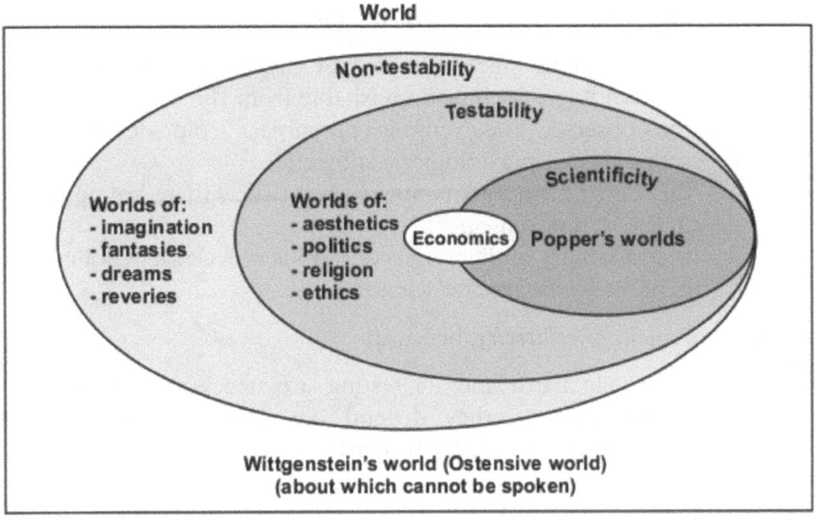

Fig. 8 Extensionality relationships between testability and scientificity (*Source* author)

- Popper accepts degrees of testability—a testability has a degree as great as the probability that the conjecture will be rejected by the factual in the case is greater;
- the testability must be accessible at least for two persons who are independent of each other (in fact, the accessibility should regard the entire scientific community in the field involved);
- no conjecture (or hypothesis or theory) can be verified,[32] because only two non-ambiguous results will be delivered by factual testing: a) corroboration, that is, not yet rejection; b) refutation;
- Popper invites us to become agnostic regarding the scientific (as being empirical) knowledge, because no testing will say something about the truth of our theories, but it only tells us about their falsity, or does not tell us anything about.

What's Different within the Economic Field?

There are some irreducible features in the economic (more general, in the social) field. Let's shortly list the most relevant of them.

(a) *interdisciplinarity requirement*, because:

- the economic subject is part of the economic object (it is epistemologically indistinguishable from the object);
- the observer (i.e., cognitive) subject coincides with the actional (i.e., praxiological) subject;
- the "law of motion" is not invariant (i.e., there are no laws[33] in the strong sense);
- the variability of the initial conditions is necessary (not contingent, as in the natural sciences).

(b) *requirement of relativity*, because:

- economic truth and its testing are necessarily axiologically contextual, i.e., they depend on values, which transform economic knowledge into hermeneutics;
- the "law of motion" is strongly sensitive to the initial conditions:
  - the economic kinematics are chaotic (it is punctually unpredictable);
  - the economic kinematics are not reversible (or, at least, not ergodic);
  - the economic kinematics are strongly hysteresic.

(c) *hidden causality*, because:

- most of the time, the effect precedes the cause
  - because the effect is of the purpose type (and the purpose is a kind of cause—Aristotle's causa finalis), which arises before the economic action (this last being the efficient cause);
- most of the time, the cause cannot be known (observed)
  - in the best case, the cause appears in the form of the causal mechanism (causal chain without a first cause, but only with causes with different degrees of proximity to the effect);
  - in the worst (and most frequent) case: the cause appears in the form of a simple correlation (either structural or functional, but not causal, that is, it appears in the form of a causal chain whose causes have varying degrees of proximity to the effect).[34]

(d) *causal asymmetry*, because:

- identical causes can lead, under the same conditions, to different effects (morphogenesis);
- different causes can lead, under the same conditions, to the same effect (morphostasis);
- causality is not "submerged" into trajectories (which are reversible, by changing the algebraic sign of the time variable) but into irreversible processes, governed by the law of entropy.

(e) *requirement of problematization*, because:

- there is no authentic research in economics (more generally, in the social sciences) without generating a problem (so, without having a structural, functional, or causal incompleteness);
- economic research must identify problems of a scientific type, that is, it is likely to extend the horizon of factual testable knowledge (i.e., the testing of the truth of correspondence type) or, at least, the list of hypothetical testable hypotheses or conjectures;
- the problematization implies the increase of the weight of the deductive or, at least, of the abductive character in formulating the hypotheses and in testing their veracity.

(f) *requirement of invention*, because:

- in the economy (in the social field, more generally), the invention is dominant, but not the discovery (instead, discovery is dominant in the natural sciences);
- in the economy (in the social field, more generally), the conceptualization consists, in a dominant way, in the construction of heuristic fictions (the "as if" method must be used massively);
- invention involves a much higher risk of error as compared to the discovery (in fact, any theory is, in essence, an invention; the theory has no ontological status, although Karl Popper classifies it within the "third world", i.e., the world of thinking contents objectifying;
- the construction of meta-theories (meta-explanations) is the safest way to control the information explosion (there is, however, also the categorical knowledge aimed at treating that explosion)

  - the extreme abstraction must be the final target of fundamental economic or social research;
  - the most powerful de-contextualization of the scientific result is a symptom of veracity (like the formal aesthetic aspect in the natural sciences).

(g) *requirement of problematic opening*, because:

- an authentic scientific result is the one that proposes, at the same time, new queries that it necessarily generates (otherwise, it is purely tautological);
- social research must, in essence, tend towards understanding (comprehension); in the social field, many explanations are not, cannot be, and should only be descriptions of the understanding of human behaviour; so, not the explanation is the fundamental end of the social research;
- scientific economic research must consider that the rationality of the decision and of the economic behaviour are false targets, because it is principled impossible to be achieved (the desiderative thinking always dominates the rational thinking—this last is a simple optimal adequacy of the means for purposes)[35];
- testing the truth of economic propositions (or of the economic predicates, as the case may be) remains axiologically contextualized, which generates an insurmountable gap in the Popperian falsification criterion (it is difficult to replicate the prediction context in the form of the testing experiment context);
- the isolation of an economic system as a cognitive object "breaks" the relations which must not be ignored between the "cut" system and the environment that is formed around this system;
  - these relationships cover the entire relational spectrum: they are of causal type, structural type, and functional type;
  - the cognitively isolated system is ontologically coexisting with its environment: the change of the system interacts with the change of the environment, in a complex network of mutual influences (co-evolution)[36];

- the initial conditions of any social/economic system are necessarily non-invariant (necessity arises from free will, which does not exist in the natural domain);
- induction is impossible in the social-economic field
  - any inductive result has an exclusively local validity (both in time and space);
  - or, the scientificity of a cognitive result implies its de-contextualization (at least at the level of the generality, but it would be desirable to achieve the universality)[37];
- invariants (formal or simply heuristic) are very difficult to identify (however, scientificity means, in the last and highest instance, the identification/construction of invariants);
- in the social/economic disciplines, the explanation, as a description of causality, has a more accessible and, at the same time, enough proxy: understanding/comprehending;
- social/economic logic is not always bivalent (i.e., it does not always hold the third part excluded).[38]

Ontological Conditioning of Popperian Falsifiability within Economic Field

We should be aware that Popperian falsifiability implies a kind of objectivity. Indeed, both predictions on the factuals and the descriptions of the corresponding actualized factuals must be public, that is, observable and operationally accessible to everyone or, at least, to all members of the scientific community involved.[39] This publicity consists in the following:

(a) the theory based on which the hypothesis or conjecture (i.e., the prediction) is enunciated belongs to the third world—that is, the world of the objectified inter-subjectivity. To be mentioned that this third world is located inside the "intersection" between the pure ontology (the first world) and the pure psychology (the second world);
(b) as said above, both prediction and its testing are not only communicable to other individuals (at least one more), but they are effectively communicated in a known language (most of the time, they are expressed in the jargon of the scientific field involved);

(c) it is desirable[40] that the enunciator of the prediction be autonomous from the testator of the implied factual. Such an intersubjectivity breaking is required in order to ensure the avoiding false testing; this danger is not certainly intentional, but it is psychologically to be considered because the author of a prediction loves so much his/her theory so he/she becomes unmindful of the rejection evidence and, so, can make one of the two basic errors in any testing[41];
(d) even if any economic event (as a contextualized economic phenomenon) is contingent,[42] that is, it is possible but unnecessary, it has such a strong impersonal character that it must be considered as objective in the sense of the third world.

In such an interpretation of the objectivity in the economic field (more general, in the social one), in what follows, we'll examine some of the possible epistemological vulnerabilities of the Popperian falsifiability when applied to the economic factuals. As we understand, could there are two categories of vulnerabilities from epistemological point of view: (a) caused by the rigidity of Popper's position, which based its proposal on natural sciences; (b) caused by the stubbornness with the economic discipline tried in the past and, unfortunately, still tries today to verify the preconditions of Popper's falsifiability, in a tragic tentative to transform the economic theory into a theory about molecules, or into a kind of social statistics, analogous to the Boltzmann-ian mechanical statistics.

Epistemological Vulnerabilities of Popperian Falsifiability within Economic Field

Based on the economic field peculiarities related to the natural one, as well as on the ontological specifications of Popperian falsifiability, we think six problematic issues are arising when the falsifiability testing is (intended to be) applied to the economic events: a) the problem of truth; b) the singularity/unrepeatability; c) the problem of prediction; d) the corroboration degree; e) Duhem-Quine problem; f) the ad hoc hypotheses.

(a) *the problem of truth*

Popper had in mind the correspondence-truth, as it is understood under Aristotelian tradition of logic. It is obvious that the correspondence-truth is framed within the emergence, that is, within non-deliberative (i.e., non-normative) processes. An emergent process implies the invariance of its initial conditions, as well as the invariance of the "motion law".[43] But the economic events are not emergent at all; any such event is the result of the intention and action of at least an individual. Although the economic process is the result of an interaction between the individuals and the non-anthropic environment, the non-anthropic environment cannot generate, by itself, an economic event. So, the correspondence-truth, as it is generally understood, cannot arise in the economic process, because, in a very strong sense, the economic truth is rather intentionally created than happened.[44] We can say the economic truth has not finality but it has purpose.[45] Because of the intentionality of the economic process, as well as of the purpose-oriented feature of any such economic process, we think it is required to (minimally) amend the current correspondence-truth or to (maximally) try to invent another kind of truth, framed by intentionality and purposiveness.[46] The main pressure towards such a research direction is from the following reason: once an economic process has started, the individuals involved could change their purpose, so any prediction enunciated before the starting time is no longer comparable (as the correspondence-truth requires) with the result of that process.[47] Fig. 9 specifies the idiosyncrasy of the economic event, compared with the natural one.

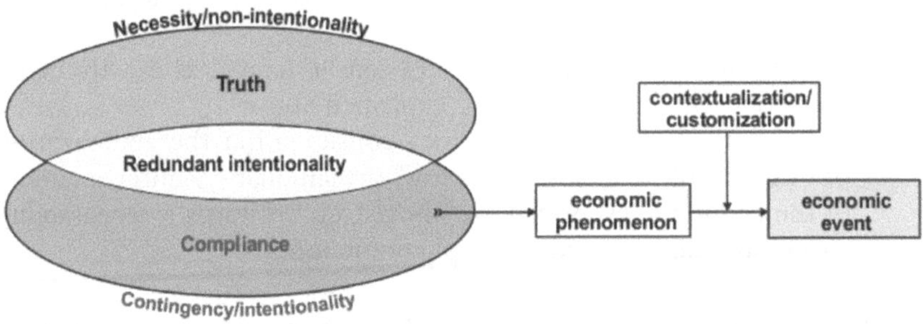

Fig. 9 Economic event is "endowed" with intentionality/purpose (*Source* author)

(b) *the singularity/unrepeatability*

Being contingent and purpose-generated, the economic event is not repeatable in a "pure" form, but only as a class of those events.[48] We could say there is a category-based repeatability, not an idiosyncratic-based one. Like a theory, which is not testable per se, but only based on its (that is, idiosyncratic) consequences, in the same way, an economic event is testable at the individual level only, not at the categorial level. Therefore, the economic event is not testable in the standard (pure, strict) Popperian sense, because:

- Popperian sense of testability (falsifiability) concerns the particular factual only (which remains repeatable, i.e., it remains non-singular);
- since there is no logically repeatable factual in the presumptive set of economic events, it follows that the economic event is not testable in a strictly Popperian sense.

However, the problem of the economic event singularity can be finer analysed:

(a) since the species can be extracted from the genus by adding at least an extra predicate, in a symmetrical way, the genus can be constructed from the species by subtracting the predicates that are not in the intersection set of all predicates of all species concerned. So, we could find a core of predicates of the economic events concerned shared by these events;
(b) such a core of common predicates can be named as exactly being the economic phenomenon, as explained above[49];
(c) any testing should then take into consideration the actualization of this core of predicates. This way, the singularity/unrepeatability of the economic event can be "moved up" towards a repeatability framed by the built economic phenomenon.

Of course, such a weakening of the falsification procedure needs a more extended examination and grounding, in order to hold the essence of the Popperian falsifiability proposal when applied in the economic field. Figure 10 shows an image of such a vulnerability.

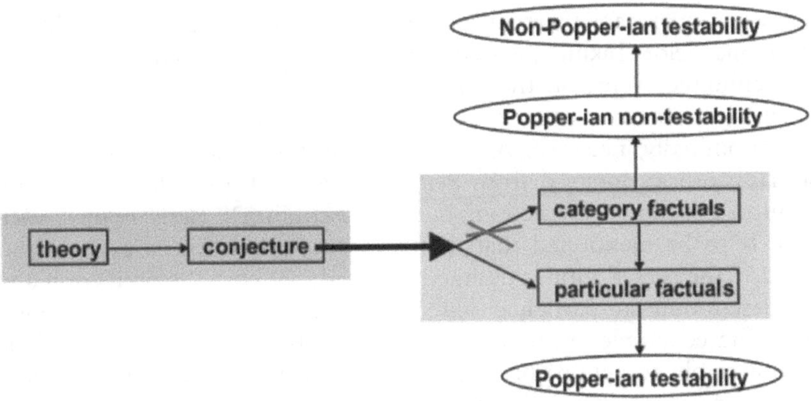

Fig. 10 Economic event is "endowed" with intentionality/purposiveness (*Source* author)

(c) *the prediction*

As it is well known, the falsifiability implies a semantic comparison between a theory-based prediction, expressed generally through a verbal statement,[50] about a given (selected) factual, and a description, expressed also, generally, through a verbal statement about the same factual. As a prediction, the factual is only presumed (has a potential or virtual statute), while as a description, the same factual comes into reality (has an actualized statute). So, to repeat: the correspondence-truth used to proceed to Popperian falsifiability involves the semantic coincidence, that is, the overlapping, between the referential addressed by the prediction and the referential addressed by the description. Be a factual denoted as F_i. Its potential (or future, or un-inspected) state is $\overline{F}_{i+1}$, while its actual (or effective) state is $\widetilde{F}_{i+1}$. The prediction, P_i, is $P_i\left(\overline{F}_{i+1}\right)$, being issued at the moment i, while the description, $D_{i\,+\,1}$, is $D_{i+1}\left(\widetilde{F}_{i+1}\right)$, being issued at the moment $(i + 1)$. At moment $i + 1$, the prediction and the description involved are semantically compared, and a result about corroboration or rejection of the prediction (and, as a consequence, of the hypothesis based on which the prediction was issued) is delivered. The essence of the above-described procedure consists of the existence of a prediction.

The question is: are there or, put else, may there be predictions in the economic field? Taking into consideration the contingent character of the economic event, on the one hand, as well as the purposiveness on which any economic event is projected, on the other hand, the answer is, undoubtedly, negative. A prediction must be built on a theory (or on a hypothesis inferred from a theory). A prediction that is built on a purpose is not a prediction, but a prescription[51] (let's note it with N_i). It to be mentioned that: (1) while the prediction is explanation-based,[52] the prescription is desirability-based; (2) both the prediction and the description are particular statements, not general or universal ones. Since the economic event (as knowable or observable hypostasis of the economic phenomenon) has a praxiological nature, in fact, the purpose is designed through a *sui generis* combination between prediction and prescription[53]—we could name such a combination as *presdiction*.

Trying to conclude, we could say that the fundamental consequence of the above mentioned comes into the non-relevance of the correspondence-truth in the economy, not only because we cannot put it into evidence, but also because this truth cannot be put into evidence independently and inter-subjective verifiably.[54] In fact, the fulfilment vs. non-fulfilment of the economic purpose is neither true nor false; it simply cannot be associated with the concept of truth. In addition, given the contingency of the economic action, the prediction is incorporated (captured) in the prescription—the Oedipus effect—so, in general, in the economy, what prevails is the prescription, not the prediction.[55]

Moreover, in the economic field, another characteristic is dominant: while, in the general epistemology, the observation (the observational statement) is theoretically contaminated, in the economic epistemology, there is another type of contamination, both of observation (observational statement) and of prediction. We propose that any observational statement in the economic field (more generally, in the social field) be considered goal-contaminated,[56] so any "prediction" is goalnessly (purposivenessly) designed.

The most important epistemological aspect of the prediction (in fact, of the prescription, respectively of the *presdiction*), which most can make vulnerable Popperian falsifiability in the economic field, is its categorial character. A purpose can only be achieved through social interaction (what we call economic action), so that purpose can no longer be particular (that is, assigned individually), but must be a commitment[57] collectively assumed, so it gets categorial valences. No individual will achieve their personal purpose, although all involved individuals will achieve their common purpose. Obviously, the categorial character of the prediction forbids the standard Popperian falsifiability. Figure 11 shows a synoptic view of the above considerations about the prediction in the economic field.

(d) *the corroboration degree*

After replacing the verification concept of the Vienna Circle with the corroboration one, Popper did not leave this concept alone. More precisely, he very analytically discussed the problem of the corroboration degrees. There was the idea that the more factual evidences corroborate a hypothesis, (more exactly, a prediction based on a given hypothesis) the more probable that hypothesis could be true. Popper's position was radical: no matter how many corroborations support the prediction (considered as being a particular logical consequence of a theory/hypothesis), the falsification degree of the theory involved does not change (more precisely, it remains maximum). In other words, the corroboration does not change the probability that the theory is true (or false). We think, however, Popper's position regarding the corroboration degree is incompatible with the economic event, because, at least:

- economic predictions are, as has been shown, *presdictions*, i.e., they are of a finalist type, based on purpose (*Nota bene*: the purpose is always contingent);

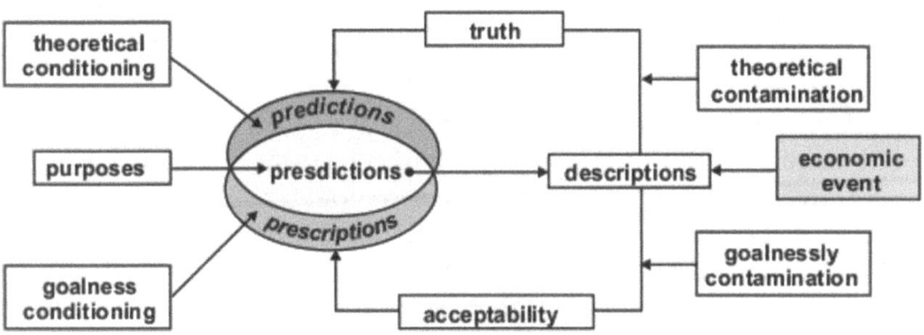

Fig. 11 *Presdictions* as "economic predictions" (*Source* author)

- therefore, economic predictions are, in essence, combinations—probably linear—between anticipations[58] (associable to predictions) and expectations[59] (associable to prescriptions);
- since expectation and confidence are relatively psychologically substitutable, it turns out that a corroboration can change (in the sense of increasing) confidence in the theory that underpinned the prediction;
- increasing confidence in the corroborated theory increases the likelihood that the theory in question will respond "affirmatively" to subsequent tests (i.e., increases the probability[60] that the theory is "true").

In our opinion (expressed on other occasions), the only kind of probability which could be "saved" for the economic modelling is Bayesian probability, which never should work in the natural field, where we have necessity only, i.e., anticipations only. Since the economic predictions (as presdictions, of course) are purpose-based, they are very sensitive to the corroboration. We could even advance the idea that, if in the field of natural events, there is a sensitivity of them to the initial conditions—which leads to the chaotic type models—in the economic field, there is a sensitivity of the economic events to the final state, that is, the purpose—which leads to the normative type models. In such a context, we believe that, if the sensitivity to the initial conditions can be modelled using chaos theory (or non-linear dynamics theory), then the sensitivity to the final state can be modelled (should be modelled) using the topological theory.[61] For reasons of conceptual symmetry, we can state here the following conjecture: *in contrast to the natural domain (where the refutation of a single particular prediction invalidates the truth of the theory involved), in the economic field, the refutation of a presdiction has the effect not of invalidating the theory involved, but of reducing the confidence in it (reducing the probability of being "true")*. In other words, refutation could mainly address the purpose established outside any theory, not the theory involved. A symmetrical conjecture could be formulated by the side of corroboration: *in contrast to the natural domain (where the corroboration of a single particular prediction does not increase the probability that the theory involved be true), in the economic field, the corroboration of a presdiction has the effect of increasing the probability that the theory involved be true, by increasing the confidence in it*. Figure 12 puts together confidence, corroboration, and probability (of type Bayes) as discussed above (*Nota bene*: by net number of corroborations must be understood the difference between the number of corroborations and the number of refutations regarding the same *presdiction*).

So, the probability curve of the truth regarding an economic prediction is a logistic depending directly on the confidence degree and indirectly on the net number of corroborations, that is, it is a functional (a function of a function). The probability increases more slowly for a small degree of confidence, then it increases decelerated after an inflexion point in the net number of corroborations (such a point is psychologically determinable). The fundamental reason, based on which, in the economic field, the net number of corroborations increases the probability that the conjectures are true, is the presence of the purpose[62] in any presdiction—but the purposes are something subjective, based on belief, and the belief can increase with the increase of the number of (net) corroborations.

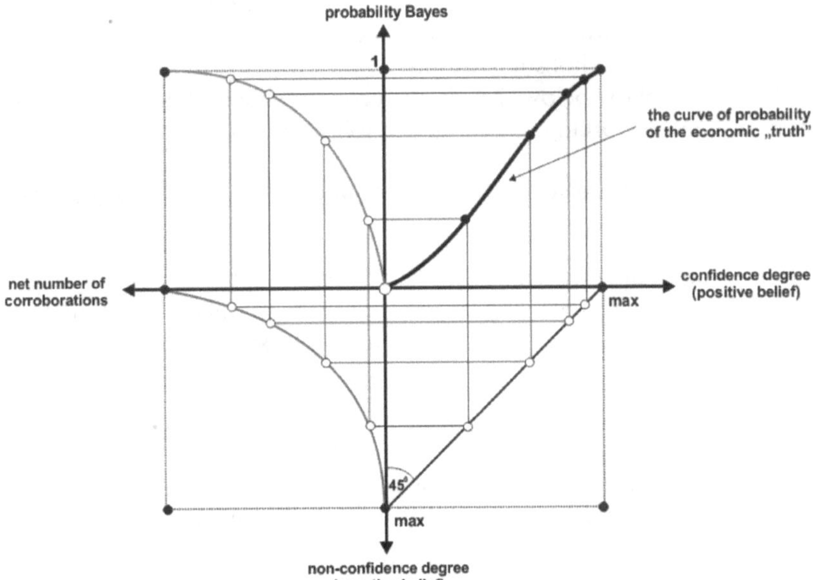

Fig. 12 Probability curve of the economic "truth" as function of the net number of corroborations (*Source* author)

(e) *Duhem-Quine thesis*

To examine the vulnerability introduced by Duhem-Quine thesis on the Popperian falsifiability, let's remember Popper's position regarding the effect of a refutation result of factual testing: *if a prediction based on a hypothesis derived from a theory is rejected, then the hypothesis is falsified*. This is a reductionist position, based on the concept of experimentum crucis. Two questions arise based on this positioning: (1) with what certainty should the refutation of that hypothesis?; (2) should the refutation be extended to the host theory of the hypothesis as a whole?

It is easy to observe that by answering the first question, the second one is, for the most part, answered too. In fact, Duhem, then Quine (1976), approached the first question. This thesis says: *no hypothesis can be denied by a falsification of the associated prediction, because, besides the hypothesis tested, other hypotheses (implicit or explicit) condition the experiment or observation*. As a result, the falsification process should be continued ad infinitum, to test all the hypotheses involved in the given prediction. This is a holistic position.

We'll try to show below that, in the economic field, the Duhem-Quine thesis is plenary working, based on the following arguments:

- the economic event is multiple-conditioned (natural, psychological, sociological, political, axiological);
  - consequently: an economic prediction is based not only on an economic type hypothesis, but also on many other auxiliary non-economic hypotheses/assumptions;
- given the non-repeatability of the economic event, it is not possible to ensure the functioning of the methodological condition of experiment named ceteris paribus; this will "break" the logical chain of separate testing of the additional hypotheses involved in the initial experiment, so it will make falsifiability vulnerable;
  - consequently: in the economic field (more generally, in the social field) there is an overdetermination of the individual,[63] which prohibits methodological individualism, so prohibits Popperian reductionism regarding the falsifiability;

Therefore, refutation of an economic presdiction cannot logically unambiguously lead to the rejection of the hypothesis that generated that presdiction. In this case, the causal overdetermination of the individual acts as a categorial cause, induced by what we could name the institutional overdetermination of the economic presdiction. Such institutional overdetermination is one of the most common forms of the Duhem-Quine thesis translated into the economic field.

Figure 13 provides a general view of the Duhem-Quine problem for the factual falsifiability in the economic field.

(f) *the* ad hoc *hypotheses*

Popper himself was conscious of the vulnerabilities induced by his punctuality in interpreting the result of factual testing as falsifiability. Consequently, he approached the problem of the so-called ad hoc hypotheses which analysts would desire to introduce after the answer provided by

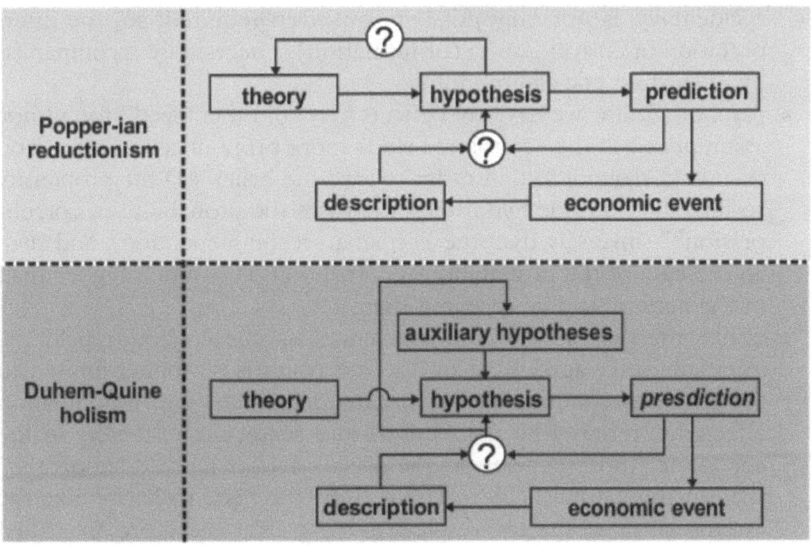

Fig. 13 Comparative view of Popper's punctual falsifiability and Duhem-Quine's holistic falsifiability (*Source* author)

factual testing in order to save the hypothesis "attacked" through rejection of the associated prediction. More precise, Popper requires that the failure of a prediction must necessarily lead to refuting the assigned hypothesis; this does not have to be "saved", however, by introducing ad hoc hypotheses[64] (either at the level of definitions, or at the level of experiment conditions, or at the interpretative level of the test results) that will relax the strength of the test. However, Popper accepts being introduced, if needed, those ad hoc assumptions that reduce the probability of corroboration of the hypothesis in question (or, equivalently, increase the probability of refuting it). So, Popper agrees to worsen the situation from the point of view of testing, not to relax it.

Regarding the economic field, we think the following could be said about the issue of the ad hoc hypotheses:

- since the interpretation of the test result is not based on the concept of correspondence-truth (as the Popperian falsifiability requires), but it is of finalist (goalness) type (i.e., it is a desirable-truth), the introduction and use of ad hoc hypotheses in a systematic way, not accidentally, is not only possible, but even required; so, the interpretation of corroboration (or refutation) is necessarily accompanied by ex post ad hoc assumptions;
- psychologically, we have two effects here: (1) the "need" for ad hoc assumptions in the economic field is more pronounced in refutation than in corroboration, in order to save the belief; (2) the propensity to introduce ad hoc hypotheses increases the probability of corroboration[65] (inversely than the Popperian recommendation), and such an increase of the probability of corroboration is much higher than in the natural field (if accepted there);
- unlike the case of the natural sciences, in the economic field the inter-subjective agreement on the test result is no longer limited to the scientific community, but is extended to the entire population affected/interested by that result—in a sense, the testability in the economic (more general, in the social) field is more "democratic" than in the natural field—consequently: the need to harmonize the interpretation of the test result is much greater and more diversified in terms of "competence", which is why the introduction of ad hoc hypotheses that evade the Popperian condition (that is, the recommendation to try so to decrease the probability of corroboration) is almost inevitable.

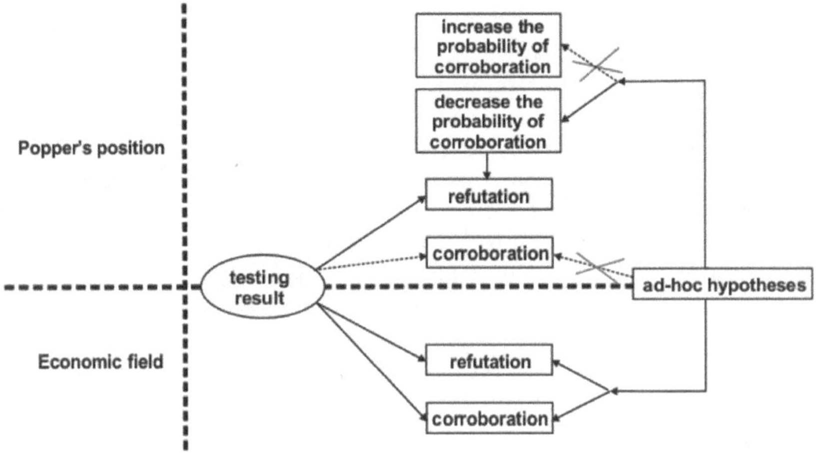

Fig. 14 Ad hoc hypotheses are necessarily working in the economic field, for both refutation and corroboration (*Source* author)

Figure 14 illustrates the above discussion.

What's to Do?

We think at least three questions should be answered regarding the above vulnerabilities examined:

(a) *firstly*, what should we understand by *truth* in the economic field? Based on the impurity of the economic prediction, which is, as already said, a presdiction, that is, a combination[66] between prediction and prescription, it seems the truth is rather normative than extrapolative. Considering that the prediction is based on explanation, that is, it has a cognitive nature, while the prescription is based on desirability, that is, it has a normative nature, we suggest a tetravalent logic of the economic truth. The basic lines of the proposal are the following:

- there are four truth values[67]:
  - *T*: nominal full achieving of the purpose, "no rest"

- $\overline{T}_{+}$: nominal failure of the purpose, but "with positive rest", that is, accompanied by the arising of unintended consequences which are appropriate[68] to the subject;
- T_{-}: nominal achievement of the purpose, but "with negative rest", that is, accompanied by the arising of unintended consequences which are not appropriate for the subject;
- $\overline{T}$: nominal failure of purpose, "no rest".

- the truth remains a kind of correspondence-truth, but such a truth is no longer inter-subjectively communicable and understandable; it gains idiosyncratic features, so only for the common core of the collective purpose (the non-empty intersection of all individual purposes) it recaptures its public falsifiability
- table of the truth values is shown in Table 11[69]:

(b) *secondly*, what should we understand by *rationality* in the economic field? Since the presdiction is not a pure prediction, we can no longer test the correspondence-truth, but what test can we? It seems we cannot test anything other than the adequacy of the assigned means to the achieved end. If the purpose is achieved, then the means[70] assigned were adequate; if it is not achieved, then the means were inadequate. But such a reason is just the epistemological content of the concept of instrumental rationality.[71] Of course, the economic process is not (and is not primarily) captured by instrumental rationality only. On the contrary, it is functioning rather under the symbolic rationality and often under the evidential rationality (Nozick, 1995). At least the symbolic rationality has

Table 11 Typology of statements in a 4 T logic

Values of occurrence	*Proposition (statement) type*
T	Performative statement ($\mathcal{S}_{[\mathrm{p}]}$)
$\overline{T}_{+}$	Convenient non-performative statement ($\mathcal{S}_{[\overline{\mathrm{p}}\mathrm{c}]}$)
T_{-}	Performative non-convenient statement ($\mathcal{S}_{[\mathrm{p}\overline{\mathrm{c}}]}$)
$\overline{T}$	Non-performative statement ($\mathcal{S}_{[\overline{\mathrm{p}}]}$)

Source author

no interference with the instrumental rationality. Moreover, while the instrumental rationality provides the assignment of the means to the pre-existing purpose, the symbolic rationality generates, in a non-inferential way, just the purposes in case. The non-inferential way signifies that the purposes are "derived" directly from values, that is, from belief. We can say, without any risk of error, the purposes are not...rational (of course, related to the instrumental rationality).

(c) *thirdly*, what should we understand by *scientificity* in the economic field? It is obvious that the economic theory does not match the sufficiency predicates for a strong scientificity.[72] The scientificity refers only to the theoretical aspect of human action (or activity). Therefore, we will not seek to identify this predicate in either the praxiological or practical[73] action of individuals (or of the social groups). Just as there is only one distinct type of human action, it means that scientificity refers to the theoretical action of individuals (in Table 12, the abstract structure of the human action is rendered[74]). This means that scientificity can be (or, after the case, cannot be) a property only if it is associated with that type of human activity that addresses the object-object[75] relationship. In the other two types of human activity, the very invocation of scientificity (irrespective of whether or not the property is detected) is meaningless. This position should not be interpreted in the sense of a positivism (neither absolute nor relative), because we have not invoked either the factual testability of the sentences describing the property in question, or the validity (either logical or grammatical) of the formation of the propositions in question.

So, from the perspective of the strong scientificity (primarily represented by physics), Economics is not scientific. We believe Economics should be considered as a praxeology as Fig. 11 indicates and, in such a qualification, it must be reconstructed by extracting it from the row of elucidating the object, from the columns of theoretical signification (object-object relationships), and from the column of practical signification (subject-subject relationships), that is, by coming back to von Mises old and visionary suggestion (Mises, 1998).

Additional comments

Table 12 Scientificity is a predicate of the object-object relationship which concerns the object elucidation

Relationship Elucidation of	*Object-object (O-O)*	*Subject-object (S-O)*	*Subject-subject (S-S)*
The object	**Sciences** –physics –biology –cosmology –chemistry	**Arts** –music –painting –sculpture –literature –architecture	**Hermeneutics** –criticism –politics –history
The subject	**Logics** –logic –accounting –mathematics –linguistics	**Praxiologies** –economics –sociology –psychology –theoretical philosophy	**Ethics** –religion –morals –social philosophy

Source author

Basically, the possibility of the teleological truth can be inferred from a short discussion on the concept of knowledge, scientific knowledge, and languages involved, as follows.

1. *Knowledge*

To get the concept of knowledge, it is needed to travel the road from Nature cu Culture, so to speak. The first step, here, is the perception of signals, where the perception "device" belongs to the subject,[76] and the signals can belong both to the subject (the same or other) and to Nature, where by Nature is understood both the non-anthropogenic and anthropogenic environment. Signals refer to any change in the *statu quo* so that the mentioned change is perceived by the subject. The sufficient condition that a signal be perceived is the following: the signal in question must bear a sign. In fact, a sign arises when a change in the *statu quo* arises too. Let us introduce some notations:

- (S): the set of signals
- (C): the set of changes that are signalled through the signals
- (s): the set of signs that are perceived by the subject

So, there are the following relationships among the mentioned sets:

$$(s) \subseteq (C) \subseteq (S)$$

The subject can perceive the signs if and only if those signs are already registered in a "list" of signs which the subject holds, generally based on own experience (a posteriori signs) or based on the Kantian forms of intuition[77] (a priori signs). When a signal affects the subject's (six) senses, he/she compares the signs in the signal with the signs in the list and, if he/she finds in the list the sign of the signal, then the sign in the case is perceived. In the contrary case, the sign is either ignored or added to the list as a new sign. So, that list is permanently actualized by the very daily experience.

The perception is "transferred" from the senses to the intellect, where they become concepts. The concepts are then integrated into a reasoning or chains of reasonings. A reasoning is a proposition expressed linguistically (either verbal or formal) about reality (things, properties, relationships). What we call cognizance (*Nota bene*: a cognizance is an "individual" of the knowledge population) is the very content of a proposition about reality. A set of cognisances, ordered and structured according to a theoretical/metaphysical/theological/artistic framework (for example, a system of axioms), constitutes what is called knowledge. For the moment, both cognizance and knowledge are just an opinion, more or less sophisticated, about reality. To become an episteme, the opinion must be factually testable. Even corroborated through effective testing, the episteme is always provisional, since it could always be refuted in future.

In fact, the concept of knowledge that we have in mind in this communication is the common one in epistemology, namely the one based on ἐπιστήμη (epistēmē), and opposed to δόξα (doxa), that is, verifying the four logical conditions (or sufficiency predicates) for epistēmē: (1) there is an opinionator; (2) there is an opinion expressed by the opinionator in a sentence (usually verbal); (3) the opinion is true; (4) the opinion is well-founded.[78]

In front of knowledge, there is always, in the first instance, only one of the three hypostases of reality (things, properties, relations), namely the relationship—both things and properties in the three categories of reality[79] are revealed (and relevant) exclusively through the perception, respectively the knowledge of the relations: between things, between properties, between relations (second-order relations), between things and properties, between things and relations, between properties and relations. The cognitive primitivity of the relationship leads us to a typology of knowledge (i.e., to categories of knowledge) precisely from this perspective. So, logically, there are five categories of knowledge, organized as follows Table 13.

Each category of knowledge seeks/obtains a regional truth, specific to that category of knowledge, so there can be five types of truth—one for the scientific order (or language) Λ^0, one for the scientific order Λ^1, and three for the scientific order Λ^2. The teleological truth is specific to the societal/social/economic field, and is associated with the language of type Λ^1.

Scientific research

The scientific research (*SR*) is a very specific action/activity, either at the individual or societal level, which is characterized by the following sufficiency predicates:

1. (*P*) has as purpose to acquire scientific knowledge of reality[80];
2. (*R*) model of rationality concerning the object of research;
3. (*M*) unfolds based on a pre-established methodology of research, usually of a deductive (or, at least, an abductive) approach.

Non-mandatorily, the scientific research proceeds, regularly, inside a cognitive paradigm (*CP*), either explicitly or implicitly (Kuhn, 2012; Dinga et al., 2022), or following a (specific) research program[81] (*RP*) (Lakatos, 1980). Consequently, the hard core of the definition of scientific research is delivered by the logical conjunction (the *PRM* framework):

$$\overline{SR} \leftarrow (P) \bigwedge (R) \bigwedge (M)$$

while the complete definition will add the two contingent predicates:

$$SR = (\overline{SR}) \bigcup \left\{ (CP) \bigvee (RP) \bigvee \left[(CP) \bigwedge (RP) \right] \right\}$$

Scientific knowledge

Table 13 Knowledge categories

Denomination	*Finality/truth*	*Identitary condition*	*Relation targeted*	*Way of validation*	*Popper's world*	*Language (scientific order)*
Theoretical knowledge	Correspondence-truth	Factual testability	Object-object	Niche inter-subjective vote	1	Λ^0
Artistic knowledge	Possible truth	Adhesion	Subject-subject	General inter-subjective vote	2	Λ^2
Metaphysical knowledge	Plausible truth	Adhesion	Subject-subject	General inter-subjective vote	2	Λ^2
Praxiological knowledge	Teleological truth	Successful	Subject-object	Praxiological replication	3	Λ^1
Practical knowledge	Accepted truth	Belief	Subject-subject	General inter-subjective vote	3	Λ^2

Sursa Autorul

The scientific knowledge (*SK*) is, obviously, a species of knowledge. So, the proximal genus of the scientific knowledge is the (general) knowledge. To get the definition of the scientific knowledge, we must identify, based on Ockham's razor, the specific differences.[82] I think the following specific differences should be retained:

1. (*A*) is an artefact, that is, it is objectified in one way or another, usually by communication at the society level[83];
2. (*V*) is inter-subjectively validated, by the intermediation of a "vote" within the scientific community, regularly inside the cognitive paradigm concerned;
3. (*T*) is factually testable. It is important, here, to provide two important considerations:
   - a (presumptive) scientific knowledge is not mandatorily required to be actually tested, but it is sufficient to provide a convincing proof (demonstration) that it is testable, so the mark of the scientificity is simply the (factual) testability;
   - there is a difference between the concepts factual and empirical—while the factual is a repeatable event (phenomenon), the empirical is a singular one. It is obvious that the testability is concerned with factual, not empirical; for example, the corroboration of a prediction by the assigned factual must allow the possibility that factual refute the same prediction in the future, which is impossible for an empirical event to do.

Nota bene 1: there is no crisp overlapping between the scientific research and scientific knowledge; the scientific knowledge can also be acquired outside scientific research (for example, by the intermediation of intuition), and, in turn, the scientific research can also acquire non-scientific knowledge. However, most of the scientific research provides scientific knowledge, and most of the scientific knowledge is provided by scientific research.

Nota bene 2: according to the specific difference (*T*), the scientific knowledge obeys agnosticism.

Consequently, the scientific knowledge (*SK*) is delivered by that knowledge which cumulatively verifies the three sufficiency predicates. If we denote the (general) knowledge with *K*, then we can write:

$$SK = (K) \bigwedge (A) \bigwedge (V) \bigwedge (T)$$

which means that the non-scientific knowledge ($\overline{S}K$) can be formally described as follows:

$$\overline{S}K = (K) \wedge \{(\overline{A}) \vee (\overline{V}) \vee (\overline{T}) \vee [(\overline{A}) \wedge (\overline{V})] \vee [(\overline{A}) \wedge (\overline{T})] \vee [(\overline{V}) \wedge (\overline{T})] \vee [(\overline{A}) \wedge (\overline{V}) \wedge (\overline{T})]\}$$

Notes

1. The concept of the invisible hand was coined by Adam Smith (2005).
2. The property is called *ultimate* means *of last resort*.
3. In other words, we can say that happy individuals make a happy society, but we cannot say the inverse, except in accidental cases, not principled ones.
4. Of course, there are always societal projects that do not belong to the elite, but to isolated individuals (regularly philosophers, especially social philosophers) who reflect on a better social/societal order—Augustin, Campanella, Kant, and so on.
5. The difference between experiment and experience is the following: the experiment unfolds in vitro (experimental time, that is, accelerated), while the experience unfolds in vivo (real time, that is, at its common rate). For example, it would maybe have been better if Nazism or Communism had been experimented with (in a... laboratory) before being effectively implemented as societal orders.
6. I.e., unexpected, undesirable, unanticipated.
7. The so-called adverse (or even, in some contexts, perverse) effects.
8. I remind that if the municipality intends to arrange an alley in the park, it should wait to see where people across the park and then arrange the alley exactly on the "alley" indicated by people. The reason is that wherever the alley is arranged in the park, people will traverse the park on the old road. This example is very instructive, for example, in the case of designing the fiscal policy—here would function, in fact, an inverse nudge, from the people to the state. *Nota bene*: maybe Mr. Richard Thaler will complete his theory from a symmetrical perspective!
9. The teleological truth is generated by the desiderative thinking, i.e., by the purposes.

10. As we see will next, in the case discussed in this book, we have binomial ($n = 2$) evolutionary processes which are integrated into a quadrinomial ($n = 4$) process.
11. We have, here, another manifestation of the "law of returning to the average", so ingeniously exploited by Daniel Kahneman (Nobel laureate).
12. Of course, within the whole constellation of the relationships between humans and the non-anthropogenic environment.
13. A generic perturbation is, by definition, a cause for changes in the *statu quo* of the system targeted by that perturbation, so that even an improvement in that *statu quo* constitutes also a change, so a mutation.
14. Although we separate the resources from the population, this is somewhat unrealistic, since the population is a (special) resource by itself. However, it cannot be rejected that, from a logical point of view, the resources are "opposed" to population in the very (individual) life functioning.
15. At this point, by science, I understand the theoretical science, i.e., that science which is interested only in the relationships object–object. The practical science (which is interested in the relationships subject–subject), I will discuss at the humanities (at the third binomial).
16. Of course, at the societal level, no binomial is closed, but, for the moment, all the binomials must be considered closed to themselves in order to identify the principles and mechanisms to provide their own equilibrium.
17. Again, here, in the sense of possibility, neither of objective probability nor Bayesian probability.
18. It is worth mentioning that the opinions provided address the societal field of the symbolic species; they cannot be, perhaps, extended either to biological species or to the logical ones.
19. Such an assessment is valid both for the phylogenetic development and for the ontogenetic evolution.
20. It is easy to show that any non-verbal statement, for example, a mathematical enunciation like $E = mc^2$, is, in fact, an abbreviation of the same content expressed verbally.
21. This is the well-known position of Wittgenstein (see *Tractatus Logico-Philosophicus*, translated by Humanitas Publishing House, second edition, 2012). His positioning is larger than that of the

Vienna Circle (the logical empiricists required the statement's content—that is, the statement's referential—be not only possible in the world, but verifiable through empirical experience in the world). Of course, there could are statements about possible facts which are situated outside any experience, so the Vienna Circle's positioning is more restrictive —from the modal category of possible it extracts the category of experiential only.

22. The equivalence between necessity and a prior*ism* of a statement is not non-problematic (see, for example, the objections formulated by Saul Kripke, which indicated counterexamples of contingent *a priori* statements), but, in this study, it will be accepted, together with the equivalence between contingency and *a posteriorism*.
23. We do not extend here the discussion beyond the binary logic, because it is not needed by the purpose of the paper.
24. To be mentioned that the internality in this case is not the same as the internality required by Wittgenstein in order to put into evidence the sense of a statement. It can be said that the internality in the case of the internal coherence truth is not a necessary internality, but a contingent one.
25. The term *state* should be taken in its largest meaning, that is, its referentials could equally be: events, structures, causalities, processes, and so on, which can be associated with the reality (objective, subjective, or objectified by the inter-subjective relationships, so the third Popperian worlds).
26. For example, the statement is true or false, but not undetermined (remember we are in a world in which the binary logic is working).
27. Remember that testability did not require publicity—a testable statement holds its testability even if a single individual formulates the statement in case and nobody knows about it.
28. For example, a religious statement, addressing a religious feeling, is comprehensible for the author of that statement only (because the religious feelings cannot be "translated" for others), so that statement is not scientific, but it is still testable.
29. By verifying the scientificity, a statement acquires the status of a scientific statement. The same about testability.
30. Although Popper sententiously stated that testability is equivalent to scientificity (and also with falsifiability), we believe that the testability and scientificity are not semantically (that is, from the perspective of their extensions) equivalent at all. Regarding

the relationships between testability and falsifiability, we'll address them further.

31. By conjecture is understood a statement, generally verbally expressed and logically and grammatically valid, about a non-inspected or a future factual (that is, an event as hypostasis of the phenomenon concerned).
32. Popper delimits from the Vienna Circle both regarding verificationism and confirmabilism. Although regarding verificationism, his arguments are convincing, regarding confirmabilism he did not provide explicit positioning, but his position could be inferred from the fact that his falsifiability does not have a potential character, as the confirmabilism does, but an actual one.
33. Of course, there could be deep enough correlations among phenomena (what the econometricians are searching) or even serial "laws" (see the suggestion of the Romanian historian A.D. Xenopol), but without accepting general/universal social laws. What are called *economic laws* (e.g., the law of demand) are metaphors for some observable regularities whose primitive causes (still) remain unknown.
34. Wherever we have a causal chain, it is about correlation and not about causal explanation.
35. See, here, the instrumental rationality addressed by Robert Nozick.
36. See, here, the composition error (e.g., saving paradox), Lucas's criticism, the impossibility of aggregating individual indicators or hierarchies of preferences (Arrow, Peacock).
37. See, here, the paradox of Russell's hen or the paradox of Hempel's ravens, both regarding the possibility for the induction to generate the truth value: false.
38. So, in the social process, the subject is always, partially, object too (that is, instead $A \bigvee \overline{A}$, we have $A \bigwedge \overline{A}$).
39. In the manner in which the Kuhnian concept of paradigm requires the "inhabitants" of a given paradigm (Kuhn, 2012).
40. Such a condition of publicity is not so strong and, in fact, it is not absolutely required, but, in the last case, we need a guarantee about the honesty of the testator, which could coincide with the enunciator regarding a given factual testing.
41. Remember: (a) the *error of order 1*—to believe a true hypothesis (that is, a true evidence) is false; (b) *the error of order 2*—to believe a false hypothesis (that is, a false evidence) is true.

42. The contingency of the economic event is, of course, the…necessary result of the free will which human beings are endowed with. Based on Wittgenstein's allegations, the sense of a statement is provided by its contingency, once the contingency implies the possibility.
43. By translating these invariances into the "physiology" of the syllogism, we get the condition of the invariance inside the major premise (or inside the invariance of the covering law).
44. The correspondence truth is associable only with the necessary events or with those where the intentionality is redundant in relation to the necessity.
45. By purpose must be understood that "finality" is contingent. Since the contingency can be imposed by free will only (which, in turn, is exclusively associated with the human being), we can conclude that the "economic truth" could be another "animal" than the standard correspondence truth.
46. For example, the "economic truth" could also have two values of truth (that is, it could work too under a bi-valent logic), but not anymore "true" or "false". These truth values could be "achieved" or "non-achieved", "acceptable" or "non-acceptable", "desirable" or "non-desirable", and so on.
47. Do remember, also, the Oedipus effect which acts even through the prediction enunciated and known by the individuals involved in the factual aimed at by the prediction in the case.
48. A given class of events is generally named a phenomenon.
49. Such a procedure is logically equivalent to that of Imre Lakatos's proposal to "save" Popperian falsifiability from its too big sensitivity to any factual rejection of hypotheses/conjectures.
50. Remember that any non-verbal statement (like an equation—e.g., Fermat's conjecture) is also, in the last instance, verbally based.
51. The prescription could be defined shortly as: a statement putting a rule regarding the description of an objective of activity, which is not an emergent event but a deliberative/planned/represented one (by an emergent event must be understood: a state which happens, so it is not produced—e.g., market equilibrium, through "invisible hand"mechanism).
52. The explanation is a general causal statement, not a particular one; that is, it is a coverage law so logically, the explanation is the major premise in a generic syllogism. The prediction always

concerns a particular event, under a coverage law, not a categorial one, so the prediction stays as a minor premise in a generic syllogism. Somehow, the prediction is a future particularization (contextualization) of the past (general) explanation.

53. If the economic action has a great dependence on the non-anthropogenic nature, the weight of the prediction into the presdiction increases, otherwise, the weight of the prescription into the presdiction increases. In the moment when the *presdiction* is enunciated, there is a linear combination between prediction and prescription, analogously with the linear superposition of the microstates in Quantum Mechanics. Moving further the analogy, when the economic factual event is observed, all the "superposed" states of that event collapse into a single state which the observer unambiguously records.
54. Indeed, different individuals could have different purposes within the same economic process.
55. But why have we not, in the economic field, prescriptions only? The reason comes from the praxiological statute of the economic process, that is, the interactions between human beings and their non-anthropic environment—the non-anthropic environment introduces into the presdiction the prediction's side, while the human beings' purposiveness introduces into the presdiction the prescription's side.
56. A rudiment of this idea can be found in Kuhn's concept of paradigm (see his sub-concepts of puzzle, respectively of anomaly). Unfortunately, Kuhn does not realize this epistemological aspect, but only leads to the last logical consequences his his own concept of paradigm.
57. The concept of commitment has here the signification established by Amartya Sen (see his work *On the Ethics and Economics*, Blackwell Publishing, second edition, 1988), that is, a special engagement, most of the time of a moral kind, towards membership groups.
58. Anticipations are results necessarily inferred from a model of rationality; that is, they are not contingent once the model of rationality is selected. In other words, the anticipations have nothing to do with free will, the purposes, and so on; they are completely and externally binding (or, equivalently, they are objective, related to the given model of rationality).

59. Expectations are, on the contrary, completely subjective. They are internal to the subject and are not based on a model of rationality. In fact, the expectations are desirabilities, are contingent, and are generated through free will (*Nota bene*: the free will is the capacity/ability to oppose the "social necessity", not the "natural necessity").
60. We talk here about, of course, a Bayesian probability, while Popper considered an objective probability (based on archives). The objective probability could be associated with anticipations, while subjective probability (like Bayesian probability) could be associated with expectations.
61. About the appropriateness of the topological theory (more exactly, the algebraic topology) for the economic modelling, we'll come back with another intervention.
62. In a larger logical approach, the presence of purpose inside the economic presdiction is similar to the presence of an implicit assumption which, according to Duhem-Quine thesis, must itself be corroborated. So, our suggestion regarding the structure of the economic presdiction could be interpreted as a... theoretical corroboration, for the economic field, of the Duhem-Quine thesis.
63. For example, the economic institutions (more generally, social institutions) act causally (or, at least, conditionally) on individual economic action and, also, on the collective economic action, which implies a common purpose.
64. To be aware that Duhem-Quine auxiliary hypotheses, above discussed, have nothing to do with the Popperian ad hoc hypotheses.
65. Again, because in the economic field we have to do with the desirable truth, not with the correspondence truth.
66. We think a linear combination, by analogy with the linear superposition of the states in the Quantum Mechanics world, between prediction and prescription could easily be modelled, even from a quantitative perspective.
67. Such a logic could be named a teleological logic (abbreviated, a 4 T logic).
68. Somewhat on the same line of thinking is the proposal of James G. March and Johan P. Olsen (see their paper, *The logic of appropriateness*, ARENA Working Papers WP 04/09, Centre for European Studies, University of Oslo) applied to political institutions (so to

a very narrow area of the social field) by combining the cognitive rules with the normative ones. However, the concept of normativity in March and Olsen's paper is viewed in a very particular hypostasis, that is, as codified rules of the institutional framework, while our view is much larger and much more general.

69. We would want to replace the term *truth* with the term *occurrence* when the economic field is involved in the process of testing.
70. By this concept, we understand the praxiological referential here, that is, all operational means which have the capacity to contribute to achieving the purpose: strategies, economic resources, commitments (in Amartya Sen's sense, as already claimed), values, etc.
71. See, about the concept of instrumental rationality, the exciting book of Robert Nozick, *The Nature of Rationality*, Princeton University Press, 1995 (unfortunately not yet translated into Romanian).
72. We do not develop here a discussion about the concept of strong vs. weak scientificity (the issue was been exposed in other our works), but, for example, the economic theory is not analytical (in the sense of Nicholas Georgescu-Roegen, not of Descartes or Kant), that is, its "laws" are not applicable symmetrically to any individual of the economic objects (which includes the economic subjects as well).
73. As has already been pointed out, we need to distinguish between practical action and praxiological one: while practical action refers to action involving subject-subject relationships (for example, political or religious action), praxiological action refers to actions aimed at producing change in the world (i.e., state changes in the world), so is interested in subject-object relationships. Of course, there are some semantic overlaps: for example, a change in the state of the intended world through the development of subject-subject relationships (i.e., a practical action, for example, through performative or perlocutionary enunciations) is, at the same time, a praxiological one. However, there may be practical actions (in the sense that are retained here) that are not praxiological in nature (for example, Platonic love relationships).
74. Interesting is the position of Jürgen Habermas, who proposes a classification of sciences based on the "leading interest in knowledge". Thus, it distinguishes a *technical* criterion (leading to analytical-empirical sciences), a *practical* criterion (leading to the

historical-hermeneutical sciences) and an *emancipatory* criterion (leading to critical sciences). It can be noted that our opinion proposes a foundation for the very criteria of classifying the sciences (which Habermas does not do, assuming directly the three classes mentioned), namely, the subject-object relationship. The element that can establish a connection with Habermas's proposal is the "interest" of elucidation, which can be either the object or the subject (see Fig. 7).

75. Thus, we implicitly understand that human activity in relation to the object-object relation takes place in the so-called von Newman conditions, i.e., the theoretical (cognitive) action of the subject does not disturb either the object under examination or its relation to other objects. The special Quantum Mechanics situation (Heisenberg‘s imprecise or no-determination relationship) is, probably, an intrinsic property of the object-object relationship, even if it is only revealed by conducting a measurement experiment, so it cannot be considered a disturbance of the object by the subject. Rather, here the entanglement could be a good explanation of such imprecision of the conjugated (so, entangled) mathematical operators, which stay for the quantum entities.
76. I narrow the discussion to the human being, here.
77. The basic forms of intuition, that are transcendental, are: space and time, based on which the entire experience is possible and structured.
78. The problem of the foundation of opinion is, of course, distinct from the problem of the truth of opinion—while the truth of opinion requires an external "term" (the factual or coherence or inter-personal vote), in order to be validated, the foundation of opinion requires an internal "term", namely the belief of the opinioner, considered in the broadest sense of the concept of belief. The problem of the foundation or justification of opinion is an epistemological issue in itself and we will not develop it here.
79. Category 1 (Popper's world 1)—objective reality (non-artefacts), category 2 (Popper's world 2)—subjective reality (subjectivities), category 3 (Popper's world 3)—objectified reality (artefacts of any nature, e.g., this essay).
80. The reality is composed of three "areas": (a) the objective reality—it is independent from the subject (Popper's first world); (b) subjective reality—it is exclusively dependent on the subject

(Popper's second world); (c) objectified reality—artefacts, of any nature, of the individual and society, the so-called world of the objective content of the thought (Popper's third world).

81. The basic supposition of Lakatos's proposal of the concept of research program is that there is a difference between fallibilism and falsifiabilism. *Nota bene*: such a distinction was not made by Kuhn, or Popper.
82. Logically, the proximal genus together with the specific differences constitutes exactly the content of the concept of sufficiency predicates.
83. Or, equivalently, belongs to Popper's third world.

References

Dinga, E. (2024). On Cyclicality and Intrinsic Rhythm in Time Series. In C. Oprean-Stan (Ed.), *Chapter in the book. Application of novel research methods, the study of current economic phenomena*. Peter Lang.

Dinga, E. (2025). *Economic resilience during overlapped crises–Antifragility, sustainability and Autopoieticity*. Palgrave Macmillan–Springer Nature.

Dinga, E., Oprean-Stan, C., & Tănăsescu, C. R. (2025). *About the Two-Handed Model of Sustainability*. In C. R. Tănăsescu, C. Oprean-Stan, S. O. Idowu, & B. D. Diaz (Eds.), *Advancements in sustainable development*. Springer Nature.

Dinga, E., Oprea-Stan, C., Tănăsescu, R. C., Brătian, V., & Ionescu, G.-M. (2022). *Financial market analysis and behaviour. The adaptive preference hypothesis*. Routledge Taylor & Francis Group.

Kuhn, T. (2012). *The structure of scientific revolutions*. The University of Chicago.

Lakatos, I. (1980). In J. Worrall & G. Currie (Eds.), *The methodology of scientific research Programmes: Vol. 1*. Cambridge University Press.

Mises, L. v. (1998). *The human action. A treatise on economics*. Ludwig von Mises Institute, Auburn, Alabama.

Nozick, R. (1995). *The nature of rationality*. Princeton University Press.

Quine, W. V. O. (1976). Two dogmas of empiricism. In *Can theory be refuted?* Springer.

Smith, A. (2005). *An inquiry into the nature and causes of the wealth of nations*. Pennsylvania State University.

Wittgenstein, L. (2010). *Tractatus Logico-Philosophicus*. E-book. https://www.adamwalanus.pl/2015/Tractatus.pdf

Index

E. Dinga, *The Economics of Social Justice and Societal Evolution*,
https://doi.org/10.1007/978-3-032-24055-2

P

Q

R

FSC
www.fsc.org
MIX
Papier | Fördert
gute Waldnutzung
FSC® C083411

Zeitfracht Medien GmbH
Ferdinand-Jühlke-Straße 7
99095 Erfurt, Deutschland
produktsicherheit@kolibri360.de